ORDEAL
BY
FIRE

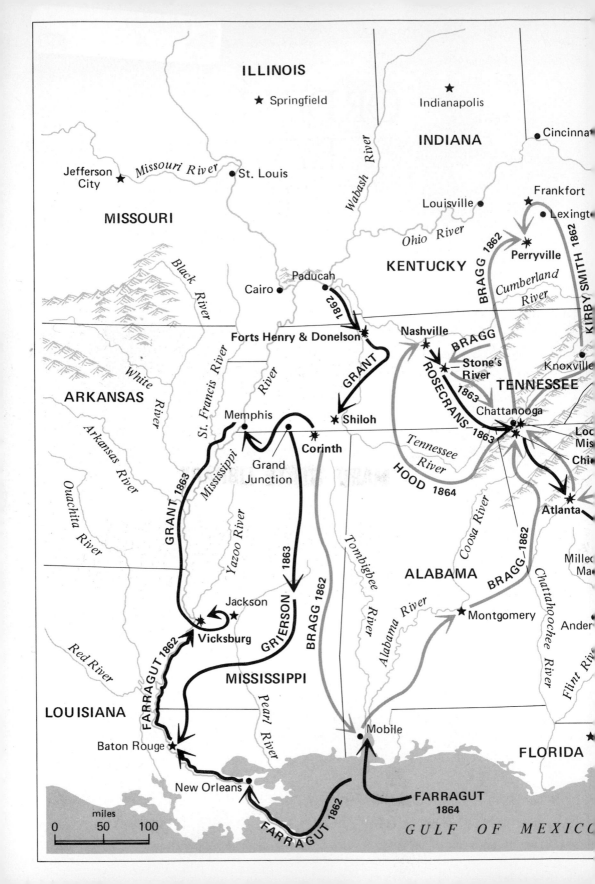

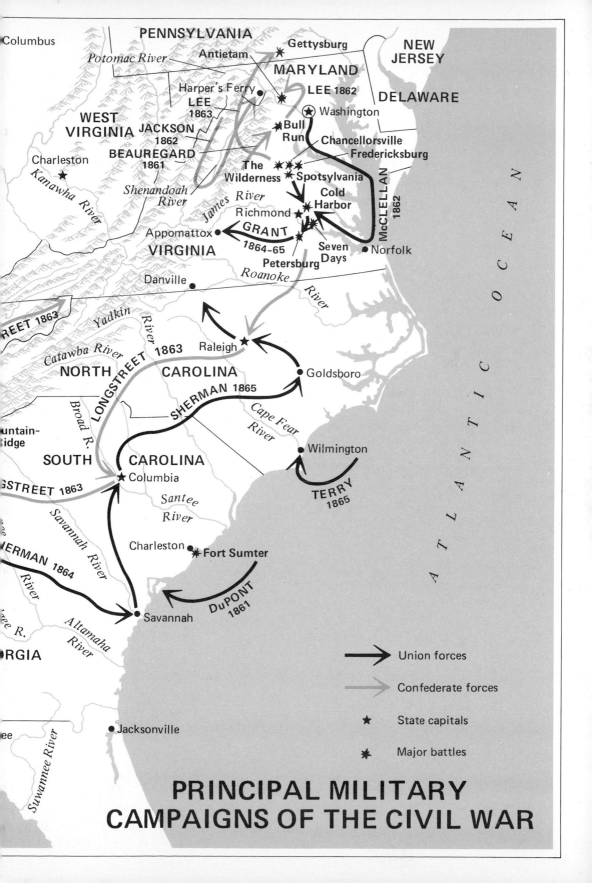

PRINCIPAL MILITARY
CAMPAIGNS OF THE CIVIL WAR

Columbus

PENNSYLVANIA

Potomac River

Antietam

Gettysburg

MARYLAND

NEW
JERSEY

Harper's Ferry

LEE
1863

LEE 1862

DELAWARE

WEST
VIRGINIA

JACKSON
1862

Washington

BEAUREGARD
1861

Bull
Run

Chancellorsville

Fredericksburg

Charleston

Kanawha River

The
Wilderness

Spotsylvania

*Shenandoah
River*

James River

Cold
Harbor

McCLELLAN
1862

Richmond

Appomattox

GRANT
1864–65

Seven
Days

Norfolk

VIRGINIA

Petersburg

Danville

Roanoke River

REET 1863

Yadkin River

Catawba River

Raleigh

NORTH   CAROLINA

LONGSTREET 1863

Goldsboro

untain-
idge

Broad R.

SHERMAN 1865

*Cape Fear
River*

SOUTH   CAROLINA

GSTREET 1863

Columbia

Wilmington

*Santee
River*

TERRY
1865

Savannah River

Charleston

Fort Sumter

ERMAN 1864

DuPONT
1861

River

Savannah

RGIA

*Altamaha
River*

ee R.

A T L A N T I C   O C E A N

Jacksonville

ee

Suwannee River

→	Union forces
→	Confederate forces
★	State capitals
✳	Major battles

ORDEAL BY FIRE

VOLUME II
THE CIVIL WAR

James M. McPherson

Princeton University

Alfred A. Knopf — New York

THIS IS A BORZOI BOOK
PUBLISHED BY ALFRED A. KNOPF, INC.

First Edition

987654321

Library of Congress Cataloging in Publication Data

McPherson, James M.
  Ordeal by fire.
    Bibliography: p.
    Includes index.
    1. United States—History—Civil War, 1861–1865—Causes. 2. United States—History—Civil War, 1861–1865. 3. United States—History—1865–1898. 4. Reconstruction. I. Title.
E468.M23   973.7   81-11832
ISBN 0-394-35812-0 (pbk.: v. 2)   AACR2

Manufactured in the United States of America

Design by James M. Wall

For Jenny

A Note on This Paperback Edition

This volume is part of a separate printing of *Ordeal By Fire*, not a new or revised edition. Many teachers who have used the full edition of *Ordeal By Fire* have suggested the publication of each of its three parts—"The Coming of War"; "The Civil War"; and "Reconstruction"—as separate volumes for adaptation to various types and structures of courses. This edition, then, is intended as a convenience for those instructors and students who wish to use one part or another of *Ordeal By Fire* rather than the full edition. The pagination of the full edition is retained here, but the table of contents, bibliography, and index cover only the material in this volume.

Preface

The Civil War is the central event in the American historical consciousness. While the Revolution of 1776–1783 created the United States, the Civil War of 1861–1865 preserved this creation from destruction and determined, in large measure, what sort of nation it would be. The war settled two fundamental issues for the United States: whether it was to be a nation with a sovereign national government, or a dissoluble confederation of sovereign states; and whether this nation, born of a declaration that all men are created with an equal right to liberty, was to continue to exist as the largest slaveholding country in the world. The Constitution of 1789 had left these issues unresolved. By 1861 there was no way around them; one way or another, a solution had to be found.

The Civil War shaped the institutions of modern America. It did so at the cost of 620,000 soldier deaths—almost equal to the number of American deaths in all the rest of the nation's wars combined. The Civil War was the largest and most destructive conflict in the Western world between 1815 and 1914. It was a total war. It mobilized the total resources of the two societies that fought it, and utterly devastated the resources of the loser. The principal issues of the war, sovereignty and freedom, proved to be uncompromisable. All efforts for a negotiated peace failed, and the war ended—could only have ended—in unconditional surrender. The war destroyed not only slavery and the Confederacy, but also the socioeconomic foundations on which these institutions had been built.

This totality of effort and consequence, this high drama of great events with its heroes and knaves, its triumph and tragedy, has produced a continuing scholarly and popular interest in the Civil War that testifies to its centrality in our historical consciousness. More books have been written about this war than about any other aspect of American history. Nearly 800 Civil War regimental histories have been published, compared with a mere handful for the Revolution. Civil War "buffs" outnumber those of other American wars by a wide margin. Millions of people each year visit Civil War battlefield sites and parks. Civil War roundtables persist into the late twentieth century. The subjects of slavery, emancipation, and the impact of the war on both blacks and whites in the South are among the most active and fruitful fields of American historical scholarship.

This volume is intended for use in college courses in American history. It can be assigned in conjunction with the author's preceding and/or succeeding volumes in the trilogy on America's *Ordeal By Fire:* Volume 1: *The Coming of War;* and Volume 3: *Reconstruction.* Or it can be assigned separately in any of a number of American history courses, including the survey.

The Civil War occurred at the dawn of photography, and the images of agony, suffering, endurance, perseverance, resignation, death, dedication, and triumph that leap out from the remarkable wet-plate photographs of that era are literally worth a thousand words. This book contains sixty-four wartime photographs, which are printed on or near the pages in the text that discuss the events or people they depict. Many of the photographs are accompanied by brief essays explaining their setting and significance. In addition, to help readers understand military campaigns and battles, the book includes twenty-nine maps, also located on the pages where these battles are described. For readers unfamiliar with the military terminology of the Civil War era, there is a glossary that defines these terms.

Men and women who lived through the Civil War knew that they had experienced the most crucial epoch in the nation's history. No other generation of Americans shared the intensity of this experience, the trauma of disaster, the euphoria of triumph. "I doubt whether any of us will ever be able to live contented again in times of peace and laziness," wrote young Henry Adams in the midst of the war. "One does every day, and without a second thought, what at another time would be the event of a year, perhaps of a life. . . . Our generation has been stirred up from its lowest layers and there is that in its history which will stamp every member of it until we are all in our graves. We cannot be commonplace." Twenty years later Oliver Wendell Holmes, Jr., a thrice-wounded veteran of the war, reminisced that "in our youth our hearts were touched with fire. It was given to us to learn at the outset that life is a profound and passionate thing." This book attempts to recapture the profound passion of those years in which the United States, as Abraham Lincoln said at Gettysburg, was transformed by "a new birth of freedom."

Princeton, New Jersey   James M. McPherson

Acknowledgments

A good many people and institutions have helped me produce this book. Students, colleagues, and lecture audiences over the years have knowingly or unknowingly helped to shape my knowledge and understanding of this era. The resources and staffs of the Princeton University Library and the Henry E. Huntington Library were indispensable. I am especially indebted to Martin Ridge, the late Ray Billington, James Thorpe, Virginia Renner, and Noelle Jackson for making my year of research and writing at the Huntington Library so pleasant and productive. Thanks must also go to the National Endowment for the Humanities and to Princeton University, which provided the funds and a leave for my year at the Huntington. In addition to the Huntington and Princeton Libraries, I wish to thank the following libraries and archives for permission to publish copies of photographs in their possession, and to thank their staffs for assistance in photo research: the Library of Congress, the United States Army Military History Institute, the Chicago Historical Society, and the Edward G. Miner Library of the University of Rochester Medical Center.

Several colleagues and friends read drafts of these chapters and made fruitful suggestions for improvement. For their careful and honest reading, I am indebted to Stephen E. Ambrose, Richard N. Current, Michael F. Holt, Peyton McCrary, Eric L. McKitrick, and Emory Thomas. I also owe thanks to members of the editorial staff at Alfred A. Knopf, especially to David C. Follmer, who as history editor for the college department first suggested the project from which this book grew and who faithfully supported it from the beginning, to his successor Christopher J. Rogers, who has shepherded this paperback edition to completion, and to James Kwalwasser, who gave the project more editorial time, effort, care, and enthusiasm than the most demanding author could expect. I am grateful to Louis Masur for his checking of quotations and references, and to my wife Patricia for her time and patience in helping me with the tedious task of reading proofs. Writing this book has been an intellectually rewarding experience, and all of these people have helped in various ways to enrich the experience.

Contents

————

Twenty-one/Behind the Lines   369

Twenty-two/Wartime Reconstruction and the Freedmen   391

Twenty-three/Military Stalemate, 1864   409

Twenty-four/The Third Turning Point: The Reelection of Lincoln   437

Twenty-five/The End of the Confederacy   459

PHOTOGRAPHS

MAPS

TABLES

FIGURES

ORDEAL
BY
FIRE

VOLUME II
THE CIVIL WAR

Ten

A Brothers' War:
The Upper South

THE CONFLICT TAKES SHAPE

The day after the surrender of Fort Sumter, Lincoln called 75,000 state militia into federal service for ninety days to put down an insurrection "too powerful to be suppressed by the ordinary course of judicial proceedings."[1] With these words the President accepted the South's challenge to civil war, a war that would last not ninety days but four years and would destroy the Old South, transform the Union it preserved, and cost at least 620,000 lives.

During the weeks after the fall of Sumter, war fever swept both North and South. "The heather is on fire," wrote an awestruck Boston merchant as bands blared, flags waved, orators thundered, and people cheered. "I never before knew what a popular excitement can be." A New Yorker who was astonished by the huge Union rallies in his city wrote: "It seems as if we never were alive till now; never had a country till now." A correspondent of the London *Times* traveling through the South saw immense crowds with "flushed faces, wild eyes, screaming mouths," whose rebel yells competed in volume with bands playing "Dixie."[2]

The bombardment of Sumter united a divided North. Stephen Douglas rose from his sickbed to call on Lincoln and assure him of Democratic support for a war to preserve the Union. "There can be no neutrals in this war," said Douglas; *"only patriots—or traitors."* At the other end of the political spectrum, abolitionists who had opposed all attempts to coax the departing states back by compromise now acclaimed the effort to bring them back by force. Even though the states to be brought back had slavery, abolitionists believed that the institution would not survive the conflict. Amid the feverish war preparations in Washington, one abolitionist wrote: "I hear Old John Brown knocking on the lid of his coffin & shouting 'Let me out,' 'let me out!' The doom of slavery is at hand. It is to be wiped out in blood. Amen!"[3] In the difference between the Democrats' support for a war to restore the old Union and the abolitionists' vision of a war to create a new one lay the seeds of a bitter harvest. But in April 1861 the North was united as never before or since.

From Northern governors came a zealous response to Lincoln's call for troops. Nearly every state offered to send more men than were requested. But owing to the rundown condition of the militia in several states, many of these men were lacking in organization, training, arms, and equipment. One state ready immediately to send more than patriotic telegrams was Massachusetts. Governor John Andrew, who had foreseen war sooner than most of his contemporaries, had put the Massachusetts militia in shape for mobilization months before the firing on Sumter. When Lincoln's call came, he responded: "Dispatch received. By what route shall we send?" Two days later, April 17, he wired the War Department: "Two of our regiments will start this afternoon—one for Washington, the other for Fort Monroe; a third will be dispatched tomorrow, and the fourth before the end of the week."[4]

Lincoln's call for militia requisitioned a quota of troops from each loyal state. The governors of six of the eight slave states still in the Union sent defiant refusals. "Tennessee will furnish not a single man for the purpose of coercion," declared its governor, "but fifty thousand if necessary for the defense of our rights and those of our Southern brothers." Virginia's governor telegraphed the President that since he had "chosen to inaugurate civil war," Virginia would join her sister states to the South. From North Carolina and Arkansas came similar replies, while the secession-minded governors of Kentucky and Missouri also refused to comply with Lincoln's call.[5]

The governors of Tennessee, Virginia, North Carolina, and Arkansas were, for the most part, expressing the popular will of their states. A majority of people in these states were bound by ties of culture and ideology to the lower South. They were conditional Unionists only so long as Lincoln did nothing to "coerce" the Confederacy; when forced to a choice, they chose southernism over nationalism. On April 15, a cheering crowd in Richmond ran up a Confederate flag, dragged cannon from the state arsenal to the Capitol, and fired a one-hundred-gun salute to the flag. Similar scenes took place in Raleigh, Nashville, and Little Rock. On April 17 the Virginia state convention, still in session after two months of futile compromise efforts, passed a secession ordinance by a vote of 88 to 55. Arkansas followed on May 6 by a vote of 69 to 1; North Carolina voted unanimously on May 20 to secede. In Tennessee, where voters had earlier rejected the calling of a state convention, the legislature resolved to enter the Confederacy, an action ratified in a popular referendum on June 8 by a majority of more than two to one.

The allegiance of these four states was of great importance to the Confederacy. Virginia, Tennessee, and North Carolina ranked first, second, and third in white population among the eleven Confederate states. Along with Arkansas, these upper-South states possessed more than half of the manufacturing capacity of the Confederacy, produced half of its food crops, contained nearly half of its horses and mules, and furnished more than two-fifths of the men in the Confederate armies. Without the upper South, the Confederacy could scarcely have been a viable military power.

But large pockets of Union sentiment remained in the upland and mountain counties of these late-seceding states. Traditionally hostile to the slaveholding lowlands, eastern Tennessee and western Virginia voted strongly against secession even after the firing on Sumter. In Knoxville, the blunt-spoken editor William G. "Parson" Brownlow vowed to "fight the Secession leaders till Hell freezes over, and then fight them on the ice."[6] Senator Andrew Johnson of Tennessee refused to go with his state and remained in the U.S. Senate, the only senator from a Confederate state to do so. After Confederate Tennessee had held special congressional elections in August 1861, the victorious Unionist candidates from three east Tennessee districts went to Washington instead of Richmond and took their seats in the Union Congress. Three congressmen from Virginia west of the Shenandoah Valley also remained loyal. Unionists in these areas plus those in the rest of the Appalachian uplands—extending all the way to northern Alabama—were a thorn in the flesh of the Confederacy.

THE FIRST CLASHES

Even before Virginia and North Carolina had officially seceded, state troops moved to seize federal property within their borders. When a thousand Virginia militia appeared on the heights above Harper's Ferry on April 18, the U.S. army garrison of forty-seven men fled after setting fire to the arsenal and armory. The Virginians moved in quickly and saved much of the rifle-making machinery from destruction. Meanwhile several thousand Virginia militia entrained for Norfolk to seize the Gosport Navy Yard, largest shipbuilding and repair facility in the South. The elderly commander of this post, confused by vague orders from Washington, decided to abandon the yard and destroy its facilities before the militia could overwhelm his handful of sailors and marines. On the night of April 20 the Federals tried to burn the half-dozen warships in the yard, blow up the dry dock, and spike the 1,200 cannon. But in their haste they made a poor job of it, and the Virginians captured most of the machinery and artillery in good condition. The cannon were soon on their way to forts throughout the South, while the Confederate navy began the task of raising and refitting a powerful steam frigate that had been burned to the waterline, the *U.S.S. Merrimack.*

The ease with which these key points had been seized showed the vulnerability of Union installations in the upper South. Surrounded by slave states and full of Confederate sympathizers, Washington also feared a secessionist *coup d'état* during the tense days of April 1861. Secession sentiment was strong in Maryland. On April 19 a mob in Baltimore attacked several companies of the 6th Massachusetts Regiment, Governor Andrew's first militia unit en route to Washington. The soldiers returned the fire. When the melee was over, four soldiers and twelve Baltimoreans lay dead and many wounded. The battered regiment arrived in Washington that evening, while behind them enraged Marylanders burned railroad bridges and tore down telegraph wires, cutting the capital off from the North.

Exultant at this turn of events, the *Richmond Examiner* urged Virginians to march into Washington and clean out "that filthy cage of unclean birds." The Confederate secretary of war predicted that his country's flag would fly over the U.S. Capitol by May 1.[7] More Northern troops were reported on the way to Washington, but having no communication with the outside world the government did not know where they were. Finally on April 25 a troop train puffed into the capital carrying the crack 7th New York Regiment, followed by other trains full of militia from Rhode Island and Massachusetts. Resourceful Benjamin Butler, a Massachusetts Democrat whom Andrew had reluctantly appointed commander of the state's four militia regiments, had detrained the 8th Massachusetts at the head of Chesapeake Bay, commandeered a steamer, brought his troops to Annapolis, and put mechanics and railwaymen from the regiment to work repairing the damaged rolling stock and branch line from Annapolis to Washington. By the end of April ten thousand troops were in the capital, most of them having arrived over Butler's route.

THE EASTERN BORDER STATES: MARYLAND AND DELAWARE

Washington was safe for the moment, but the problem of Maryland remained. Pro-Confederate units in the state were arming and drilling. Public pressure forced Unionist Governor Thomas Hicks to call the legislature into session. Lincoln decided that drastic measures were necessary to forestall disaster, for no government could function if its capital was surrounded by enemy territory. He suspended the writ of *habeas corpus* (virtually equivalent to declaring martial law) in part of Maryland. Federal troops occupied Baltimore and other important points. Intimidated by this show of force and by the rising tide of Union sentiment in the western counties, the legislature rejected secession.

Nevertheless, Maryland remained a divided state. While more than 30,000 white men (and 9,000 blacks) from the state fought in the Union army and navy, an estimated 20,000 went South to fight for the Confederacy. The Union government arrested many Maryland citizens for pro-Confederate activities. One of these, John Merryman, appealed for release under a writ of *habeas corpus* in May 1861. Sitting as a circuit judge in this case, Chief Justice Roger Taney issued the writ in a ruling, *ex parte Merryman*, which denied the President's power to suspend *habeas corpus*. In refusing to obey Taney's injunction, Lincoln pointed to Article I, Section 9, of the Constitution, which authorized suspension of the writ "when in Cases of Rebellion or Invasion the public Safety may require it." Taney insisted that only Congress possessed this power, but Lincoln commanded the army and his interpretation prevailed.

Although Delaware contained numerous Southern sympathizers, the state's adherence to the Union was never in serious doubt. Slavery had virtually ceased to exist there (fewer than 1,800 of Delaware's 20,000 blacks were slaves). The economy of the most populous part of the state, Wilmington and environs, was oriented toward Pennsylvania. The governor was a Unionist, and the legislature on January 3, 1861, decisively rejected secession. Delaware furnished about

10,000 white men and 1,000 black men to the Union army and navy; probably not more than 1,000 men from the state fought for the Confederacy.

THE WESTERN BORDER STATES: KENTUCKY AND MISSOURI

War brought bitter divisions and cruel violence to Kentucky and Missouri. Just as control of Maryland was vital to the security of Washington, control of these western border states was crucial for the war in the West. Missouri had a larger white population than any other slave state, while Kentucky had a larger white population than any Confederate state save Virginia. They possessed resources on a comparable scale. The Mississippi-Missouri river network added to the military importance of Missouri, while the confluence of the Ohio, Mississippi, Tennessee, and Cumberland rivers on the borders of Kentucky made the state a vital military nexus for the movement of troops and supplies. Lincoln reportedly said that while he hoped to have God on his side, he must have Kentucky.

Kentucky

Nowhere was the phrase "a brothers' war" more apt than in Kentucky. It was the native state of both Abraham Lincoln and Jefferson Davis. Heir to Henry Clay's nationalism, it was also drawn toward the South by ties of slavery and kinship. Kentucky regiments fought each other on battlefields from Shiloh to Atlanta. Three of Henry Clay's grandsons fought for the Union and four enlisted in the Confederate army. One son of Senator John J. Crittenden became a general in the Union army and the other a general in the Confederate army. The other senator from Kentucky in 1861, John C. Breckinridge, resigned his seat to join the Confederate army, where he rose to major general. Three of his sons also fought for the Confederacy, while two Kentucky cousins joined the Union army. Four of Mrs. Lincoln's brothers and three brothers-in-law, one of them a general, served in the Confederate army.

Pulled both ways, Kentucky at first tried to remain neutral. Governor Beriah Magoffin responded to Lincoln's call for troops with a statement that Kentucky would send no men "for the wicked purpose of subduing her sister Southern States." Mindful of Union sentiment in large parts of the state, however, Magoffin also refused a request from Jefferson Davis for troops. Called into special session, the legislature issued a neutrality proclamation warning both the Union and the Confederacy against sending troops into or through the state.

For the time being, both Lincoln and Davis decided to respect Kentucky's neutrality, for it was clear that whichever side violated this neutrality would drive the state into the arms of the other. The tactics Lincoln had used in Maryland would be counterproductive here. But the state soon became a rich source of horses, mules, leather, grain, and meat for Confederate forces mobilizing south of its border. The Louisville and Nashville Railroad served as a conduit for a brisk trade in military supplies to the South. Governor Magoffin secretly allowed Southern agents to begin recruiting in the state. Many

Kentuckians slipped over the Tennessee border to join the Confederate army.

Lincoln's hands-off policy may have benefited the Confederacy militarily, but it paid handsome political dividends for the Union. Kentucky held three special elections in 1861: for a border-state convention in May, for a special session of Congress in June, and for the state legislature in August. Unionists won solid majorities in every election. Meanwhile the partisans of each side were arming to prevent a coup by the other. Magoffin organized Confederate sympathizers into "state guard" regiments. Unionists countered by organizing "home guards." Lincoln authorized five thousand rifles for the home guards, and the Unionists secretly ferried these weapons across the Ohio River at night. The President also sent Robert Anderson, the defender of Fort Sumter and a native of Kentucky, to Cincinnati to receive Kentucky volunteers into the Union army.

As both sides built up their forces on the borders and as state guards confronted home guards inside the state, the days of Kentucky's neutrality appeared to be numbered. Several Union regiments under the command of General Ulysses S. Grant were poised just across the Ohio River at Cairo, Illinois. Fearing that these regiments were about to seize the strategic heights commanding the Mississippi River at Columbus, Kentucky, Confederate General Leonidas Polk decided to steal a march on them by occupying Columbus himself. His troops did so on September 3. Polk's fears were well-founded, and his move was militarily sound. But by moving first he committed a political blunder. Kentucky's Unionist legislature denounced the Confederate "invaders" and invited the U.S. government to drive them out. On September 6 Grant obligingly occupied Paducah and Southland, at the mouths of the Tennessee and Cumberland rivers. A taciturn man whose iron will and quiet efficiency compelled obedience and got things done, Grant belied his reputation as a drunk and a drifter. His occupation of these key river points boded ill for the Confederacy.

The war that Kentucky had vainly hoped to avoid by neutrality was now at its doorstep. The state officially remained in the Union, even though in November 1861 its secessionist minority called a convention, passed an ordinance of secession, and "joined" the Confederacy. During the war nearly 50,000 Kentucky whites (and 24,000 blacks) fought in the Union army, while an estimated 35,000 served in the Confederate ranks.

Missouri

A quite different series of events kept Missouri in the Union. It would scarcely stretch the truth to say that the Civil War began along the Missouri-Kansas border in 1854 and lasted there eleven years instead of four. Many of the border ruffians continued their battle for slavery as members of the Confederate army, while the free-state Kansas "jayhawkers" donned Federal uniforms in 1861.*A former leader of the border ruffians, Claiborne Jackson, had been elected governor of Missouri

*For the border ruffians, see pp. 92–93. The jayhawkers (from the name of an imaginary bird) were the free-soil counterparts of the border ruffians. They practiced the same guerrilla tactics of hit-and-run attacks, ambush, and terrorism as their enemies, which helped make the war in Missouri a particularly vicious affair.

in 1860. When Lincoln called for militia from the state, Jackson sent a defiant reply: "Your requisition is illegal, unconstitutional, revolutionary, inhuman, diabolical, and cannot be complied with."[8] The governor moved quickly to place Missouri in the Confederacy before Unionist elements could organize. He took control of the St. Louis police and began to mobilize the militia under pro-Confederate officers. On April 21 some of these troops seized the U.S. arsenal at Liberty, near Kansas City. But Jackson had a bigger prize in mind—the arsenal in St. Louis, which held 60,000 muskets and other military equipment. He secretly asked Jefferson Davis for a battery of artillery to use against the arsenal. Davis complied, and on May 8 boxes marked "marble" but containing four cannons and ammunition arrived at St. Louis from downriver.

But Jackson had reckoned without two antagonists even more determined than he. The acting commander of the St. Louis arsenal was Captain Nathaniel Lyon of the 2nd U.S. Infantry. Lyon was a wiry, hard-bitten Connecticut Yankee who had acquired strong anti-Southern convictions when stationed in Kansas before the war. His aggressive Unionism was backed by Francis P. Blair, Jr., a congressman from Missouri and brother of Lincoln's postmaster general. Lyon and Blair arranged for the removal of most of the muskets across the river to Illinois and kept the rest to arm volunteer regiments organized mainly by the German-American population of St. Louis, the backbone of Unionism in Missouri. Lyon mustered four of these regiments into Federal service. On May 10 he led them with two companies of regulars to surround the pro-Confederate militia camp. Outnumbered, the militia surrendered. As the prisoners were marched through St. Louis a crowd gathered. Growing increasingly raucous, members of the crowd cheered for Jefferson Davis, threw stones at the "Hessians," and threatened them with revolvers. Finally a drunken man shot an officer, whereupon the soldiers opened fire. When it was over, twenty-eight people lay dead or dying. That night mobs roamed the streets, and next day another affray broke out in which at least six more people were killed.

This affair blew the lid off Missouri. Many conditional Unionists went over to secession, including former Governor Sterling Price, who assumed command of the pro-Southern troops. The legislature adopted Governor Jackson's proposals to put the state on a war footing. On the other side, Lyon was promoted to brigadier general and given command of the 10,000 Union troops now in Missouri. In a stormy meeting with Price on June 11, Lyon ended the armed truce that had prevailed while moderates tried to work out a Kentucky-style "neutrality" for Missouri. "Rather than concede to the State of Missouri for one single instant the right to dictate to my Government," Lyon told the aristocratic, Virginia-born Price, "I would see you . . . and every man, woman, and child in the State dead and buried. This means war."[9]

Lyon moved his troops up the Missouri River to the capital, Jefferson City. Price retreated farther upriver to Boonville. Lyon pursued him with 1,700 men, and in a skirmish on June 17 he routed Price's militia and drove them in disarray to the southwest corner of the state. There they hoped to regroup, arm new recruits, and combine with Confederate troops from Arkansas to win Missouri for the South. Meanwhile the state convention, which had adjourned in March after rejecting a secession ordinance, reassembled and assumed the functions of a legislature. It declared the governorship vacant and appointed a new governor. Claiborne Jackson retaliated by forming a pro-Confederate shadow government, which was officially recognized by the Confederacy in November.

On July 25, John C. Frémont arrived in St. Louis as commander of the Union's Western Department. As a former explorer of the Rockies, hero of California's Bear Flag Revolt, and first Republican presidential candidate, Frémont had both military experience and political connections. But the chaotic situation in Missouri proved too much for him. Guerrilla warfare raged in all parts of the state. Two Confederate armies were gathering on the southern border for an invasion. Four days after Frémont arrived, a Rebel force of 6,000 crossed the Mississippi from Tennessee and occupied New Madrid, where they threatened the Union garrison at the river junction of Cairo, Illinois.

Frémont decided to reinforce Cairo, but to do so he had to withhold reinforcements from Nathaniel Lyon's army of 6,000 men at Springfield in southwest Missouri. Short of supplies, distant from his base, the enlistment time of the ninety-day regiments that comprised half his force about to expire, Lyon confronted a motley Southern army composed of Sterling Price's Missourians plus Confederates under General Ben McCulloch, a former Texas Ranger. Since this force numbered more than twice as many men as his own, Lyon's only choice seemed to be retreat. But he was loath to give up southern Missouri without a fight. Aggressive and impetuous, Lyon decided to make a surprise attack on the Confederate camp at Wilson's Creek, ten miles from Springfield. Boldly splitting his small army, he sent 1,200 men under General Franz Sigel on a flanking march to attack the Confederate rear while he himself with 4,200 men hit them in front. The two groups attacked at dawn August 10. The advantage of surprise gave the Federals an edge at first. The poorly armed Rebels fell back between the Union pincers. But at a critical point Sigel, seeing a regiment in blue uniforms (the Union color) emerge from the smoke in his front and assuming that Lyon had broken through the Confederate line, ordered his men to hold their fire. The men in blue were not Yankees, however, but a Louisiana regiment that, like many others on both sides in the early months of the war, had clothed itself in uniforms of a color and style of its own choosing. The Louisianians, unopposed, cut down Sigel's force with a withering fire and routed it from the field. Lyon's own command, now outnumbered three to one, held on desperately in the face of repeated counterattacks. But they lost many men and began to run short of ammunition. After Lyon had been killed, the top-ranking Federal officer left unwounded on the field (a major) decided to order a retreat. The Unionists trudged back to Springfield and then one hundred miles northward to the railhead supply base at Rolla.

Confederate victory in this small but vicious battle of Wilson's Creek (each side suffered more than 1,200 casualties) exposed southern and western Missouri to Confederate invasion. Marching northward with 10,000 men and gathering recruits as he moved, Price went all the way to the Missouri River, where with 18,000 troops he laid siege to the 3,500-man Union garrison at Lexington. Frémont could spare few men from the task of fighting guerrillas, but he managed

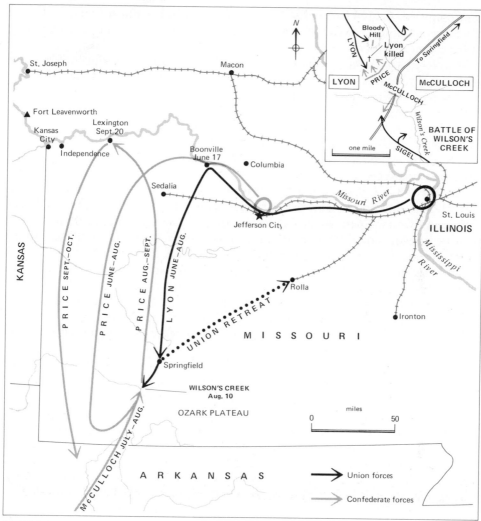

MISSOURI, 1861

to scrape together two small brigades to reinforce Lexington. They were too little and too late. The garrison surrendered on September 20.

In two months Frémont had lost nearly half of Missouri. And military reverses were not his only problem. As commander of a department he faced complex administrative problems with little help from Washington a thousand miles away. War contracts must be let; supplies, arms, horses, and wagons must be obtained in a hurry; gunboats for the river navy must be built; new recruits must be organized and trained; transport bottlenecks must be overcome; Rebel sympathizers must be watched; and quarreling factions of Unionists must be kept in line. Frémont was not equal to the task. Honest himself, he was overwhelmed by contractors eager to make profits from the army's needs. Reports of graft became commonplace. Congressman Blair, the most powerful political figure in Union Missouri and now a colonel as well, turned against Frémont and began scheming to have him removed.

Distracted by these problems and bedeviled by the increasing boldness of guerrillas, Frémont took a desperate step. On August 30 he issued an order that put the whole state under martial law, proclaimed the death penalty for guerrillas captured behind Union lines, and confiscated the property and freed the slaves of all Confederate sympathizers in Missouri. This order stirred up a hornet's nest. Abolitionists and many Republicans lionized Frémont as one general who knew how to destroy the taproot of rebellion. But a guerrilla commander in southeast Missouri announced that for every one of his men executed by the Yankees he would "HANG, DRAW AND QUARTER a minion of said Abraham Lincoln."[10] Slaveholding Unionists from Missouri to Maryland threatened to defect if Frémont's emancipation edict was carried out. Vitally concerned with maintaining the allegiance of the border states, Lincoln believed that he could not afford to let Frémont's action stand. He told the general that he must execute no guerrillas without prior approval from Washington and suggested privately that he modify his confiscation and emancipation edict to make it conform with the confiscation act enacted by Congress on August 6 (see p. 268), which authorized the seizure only of property and slaves used directly in the Confederate war effort. Frémont refused, whereupon Lincoln publicly ordered him to modify the proclamation.

The President also decided to make a change of command in Missouri, where the war contract scandals had become notorious. Knowing that he could save himself only by military success, Frémont gathered 38,000 troops and took personal command of them. The Federals drove Price's army almost to the Arkansas line once again. But as Frémont was preparing for a showdown battle, an order relieving him of command reached his headquarters on November 2. His successor, believing the army overextended, ordered a retreat to its bases in central Missouri. On November 19, General Henry W. Halleck took control of the newly created Department of Missouri (which also included western Kentucky, bringing Grant under Halleck's command). A military scholar who had written and translated several works on strategy (which earned him the sobriquet "Old Brains"), Halleck was a cautious general who waged war by the book. He possessed the administrative capacity that Frémont lacked and soon brought order out of the organizational chaos in Missouri.

In the course of the war about 80,000 white Missourians (and 8,000 blacks) served in the Union armies, while at least 30,000 joined the Confederates and another 3,000 or more fought as Southern guerrillas. Among the latter was the notorious William Quantrill, whose band at one time or another included such desperadoes as Cole Younger and Frank and Jesse James. These guerrilla bands wreaked havoc out of all proportion to their numbers. Counterguerrilla forces sprang up among the Kansas jayhawkers, whose raids across the border continued the vicious warfare of Bleeding Kansas days. Although peripheral to the principal military campaigns of the war, Missouri suffered more than any other state from raids, skirmishes, and guerrilla actions.

Each through a different process, then, the four border slave states remained in the Union, though a substantial minority of their people supported the Confederacy. The war itself created a fifth Union border state: West Virginia.

WEST VIRGINIA

The western portion of the state of Virginia was strategically important because the Baltimore and Ohio Railroad (the B&O) and the Ohio River ran through it or along its border for two hundred miles. The Confederates struck first in this vital area by cutting the B&O west of Harper's Ferry in May 1861. The task of driving them out fell to General George B. McClellan, who organized 20,000 troops in Ohio and sent a vanguard across the river in late May. This force occupied Grafton on the B&O and then moved fifteen miles south to rout a small Confederate outpost at Philippi on June 3. The Confederates sent reinforcements to western Virginia under General Robert Garnett, who fortified two passes through the mountains twenty miles south of Philippi. Meanwhile the Confederate garrison at Harper's Ferry, menaced by the Federal advance in its rear and by the buildup of another Union force across the Potomac in its front, retreated to a more defensible position near Winchester.

Union forces now controlled the B&O, but McClellan's plans had evolved beyond merely regaining the railroad. With 12,000 men he advanced in two columns against Garnett's 5,000. While one Union column demonstrated against the most strongly defended pass at Laurel Mountain, the other assaulted the Confederate position at Rich Mountain on July 11. Accepting the battle plan suggested by General William S. Rosecrans, McClellan sent Rosecrans's brigade to circle around and assail the Rebels from the rear while the main force attacked in front. Rosecrans did his job well, smashing through the Confederate defenses and driving the survivors into the town of Beverly, where more than 550 surrendered. The weakness of McClellan's frontal attack allowed the rest to escape northward, where they joined the other Confederate force retreating from Laurel Mountain. On July 13, the pursuing Federals fell on the Confederate rear guard at Carrick's Ford, where Garnett was killed trying to rally his broken regiments.

At a cost of fewer than a hundred casualties, the Federals had inflicted ten times that number of losses on the Confederates, including seven hundred prisoners. The defeated Southern army fled eastward, leaving most of Virginia west of the Alleghenies under Union control. Although much of the credit for these victories belonged to McClellan's subordinates, especially Rosecrans, McClellan proved adept at writing dispatches reflecting glory on himself. The Northern press lauded the thirty-four-year-old general as a "Young Napoleon" who would roll up the Confederate flank in the mountains and drive all the way to Richmond. McClellan's army was too small for this, however, even if the formidable problems of transport and supply across the rugged Alleghenies could have been solved. Most of McClellan's troops were needed to protect the railroad and other key points against guerrilla and cavalry raids and to prepare for an expected Confederate counterstroke.

The Richmond government sent Robert E. Lee to regain western Virginia. One

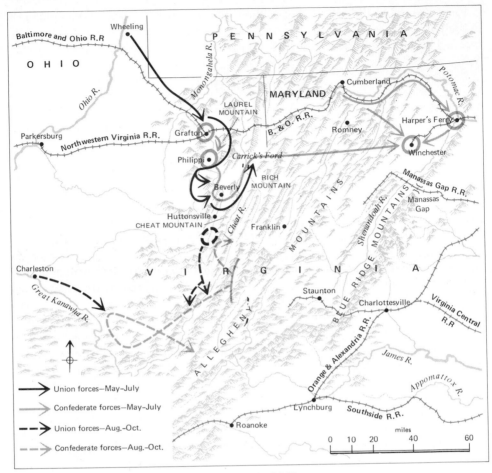

OPERATIONS IN WESTERN VIRGINIA, 1861

of the most promising officers in the old army, Lee on April 18 had declined Lincoln's offer of command of the Union armies and had resigned his commission two days later. Lee was lukewarm toward slavery and opposed to secession; but he was unwilling to "raise my hand against my birthplace." He chose state over nation. After an interval as a desk general in Richmond, he went west to the mountains on July 28 to assume overall command of the 15,000 reorganizing Confederate troops facing about 11,000 Federals now occupying trans-Allegheny Virginia. Lee decided to attack a Union brigade dug in at the Cheat Mountain pass through which ran the turnpike connecting Staunton in the Shenandoah Valley with Parkersburg on the Ohio River. Hampered by heavy rains and by epidemics of measles and typhoid that put a third of his men on the sick list, Lee's complicated enveloping maneuver fizzled on September 12 and he fell back without a battle.

Lee then moved south to the Kanawha Valley to take charge of the brigades under Generals John Floyd and Henry Wise, Virginia politicians who spent more energy feuding with each other than fighting the enemy. Lee straightened out their conflict by getting Wise recalled to Richmond. But his plan to trap a Union force under Rosecrans failed when Rosecrans pulled back to a defensive position too strong for Lee to attack. Disease, mud, feuding generals, and supply problems over terrible mountain roads had defeated Lee. Although he kept Rosecrans out of the Shenandoah Valley, his three months' expedition was counted a failure. Southern newspapers called him "Granny Lee" and criticized him for having failed even to bring the Yankees to battle, much less to disturb their control of western Virginia. Lee's first campaign almost ruined his reputation before it had a chance to become established.

The Union's military success in western Virginia had important political consequences. Few residents of this region owned slaves. For decades they had complained of overtaxation and underrepresentation in the state government. They had little in common with the "tidewater aristocrats." Their economy and culture were oriented toward Ohio and Pennsylvania. When Virginia seceded from the Union, many of the trans-Allegheny convention delegates returned home determined to secede from Virginia. They arrived to find mass meetings demanding the same thing. Many northwestern Virginians welcomed the Union troops as liberators. At the second of two conventions in Wheeling representing thirty-four trans-Allegheny counties, delegates on June 19 voted to constitute themselves the legitimate government of Virginia. This convention later passed an ordinance calling a constitutional convention to meet in Wheeling in November 1861 to form a new state to be named Kanawha (later changed to West Virginia). This action was ratified by a popular referendum in which only those who took a Unionist oath could vote. In May 1862 a Unionist "legislature," which theoretically represented all of Virginia but in reality represented primarily the western counties, gave its approval to the creation of the new state. This technically fulfilled the stipulation of the U.S. Constitution (Article IV, Section 3) that no new state can be formed within the boundaries of an existing state without the consent of the latter's legislature.

Despite these irregular proceedings, the Union Congress finally admitted West Virginia as a state in 1863 (after requiring the abolition of slavery therein). This new state contained fifty counties, nearly half of which, however, probably had a pro-Southern majority that would have preferred to remain part of Confederate Virginia. West Virginia contributed about 25,000 men to the Union army, though many of these remained tied down by Rebel guerrilla bands that roamed the mountains throughout the war. Perhaps 15,000 West Virginians fought for the Confederacy. Like Missouri, West Virginia carried on its own civil war within the larger conflict.

EAST TENNESSEE

The Lincoln administration hoped to provoke a Unionist uprising in east Tennessee to restore that region to the Union on the West Virginia model. Soon after Union military forces had occupied northern Kentucky in September 1861, Federal agents established contact with east Tennessee Unionists to coordinate a local uprising with an invasion by Northern troops through the Cumberland Gap from

Kentucky. The commander of the small invading army was General George H. Thomas, a Virginian who had remained loyal to the Union.

Right on schedule at the end of October the Tennessee Unionists began burning bridges, attacking Confederate supply lines, and softening up the opposition for their Northern liberators. But the Yankees did not come. Nervous about an expected Confederate thrust in central Kentucky, the commander of the Union's Department of the Ohio, General Don Carlos Buell, canceled Thomas's invasion. The roads were terrible, said Buell, the mountains rugged, winter was coming on, and a Union occupying force could not be sustained in this difficult country even if it could get there. The true line of operations, he insisted, was along the rivers against central and west Tennessee. Without support from the outside, the east Tennessee resistance collapsed in November. Confederate soldiers rounded up scores of Unionists, executed five, and imprisoned the rest.

Buell's pessimism about a winter offensive was justified. But continuing pressure from the administration caused him reluctantly to order Thomas southward in January 1862. Winter rains mired Thomas's wagons and artillery axle-deep in mud, on roads little better than Indian paths. A fifth of his 5,000 men fell out sick or as stragglers in the ninety-mile march to Logan's Cross-Roads, which was still eighty miles short of the Cumberland Gap. At Logan's Cross-Roads, a Confederate force of 4,000 under Generals George Crittenden and Felix Zollicoffer struck Thomas in a surprise dawn attack January 19. Although pushed back at first, the Federals rallied in a spirited counterattack that killed Zollicoffer and routed the Rebels. It was a decisive tactical victory for Thomas but its strategic consequences were negligible. The wild mountains south of the Cumberland River made a farther advance impossible during the winter. By spring the important campaigns in west Tennessee diverted Federal attention to that theater. To Lincoln's sorrow, east Tennessee was fated to remain under Confederate control for another year and a half.

On balance, the outcome of the crucial struggle for the upper South in 1861 probably favored the Union. Although four of these states (Virginia, North Carolina, Tennessee, and Arkansas) went over to the Confederacy, they were offset by the five border states (including West Virginia) of equal population that declared for the Union. The production of food, draft animals, iron, lead, salt, and other items of military importance was greater in the five Union than in the four Confederate states. Union control of northern Kentucky and Missouri provided strategic access to the major river systems in the western war theater. This enabled the North to launch its victorious river-borne invasions deep into Confederate territory during 1862. And while close to 100,000 men from the Union border states fought for the Confederacy, this was not much in excess of the 45,000 whites and an equal number of blacks from the upper-South Confederate states who eventually served in the Union armies.

In the spring of 1861, however, most of these developments lay in the future. The main concern of both sides in these early months of the war was to mobilize, train, and equip their armies and navies, and to develop a strategy for using them.

Eleven

Mobilizing for War

ORGANIZING THE ARMED FORCES

Unreadiness for War

Seldom has a country been less prepared for a major war than the United States was in 1861. The tiny regular army—fewer than 16,000 men—was scattered in small units all over the country, mostly west of the Mississippi. Nearly a third of the army's officers were resigning to join the Confederacy. The War Department in Washington drowsed in peacetime routine. All but one of the officers commanding the eight army bureaus had been in service since the War of 1812. General-in-Chief Winfield Scott was seventy-four years old and suffered from dropsy and vertigo. There was nothing resembling a general staff. There were no accurate military maps. When General Henry W. Halleck began to direct operations in the western theater in 1862, he used maps obtained from a bookstore. West Point was a good school, but its strong points were engineering, mathematics, and fortifications. Its students learned little of strategy, staff work, or the tactical command of troops in the field. Many of the Point's graduates, including George B. McClellan, Ulysses S. Grant, William T. Sherman, Thomas J. Jackson, Jefferson Davis, and Braxton Bragg, had resigned from the army to pursue civilian careers.

The navy was scarcely in better shape. Only forty-two of its ninety ships were in commission. Most of these were on station in distant waters; only three were available for immediate service along the American coast. Trained for deep-water operations, the navy had little experience with the coastal and inshore work that would be required of it during the Civil War. Indeed, its officers knew the coastal defenses and forts of foreign nations better than those of the South, for they had never contemplated operations against their own ports!

In theory, the state militias formed a ready reserve of all men of military age. But practice fell ludicrously short of theory. The militia had always been somewhat unreliable in war; by the 1830s it had become a peacetime joke. Militia musters were the occasion for a drinking holiday. Rare was the company that took seriously the idea of drilling. Several militia regiments were called up during the Mexican War, but they saw little action because the principal reliance in that conflict was on volunteer regiments. By the 1850s the volunteer principle had largely replaced the concept of universal obligation for militia service. Socially elite volunteer companies sprang up in both North and South. Recognizing the inevitable, several states incorporated these units into the militia structure, making the militia for all practical purposes voluntary and selective rather than compulsory and universal. Being primarily social rather than military societies, few of these volunteer companies acquired any real training or discipline. Nevertheless it was they who first answered the call to arms in 1861.

On both sides the notion prevailed that the war to be fought by these citizen soldiers would be a short one. The active phase of the Mexican War, which served as a reference point for Americans, had lasted only sixteen months and had resulted in the conquest of a country larger than the Confederacy. A more recent example, the Franco-Austrian War of 1859, had lasted less than three months. After Sumter fell, the *New York Times* predicted that this "local commotion" in the South would be put down "in thirty days." The *Chicago Tribune* thought it might take two or three months. General Winfield Scott, less optimistic than most, was confident of success by the spring of 1862. Confederate estimates were even more unrealistic. Many Southerners felt contempt for Yankees as "vulgar, fanatical, cheating counter-jumpers." Northerners were cowards: "just throw three or four shells among those blue-bellied Yankees," said a North Carolinian, "and they'll scatter like sheep." Many Southerners believed that one Rebel could lick ten Yankees because "the Yankee army is filled up with the scum of creation and ours with the best blood of the grand old Southland."[1]

Of course not everyone in the South or North lived in this dreamland. Jefferson Davis and his vice president, Alexander Stephens, tried to warn their followers that it would be a long, hard war. Just after the fall of Sumter, William T. Sherman wrote: "I think it is to be a long war—very long—much longer than any politician thinks." On Lincoln's call for 75,000 three-months militiamen, Sherman commented: "You might as well attempt to put out the flames of a burning house with a squirt-gun."[2]

But such were minority opinions amid the ebullient enthusiasm that existed in the spring of 1861. Men on both sides rushed to enlist before the war was over. They had only the vaguest and most romantic notions of what war was like. Their vision was of bands, banners, massed formations marching in brilliant sunshine over open fields to glorious victories in which death, if it came, would be painless and honorable. Few could envisage the mud or choking dust, the bone-deep fatigue, the searing thirst and gnawing hunger, the bitter cold or enervating heat of the march or bivouac; the boredom of camp life; the gut-tearing pain of dysentery or the delirious ravings of typhoid in a primitive army hospital; the smoke, noise, confusion, and terror of battle; the blood and screams and amputated limbs of the surgeon's tent. Even those who foresaw a long war could scarcely conceive of the massive mobilization of men and resources this war would require or the savage destruction of men and resources it would accomplish.

Recruitment and Supply

Lincoln realized that three-months militiamen would be inadequate for even a short war. On May 3 the President called for 42,000 three-year volunteers, expanded the regular army by authorizing an additional 23,000 men, and directed the recruitment of 18,000 sailors for the navy. Lincoln's only legal authorization for these measures was his emergency war powers as Commander in Chief, but he expected Congress to ratify his actions at its special session beginning July 4. Congress did so. In his message to the special session, Lincoln also asked for authority to raise at least 400,000 additional volunteers; Congress approved 500,-000; and in the end more than 700,000 men enlisted, most of them for three years, under these presidential and congressional actions of 1861. Some of the three-months regiments reenlisted for three years; many individuals in other militia units reenlisted in the new three-year regiments after expiration of their initial service.

The process of raising a three-year regiment went something like this: Prominent citizens opened a recruiting office and organized recruiting rallies. When approximately one hundred men had signed up, they were formed into a company; ten companies were then enrolled as a regiment. In accordance with long-standing militia and volunteer tradition, the men in most companies elected the company officers (captain and lieutenants); these in turn elected the regimental officers (colonel, lieutenant colonel, and major). The state governor officially commissioned the regimental officers but usually appointed those elected by the junior officers. In practice, the selection of officers at all levels was often predetermined by their role in organizing a company or by their political influence. The election of officers was often a *pro forma* ratification of their leadership. The principal basis for recruitment and organization was geography. Companies and sometimes entire regiments came from the same township, county, or city. Ethnicity was also an affinity basis for numerous regiments in the Union army. Many regiments and sometimes whole brigades were composed primarily of German-Americans or Irish-Americans.

In the early months of the war, states or localities provided uniforms and other equipment. This led to a motley variety of colors and types of uniforms, ranging from the standard dark blue jacket and light blue trousers of the regular army to the gaudy "Zouave" colors based on the uniforms of the renowned French colonial regiments of Algeria. Some Union regiments at first wore gray uniforms (and some Confederates initially wore blue), leading to tragic mix-ups in the early battles. Not until 1862 were Union soldiers consistently uniformed in blue.

The process of Northern recruitment was marked by great energy at the local level and decreasing efficiency at each step up the ladder to the War Department. It was a do-it-yourself mobilization. Secretary of War Simon Cameron was overwhelmed by his task. As the regiments poured in to state rendezvous points or training camps, shortages and confusion abounded. In a November 1861 report from his base at Cairo, Illinois, General Ulysses S. Grant complained of "a great deficiency in transportation. I have no ambulances. The clothing received has been almost universally of an inferior quality and deficient in quantity. . . . The quartermaster's department has been carried on with so little funds that government credit has become exhausted." Grant's superior in St. Louis, General Henry W. Halleck, put it succinctly: "Affairs here are in complete chaos."[3]

The need to sign war contracts hurriedly in 1861 led to scandals and charges

(Reproduced from the Collections of the Library of Congress)

These pictures show typical Confederate and Union volunteer
infantry companies in the early months of the war. The above
photograph is of Co. K of the 4th Georgia Infantry in April 1861.
Note the seven stars in the Confederate flag, indicating that the
photograph was taken before the secession of the upper-South states.
This "Stars and Bars" flag remained the official flag of the

of profiteering. A few clothing contractors supplied uniforms made from pressed scraps of shredded wool, called "shoddy," which fell apart after a few weeks' wear. Not until Congress set up a watchdog committee and Edwin M. Stanton replaced the blundering Cameron as war secretary in January 1862 did order and efficiency govern the business of contracts and supply for the Union army. By 1862 the Northern forces would become the best-equipped armies in the world's history, but a society unprepared for war required a full year to gear up for the conflict.

In some respects, the South mobilized more quickly than the North. Although the Confederacy began with no regular army or navy and few resources to create the latter, the South's numerous volunteer companies put themselves on a war footing as soon as their states seceded. On March 6, 1861, more than five weeks before the

(Reproduced from the Collections of the Library of Congress)

Confederacy. But its arrangement of stars and bars caused it to become confused with the Stars and Stripes of the U.S. flag in the first battle of Bull Run. Confederate General Beauregard therefore devised a battle flag based on the St. Andrew's cross, and it was this battle flag that has come down through history as the familiar banner of the Confederacy. The photograph on this page shows Co. K of the 6th Vermont Infantry at the regiment's training camp near Washington in the fall of 1861. Note the healthy, spit-and-polish appearance of both companies before they saw combat. Still, by the time these pictures were taken, their numbers had been reduced, the Georgia company to 80 percent, and the Vermont company to 60 percent of its initial complement of 100 men. The 6th Vermont was part of the Vermont Brigade, which would suffer greater losses than any other Union brigade. More than one-fourth of the men in the 6th Vermont would die in the war.

firing on Sumter, the Confederate Congress authorized 100,000 volunteers. Two more laws in May provided for an additional 400,000 men. Although the South's manpower pool was less than one-third as large as the North's, the Confederacy had nearly two-thirds as many men under arms as the Union by July 1861.

The recruiting process followed pretty much the same pattern in the South as in the North. Localities and states took the initiative, swamping the War Department with more volunteers than it could equip. More than 150,000 muskets were stored in the U.S. arsenals seized by the seceding states, but most of these were obsolete and many were unserviceable. Confederate volunteers often brought their own weapons. Many companies initially carried shotguns, hunting rifles, and ancient flintlock muskets. Each regiment also uniformed itself in 1861, and the range of styles and colors was as great as in the Union army. The Confederate government adopted cadet gray as the official uniform color but was never able to clothe its armies uniformly. Many soldiers wore no distinguishable uniform at all; the most common hue was "butternut," a dust-brown color produced by a dye made from butternut bark or walnut hulls.

Army Organization

The Union and Confederate armies were similar in organization. The basic unit was the regiment; the three combat arms were infantry, artillery, and cavalry. The infantry was the backbone of both armies. The Union raised during the war the equivalent of 2,047 regiments: 1,696 infantry; 272 cavalry; and 78 artillery. The number of regiments or equivalents in the Confederacy is unknown because of the loss or destruction of records, but estimates range from 764 to 1,000.

· Each of the ten companies in an infantry regiment had an official strength of eighty-two privates, thirteen sergeants and corporals, two lieutenants (some Confederate regiments had three), and a captain. The regiment itself was commanded by a colonel, with a lieutenent colonel and major as second and third in command plus a small regimental staff. Thus the official strength of an infantry regiment was about 1,000 men. When first enrolled, most regiments came close to this total. But sickness, casualties, and desertions soon reduced this number. By the second year of the war, the average combat strength of veteran regiments on both sides was less than 500; by the third and fourth years, 350 or less. Many regiments by 1863 went into battle with fewer than 200 men.

Instead of channeling new recruits into old regiments to keep them up to strength, states preferred to organize new regiments. There were two main reasons for this: (1) each new regiment offered the governor a chance for patronage through the appointment of field officers, and provided ambitious men with commissions they could not get if they joined an old regiment with its quota of officers already filled; (2) the geographical basis of regiments created an original relationship of identity and pride between the men at the front and the folks back home that would have been weakened if new recruits from elsewhere came into the regiment. Most localities eventually recruited some new men for "their" old regiments, but never enough to maintain anything near full strength. Of the 421,000 new three-year recruits for the Union army in the summer and fall of

1862, only 50,000 went into existing regiments. Commanding generals repeatedly denounced this inefficient and costly system. But it was the price that a democratic society paid to maintain a volunteer army of citizen soldiers. With the coming of conscription, draftees and substitutes could be assigned to old regiments. Because the Confederacy resorted to conscription earlier than the Union, it kept its regiments a little closer to full strength—but the difference was marginal.

Cavalry regiments were organized in the same fashion as the infantry, except that Union regiments had twelve instead of ten companies (called "troops" in the cavalry). The artillery was of two basic kinds: heavy artillery posted in permanent fortifications, and light or field artillery attached to mobile armies. Since the Confederates rarely attacked Union forts after the fall of Sumter, several Union "heavy" regiments were converted to infantry in the latter part of the war. The basic tactical unit of field artillery was the battery, composed of four to six guns with their caissons and four or six horses to pull each gun and caisson. The battery was commanded by a captain and was comparable in size to an infantry company. But unlike the latter, it was generally kept near full strength because of the need for enough men to fire the guns and manage the equipment.

Infantry and sometimes cavalry regiments were grouped into brigades commanded by a brigadier general. Initially composed of four regiments, brigades expanded to five or six later in the war, as the size of regiments decreased. Three or four brigades were grouped into divisions. The division commander was usually a major general. In the first year or so of the war, armies consisted of two or more divisions. But in 1862 both sides adopted the corps organization for larger armies. Composed of two or more divisions (usually three), an army corps was normally commanded by a lieutenant general in the Confederacy but by a major general in the Union (except for Grant in 1864–1865, the North had no higher rank than major general). Artillery batteries were grouped with brigades, divisions, or corps as the tactical situation required.

There was one interesting difference between the Union and Confederate armies. The Union government supplied the horses for its cavalry and artillery. The South expected men in these branches to provide their own horses. This tended to create class distinctions in the Confederate army, especially between the cavalry and infantry, since not every man could afford a cavalry mount. To a degree, the Confederacy preserved the medieval tradition of the cavalry ("chevaliers" or knights) as the preserve of the aristocracy. The actual practice was more egalitarian, however, especially in the western Confederate armies, where if a man did not own a horse he had a good chance of stealing one or capturing it from the enemy. Nathan Bedford Forrest's troopers scarcely fit one's idea of an aristocracy. Horse-stealing expeditions were an important cavalry function, which Forrest's men elevated to a fine art.

Leadership and Training

In most respects the Confederate army was fully as democratic as its enemy, perhaps more so. Johnny Reb also elected his company officers, and sometimes his regimental officers too. Professional army men in both North and South

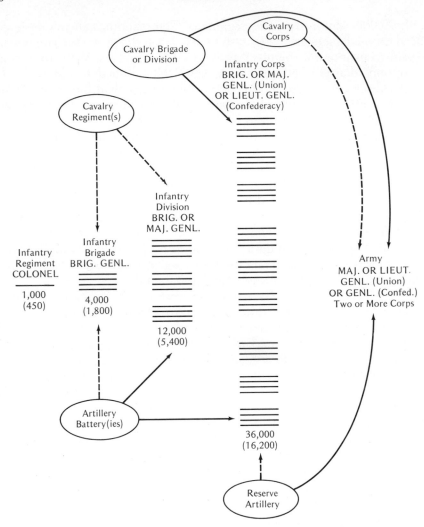

Normal commanding officer of each unit appears in capital letters. Numbers below each unit indicate full quota of men; numbers in parentheses indicate typical size of combat units by second year of war. (By the last two years of the war, brigades often contained five or six regiments; divisions sometimes contained four brigades; and corps sometimes contained four divisions.) Arrows indicate attachment of artillery and cavalry to infantry units; broken arrows indicate occasional attachments to these units. Cavalry often operated independently of infantry units.

Figure 11.1   ORGANIZATION OF UNION AND CONFEDERATE ARMIES

deplored this practice. But in a volunteer army whose privates were accustomed to electing their governors, congressmen, and presidents, the logic of electing their army leaders seemed unassailable. As Jefferson Davis put it, "the troops were drawn from civil life. . . . Who so capable to judge the fitness to command a company, a battalion or a regiment as the men composing it?" It was part of the American creed that any intelligent citizen could learn the skills of statesman or soldier. Most civilians believed that the average lawyer or businessman could "give an average army officer all the advantage of his special training, at the start, and yet beat him at his own trade in a year."[4]

One can readily imagine the impact of this system on discipline. Privates tended at first to obey only those orders they considered reasonable. Men who regarded themselves as equals of their neighbors at home were slow to change their minds just because the neighbor now wore shoulder straps. Officers were reluctant to enforce discipline if it meant that they might be voted out of their commission or might lose the election for county attorney after the war. All too often, officers deserved the contempt of their men. Many officers knew little or nothing about training or commanding soldiers. "Col. Roberts has showed himself to be ignorant of the most simple company movements," wrote a Pennsylvania soldier in 1861. "There is a total lack of system about our regiment. . . . We can only be justly called a mob & one not fit to face the enemy." But the enemy was in no better shape, if one is to believe Confederate professionals. General Joseph E. Johnston, commanding the Southern garrison at Harper's Ferry, complained in June 1861 that his officers and men were so lacking in "discipline and instruction" that it would be "difficult to use them in the field." Of one regiment Johnston said: "I would not give one company of regulars for the whole regiment."[5]

Recognizing the need for minimum standards of officer competence, the Union army in July 1861 instituted an examination for officers. Those who failed were to be replaced by others who had passed. Although this examination did not end the election of officers in new regiments, it did something toward ensuring that those elected met certain standards. Promotion within the ranks of old regiments was generally earned by merit, not election, though the continuing role of state governors in the appointment of officers meant that politics would never be absent from the process. By 1863 the Union army had virtually ended the practice of electing officers. The Confederates were slower to give it up. Although the South established officer examinations in October 1862, not until the war was almost over did the Confederate Congress abolish the practice of allowing companies to elect their officers.

Nevertheless, Confederate officers were probably of higher caliber than their Union counterparts during the first year or two of the war. The South's military tradition and its large number of graduates from such academies as Virginia Military Institute provided a reservoir of trained leaders. Half of the officers in Virginia regiments in 1861 were VMI graduates; 1,702 of the 1,902 men who had ever attended VMI served in the Confederate army. Almost the same could be said of graduates of military academies in other Southern states. The North could not match this; most company and regimental officers for the Union had to learn their work on the job.

The 313 officers who resigned from the regular U.S. army in 1861 to fight for the South also gave Confederate armies a core of professional leadership. Of course the other 767 regular army officers stayed with the Union. But because of a policy decision by General Winfield Scott, most of them remained in the regular army instead of being dispersed among the volunteer regiments to provide a cadre of professional instructors and officers. Scott wanted to preserve the tactical existence of the only force he considered wholly reliable—the regulars—as a model for the volunteer army rather than as leaders of it. Eventually several hundred regular army officers were allowed to join the volunteer forces, but many others went through the war as captains or lieutenants in the tiny regular army while volunteer regiments blundered along under colonels from civilian life. The South got a big jump on the North in utilizing trained officers to leaven its volunteer armies.

The majority of generals on both sides came from civilian life. Of the 583 men who attained the rank of general in the Union army, only 194 (33 percent) were in the regular army when the war began. Another 70 (14 percent) had attended West Point or other military schools. In the Confederacy, 125 (29 percent) of the 425 generals came from the regular army, and another 69 (16 percent) had attended military academies, including West Point.

The nonprofessionals in both armies can be divided into two groups: the "political generals," who were appointed because of their influence and connections; and a larger group of "civilian generals," who started at lower ranks and achieved promotion largely through merit. The political generals acquired a reputation—partly deserved—for military incompetence. Although the South had its share of such men—one thinks of John Floyd, Gideon Pillow, Henry Wise, and Robert Toombs—the phrase "political general" usually referred to Northerners such as Benjamin Butler, Nathaniel Banks, John McClernand, Francis Blair, Jr., and others. Powerful political figures, several of them prewar Democrats, they were appointed in order to attract various Northern constituencies to support of the war. Some of them received their commissions as rewards for raising large numbers of volunteers. Others obtained appointment because of sponsorship by important governors or congressmen. Some were leaders of ethnic groups: Franz Sigel and Carl Schurz, for example, received commissions because of their prominence in the German-American community, while Thomas Meagher, commander of the "Irish Brigade," helped to rally his countrymen for the cause.

Political generals formed the counterpart at the command level of elected officers at the company level—both were necessary in the citizen armies of a democratic society. Professional soldiers did not like this situation but reluctantly accepted the necessity. "It seems but little better than murder to give important commands to such men as Banks, Butler, McClernand, Sigel and Lew Wallace," sighed General Halleck after he became chief of staff, "yet it seems impossible to prevent it."[6] And the system of political patronage produced good as well as evil. Grant's initial appointment as brigadier general came through the influence of his friend Elihu Washburne, a congressman from Illinois. Sherman's appointment to the same rank was aided by political connections that included his brother John, senator from Ohio. Some of the most political of generals developed into first-class soldiers, while many West Pointers proved to be spectacular failures. And in any case, professionals held most of the top commands: in fifty-five of the sixty largest battles, West Pointers exercised overall strategic command of both armies; in the other five, a professional commanded one of the two armies. In both

North and South, some politicians and army nonprofessionals complained that the "West Point clique" formed a closed corporation that denied promotions to able outsiders.

During the first year of war, most officers and men alike were raw recruits. By the standards of European armies the American levies were little more than armed mobs. Officers had to teach themselves before they could train their men. Civil War literature abounds with stories of colonels and captains burning the midnight oil studying manuals on drill and tactics to stay one step ahead of their men. This practice went right to the top in the North, for Abraham Lincoln read numerous books on strategy in an effort to learn his job as Commander in Chief. Eventually these American volunteer armies became tough, battle-wise veterans—perhaps equal to any European army in military skills and superior in motivation, for as citizens and voters (most of them), with higher levels of literacy than any previous armies in history, they had a better idea of what they were fighting for.

The egalitarian ethos of these citizen armies also meant that officers must be leaders rather than merely commanders. Although the Civil War had its share of rear-echelon commanders, the successful officers led their men from the front, not the rear. Battle casualties were proportionately higher among officers than among enlisted men in both armies. Eighteen percent of all Confederate generals were killed in action, compared with 12 percent for the Confederate army as a whole. Eight percent of the Union generals suffered battle deaths, compared with 5½ percent for the entire army.

THE NAVIES AND THE BLOCKADE

The Confederate Navy

If the Confederate army was better prepared than its enemy at the outset, the reverse was true of the navies. Indeed, the Confederacy scarcely had a navy. Of the U.S. navy's 1,457 officers and 7,600 seamen in 1861, only 259 officers and a handful of men defected to the Confederacy. Southerners were a martial but not a maritime people. The main shipbuilding facilities were in the North; the merchant marine was Northern-owned; most of the merchant seamen were Yankees. Under the circumstances, Confederate Secretary of the Navy Stephen Mallory did a remarkable job in creating a navy from scratch. The South built or acquired more than 130 vessels during the conflict, most of them small craft mounting only one or a few guns. But by the end of the war, 37 armored warships had been built or were under construction. Several of these were "rams," with heavy iron prows designed to ram and sink enemy ships. Such was the South's lack of industrial facilities, however, that not a single machine shop in the Confederacy was capable of building an engine large enough to power these ships adequately, and most of the rams never saw action.

But the Confederacy did contribute several technological innovations to naval warfare. The rebuilding of the captured *Merrimack* as the first ironclad warship to see combat action is well known. The South also developed various naval mines

Confederate Ironclad Ram *Atlanta*. The *Atlanta* was typical of
armored Confederate ships, with an iron prow below the waterline to
rip holes in Union wooden warships. This picture was taken after the
Atlanta's capture on the Savannah River; the men posing on deck are
Union sailors. *(Reproduced from the Collections of the Library of Congress)*

(which were called "torpedoes"), which sank or damaged forty-three Union warships. The Confederates built several "torpedo boats," small half-submersed cigar-
shaped vessels carrying a contact mine on a spar extending in front of the bow.
The South also built the world's first combat submarine, the *C.S.S. Hunley,* which
sank to the bottom with loss of its crew three times in trials before torpedoing
a Union blockade ship off Charleston on February 17, 1864, sending both the
blockader and the *Hunley* to the bottom.

The most spectacular activity of the Confederate navy was commerce raiding.
At first this ancient form of official piracy was carried out by privateers (privately
owned ships commissioned by a belligerent government to capture enemy merchant ships). On April 17, 1861, Jefferson Davis offered letters of marque to any
ships that wished to prey upon Yankee commerce. Numerous privateers were soon
darting out of coves along the Southern coast to snatch unarmed merchantmen.

Refusing to recognize the Confederacy as a legitimate government, Lincoln
retaliated with a proclamation stating that captured privateer crews would be
hanged as pirates. Davis came right back with a declaration that for every man
so executed, a Union prisoner of war would be similarly treated. By the fall of 1861
several captured privateer crews languished in Northern jails awaiting trial. Although judges and juries showed a reluctance to convict, the crew of the *Jeff Davis,*
most notorious of the privateers, was convicted and sentenced to death in Phila-

delphia. True to his word, Davis had lots drawn among Union POWs, and the losers—including a grandson of Paul Revere—were readied for hanging if the Philadelphia sentence was carried out. Lincoln hesitated and finally backed down. He announced on February 3, 1862, that privateer crews would be treated as prisoners of war.

But by this time the Union blockade and the refusal of neutral ports to admit prizes taken by privateers had put an end to privateering. Commerce raiding was taken over by Confederate naval cruisers, which unlike privateers usually destroyed their prizes instead of selling them. Sleek, fast, and heavily armed, twenty such Rebel cruisers roamed the seas searching out Yankee merchantmen. Several of these cruisers were built in Britain. The most famous was the *Alabama*, built at Liverpool and manned mostly by British sailors. Its captain was Raphael Semmes, an Alabamian who resigned from the U.S. navy to become the Confederacy's premier maritime hero. From September 1862 until sunk by the *U.S.S. Kearsarge* off Cherbourg, France, on June 19, 1864, the *Alabama* destroyed at least sixty-two merchant vessels and one ship of the U.S. navy. Other famous raiders were the *Sumter,* the *Florida,* and the *Shenandoah.* Their exploits crippled the U.S. merchant marine, which never recovered. The raiders destroyed 257 merchant ships and whalers, caused the transfer of at least 700 others to foreign flags, and forced most of the rest to remain in port. These were impressive achievements for a handful of ships, but they had a negligible impact on the outcome of the war.

The Union Navy

The Confederate navy was unable to challenge the enemy where it mattered most —on the coasts and rivers of the South. Union naval power was a decisive factor in the war. Although few ships were available for immediate service at the outset, Secretary of the Navy Gideon Welles and his dynamic Assistant Secretary, Gustavus V. Fox, both New Englanders, quickly chartered or purchased civilian vessels for conversion to warships and began contracting for the construction of new vessels. By the last year of the war, the 42 warships of 1861 had grown into the world's largest navy—a powerful fleet of 671 ships of all types, from shallow-draft river gunboats to ironclad monitors. These ships maintained a blockade of 3,500 miles of coastline, forced the surrender of Confederate ports from Norfolk to New Orleans, penetrated the South's river system into the heart of the Confederacy, and protected the huge fleet of Union coastal and river supply vessels. The joint army-navy operations on Southern rivers (to be described in later chapters) that played such a decisive role in the western theater contributed a major tactical innovation to warfare. Indeed, the navy's contribution to Northern victory was far out of proportion to its numbers. About 100,000 men served in the Union navy, only 5 percent of the number in the army.

The Union navy was more professional than the army. Few civilians sought commissions afloat as political plums. Even those Americans who believed that anyone could learn the art of war on land admitted that the sea demanded more specialized skills. The navy immediately established an officers' examination board and during 1861 appointed a thousand new officers, drawn mostly from the merchant marine. Seamen were recruited from the same source. Unlike volunteer soldiers, they already knew their trade, except for gunnery. In June 1861, Welles appointed a naval strategy board, something the army never did.

The Blockade

The navy's chief task was the blockade. On April 19, Lincoln proclaimed a blockade of Confederate ports. Since international law recognized a blockade as a weapon of war between sovereign powers, this in effect granted the Confederacy the belligerent status that Lincoln simultaneously tried to deny it in his stated intention to treat privateers as pirates. The Union blockade was never wholly effective, though it became increasingly so with each month of the war. The task of patrolling all of the 189 harbors and coves in the South where cargo could be landed was impossible. But on May 1, eleven days after the declaration of blockade, the navy captured its first blockade runner. Within another three weeks all major Southern ports were under surveillance. By the end of 1864 there were 471 ships on blockade duty.

The Confederacy's need for European arms and materiel, Europe's need for Southern cotton, and the profits to be made by carrying these items through the blockade created a bonanza business for blockade runners. Some of these were old, slow cargo ships that succeeded only because of the blockade's looseness in the first year of war. As the blockade tightened, the risks increased—but so did the profits. Fast, sleek steamers were built in Britain especially for blockade running. Painted gray for low visibility and burning almost smokeless anthracite—and designed with low freeboards, shallow drafts, and raked smokestacks that could be telescoped almost to deck level—these ships repeatedly evaded Yankee blockaders to slip in and out of Southern harbors in the dark of the moon. Nassau, Bermuda, and Havana became the chief ports from which the blockade runners operated. Wilmington was their main port of entry. The numerous inlets and shoals at the mouth of the Cape Fear River below Wilmington made it the hardest Confederate port for the Union navy to patrol.

Private individuals owned most of the blockade runners; but as the war went on, the state governments and the Confederate government itself acquired an increasing number. The secretary of war tried to require privately owned runners to reserve at least one-third of their cargo space at reasonable rates for military freight. But the highest profits could be made on such items as silks, liquor, and other consumer goods, and many runners carried these in preference to arms or shoes or bacon for the army. Finally, in February 1864, the Confederate government prohibited the importation of luxury goods and required all runners to allot at least half their space to the government at fixed rates.

In July 1861, the Union navy's strategy board made a decision of far-reaching consequences. The naval bases for blockade squadrons at Hampton Roads and Key West were 600 miles or more from such enemy ports as Charleston, Savannah, and New Orleans. This meant that blockade ships spent as much time returning to their bases for coal, supplies, and repairs as they did on blockade duty. Moreover, the navy could not patrol every inlet from which blockade runners and privateers operated. Thus the strategy board planned to seize several inlets and harbors along the Southern coast to close them to blockade runners and to establish additional bases for the blockade fleet.

The first joint army-navy expedition for this purpose arrived off storm-swept Cape Hatteras August 27 with seven ships and 900 soldiers under Benjamin Butler. The fleet shelled the two forts guarding Hatteras Inlet into submission. Butler's troops occupied the forts, and the Yankees henceforth controlled the channel through which at least 100 blockade runners had passed in the previous six weeks. Two weeks later the navy seized without opposition Ship Island off Biloxi, Mississippi, and established there a base for blockade patrol of the Gulf ports.

The finest natural harbor on the Southern coast was Port Royal, South Carolina, midway between Charleston and Savannah. Port Royal was the Union navy's first choice as a base for the South Atlantic blockade fleet. Preparations for an army-navy expedition to capture it went forward in secrecy during the fall of 1861. Flag Officer (later Rear Admiral) Samuel Du Pont commanded the fleet of fourteen warships, twenty-six collier and supply vessels, and twenty-five transports to carry 12,000 soldiers and marines. Although a gale off Hatteras wrecked or crippled several transports, the remainder of the fleet arrived intact off Port Royal Sound in early November. Two forts mounting forty-three heavy guns guarded the sound, but Du Pont's warships carried more than 120 guns. Steaming between the forts in a long oval pattern on November 7, the fleet pounded them at a rate of two dozen shells per minute. Confederate General Thomas Drayton (brother of Commander Percival Drayton of the *U.S.S. Pocahantas,* one of the attacking warships) decided to abandon the ruined forts. The army and marines took possession of Port Royal and the entire string of coastal islands from Savannah almost to Charleston. The Southern white population fled to the mainland, leaving behind 10,000 slaves and hundreds of rich long-staple cotton plantations.

The Port Royal attack was a success far beyond Union expectations. Unprepared to follow it up with an invasion inland, the army consolidated its control of the islands while the navy built up a huge base. During the next few months, amphibious expeditions seized coastal points as far south as St. Augustine. Army artillery operating from an island off the coast bombarded and captured Savannah's Fort Pulaski in April, closing the harbor to blockade runners.

Nor did North Carolina escape further incursions of the blue tide. General Ambrose E. Burnside, a Rhode Islander with mutton-chop whiskers, organized a division of New Englanders accustomed to working around water and boats. In January 1862, Burnside's 11,500 men accompanied by a naval flotilla of shallow-draft gunboats, tugs, transports, and barges crossed the shoals at Hatteras Inlet and steamed up Pamlico Sound to Roanoke Island. This island controlled the channels between the Pamlico and Albemarle sounds and therefore the river outlets of every North Carolina port except Wilmington. The Confederates had fortified the island, but their 2,500 troops were hopelessly outmatched. In an amphibious attack on February 7–8, steamers towed long strings of surfboats crammed with soldiers to the shallows while gunboats stood by to cover their landing. Burnside's men poured onto the beach, fanned out, and smashed through the Rebel trenches. They took the forts in the rear while the gunboats punched through the channel obstructions in their front. It was a well-executed operation that netted 2,675 Confederate prisoners at a cost of 278 Union casualties. During the next several weeks, the bluecoats occupied mainland North Carolina ports for 150 miles up and down North Carolina's sounds.

The Monitor *and the* Merrimack

For Confederates, the news from the coast was nothing but bad all through the fall and winter of 1861–1862. But they were counting on a powerful new weapon to turn the tide. Since their seizure of the Norfolk navy yard in April 1861, the Confederates had been rebuilding the captured *Merrimack* as an ironclad ram. Work went forward slowly because of shortages, but by winter the heavily armored ship was nearing completion. She was not the world's first ironclad. The French had used iron-sheathed "floating batteries" in the Crimean War, and in 1861 the French navy had one iron ship and the British two. The Union navy in October 1861 contracted with the Swedish-born inventor John Ericsson for an entirely new type of ironclad, the *Monitor*. With a hull low on the waterline and a revolving turret mounting two guns, she looked like "a tin can on a shingle." The *Monitor* was completed in New York about the time the *Merrimack* (rechristened *Virginia*) was getting ready to sally forth from Norfolk against the Federal blockade ships at Hampton Roads.

On March 8, 1862, the *Virginia* attacked. Before dark she had destroyed two

Union Sailors on the *Monitor*. Sailors relaxing on board after their fight with the *C.S.S. Virginia*. Note the dents in the turret below the gunport, caused by the *Virginia*'s cannonballs. *(Reproduced from the Collections of the Library of Congress)*

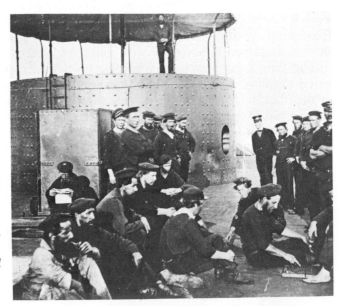

ships and run three others aground, to be finished off on the morrow. Shots from Union ships had bounced harmlessly off her armor. Panic seized Washington. But that evening the *Monitor* arrived at Hampton Roads and next morning engaged the *Virginia* in history's first combat between ironclad ships. After more than three hours of close-in fighting, in which each vessel sustained more than two dozen direct hits without suffering crippling damage, the exhausted crews broke off the duel. The *Virginia*'s threat to the Union blockade was neutralized. Though the engagement was a draw, the *Monitor* proved herself the superior ship. She was faster and more maneuverable because of a shallower draft (eleven feet as against the *Virginia*'s twenty-two); her low hull presented two-thirds less target area; and her two-gun revolving turret generated as much firepower in a given direction as the *Virginia*'s ten lighter guns. The *Virginia* had to be scuttled when Norfolk fell to the Federals in May 1862 because she was too unseaworthy to escape to open water and too deep-drafted to go up the James River. But the *Monitor* became the prototype for fifty-eight ironclad warships built or begun by the Union during the war. The Confederacy's major salt-water challenge to the Union navy had failed.

Results of the Blockade

The effectiveness of the Union blockade was hotly argued during the Civil War —and has been debated ever since. The Confederate secretary of state insisted that it was a "paper blockade" undeserving of recognition under international law. In support, several historians have cited figures or estimates showing that the South exported at least a million bales of cotton and imported 600,000 rifles, half a million pairs of shoes, and so on. In 1861 at least nine out of ten blockade runners were getting through. By 1865, the Union navy had cut this to one out of two. But for the war as a whole there were an estimated 8,500 successful trips through the blockade, while the Union navy captured or destroyed only 1,500 blockade runners. Thus, it is argued, the blockade was ineffective.[7]

But these figures can sustain an opposite interpretation. The important fact is not how many blockade runners got through, but how much cargo would have got through had there been no blockade. The million bales of cotton exported during the last three years of the war (after the voluntary Confederate cotton embargo of 1861 discussed on p. 217) contrasted with more than ten million exported in the three years prior to the war. Twenty thousand ships entered and cleared Southern harbors in the four antebellum years, most of them with much greater cargo capacity than the 8,500 blockade runners of the war years. Many blockade runners had to jettison part of their cargoes to increase speed when pursued. The blockade cut the South's seaborne trade to less than a third of normal. And war times were not normal because, lacking an industrial base, the South needed to import large quantities of materiel for its war effort. Although of minor military importance at first, the blockade in the end played a large part in the outcome of the war.

Twelve

The Balance Sheet of War

The American Civil War is often described as the first "modern" war. What this means is not always clear, for every war is more modern than the previous one. In any case, many firsts are associated with the Civil War: the first extensive use of the railroad and telegraph for military purposes, the first combat between iron-plated warships, a much greater use of rifled field artillery and of rifled small arms than ever before, the first use of repeating rifles, the experimental development of crude machine guns, the first combat use of a submarine, trench warfare on a scale that anticipated World War I, the first considerable use of airborne (balloon) observation, the first general conscription in American history, and the first extensive application of the "American system" of mass production to the manufacture of military goods.

But in many respects the Civil War was more traditional than modern—that is, it more closely resembled the Napoleonic Wars of fifty years earlier than World War I a half-century later. Despite railroads and steamboats, the armies still depended on animal-powered transport for field supply. Campaigning slowed or halted during the winter and during heavy rains because of what Napoleon had once called the "fifth element" in war—mud. Despite advances in repeating arms and in rifling, most infantrymen carried muzzleloaders, and during the war's first year most of these were smoothbores. The cavalry was still an important military arm. The modern concept of substituting firepower for men was yet in its infancy. Weapons and machines counted for much in this war—but men and horses still counted for more.

MANPOWER AND RESOURCES

In 1861 the Union states had nearly three and a half times as many white men of military age as had the Confederacy. Of course the slaves were a military asset to the South, for they could do the home-front tasks done by free men in the North and thus release an equivalent number of whites for army service. On the other hand, the North also drew on former slaves for military labor and eventually enlisted more than 150,000 of them in its armed forces. Altogether an estimated 2,100,000 men fought for the Union and 800,000 for the Confederacy (the exact number is not known because the Union records enumerate the number of enlistments, which must be adjusted to avoid the double counting of men who reenlisted, and many Confederate records were destroyed). Just over half the men of military age in the North served in the army or navy; close to four-fifths of the white men in the South did so, a *levée en masse* made possible only by the existence of slavery.

Confederate Conscription

Ironically the South, which went to war to protect individual and states' rights against centralized government, was compelled to enact military conscription a year earlier than the North. By the fall of 1861 the romantic enthusiasm that had stimulated volunteering in the early months was wearing off. "I have seen quite enough of A Soldier's life," wrote one Johnny Reb to his family, "to satisfy me that it is not what it is cracked up to be." A Confederate general wrote from the Virginia front on October 20: "The first flush of patriotism led many a man to join who now regrets it. The prospect of winter here is making the men very restless and they are beginning to resort to all sorts of means to get home."[1] More than half the Confederate soldiers on the rolls were one-year volunteers who had enlisted in the spring of 1861 (the rest were three-year men). Faced with the prospect of a large part of their armies melting away just as the Yankees launched their spring offensives in 1862, the Confederate Congress in December passed an act offering to all one-year men who would reenlist a $50 bounty, one month's furlough, and the opportunity to join new regiments with new elected officers if the reenlistees did not like their old ones. But this failed to produce enough reenlistments. In March 1862 Robert E. Lee, then serving as Jefferson Davis's military adviser, urged passage of a national conscription law as the only way to avert disaster.

The Confederate Congress complied in April with legislation making able-bodied white males (including those whose enlistments were expiring) aged eighteen to thirty-five liable to conscription for three years' service. The law exempted persons in several war-production occupations plus militia officers, civil servants, clergymen, and teachers. The last-named exemption proved full of mischief, for many new schools suddenly sprang up in excess of any apparent demand for them. A supplemental conscription law passed in October 1862 exempted one white man on any plantation with twenty or more slaves. The Confederacy also allowed drafted men to hire substitutes to serve in their stead. A practice with roots in both the European and American past (state militia drafts during the Revolution had permitted substitutes), substitution was intended to ameliorate the coerciveness of conscription. But it favored those rich enough to afford substitutes. By 1863 the going price for substitutes had risen to $6,000 in Confederate currency (about $300 in gold). Along with the "20-Negro law," substitution produced the bitter saying that it was "a rich man's war but a poor man's fight."

As Confederate manpower needs became more desperate, the conscription law was strengthened. Congress raised the upper age limit to forty-five in September 1862 and fifty (with the lower limit reduced from eighteen to seventeen) in February 1864. The substitute clause was repealed in December 1863, and men who had previously furnished substitutes became eligible for the draft. The exempt categories were trimmed (though the controversial 20-Negro provision was retained in modified form). The new conscription act of February 1864 required all men then in the army to stay in, thus making sure that the three-year men of 1861 would not go home when their enlistments expired.

So unpopular was conscription that it was impossible to enforce in some parts of the South, especially in the upcountry and mountain regions. In non-slaveholding areas the "rich man's war" theme was particularly strong. "All they want," said an Alabama hill farmer, "is to get you pupt up and go to fight for their infurnal negroes and after you do there fighting you may kiss there hine parts for o they care."[2] Draft evaders and deserters in some upcountry regions formed armed bands, killed several draft officials, and resisted all Confederate authority.

Several of the South's leading politicians also denounced the draft as being contrary to the goals the Confederacy was fighting for. "No act of the Government of the United States prior to the secession of Georgia," said that state's pugnacious Governor Joseph E. Brown, "struck a blow at constitutional liberty so fell as has been stricken by this conscription act." Brown did everything he could to frustrate the draft. He appointed large numbers of Georgians to the exempt positions of civil servant and militia officer. The state militia became so top-heavy with officers that a disgusted Confederate general described a typical militia company as containing "3 field officers, 4 staff officers, 10 captains, 30 lieutenants, and 1 private with a misery in his bowels."[3] Other governors, particularly Zebulon Vance of North Carolina, also resisted the draft on libertarian and states' rights grounds. Their opposition became part of a larger conflict between states' rights and centralization that hampered the Confederate war effort.

But despite opposition, despite inefficiency and fraud in its enforcement, conscription did produce men for the Confederate armies. Without the draft the South could scarcely have carried the war past 1862, for in addition to bringing new men into the army it kept the veterans from leaving. A total of perhaps 120,000 draftees served in the Confederate army, while an estimated 70,000 men provided substitutes. How many of the latter actually served in the ranks is a moot question, since many substitute papers were fraudulent. In any event, perhaps 20 percent of the Confederate soldiers were draftees and substitutes, compared with

8 percent of the Union army.* The compulsory reenlistment of volunteers in the South meant that every Confederate soldier served for the duration unless killed or discharged because of wounds or disease. In the Union, by contrast, men whose terms expired could not be drafted or compelled to reenlist. Thus while the total number of men who fought for the Union was two and a half times greater than those who fought for the Confederacy, the difference in the number of veterans in the ranks at any given time was much smaller. Since one veteran was believed to be worth at least two recruits, the Confederacy's inferiority in manpower was less than it appeared to be.

In resources necessary to wage war, however, the South was at an even greater disadvantage than in manpower. The North possessed close to 90 percent of the nation's industrial capacity. In certain industries vital to military production, Union superiority was even more decisive. According to the 1860 census, the North had eleven times as many ships and boats as the South, produced fifteen times as much iron, seventeen times as many textile goods, twenty-four times as many locomotives, and thirty-two times as many firearms (though an important market for the last had always been the South). In food production, the Northern superiority was little better than two to one (or about the same per capita as the South). But the Union had more than twice the density of railroad mileage per square mile and several times the amount of rolling stock. The South's inferiority in railroads, intensified by a lack of replacement capacity, produced transportation bottlenecks that created frequent shortages of food and supplies at the front. The North's advantage in horses and mules was less than two to one, but many of the Confederacy's animals were in portions of the upper South soon overrun by Union armies.

CONFEDERATE ADVANTAGES

With all these disadvantages, how could Southerners expect to win? "Something more than numbers make armies," wrote a Confederate journalist. "Against the vast superiority of the North in material resources," he insisted, the South had "a set-off in certain advantages."[4]

War Aims and Morale

The most important advantage stemmed from the contrasting war aims of the two sides. To "win," the Confederates did not need to invade the North or to destroy its armies; they needed only to stand on the defensive and to prevent the North from destroying Southern armies. Southerners looked for inspiration to the American Revolution, when Britain's relative material superiority was even greater than the North's in 1861. They also looked to other successful revolutions by small countries. All the power of Spain under Philip II could not stamp out rebellion in the Netherlands. The legions of Austria marched in vain against tiny Switzer-

*For a discussion of the Union draft, see pp. 355–57

land. Like those liberty-loving rebels, said Jefferson Davis in his first war message to the Confederate Congress April 26, 1861, "we seek no conquest, no aggrandizement, no concession of any kind from the States with which we were late confederated; all we ask is to be let alone."[5]

To win the war, the North had to invade, conquer, and destroy the South's capacity and will to resist. Invasion and conquest are logistically far more difficult than defense of one's territory. Recalling their own army's experience in 1776, British military experts in 1861 agreed that a country as large as the Confederacy could not be conquered. "It is one thing to drive the rebels from the south bank of the Potomac, or even to occupy Richmond," observed the London *Times* early in the war, "but another to reduce and hold in permanent subjection a tract of country nearly as large as Russia in Europe. . . . No war of independence ever terminated unsuccessfully except where the disparity of force was far greater than it is in this case. . . . Just as England during the revolution had to give up conquering the colonies so the North will have to give up conquering the South."[6]

The intangible but vital factor of morale favored an army fighting in defense of its homeland. "We shall have the enormous advantage of fighting on our own territory and for our very existence," wrote Confederate leaders. "All the world over are not one million of men defending themselves at home against invasion, stronger in a mere military point of view, than five millions [invading] a foreign country?"[7] When the Confederates became the invaders, this morale advantage went over to the Yankees. On the first day of the battle of Gettysburg a Union officer wrote: "Our men are three times as Enthusiastic as they have been in Virginia. The idea that Pennsylvania is invaded and that we are fighting on our own soil proper, influences them strongly." On the Confederate retreat to Virginia after Gettysburg, one of Lee's staff officers said that "our men, it must be confessed, are far better satisfied when operating on this [south] side of the Potomac. . . . They are not accustomed to operating in a country where the people are inimical to them, and certainly every one of them is today worth twice as much as he was three days ago."[8]

Geography and Logistics

One of the South's important military advantages was geography. The Confederacy covered a large territory—750,000 square miles—twice as large as the thirteen colonies in 1776. The topography in the eastern part of the Confederacy favored the defense against invasion. The Appalachian chain was a formidable barrier that resisted penetration until Sherman's invasion of Georgia in 1864. The Shenandoah Valley of Virginia formed a natural route of invasion, but this favored the Confederacy rather than the Union because it ran southwest, away from Richmond and the main battle theater in Virginia. Indeed, the Confederacy used the valley three times for invasions or threats against the North (Jackson in 1862, Lee in his Gettysburg campaign in 1863, and Jubal Early in 1864), for in that direction the valley pointed toward important Northern cities, including Washington itself. Much of the South was heavily wooded, providing cover for armies operating on

The photo above shows the result of a Rebel raid on a Union rail supply line in Virginia. Yankee repair crews have already relaid the ripped-up tracks but have not yet cleared away the overturned locomotive and cars. The photo on the right shows a Union-rebuilt railroad bridge over Potomac Creek in Virginia. President Lincoln admired the proficiency of the army engineer corps in constructing trestles out of what appeared to be "nothing but bean-poles and corn-stalks."

(Reproduced from the Collections of the Library of Congress)

(Reproduced from the Collections of the Library of Congress)

the defensive. Between Washington and Richmond, six rivers and numerous streams ran from west to east, each of them a line of defense. In the western portion of the Confederacy, by contrast, the river system favored an invading force. The Cumberland and Tennessee rivers were highways of invasion into Tennessee, northern Mississippi, and northern Alabama, while the Mississippi River was an arrow thrust into the heart of the lower South.

But away from the rivers an invading force was dependent on railroads or roads, and railroads were especially vulnerable to guerrillas and cavalry, who developed the destruction of trackage, bridges, and rolling stock into a fine art. The Union engineer corps became equally adept at repairing the damage (a Yankee construction battalion once built an 800-foot bridge containing 400,000 board feet of lumber in four and a half days from trees to trestle), but Northern military movements were repeatedly delayed or stopped by the destruction of supply lines in their rear. In this way, a few hundred guerrillas or cavalry could neutralize an entire army and force it to detach thousands of men to guard its communications.

Once an army moved away from its railhead or river-landing supply base, its marching men, artillery, and supply wagons had to move by road. Union armies campaigning in the South averaged one wagon for every forty men and one horse or mule for every two or three men. An invading army of 100,000 men would thus be encumbered with 2,500 wagons and at least 35,000 animals and would consume 600 tons or more of supplies each day. The South's wretched roads became an important Confederate military asset. Most of them were dirt tracks without ditches or anything else to prevent them from becoming impassable in wet weather. Wagons and artillery often sank to the axles, especially in Virginia, where the red clay soil formed a mud with the character almost of quicksand. Civil War literature is full of mud stories. A Union officer in the Virginia peninsula campaign of 1862 insisted that he saw an army mule sink out of sight except for its ears—though he admitted that "it was a small mule."

Of course the roads were as bad for the Rebels as for the Yankees. But an army operating in its own territory is closer to its base and needs fewer wagons because it can gather much of its food and forage from the friendly countryside. Then, too, Johnny Reb traveled lighter than Billy Yank. Carrying his few necessities in a blanket roll rather than a knapsack, getting along without a shelter tent, subsisting on less food, the Confederate infantryman usually marched with thirty to forty pounds of equipment including rifle and ammunition. The fully equipped Union soldier carried about fifty pounds. The very abundance of Northern war production encouraged some Union generals to requisition so lavishly that their troops became bogged down in their own supplies. "This expanding, and piling up of *impedimenta*," an exasperated Lincoln told one general, "has been, so far, almost our ruin." Not until 1864 did some Northern commanders learn the dictum expressed two years earlier by Confederate General Richard Ewell: "The road to glory cannot be followed with much baggage."[9]

The deeper the Union army penetrated into enemy territory, the longer became its supply lines and the greater became the necessity to detach troops to guard these lines. By the time Sherman reached Atlanta in 1864 only half of his total forces were at the front; the rest were strung out along his 470-mile rail lifeline back through Chattanooga and Nashville to Louisville. As an invading power, the Union army also had to assign large numbers of troops to occupation duties.

For these reasons, scarcely half of the 611,000 men present for duty in the Union armies at the beginning of 1864 were available for front-line combat service, while probably three-fourths of the Confederate total of 278,000 were so available. Thus the usual Southern explanation for defeat ("They never whipped us, Sir, unless they were four to one. If we had anything like a fair chance, or less disparity of numbers, we should have won our cause and established our independence"[10]) requires some modification. Indeed, one writer has maintained that in the war's fifty main battles, the number of Union combat soldiers averaged only 2 percent more than the enemy.[11] This probably understates Union numerical superiority. A calculation based on the sixty battles listed in the best statistical study of the subject shows that the Union armies averaged 37 percent more men than the Confederates.[12] But even this was a far cry from the "overwhelming numbers" portrayed in much Civil War historiography.

Other advantages accruing to the Confederacy from fighting on the defensive were interior lines of communication, better knowledge of topography and roads, and a superior intelligence network. The term "interior lines" means simply that armies fighting within a defensive arc can shift troops from one point to another over shorter distances than invading armies operating outside the perimeter of the arc. Several instances of this occurred in the Virginia theater. Most notable was Lee's transfer of his army from the peninsula to the Rappahannock in July–August 1862, a distance of about seventy-five miles, while the Union Army of the Potomac had to travel three times as far, partly by water. Some of these Union troops arrived too late to participate in the second battle of Bull Run.

The South was laced with obscure country roads not marked on any map. Only local knowledge could guide troops along these roads, many of which ran through thick woods that could shield the movement from the enemy but where a wrong turn could get a division hopelessly lost. Here the Confederates had a significant advantage. Rebel units used such roads to launch surprise attacks on the enemy. The outstanding example was Jackson's flank attack at Chancellorsville after a day-long march on a narrow track used to haul wood for a charcoal iron furnace, guided by the son of the furnace owner. Numerous examples could also be cited of Union troops getting lost on similar roads because of inaccurate or nonexistent maps.

"If I were mindful only of my own glory," wrote Frederick the Great of Prussia, "I would choose always to make war in my own country, for there every man is a spy, and the enemy can make no movement of which I am not informed."[13] Robert E. Lee could have said the same. Operating amid a hostile population, the Union army was at a distinct disadvantage in the matter of military intelligence. Even the women and children, reported a Northern officer, "vied with each other in schemes and ruses by which to discover and convey to the enemy facts which we strove to conceal."[14] Confederate officers often treated information obtained in this way with a grain of salt and relied mainly on their excellent cavalry for intelligence. But the cavalry, of course, functioned more effectively among a friendly than a hostile population. And many examples of important information conveyed by civilian spies could be cited. The best known is the work of Belle Boyd during Jackson's Shenandoah Valley campaign of 1862.

CONFEDERATE GUERRILLAS

There is disagreement among historians about the impact of Southern guerrillas on the war. Bruce Catton wrote that the numerous guerrilla attacks "befuddled the Federal high command, kept the invaders from getting accurate information about the strength and position of their opponents, disrupted supply and commu- nication lines, and . . . went a long way to nullify the heavy advantage in numbers which the Federals possessed." The biographer of partisan leader John Singleton Mosby claims that the operations of guerrillas behind Union lines in Virginia in 1864 were "responsible largely for the war's extension into 1865."[15] But other historians maintain that partisan bands did the Confederate cause more harm than good. They drained potential manpower from the organized armies, it is claimed, and by their savage attacks on civilians and rear-area military personnel they discredited the Southern cause and provoked ruthless reprisals. The credit for successful raids on Union supply lines, according to this interpretation, belongs less to guerrillas than to cavalry troops under such commanders as Nathan Bedford Forrest and John Hunt Morgan.[16]

The truth probably lies somewhere between the two assertions. Although the claim that guerrillas prolonged the war by a year is an exaggeration, Mosby's band did give Union commanders no end of trouble and did handicap Federal opera- tions in the Shenandoah Valley (see pp. 424 and 444). Partisan bands in other theaters also wreaked havoc behind Union lines. The assertion that it was Confed- erate cavalry, not guerrillas, that accomplished these things fails to recognize that there was sometimes little if any difference between the two categories. Nearly all guerrillas were mounted, and most of them had some sort of relationship with the Confederate army as "rangers." Many of the troopers who rode with Morgan, Forrest, and other cavalry generals were local men who melted back into the civilian population in classic guerrilla fashion after a raid.

Guerrilla warfare had a glamorous reputation in the South, stemming from the exploits of the "Swamp Fox," Francis Marion, during the Revolution. With the blessing of the Confederate War Department, several ranger companies sprang up in 1861—especially in western Virginia, where they harassed Union occupa- tion troops and repeatedly cut the B&O. Confederate generals in Missouri and Arkansas encouraged the early operations of William Quantrill and other guerrilla leaders. Union generals organized counterinsurgency units to track down and destroy Rebel guerrilla bands, but as in more recent wars these efforts met with more frustration than success.

In April 1862 the Southern Congress authorized the official formation of partisan ranger companies, which were to be enrolled as units of the Confederate army. Mosby's rangers were the most famous of these companies. Mosby's exploits (which included the capture of a Union general in his bed only ten miles from

John Singleton Mosby and Members of His Partisan Band. Mosby is the beardless, hatless man standing near the center. *(Reproduced from the Collections of the Library of Congress)*

Washington) became legendary, earning him the praise of J. E. B. Stuart and Robert E. Lee. Unlike some other guerrilla outfits, Mosby's men usually wore Confederate uniforms, though they frequently concealed them under captured Union overcoats that enabled them to get through Yankee lines at will.

Despite the apparent success of ranger companies, several Confederate leaders by 1863 began to question their value. Many potential army recruits preferred to join these companies with their easy discipline, adventurous life, and prospects for loot. A good many guerrilla units were no better than "bushwhackers" (the Federals' term for them) who, in the words of a Union officer, "kill for the sake of killing and plunder for the love of gain."[17] Most notorious of the bushwhackers was Quantrill, who held a commission as captain in the Confederate army. In August 1863 he led his men on a raid into Lawrence, Kansas, the old free soil stronghold. He burned the defenseless town and murdered 183 male civilians in cold blood. This and other infamous raids by Missouri partisans gave all guerrillas a bushwhacker image. In January 1864, the Confederate Congress repealed the law authorizing partisan units and ordered their merger with regular commands. But this was a paper change only, for most ranger units continued to function.

The question of how to treat captured guerrillas vexed the Union government.

Early in the war several generals threatened to execute them, but this only produced retaliatory threats of an eye-for-an-eye execution of captured Yankees. In 1862 the Union War Department decided to treat partisans as ordinary prisoners of war so long as they were officially authorized by the Confederacy. But as the guerrillas escalated their violence and as more of them operated without uniforms or official sanction, Union commanders sometimes had them shot when captured. In July 1864 the Northern Congress approved this practice. When Philip Sheridan took command of Union forces in the Shenandoah Valley in August 1864, Grant told him: "Where any of Mosby's men are caught hang them without trial."[18] One of Sheridan's cavalry commanders, George A. Custer, executed six guerrillas, whereupon Mosby had six captured troopers from Custer's brigade draw lots and go before a firing squad.

Probably no more than 10,000 men (not including official cavalry units) functioned as guerrillas in the Confederacy. It can be plausibly argued that they did more damage to the Union war effort than an equal number of front-line soldiers. In the fashion of guerrillas in other wars, they tied down several times their number of regular soldiers in guard duty or search-and-destroy missions. But whatever their military value, it is certain that guerrilla raids and Union reprisals increased the hatred and violence that made the Civil War a total war—a war of peoples as well as of armies.

MEN AND ARMS

With all the advantages of fighting a defensive war on its own territory, in which stalemate would be victory, perhaps the South was right in its belief that one Southerner could whip ten Yankees—or at least three. And in the war's early stages, the average Confederate cavalryman or infantryman probably *was* a better soldier than his enemy. Most Southern boys learned to ride and hunt as an essential part of growing up. Most Rebel soldiers did not have to be taught to shoot; many Yankees did. Martial values were more central to Southern than to Northern culture. The South's less modernized society proved a military advantage during the first half of a war in which the traditional martial qualities of man and horse gave way slowly to the modernized superiority of industry and the iron horse.

Cavalry

The Confederacy enjoyed its greatest early superiority in the cavalry. The mounted arm illustrated Karl von Clausewitz's* dictum that a nation will fight a war that resembles its social system. Lack of good roads in the South had com-

---

*A Prussian military officer (who rose to the rank of general) of the early nineteenth century. A brilliant strategist, von Clausewitz achieved renown as the author of *Vom Kriege* (3 vols., 1833) and several other texts of military science.

pelled Southerners to ride from childhood, while most Northerners traveled on wheels *drawn* by horses. It took longer to train a cavalryman than an infantry or artillery soldier. A majority of the cavalry officers in the regular army had been Southerners. In leadership, horsemanship, and the equally important matter of taking care of horses, the Confederate trooper had a tremendous head start. The cavalry attracted the devil-may-care element of the South. General Sherman best described this element:

> The young bloods of the South; sons of planters, lawyers about towns, good billiard-players and sportsmen. . . . They hate Yankees *per se,* and don't bother their brains about the past, present, or future. As long as they have good horses, plenty of forage, and an open country, they are happy. . . . They are splendid riders, first-rate shots, and utterly reckless. . . . They are the best cavalry in the world.[19]

During the first two years of the war, Confederate troopers rode circles around Yankee horsemen, who, in the exaggerated words of a British observer, could "scarcely sit their horses even when trotting."[20] This was no small matter, for though cavalry were soon to become obsolete, they still performed vital functions during the Civil War. They were the eyes of the army. Their primary tasks were to obtain information about the size and movements of enemy forces while screening their own army from similar efforts by enemy cavalry. This reconnaissance function became particularly important in the wooded terrain of the South. It was in this task especially that the Rebel cavalry outshone the Yankees during the war's first two years. Another function of cavalry was to patrol the front or flanks of a marching or fighting army, to prevent surprise attacks and detect enemy flanking movements. In this job too the Confederate cavalry performed better during the early part of the war. The logistical importance of the railroad also enhanced the cavalry's role as a raiding force deep in the enemy's rear.

The saber was becoming little more than a ceremonial arm, and some troopers did not bother to carry one. The principal cavalry weapon was the breechloading carbine. Since carbines were in short supply in the South, many Rebel cavalrymen carried shotguns. Most troopers also carried revolvers. Cavalry units did some of their actual fighting on foot, having used their horses mainly as a means of rapid transportation to the scene of action. The Civil War produced new developments in dismounted cavalry tactics. Forrest was one of the principal innovators in this sphere. Sheridan carried the concept further when he took command of the Army of the Potomac's cavalry in 1864. Although the cavalry did less heavy fighting than the infantry, the foot soldier's half-sneering, half-envious question, "Whoever saw a dead cavalryman?" did not reflect reality. By late 1863 several Union cavalry brigades were armed with seven-shot repeating carbines, which greatly increased their firepower and made them more than a match, fighting dismounted, for an equal number of infantry. This increased firepower plus improved horsemanship, leadership, and experience brought Union cavalry to a par with Confederate horsemen by 1863 and gave them the edge, man for man, in the last year of the war.

Artillery

Just as the Confederacy's initial cavalry supremacy reflected the premodern aspects of Southern society, so the Union's superior artillery throughout the war reflected the technological ascendancy of the North. The industrial capacity for manufacturing cannon, shells, powder, and fuses was of course greater in the North than in the South. Artillery officers in the old army had been mostly Northern-born. The mathematical aptitude and training necessary to calculate range and elevation existed more widely in the North.

During the first two years of the war, the Confederacy captured more artillery than it manufactured or imported. These captures included not only the heavy ordnance seized from forts and from the Norfolk navy yard at the time of secession, but also field artillery captured in battle. By 1863, however, the South was producing most of its own artillery, chiefly at the Tredegar Iron Works in Richmond. The Confederacy manufactured nearly 3,000 cannon (compared with more than 7,000 in the Union) and built from scratch one of the world's largest gunpowder mills at Augusta, Georgia. But many of the Southern-built cannon were defective and prone to crack. Shell fuses were also unreliable (so were Union fuses, but less so), causing most shells to explode too soon, too late, or not at all.

Civil War cannon were of two basic types: smoothbore and rifled. Rifled artillery was new; a few rifled pieces had been used in the Franco-Austrian War of 1859, but the Civil War produced their first widespread use. Rifled barrels gave the projectiles greater distance, velocity, and accuracy (see the discussion of rifling on p. 193). Nearly half of the Union cannon and about one-third of the Confederate cannon were rifled. Artillery projectiles were of three basic kinds: shells and solid shot for long-range work and case shot (canister or grape) for close-in defense against attacking infantry. Case shot was contained in shells that exploded to spray hundreds of small bullets (canister) or nine golf-ball-sized shot (grape). The effect of a cannon firing case shot into troops at close range was like that of a huge sawed-off shotgun. Despite the greater power and accuracy of rifled cannon, the twelve-pound smoothbore Napoleon remained the artillerists' favorite gun; the unreliability of shell fuses limited the value of longer-range rifled guns, and the versatile Napoleons, which could fire any kind of projectile, were the best for case shot.

The first crude predecessors of the machine gun were developed during the Civil War. For the Confederacy, Captain R. S. Williams invented a gun operated by a revolving camshaft that fed bullets from a hopper into the breech at the rate of twenty per minute. This gun was evidently used in combat as early as 1862. At least two dozen were built, but they were prone to malfunction and saw little action. The same was true of two types of rapid-fire guns developed in the North, the "coffee-mill gun" (so labeled by Lincoln because its feeder mechanism resembled a coffee grinder) and the Gatling gun, invented by Richard Gatling of Indiana. The multiple-barreled Gatling gun could fire 250 shots a minute—when it worked—and became the model for the postwar evolution of the modern machine gun. But its unreliability prevented significant combat use during the war itself.

A Union Battery Posing in Action Stations for the Photographer in Virginia, 1863. *(Reproduced from the Collections of the Library of Congress)*

Infantry

Despite the cavalry's glamor and the artillery's power, the infantry was by far the most important branch of Civil War armies. Combat troops in the Union army consisted of 80 percent infantry, less than 15 percent cavalry, and about 6 percent artillery. In the Confederate army, the proportion of artillery was the same, cavalry was higher at nearly 20 percent, and infantry was lower at 75 percent. The infantry inflicted and suffered 80 to 90 percent of the battle casualties. The infantry's relative importance was greater in the Civil War than in any other war. This was so because the rifle had replaced the smoothbore musket as the infantry weapon.

The Rifle

For centuries men had known that by cutting spiraled grooves inside a musket barrel to impart spin to the bullet, they could increase its range and accuracy.* Hunting weapons were usually rifled, and some eighteenth-century armies contained special rifle regiments. But the smoothbore remained the principal infantry weapon until the 1850s. Why? Because a bullet large enough to "take" the rifling was hard to ram down the barrel of a muzzleloading weapon. After a rifle had been

---

*To illustrate the principle: without spin, a bullet might behave as erratically as a knuckle-ball in baseball.

fired a few times, the residue from the black powder built up in the grooves and made the gun impossible to load without cleaning. Since rapid loading and the reliability of repeated and prolonged firing were essential in a military weapon, the rifle could be used only for specialized purposes.

Gun designers had long been experimenting with methods to overcome these difficulties. The man given credit for solving the problem was French army Captain Claude E. Minié, who in the 1840s invented an elongated bullet with an iron or wooden plug in the base that expanded when fired, to take the rifling. The bullet was of slightly smaller caliber than the barrel and thus could be easily loaded; the expanding base kept the grooves clean as it shot through the barrel. The Minié ball was expensive and prone to malfunction because of its wooden or iron base; the famous "minie ball" of Civil War rifles was developed by an American, James H. Burton, at the Harper's Ferry armory. Instead of a plug, it had a cavity in the base which was expanded by gas from the powder explosion that fired the bullet.

This simple invention revolutionized military tactics. The maximum range of a smoothbore musket was about 250 yards, but a soldier could scarcely count on hitting anything at over 80 yards. In 1861, experienced marksmen in an Illinois regiment fired 160 shots from a smoothbore at a flour barrel 180 yards away and registered only four hits. By contrast, the new Springfield and Enfield rifles had a maximum range of more than 1,000 yards and an effective range of about 400 yards. After a New Hampshire regiment received Springfields in October 1861 a private wrote home to his parents: "We went out the other day to try them We fired 600 yds and we put 360 balls into a mark the size of old Jeff."[21] This fivefold increase in range greatly strengthened the infantry vis-à-vis the cavalry and artillery. It became suicidal for cavalry to charge infantry, for most of the horses and many of their riders would be shot down before they reached the infantry. The Napoleonic tactics of advancing field artillery along with or ahead of charging infantry would no longer work, for the cannoneers and horses would be picked off before the artillery got close enough to do much damage.

The rifle gave the tactical defense a big advantage over the offense. Traditional tactics had favored compact frontal assaults by infantry against defensive positions. The defenders would have time for only one or two volleys with their smoothbore muskets before the attackers were upon them with bayonets. But with rifles, the defenders could hit attackers five times farther away than previously. Rarely did a charging line get close enough to use the bayonet (fewer than 1 percent of Civil War wounds were caused by bayonets). But commanders whose West Point textbooks had taught Napoleonic tactics and whose previous experience had been in the Mexican War, where compact assaults usually succeeded, were slow to appreciate the new power of the rifle. Generals on both sides, as late as 1864, ordered frontal attacks that were beaten back with fearful slaughter.

The defense also benefited from the evolution of trench warfare in the last two years of the conflict. Field trenches were not new, of course, but the advent of the rifle drove troops to seek cover more than ever before. By 1863 the men of both armies were constructing trenches and breastworks at virtually every place

Civil War Trenches. This photograph shows part of the Confederate
entrenchments protecting Atlanta in 1864. The soldiers posing here
are members of Sherman's army after they had captured Atlanta.
(Reproduced from the Collections of the Library of Congress)

of deployment. The campaigns of 1864–1865 left the countryside of Virginia and
Georgia scarred as if a race of giant moles had burrowed through it. Good troops
in good trenches could hold them against three or four times as many attacking
troops. The rifle and the trench ruled the later Civil War battlefields as thoroughly
as the machine gun and trench ruled those of World War I.

In 1861, however, most regiments on both sides carried smoothbores, for when
the war began there were barely enough rifles to equip the tiny regular army. The
Union and Confederate governments, several state governments, and some private firms sent agents to Europe, where they engaged in a bidding contest for the
surplus arms of Britain and the Continent. Altogether the Union government and
Northern states bought more than a million muskets and rifles in Europe, some
worthless but most serviceable. By 1863, the domestic arms industry was turning
out enough rifles for the Union army, so foreign purchases came to an end. The
U.S. armory at Springfield, Massachusetts, produced nearly 800,000 rifles; private
manufacturers made an additional 900,000 of the Springfield model. Northern
factories and government armories turned out more than two and a half million
small arms of all types during the Civil War, an unprecedented achievement that
testified to the modernized efficiency of the arms industry.

The Confederacy could not come close to matching this output. Total Confederate domestic production of rifles is unknown, but it probably did not exceed

250,000. In addition the South imported 600,000 rifles, a large portion of them Enfields. In the war's first year, the Confederacy was starved for weapons; during 1862, victorious Rebel armies captured 100,000 Union rifles and blockade runners brought in nearly 200,000 more, ending the South's small-arms famine. By 1863 most infantrymen on both sides were armed with modern rifles.

"Modern" they may have been, but they were still single-shot muzzleloaders. To load this weapon was a complicated procedure: the soldier took a paper-wrapped cartridge containing bullet and powder from his cartridge pouch; tore open the paper with his teeth; poured the powder down the barrel; put the bullet in the barrel; rammed bullet and powder down with the ramrod; half-cocked the hammer; put a percussion cap on the nipple; cocked the hammer; aimed; and fired. An experienced soldier could get off two or three shots a minute. But in the noise and excitement of battle, many soldiers failed to do one or more of these steps properly, and the gun misfired. The exhausted or distracted soldier might fail to realize this, might ram down another load and misfire a second, third, or even several times. After the battle of Gettysburg, 24,000 loaded rifles were found on the field. Half of them had two bullets in the barrel, 6,000 had three or more loads, and one famous specimen had twenty-three loads jammed down the barrel. Even if a soldier did everything correctly, he normally had to stand or kneel to load his rifle (though some agile men learned how to load while lying on their backs), thereby exposing himself to enemy fire.

The obvious solution to these problems was a rifle that could be loaded at the breech. Military breechloaders had existed for many years. But they were plagued by problems, chiefly the escape of powder gas through the breech, which caused the gun to malfunction as the barrel heated with rapid use. In the 1850s several inventors (including Ambrose E. Burnside, who became a Union general) developed copper cartridges or other devices that largely solved the problem of escaping gas. The Union cavalry received breechloading carbines as fast as they could be produced, and some Rebel horsemen also carried them when they could get them by capture or from the limited production of the Richmond armory. Ingenious Connecticut Yankees also invented breechloading repeaters. The most successful was the Spencer seven-shot carbine, fed by a springloaded clip in the stock, which became the favorite weapon of Yankee troopers in 1864–1865.

The breechloading and repeating techniques could be applied to rifles as well as carbines (the main differences between the two were the rifle's longer barrel and heavier powder charge). But the U.S. Ordnance Bureau was slow to accept the idea of breechloaders for the infantry. Angry progressives referred to Ordnance Bureau Chief James Ripley as "Ripley Van Winkle" because of his opposition to breechloading rifles. Several historians have maintained that if Ripley had contracted for large numbers of breechloaders and repeaters in 1861–1862, the war might have been shortened by a year or more. As it was, few breechloading infantry rifles were produced before Lincoln forced Ripley to retire in September 1863.[22]

But there is another side to this question. The initial skepticism of Ripley and other officers toward breechloaders and repeaters was not wholly unfounded. They argued that (1) the new weapons had not yet proven themselves in 1861–1862, and it would be foolish to divert resources from the production of muzzleloaders like the Springfield until all troops had been armed with these reliable weapons; (2) because of European purchases and domestic production of several types of muzzleloaders, the Ordnance Bureau had trouble enough supplying different regiments with the right kinds of ammunition without having to supply ammunition also for the dozen or so different breechloaders then in existence; (3) soldiers firing breechloaders might waste ammunition, thereby exacerbating the already serious logistics problem. Although it turned out in the end that men armed with breechloaders and repeaters became more efficient and accurate in their fire than before, there was enough wild and wasteful shooting early in the war to lend credence to this argument. And despite the disadvantages of muzzleloaders, the Springfield and Enfield were deadly weapons, as the carnage of Civil War battlefields cruelly attested.

Nevertheless, part of the indictment against Ripley is valid: despite malfunction problems, the breechloaders were better weapons, and more of them could have been produced earlier had it not been for Ripley's opposition. Altogether about 100,000 Sharps single-shot breechloaders (90,000 carbines and 10,000 rifles), 55,000 Burnside single-shot carbines, 85,000 Spencer seven-shot carbines and rifles, and at least 100,000 breechloaders and repeaters of other types were manufactured for the Union army. They gave Yankee soldiers who carried them a powerful advantage in the war's later stages.

Southern and Northern War Production and Supply

Although often less well armed than their enemies, Confederate soldiers did not suffer from ordnance shortages after 1862. The Confederate Ordnance Bureau was the one success story of Confederate logistics. The architect of this success, Chief of Ordnance Josiah Gorgas, was a native of Pennsylvania and a West Point graduate who had married a Southern woman. Starting with almost nothing except the Tredegar Iron Works in Richmond, Gorgas created dozens of factories that turned out large quantities of powder and ammunition. He was a genius at improvisation. Appeals went out to Southern churches and plantations to turn in their bells to be melted down and recast into cannon. Southern women saved the contents of chamber pots to be leached for niter to produce gunpowder. Army officers gleaned battlefields to retrieve and recycle lead for bullets. Ordnance officials scoured the countryside for stills, which were melted down to obtain copper for rifle percussion caps. Gorgas's achievement is best described in his own words: "From being the worst supplied of the Bureaus of the War Department," he wrote in his diary on April 8, 1864, the Ordnance Bureau

is now the best. Large arsenals have been organized at Richmond, Fayetteville, Augusta, Charleston, Columbus, Macon, Atlanta and Selma. . . . A superb powder mill has been built at Augusta. . . . Lead-smelting works were established by me at Petersburgh. . . . A cannon foundry established at Macon for heavy guns, and bronze foundries at Macon, Columbus,

Ga., and Augusta; a foundry for shot and shell at Salisbury, N.C. . . . a manufactory of carbines has been built up here [Richmond]; a rifle factory at Asheville (transferred to Columbia, S.C.). . . . Where three years ago we were not making a gun, a pistol nor a sabre, no shot nor shell (except at the Tredegar Works)—a pound of powder—we now make all these in quantities to meet the demands of our large armies.[23]

But when we turn from ordnance to the commissary and quartermaster bureaus of the Confederacy, a far different picture emerges. If an army marches on its stomach, as Napoleon said, the mobility of Rebel soldiers was all the more marvelous, for they seldom had enough to eat. The deterioration of Southern railroads, the disorganization of the economy by runaway inflation, and the inefficiency of Commissary General Lucius Northrop (who was said to retain his post only because of favoritism by President Davis) all combined to make food supply one of the Confederacy's worst problems. During the winter of 1862–1863, the daily ration in Lee's army was reduced to four ounces of bacon, eighteen ounces of cornmeal, and an occasional handful of rice or black-eyed peas. Thousands of men suffered from scurvy, which disappeared only when the arrival of spring enabled the soldiers to eat sassafras roots and wild onions. In January 1864, Lee wrote: "Unless there is a change, I fear the army cannot be kept effective and cannot be kept together."[24]

Men can fight in rags, and many Rebels did. But it is hard to march twenty miles a day or stand picket duty in winter without shoes. Yet Confederate soldiers did that also. At almost any given time some of the Southern soldiers were shoeless. When Lee's army invaded Maryland in 1862, several thousand stragglers stayed behind, mainly because they could not march on the macadamized Maryland roads in bare feet. These men might have made a difference had they been present at the battle of Antietam.

Union soldiers also sometimes suffered from lack of proper food. During the winter of 1862–1863, corruption and inefficiency in the Commissary Department caused food shortages and scurvy in the Army of the Potomac. But most of the time Billy Yank was abundantly supplied. Quartermaster General Montgomery Meigs was a superb administrator. Northern industry and agriculture poured out uniforms, overcoats, shoes, pork and "hardtack" (a three-inch square of hard bread that formed the staple of Union rations), and other items in such abundance that Yankee soldiers became prodigal of their provisions. "A French army of half the size of ours could be supplied with what we waste," confessed one Union general.[25]

In the end, the greater resources and productivity of the Northern economy enabled Union forces to overcome the Confederacy's advantages of fighting a defensive war in its own territory. Man for man, the Yankee soldier was no better than the Rebel; at first he may not have been as good. But there were more Yankees than Rebels and they were better armed and supplied.

FINANCING THE WAR: THE CONFEDERACY

The most serious deficiency of the Confederate economy was its financial structure. With its capital invested primarily in land and slaves, the South had not developed a fiscal system capable of meeting the demands of a wartime economy. Forced to print paper money to prime its monetary pump, the Confederacy set in motion a dizzying spiral of inflation that could not be stopped.

This was one of the war's cruel ironies, for Confederate Secretary of the Treasury Christopher Memminger was a hard-money advocate who considered the printing press "the most dangerous of all methods of raising money."[26] Of the three methods to finance the war—taxation, loans, and treasury notes (paper money)—Memminger preferred the first. But the Confederate Congress was wary of imposing new taxes. For thirty-five years Americans had paid no internal taxes to the federal government, whose modest prewar budgets had been funded by tariffs and the proceeds of land sales. Believing that the war would be short and that heavy taxes would diminish patriotic ardor, Southern lawmakers passed no general tax measure until August 1861. The small direct property tax then levied was weakened by offering the states a 10 percent reduction of their quotas if they paid the Confederate Treasury by April 1, 1862. All but three states did so not by collecting the tax but by floating state loans!

More palatable than taxes were bond issues, to be repaid by future generations who would presumably enjoy the benefits of independence won by the sacrifices of the war generation. The Confederacy's first bonds ($15 million) were fully subscribed in the patriotic fervor of 1861. But this loan soaked up most of the available specie in the South without coming close to meeting mounting costs. The shortage of capital spawned the ingenious idea of a "produce loan," which would enable farmers to pledge the proceeds from part of their crop in return for bonds equal to the market price of their pledge. First authorized in a $50 million bond issue of May 1861, the produce loan was expanded to $100 million in August. But the response was disappointing. Pledges were slow to come in, and the government had trouble collecting them. The mushrooming price of cotton encouraged planters to hold their crop for higher prices and even to smuggle it through enemy lines for Yankee gold. From the produce loan, the Confederacy realized only $34 million—most of it late in the war, when the currency had so far depreciated as to be almost worthless.

To fill the monetary gap, Congress authorized $119 million of treasury notes in 1861 and $400 million in 1862. Once begun on this scale, the printing of money became like liquor to an alcoholic—the more printed, the more needed to achieve the same result. When coupled with the shortages caused by the blockade, by Union invasions, and by the deterioration of Southern railroads, these issues of paper money drove the price index up to 762 by the beginning of 1863 (January 1861 = 100). State and city governments added to the flood of paper money by printing their own notes. Counterfeiting of the crudely printed Confederate notes became widespread. The South moved toward a barter economy as creditors required payment in goods rather than in depreciated currency. Farmers complained that their crops were impressed by army commissary officers at far below the market value. Wages lagged behind prices: real wages in the South declined by at least 65 percent during the war. City dwellers could not afford skyrocketing food prices and rents, and food riots broke out in several cities during 1863.

By 1863, everyone realized that the printing press was a major cause of inflation.

Newspapers that had opposed high taxes in 1861 reversed themselves and presented the strange spectacle of a people begging to be taxed. Congress responded with the passage on April 24, 1863, of a remarkably comprehensive tax bill. It included: an 8 percent sales tax on consumer goods, a 10 percent profits tax on wholesalers, excise taxes, a license tax on businesses and professions (a later amendment added a 5 percent levy on land and slaves), and a graduated income tax ranging from 1 percent on incomes between $1,000 and $1,500 up to 15 percent on incomes over $10,000. A unique additional feature was the "tax in kind" on agricultural products. After reserving specified amounts of food crops for their own families, farmers were required to pay one-tenth of their remaining crops to the government.

These taxes were a failure. Evasion was widespread and enforcement erratic, under the pressures of Union invasion and the breakdown of Confederate authority. In two years the money taxes yielded only $119 million in badly depreciated currency. The tax in kind yielded products valued at only $62 million. This latter tax was particularly unpopular. Farmers living near the war theaters or near railroads found their full quotas seized by tax agents, while those remote from armies or transportation paid little or nothing. And when some tax-in-kind food crops rotted in government warehouses for want of transportation, the bitterness of farmers knew no bounds.

After the Confederate military defeats at Gettysburg and Vicksburg in July 1863, inflation became even worse. The only remedy seemed to be to run the printing presses faster. By the spring of 1864 it took $46 to buy what $1 had bought three years earlier. The Confederate Congress tried to reverse the trend by requiring treasury notes to be converted to low-interest bonds (in effect a forced loan) or exchanged for new notes at the rate of three old notes for two new ones. This partial repudiation did stabilize the currency for several months, but only at the cost of destroying whatever faith was left in Confederate finances. By the spring of 1865 prices had risen to ninety-two times their prewar level.

Unsound financial policies were one cause of Confederate defeat. Reliance on taxes for less than 5 percent of government revenues and on loans for 35–40 percent, leaving the remaining 60 percent to be created as fiat money, was a sure-fire recipe for disaster. It sapped civilian morale and embittered large segments of the population. Runaway inflation was in effect a form of confiscatory taxation that fell most heavily on the poor. But the Confederate Congress and Treasury do not deserve all the blame. Factors beyond their control—the Union blockade, Northern military victories, the refusal of European governments to recognize the Confederacy—were also responsible. The chief culprit, however, was the South's unbalanced agricultural economy, which was just not equal to the demands of modern, total war.

FINANCING THE WAR: THE UNION

At first the Union government seemed little better prepared than the Confederacy to finance a major war. The depression following the Panic of 1857 had reduced tax revenues. Just as the economy was recovering, the secession crisis plunged it into another recession. For the first time since the War of 1812, the federal budget had run a deficit for four consecutive years. When Lincoln became President, the national debt was higher than ever before, government bonds were selling below par, and the Treasury was nearly empty. The new Secretary of the Treasury, Salmon P. Chase, had been appointed not because of his financial knowledge (which was minimal) but because of his political influence.

Even if Chase had been a financial genius, the monetary system of the United States in 1861 would have been hard to mobilize for war. Although the North had one of the world's most advanced economies, Jacksonian Democrats had saddled the federal government with an antiquated financial structure. The Independent Treasury Act of 1846 had prohibited the government from depositing its funds in banks and had required all payments to or by the government to be made in specie. This had climaxed the campaign, begun fifteen years earlier, to destroy the Second Bank of the United States and to divorce the federal government from the country's banking and monetary system. Chartered by the separate states, banks and the banknotes that they circulated as currency varied widely in soundness. In 1861, seven thousand different kinds of banknotes were circulating, many of them counterfeit and others virtually worthless because the issuing bank had gone bankrupt. Out of this monetary chaos had emerged a degree of order and strength in the private sector, for the sound banks functioned mainly on a demand deposit basis (similar to the modern checking account), and the banknotes of even the less sound banks provided a medium of exchange that circulated at various rates of discount. But the federal government continued to operate in a monetary horse-and-buggy age: "tons of gold had to be hauled to and fro in dray-loads, with horses and heavers doing by the hour what bookkeepers could do in a moment."[27]

Such a system was perhaps acceptable in peacetime, when the federal government played a small role in the economy. The government's annual budgets in the 1850s averaged less than 2 percent of the gross national product (compared with 22 percent today). But the Civil War changed all that. Government expenditures jumped to an average of 15 percent of the gross national product during the war. The conflict forcibly modernized the government's monetary structure. While the South's economy proved unequal to the demands of total war, the underlying strength of the Northern economy enabled the Union to emerge in 1865 with a sounder financial system than before.

During the first year of fighting, however, the Union Treasury was in bad shape. In August 1861, Congress did take the unprecedented step of levying an income tax of 3 percent on incomes over $800. But this tax was not to be collected until the beginning of 1863. Meanwhile, the Treasury had to rely mainly on the borrowing authority granted by Congress. The government had traditionally gone to eastern banks for the short-term loans needed to carry on ordinary business. Chase wanted to change this and to offer bonds directly to the public. A people's war should be sustained by the people's loans. Here was the germ of the great bond drives of the two world wars in the twentieth century. But in the Civil War this novel idea got off to a slow start. The banks underwrote the first $150 million loan in the fall of 1861. Jay Cooke's small banking house in Philadelphia successfully promoted the public subscription of these bonds. But elsewhere public sales were poor. The average citizen had never seen a government bond, much less thought of buying one. Moreover, the bonds had to be paid for in specie, and few people possessed any spare gold.

The specie problem also plagued the banks. Their reserves threatened to fall below the requirements necessary to support their notes and demand deposits. Then in November 1861 a potentially disastrous diplomatic crisis erupted between the North and Britain over the seizure of Confederate envoys traveling on the British ship *Trent* (see pp. 219–220). Stocks and bonds fell, gold and silver went into hoarding or left the country, and the North seemed to be heading toward another financial panic. Peaceful settlement of the *Trent* affair did little to ease the crisis. On December 30 all banks and the Treasury suspended specie payments. For a while soldiers and government contractors were not paid, and banks did not redeem their notes in gold. To pessimists it looked like the North was about to lose the war by default.

Creation of the Greenbacks

But Congress resolved the crisis in a way that was to have profound consequences for the nation's future monetary history. Three main proposals emerged during the congressional debate. Chase proposed to create a national banking system that would enable banks to issue notes backed by government bonds, which in turn would be backed by Treasury reserves. This was a far-reaching suggestion that eventually bore fruit, but it could not go into effect soon enough to meet the emergency of early 1862. Several bankers put forward a second alternative: a new issue of bonds to be sold "at the market"—that is, at whatever price they would bring, even if it meant selling them below par. This would bring specie out of hoarding, begin the flow of money, and supply the government with necessary funds. It would also make large profits for bankers and investors, who would buy at a discount and eventually receive par value plus interest. Thus Congress rejected the idea. The third proposal was to do what the Confederacy was already doing —to print fiat money. This was the alternative chosen by Congress, which on February 25, 1862, passed the Legal Tender Act authorizing the issue of $150 million in treasury notes—the famous greenbacks.

Congress enacted this law only after a great deal of soul-searching. Was it constitutional? Was it a violation of contract to make greenbacks legal tender to pay debts previously contracted? Was it wise? Would the greenbacks depreciate as the continentals had done in the Revolution or as Confederate notes were depreciating? Were the greenbacks not immoral? "By common consent of the nations," said a banker, "gold and silver are the only true measure of value. These metals were prepared by the Almighty for this very purpose." Democrats in Congress voted against the Legal Tender Act by a three-to-one margin because, as one of them said, it launched the country "upon an ocean of experiment upon

which the wise men who administered the government before we came into power
. . . would not permit it even to enter."[28] More open to experimentation, Republicans voted three to one in favor of the act. But many of them did so with misgivings. "It shocks all my notions of political, moral, and national honor," said William Pitt Fessenden, chairman of the Senate Finance Committee. "The thing is wrong in itself, but to leave the government without resources at such a crisis is not to be thought of." Chase, a hard-money man at heart, came to reluctant support of the bill only because *immediate action is of great importance. The Treasury is nearly empty.*"[29]

The Legal Tender Act fulfilled the hopes without confirming the fears of those who passed it. It gave the government money to pay its obligations, ended the banking crisis, and injected a circulating medium into the specie-starved economy. Although the greenbacks gradually depreciated in relation to gold, the Union did not experience the runaway inflation that ruined Confederate finance. Why not? First, the Union greenbacks, unlike Confederate notes, were made *legal tender,* receivable for all debts public or private except import duties and interest on the national debt. Banks, contractors, merchants, and the government itself had to accept greenbacks as lawful money at their face value, with the exceptions noted. Some Republican congressmen who opposed these exceptions asked why bondholders should receive interest in gold while soldiers who risked their lives were paid with paper money. But supporters of interest payments in gold argued that such a policy was necessary to attract foreign and domestic investors to buy at par the $500 million of 6 percent bonds authorized in February 1862. This argument was undoubtedly correct, for without the promise of interest in gold as a hedge against inflation these bonds could not have been sold at par.* The requirement that import duties be paid in specie guaranteed the government the means to maintain interest payments in gold.

The fortuitous timing of the greenback issues was a second reason for their success. Union military and naval victories in the winter and spring of 1862 (see pp. 222–234) lifted Northern morale and helped to float the greenbacks on a newly buoyant mood. A third reason why Union greenbacks depreciated less than any previous fiat money was Congress's belated recognition that new and heavy war taxes must be levied. The revenue measure signed by Lincoln on July 1, 1862, taxed practically everything: it imposed an income tax of 3 percent on incomes from $600 to $10,000 and 5 percent on those above $10,000 (revised upward in 1864 to 5 percent on incomes over $600 rising to 10 percent on those over $10,000); it laid excise taxes on everything from tobacco and liquor to yachts and billiard tables; and it levied license taxes, stamp taxes, inheritance taxes, and value-added taxes on hundreds of products. It also increased the tariff, to protect manufacturers from the added costs imposed by internal taxes. These levies raised more than $600 million in the last three years of the war. Along with $1.5 billion of bonds sold during the same period, the taxes soaked up part of the inflationary

---

*The question of whether the principal of the bonds should also be paid in gold caused considerable controversy after the war. The Republicans insisted that it should, and they carried their point. See pp. 541 and 547.

pressures of the war economy—even though three subsequent greenback issues raised the total amount of this currency to $447 million.

War Bonds

The U.S. Treasury marketed a bewildering variety of war bonds. The most common were the famous "five-twenty" bonds (redeemable in not less than five and not more than twenty years) at 6 percent, of which more than $600 million were sold. But during the summer of 1862 these bonds were not selling well. Confederate military victories in Virginia offset earlier Union gains in the West. European recognition of the Confederacy appeared imminent. And the 6 percent interest on the bonds was not attractive to investors so long as the future seemed cloudy. By late summer, the Treasury faced a crisis almost as grave as in January. At this juncture, Chase appointed Jay Cooke as a special agent to market the lagging five-twenties. Cooke attacked the problem with energy and skill. He flooded the newspapers with advertisements that appealed both to patriotism and to profit. He organized 2,500 subagents who sold bonds in every corner of the North. Cooke democratized the purchase of government securities. Nearly a million Northerners —one out of every four families—bought war bonds. This helped to bind the average person not only to the war effort but also to the modernizing capitalist system by which it was financed. It also helped Cooke's banking house become one of the country's leading financial institutions.

National Banks

From the experience of Civil War finance developed the national banking system, which remained the backbone of the American monetary structure until superseded by the Federal Reserve system in 1913. The creation of national banks sprang from several motives: the need to create a market for war bonds, the desire of Whiggish Republicans to resurrect the centralized banking structure destroyed by the Jacksonians, and the desire of many leaders of the financial community, especially in the Northeast, to create a more stable banknote currency. In February 1863, Congress passed the National Bank Act (supplemented by a second act in June 1864), which established criteria by which a bank could obtain a federal charter and issue national banknotes in an amount up to 90 percent of the value of the U.S. bonds that it held. Designed to replace the plethora of state banks and banknotes with a uniform national system, this legislation was supported by 78 percent of the congressional Republicans, who narrowly overcame the 91 percent of the Democrats voting against it.

The chartering of national banks proceeded slowly at first, for many state banks saw no advantage in joining the federal system. By the end of 1864, fewer than five hundred national banks had been chartered while more than a thousand state banks were still doing business. Under the impulse of a triumphant nationalism, Congress in March 1865 enacted a tax of 10 percent on state banknotes. This soon accomplished its purpose of driving these notes out of circulation and forcing most state banks to apply for federal charters. By the end of 1865, the 1,294 national banks had five times the assets of the 349 state banks still in existence. By 1873 state banknotes had virtually disappeared.*

Whereas the Confederacy raised 60 percent of its funds by printing paper money and less than 5 percent by taxes, Union war finances included 13 percent paper money and 21 percent taxes. While the Confederacy suffered an inflation rate exceeding 9,000 percent, the cost of living rose about 80 percent in the North and fell gradually but steadily after the war was over.† This compares with 80 percent inflation in World War I and 72 percent in World War II. Because wages rose at a slower rate than prices during the Civil War, real wages declined by about 20 percent in the North, but they returned to the prewar level by 1866 and continued to rise thereafter. Without rationing or price controls, the Union government successfully financed the war after overcoming the inexperience and crises of the first year. Northern people suffered no serious shortages of food or other necessities except cotton cloth. To a remarkable degree, the Northern economy was able to produce both guns and butter.

*But not state banks. Indeed, by 1873 their number had grown to 1,330 and their assets totaled nearly half as much as the assets held by the 1,968 national banks. The requirement that national banks must purchase U.S. bonds in an amount equivalent to at least one-third of their capital discouraged many smaller banks, especially in the West and South, from applying for a national charter. Most of the national banks were therefore concentrated in the Northeast, and this fact, combined with the limitation of national banknotes to $300 million (later increased slightly), created a severe regional maldistribution of banknote currency that hurt the economy of the West and South and produced postwar demands in these regions for monetary reform and inflation.

†The inflation rate was distinct from the gold premium, another index of currency depreciation. The former measured changes in what a dollar would buy; the latter measured fluctuations in the value of a dollar in relation to the value of gold. Although this fluctuation had some impact on domestic prices, it mainly reflected the international status of the dollar. With the suspension of specie payments and the creation of the greenbacks in 1862, the United States in effect went off the gold standard, though it still used gold for international trade. The gold value of the dollar fluctuated wildly in response to changes in the military situation. The price of gold soared to 284 (i.e., it took $2.84 in currency to purchase a dollar of gold) in July 1864, when Grant and Sherman seemed stymied before Petersburg and Atlanta, and Confederate General Jubal Early led a raid to the very outskirts of Washington. By the end of the war gold had dropped to 127.

Thirteen

The War at Home and Abroad

THE FIRST BATTLE OF BULL RUN

One of the war's most consequential strategic developments was a political decision. On May 21 the Confederate Congress accepted Virginia's invitation to move the capital from overcrowded, wilting Montgomery to the bustling industrial and commercial center of Richmond. By locating their capital a hundred miles from Washington, the Confederates made northern Virginia the war's main battle theater. Although Richmond would have been a focal point of conflict in any case because of its industrial importance, its political significance concentrated most Confederate strategic thinking on the Virginia theater at the expense of the West, where in the end the South lost the war.

If a defensive strategy accorded with Southern war aims, the North's determination to restore the Union required some sort of offensive plan. On May 3 General in Chief Winfield Scott proposed such a plan. He would cordon the Confederacy on all sides with a blockade by sea and by the dispatch of an invasion flotilla down the Mississippi to the Gulf. This would "envelop the insurgent states and bring them to terms with less bloodshed than by any other plan."[1]

Although the blockade already existed and Scott's proposed move down the Mississippi anticipated the later course of the war in the West, two things were wrong with his plan in 1861. First, having sealed off the South, Scott planned to stay put and wait for the Confederacy to die of suffocation and for Southern Unionists to regain power. A Virginian himself, Scott still cherished the illusion that his Southern brethren would come to their senses if the North acted firmly but with restraint. Second, Scott's plan would take time—five months to build the gunboats and train the soldiers; several more months for them to fight their way downriver and for the blockade to become effective. But Northern faith in Southern Unionism had worn thin, and public opinion clamored for an immediate invasion to "crush" the rebellion. When details of Scott's proposal leaked out, newspapers derisively labeled it "The Anaconda Plan." Editors called for action. On June 26 the powerful *New York Tribune* put the slogan "Forward to Richmond" on its masthead and kept it there day after day, thundering editorially that the Rebel Congress must not be allowed to meet on July 20.

The main Union army of 35,000 men under General Irvin McDowell was encamped across the Potomac from Washington. Twenty-five miles away a Confederate force of 20,000 under General Beauregard deployed on the south bank of Bull Run covering the key rail junction at Manassas. Fifty miles to the northwest, in the Shenandoah Valley, 12,000 Rebels under General Joseph E. Johnston, former Quartermaster General of the U.S. Army and now the ranking officer of the Confederacy, confronted a Union force half again as large under General Robert Patterson, a 69-year-old veteran of the War of 1812. Lincoln ordered McDowell to draw up a plan for an attack on Beauregard's army at Manassas. A former major in the regular army, McDowell had never commanded so much as a squad in battle. But he had experience in staff work; he had taught tactics at West Point; and the plan he submitted was a good one—for veteran troops. While Patterson advanced against Johnston's forces in the valley to prevent them from reinforcing Beauregard, McDowell would march from Washington, feint against the strongly held fords and bridges on Bull Run, and send a large column around the Confederate defenses to cross the river and attack their flank. Lincoln liked the plan, but McDowell protested that he needed more time—several weeks at least—to train and discipline his raw troops. Lincoln could not wait. "You are green, it is true," he said, "but they are green also; you are all green alike." The President told McDowell to get moving.[2]

McDowell issued orders for the advance to begin on July 16, but things went wrong from the start—as he had feared. Confused by ambiguous orders from Washington, Patterson demonstrated half-heartedly against Johnston in the valley and then pulled back. Meanwhile the Confederates had learned of McDowell's plans from Rose O'Neal Greenhow, head of a Confederate spy ring in Washington. Jefferson Davis ordered Johnston to entrain most of his troops on the Manassas Gap Railroad and bring them to reinforce Beauregard. Johnston left a cavalry screen under Colonel James E. B. (Jeb) Stuart to deceive Patterson and marched most of his army to the railhead. So befuddled was Patterson by Stuart's aggressive maneuvers that he did not even discover Johnston's departure until July 20. By then all but one of the Confederate valley brigades had arrived at Manassas. Patterson's failure to hold Johnston in the valley proved to be of crucial importance in the upcoming battle. It also illustrated three of the Confederate advantages discussed in the previous chapter: superior intelligence sources, better cavalry, and the ability to move troops on interior lines.

Despite all this, the Federals might have kept the advantage if McDowell had been able to move as fast as planned. But his march from Alexandria to Bull Run turned into a nightmare of confusion and delays, which illustrated the military axiom that march discipline is harder to achieve with half-trained troops than is battle discipline. Soldiers had to halt in the July heat for hours at a time while problems up ahead bogged down the whole line. Troops fell out of line to pick blackberries or to take a nap in the shade. Inexperienced officers did not know how to keep thousands of men under control. It took two and a half days for the army to move twenty-two miles, a distance that veterans later in the war could march in a day. The need to reissue rations and ammunition consumed or lost by careless troops and the necessity for reconnaissance in this little-known, ill-mapped terrain caused further delays. McDowell was finally ready for action on Sunday, July 21. On that day carriages from Washington filled with congressmen and assorted spectators drove out to "see the Rebels get whipped."

McDowell's flanking column of 12,000 men roused themselves at 2 A.M., stumbled through the underbrush in the dark, and deployed after crossing the Sudley Springs ford three hours behind schedule. In the meantime, other Union brigades feinted against the stone bridge over Bull Run and the fords downstream to hold the Confederates there while the flanking force rolled them up. At first it worked, despite all the delays. Union regiments came scrambling across the fields north of the Warrenton turnpike, attacking disjointedly but driving before them the outnumbered Confederates, who had changed front to meet this threat to their left flank. Other Union troops forded the river to join the assault. To their crumbling left the Confederates rushed reinforcements, including a brigade under Virginian Thomas J. Jackson, who took a defensive position on Henry House Hill. By noon the Rebels had been forced back to this hill. Attempting to reform his shattered brigade of South Carolinians, General Barnard Bee pointed toward Jackson's troops. "Look!" he shouted. "There is Jackson standing like a stone wall! Rally behind the Virginians!" Rally they did, even though Bee himself was killed. Thus was the legend of "Stonewall" Jackson born.

As Beauregard and Johnston arrived at Henry House Hill to direct their regrouping forces in person, the Union troops, jubilant but disorganized by their success, paused to reform for a renewed assault. Then for two hours, from 2 to 4 P.M., heavy fighting surged back and forth across the hill. At one point the confusion caused by a multiplicity of uniforms crippled a Union attack. A blueclad regiment moved out of the woods toward two Union artillery batteries. Thinking they were supporting infantry, the Federals held their fire until the regiment, which turned out to be the 33rd Virginia, suddenly leveled their muskets and fired a volley at point-blank range, killing many of the gunners and knocking out the batteries. The fighting raged on, but the steam went out of the Union advance in that sector. McDowell was in the thick of the fighting, personally giving orders to brigades, even regiments, but in this display of courage he neglected the duties of overall command and failed to order up two reserve brigades resting in the rear.

Beauregard and Johnston, by contrast, now had firm control of their army, including the last brigade from the valley, just off the train at Manassas and marching into line at 4 P.M. Bolstered by these and other reinforcements, Beauregard ordered a counterattack with his fresh troops. The Southerners charged forward with the rebel yell on their lips. A high-pitched, wailing scream, this

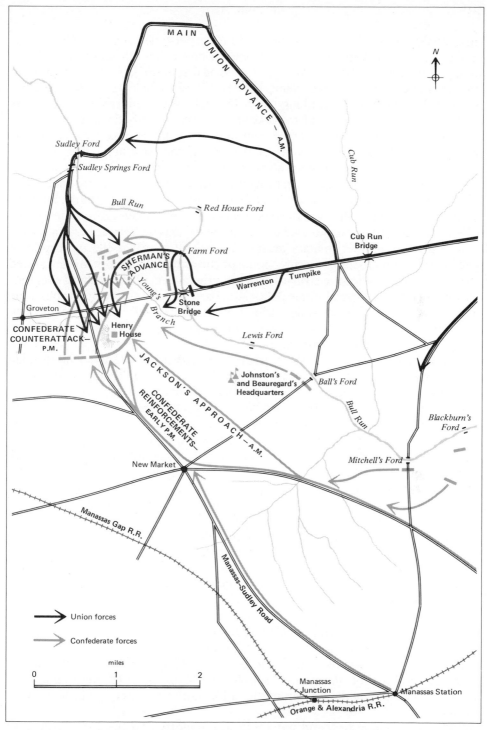

THE FIRST BATTLE OF BULL RUN, JULY 21, 1861

famous yell served the same function as the deeper-toned shout uttered by the Yankee soldiers in battle—it relieved tension and created a sense of solidarity among comrades. Of unknown origin (some said it came from the fox hunter's cry, others likened it to a hog-calling halloo), the rebel yell was by all accounts a fearsome thing. "There is nothing like it this side of the infernal region," wrote a Union veteran. "The peculiar corkscrew sensation that it sends down your backbone under these circumstances can never be told. You have to feel it, and if you say you did not feel it, and heard the yell, you have *never* been there."[3]

In the face of this screaming counterattack the exhausted Yankees, many of whom had been marching and fighting with little food or water for more than thirteen hours on an exceptionally hot July day, gave way—slowly at first, but with increasing disorder as they were forced back across Bull Run. As the sun dipped toward the horizon, panic infected many bluecoats, and the retreat became a rout. This illustrated another military maxim: an orderly retreat is the most difficult maneuver for raw troops to execute. Some of the army vehicles became entangled with the carriages of frantic civilians caught in the melee. One Northern congressman was captured; several other politicians tried to rally the fugitives but were pushed aside by wild-eyed soldiers who wanted only to get away. All night long the men streamed back toward Washington, making far better time in their retreat than they had in their advance.

The battle of Bull Run (or the battle of Manassas, as the Confederates called it) was a decisive tactical victory for the South. Of the 18,000 men on each side actually engaged (several brigades on both sides did not see action), 387 Confederates and 481 Yankees were killed, 1,582 and 1,011 respectively were wounded, and about 1,200 Northerners were missing, mostly captured. In Civil War battles, about one-seventh of the wounded later died of their injuries; so the total of killed and mortally wounded came to about 600 on each side. Although this was a small battle by later Civil War standards, it was by far the largest and most costly in American history up to that time.

When Jefferson Davis himself arrived on the Bull Run battlefield at the climax of victory, he urged Johnston and Beauregard to push on to Washington. But Johnston believed that his army was "more disorganized by victory than that of the United States by defeat."[4] A controversy later developed in the South over responsibility for the failure to follow up the victory. Beauregard blamed Davis for vetoing an advance, but in fact the opposite appears to have been the case. In any event, the Confederates could hardly have taken Washington. McDowell formed a strong rear guard of fresh troops at Centreville, which probably could have checked an enemy advance. Other Union soldiers rallied in the fortifications along the Potomac, a formidable barrier. A drenching rain the day after the battle turned roads into bottomless mud. Moreover, the Confederates did not have the logistical capacity for an advance; supplies at Manassas itself were almost exhausted, and some men went without food for more than twenty-four hours after the battle.

Bull Run made a profound impact on the country. To the Confederates, it seemed to confirm that one Southerner could whip ten Yankees—even though the numbers were equal and the Rebels had come within an ace of being whipped themselves. They had stood on the defensive for most of the battle, always an advantage but especially so with inexperienced troops. Nevertheless, this first decisive Confederate victory instilled Southern troops in Virginia with a confidence that gave them a psychological edge in future battles. More important, perhaps, it created a gnawing sense of inferiority among some Union officers and soldiers in this theater. Perhaps the Rebels were better fighters than the Yankees after all, just as Southerners had always claimed. This potential inferiority complex would prove to have significant military consequences in the eastern theater during the next two years.

McCLELLAN AND THE ARMY OF THE POTOMAC

The tonic of triumph stimulated overconfidence on the Southern home front, causing many to believe that the war was over. At the same time, however, the shock of defeat jolted the North into reality. A mood of grim determination replaced the incandescent optimism of the spring. If Southerners thought the Yankees would quit after one licking, they soon learned differently. Three-year volunteers flooded Northern recruiting offices. The administration moved quickly to reshuffle the top command in the East. George B. McClellan, fresh from his successes in western Virginia, was brought to Washington as commander of the newly named Army of the Potomac. McDowell suffered demotion to a division commander, and Patterson, who had failed to keep Johnston in the valley, was replaced by the Massachusetts political general, Nathaniel P. Banks.

Only thirty-four years old, McClellan had served with distinction in the Mexican War, had studied military methods in Europe, and from 1857 to 1861 had been successively a chief engineer, vice president, and president of midwestern railroads. McClellan later wrote that when he arrived in Washington on July 26, he "found no army to command—only a mere collection of regiments cowering on the banks of the Potomac, some perfectly raw, others dispirited by the recent defeat."[5] Though this was an exaggeration, the situation was bad enough. McClellan took hold with a firm hand to reorganize and train these troops. Unfit officers found themselves discharged; enlisted men found themselves under a rigorous discipline that turned them from recruits into soldiers. They regained some of the pride lost at Bull Run. An excellent organizer, McClellan was just what the army needed in 1861.

The press hailed McClellan as the man to save the country. Some enthusiasts talked of him as the next president (he was a Democrat). The adulation went to McClellan's head. He came to regard himself not as the subordinate of the President and of the general in chief but as their master. In letters to his wife and friends, McClellan unconsciously revealed his messiah complex. "I receive letter after letter, have conversation after conversation, calling on me to save the nation, alluding to the presidency, dictatorship, etc.," he wrote. "By some strange operation of magic I have become the power of the land. . . . God has placed a great work in my hands. . . . I was called to it; my previous life seems to have been unwittingly directed to this great end." His soldiers reinforced McClellan's ego. "You have no idea how the men brighten up now when I go among them," he wrote to his wife. "You never heard such yelling. . . . I can see every eye glisten." As for Lincoln and General in Chief Scott, McClellan wrote:

> I am leaving nothing undone to increase our force; but the old general always comes in the way. . . . The people call on me to save the country. I must save it, and cannot respect anything that is in the way. . . . The President is an idiot and the old General is in his dotage. . . . If [Scott] *cannot* be taken out of my path I will not retain my position but will resign and let the administration take care of itself.[6]

On November 1 Scott finally resigned and McClellan took his place. When Lincoln warned McClellan that the dual jobs of general in chief and commander of the Army of the Potomac would be taxing, the general replied: "I can do it all."[7]

The three months after Bull Run saw no important action in the Virginia theater. While McClellan trained his growing army (120,000 men by October), Johnston was doing the same with fewer than 50,000 Confederates at Centreville. The Rebels pushed their outposts to within sight of Washington, where pickets of both armies watched each other and occasionally traded shots. It was during this period that a Northern woman wrote the poem "All Quiet Along the Potomac," which a Southern composer set to music. Its haunting strains and sentimental lyrics made it one of the most popular war songs on both sides of the Potomac.

These were McClellan's honeymoon months with Northern public opinion. But as the fine, clear days of October passed and McClellan made no move with his "magnificent army," the administration and the public began to grow impatient. McClellan had begun to exhibit the weaknesses that would ultimately bring about his downfall. His first defect was perfectionism. He was superb at preparation, but the preparation was never complete enough to satisfy him. The army was perpetually *almost* ready to move. Linked to this was McClellan's chronic exaggeration of the forces opposing him. At a time when Johnston had only 41,000 men ready for duty, McClellan estimated enemy numbers at 150,000 and used this as a reason for delay until he could build up his own force to 200,000. McClellan's intelligence service, headed by Allan Pinkerton of the famous Pinkerton detective agency, fed the general's fears by constantly overestimating the size of Confederate forces. But McClellan believed what he wanted to believe. He too had absorbed notions of the South's martial superiority, which caused him always to magnify the strength of the enemy.

McClellan lacked that mental and moral courage required of great generals, the will to *act*, the willingness to confront that terrible moment of truth. To cover his weaknesses, he had an unhappy tendency to seek scapegoats. "I am here in a terrible place," he wrote his wife. "The enemy have three or four times my force; the President, the old general, cannot or will not see the true state of affairs. . . . I am thwarted and deceived . . . at every turn."[8]

McClellan's low opinion of Lincoln caused him to commit serious errors of

George B. McClellan
and His Wife, Ellen
Marcy McClellan.
McClellan expressed his
frank and unflattering
judgments of Lincoln,
Stanton, and
Republicans in letters to
his wife. Her father was
a general on McClellan's
staff. *(Reproduced from
the Collections of the
Library of Congress)*

judgment. For one thing, he failed to keep the administration informed of his plans. When pressed about his reasons for inaction, he replied petulantly or not at all. Privately, he described the cabinet as "geese" and the President as "the original gorilla." Once when Lincoln wished to learn something of McClellan's plans, the general made himself scarce "to dodge all enemies in the shape of 'browsing' Presidents, etc." A few evenings later, in November 1861, Lincoln and Secretary of State Seward called on McClellan and were informed that the general was out, but would be home soon. When McClellan returned and learned of his visitors he ignored them and went upstairs. Lincoln and Seward waited another half hour until a servant finally deigned to inform them that the general had gone to bed.[9]

McClellan made no secret of his contempt for abolitionists and radical Republicans. A year earlier, his closest political friends had been Breckinridge Democrats. His proslavery leanings and his refusal to strike the Rebels a blow aroused dark thoughts among some Republicans. Montgomery Blair said on October 1 that "Lincoln himself begins to think he smells a rat." Suspicions of McClellan's loyalty to the Northern cause were unfounded. But he did appoint fellow Demo-

Secret Service Agents, Army of the Potomac. The man in the
checkered shirt is Allan Pinkerton, known during the war by the alias
E. J. Allen. His exaggerated reports of Confederate strength
reinforced McClellan's defensive caution.   *(Copied from original in
Princeton University Library)*

crats to several important staff positions. Like himself, they wanted to restore the
Union on the basis of something like the Crittenden Compromise. They were
"soft" on slavery, and in a sense they were soft on the South as well. Having
attended West Point and served in the old army with Southern officers (several
Confederate generals "were once my most intimate friends," wrote McClellan in
November 1861), they could not share the Republicans' aggressive free-labor
ideology. They did not want to fight the kind of war the abolitionists and radicals
were beginning to demand—a war to destroy slavery and to reshape the South in
the free soil image. "Help me to dodge the nigger," McClellan wrote to an
influential Democratic friend. "*I* am fighting to preserve the integrity of the
Union. . . . To gain that end we cannot afford to mix up the negro question."[10]

Thus did McClellan's personality and politics become mixed up with questions
of military strategy and war aims. A dangerous polarization developed between top
echelons of the army and of the Republican party. The Army of the Potomac
became politicized, with serious consequences for its future effectiveness.

These developments came to a head in the battle of Ball's Bluff and its after-math. This battle occurred when McClellan ordered General Charles P. Stone to send part of his division on a reconnaissance in force across the Potomac toward Leesburg, Virginia, to determine the strength and movements of a Confederate brigade there. Stone did so on October 21. The Rebels ambushed the blue regiments and forced them down the steep bluff into the river, where several men were shot or drowned as they tried to swim to safety. More than 200 Federals were killed and wounded, and 700 captured. One of the killed was Colonel Edward Baker, commander of the reconnaissance and also a Republican senator from Oregon and a close friend of President Lincoln. It was a humiliating defeat, although of little military consequence. Its political consequences, however, were large. In December 1861, Congress created a joint committee to investigate "the conduct of the present war," especially Ball's Bluff and Bull Run. Dominated by radical Republicans, the Committee on the Conduct of the War was productive of both good and evil. It investigated army medical services, illegal trade with the enemy, and war contracts, and helped to bring about greater efficiency and honesty in such matters. But it also harassed Democratic generals and intensified the political tensions infecting the Army of the Potomac.

General Stone was the committee's first target. A West Pointer and a Democrat from Massachusetts, Stone had ordered the return to their masters of fugitive slaves who came into his lines. For this he was reprimanded by Governor Andrew and denounced on the Senate floor by Charles Sumner. Stone was also reported to have been in contact with Confederate officers at Leesburg. Was he disloyal? Had he deliberately sent Baker and the Union troops into a trap at Ball's Bluff? The committee investigated all sorts of rumors against Stone. Although the general's convictions were undoubtedly proslavery and he may have maintained ill-advised contacts with Confederate friends, none of the stories of his disloyalty was ever proven. The committee bullied Stone, refused to let him cross-examine witnesses, and did not even inform him of the specific charges against him. Without receiving a trial or a military inquiry, he was imprisoned in February 1862 for six months. Though he was later restored to minor commands, his career was ruined.

EUROPE AND THE WAR

The American Civil War proved an exception to the rule that large-scale internal wars become international wars. Although the South sought foreign intervention and European powers were tempted to fish in troubled American waters, the Confederacy failed to achieve even diplomatic recognition by a single foreign government. Many factors were responsible for this failure: the skill of Northern diplomacy, the diversion of European interests to international crises in Poland and Denmark, the antislavery sentiments of most Europeans, British and French fears of the consequences of a war with the North, and others. But the most important single factor was the inability of Confederate arms to win enough consecutive victories to convince European governments that the South could sustain its independence. Diplomatic success was contingent upon military success. The rhythm of foreign policy was dictated by the outcome of battles. Confederate military prowess came close to winning foreign intervention in the fall of 1862, but the Union victory at Antietam in September kept the fruits of diplomatic recognition just beyond the Southern grasp.

European attitudes toward the American war are often summarized by a series of generalizations. The upper classes, especially in Britain, are said to have been pro-Confederate because of an affinity between Southern planters and the European aristocracy. The British textile industry depended on Southern cotton. English manufacturers and shipping merchants welcomed the discomfiture of their Yankee competitors. European governments were not sorry to see the weakening of the North American republic whose remarkable growth threatened their own Western Hemisphere interests. The European ruling classes looked with pleasure on the downfall of the American democratic experiment, whose success inspired emulation by the restless masses in their own lands. The working classes and the liberal middle class, on the other hand, are said to have sympathized with the North as the great symbol of republicanism and progressivism in the world. Victory for the Union would be a triumph of free labor and democracy whose impact would advance the cause of liberalism in Europe; but the success of the Confederacy would represent the triumph of slavery and reaction.

Although they contain much truth, these generalizations are oversimplified. Recent research has uncovered crosscurrents and ambivalences in European attitudes. While it was true that British workers in general sympathized with the North, unemployment in the textile industry of Lancashire caused many laborers there to favor intervention in behalf of the South to obtain cotton. On the other hand, many British manufacturers and merchants found the wartime North to be a profitable customer rather than a rival. Some European liberals saw no moral advantage in the Union cause so long as the North fought only for Union and not for emancipation. At the same time, as rebels against an established government, the Southern gentry inspired apprehension as well as admiration among European ruling classes. Although some British statesmen secretly hoped for the downfall of the Yankee republic, others feared that the resulting power vacuum would spawn intrigue and instability in the Western Hemisphere. The French ruler Napoleon III did take advantage of the American conflict to create a puppet monarchy in Mexico. But in the tradition of balance-of-power politics, France was no more eager than Russia to see a decline in American maritime strength, which had functioned as a counterweight to British naval supremacy.

Considerations of power and national self-interest, more than of ideology or public opinion, ultimately determined European policy toward the Civil War. And in the evolution of this policy Britain was the country that really mattered. As the world's leading industrial and naval power, Britain's interests were the most affected by the American war, and Britain was also the nation best equipped to intervene. Napoleon toyed with the idea of unilateral intervention, but in the end he refused to take any action (except in Mexico) without British cooperation.

THE KING COTTON ILLUSION

In 1861 the South based its foreign policy on the theory that cotton was king. According to this theory, the British and French economies depended heavily on cotton. Four-fifths of Britain's cotton supply came from the South. Any interruption of this supply would disrupt the British economy, reduce the workers to starvation, and bring down the government. Britain would be forced to break the blockade and thereby to provoke a war with the North that would ensure Confederate independence.

"What would happen if no cotton was furnished for three years?" Senator James Hammond of South Carolina had asked rhetorically in his famous "King Cotton" speech of 1858. "England would topple headlong and carry the whole civilized world with her, save the South. No, you dare not make war on cotton. No power on earth dares to make war upon it. Cotton is king!" Few Confederates in 1861 doubted the logic of this argument. Mississippi's governor told a British war correspondent that "the sovereign State of Mississippi can do a great deal better without England than England can do without her." "Why sir," said another Southerner, "we have only to shut off your supply of cotton for a few weeks and we can create a revolution in Great Britain." A Charleston merchant was confident that if the Union blockade reduced British imports of cotton, "you'll just send their ships to the bottom and recognize us. That will be before Autumn, I think."[11]

Confederates did not intend to rely on the Union blockade alone to invoke the sovereignty of King Cotton. Southern committees of public safety imposed an embargo on the export of cotton. Although never officially endorsed by the Confederate Congress, the cotton embargo enjoyed wide support in the South and was enforced with thoroughness. Most of the 1860 crop had already been shipped, but most of the 1861 crop stayed in the South. In 1862 Southern planters sowed only one-third of the usual cotton crop and gave over their remaining acres to food production. The 1863 and 1864 crops were even smaller, less than one-eighth the prewar average. British imports from the Confederacy in 1862 were about 1 percent of the 1860 level.

But unfortunately for the King Cotton theory the bumper crops of the late 1850s had created an oversupply of raw cotton and cotton products. By a cruel irony, the cotton embargo of 1861 actually benefited British textile firms suffering from a glutted market. Not until the latter half of 1862 did the much-touted cotton famine seriously affect Britain and France.

Even without the fortuitous circumstance of a cotton surplus in 1861, the embargo probably would not have produced British intervention. The world's most powerful nation was not likely to submit to economic blackmail. King Cotton's sovereignty was an illusion. The British developed alternative sources of cotton in India and Egypt. Although the quality of this cotton was poorer than that of Southern cotton and its quantity far less at first, by 1864 British cotton imports had risen to nearly three-quarters of the antebellum average. Most of this came from India and Egypt, but some came from Southern ports now in Union hands and some from the Confederacy itself. By 1863 the South had reversed its embargo policy and was trying desperately to ship cotton through the tightening blockade to pay for military imports.

The economic motives for British intervention were highest in late 1862, when the cotton famine was at its worst and thousands of Lancashire workers were suffering. But if this sector of the British economy was temporarily depressed by the American war, other sectors were booming. Even before the war, textiles had been losing their central importance in Britain. Union and Confederate war purchases stimulated the rapidly growing iron and shipbuilding and munitions industries. Linen and woollen production took up part of the slack in cotton textiles. The wartime boom in these sectors absorbed many unemployed cotton workers. An increase of poor relief tided over the rest until cotton textiles recovered in 1863. It turned out after all that Mississippi needed England more than England needed Mississippi.

THE BLOCKADE AND FOREIGN RELATIONS

The Union blockade emerged as the central diplomatic issue of the war's first year —not because of its economic effects but because of its legal and political implications. Lincoln's proclamation of a blockade undermined his insistence that the war was a mere domestic insurrection, since a blockade was a weapon of war between sovereign states. On May 13, 1861, the British government issued a proclamation of neutrality, thus granting belligerent status to the Confederacy. Other European nations followed suit. The recognition of belligerency gave the South the right to contract loans and purchase supplies in neutral nations and to exercise belligerent rights on the high seas. This produced anger in the North and jubilation in the South, for both sides considered it a prelude to diplomatic recognition of the Confederacy. But in truth the British had little choice but to recognize Confederate belligerency. European ministers professed astonishment at the Northern outburst. As British Foreign Secretary Lord John Russell put it, "the question of belligerent rights is one, not of principle, but of fact."[12]

Contrary to Northern fears and Southern hopes, the recognition of belligerency was not a first step toward diplomatic recognition. In fact, the European proclamations of neutrality favored the Union in the long run, for they constituted official acceptance of the blockade. Under international law a blockade must be physically effective to be legally binding on neutral powers. But "physically effective" was a matter of definition. Did it mean that every port must be sealed off by an impenetrable cordon of warships? As a neutral power in previous European wars, the United States had insisted that it meant precisely that. But as the world's leading naval power, Britain had always maintained that a blockade was legal if patrolling warships made an effort to prevent vessels from entering or leaving enemy ports. These differing interpretations had helped bring the two nations to war in 1812. But now the roles were reversed: the United States was a naval belligerent and Britain the foremost neutral. The Union took the traditional British position on the question of the blockade's effectiveness, while the Confederacy reiterated the traditional American position. Britain could have found grounds to declare the blockade illegal had it chosen to do so, for Confederate envoys presented long lists of ships that had run the blockade. But the British government had no desire to create a precedent that could boomerang against their navy in a future war. On February 15, 1862, Foreign Secretary Lord Russell pronounced the Union blockade legal so long as warships patrolled a port in strength "sufficient really to prevent access to it or create an evident danger of entering or leaving it." The Union blockade certainly met this criterion.[13]

In previous wars, the British navy had developed the doctrine of "continuous voyage" to justify the seizure of cargoes on ships plying between neutral ports if there was reason to believe that these cargoes were destined ultimately for an enemy port. The United States had rejected this doctrine a half-century earlier, but now the Union navy carried it even further than Britain had done. War materiel destined for the Confederacy usually proceeded from a European port to another neutral port near the Southern coast. There it was transferred to blockade runners. Union warships began to seize British merchant ships before they reached Nassau, Havana, and other transshipment ports. In the *Springbok* case (1863), a New York prize court upheld the seizure of the British ship *Springbok*, bound for a neutral port, on the grounds that its cargo was destined ultimately for the Confederacy. Despite furious protests from merchants, the British government took no action except to record the precedent.

In 1863 the Union navy extended the continuous voyage principle to ground transportation. By that year one of the busiest neutral ports for Confederate goods was Matamoras, a Mexican city just across the mouth of the Rio Grande from Texas. In February 1863 the navy seized the British ship *Peterhoff* near St. Thomas in the Caribbean. Bound for Matamoras, the *Peterhoff* carried supplies and other war contraband. A prize court upheld the seizure because of evidence that this materiel would have been transshipped by land across the border into the Confederacy. Once again the British press clamored for retaliation against the arrogant Yankees, but the government accepted the American doctrine of "continuous transportation" and stored up the precedent for future use. A half-century later, during the early years of World War I, this particular chicken came home to roost when Britain applied the doctrine of continuous transportation against American exports to neutral Holland of war goods destined ultimately for Germany.

THE *TRENT* AFFAIR

One case of Union interference with a British ship did come close to causing an Anglo-American war. On November 8, 1861, the *U.S.S. San Jacinto* stopped the British mail packet *Trent*, bound from Havana to St. Thomas. On board the *Trent* were James Mason of Virginia and John Slidell of Louisiana, Confederate commissioners traveling to London and Paris. Captain Charles Wilkes of the *San Jacinto* sent a boarding party to apprehend Mason and Slidell, and then carried them away to a Union prison in Boston. This event caused celebration in the North and turned Wilkes into a hero. The House of Representatives voted him a special medal. But when the news reached England, press and public reacted with violent anger. Prime Minister Viscount Palmerston told a tense cabinet: "You may stand for this but damned if I will!"[14] The British navy dispatched reinforcements to its North American squadron. The army made ready to send an expeditionary force to Canada. War talk was common on both sides of the Atlantic.

But neither side could profit by such a war, and both soon realized it. The British government prepared a tough note (but not an ultimatum) demanding an apology and the release of Mason and Slidell. Prince Albert, almost on his death-bed, softened the note by adding a suggestion that perhaps Wilkes's action had been unauthorized. This provided the Union government a way to give in without losing face. Wilkes had in fact acted on his own. The legality of his action was clouded by the ambiguities of international law. The right of search and seizure of contraband on the high seas was well established. But whether diplomats were "contraband" was less clear. If Wilkes had put a prize crew on board the *Trent* and brought it before a prize court, the British would have had no case against the United States. Secretary of State Seward made use of this technicality to admit that Wilkes had acted wrongly. Lincoln ordered the release of Mason and Slidell, and the British accepted this in lieu of an apology. The crisis was over. Mason and Slidell proceeded to London and Paris, where they spent a futile three years trying to win foreign recognition and intervention.

Fourteen

The Springtime
of Northern Hope

Although Union arms would soon win a string of stirring victories, January 1862 was a month of gloom in Washington. The release of Mason and Slidell in the aftermath of the *Trent* affair had produced a feeling of letdown. Northern banks and the U.S. Treasury had just suspended specie payments (see p. 202). News of war contract scandals dominated front pages. The Army of the Potomac had done nothing significant for six months except to send four regiments to disaster at Ball's Bluff, and now General McClellan had fallen ill with typhoid fever. Even General George Thomas's victory at Logan's Cross-Roads in Kentucky (see p. 162) did little to brighten the gloom, for it produced no further advance. On the back of a letter from General Henry Halleck, commander of the Department of Missouri, explaining why Halleck's troops could not make a forward move along the Mississippi, Lincoln wrote: "It is exceedingly discouraging. As everywhere else, nothing can be done." The despondent President dropped into the office of Quartermaster General Montgomery Meigs one day and said: "General, what shall I do? The people are impatient; Chase has no money . . . the General of the Army has typhoid fever. The bottom is out of the tub. What shall I do?"[1]

On January 27, Lincoln issued "General War Order No. 1" directing a forward movement of all armies on February 22 (Washington's birthday). A rather clumsy device which Lincoln hoped would assuage public impatience and prod McClellan, this order had no military effect. But it did force McClellan to tell Lincoln of his plan to transport the Army of the Potomac by water down the Chesapeake Bay to land them for a flank attack on the Confederate troops at Centreville and Fredericksburg. While Lincoln was mulling over this plan, dramatic news arrived from the West.

FORTS HENRY AND DONELSON

The Confederate government in 1861 had appointed Albert Sidney Johnston (not to be confused with Joseph E. Johnston in Virginia) commander of its Western Department. A Kentuckian and one of the highest-ranking officers in the old army, Johnston had been offered a top Union command but had chosen to go with the South. When Union troops under Don Carlos Buell and Ulysses S. Grant occupied northern Kentucky in the fall of 1861, Johnston established a defensive line through the southern part of the state anchored by concentrations of forces at Bowling Green and at Columbus, on the Mississippi River. Buell planned a spring campaign against Bowling Green, but while he planned, Grant acted.

The weakest links in Johnston's line were Forts Henry and Donelson, twelve miles apart on the Tennessee and Cumberland rivers just south of the Kentucky-Tennessee border. A Union fleet of three wooden and four iron-armored gunboats (with more under construction) gave the Yankees control of the rivers. Commanding this fleet was Flag Officer Andrew Foote, a tough, teetotaling Connecticut Yankee who saw eye to eye with Grant about the strategic importance of Forts Henry and Donelson. Halleck saw it too, and authorized Grant to attack Fort Henry. Accompanied by the fleet, Grant brought 15,000 men up the Tennessee River (southward), landed them four miles below the fort, and prepared to attack it in the rear while the fleet shelled it from the river. As it turned out, the gunboats did the job alone before the infantry arrived on the scene. Fort Henry was badly sited on low ground, threatened almost as much by the rising river as by the approaching Yankees. At 1 P.M. on February 6, Foote's gunboats opened a heavy bombardment; the fort replied valiantly and disabled one ironclad with a shot into the boiler. But the Rebels were outgunned. After most of the garrison had escaped by land to Fort Donelson, the Confederate commander surrendered in midafternoon.

The consequences of this brief action were momentous. The Union gunboats now ranged all the way up the Tennessee to Florence, Alabama. Grant organized his troops for the overland march against Donelson while the ironclads steamed back downriver and up the Cumberland for another joint effort with the army. Johnston faced a desperate dilemma. His defensive line was pierced; his rail link between Bowling Green and Memphis was cut by Federal control of the Tennessee River; the Confederate stronghold at Columbus on the Mississippi was flanked by Grant at Fort Henry. If Donelson also fell, Johnston's main force at Bowling Green would have Grant in its rear while facing Buell in front, and Nashville itself could not be held. If he put every available man into Fort Donelson he risked losing them; if he retreated to a new defensive line in central Tennessee, Donelson's small garrison would fall like a ripe plum into Grant's lap. Johnston compromised by sending half of his troops from Bowling Green to Donelson, which brought the force there to 17,000 men, and retreating with the rest toward Nashville. The general who took command at Donelson was none other than John B. Floyd, the Virginia politician who had been sent to Kentucky after his failure in western Virginia.

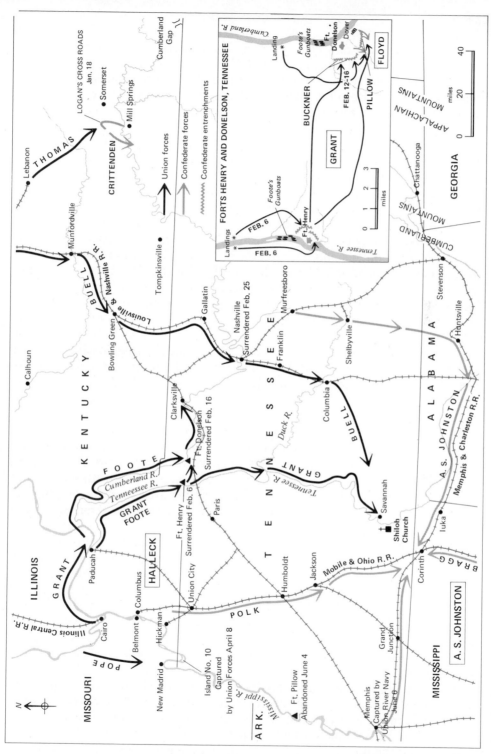

KENTUCKY AND TENNESSEE, WINTER AND SPRING 1862

FORTS HENRY AND DONELSON, TENNESSEE

Union forces

Confederate forces

Confederate entrenchments

Grant's confident forces converged on Donelson, where reinforcements increased his army to 27,000 men. Grant planned to have these troops surround the fort on the land side while Foote's flotilla pounded it into submission as it had done to Fort Henry. But Donelson proved a much tougher prospect. The fifteen-acre earthwork fort protected a dozen heavy guns sited on a bluff above the river. Outside the fort ran a circle of trenches along ridges overlooking steep wooded ravines. Good troops should have been able to hold these trenches against at least twice their number if the fearsome gunboats could be kept at bay. The battle began auspiciously for the Confederates. They repulsed a premature Federal infantry probe on February 13. Next day the armored gunboats moved up to the attack, but these monsters turned out not to be invincible after all. Well-aimed fire by the Rebel batteries damaged three of them after a fierce duel, and the wounded Foote (he later died of his wound) called off the attack.

Although the Confederates had won the first round, Floyd and his subordinates still considered themselves to be in a bad fix. The Yankees had them besieged by land and water; surrender seemed only a matter of time. That night a council of Confederate officers decided to try a breakout attack on the morning of February 15 to enable the garrison to escape. As the Union soldiers on the right wing were getting ready for breakfast, 10,000 screaming Rebels suddenly burst from the woods with muskets blazing. After several hours of hard fighting, in which Colonel Nathan Bedford Forrest's battalion of dismounted cavalry particularly distinguished itself, the Southerners forced back the Union right and opened the road to Nashville.

What happened next has been the subject of controversy. Having opened the escape route, Confederate General Gideon J. Pillow ordered his men back to the trenches, and after some hesitation Floyd approved the order. Some historians consider this action inexplicable; others believe that the Rebel commanders, having succeeded in their plan, suddenly lost their nerve. The truth seems to be that the Confederate soldiers, exhausted and disorganized by their long fight in subfreezing weather, needed a pause to regroup and to fetch their equipment before marching away.

But this pause proved fatal. Grant had been absent during the fighting, conferring with Foote on his flagboat three miles downstream where the wind had blown the noise of battle away from him. Returning to find his right wing routed, he faced the crisis calmly. Reasoning that the Confederates must have weakened their own right to attack his, Grant ordered his left division to assault the trenches in their front. With a yell, Iowa and Indiana boys carried the first line of thinly held trenches while Grant on the right personally helped regroup the demoralized Illinois regiments for a counterattack that regained most of what they had lost in the morning.

During the night of February 15–16, Confederate officers once again held a council of war and decided, over Forrest's bitter objections, to surrender. Facing possible indictment for fraud and treason for actions he had committed as secretary of war under Buchanan, Floyd turned the command over to Pillow. Pillow, who as a politician was also apprehensive about falling into Federal hands, turned his command over to General Simon B. Buckner, who was not amused by these antics. While Floyd and Pillow escaped with 2,500 men in boats and Forrest led his 700 troopers out through a flooded road, Buckner prepared to surrender the remaining 13,000. Ironically, Buckner had once lent money to Grant when he was down and out in the old army. But when Buckner requested the terms of surrender, Grant would offer no favors in return. He replied: "No terms except an unconditional and immediate surrender can be accepted. I propose to move immediately upon your works."[2]

These words made Grant famous. But the consequences of his triumph at Donelson were more than personal. The fall of the fort lifted morale in the North and depressed it in the South. From London, Confederate envoy James Mason wrote that "the late reverses at Fort Henry and Fort Donelson have had an unfortunate effect on the minds of our friends here."[3] Worse was yet to come. With the Cumberland River now controlled by the Union navy, Nashville was no longer tenable, and the Confederates evacuated it on February 23. An important industrial and transport center, the city was also the first Confederate state capital to fall to the Yankees.

What was left of Albert Sidney Johnston's command retreated to the rail junction of Corinth in northern Mississippi. There they were joined by the garrison that had evacuated Columbus, Kentucky, and by reinforcements from the lower South. In March, Grant established his forward base at Pittsburg Landing on the Tennessee River only twenty miles from Corinth. He was reinforced by three new divisions, one of them commanded by William Tecumseh Sherman. Halleck was now in overall command of the Tennessee-Missouri theater. He ordered Buell's Army of the Ohio forward from Nashville to join Grant's Army of West Tennessee for a joint offensive of 75,000 Union troops against the 45,000 Confederates now concentrated at Corinth.

THE BATTLE OF SHILOH

But Johnston had no intention of waiting for Grant to attack him. Joined by General Beauregard, who had been sent west after quarreling with Jefferson Davis in Virginia, Johnston proposed to regain the initiative by a sudden strike at Grant's 40,000 men before they could be reinforced by Buell, who was delayed by flooded rivers and destroyed bridges. Johnston had one big advantage—no one on the Union side expected him to take the offensive. The loss of Donelson and the subsequent Confederate retreat had convinced Grant that the Rebel army was demoralized. At Pittsburg Landing the Yankee troops spent their time drilling instead of entrenching, for their commanders were so offensive-minded that they took no defensive precautions.

Johnston planned to march his army from Corinth to a bivouac near Federal lines, from where he would launch a dawn attack on April 4. But from the outset things went wrong. Johnston learned what McDowell had learned at Bull Run nine months earlier—that a large body of green troops could not move quickly from one place to another. The Confederates consumed three days in this march of eighteen miles. Certain that the advantage of surprise had been lost and that Buell had joined Grant by now, Beauregard wanted to call the whole thing off and return to Corinth. By all odds he should have been right. The Confederates had made a great deal of noise getting into position. They had skirmished with cavalry pickets in front of Sherman's division. Grant knew that the Rebels were up to something, perhaps an attack on his detached division five miles downriver at Crump's landing, but he telegraphed Halleck that he had "scarcely the faintest idea of an attack (a general one) being made upon us." To a nervous colonel in his division who reported a Rebel build-up in the woods, Sherman said contemptuously: "Take your damned regiment back to Ohio. Beauregard is not such a fool as to leave his base of operations and attack us in ours. There is no enemy nearer than Corinth." But at that very moment, two miles away, Johnston was making his decision. Having finally got his army close to the enemy, he would not hear of retreat. "I would fight them if they were a million," Johnston told his corps commanders on the evening of April 5. "Gentlemen, we shall attack at daylight tomorrow."[4]

Next morning the first wave of the Rebel assault hit Sherman's camps near a small log church named Shiloh. The Yankees were not taken entirely by surprise, as some newspaper reports later stated. Union patrols had gone forward at first light, had encountered Confederate skirmishers, and had fallen back noisily toward their own lines, giving the two front divisions (those of Sherman and of Benjamin Prentiss, which were both composed of green troops) time to brace themselves for the gray wave coming toward them.

During that long day the 40,000 Confederates drove back the 33,000 Federals (Grant's detached division did not arrive on the field until dark) slowly but surely, with appalling losses on both sides. Brigades and regiments lost cohesion in the thick woods and small clearings, and the battle broke down into a series of vicious fire fights. Breakfasting at his headquarters seven miles downriver, Grant heard the sound of the firing. He ordered the vanguard of Buell's arriving troops forward to the battlefield, commandeered a steamboat, and hastened to the front, where in cooperation with his division commanders, he labored to shore up faltering blue lines. By midafternoon a pattern had emerged. Both Union flanks had been bent backward, but Prentiss, with the remnants of his division and parts of others, held a line in the center along a sunken road that Confederates aptly named "the hornet's nest." While personally directing one of the attacks near this sector, Johnston fell mortally wounded. Beauregard took command. Instead of containing and bypassing the hornet's nest, the Southerners brought up sixty-two guns and loosed an artillery barrage in an attempt to break the Yankee center. The relentless Rebels finally surrounded Prentiss, who surrendered his 2,200 survivors in late afternoon, having gained time for Grant to establish a strong defensive line along the ridge at Pittsburg Landing. Toward evening the first brigade of Buell's army crossed the river to join Grant; two gunboats and fifty guns on the ridge poured a heavy artillery fire into Confederate ranks; and Beauregard sensibly decided against sending his exhausted troops on one final twilight assault.

The Rebels had driven the bluecoats back more than two miles but had failed

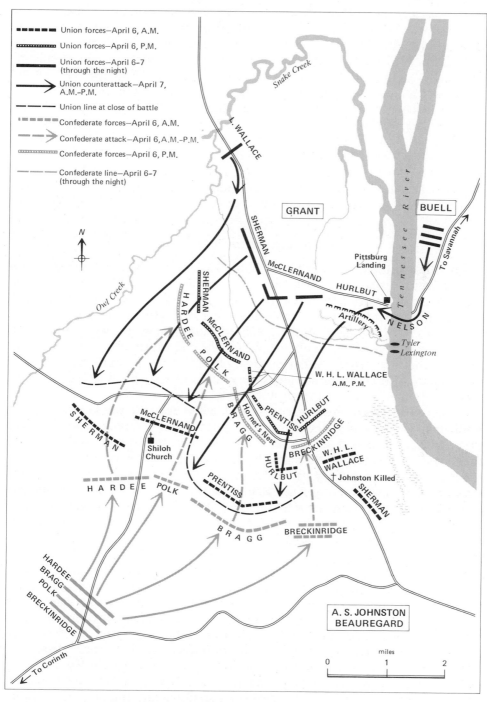

THE BATTLE OF SHILOH, APRIL 6–7, 1862

to achieve a breakthrough. And now the odds were with Grant. His missing division finally arrived from downriver, while three of Buell's divisions crossed during the night. On the morrow Grant's strength would be augmented by 25,000 fresh troops, while the Confederates could expect no reinforcements. During the night lightning flashed and rain fell on the 2,000 dead and 10,000 wounded lying on the battlefield. Few soldiers on either side could sleep. The gunboats lobbed eight-inch shells into the bivouacs of exhausted Confederates all night long. When sodden morning finally came, the determined Yankees counterattacked all along the line. Yard by yard they pushed the Rebels back over yesterday's battleground until in midafternoon Beauregard broke off resistance and began a weary retreat through the mud to Corinth. The Federals seemed satisfied to regain their original camps and made only a feeble pursuit, which was checked by Forrest's cavalry.

Retreat and Pursuit after Battle

A number of historians have criticized Grant's failure to follow up his victory with a vigorous blow that might have destroyed the Rebel army. It is true that the Confederates were in a bad way on the retreat to Corinth. One corps commander, Braxton Bragg, wrote on the morning after the battle: "Our condition is horrible. Troops utterly disorganized and demoralized. Road almost impassable. No provisions and no forage."[5] But as after Bull Run, the victors were as disorganized and spent as the vanquished. Although some of Buell's troops were comparatively fresh, Grant himself could not give orders to them, and Buell lacked the killer instinct.

Pursuit of a beaten enemy after a major Civil War battle was never as easy as it might appear on paper. The soldiers were emotionally and physically exhausted. Often they had marched many miles before fighting and had eaten and slept little for several days. So long as the action was at its height, the flow of adrenalin kept them going, but the slightest pause after hours of fighting produced an emotional letdown and an overpowering thirst that made the search for water a top priority. A Union soldier wrote home after Shiloh: "We chased them one-quarter mile, when we halted . . . and threw ourselves on the ground and rested. Oh, mother, how tired I was, now the excitement of the action was over. . . . The dead and wounded lay in piles. I gave water to some poor wounded men, and then sought food in an abandoned camp near us." After another battle one of the survivors said: "I never saw so many broken down and exhausted men in all my life. I was sick as a horse, and as wet with blood and sweat as I could be, and many of our men were vomiting with excessive fatigue. . . . Our tongues were parched and cracked for water, and our faces blackened with powder and smoke."[6]

A beaten army usually had an incentive to retreat quickly despite fatigue, but it was harder to motivate the victors to further exertion. After a few battles— notably Antietam and Gettysburg—the Union armies had fresh reserves of veteran troops who should have been used in vigorous pursuit. But most of the time, as at Shiloh, the men were too fought-out to do anything but rest and marvel upon their survival. And during or after many Civil War battles, as at Shiloh, rain churned the roads into mud, hindering pursuit.

Shiloh was the most ghastly bloodbath in the history of the Western Hemisphere thus far, though later Civil War battles would put it in seventh place in this respect. More than 1,700 men were killed and 8,000 wounded on *each* side. Of the 16,500 total wounded, over 2,000 more men would soon die. Shiloh was America's baptism in total war. "O it was too shocking too horrible," wrote one Confederate survivor. "God grant that I may never be the partaker in such scenes again. . . . When released from this I shall ever be an advocate of peace."[7]

OTHER UNION TRIUMPHS IN THE WEST

For a time in the spring of 1862 the Confederacy appeared to be finished. Four hundred miles west of Shiloh and one month earlier, Union victory in the battle of Pea Ridge had cleared the Rebels (except for guerrillas) out of Missouri and achieved Union control of northern Arkansas. After Frémont's departure from Missouri in November 1861 (see pp. 157–158), General Samuel R. Curtis had taken field command of the main Union army in the state. In a winter campaign, Curtis's 12,000 men maneuvered Sterling Price's 8,000 Confederate Missourians into Arkansas, where Price once again linked up with Ben McCulloch's small army. The combined Rebel force of 16,000 men (including three Cherokee Indian regiments)* came under the overall command of the aggressive Earl Van Dorn. Curtis had deployed his bluecoats just south of Pea Ridge in northern Arkansas. Avoiding a frontal attack, Van Dorn executed an all-night flanking march around the north side of Pea Ridge and fell upon the Federal rear on the morning of March 7. Curtis's scouts had warned him of the Confederate maneuver, so he faced his army about to receive the attack. His artillery dispersed the Cherokee regiments, a sharpshooter killed General McCulloch, and the blue lines held against repeated infantry assaults by superior numbers. Next morning, correctly judging that Van Dorn was running short of ammunition, Curtis counterattacked and scattered the Rebels in several directions.

With the Confederates in retreat both east and west of the Mississippi, it was time to secure the great river itself. The Rebels had fortified Island No. 10 on the Mississippi (see map on p. 223), where the river made a large **S** curve near

---

*The Cherokees were the largest of the five "civilized tribes" (the others were the Chickasaws, Choctaws, Creeks, and Seminoles). Earlier in the century, whites in the Southeastern states had driven most of these Indians from their ancestral lands, and the government had resettled them in the Indian Territory (present-day Oklahoma). In 1861 the Confederacy negotiated treaties of alliance with certain chiefs of the five tribes, who sent delegates to the Confederate Congress and furnished troops to the Southern army. But about half of the Indians in the civilized tribes remained loyal to the Union. In general, the full-blooded Indians stayed with the Union and the "half-breeds" went with the Confederacy. Some of the latter owned Negro slaves. Most of the fighting of pro-Union against pro-Confederate Indians was confined to the Indian Territory; the battle of Pea Ridge was the main exception. The Cherokee leader Stand Watie rose to the rank of brigadier general in the Confederate army, and did not surrender his troops to the Union until a month after the last of the other Confederate armies had surrendered.

the Kentucky-Tennessee border. So long as the Confederates held this island, no Yankee boats could go down the river. Halleck ordered General John Pope to organize 20,000 troops into an Army of the Mississippi to cooperate with the river navy in a campaign to take Island No. 10. Pope drove the Confederates away from the Missouri side of the river; his engineers cut a canal through the swamps so that transports could bypass the island; two of the armored gunboats fought their way past the island batteries; then Pope used the gunboats and transports to ferry his men across the river below the island, where they seized the Tennessee bank. Trapped by Yankee troops and gunboats on all sides, the 7,000-man garrison surrendered itself and 150 heavy guns on April 8—the same day that beaten Confederates were stumbling through the mud from Shiloh to Corinth.

The Fall of New Orleans

Even as the North celebrated these victories in Tennessee, news came from the lower South of a stunning naval achievement—the capture of New Orleans. Believing that the main Federal threat to the lower Mississippi would come from upriver, the Confederate high command had stripped the Gulf coast of troops (who fought at Shiloh) and had sent eight Rebel gunboats northward to confront the Union river fleet above Memphis. This left only 3,000 militia to defend New Orleans by land and two uncompleted ironclads, a few armed steamboats, and two forts flanking the river seventy miles below the city to defend it against a thrust from the Gulf. It was the South's bad luck that this was the way the Federals came and that the expedition was led by the most remarkable naval commander of the war, David G. Farragut.

Tennessee-born and married to a Virginian, Farragut nevertheless remained loyal to the stars and stripes. Sixty years old at the outbreak of the Civil War, he had joined the navy as a midshipman at the age of nine and had fought in the War of 1812 and the Mexican War. A combative man, Farragut believed in carrying the war as far inland as water would float his ships. In 1862 his Gulf Expeditionary Force consisted of twenty-four wooden warships carrying 245 guns, nineteen mortar boats, and 15,000 soldiers under the command of Benjamin Butler. In mid-April the fleet moved upriver to the forts below New Orleans. There the mortar boats under the command of Commodore David D. Porter commenced a week-long bombardment that fired 17,000 thirteen-inch shells without putting the forts out of action. Growing impatient with these spectacular but ineffective fireworks, Farragut decided to run his ships past the forts. At 2 A.M. on April 24, the fleet weighed anchor and moved single file up the channel against a three-knot current. The forts opened fire with 100 guns; the ships replied with their broadsides; the intrepid Confederate fleet tried to ram some of the Union ships and to push fire rafts against others (they almost set Farragut's flagship afire). One of the Union officers described the scene as resembling "all the earthquakes in the world and all the thunder and lightning storms together, in a space of two miles, all going off at once."[8] Despite the sound and the fury, Farragut got

Admiral David G.
Farragut *(Reproduced
from the Collections of the
Library of Congress)*

through with only one ship sunk and three disabled. He steamed up to New Orleans, where the helpless militia fled from the fleet's guns without firing a shot. The city surrendered to Farragut on April 27. Downriver, the troops in the two Confederate forts mutinied and surrendered to Butler, who left a regiment to garrison them and brought the rest of his men up to occupy the South's largest city and principal port.

Farragut did not rest on his laurels. He sent seven ships on up the river where Baton Rouge became the second state capital to fall, surrendering like New Orleans, with Union ships' guns trained on its streets. Natchez also surrendered without resistance, but Vicksburg—with its heavy guns sited high on the bluff— refused to yield, and Farragut dropped back downriver. From New Orleans to Vicksburg, the Mississippi was a 400-mile Union highway by the end of May. Not to be outdone, the river fleet in the north fought its way down to Memphis, where on June 6 Federal ironclads and rams sank or captured seven of the eight boats in the Confederate river fleet while the unhappy citizens of Memphis watched from the bluffs. The city then surrendered.

The Pace of Union Triumphs Slows

While the U.S. navy was winning this series of dazzling victories, what were the western armies doing? After Shiloh the Confederates concentrated all available men at Corinth, bringing their total strength up to 70,000 men, of whom a quarter were on the sicklist. Halleck brought together more than 100,000 Federals on the old Shiloh battlefield, took personal command of them, and began a slow, methodical advance on Corinth. A textbook soldier, Halleck believed more in the eight-

U.S.S. Pensacola. A twenty-three gun steam sloop, the
Pensacola was a typical wooden ship of the salt-water Union navy.
Using steam for speed and combat, she could switch to sails for
long-distance cruising. Farragut preferred wooden ships to the
new ironclads, contending that a shot could pass clean through a
wooden ship and do less damage than when penetrating an
ironclad. Whatever the merit of this argument, the *Pensacola* was
the second ship in Farragut's line during the run past the
forts below New Orleans. She took many direct hits but kept
on going.   *(Reproduced from the Collections of the Library of
Congress)*

eenth-century idea of capturing "strategic points" than in destroying the enemy's
army. Thus the vital rail junction at Corinth was his objective. If Beauregard
would evacuate the place without a fight, Halleck would be happy. Beauregard did,
slipping away at the end of May in what Halleck regarded as a Union triumph
but Grant considered a disaster, for he believed that a determined effort might
have destroyed part of the Confederate army.

At this time, however, Grant was under a cloud. He had never lost his reputation from the old army days as a heavy drinker, and after he had achieved
prominence at Donelson, rumors of his drinking began to circulate again. After
Shiloh, whispers made the rounds that the Union army had been surprised there

because its commander was drunk. Lincoln was not taken in by these unfounded reports.* To one visitor bearing such a tale, the President said: "I can't spare this man; he fights."[9]

But Halleck evidently thought he could spare him, for in the Corinth campaign he put Grant on the shelf by appointing him second in command and giving him nothing to do. Grant requested a transfer and even considered resigning from the army, but at Sherman's urging he stayed on. After Halleck went east in July, Grant took command of all Union forces in western Tennessee and northern Mississippi.

Before then, however, Halleck had divided his large army into several parts. Buell took 35,000 men to begin a frustrating (and in the end unsuccessful) campaign against Chattanooga. Other troops went to Arkansas to deal with new Confederate moves there. The rest dispersed to occupy cities and guard lines of communication in the 45,000 square miles of Confederate territory they had conquered in the past four months. Many historians have been critical of Halleck's policy of dispersal. They argue that if 50,000 men had been kept together after capturing Corinth they could have marched southward to take Vicksburg, Jackson, even Mobile. The argument has some merit. But it slights the need to detach large numbers of troops to guard supply lines, to administer occupied cities, and to deal with all the problems of conquered territory. It also overlooks the problem of disease in a deep-South summer campaign.

The Confederates at Corinth had suffered fearfully from sickness in the spring of 1862. The Union army encountered similar problems during its campaign against Corinth. Several generals, including Halleck, Pope, and Sherman, fell ill (Sherman with malaria) after the Federals had occupied the city. Disease also plagued the initial Union campaign against Vicksburg.

In June 1862, Farragut again brought his fleet and 3,200 army troops upriver with orders to take Vicksburg. The Union river fleet came down from Memphis to help. Defending Vicksburg were sixty heavy guns and 10,000 soldiers under Van Dorn. The navy's mortars and guns pounded the defenses day after day, with little effect. The army troops dug a canal across a neck of land formed by a hairpin bend in the river, in the hope that the current would widen it into a new channel to enable Northern shipping to bypass Vicksburg. But the river refused to cooperate. Shielded on three sides by the river and by impassable swamps, Vicksburg could be attacked by land only from the east, where it was protected by a high ridge. Not only would the number of troops needed for such an attack be large and the problem of supplying them formidable, but two-thirds of the Union

---

*The stories about Grant's drinking were an example of the way in which rumors about famous people, built on a tiny substratum of truth, are ballooned by newspapers and gossip into "fact." In 1854 Captain Grant, stationed at a California military outpost, apparently began drinking heavily in an attempt to overcome boredom and loneliness for his wife and children. He resigned from the army to avoid a court martial for neglect of duty, and tried a variety of occupations without notable success until he joined the army again as colonel of an Illinois volunteer regiment in 1861. In his rise to three-star rank by 1864, Grant inspired jealousy in the hearts of many other ambitious officers, who helped spread the stories of his drinking. According to Grant's biographer, the renowned Civil War historian Bruce Catton, Grant imbibed very little during the war—less than most other generals in the Union army—and his ability to perform his duties was never impaired by alcohol. See Catton, *Grant Moves South* (Boston, 1960), pp. 95–97, 462–65.

soldiers and sailors already on hand were prostrated by malaria, dysentery, and typhoid. With hundreds of men dying of disease and the river level falling (endangering Farragut's deep-water ships), the Federals gave up the first Vicksburg campaign at the end of July. Farragut withdrew southward, the river fleet northward, and for the time being the Confederates owned the Mississippi for 200 miles between Vicksburg and Port Hudson, Louisiana, which they also fortified.

Despite the failure to capture Vicksburg in 1862, the four months from the fall of Fort Henry on February 6 to the fall of Memphis on June 6 were a period of remarkable Union success in the West. "Every blow tells fearfully against the rebellion," exulted the *New York Tribune* on May 23, 1862. "The rebels themselves are panic-stricken, or despondent. It now requires no very far reaching prophet to predict the end of this struggle."

The Rebels were indeed despondent in May 1862. Not only had they been pushed back in the West, but in the East McClellan's 100,000-strong Army of the Potomac was within five miles of Richmond. Other Union forces in Virginia outnumbered the Confederates on every front and seemed poised for advances that would crush the rebellion before the Fourth of July. But by that date the brilliant generalship of Lee and Jackson had turned the tide in Virginia and ended Northern hopes for quick victory.

Fifteen

Jackson and Lee Strike Back

THE PENINSULA AND VALLEY CAMPAIGNS IN VIRGINIA

With the approach of Virginia's spring in 1862, General McClellan planned an elaborate flanking maneuver with the Army of the Potomac against the Confederates at Centreville to avoid a costly frontal attack. Anticipating such a move, Confederate commander Joseph E. Johnston spoiled it in early March by retreating forty miles southward to Culpeper. There, he was in a better position to protect Richmond against a threat from any direction. While McClellan pondered his next move, Northern journalists who visited the vacated Confederate lines discovered several logs painted black to resemble cannons plus other evidence that Johnston's position had not been so strong nor his army so large as McClellan had claimed. The "Quaker guns" caused McClellan much embarrassment and fed growing Republican suspicions that he really did not want to smash the Rebels. On March 11 Lincoln relieved McClellan as general in chief, on the ground that he could not exercise responsibility for all Union armies when he was about to take the field as commander of a campaigning army. This was logical, but it also carried overtones of distrust for McClellan.

With the Confederates now ensconced behind the Rappahannock River, McClellan proposed to shift his own campaign farther south by transporting the Army of the Potomac down the Chesapeake Bay to Fortress Monroe at the tip of the peninsula formed by the York and James rivers. This had the advantage of placing the army's base near Richmond with only two rivers to cross before reaching the Confederate capital. But it made Richmond instead of the Southern army the primary objective, a reversal of what Lincoln thought the priorities should be. It also had the defect, in Lincoln's eyes, of leaving Washington unprotected against a Rebel attack from the west or south. McClellan promised to leave enough troops in the vicinity of Washington to protect the capital, and also assured Lincoln that his move to the Virginia peninsula would compel the Confederates to turn southeast, away from Washington, to meet the threat to Richmond. Lincoln reluctantly approved the plan.

In late March a fleet of more than 300 vessels began ferrying 70,000 soldiers plus horses, wagons, supplies, and 300 cannon from Alexandria to Fortress Monroe. General Irvin McDowell's strong corps of 35,000 men remained at Fredericksburg with orders to march southward later to cooperate with McClellan in a joint attack on Confederate defenses guarding the lower peninsula. In addition to the Army of the Potomac, two other Union armies were operating in the Virginia theater: 25,000 men in the Shenandoah Valley under Nathaniel Banks, and another 8,000 in West Virginia under John C. Frémont, whom Lincoln had appointed to this command in response to congressional pressures. McClellan counted some of these troops among those he had left behind to protect Washington. McClellan also left fewer regiments in the actual Washington defenses than he had promised to leave, and nearly all of them were new recruits. The President became concerned for the safety of the capital and annoyed with McClellan's apparent indifference to this concern.

Believing that Banks had more than enough men in the valley to cope with Stonewall Jackson's small army there, Lincoln ordered one of Banks's divisions to Manassas, which was closer to Washington. But this reckoned without Jackson's extraordinary talents. Deeply religious, idiosyncratic, secretive, and unpredictable, Jackson proved to be one of the best generals of the Civil War. His orders were to prevent Banks from sending any part of his army from the valley to eastern Virginia. With only 4,200 men, Jackson on March 23 boldly attacked a division more than twice as large at Kernstown, a village just south of Winchester. He was repulsed with heavy losses, but this tactical defeat turned out to be a strategic victory with important consequences. Reasoning that Jackson must have more men in the valley than previously thought, Lincoln ordered all of Banks's army to remain there and detached a division from McClellan to reinforce Frémont in West Virginia. In order to keep enough troops near Washington to protect the capital, Lincoln ordered McDowell's corps to remain near Fredericksburg instead of joining McClellan's forces as originally planned.

McClellan's Advance Toward Richmond

The retention of McDowell's corps was the first of several actions that caused McClellan and his supporters to charge that the Republican administration did not want him, a Democratic general, to succeed. No evidence exists to support this charge. In any event, by the first week of April McClellan had 70,000 men (with 30,000 more soon to arrive) facing 17,000 Confederates entrenched across the lower peninsula near the old Revolutionary battlefield of Yorktown. Instead of assaulting this line, McClellan settled down for a siege. He overestimated the number of enemy troops holding the Yorktown defenses. The Confederate commander, General John B. Magruder, did his best to encourage McClellan's illusions. A lover of amateur theatricals, Magruder staged a show for the Federals. He paraded his troops back and forth and shifted his artillery around in such a way as to give the impression that he had more men than he did.

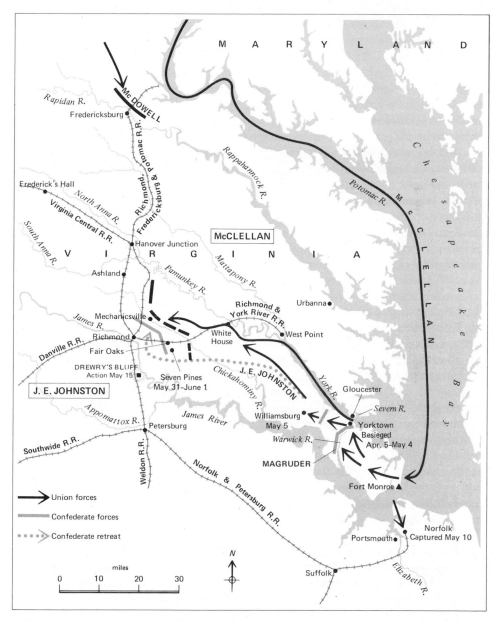

THE PENINSULA CAMPAIGN, 1862

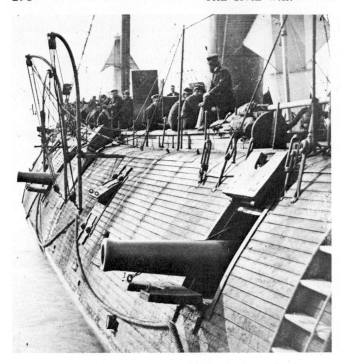

An Ironclad That Failed. Built at the same time as the *Monitor*, the *U.S.S. Galena* was a six-gun corvette plated with three-inch iron armor. During the attack on Drewry's Bluff, a ten-inch shot broke through her armor and shattered her hull, while the larger *Monitor* took similar punishment without injury. This settled the decision for the future of ironclads in favor of the more substantial *Monitor* class of ships. *(Reproduced from the Collections of the Library of Congress)*

Lincoln was disappointed with McClellan's failure to smash through the Yorktown defenses before Johnston could shift the bulk of his army to the peninsula. On April 9 the President warned McClellan that a prolonged siege would only confirm suspicions of the general's unwillingness to fight. "It is indispensable to *you* that you strike a blow. . . . I have never written you, or spoken to you, in a greater kindness of feeling than now, nor with a fuller purpose to sustain you. . . . *But you must act."* McClellan's only action was to inch forward with his siege while Johnston brought 40,000 more men to the peninsula. After looking at the Yorktown lines, Johnston commented that "no one but McClellan could have hesitated to attack."[1]

By the beginning of May McClellan finally got his huge siege guns in position. But instead of waiting for them to pound his defenses to pieces, Johnston evacuated the trenches on the night of May 3 and pulled back toward Richmond. Several Union divisions pursued the retreating Rebels and attacked the rear guard at Williamsburg on May 5. After sharp fighting, the Confederates withdrew during the night, having delayed the pursuit long enough to protect the retreating supply wagons. Further Union pursuit bogged down in heavy rains that turned the roads into a morass. The rains persisted for nearly a month, during which there was much sickness, much corduroying (laying of planks or logs) of bottomless roads, much building of bridges over swollen creeks, and much cursing—but little fighting.

The Confederate retreat compelled the evacuation of Norfolk, which opened the James River to Union warships. Five gunboats including the *Monitor* steamed up the river on May 15 to attack the Confederate fort at Drewry's Bluff, seven miles below Richmond. The government prepared to evacuate the capital, but the Union navy took a beating at Drewry's Bluff. The *Monitor*'s guns could not be elevated enough to hit the Confederate artillery on the bluff 100 feet above; the other gunboats suffered heavy damage from the Rebel guns and from sharpshooters along the banks who picked off Yankee sailors on the decks. If Richmond was to be taken, McClellan's army would have to take it.

By May 20 Johnston had established a defensive line five miles from the city, where 60,000 Confederates faced 100,000 Federals. Citing the reports of Allan Pinkerton's agents, McClellan estimated Johnston's army at 150,000 and demanded reinforcements before he would attack. Lincoln promised him McDowell's 40,000 men, who could now march down from Fredericksburg to link up with McClellan's right wing while still remaining between the Confederate army and Washington. But once again Stonewall Jackson's exploits in the Shenandoah Valley upset the Federal campaign against Richmond.

Jackson in the Valley

After the battle of Kernstown in March, Jackson had withdrawn up the valley (southward) while Banks followed cautiously, harassed by Rebel guerrillas and cavalry raids. By late April, Jackson had recruited new troops and had been reinforced by a division under General Richard Ewell, bringing his total strength to 17,000 facing Banks's 15,000 to the north (one of Banks's divisions had been recalled to reinforce the campaign against Richmond) and Frémont's 15,000 scattered at several points to the west. From Richmond, Robert E. Lee, now serving as Jefferson Davis's military adviser, suggested to Jackson another diversionary attack in the valley that would prevent further Union reinforcements being sent to the Richmond front. Jackson was just the man to turn such a suggestion into action. Keeping his plans secret even from his own officers to prevent leaks, he marched half his troops *eastward* across the Blue Ridge and put them on trains near Charlottesville, which then carried them back west to Staunton, an important supply base threatened by part of Frémont's army. Having mystified the enemy by this zigzag movement, Jackson drove two of Frémont's brigades northward after a sharp engagement in the mountains west of Staunton on May 8.

While guerrilla bands kept Frémont off balance, Jackson turned eastward again to discover that still another of Banks's divisions had been ordered to join McDowell for the expected linkup with McClellan. Since this was just what Jackson wanted to prevent, he moved quickly to attack Banks. Reduced to 8,000 men, Banks retreated down the valley turnpike to Strasburg and sent one regiment to Front Royal to guard the head of the Luray Valley. Jackson feinted as if to follow Banks to Strasburg, but suddenly swerved eastward to cross Massanutten Mountain to Luray, where he picked up Ewell's division and marched to Front Royal to overwhelm the Union garrison there on May 23. In all these movements,

Jackson's devil-may-care cavalry under Turner Ashby screened the maneuvers (that is, prevented Union cavalry from getting close enough to find out what Jackson was up to) with great success. The Rebel infantry marched so fast and far in this campaign that they became known as "Jackson's foot cavalry."

Confused by the swiftness and secrecy of Jackson's movements, Banks was surprised by the Front Royal attack. The Confederates were now on his flank ten miles away with a force twice as large as his own. Jackson urged his troops forward to cut off Banks's retreat to his base at Winchester, but the weary foot cavalry, having marched seventy miles on bad roads in the preceding four days, moved slowly for once. Banks got most of his army into position at Winchester, but Jackson followed relentlessly with a night march and attacked at dawn May 25. After a brief resistance, the Federals broke. The remnants of Banks's force streamed northward toward the Potomac. Jackson hoped to pursue and annihilate the enemy, but his exhausted infantry could go no farther and Ashby's ill-disciplined cavalry had dissolved as a fighting force after looting captured Yankee supplies. Although Banks got most of his men across the Potomac, Jackson's army had captured, wounded, or killed 3,000 Federals and had seized a bonanza of wagons, supplies, medicine, guns, and horses.

Exaggerated reports of Banks's rout caused panic in the North. Jackson was reported to be crossing the Potomac with 40,000 men to march on Washington. Lincoln did not believe this. His response was spurred not by a fear for the capital but by a desire to trap and destroy Jackson's force before it could withdraw up the valley. The President once again suspended McDowell's move toward Richmond and ordered him to send 20,000 men to Strasburg to get in Jackson's rear. He ordered Frémont to move with 15,000 men from the Alleghenies to the valley turnpike at Harrisonburg to block Jackson there if he got that far. He told Banks to reorganize his command and recross the Potomac to pursue Jackson from the north. If all went well on this military chessboard, Jackson's force would be trapped by 40,000 converging Federals.

Lincoln has been criticized for playing into Lee's and Jackson's hands, since the object of Jackson's valley campaign was to prevent McDowell from reinforcing McClellan. But Lincoln's decision to destroy Jackson first can be defended as a sound military plan. In the end it failed because his generals moved too slowly and did not coordinate their movements. Frémont approached Strasburg from the west instead of from the south as Lincoln had directed. On May 30 Frémont and General James Shields, commander of McDowell's lead division, were only twenty miles apart and converging with 25,000 men on Jackson's escape route through Strasburg. Both were closer to Strasburg than the Confederates were. But while the Union forces were slowed by muddy roads, by Confederate cavalry demonstrations, and by lack of aggressiveness, Jackson's army escaped by forced marches southward on the macadamized valley pike before the trap could be sprung.

Frémont and Shields chased Jackson southward by separate roads on either side of Massanutten Mountain. Confederate cavalry beat the Union horsemen to three key bridges in the Luray Valley, which they burned, delaying Shields' pursuit, while Jackson's rear guard burned a bridge on the valley pike to slow Frémont.

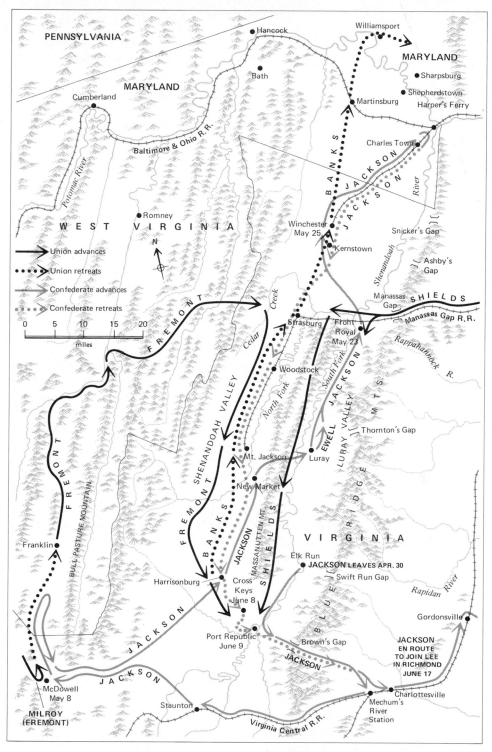

JACKSON'S SHENANDOAH VALLEY CAMPAIGN, MAY–JUNE 1862

The only remaining bridge where the two Union armies could link up was at Port Republic, a village sixty miles south of Strasburg. Jackson arrived there first and secured the bridge with his own division while leaving Ewell's 6,500 men to confront Frémont's 12,000 at Cross Keys, another village a few miles to the north. There Frémont attacked Ewell feebly on June 8, sending in only five of his twenty-four regiments before lapsing into an ineffective artillery bombardment. Next day Jackson brought half of Ewell's men to Port Republic to participate in an attack on two brigades of Shields' division. Outnumbering the Federals two to one, Jackson hoped to dispose of them quickly and then turn around for an attack on Frémont. It did not work out that way. Shields' men proved tougher than expected. Jackson drove them away only after hours of heavy fighting that left his army too bruised to go after Frémont. The Confederates withdrew to the Blue Ridge, burning the Port Republic bridge to delay any pursuit by Frémont.

Jackson's valley campaign is still studied in military schools as an example of how a small army utilizing geography and mobility can achieve numerical battlefield supremacy over larger but divided enemy forces. In a period of one month (May 8–June 9), Jackson's army of 17,000 men marched 350 miles, fought and won four battles against three separate armies whose combined numbers were twice their own, inflicted twice as many casualties as they suffered, captured large quantities of much-needed materiel, and immobilized nearly 60,000 Union troops. Three times Jackson caused Lincoln to suspend plans for McDowell's full corps to reinforce McClellan: in March after the battle of Kernstown, in May after the battle of Winchester, and again in June after Port Republic. Although one of McDowell's divisions finally did join McClellan, three others remained in or near the Shenandoah Valley to deal with whatever the fearsome Jackson decided to do next. McClellan later told the congressional Committee on the Conduct of the War that "had the command of General McDowell joined the Army of the Potomac in the month of May . . . we would have had Richmond within a week."[2] Though one may well doubt this in view of McClellan's reluctance to attack regardless of how many troops he had, it remains true that Jackson's valley campaign accomplished everything Lee and Davis had hoped it would. It also extended the streak of Confederate victories in Virginia that gave the Rebels a psychological edge over the enemy.

The Battle of Seven Pines

While Jackson was escaping Lincoln's trap at Strasburg on May 31, the armies on the peninsula were fighting a major battle five miles from Richmond. The Chickahominy River flowed between Richmond and McClellan's supply base on the York River. To protect this base and to link his right wing with the expected advance of McDowell's corps from the north, McClellan had posted his troops in such a way that the two wings of his army were divided by the Chickahominy. Bordered by swampy ground in the best of times, the river had been turned into a raging torrent by May's heavy rains. A tremendous storm on May 30 threatened to wipe out the four bridges that formed the only links between the two halves of the Union army. Taking advantage of this storm, Johnston on May 31 hurled two-thirds of his army against one of the two Union corps south of the river.

If well executed, this attack might have dealt McClellan a crippling blow. But verbal instead of written orders led to confusion on the Southern side. Johnston's battle plan required an advance of three divisions from three different directions. This proved too complicated for his inexperienced and undermanned staff to handle. General James Longstreet's division took a wrong road and became tangled with another Confederate division. The attack scheduled for dawn was not launched until afternoon. Several brigades never got into action, and others went in piecemeal. This gave Union generals time to bring up reinforcements. McClellan ordered General Edwin Sumner, a leather-lunged veteran of forty-two years in the pre-Civil War army, to bring his corps across the Chickahominy and shore up the Union flank. Despite water coursing knee-deep over the bridge, tough old "Bull" Sumner got his men and even his artillery across. His lead division counterattacked the Rebels and stopped their advance at nightfall. Next morning the Confederates renewed the assault with even less success than the previous day. By afternoon they had been driven back almost to their starting point along the road between Seven Pines and Fair Oaks (the battle is known by both names). It had been a confused, bloody conflict, fought in woods and swamps where coordination was impossible and where some wounded soldiers drowned as they sank into the sloughs. With about 42,000 men engaged on each side, the Rebels suffered 6,000 casualties and the Yankees 5,000.

The battle had no important strategic consequences, but it did have a profound impact on the top commanders of both sides. McClellan was unnerved by the sight of "mangled corpses" strewn over the battlefield. "Victory has no charms for me when purchased at such a cost," he wrote. McClellan's concern for his men was one cause of his popularity with them. But as one historian has remarked, "McClellan's affection for his soldiers was a dangerous emotion. It made him forget the hard fact that soldiers exist to fight and possibly to die."[3] It reinforced his preference for maneuver and siege rather than battle.

If Seven Pines accentuated the Union commander's caution, it had the opposite effect on Confederate leadership. General Johnston was wounded during the first day's fighting. His replacement was Robert E. Lee. Because Lee had not distinguished himself earlier in western Virginia (see pp. 159–161), his appointment evoked few cheers in the South. McClellan appraised his new opponent as "cautious and weak under grave responsibility . . . wanting in moral firmness when pressed by heavy responsibility . . . likely to be timid and irresolute in action." But a Southern officer who knew Lee well noted that despite his quiet demeanor and aristocratic bearing, he was a man of daring. "His name might be Audacity. He will take more chances, and take them quicker than any other general in this country."[4]

Lee named his command the Army of Northern Virginia. He began immediately to plan an offensive against McClellan's superior numbers. On June 12 he sent General J. E. B. Stuart on a cavalry reconnaissance to discover McClellan's exact position. A bold, dashing, romantic figure, the very image of a cavalier,

Stuart was a superb cavalry leader. Not only did he get the information Lee wanted; he also rode completely around McClellan's army, a three-day adventure in which 1,200 men circled an enemy of 100,000, captured prisoners, destroyed Union supplies, outwitted pursuing enemy cavalry, and returned with the loss of only one man. Stuart told Lee that McClellan's right flank was "in the air" (unprotected by any natural barrier such as a river or mountain) and vulnerable to envelopment.

THE SEVEN DAYS BATTLES

McClellan had moved most of his army south of the Chickahominy, leaving only Fitz-John Porter's reinforced corps of 30,000 on the north bank. Lee decided to launch an attack on this corps. To do so, he planned to bring Jackson's army from the valley to fall on Porter's flank with 18,000 men while 45,000 of the peninsula troops crossed the Chickahominy to assault his front. The risk in this was that while he reinforced his own left to assault McClellan's right, the 70,000 Federals south of the Chickahominy might smash through the remaining 25,000 Confederates in front of them. But knowing McClellan, Lee considered the risk worth taking. To mislead the Yankees, Lee first sent a division to Jackson ninety miles to the west. Federal intelligence duly reported the move. But at the same time, traveling with all possible secrecy by rail and road, Jackson was moving his men to a point just north of Richmond from which he could coordinate his attack with Lee's.

What was McClellan doing all this time? Almost daily for two weeks he had been promising Lincoln that he would begin an advance as soon as the weather improved and the "necessary preliminaries" had been completed, but in the meantime, he asked, couldn't the government send him more men? His complaints about lack of support and reinforcements had little foundation. Though he never received McDowell's entire corps (see p. 242), one of its larger divisions had reached him, and since April his original army had been reinforced by a total of 35,000 men. On June 20 he had nearly 100,000 combat troops. Even after Jackson arrived, the Confederates would have fewer than 90,000 soldiers, yet McClellan's wretched intelligence service inflated this to 200,000—which he cited as a reason for delay. Nevertheless, on June 25 McClellan made a reconnaissance in force—which was evidently the beginning of his long-promised offensive.

But the next day Lee launched his attack across the Chickahominy. From then on the Rebels had the initiative. At first, though, little went right with their offensive—and surprisingly, the fault lay mainly with Jackson. Lee's plan had called for Jackson's three divisions to fall on Porter's right and rear, which would be a signal for the divisions from Lee's army to assault the Union front near the village of Mechanicsville. But Jackson's famed foot cavalry never got to the battlefield on June 26. Tired of waiting, the lead Confederate division in the center under A. P. Hill attacked in midafternoon, drove the Union pickets from Mechanicsville, but were then mowed down with heavy loss by bluecoats posted behind a boggy creek east of the village. Less than three miles away Jackson heard

Robert E. Lee *(Reproduced from the Collections of the Library of Congress)*

Thomas J. (Stonewall) Jackson *(Reproduced from the Collections of the Library of Congress)*

Three Generals Who Turned the War Around in 1862

J. E. B. (Jeb) Stuart *(Reproduced from the Collections of the Library of Congress)*

the firing but did not come to Hill's aid. Jackson's strange behavior on this and subsequent days of what became known as the Seven Days battles has been explained in various ways. Union burning of bridges and felling of trees across the already bad roads are said to have slowed his march to Mechanicsville; Lee's orders are said to have been vague and Confederate staff work inadequate; Jackson's troops were weary from their valley campaign and the subsequent march to Richmond; Jackson himself was exhausted and lethargic after several near-sleepless nights. Whatever the reason, Jackson did not exhibit the same drive on the peninsula as he had in the valley.

During the night of June 26–27, Porter pulled his corps back to a strong line behind Boatswain's Swamp, just east of Gaines' Mill. Lee followed and launched an all-out assault with 57,000 men against Porter's reinforced 34,000 on the afternoon of June 27. Once again Jackson was slow getting into position on the Confederate left, and Lee's center divisions were repeatedly hurled back until a final attack all along the line at sundown pierced the blue defenses. Porter withdrew across the Chickahominy during the night.

What had the troops south of the river been doing while this fighting went on to the north? Once again John Magruder's theatrical talents were called into play. Lee told him to maneuver and demonstrate in such a way as to make McClellan think that he planned to attack. Magruder repeated his Yorktown performance. His artillery boomed out; his infantry marched and countermarched; officers stood in the woods within hearing of Union lines and shouted orders to imaginary regiments; some units made brief sallies against Yankee positions. The ruse worked. Indeed, McClellan telegraphed Washington that he had been "attacked by greatly superior numbers" on *both* sides of the Chickahominy—though in fact he had a numerical superiority of two and a half to one south of the river.[5]

McClellan decided to transfer his base across the peninsula to the more secure James River. He issued orders that night for the army to retreat southward to the James. He then sent a dispatch to Secretary of War Stanton which revealed that the events of the day had unhinged him:

> I have lost this battle because my force was too small. . . . The government must not and cannot hold me responsible for the result. . . . I have seen too many dead and wounded comrades to feel otherwise than that this Government has not sustained this army. . . . If I save this army now, I tell you plainly that I owe no thanks to you or to any other persons in Washington. You have done your best to sacrifice this army.[6]*

The man who wrote these words was a beaten general. No matter that he commanded an army superior in numbers and equipment to its enemy. Napoleon had said that in warfare it was not men who really counted, but *the man*—the commanding general. McClellan was proving it.

Lee intended to strike the Union army in the flank and rear during its withdrawal across the peninsula. His plans were excellent on paper but too complicated

---

*An amazed colonel in the telegraph office deleted the last two sentences before sending the dispatch to Stanton.

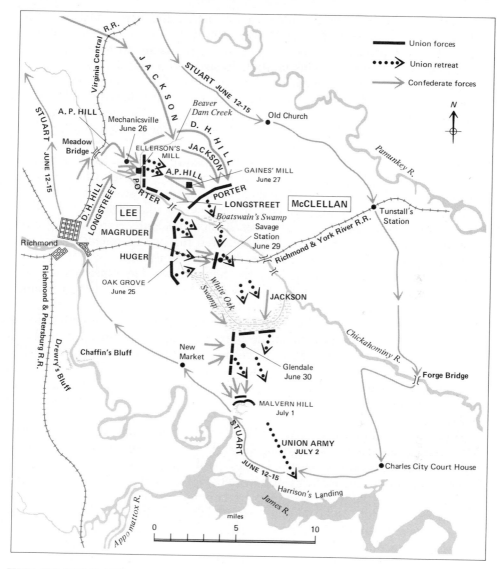

THE SEVEN DAYS BATTLES, JUNE 25–JULY 1, 1862

for his division commanders to execute. Twice they attacked portions of the
retreating bluecoats—at Savage Station on June 29 and at Glendale on June 30.
Each time the Confederates failed to coordinate their attacks; at Glendale they
managed to get only two of eight divisions into action. Twice more Jackson tarried
—once by spending all day building a bridge over the Chickahominy instead of
fording it (the river had dropped); and once by allowing himself to be held by
artillery and a broken bridge in the White Oak Swamp instead of throwing his
divisions across the fords and onto the Union flank at Glendale.

On July 1 the Federals established a formidable line across Malvern Hill, a 150-foot high slope flanked by deep ravines and with a long, open field of fire in front. The blue artillery placed 100 guns across the front, with another 150 on the flanks and in reserve. This position looked too strong to attack, but Lee thought that the litter of abandoned equipment left behind by the retreating Yankees indicated demoralization. One more push, he believed, might destroy them before they reached the James and the protection of their gunboats. Confederate batteries loosed an artillery barrage to soften up the position, but the Union guns knocked them out with counter-battery fire of surgical efficiency. Lee decided to order an infantry assault anyway. What followed, in Confederate General Daniel H. Hill's words, "was not war—it was murder."[7] Attack after attack was cut to pieces by Union cannon firing shells and canister. Northern artillery superiority counted for more at Malvern Hill than in any other battle of the war. Indeed, for the only time on either side in the war, half of the Confederate casualties were caused by artillery fire. Afterward, Hill declared that with Confederate infantry and Yankee artillery he could whip any army in the world.

Malvern Hill was the last battle of the Seven Days. The bluecoats retreated to rest and refit at Harrison's Landing, while the Rebels licked their wounds. Although Lee's achievement during his first month of command was extraordinary, he was disappointed that McClellan had gotten away without suffering greater damage. In an uncharacteristic burst of temper, Lee snapped at one of his generals that this had happened "because I cannot have my orders carried out."[8] Lee subsequently corrected the weaknesses in his staff and command structure by transferring several generals out of the Virginia theater and grouping the army's eight infantry divisions into two corps under Longstreet and Jackson.

Whatever defects had existed in the Southern command were exceeded by McClellan's deficiencies as a fighting general. In all the Seven Days, the Union army actually lost only one battle—Gaines' Mill—and the Confederates suffered 20,000 casualties to the Federals' 16,500 (6,000 of the latter were missing, mostly captured; if killed and wounded only are counted, Southern losses were nearly 20,000 and Northern about 11,000). After Malvern Hill the Confederates were hurting badly. Several Union generals, including even McClellan's protégé Fitz-John Porter, recommended a counterattack. When McClellan instead ordered a retreat to Harrison's Landing, hot-tempered division commander Philip Kearny was reported to have said: "We ought instead of retreating to follow up the enemy and take Richmond. . . . I say to you all, such an order can only be prompted by cowardice or treason."[9]

Among the Dead and the Living

Like Shiloh in the West, the Seven Days inaugurated total war in the East. Gone forever was the light-hearted romanticism with which so many Yanks and Rebs had marched off to war. The colonel of a New York Zouave regiment (see p. 165) wrote after returning from the fighting on the peninsula:

What a contrast between the departure and the return! We had started out in the spring gay, smart, well provided with everything. The drums beat, the bugles sounded, the flag with its folds of immaculate silk glistened in the sunshine. And we were returning before the autumn, sad, weary, covered with mud, with uniforms in rags. . . . Where were the red pantaloons? Where were the Zouave jackets? [Where were] those who had worn them? . . . Killed at Williamsburg, killed at Fair Oaks, killed at Glendale, killed at Malvern Hill; wounded or sick in the hospitals.[10]

Soldiers who served on burial details after battles sometimes wrote horribly eloquent descriptions of the experience: "The sights and smells that assailed us were simply indescribable—corpses swollen to twice their original size, some of them actually burst asunder with the pressure of foul gases and vapors. The odors were so nauseating . . . that in a short time we all sickened and were lying with our mouths close to the ground, most of us vomiting profusely." But many men became hardened to the sight of death. "We dont mind the sight of dead men no more than if they was dead Hogs," wrote one Yankee, while a reflective Rebel mused: "I cannot describe the change nor do I know when it took place, yet I know that there is a change for I look on the carcass of a man now with pretty much such feeling as I would were it a horse or hog."[11] The boys of '61 had become the veterans of '62.

As the war became grimmer and more destructive, the attitudes of soldiers on both sides toward each other evolved into something of a paradox. On the one hand, the level of hatred escalated with the level of killing. After the Seven Days, a Virginia private wrote in his diary: "May God avenge us of our infernal enemies. . . . 'Forgive your enemies' is the Divine precept [but] how can one forgive such enemies as we are contending against? Despoiling us of our property, driving us from our homes & friends and slaying our best citizens on the field are hard crimes to forgive." Another Rebel wrote to his wife in the spring of 1862: "Teach my children to hate them with that bitter hatred that will never permit them to meet under any circumstances without seeking to destroy each other." As the invaders rather than the invaded, Yankee soldiers less often expressed such naked hatred. But Billy Yank was capable of savage ferocity. During the peninsula campaign many stories of Rebel atrocities against prisoners and wounded men circulated in Union camps. Believing such stories, a New York regiment swore that they would retaliate in kind. When a Confederate picket whose surrender they had demanded shot one of them, the enraged New Yorkers seized him and, as an observer reported, "put a rope around his neck and hoisted him on a tree, made a target of his suspended body, then cut him down, bayoneted him in a dozen places, then dragged him to the road where they watched till long trains of wagons made a jelly of his remains."[12]

On the other hand, the fraternization between Johnny Reb and Billy Yank has become legendary. Speaking the same language, sharing a common history and many aspects of a common culture, calling each other—in some cases literally— brother or cousin, Yanks and Rebs sometimes stacked muskets during quiet times and swapped tobacco (scarce in the North) for coffee (almost unobtainable in the South), played cards, and mutually cursed their officers or the politicians who had

(U.S. Army Military History Institute)

The Veterans of '62. At right: Confederate soldiers, with a slave, in camp. Below: Union infantrymen taking a rest break. Compare these photographs with those of Georgia and Vermont recruits on pp. 166–167.

(Reproduced from the Collections of the Library of Congress)

caused the war. A typical incident occurred on July 4 in a patch of blackberries between the picket lines near Malvern Hill. "Our boys and the Yanks made a bargain not to fire at each other," a Southern private wrote, "and went out in the field, leaving one man on each post with the arms, and gathered berries together and talked over the fight, traded tobacco and coffee and exchanged newspapers as peacefully and kindly as if they had not been engaged for the last seven days in butchering each other."[13] Such incidents—and there were many—symbolized the irony and tragedy of civil war.

THE UNION ARMY AND TOTAL WAR

McClellan's failure in front of Richmond plunged Northern opinion from springtime heights of euphoria to summertime depths of despair. "The feeling of despondency here is very great," reported a prominent New Yorker in July. Democrats attacked Lincoln and Stanton for not sustaining McClellan; many Republicans denounced McClellan as a proslavery traitor and Lincoln as a dolt for keeping him in command. The President was downhearted, but he refused to panic. "I expect to maintain this contest until successful, or till I die, or am conquered, or my term expires, or Congress or the country forsakes me," he declared.[14] Gone were the hopes for a peace of reconciliation. Neither side would compromise; neither side would back down; neither side would give up until forced to do so by utter, devastating, total defeat.

A year earlier, the Union defeat at Bull Run had shocked the North into a grimmer, more determined commitment to victory. Thousands of new recruits had flocked to the colors, and the government had reorganized the command structure. In 1862, after the Seven Days, the pattern repeated itself, but this time the response of the Northern public was considerably less united and confident.

The first task was to recruit new levies to reinforce the armies for renewed offensives. Fearing that a call for recruits after the retreat in Virginia would be interpreted as a sign of panic, Lincoln arranged for Northern governors to "request" the President to call upon the states for 300,000 new three-year volunteers so that "the recent successes of Federal arms may be followed up." Lincoln did so on July 2, assigning each state a quota based on population.[15] Once again, would-be colonels and captains traveled through their counties and urged men to sign up to fight for God and country. The New York abolitionist James S. Gibbons, who though a Quaker possessed "a reasonable leaning toward wrath in cases of emergency," wrote a patriotic song to be sung at recruiting rallies: "We are Coming, Father Abraham, Three Hundred Thousand More."

But this time the 300,000 were slow to come forward. War weariness had replaced war enthusiasm. Several newspapers urged conscription. But so strong was the hostility to a draft that the government decided to exhaust every alternative first. Nevertheless, it became necessary to institute a quasi-draft in the fall of 1862. On August 4, Secretary of War Stanton issued a requisition on the states for 300,000 nine-month militiamen (this was in addition to the three-year volunteers called for a month earlier). Invoking a provision of the recently passed Militia Act (July 17), Stanton announced that states failing to meet their quotas would be subject to a militia draft. Under the complicated regulations issued by the War Department, each three-year recruit above a state's volunteer quota was equal to four nine-month men against its militia quota. This provision was designed to put pressure on the states to stimulate volunteering in order to avoid a draft. For the most part it worked—but clumsily and with warnings of trouble ahead. Most states eventually met their quotas, though some had to resort to a state militia draft to do so. This produced antidraft violence in several areas, especially among Irish-Americans in the Pennsylvania coalfields and German-Americans in Wisconsin. Some states allowed drafted men to hire substitutes. Several states and locali-

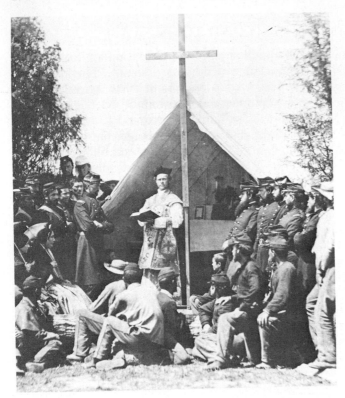

How Folks at Home Thought Soldiers Spent Their Spare Time. This photo portrays Sunday morning mass in May 1861 for the 69th New York Infantry, an Irish regiment. The regiment was camped near Washington, which explains the presence of women. *(Reproduced from the Collections of the Library of Congress)*

ties paid bounties of $100 or more to three-year volunteers. They justified the bounties as a means to provide support for the families of men who left good jobs to join the army. But these payments introduced a mercenary factor into volunteering that would become worse as time went on. The calls of July and August 1862 ultimately produced 421,000 three-year volunteers and 87,000 nine-month militiamen. This was accomplished without national conscription, but only because of the implied threat of conscription.

These measures raised fresh levies for the army. But what about new leaders to command them? In June, Lincoln had summoned John Pope from Mississippi to take command of the newly created Army of Virginia, formed from the separate armies of Frémont, Banks, and McDowell, which had made such a poor showing against Jackson in the Shenandoah Valley. Successful in the western theater, Pope had also won the support of radical Republicans with statements criticizing McClellan and opposing slavery. But Pope got off on the wrong foot with his new command. On July 14, he issued an address to the troops comparing the eastern armies unfavorably with those in the West, "where we have always seen the backs of our enemies." He wanted the Army of Virginia to discard such ideas as "taking strong positions and holding them" or securing "lines of retreat. Let us study the probable lines of retreat of our opponents, and leave our own to take care of themselves. Let us look before us and not behind. Success and glory are in the

How Soldiers Really Spent Their Spare Time. This photo shows soldiers of the 56th Massachusetts Infantry playing cards. Gambling was the most common pastime in the army. The rear areas of battlefields were always littered with playing cards and dice thrown away by soldiers turned suddenly penitent in the face of battle and possible death. *(Massachusetts Commandery Military Order of the Loyal Legion and the U.S. Army Military History Institute)*

advance, disaster and shame lurk in the rear."[16] Whether or not Stanton wrote these words, as Pope later claimed, they were hardly the best way to win the loyalty of eastern soldiers.

Pope's next act also raised hackles. He announced that his army would confiscate rebel property for its own use when necessary, would execute guerrillas and hold citizens responsible for aiding and abetting them, and would drive out of Union lines those citizens who refused allegiance to the United States and treat them as spies if they returned. These harsh orders made Pope a hated man in the Confederacy, where they were regarded as confirmation of Yankee inclinations toward pillage and murder. Robert E. Lee wrote that "this miscreant Pope" must be "suppressed." He could forgive one of his nephews for siding with the Union, said Lee, but he could never forgive him for joining Pope's staff.[17]

Although Pope's orders concerning guerrillas and civilians were not enforced, those concerning Rebel property were being carried out by this and other Union armies, with or without specific orders. Civilian property in the path of invading armies became a prime target of total war. The campaigns in northern Virginia during the next several months left whole counties devastated. If a bridge was out, construction battalions did not hesitate to tear down the nearest house or barn to rebuild it. All the trees and fence rails for miles disappeared to feed soldiers' campfires. No farmer's livestock or corn crib was safe. Even in McClellan's command, soldiers pillaged some of the fine old plantation homes on the James River. Although Southern legend has magnified the wanton destruction committed by Yankee invaders, the reality was bad enough. Soldiers justified their behavior with the argument that it made no sense to fight a war against traitors while leaving their property untouched. This was unassailable logic. The same logic underlay a confiscation act passed by Congress on July 17, 1862 (see p. 271). It also underlay the orders that went out from Washington to General Grant in August:

> It is very desirable that you should clear out West Tennessee and North Mississippi of all organized enemies. If necessary, take up all active sympathizers, and either hold them as prisoners or put them beyond our lines. Handle that class without gloves, and take their property for public use. As soon as the corn gets fit for forage get all the supplies you can from the rebels in Mississippi. It is time that they should begin to feel the presence of the war.[18]

One Union general who did not agree with this method of waging war was McClellan. On July 8, Lincoln came to Harrison's Landing to see for himself the condition of the Army of the Potomac after the Seven Days. Following the consultations, McClellan handed Lincoln a letter outlining his views on the proper conduct of the war. "It should not be a war looking to the subjugation of the people of any State," he wrote. "Neither confiscation of property, political execution of persons, territorial organization of States, or forcible abolition of slavery should be contemplated for a moment. . . . A declaration of radical views, especially upon slavery, will rapidly disintegrate our present armies."[19]

Lincoln said nothing as he read this document. But it is not hard to infer what he thought. McClellan's views were similar to Lincoln's own views—six months earlier. But much had changed in those six months. The war had taken on a remorseless quality. Lincoln had already decided to draft an emancipation proclamation (see p. 272). McClellan's ideas on war aims and policy were becoming anachronistic. Worse still, they seemed to be a bid for the Democratic presidential nomination two years hence. Prominent New York Democrats were already sounding out McClellan on this question. The general's expressed preference for a "soft" war underscored Republican suspicions that his heart was not in the cause. If Lincoln wanted an aggressive, hard-hitting general, one who believed that the war could be won only by grim, no-holds-barred fighting, it appeared that McClellan was not the man.

THE SECOND BATTLE OF BULL RUN

On July 11, Lincoln called Halleck from the West to become general in chief of all the armies. McClellan considered this a slap in the face, for he now would have to serve under a man "whom I know to be my inferior."[20] Lincoln hoped that "Old Brains" would coordinate the strategies of all Union armies and plan bold new offensives. But in this he was to be disappointed. Halleck turned out to be pedantic, fussy, and unimaginative. He soon settled into the routine of office work and seldom undertook the tasks of strategic planning and command for which Lincoln had brought him to Washington. The President later described Halleck as "little more . . . than a first-rate clerk." Yet Halleck's talents should not be dismissed too lightly. He was an efficient administrator. He could translate the

War Department's civilian directives into military language for the generals, and translate military reports into language that the government could understand. His orders and reports were clear and precise. These were important abilities in the mushrooming wartime military bureaucracy. A clerk Halleck may have been, but at least he was a first-rate clerk.[21]

The first problem facing Halleck was what to do with McClellan's army of 90,000 at Harrison's Landing. Give me 50,000 reinforcements, said McClellan, and I will take Richmond. Soon he upped the request to 100,000 and estimated that Lee had 200,000 men facing him. Sadly disillusioned, Lincoln told a cabinet member that if he gave McClellan 200,000 men the general would suddenly discover that Lee had 400,000. Lincoln had hoped that a simultaneous advance on Richmond by McClellan's 90,000 from the east and Pope's 45,000 from the north would catch Lee's army in a giant pincers. But Pope and McClellan despised each other; McClellan showed few signs of advancing; and his army was being crippled by illness, with the worst part of the sickly season on the swampy peninsula still to come. Lincoln and Halleck finally decided to withdraw the Army of the Potomac from the peninsula and send it by water to reinforce Pope for an offensive from the north.

McClellan protested bitterly against this decision. His opposition to it and his contempt for the administration* did not augur well for the speed and efficiency with which he would carry out the task of reinforcing a general he disdained. And since many of his officers and men shared these opinions, it was a serious question how well they would fight under Pope when they reached him.

Even before McClellan received his orders to withdraw from the peninsula, Lee had sent Jackson with 24,000 men to counter Pope's southward thrust. Hoping to repeat his valley tactics, Jackson decided to pounce on two advanced Union divisions commanded by his old adversary Banks before the rest of the Union forces could concentrate. But this time Banks attacked first, at Cedar Mountain on August 9. In the early fighting, the outnumbered Yankees pushed the Rebels back and even routed the famous Stonewall Brigade, Jackson's original command. But Jackson brought up reinforcements and punished the bluecoats severely.

After this engagement, Lee gambled that McClellan really was leaving the peninsula for good. He took another 30,000 troops northward to engage Pope in a showdown battle before the Army of the Potomac could reinforce him. In ten days of maneuvering Lee drove the Federals back across the Rappahannock but failed to create a favorable opportunity for attack. With the advance divisions of McClellan's army now joining Pope, Lee decided on a typically bold but danger-ous maneuver. He split his army in half and sent Jackson's corps on a wide flanking march around Pope's right to sever his supply line. In two days (August 25–26)

*At this time McClellan was writing privately that Lincoln "was an old stick, and of pretty poor timber at that," Stanton was an "unmitigated scoundrel," and the administration as a whole was "a set of heartless villains. . . . I cannot express to you the infinite contempt I feel for these people." (McClellan to Mrs. McClellan, July 13, 17, 18, McClellan Papers, Library of Congress; McClellan to Samuel L. M. Barlow, July 15, S. L. M. Barlow Papers, Henry E. Huntington Library.)

Wreckage Left by Jackson's Troops at the Union Supply Base,
Manassas, Virginia, 1862   *(Reproduced from the Collections of the Library*
of Congress)

Jackson's foot cavalry legged more than fifty miles to fall on the huge Union supply depot at Manassas. It was one of the war's great marches. Jackson was back in stride. His hungry and footsore soldiers seized all the Union supplies they could eat or carry away and put the rest to the torch. (See map on p. 258).

Pope hoped to turn this disaster into an opportunity to smash Jackson before Lee with Longstreet's corps could join him. But first he had to find Jackson. The wily Stonewall moved his three divisions by separate routes from Manassas to a wooded ridge just west of the old Bull Run battlefield. As a succession of contradictory reports of the Rebels' whereabouts poured into Pope's headquarters on August 28, he issued confusing and contradictory orders in a vain attempt to run Jackson to earth. The seemingly pointless marching and countermarching caused officers and men, especially those in Fitz-John Porter's corps from the Army of the Potomac, to curse Pope as a blunderer. A proslavery Democrat like McClellan, Porter felt even more hostile than his chief toward Pope and the antislavery Republicans who backed him. Two weeks earlier Porter had written to a Democratic editor that the administration had botched the Virginia campaign so badly that it deserved to fail. He concluded with a shocking statement: "Would that this army was in Washington to rid us of incumbents ruining our country."[22]

At sunset on August 28, one of Pope's divisions found Jackson. As this division marched unaware next to the Confederates hiding in the woods, Jackson could not resist the temptation to attack them. In a fierce, stand-up battle along the Warrenton turnpike, the bluecoats stood off twice their numbers until dark. Once again a flurry of orders went out to Federal units, which at dawn on August 29 began to concentrate in front of Jackson. The Southerners had taken position along the cuts and fills of an unfinished railroad. As Pope's divisions arrived in Jackson's front during the day, the Union general hurled them piecemeal against the Rebel defenses. Porter's corps came up on the Union left in a position to move against Jackson's flank, but having no specific orders and misled by a dust cloud that Stuart's cavalry kicked up to convince him that a strong body of infantry was in his front, Porter did nothing. Although not there yet, infantry support was on its way to Jackson, for Pope had neglected to send a strong force to block Thoroughfare Gap, through which Longstreet's corps had forced its way the previous evening. At midday on August 29, Longstreet (accompanied by Lee) did arrive in front of Porter. Not realizing that these enemy troops had come up, Pope belatedly ordered Porter to attack Jackson's flank in late afternoon. Finding it impossible to obey because of Longstreet's presence, Porter stayed put. For this he was later court-martialed and cashiered from the service.*

By nightfall on August 29, the right half of the Union army had battered itself in six bloody assaults against Jackson's corps while the other halves of both armies had remained idle. That night the Confederates pulled back some units to strengthen their lines and to prepare for another flanking maneuver the next day. Still unaware that Longstreet's 30,000 men were on the field, Pope misinterpreted these moves as a preparation for a retreat. About noon on August 30, he sent forward his own advance divisions to cut off the supposed retreat, but they quickly found Jackson in line and ready. Once again vicious fighting raged along the unfinished railroad. Some Confederate regiments ran short of ammunition and hurled rocks at the Yankees. The bluecoated attackers penetrated the Southern line at several points, forcing Jackson to call for help. At this moment Lee ordered Longstreet to counterattack with his entire corps against the Union left. With a mighty rebel yell, Longstreet's men swept forward against little opposition, for Pope had stripped the Federal left to reinforce the assault on Jackson. Longstreet's counterattack forced the whole Union line back more than a mile, where a

*Until November, Porter remained in command of the Army of the Potomac's 5th Corps. The court-martial trial took place in December 1862 and January 1863. Pope accused Porter of deliberately disobeying the attack order. Porter contended that he could not obey the order because Longstreet's troops were in his front and connecting with Jackson's flank. This was in fact true, though the court-martial board did not know it at the time. Only with the capture of Confederate records and the testimony of Southern officers after the war did the truth become known. After a great deal of controversy, Porter finally won a reversal of the court-martial verdict in 1886. The controversy has continued for a century. To some degree, Porter was the victim of Republican hostility toward McClellanite officers. But Porter's own undisguised hostility toward Pope, toward Republicans, and toward emancipation, as well as his failure to do anything at all with his 11,000 men on August 29 while the battle raged nearby, left him open to the just suspicion that he did less than he might have done to cooperate with Pope. (Otto Eisenschiml, *The Celebrated Case of Fitz-John Porter* [Indianapolis, 1950]; Kenneth P. Williams, *Lincoln Finds a General*, 5 vols. [New York, 1949–1959], I, 324–30, II, 785–89; Bruce Catton, *Terrible Swift Sword* [Garden City, N.Y., 1963], pp. 522–23.)

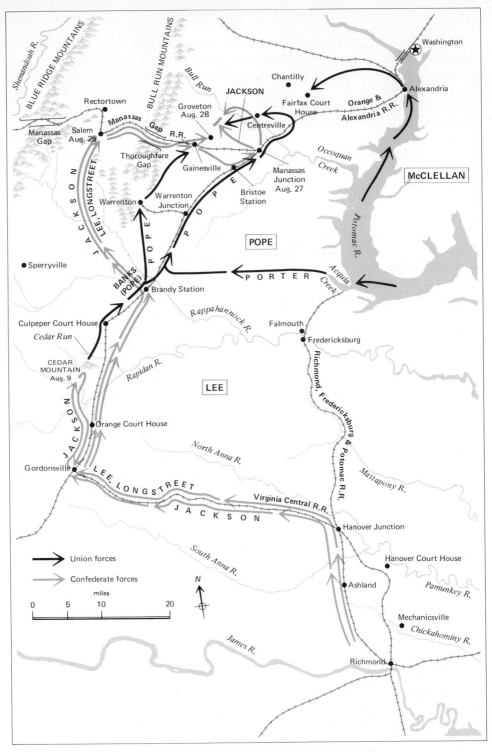

THE CAMPAIGN OF SECOND BULL RUN, AUGUST 1862

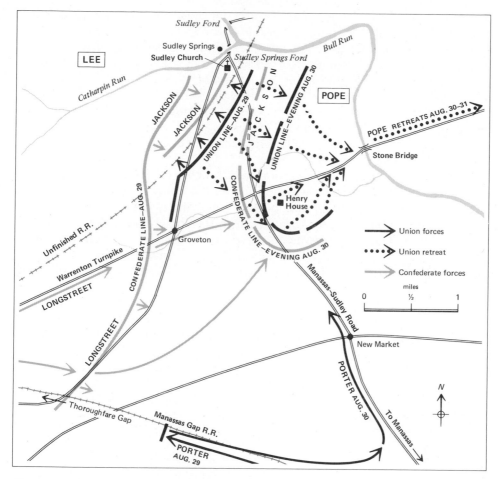

THE SECOND BATTLE OF BULL RUN, AUGUST 29–30, 1862

desperate twilight stand on Henry House Hill finally halted the Confederates. During the night the dispirited, defeated Union troops retreated wearily to Centreville. Instead of following directly, Lee sent Jackson's tired, hungry men on another wide flanking march around Pope's right through a drenching rainstorm. On September 1 these troops ran into two Union divisions, who stopped them at Chantilly in a sharp clash during a torrential downpour. Meanwhile, Pope pulled the rest of his army back to the Washington defenses.

Once again the Union army had suffered a humiliating defeat near Manassas. With just over 50,000 men Lee had inflicted 16,000 casualties on Pope's 60,000 at a cost of only 9,200 casualties to the Confederates. The defeat was all the more shocking to the North because it came on the heels of boastful dispatches from Pope that he was about to "bag" Jackson. Bitter recriminations followed the battle. Pope blamed McClellan and Porter for lack of cooperation. McClellan himself had been at Alexandria, where he had resisted Halleck's orders to send one of his corps to Pope as fast as possible. While the battle raged to the south on August 29, McClellan suggested to Lincoln that the best course might be to concentrate all available troops for the defense of Washington and "leave Pope to get out of his scrape" by himself. After the battle, Lincoln told his private secretary that McClellan's behavior had been "unpardonable." He "wanted Pope defeated." Four of the seven cabinet members signed a letter asking Lincoln to dismiss McClellan. Stanton thought McClellan ought to be court-martialed and Chase said he should be shot.[23]

But McClellan was neither shot nor fired. Lincoln retained him in command of the Army of the Potomac, which absorbed the Army of Virginia, while the luckless Pope was exiled to an unimportant command in the Midwest. Republicans found this a bitter pill to swallow. But in the circumstances Lincoln felt he had no choice. The army was demoralized and almost on the edge of mutiny against Pope, whom many soldiers considered responsible for their defeat. Although Lincoln had lost confidence in McClellan and had even tried to offer the top command to Ambrose E. Burnside (who declined), he knew that McClellan was the only man who could reorganize the army and restore its morale. Admitting that McClellan had "acted badly" in "breaking down Pope without regard to the consequences to the country," the President told confidants that "there is no remedy. McClellan has the army with him." No one else could "lick these troops of ours into shape half as well as he. . . . If he can't fight himself, he excels in making others ready to fight."[24] And this was all the more imperative, for Lee was taking his ragged, awesome butternut scarecrows across the Potomac to invade Maryland, in a campaign that was to have fateful consequences for the future of the country and of slavery.

Sixteen

Slavery and the War: Northern Politics, 1861-1862

The military, diplomatic, and political maneuvers during the first two years of the war took place in the sometimes unacknowledged context of the slavery issue. Slavery was the fundamental cause of the sectional conflict that had led to war. The South had seceded to protect its peculiar institution from the perceived Republican threat to its future. Although a significant amount of internal disaffection existed in the Confederacy, the North suffered more disunity over war aims than the South. The South fought for independence. So long as the North fought simply for restoration of the Union, Northern unity was impressive. But the hard question of what kind of Union was to be restored soon divided the North. Was it to be a Union without slavery, as abolitionists and radical Republicans hoped? Or "the Union as it was, the Constitution as it is," as Democrats insisted? Was the South to be *restored* to the Union with its rights and power intact, or *reconstructed* in the image of the free-labor North? Disagreement about ends soon became disagreement about means as well. Was it to be a total war fought for total victory, or a limited war looking toward an early peace conference to restore the Union through compromise?

WAR AIMS AND POLITICS IN THE NORTH

Lincoln's Leadership

Northern unity in the spring and summer of 1861 had been fragile along several political fault lines. The Republican party was a coalition of men who a few years earlier had been Whigs, Democrats, Know-Nothings, Free Soilers, or abolitionists. Northern Democrats still bore the scars of battles between the Douglas and

261

Buchanan wings of the party. In the loyal border states, several factions competed for leadership of the new "Unionist" parties. Lincoln's task was to mold these disparate elements into a government that could win the war at the same time that it defined what victory would mean. This proved to be a difficult task, almost an impossible one. Lincoln's greatness as a war leader resulted from his success in accomplishing this task.

When contemporaries asked Lincoln what his policy was on one issue or another, he sometimes replied: "My policy is to have no policy." To the exasperated questioner this answer seemed flippant or evasive. Lincoln did not mean it that way. He did have a policy—to win the war and restore the Union. But since the questioners often represented sharply opposed viewpoints on how to do this, he knew that to answer their questions about specific issues prematurely might destroy the delicate balance of support for the war effort. Lincoln was a master of timing. He knew how to make a series of small decisions that laid the groundwork for a large decision. He knew how to wait for the right moment to announce major policies such as emancipation, in the meantime enduring the criticisms of those who denounced his weak leadership. To abolitionists he appeared to move too slowly; for conservatives he moved much too fast. But as the President himself once told a subordinate, if half the people think you have gone too far and the other half not far enough, you have probably done just about right.

Lincoln's relations with his cabinet provide a good example of his leadership. The cabinet represented every Republican viewpoint from border-state conservatism (Attorney General Edward Bates) to antislavery radicalism (Secretary of the Treasury Chase). It contained former Whigs (Seward, Bates, Secretary of the Interior Caleb Smith, and Lincoln himself), former Democrats (Secretary of the Navy Gideon Welles and Postmaster General Montgomery Blair), a Free Soiler (Chase), and Secretary of War Simon Cameron, a former Democrat who had occasionally collaborated with Whigs and Know-Nothings. Considered too radical on the slavery issue for the presidential nomination in 1861, Seward became one of the most conservative members of the cabinet during the war. Edwin M. Stanton, who replaced the inept Cameron in January 1862, was a former Buchanan Democrat who became, next to Chase, the most radical member of the cabinet. Four cabinet officers—Seward, Chase, Bates, and Cameron—had been Lincoln's rivals for the presidential nomination in 1860. Chase continued his quest for the highest office after joining the cabinet. Full of ambition and pride (a senator once said that "Chase is a good man, but his theology is unsound. He thinks there is a fourth person in the Trinity"), Chase built up a cadre of political lieutenants in the Treasury Department who worked for his presidential nomination in 1864. He also intrigued with Lincoln's Republican critics in Congress. Cutting across these currents of ideology and politics were long-standing personal rivalries between several pairs of individuals in the cabinet.

Such a cabinet promised discord rather than harmony. But with tact, patience, and a sense of humor, the President welded them into an effective team. On purely administrative matters, Lincoln allowed each secretary to run his own department. But on matters of policy, the President made the important decisions. He announced, rather than presented to the cabinet for debate, such important actions as the Emancipation Proclamation and the appointment or dismissal of army commanders. Chase complained that on vital war issues the cabinet as a whole was "so rarely consulted that they might as well not be consulted at all." Lincoln preferred to confer individually with cabinet members on such issues. He worked most closely with Stanton and Seward. The President's unique blend of firmness and deference, the iron fist of decision clothed in the velvet glove of humor and tact, enabled him to dominate his subordinates without the appearance of domination. "The relations between him and his Secretaries were perfectly cordial always and unaffected," recalled the assistant secretary of war, "without any appearance of his thinking himself the boss, but it was always his will, his order, that determined a decision."[1]

Lincoln's relations with Congress exhibited the same combination of deference and firmness. On matters of finance and domestic legislation unconnected with the war he deferred to congressional leadership. In this respect he fitted the Whig tradition of a weak executive. But in all matters relating to the war and reconstruction, Lincoln exercised more power than perhaps any other president. His interpretation of the president's war powers was breathtakingly broad. "I conceive that I may in an emergency do things on military grounds which cannot be done constitutionally by Congress," he said.[2] Since his entire presidency was a time of emergency, he did many things that caused Democrats and even some Republicans to denounce his "tyranny" and "dictatorship."

Lincoln's actions during the first eighty days of the war established the tone for his use of executive power. Instead of calling Congress into immediate session after the bombardment of Fort Sumter (as Jefferson Davis did), he called them to meet July 4. In the meantime Lincoln took a number of bold steps on his own authority. His proclamation of blockade on April 19 was in effect a declaration of war.* By executive order on May 3 he expanded the regular army and navy beyond the number authorized by law. He also issued a call for three-year volunteers, normally a congressional prerogative. In four proclamations from April to July, Lincoln suspended the writ of *habeas corpus* in various parts of the country. He also turned over $2 million to a New York committee for "military measures necessary for the defence and support of the government" despite the Constitution's enjoinder that "no money shall be drawn from the Treasury, but in Consequence of Appropriations made by Law" (Article I, Section 7).[3]

The special session of Congress in the summer of 1861 retroactively approved Lincoln's executive actions to mobilize and increase the army "as if they had been done under the previous express authority" of Congress.[4] Two-thirds of the Democrats and border-state Unionists either abstained or voted with the Republi-

---

*The legality of this proclamation came before the Supreme Court in 1863 in the *Prize Cases* (67 U.S. 35). Plaintiffs argued that ships seized for violation of the blockade before July 13, 1861, when Congress declared the existence of a state of war, had been captured illegally. By a vote of five to four the Court upheld the President's action as legal under his emergency war powers. Three of the five justices in the majority were Lincoln appointees. Chief Justice Taney issued a dissent maintaining that the power to suppress insurrection was not the power to wage war.

can majority. Most Democrats also voted for measures to raise additional troops and to finance the war.* The opposition party had not yet divided into the factions later known as War Democrats and Peace Democrats. The germ of that division was present in the minds of Democrats who opposed or reluctantly supported some of the war measures. But thus far the spirit of bipartisanship prevailed.

The Meaning of Union

It prevailed because for most Northerners, Republicans and Democrats alike, the concept of Union was endowed with such transcendent values as to amount almost to a religion. The rebellion "has outraged the Constitution, set at defiance all law, and trampled under foot that flag which has been the glorious and consecrated symbol of American Liberty," declared a Chicago newspaper. Four years later, in his second inaugural address, Lincoln summarized the meaning of the war with these words: "Both parties deprecated war; but one of them would *make* war rather than let the nation survive; and the other would *accept* war rather than let it perish. And the war came."[5]

In the mid-nineteenth century, liberalism and nationalism were fused in both Europe and America. The revolutions of 1848 in Europe were uprisings of liberalism *and* nationalism. In Lincoln's view, the South's fight for slavery linked it with the forces of reaction in Europe. In the Old World, imperial government sought to stamp out nationalism from above; in the United States, particularist forces tried to destroy it from within; in both the Old World and the New, tradition and privilege threatened democratic nationalism. "This is essentially a People's contest," said Lincoln in 1861.

> On the side of the Union it is a struggle for maintaining in the world that form and substance of government whose leading object is to elevate the condition of men . . . to afford all an unfettered start, and a fair chance in the race of life. . . . The central idea pervading this struggle is the necessity . . . of proving that popular government is not an absurdity. We must settle this question now, whether in a free government the minority have the right to break up the government whenever they choose.[6]

The struggle is "not altogether for today," continued Lincoln; "it is for a vast future." It "embraces more than the fate of these United States. It presents to the whole family of man the question whether," as Lincoln expressed it in the Gettysburg Address two years later, a nation "conceived in Liberty, and dedicated to the proposition that all men are created equal . . . can long endure."[7] European liberals were fired by the same vision of the Union cause. The triumph of the Confederacy, wrote John Stuart Mill, "would be a victory of the powers of evil which would give courage to the enemies of progress and damp the spirits of its

---

*Because of the confused nature of party allegiances in the border states, the precise number of Republicans and Democrats in this Congress is hard to specify. In the House there were 106 Republicans, 42 Democrats, and 28 "Unionists," mostly from the border states. The Senate contained 31 Republicans, 10 Democrats, and 6 Unionists.

friends all over the civilized world. [The American war is] destined to be a turning point, for good or evil, of the course of human affairs."[8]

This vision—though misty and often inarticulate—helped to unite the North in 1861. It soon burst forth in song. The most popular song in the Union army was "John Brown's Body," set to the tune of a familiar camp-meeting hymn. First sung by a Massachusetts regiment in the spring of 1861, the song spread through all Union armies by the year's end. Its sprightly rhythm made it a perfect marching song. It was adaptable to any number of extemporized verses—profane or religious, ribald or sublime. The most popular version spoke of John Brown's body moldering in the grave, of his departure to become a soldier in the army of the Lord, and of hanging Jeff Davis on a sour apple tree. No matter what the verse, the chorus always ended with John Brown's soul marching on.

It remained for Julia Ward Howe, whose husband Samuel Gridley Howe had aided the real John Brown, to enshrine this song in the national literature. After visiting an army camp near Washington in November 1861, she awoke in the middle of the night with a creative urge to write down the words of "The Battle Hymn of the Republic." Upon publication in the *Atlantic Monthly*, this exalted version of the John Brown song also became popular, though the idea of hanging Jeff Davis on a sour apple tree remained more fashionable in the army than the concept of trampling out the vintage where the grapes of wrath were stored. The words of the "Battle Hymn," next to those of the Gettysburg Address, have come down through the years as the noblest expression of what the North was fighting for. Both somehow gave meaning to the power of God's terrible swift sword, which had struck down so many men who had given their last full measure of devotion that freedom might live.

THE SLAVERY ISSUE

The problem with this lofty rhetoric of dying to make men free was that in 1861 the North was fighting for the restoration of a slaveholding Union. In his July 4 message to Congress, Lincoln reiterated the inaugural pledge that he had "no purpose, directly or indirectly, to interfere with slavery in the States where it exists." Three weeks later, Congress passed almost unanimously the Crittenden-Johnson resolution affirming that the war was being fought not for the purpose "of overthrowing or interfering with the rights or established institutions of those States," but only "to defend and maintain the supremacy of the Constitution and to preserve the Union."[9] Little wonder that, at this stage of the war, disillusioned European liberals began to ask: Since "the North does not proclaim abolition and never pretended to fight for anti-slavery," how "can we be fairly called upon to sympathize so warmly with the Federal cause?"[10]

Most of the congressional Republicans who voted for the Crittenden-Johnson resolution were of course antislavery men. Lincoln also had more than once branded slavery "an unqualified evil to the negro, the white man, and to the State. . . . The monstrous injustice of slavery . . . deprives our republican example of its just influence in the world—enables the enemies of free institutions, with plausibility, to taunt us as hypocrites."[11]

Precisely. So why did Lincoln not respond to this taunt by proclaiming the war to be fought for freedom as well as for Union? Because as President of *all* the states, he still considered himself bound by the constitutional guarantee of slavery in the states. The Union government fought the war on the theory that, secession being illegal, the Confederate states were still legally in the Union although temporarily under control of insurrectionists. The need to retain the loyalty of the border slave states was another factor in Lincoln's and Congress's assurances on slavery. Beyond that was the desire for bipartisan support of the war. Nearly half of the voters in the free states had cast anti-Lincoln ballots in the 1861 election. The Northern Democrats were a proslavery party. Any sign of an antislavery war policy in 1861 might divide the North and alienate most Democrats.

The Antislavery Argument

Abolitionists and some Republicans disagreed with this analysis. Several prominent antislavery congressmen abstained or voted against the Crittenden-Johnson resolution. For most abolitionists, freedom for the slaves was a more important value than Union. Now that the "covenant of death" had been broken by Southern secession, Garrisonian abolitionists supported the war for the Union because they believed that the "death grapple with the Southern slave oligarchy" must become a death grapple with slavery itself. As the black leader Frederick Douglass put it in May 1861: "The American people and the Government at Washington may refuse to recognize it for a time; but the 'inexorable logic of events' will force it upon them in the end; that the war now being waged in this land is a war for and against slavery."[12]

But since the North was fighting for a Constitution that protected slavery, emancipationists had to find extraconstitutional reasons for a blow against bondage—reasons compelling enough to overcome the inertia of indifference, conservatism, and racism that had for so long sustained Northern toleration of slavery. Abolitionists quickly hit upon the "military necessity" argument for emancipation. By insisting that slavery was crucial to the Southern war effort and its abolition necessary for Northern success, they hoped to put their cause on the broadest possible platform—a platform that could appeal to all Unionists whether Republican or Democrat, radical or conservative, egalitarian or racist. Although they themselves wanted emancipation for reasons of justice and morality, they avoided these themes in their early wartime rhetoric. "You will observe that I propose no crusade for abolition," wrote Charles Sumner in November 1861. Emancipation "is to be presented strictly as a measure of military necessity . . . rather than on grounds of philanthropy. . . . Abolition is not to be the object of the war, but simply one of its agencies."[13]

It was easy enough to prove slavery's military value to the Confederacy. The three and a half million slaves in the eleven Confederate states constituted nearly 40 percent of their population and a majority of their labor force. Southern newspapers boasted that slavery was "a tower of strength to the Confederacy" because it enabled her "to place in the field a force so much larger in proportion to her white population than the North."[14] More than half the workers in Confederate iron, salt, and lead mines were slaves. By 1864, blacks constituted one-third the labor force at the Tredegar iron works in Richmond and three-quarters of the naval works in Selma, two of the Confederacy's main ordnance plants. At least half the nurses in Confederate military hospitals were black. Slaves worked as cooks, servants, teamsters, construction laborers, and even musicians in the Confederate armies. So important were slaves in all these capacities that the military authorities impressed them into service from the beginning of the war, well before the Confederacy began drafting white men into the army. Well might Frederick Douglass exclaim that "the very stomach of this rebellion is the negro in the form of a slave. Arrest that hoe in the hands of the negro, and you smite the rebellion in the very seat of its life."[15]

Abolitionists maintained that emancipation could be accomplished under the "laws of war." With the proclamation of the blockade and the decision to treat Rebel captives as prisoners of war, the conflict had taken on the character of a war rather than a mere domestic insurrection. Slavery in the Confederate states, insisted abolitionists, no longer enjoyed constitutional protection but came instead under international law. The confiscation of enemy property was a belligerent right recognized by international law. Slaves were enemy property; some of this property was being used in direct aid of the rebellion and was therefore doubly liable to confiscation.

The first move toward applying this theory came in May 1861 from an unlikely source: General Benjamin Butler, a former Breckinridge Democrat now in command of Union troops at Fortress Monroe on the Virginia coast. A shrewd politician, Butler had felt the antislavery wind blowing from his home state of Massachusetts and was ready for the first step in his pilgrimage to the radical wing of the Republican party. When three slaves who had been working on Confederate fortifications escaped to Butler's lines on May 23, he refused to return them to their masters and labeled them "contraband of war." This phrase caught on, and for the rest of the war slaves who came within Union lines were known as contrabands. Word soon got around among slaves on the Virginia peninsula. By August, a thousand contrabands were in Butler's camps, and abolitionists were making plans to establish schools and send missionary teachers to them.

The belligerent right of confiscation was incorporated into a law signed by Lincoln on August 6, 1861, which authorized the seizure of all property, including slaves, used in military aid of the rebellion. This confiscation act applied to only a handful of slaves then within reach of Union forces, and it did not specifically emancipate them. But like Butler's contraband policy, it was the thin edge of the wedge of emancipation. It also marked a departure from the Crittenden-Johnson resolution passed only two weeks earlier. During those two weeks the meaning of Union defeat at Bull Run had sunk in. The war was not going to be short and easy. The resulting reassessment of war policies produced a harder attitude toward the slaveholders' rebellion. Most Republicans were now willing to consider at least limited steps against slavery as a means of victory if not yet as an end in itself.

Arrival of Contrabands in Union Lines   *(Reproduced from the Collections of the Library of Congress)*

But Democrats were not. Congress passed the confiscation act by a party-line vote, with all but six Republicans in favor and all but three Democrats opposed. It was the first real breach in the bipartisan war front.

As the conflict moved toward total war in subsequent months, this breach became wider. The slavery issue dominated the 1861–1862 session of the Union Congress. When the Congress reassembled in December 1861, fifty-three House Republicans who had voted for the Crittenden-Johnson resolution in July changed their votes, and the House thereby refused to reaffirm the resolution. The question of what to do about slavery not only divided Republicans from Democrats but also served increasingly to define the differences among three factions in the Republican party: conservative, moderate, and radical.

Slavery and the Republican Party

All Republicans were in some sense antislavery. But differences of degree did exist. Conservatives hoped for the ultimate demise of bondage, but they were gradualists, believing in voluntary action by the states rather than in coercive federal action, and preferred to link emancipation with the colonization of freed slaves abroad. The radicals were deep-dyed antislavery advocates who wanted to abolish the institution immediately, through the war power of the national government. The moderates were a less easily defined group. They disliked slavery and hoped to see it abolished sooner rather than later, but they feared the social consequences of precipitate action. Early in the war they were hard to distinguish from the conservatives, but the imperatives of total war drove them ever closer to the radicals as the intensity of the conflict increased.

The foremost moderate was of course Lincoln himself, who said in his first annual message to Congress on December 3, 1861: "In considering the policy to be adopted for suppressing the insurrection, I have been anxious and careful that the inevitable conflict for this purpose shall not degenerate into a violent and remorseless revolutionary struggle."[16] The President's gradualist temperament and his pragmatic conviction that most Northerners, as well as the border-state Unionists, would not tolerate radical action against slavery had lain behind his modification of General Frémont's emancipation order in Missouri in September 1861 (see p. 158). For the same reasons, Lincoln took another action in December that angered radicals. Without consulting the President, Secretary of War Cameron had included in his report to Congress a section endorsing the freeing and arming of slaves who came into Union lines. When Lincoln learned of this, he ordered the report recalled and the section deleted. Within weeks Cameron, like Frémont before him, was removed from his post. In both cases, lax administration and corruption in war contracts were the principal reasons for removal. But to radicals it appeared that vigorous antislavery men were being combed out of the government and the army while proslavery generals such as McClellan and Buell were riding high.

Unlike Lincoln, abolitionists and radical Republicans did believe in a "remorse-less and revolutionary" war. An abolitionist editor wanted the Civil War to become "the glorious Second American Revolution" to complete the unfinished business of the first—"a National Abolition of Slavery."[17] In an editorial on January 24, 1862, that must have chilled the hearts of conservatives, the *New York Tribune* compared the crisis of the Union to the crisis of France during the Revolution of 1789. Beset by internal factions and threatened by counterrevolution within and foreign intervention without, the French Republic survived only by exporting the revolution to all Europe. "Like the French leaders of 1793," said the *Tribune,* "we must offer liberty and protection to the oppressed, and war to the oppressors." The most radical of the congressional Republicans, Thaddeus Stevens, was equally outspoken. "Free every slave—slay every traitor—burn every Rebel mansion, if these things be necessary to preserve this temple of freedom," said Stevens. We must "treat this [war] as a radical revolution, and remodel our institutions."[18]

Although the radicals never constituted a majority of Republicans, they were the most aggressive faction in the party. A vigorous, determined minority with a clear vision of what it wants and how to get it always has an advantage, especially in time of crisis. The radicals controlled key committee chairmanships in Congress. In the Senate, Charles Sumner and Henry Wilson of Massachusetts were chairmen respectively of the Committee on Foreign Affairs and the Committee on Military Affairs, John P. Hale of New Hampshire chaired the Naval Affairs Committee, Zachariah Chandler of Michigan headed the Committee on Commerce, and Benjamin Wade of Ohio served as chairman of both the Committee on Territories and the Joint Committee on the Conduct of the War. In the House, the radical Pennsylvanians Galusha Grow and Thaddeus Stevens held the two most important positions—Speaker and chairman of the Ways and Means Committee. Several moderate Republican senators who usually supported radical positions in 1862 also held important committee chairmanships, notably Lyman Trumbull of Illinois (Judiciary Committee) and William Pitt Fessenden of Maine (Finance Committee).

New England was the mother of congressional radicalism. Of the ten most prominent radicals in the House, five (including Stevens and Grow) had been born and raised in New England. In the Senate, eight of the twelve radicals and nine of the thirteen moderates, but only two of the seven conservative Republicans, were natives of New England. The influence of New England in the Senate was extraordinary. Senators from that region held eleven committee chairmanships, and men born in New England chaired five of the eleven remaining committees. Only one New England senator did not hold a committee chairmanship. New England had been the taproot of abolitionism and the cutting edge of modernization in the antebellum era; now the region also played a dominant role in forging the modernizing, antislavery legislation of the Civil War.

Congress and Slavery

Congress could not have escaped the question of slavery in 1861–1862 even if it had wanted to. The Union navy's conquest of the South Carolina coastal islands had brought 10,000 contrabands within Union lines; hundreds of others were trickling in weekly wherever blueclad troops were encamped in slave territory; the Union advances in Tennessee and Louisiana brought in scores of thousands more. The legal status of these contrabands remained unclear, but some Northern commanders in Virginia and South Carolina were already treating them as free people. On the other hand, Union generals in the border states returned fugitives claimed by loyal masters, and General Halleck in Missouri issued an order excluding contrabands from his lines altogether. Without guidance from Washington, the contraband question in military zones was mired in confusion and contradiction.

Congressional Republicans attacked slavery on several fronts. By mid-January no less than seven different bills dealing with emancipation and confiscation of Rebel property had been reported out of committees. The first action was a new article of war enacted March 13; it prohibited army officers, under pain of court-martial, from returning fugitive slaves to their masters. Next on the agenda, April 16, came the abolition of slavery in the District of Columbia, with an average compensation to owners of $300 per slave. This was followed by legislation to create schools for black children in Washington and to permit blacks to testify in District of Columbia courts. In June, Congress prohibited slavery in all territories and ratified a new treaty with Britain for more effective suppression of the Atlantic slave trade.

Important as these acts were, they only nibbled at the edges of slavery. More far-reaching was a bill for the confiscation of Confederate-owned property. This was a total-war measure based on the "laws of war" and the constitutional power of Congress to punish treason (Article III, Section 3). As finally enacted on July 17, this second confiscation act authorized the seizure of the property of persons in rebellion against the United States and specified that all of their slaves who came within Union lines "shall be deemed captives of war and shall be forever free."[19]

This measure went far beyond the first confiscation act of the previous August. It altered the character and purpose of the war. Yet in practical terms both its immediate and long-term effects were marginal. Confiscation and emancipation under the law would depend on legal proceedings to determine whether owners had been engaged in rebellion. And because Lincoln believed that the question of wartime emancipation must be handled by the president as commander in chief, he took little action under the second confiscation act as such. The emancipation provisions of the act were soon overshadowed by the President's own executive acts against slavery.

Lincoln and Slavery

For several months in the spring and summer of 1862, however, it appeared that Lincoln intended to do nothing against slavery. In May General David Hunter, commander of Union forces occupying islands and enclaves along the south Atlantic coast, issued an order emancipating all slaves in the "Department of the South," theoretically including all of South Carolina, Georgia, and Florida. Lincoln revoked the order, stating that he reserved to himself the authority to make such a momentous decision. Abolitionists and radicals condemned the President. "Stumbling," "halting," "prevaricating," "irresolute," "weak," "besotted," were some of the adjectives they applied to Lincoln. "He has evidently not a drop of anti-slavery blood in his veins," wrote William Lloyd Garrison. "A curse on that [border-state] 'loyalty' which is retained only by allowing it to control the policy of the Administration!"[20]

Garrison was wrong. By the spring of 1862, Lincoln had become convinced that the war must end slavery. But he still wished to achieve emancipation gradually, with the least possible amount of revolutionary disruption. This helps to explain his proposal in 1862 for voluntary border-state emancipation. On March 6, the President had sent a special message to Congress recommending the passage of a joint resolution offering financial aid to any state "which may adopt gradual abolishment of slavery." Congress passed the resolution, with Republicans unanimously in favor and Democrats 85 percent opposed. But border-state spokesmen complained of federal coercion, bickered about the amount of proposed compensation and about Congress's constitutional right to appropriate funds for this purpose, and expressed fears of race war and economic ruin even if emancipation took place gradually over a thirty-year period as Lincoln had suggested. Disappointed, the President again appealed to the border states in May 1862. If they adopted his plan, said Lincoln, the changes produced by emancipation "would come gently as the dews of heaven, not rending or wrecking anything." But if they did nothing the radicals would preempt the ground. "You cannot," admonished the President, "be blind to the signs of the times."[21]

But the border-state representatives remained blind to the signs, despite the increasing momentum of emancipation sentiment in the North. "The great phenomenon of the year," observed a conservative Boston newspaper in the summer of 1862, "is the great intensity which this [emancipation] resolution has acquired. A year ago men might have faltered at the thought of proceeding to this extremity in any event. The majority do not now seek it, but, we say advisedly, they are in great measure prepared for it." On July 12, Lincoln once more brought border-state representatives to the White House. This time his plea for cooperation was backed by a blunt warning: "The incidents of the war can not be avoided. If the war continue long . . . the institution in your states will be extinguished by mere friction and abrasion . . . and you will have nothing valuable in lieu of it." In revoking General Hunter's emancipation edict "I gave dissatisfaction, if not offense, to many whose support the country cannot afford to lose. And this is not the end of it. The pressure, in this direction is still upon me, and is increasing. By conceding what I ask, you can relieve me." Lincoln's plea again fell on deaf ears. By a vote of 20 to 9, the border-state representatives rejected his plan.[22]

That evening Lincoln made up his mind to issue an emancipation proclamation that he had begun drafting several days earlier, after McClellan had been driven back from Richmond in the Seven Days battles. The President had come to the conclusion stated a year earlier by Frederick Douglass that "to fight against slaveholders, without fighting against slavery, is but a half-hearted business, and paralyzes the hands engaged in it." On July 13 Lincoln privately told Seward and Welles of his decision. On July 22 he convened the cabinet to inform his ministers officially. Montgomery Blair, the Postmaster General, opposed the issuance of a proclamation, for he feared that it might throw the fall elections to the Democrats. All other cabinet members endorsed it with varying degrees of enthusiasm. But Seward pointed out that because of the "depression of the public mind, consequent upon our [military] reverses," the proclamation "may be viewed as the last measure of an exhausted Government, a cry for help." He suggested that Lincoln "postpone its issue until you can give it to the country supported by military success."[23]

Lincoln accepted Seward's shrewd advice. But the wait turned out to be two long, agonizing months during which Northern morale dropped to its lowest point thus far, public opinion became further polarized on the issue of slavery, and the army in Virginia suffered its second ignominious defeat at Bull Run.

THE COPPERHEADS

The war placed Northern Democrats in a difficult position. The party gradually divided into "war" and "peace" wings. The War Democrats generally supported whatever military measures seemed necessary to defeat the Confederacy. Some War Democrats became Republicans, and a few—such as General Benjamin Butler and Secretary of War Edwin M. Stanton—eventually moved all the way to the radical wing of the party. The Peace Democrats initially supported the preservation of the Union by military force. But as the conflict moved toward total war, they began to denounce the Republicans' determination to destroy and remake the South in the Northern free-labor mold. Opposition to Republican war policies sometimes became opposition to a continuation of the war itself. This was not necessarily a pro-Confederate position, despite Republican efforts to portray it as such. Peace Democrats urged restoration of the Union through negotiation and compromise, but at times the more hot-headed among them spoke or acted in such a way as to give substance to Republican charges of disloyalty. The relative strength of the "peace" and "war" factions within the Democratic party fluctuated with Northern fortunes in the war. On many vital issues, however, such as emancipation and military arrests, both factions united in opposition to the administration.

As Northern morale plummeted during the summer of 1862, the hopes of the Peace Democrats, or Copperheads, rose correspondingly. Like so many political labels, "Copperhead" was a term of reproach invented by opponents. In the fall of 1861 some Republican newspapers in Ohio likened antiwar Democrats to the poisonous copperhead snake. The term soon caught on and was often applied indiscriminately to all Democrats; but it is used here interchangeably with Peace Democrats only. Although the Copperheads drew support from every socioeconomic group in the North, their greatest strength was concentrated among the Butternuts of the southern Midwest and the immigrant Catholics of the cities. Both of these groups disliked blacks, abolitionists, temperance reformers, New England Yankees, and the modernizing changes that were upsetting the traditional bases of their culture. As the war took on the dimensions of a Republican antislavery crusade, the Butternuts and ethnic Catholics became increasingly antiwar.

Economic issues continued during the war to exacerbate the anti–New England sentiments of the southern Midwest. The region's representatives in Congress voted solidly against the national bank acts, income tax and tariff legislation, and other wartime financial measures. They revived Jacksonian rhetoric to denounce "this monstrous Bank Bill" and "the money monopoly of New England." "The design is to destroy the fixed institutions of the States, and to build up a central moneyed despotism," said one Midwestern Democrat in 1863; another asked: "Shall we sink down as serfs to the heartless, speculative Yankee for all time to come—swindled by his tariffs, robbed by his taxes, skinned by his railroad monopolies?"[24]

Ethnocultural hostilities reinforced these anti–New England economic attitudes. It was the "Constitution-breaking, law-defying, negro-loving Pharaseeism of New England" that had driven the South to secession, said Congressman Samuel S. Cox of Ohio in 1863. The Yankee "tendency to make government a moral reform association . . . is the especial curse of the nation at the present time." Much of the Roman Catholic press joined this attack on the "New England Negrophiles" and "canting Abolition Puritans [who] brought on this war."[25]

There was much talk in the southern Midwest of organizing the region into a

"Northwest Confederacy" to make peace with the South and to reconstruct the old Union with New England left out. Although in hindsight such a project appears fantastic, it was seriously proposed during the war. "The erection of the States watered by the Mississippi and its tributaries into an independent Republic," said Cox, "is the talk of every other western man."[26] Confederate agents worked quietly to encourage antiwar sentiment in the Midwest. The Knights of the Golden Circle (the secret society formed in the 1850s to promote Southern expansion into the Caribbean) organized chapters in the Midwest to promote the Northwest Confederacy. Although Republicans exaggerated the extent of such activity in their attempt to stigmatize the Democrats as disloyal, the existence of the Knights of the Golden Circle and similar societies was not a myth.

The radical changes set into motion by Republican war policies threatened Copperhead values and traditions. This was why Peace Democrats adopted the slogan "The Constitution as it is and the Union as it was." Continuation of the war, they said, would produce "terrible social change and revolution." The "most radical, revolutionary, and disorganizing doctrines" were "brought into vogue by the war; doctrines which sweep away the whole fabric of our institutions." The foremost Copperhead was Congressman Clement L. Vallandigham of Ohio, descendant of a Virginia family and married to the daughter of a Maryland planter. Vallandigham knew what kind of Union he wanted restored. "It is the desire of my heart," he wrote, "to restore the Union, the Federal Union as it was forty years ago." But if this Republican war continued, he said in January 1863, "I see nothing before us but universal political and social revolution, anarchy and bloodshed, compared with which the Reign of Terror in France was a merciful visitation."[27]

Democrats and Emancipation

Opposition to emancipation became the chief rallying cry not only of Copperheads but of nearly all Democrats. "We mean that the United States . . . shall be the white man's home . . . and the nigger shall never be his equal," said a Democratic senator in a typical statement. A wealthy and powerful New York Democrat declared that "the verdict of impartial history will surely put Jeff Davis, bad as he is, far above the abolition herd who have brought this revolution upon us." And Archbishop John Hughes of New York announced that Catholics "are willing to fight to the death for the support of the constitution, the government, and the laws of the country. But if . . . they are to fight for the abolition of slavery, then, indeed, they will turn away in disgust from the discharge of what would otherwise be a patriotic duty."[28] Rarely in American history has an issue so sharply polarized political parties as emancipation polarized them in 1862. This can be demonstrated by an analysis of congressional votes on four antislavery measures in 1862: the article of war forbidding the return of fugitives, emancipation in the District of Columbia, prohibition of slavery in the territories, and the second confiscation act. Senate and House Republican votes on these bills were 99 percent aye, while Democratic votes were 96 percent nay. Given the persistence of antiabolition and antiblack sentiments among the constituents of many Republican congressmen, this virtually unanimous support of emancipation measures testified to the power of ideology and the pressures of total war to overcome "politics as usual." But it also promised trouble for Republicans at the polls in the fall of 1862, as Montgomery Blair had warned (see p. 272).

Racial fears motivated the antiabolition sentiments of many Northern whites. The Democratic press exploited these fears. It dwelt on the theme that emancipation would turn loose a flood of freed blacks into the North. "The hundreds of thousands, if not millions of slaves [the confiscation act] will emancipate will come North and West," proclaimed the *Cincinnati Enquirer,* "and will either be competitors with our white mechanics and laborers, degrading them by the competition, or they will have to be supported as paupers and criminals at the public expense." Other editors warned of the "two or three million semi-savages" who would come North to mix with "the sons and daughters" of white workingmen. A New York Democratic newspaper ran frequent stories and editorials under such headlines as "White Supremacy or Negro Amalgamation?" "Can Niggers Conquer Americans?" "Shall the Negroes Come North?" "Shall the Working Classes be Equalized with Negroes?" And a German-language newspaper in Milwaukee issued a call to action: "Workingmen! Be Careful! Organize yourselves against this element which threatens your impoverishment and annihilation."[29]

With such advice from their leaders, it was little wonder that in 1862 white laborers erupted into mob violence against blacks in a half-dozen cities across the North. Most of the rioters were Irish Americans, who attacked black employees or strikebreakers in such occupations as stevedore and deckhand. The mobs sometimes surged into black neighborhoods and assaulted people on the streets and in their homes. In southern Illinois, Butternut farmers and farmhands attacked contrabands who had been brought in from Tennessee to help with the harvest.

Fears of emancipation were not confined to Butternuts and Irish. Republicans ruefully admitted that large parts of the North were infected with racism. "Our people hate the Negro with a perfect if not a supreme hatred," said Congressman George Julian of Indiana. Senator Lyman Trumbull of Illinois conceded that "there is a very great aversion in the West—I know it to be so in my State—against having free negroes come among us. Our people want nothing to do with the negro."[30] The same could be said of many soldiers who would be required to fight to free the slaves, if the Republican antislavery policy was to succeed.

THE UNION ARMY AND EMANCIPATION

The racial sentiments of Northern soldiers reflected the society from which they came. Although some men had joined the army to fight against slavery, a careful scholar who studied thousands of letters and diaries of Union soldiers concluded that no more than "one soldier in ten at any time during the conflict had any real interest in emancipation per se."[31] Many men agreed with the soldier who wrote: "I came out to fight for the restoration of the Union and to keep slavery [from] going into the territories & not to free the niggers." Some Northern soldiers made no bones about their racism. "I think the best way to settle the question of what to do with the darkies," wrote a New Yorker in 1861, "would be to shoot them."[32]

As time went on, however, the demands of a total war in which white Southerners were enemies and black Southerners were potential allies converted most Yankee soldiers to a belief in emancipation—if not as an act of justice, at least as a necessity of war. A Minnesota soldier wrote in March 1863:

> I have never been in favor of the abolition of slavery until since this war has detirmend me in the conviction that it is a greater sin than our Government is able to stand—and now I go in for a war of emancipation. . . . I am satesfied that slavery is . . . an institution that belonged to the dark ages—and that it ill becomes a nation of our standing to perpetuate the barbarous practice. It is opposed to the Spirit of the age—and in my opinion this Rebelion is but the death strugle of the overgrown monster.[33]

Contrabands welcomed Yankee soldiers as liberators, gave them food, showed them where valuables were hidden at abandoned plantations, served as guides and scouts and spies for the invading forces. Slaves often sheltered escaped Union prisoners of war and helped them on their way back to Northern lines. This friendliness was bound to affect the attitudes of Northern soldiers, some of whom repaid it by teaching contrabands to read and write or by helping them in other ways. An antislavery company of Ohio soldiers took up a collection to send a promising contraband to Oberlin College. Other freed slaves received similar help to go North.

Most of the positive references to blacks in soldiers' letters date from the second half of the war, and the majority were written by men from New England and other antislavery areas of the upper North. Social class also made a difference in racial attitudes: officers and men with a fair amount of education were more likely to be antislavery than privates and men with less schooling. Among the latter, especially in the first two years of war, crude racism was the rule. These soldiers often treated with cruel callousness the slaves who naively welcomed them as liberators. A trooper stationed in South Carolina wrote in November 1861: "About 8–10 soldiers from the New York 47th Regiment chased some Negro women but they escaped, so they took a Negro girl about 7–9 years old, and raped her." A Connecticut soldier wrote from Virginia that some of his messmates had grabbed "two niger wenches . . . turned them upon their heads, & put tobacco, chips, sticks, lighted cigars & sand into their behinds."[34]

COLONIZATION OF FREED SLAVES

In sum, although the Yankee army eventually became an army of liberation, many of its members were at best reluctant liberators. An Illinois soldier who approved of emancipation nevertheless declared in October 1862 that "I am not in favor of freeing the negroes and leaving them to run free and mingle among us nether is Sutch the intention of Old Abe but we will Send them off and colonize them."[35]

Such indeed was Lincoln's expressed intention at that time. The President had invited five Washington black leaders to the White House on August 14, 1862, and urged them to consider the idea of emigration. Slavery was "the greatest wrong inflicted on any people," Lincoln told the delegation. But even if the institution were abolished, racial differences and prejudices would remain. "Your race suffer very greatly, many of them, by living among us, while ours suffer by your presence." Black people had little chance for equality in the United States. More than that, "there is an unwillingness on the part of our people, harsh as it may be, for you free colored people to remain with us. . . . I do not mean to discuss this, but to propose it as a fact with which we have to deal. I cannot alter it if I would. . . . It is better for us both, therefore, to be separated." Lincoln implored his listeners to recruit several hundred fellow blacks for a pilot colonization project to demonstrate the feasibility of this "solution" of the race problem.[36]

Northern blacks and abolitionists predictably condemned the President's proposal. For thirty years they had been fighting colonization and they were not about to stop now, on the eve of victory for their cause. The wealthy Philadelphia black abolitionist Robert Purvis bluntly addressed Lincoln in print: "It is in vain you talk to me of 'two races' and their 'mutual antagonism.' In the matter of rights, there is but one race, and that is the *human race.* . . . Sir, this is our country as much as it is yours, and we will not leave it." Most radical Republicans expressed the same viewpoint, at least in private. Chase complained in his diary of the racism inherent in Lincoln's proposal. "How much better would be a manly protest against prejudice against color!—and a wise effort to give freemen homes in America."[37]

But this was still a minority opinion in the North. From Thomas Jefferson to Abraham Lincoln, America's foremost statesmen had come to a similar conclusion: emancipation could work only if the freed slaves were colonized abroad. Otherwise, the South would endure the horrors of race war and the freed people would either suffer extermination or degenerate into a vicious class of welfare clients. The actual prospect of emancipation in 1862 intensified these concerns. Abolitionists "may prattle as they wish about the end of slavery being the end of strife," warned a Boston conservative, but "the great difficulty will then but begin! The question is the profound and awful one of race."[38]

Whatever its substantive merits, colonization was good politics. Having made up his mind to issue an emancipation proclamation, Lincoln thought it best to sugar-coat this strong pill with colonization. Even some radicals accepted this reasoning. "I believe practically [colonization] is a damn humbug," said one, "but it will take with the people."[39] Congress appropriated $600,000 in 1862 to finance the voluntary colonization of freed slaves. Radical Republicans initially opposed this, but half of them eventually changed their minds when it became clear that the appropriation was necessary to ensure passage of the confiscation act of 1862.

In the end, colonization did turn out to be a humbug. Lincoln managed to recruit 450 blacks for settlement on an island off the coast of Haiti. But the colony suffered from smallpox and from the malfeasance of the white promoter who had contracted with the government to manage the venture. The administration admitted its mistake in 1864 and sent a naval vessel to bring back the 368 survivors. By then the momentum of war had carried Northern opinion beyond the conservatism of 1862, and no more was heard of colonization. An abolitionist pronounced a fitting epitaph upon this sorry episode: "Thus does the boasted wisdom of 'Conservatism' turn out to be folly, while the 'fanaticism' of the 'crazy Radicals' is proved by experience to be the highest wisdom."[40]

LINCOLN'S CIRCUMLOCUTION ON EMANCIPATION, AUGUST–SEPTEMBER 1862

A strategy of caution and indirection governed Lincoln's public statements during the ten weeks between his decision to issue an emancipation proclamation and the date he actually did so. During this interval of plunging Northern morale, radicals attacked Lincoln from the left for his retention of McClellan in command and his refusal to proclaim emancipation, while Democrats sniped at the President from the right and hoped for victory in the fall elections. Through it all Lincoln remained outwardly calm and noncommittal. He refused to disclose the emancipation proclamation prematurely, lest it drive conservatives and War Democrats into the arms of the Copperheads. At the same time he threw out hints of what was coming, lest the radicals desert him completely. Never was Lincoln's sense of timing better demonstrated than in these difficult late summer days of 1862.

An example of Lincoln's strategy was his reply on August 22 to Horace Greeley's open letter in the *New York Tribune* entitled "The Prayer of Twenty Millions." Greeley complained that the "Union cause has suffered from a mistaken deference to Rebel Slavery." He implored Lincoln to turn the war into a crusade for freedom. In an unusual public response, the President carefully explained: "My paramount object in this struggle *is* to save the Union, and is *not* either to save or to destroy slavery. If I could save the Union without freeing *any* slave I would do it, and if I could save it by freeing *all* the slaves I would do it; and if I could save it by freeing some and leaving others alone, I would also do that." In closing, Lincoln stated that this represented his "view of *official* duty; and I intend no modification of my oft-expressed personal wish that all men everywhere could be free."[41] Here was something for both conservatives and radicals: an assertion that Union, not emancipation, was the Northern war aim; but also a hint that emancipation might become necessary to save the Union.

Lincoln similarly balanced the pros and cons of emancipation in his September 13 reply to a group of Chicago clergymen who had borne to Washington a petition for freedom. The President agreed that "slavery is the root of the rebellion, or at least its *sine qua non.*" He also agreed that "emancipation would help us in Europe, and convince them that we are incited by something more than ambition. . . . And then unquestionably it would weaken the rebels by drawing off their laborers, which is of great importance." On the other hand, with Confederate armies on the offensive and Union armies reeling backwards, "what *good* would a proclamation of emancipation from me do? . . . I do not want to issue a document that the whole world will necessarily see must be inoperative, like the

Pope's bull against the comet! Would *my* word free the slaves, when I cannot even enforce the Constitution in the rebel states?"[42]

Here again was something for both sides. Lincoln's statements could be read as indicating that he believed an emancipation edict useless. But with his actual proclamation tucked away in a desk drawer as he spoke, what the President really meant was that a proclamation would be useless until Union arms won a big victory. Then, perhaps, he could enforce emancipation *and* the Constitution in the South. For as Lincoln met with the Chicago delegation, his mind was preoccupied with the fateful military drama unfolding in Maryland.

Seventeen

The First Turning Point: Antietam and Emancipation

THE BATTLE OF ANTIETAM

Under ordinary circumstances, Lee's victorious but exhausted army should have gone into camp for rest and refitting after Second Bull Run. Food was low, thousands of men were shoeless, and the Union forces in his front were nearly twice as large as his own. But Lee had beaten the odds before by taking great risks; he now proposed to take a greater one in a bold campaign to win Maryland for the Confederacy, earn diplomatic recognition from Britain and France, and perhaps even force the Union to sue for peace. An invasion of the North would also take the armies out of war-ravaged Virginia during the fall harvest and enable the hungry Rebel soldiers to live off the enemy's country for a time.

Screened by Stuart's cavalry, the Army of Northern Virginia, on September 4, 1862, began splashing across the Potomac forty miles upriver from Washington. But already thousands of men were falling behind because they lacked shoes or because they were sick from eating green corn and green apples. Many others would drop out from exhaustion or bloody feet before the showdown battle. The Confederates concentrated at Frederick on September 7. Disappointingly few Marylanders flocked to the Rebel standard, for western Maryland was Unionist in sentiment. Lee hoped to move west of South Mountain (an extension of the Blue Ridge into Maryland) to open a supply line into the Shenandoah Valley. Before he could do so, however, he needed to eliminate the 10,000-man Union garrison at Harper's Ferry. On September 9 he ordered Jackson's corps and portions of Longstreet's to converge on Harper's Ferry and capture it. After accomplishing this, they were to rejoin the rest of the army for a planned move to cut the Pennsylvania Railroad at Harrisburg. Once again—for the third time in three campaigns—Lee divided his army, contrary to the maxims of military textbooks. It had worked before because Lee's appraisals of his opponent's defects had been accurate. Counting on McClellan's slowness, he expected to reunite the army before the Federals caught up with him.

Meanwhile McClellan had whipped the Army of the Potomac back into shape and was moving northward with 80,000 men to locate the Rebels, whose numbers he estimated at 120,000 (two and a half times their actual strength). On September 13, McClellan had a stroke of luck such as few generals have ever had. In an abandoned Confederate encampment at Frederick, a Union corporal found a copy of Lee's orders wrapped around three cigars, lost by a careless Southern officer. The orders gave McClellan a clear picture of the whereabouts of Lee's army, divided into five parts: three separate columns converging on Harper's Ferry; two divisions at Hagerstown; and another division at Boonsboro, near Turner's Gap, where the National Road crossed South Mountain. Each of the five parts was at least eight or ten miles from any of the others; the two most widely separated parts were thirty miles from each other with the Potomac between them; McClellan with most of his army was only twelve miles from the nearest Confederate unit. As historian Bruce Catton has written, "no Civil War general was ever given so fair a chance to destroy the opposing army one piece at a time." McClellan was jubilant. To one of his generals he said, "Here is a paper with which if I cannot whip 'Bobbie Lee,' I will be willing to go home."[1]

But instead of marching immediately to force the gaps through South Mountain and fall on Lee's scattered divisions, McClellan waited sixteen hours before moving. By the time two of his corps reached Turner's Gap and another arrived at Crampton's Gap five miles to the south, Lee had been warned and had rushed troops to defend the passes. Union General William B. Franklin's 6th Corps pushed through Crampton's Gap on the afternoon of September 14 and rolled southward toward Maryland Heights overlooking Harper's Ferry, but then stopped timidly when some of the Confederate brigades besieging the Ferry turned to meet them. Meanwhile, after a fierce day-long battle at Turner's Gap, in which the outnumbered Confederates suffered 2,700 casualties to the Union's 1,800, Lee withdrew toward the village of Sharpsburg. His invasion plans were wrecked, but McClellan's slowness had given him an extra day to extricate his scattered army from destruction. Lee prepared orders for a retreat to Virginia. But when he learned that Jackson's troops had captured Harper's Ferry and its garrison on the morning of September 15, he changed his mind and ordered the army to concentrate and accept battle at Sharpsburg.

The ensuing battle of Antietam (or Sharpsburg, as the South called it) was a story of desperate defense by the Confederates and missed opportunities by the Federals. Lee's troops occupied the low ridge just east of the village running north and south four miles, with his left flank on the Potomac and his right on Antietam Creek. For some reason (perhaps because they lacked spades and axes) the Confederates did not entrench, a neglect that would be unthinkable a year later. Because of straggling and because of his losses at South Mountain, Lee had fewer than 45,000 men to face McClellan's 75,000. And on the afternoon of September 15, before Jackson could join him from Harper's Ferry, Lee had only 19,000 troops at Sharpsburg. But again McClellan moved cautiously, and the chance for an attack with overwhelming numbers on the 15th slipped away. Next morning

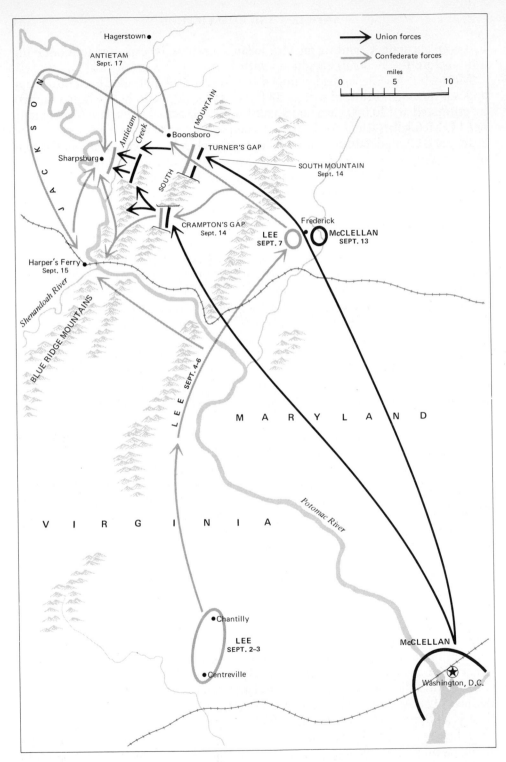

Hagerstown ●

ANTIETAM
Sept. 17

MOUNTAIN

J A C K S O N

Antietam Creek

● Boonsboro

TURNER'S GAP

SOUTH MOUNTAIN
Sept. 14

Sharpsburg ●

SOUTH

Frederick

CRAMPTON'S GAP
Sept. 14

LEE
SEPT. 7

McCLELLAN
SEPT. 13

Harper's Ferry ●
Sept. 15

Shenandoah River

BLUE RIDGE MOUNTAINS

LEE SEPT. 4-6

M A R Y L A N D

V I R G I N I A

Potomac River

● Chantilly

LEE
SEPT. 2–3

● Centreville

McCLELLAN

Washington, D.C.

→ Union forces
→ Confederate forces

miles
0   5   10

LEE'S INVASION OF MARYLAND, 1862

Jackson's divisions started arriving from Harper's Ferry, but still the Federals did not attack, despite having more than 60,000 men on the ground to Lee's 30,000. The hours ticked away while McClellan matured plans for an attack on the morrow, by which time all of McClellan's troops and all but A. P. Hill's division of Lee's army (which had stayed at Harper's Ferry to supervise the surrender) would be in line.

The Union 1st and 12th corps under Joseph Hooker and Joseph Mansfield crossed the Antietam on the afternoon of September 16 and prepared to assault next day the Confederate left, held by Jackson. The 9th Corps under Burnside was to force its way across the creek on the Confederate right. The other three Union corps would be held in reserve to reinforce these attacks and to smash through the Confederate center when and if Lee weakened it to reinforce both wings.

It was a good battle plan. Hooker got it off to a good start with a furious attack at dawn in which he lived up to his sobriquet of Fighting Joe. His 12,000 men swept forward from a grove known ever after as the North Woods. Artillery and musketry blasted a forty-acre cornfield in which Confederate infantry were hiding. "In the time I am writing," Hooker later reported, "every stalk of corn in the northern and greater part of the field was cut as closely as with a knife, and the slain lay in rows precisely as they had stood in their ranks a few minutes before. It was never my fortune to witness a more bloody, dismal battlefield."[2] Many other participants who later wrote of this battle agreed that the fighting was the most intense of their experience. A half-savage "fighting madness" took possession of men and drove them to acts of courage or desperation beyond human ken. The blue brigades surged through the cornfield and up to the edge of the West Woods near a small whitewashed church of the pacifist Dunkard sect. There John B. Hood's gray division finally stopped the Federals and drove them back across the cornfield. Soon afterward, fresh Union troops from Mansfield's corps charged from the East Woods through the cornfield and pushed the broken Confederate lines into and through the West Woods. But once more the Union attack ran out of steam as men went down by the hundreds. Mansfield was killed and Hooker wounded, and most of their shattered divisions pulled back to reorganize after three hours of unmitigated hell. In midmorning Union General Edwin Sumner led his 2nd Corps forward against the West Woods. His lead division had penetrated the position deeply when suddenly two Confederate divisions appeared on its flank and poured a deadly fire into the Yankee brigades, cutting down 2,200 men in twenty minutes. Then a counterattack by Jackson across the cornfield was beaten back with staggering losses. The cornfield had become a no-man's land. It was so full of bodies that, in one soldier's recollection, a man could have walked through it without stepping on the ground.

Before noon the battle on the Confederate left was over. Each side had fought the other to exhaustion. Thirteen thousand men lay dead or wounded. The Union attacks had failed because they were delivered seriatim instead of simultaneously. The Confederates had had time to shift troops and to bring up reserves to meet the assaults. McClellan must bear part of the blame for this. His battle dispositions had prevented Mansfield from going in together with Hooker, while he personally

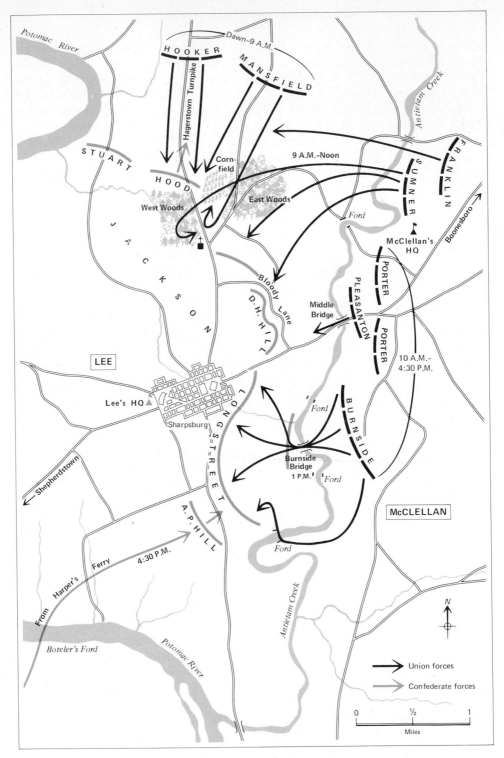

THE BATTLE OF ANTIETAM, SEPTEMBER 17, 1862

had delayed Sumner's attack for more than an hour.

McClellan was also responsible for the failure to exploit a Union breakthrough in the center. Two divisions of Sumner's corps had veered left from the assault in the West Woods and had bumped into a Confederate line at a sunken farm road, known thereafter as Bloody Lane. There for three hours the Rebels had hung on desperately in their ready-made trench until a misunderstood order allowed two Union regiments to enfilade the road and drive out those defenders not already lying dead or wounded in its tracks. The Confederate center was wide open. "There was no body of Confederate infantry in this part of the field that could have resisted a serious advance," wrote a Southern general. "When Rodes' brigade left the sunken road," added one of Longstreet's artillery officers, "Lee's army was ruined, and the end of the Confederacy was in sight."[3] Franklin was on hand with 8,000 fresh troops of his 6th Corps to exploit the breakthrough. He begged McClellan to unleash him, but the commanding general, shaken by the morning's carnage and fearing a counterattack by an army that he still believed outnumbered him, refused with the words that "it would not be prudent to make the attack."[4] Somewhat later, another Union general urged McClellan to send one division of Franklin's corps and the two uncommitted divisions of Porter's 5th Corps through the weakened Confederate center, but again McClellan refused.

Meanwhile what of Burnside on the Union left? Throughout the morning McClellan had repeatedly ordered him to push his strong 9th Corps across the Antietam and roll up the Confederate right. But this was easier said than done, for the one bridge over the creek in that sector was well covered by Confederate artillery and riflemen. Nevertheless Burnside could have done better than he did. The Antietam at that season was fordable in several places, yet Burnside had focused all his attention on the bridge. In the early afternoon some of his brigades finally found fords; at about the same time other troops forced a crossing over the bridge. But then Burnside delayed to deploy his divisions and did not begin to push forward against the weakened Confederate right until 3 P.M. For a time this blue advance swept all before it, reaching the outskirts of Sharpsburg itself, only half a mile from Lee's line of retreat to the Potomac fords. Again all seemed lost for the Confederates when suddenly, double-timing onto the field with a rebel yell, came A. P. Hill's division, which had marched seventeen miles in seven hours from Harper's Ferry. Some of Hill's veterans wore captured blue uniforms, which increased the surprise when they smashed the Federal flank and stopped the last Union advance of the day.

Night fell on a battlefield whose horrors defied description: 2,100 Yankees and 2,700 Rebels were dead, and another 18,500 (split almost evenly between the two armies) were wounded, 3,000 of them mortally. It was the bloodiest single day of the war.* Whole units on both sides were virtually wiped out; regimental and even

---

*By way of comparison: on D-Day in World War II, American forces suffered 6,000 casualties—about one-fourth the number of casualties at Antietam. More than twice as many Americans were killed or mortally wounded in combat in a single day at Antietam as in the War of 1812, the Mexican War, and the Spanish-American war *combined.*

Confederate Dead as They Fell Near the West Woods in the Battle
of Antietam   *(Reproduced from the Collections of the Library of Congress)*

These pictures reveal the horrors of war in a way that words cannot
convey. These and many other photographs of the Antietam
battlefield were taken by Alexander Gardner and James Gibson, who
worked for the famous photographer Mathew Brady, two days after
the battle. A month later the photographs went on exhibit at Brady's
studio in New York City, where thousands of people viewed these
scenes of carnage. This was the first time in American history that
the public could vicariously witness the devastation and suffering of
war. In the *New York Times* of October 20, 1862, a reporter
described the exhibit: "Mr. Brady has done something to bring home
to us the terrible reality and earnestness of war. If he has not brought
bodies and laid them in our door-yards and along streets, he has done
something very like it. . . . [But] there is one side of the picture that
the sun did not catch, one phase that has escaped photographic skill.
It is the background of widows and orphans, torn from the bosom of
their natural protectors by the red remorseless hand of Battle. . . .
Homes have been made desolate, and the light of life in thousands of
hearts has been quenched forever. All of this desolation imagination
must paint—broken hearts cannot be photographed."

Confederate Dead Near the Shell-Marked Dunkard Church
(Reproduced from the Collections of the Library of Congress)

Confederate Dead in Bloody Lane
(Reproduced from the Collections of the Library of Congress)

brigade losses of 50 percent were common. A British military observer who visited the battlefield ten days later wrote that "in about seven or eight acres of wood there is not a tree which is not full of bullets and bits of shell. It is impossible to understand how anyone could live in such a fire as there must have been here."[5]

What had been achieved by this valor and sacrifice? The battle was a tactical draw; but for the Confederates it was a strategic defeat. Lee had gone North with high hopes of ending the war at one stroke; his crippled army limped back to Virginia with these hopes shattered. Yet McClellan's failure was the greater. Several times he had had victory in his grasp only to lose it by faulty generalship and timidity. Never did more than 20,000 Federals go into action simultaneously. This allowed Lee to shift men from quiet to threatened sectors. Twenty thousand Union troops, more than a quarter of the army, were scarcely engaged at all. This makes a mockery of McClellan's statement in a letter to his wife: "Those in whose judgment I rely tell me that I fought the battle splendidly and that it was a masterpiece of art."[6]

The sun rose on September 18 to show the battered Confederates still in place. McClellan received 13,000 reinforcements during the morning. With the 20,000 previously uncommitted, this gave him more fresh men than Lee had left in his whole army. Yet McClellan did not renew the attack, and Lee escaped across the Potomac on the night of September 18. A feeble pursuit on September 20 was repulsed by the Rebel rear guard. Lee retreated unmolested to Winchester, while the Federals buried the dead and set up field hospitals for the wounded. Not for five weeks would the main body of the Army of the Potomac again cross into Virginia. Lincoln seized upon Antietam as the victory he had been waiting for to issue the Emancipation Proclamation (see p. 293). But the President was sorely disappointed by this renewed demonstration of McClellan's failure to close in on the enemy for the kill. For the moment, however, Lincoln postponed major military decisions in the eastern theater because events in the West were reaching a crisis.

THE CONFEDERATE INVASION OF KENTUCKY

After Beauregard had evacuated Corinth, Mississippi, at the end of May, his standing with Jefferson Davis had fallen even lower. Davis replaced him as commander of the Confederate Army of Mississippi with Braxton Bragg, a stern disciplinarian who had previously led a corps in this army. In July Bragg divided his army into three parts. He left 16,000 men under Earl Van Dorn and another 16,000 under Sterling Price to defend Mississippi. The remaining 30,000 he took by a roundabout rail route to Chattanooga to help Edmund Kirby Smith's 18,000 Confederate troops defend east Tennessee against Buell's advancing Army of the Ohio. Bragg arrived in Chattanooga before Buell could get there, even though the Federals had only one-fourth as far to go and had started six weeks earlier.

Buell's problems illustrated the difficulties of railroad logistics in enemy territory. Until this time, Union forces in the West had supplied themselves mainly by river. But a drought in the summer of 1862 made Buell dependent on the

railroad, which he had to rebuild as he moved eastward through northern Ala-
bama. Guerrilla raids reduced his normally slow movements to a snail's pace. A
Democrat like McClellan, Buell believed in a "soft" war and was unwilling to deal
harshly with guerrillas or to subsist his army off the countryside. As he approached
Chattanooga in July, he opened a new rail supply line through Nashville to
Louisville. But his troubles had just begun. Cavalry raids by Nathan Bedford
Forrest and John Hunt Morgan repeatedly cut this railroad and stopped Buell's
advance. The hapless Union cavalry could do little against the daredevil Rebel
horsemen, who lived off the country and melted back into the population after
a raid.

Meanwhile, when Bragg reached Chattanooga he turned to the offensive.
Jefferson Davis ordered Bragg and Kirby Smith to draw Buell out of Tennessee
by invading Kentucky. Confederate leaders believed Kentuckians to be eager for
liberation from their Yankee oppressors. The invading armies took along 15,000
extra rifles to arm the men they expected to join them. At first things went well.
The 10,000 troops with Kirby Smith by-passed the Union force holding Cumberland Gap and marched all the way to central Kentucky, where on August 30
they defeated and captured most of the Union garrison at Richmond (just south
of Lexington). With 30,000 men Bragg struck northward from Chattanooga,
moving quickly across Tennessee, and marched into Kentucky on a parallel
route 100 miles to the west of Smith. Buell had to abandon his stalled campaign
against Chattanooga and race northward to prevent the Rebels from capturing
Louisville.

Despite their apparent success, the ragged, shoeless Confederates learned in
Kentucky as in Maryland that it was one thing to invade Union territory but quite
another to stay there. Confederate soldiers were outstanding at marching and
fighting, but the South lacked the logistical capacity to convert a large-scale raid
into a genuine invasion. And despite the Confederate flags and the smiles of pretty
girls as Southern troops marched through their towns, Kentuckians proved no
more ready than Marylanders to join up. Those 15,000 rifles stayed in their
wagons. Kirby Smith did seize the state capital at Frankfort and prepared to
inaugurate a Confederate governor. But this meant little so long as Buell's army
remained in Kentucky and another 80,000 Northern recruits drilled in Louisville
and Cincinnati. Unless these soldiers and the industrial might that backed them
could somehow be eliminated, most residents of the bluegrass state would think
twice about declaring open allegiance to the Confederacy, no matter how strong
their Southern sentiments might be.

By mid-September, Buell had received three divisions of reinforcements from
Grant and now had an army of 50,000. Meanwhile the Confederates captured
another 4,000-man garrison at Munfordville, Kentucky. Criticism of Buell rose to
a crescendo in the North. Whatever the underlying weaknesses of the Confeder-
ate invasion, it appeared to be a brilliant success. The Rebels had captured 8,000
Union soldiers, had drawn another 50,000 out of Tennessee, and were threatening
Louisville and even Cincinnati. Buell seemed to have done nothing to stop them.
Halleck warned a Western officer that unless Buell "does something very soon"

he would be removed. "The Government seems determined to apply the guillo-
tine to all unsuccessful generals," continued Halleck. "It seems rather hard to do
this where the general is not at fault, but perhaps with us now, as in the French
Revolution, some harsh measures are required."7 At the end of September, Lincoln did try to replace Buell with George Thomas; but he suspended the order
when Thomas protested that commanders should not be changed on the eve of
battle.

The Battle of Perryville

Buell finally moved out to fight the Rebels. He sent two divisions on a feint toward
Frankfort, which disrupted the inauguration of the Confederate governor and
diverted Kirby Smith's troops and one division of Bragg's army from the main
battle. The rest of Buell's army moved in three columns toward Perryville, where
Bragg concentrated his remaining forces to meet them. The preliminaries of the
ensuing battle were much influenced by the search for water, for the drought had
dried up all but the larger streams. One Union corps detoured to find water; when
advance units of another reached Perryville at dusk on October 7, they immediately
attacked in a vain attempt to gain control of Doctor's Creek two miles west of town.
A brigade in Philip Sheridan's division attacked again at dawn and carried not only
the creek but the heights beyond. A small, bandy-legged man only thirty-one years
old, Sheridan possessed an indomitable will and driving force. After he had seized
the heights and held them against a counterattack, the rest of Buell's army filed into
position on the left and right to form a line six miles long.

But then the initiative went over to the Confederates, who had only 16,000
men on the field, one-third as many as Buell. General Leonidas Polk, who in
addition to commanding a corps in Bragg's army was an Episcopal bishop,
launched an all-out attack on the Union left, leaving only two brigades of infantry
and one of cavalry to demonstrate against the Union center and right. The Rebels
rolled up the green troops on the Federal left, driving them back more than a mile
and killing two generals before resistance stiffened. Sheridan meanwhile grasped
the opportunity to counterattack against the weak Confederates in his front and
sent them flying back two miles through the village of Perryville.

By nightfall, then, the troops on the northern half of the battlefield had swung
counterclockwise in a huge quarter-circle. The right half of Buell's army had not
fought at all. Through a freak of wind and atmospheric conditions (known as
acoustic shadow), they had heard nothing and did not even realize that a battle
was going on a mile or two to their left. For the same reason, Buell himself
remained unaware of the fighting until late afternoon. For those engaged (23,000
Federals, 15,000 Confederates) the casualties were heavy: 4,200 Yankees and
3,400 Rebels killed, wounded, or missing. Buell planned to attack with his whole
army next morning, but Bragg slipped away during the night to join Kirby Smith's
forces. Even united, however, the two Confederate armies were outnumbered.
They were also short of supplies, and encumbered with many sick and wounded.
In a despondent mood, Bragg decided to withdraw from Kentucky. Buell pursued

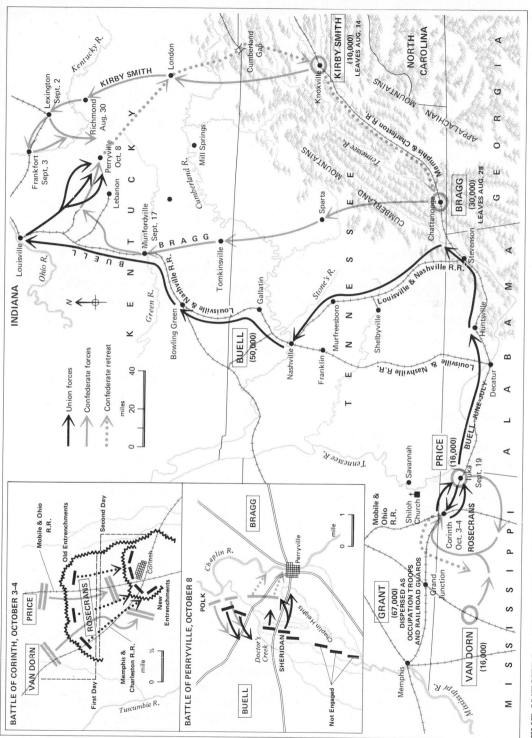

THE WESTERN THEATER, SUMMER–FALL 1862

timidly and failed to attack the retreating Confederates, despite good opportunities to do so.

THE BATTLES OF IUKA AND CORINTH

One reason for Bragg's decision to withdraw was a series of actions 300 miles away, in northern Mississippi. The mission of Van Dorn's and Price's small Confederate armies there was to keep Grant from reinforcing Buell and, if possible, to strike northward themselves in coordination with Bragg's invasion. But Grant and Rosecrans* had frustrated both objectives. Several thousand of the Union soldiers who fought at Perryville, including Sheridan, were among the reinforcements Grant had sent Buell. And in two battles—at Iuka and Corinth—Rosecrans blocked the plans of Price and Van Dorn to invade west Tennessee.

In mid-September Price occupied the town of Iuka in northeast Mississippi. Grant formed a plan to trap these 14,000 Confederates between two converging Union forces. Rosecrans with 9,000 men came up from the south, while 8,000 troops from the Army of the Mississippi under General Edward Ord approached along the railroad from the west. But the difficult procedure of bringing two separate forces together on the battlefield went awry, as it often did in those days before radio communication. Rosecrans came up late and was attacked by Price on September 19; but he held his own while an acoustic shadow kept Ord from hearing the sound of battle. That night Price, realizing that he was in a trap, escaped by an unblocked road and moved to join Van Dorn forty miles to the west, while the Federals marched back to their base at Corinth.

On October 3 the combined armies of Van Dorn and Price launched a fierce attack against an equal number of bluecoats (22,000) under Rosecrans at Corinth. After driving the Yankees back two miles in their initial thrust, the Rebels halted for the night. When they renewed the attack next morning, stiffened Union resistance cut them to pieces. The Confederates retreated southward; Rosecrans's force was too crippled for effective pursuit, and a fresh brigade sent by Grant managed only to pick up a few hundred Rebel stragglers. In the two battles of Iuka and Corinth, Union casualties totaled 3,300, and the Confederates lost 5,700 men, a quarter of their force.

From September 17 to October 8, three attempted Confederate invasions of Union territory were turned back. It was the South's most ambitious bid for victory through coordinated military offensives. Although Lee would again invade the North in June 1863, never again would all the principal Confederate armies march northward simultaneously. Although none of the three big battles—Antietam, Perryville, and Corinth—was an unequivocal Union victory, together they marked a turning point of crucial importance. They ended the chance for European recognition of the Confederacy, and they changed the character of the conflict from a war for Union to a war for Union and freedom.

*When General Pope was transferred to the eastern theater in June, Rosecrans came west to take command of the Army of the Mississippi.

Some of the Fifty-six Confederates Killed in a Charge on a Union
Battery in the Battle of Corinth, October 4, 1862   *(Reproduced from
the Collections of the Library of Congress)*

THE PRELIMINARY EMANCIPATION
PROCLAMATION

Five days after the battle of Antietam, Lincoln called the cabinet together to
announce his decision to issue the Emancipation Proclamation. For months, the
President reminded his advisers, he had tried to persuade the border states to
act against slavery. Now "we must make the forward movement" without them.
"They [will] acquiesce, if not immediately, soon; for they must be satisfied that
slavery [has] received its death-blow from slave-owners—it could not survive the
rebellion." As for Northern Democrats, Lincoln no longer cared to conciliate
them, for "their clubs would be used against us take what course we might."[8]

The edict dated September 22, 1862, was actually a preliminary proclamation,
for it declared that the slaves in states still in rebellion on January 1, 1863, "shall
be then, thenceforward, and forever free." The proclamation justified emancipation solely on grounds of military necessity, endorsed voluntary colonization of
freed slaves, and reiterated Lincoln's plea for gradual emancipation in the loyal
slave states. This conservative approach was deliberate. Still uncertain of the
country's response to such a revolutionary step, the President announced it in a

manner designed to cushion the shock and make emancipation appear a necessary means of winning the war. Most radicals and abolitionists understood this. "A poor *document*, but a mighty *act*" was Massachusetts' radical Governor John Andrew's comment on the proclamation. A Garrisonian abolitionist conceded that from a purist's viewpoint the proclamation had a number of defects. But "I cannot stop to dwell on these. Joy, gratitude, thanksgiving, renewed hope and courage fill my soul."[9]

LINCOLN AND CIVIL LIBERTIES

Two days after signing the Emancipation Proclamation, Lincoln issued a second edict; this one suspended the writ of *habeas corpus* and authorized the military arrest of "all Rebels and Insurgents, their aiders and abettors within the United States, and all persons discouraging volunteer enlistments, resisting militia drafts, or guilty of any disloyal practice."[10] Democrats denounced this action as the tyrannical twin of emancipation. The two proclamations provided the opposition with its main issues in the 1862 congressional elections. Before turning to these elections, it is necessary to examine the question of civil liberties in the wartime North.

Although no consistent policy of newspaper censorship existed during the war, the government did use its military control of the telegraph after January 1862 to regulate reporters' dispatches. The Post Office occasionally excluded "treasonable" newspapers from the mails. Generals sometimes barred certain newspapers from their departments on the ground that they provided military information to the enemy. On several occasions the government shut down particular newspapers for limited lengths of time. Most of this newspaper suppression took place in occupied portions of slave states, though a few famous cases occurred in the North itself. Northern mobs destroyed the offices and presses of several Copperhead newspapers. At least two such mobs were led by Union soldiers, who were not punished for their acts.

During 1861 the State Department was responsible for enforcing internal security. Seward organized a secret service network of agents and informers whose zeal frequently exceeded their discretion. The government arrested hundreds of men in the border states and detained them without trial. In Maryland, federal troops imprisoned several members of the legislature and a state judge. The army also arrested and punished numerous spies, saboteurs, and guerrillas in the occupied portions of the South and border states.

By executive order in February 1862, Lincoln transferred responsibility for all internal security matters to the War Department. Stanton reduced the number of arrests and established a commission to examine the cases of prisoners then being held. Most of them were released upon taking an oath of allegiance. Arrests almost ceased during the spring of 1862, when the North was confident of soon winning the war. But the reverses of summer, the mushrooming of Copperhead sentiment, and the resistance to the militia draft in the fall of 1862 produced a new wave of military arrests. Lincoln's September 24 proclamation suspending *habeas corpus* was aimed mainly at this draft resistance.

Altogether during the war, Union authorities arrested at least 15,000 civilians. Was this an excessive repression of civil liberties? Many contemporaries certainly thought so. They did not question the arrest of enemy agents and saboteurs or the military trials of guerrillas and spies in active war zones. (Some critics even sanctioned the military arrest and trial of draft evaders and of persons encouraging desertion or draft resistance, although some of these activities occurred in Northern states where the civil courts were functioning.) But they condemned the arbitrary arrest of editors, public officials, and other persons whose only crime was to write or speak against the administration's war policies or in favor of peace. Some of those arrested were victims of wild rumors of conspiracy that became an inevitable part of war psychology. Some were imprisoned for months without any charges having been brought against them. All of this seems to confirm that the administration's record on civil liberties was a bad one.

Yet there was often a thin line between verbal antiwar activities and those that were obviously treasonable. Was an inflammatory speech urging recruits to refuse to fight an "abolitionist war" an exercise of free speech, or was it aiding and abetting the enemy? Lincoln stated the question graphically: "Must I shoot a simple-minded soldier boy who deserts, while I must not touch a hair of a wily agitator who induces him to desert? . . . I think that in such a case, to silence the agitator, and save the boy, is not only constitutional, but, withal, a great mercy." The President insisted that in a time of grave emergency it was better to arrest too many than too few. "Under cover of 'Liberty of speech,' 'Liberty of the press' and 'Habeas Corpus',," he wrote, the Rebels "hoped to keep on foot amongst us a most efficient corps of spies, informers, suppliers, and aiders and abettors of their cause." The civil courts were too slow to handle these cases in the emergency; and if released on writs of *habeas corpus* to await trial, these persons would continue their treasonable activities. The purpose of military arrests was preventive, not punitive. Men were detained so they could not aid the rebellion; they were released without trial sooner or later, more sooner than later, when the danger had passed. These were strong measures, Lincoln admitted, unconstitutional in times of peace but constitutional "in cases of rebellion or invasion." "I can no more be persuaded," wrote Lincoln in one of his homely but effective metaphors, "that the government can constitutionally take no strong measure in time of rebellion, because it can be shown that the same could not be lawfully taken in time of peace, than I can be persuaded that a particular drug is not good medicine for a sick man, because it can be shown to not be good food for a well one."[11]

One of the most thorough students of wartime civil liberties defends the Lincoln administration. Most prisoners, he found, were treated well during their confinement. Most were in prison "for good reason." Most were released after relatively short detentions unless convicted for actual crimes such as espionage or treason. When military commissions tried civilians, it was usually for a military crime committed in a war zone. (The notable exceptions of the Vallandigham and Milligan cases are discussed in Chapters 20 and 24.) The overwhelming majority of the 15,000 arrests occurred in the occupied South or in the border states that because of guerrilla activity and espionage were really part of the war zone. "Considering the imperative demands of the emergency, a fair amount of restraint was shown in the making of arrests. . . . The Government smarted under great abuse without passing an Espionage Act or a Sedition Law. Freedom of speech was preserved to the point of permitting the most disloyal utterances."[12] Although troops patrolled the polls in border states to exclude voters who had not taken an oath of allegiance, free elections took place throughout the war, administration candidates often suffered defeat, and for a time in 1864 it appeared that Lincoln himself would not be reelected. Compared with the draconian enforcement of espionage and sedition laws in World War I and the internment of Japanese Americans during World War II, the infringement of civil liberties during the much greater internal crisis of 1861–1865 seems mild indeed. Be that as it may, Democrats made political capital out of "arbitrary arrests" in the 1862 elections. Resentment of the militia draft also worked in their favor. But the most important single issue, judged by the volume of rhetoric, was the Emancipation Proclamation.

THE ELECTIONS OF 1862 IN THE NORTH

Democrats called on voters to repudiate the Republicans before Lincoln could issue the final emancipation proclamation on January 1. In New York, where Democratic gubernatorial candidate Horatio Seymour hoped the election would catapult him into national prominence, party organs announced that "a vote for Seymour is a vote to protect our white laborers against the association and competition of Southern negroes." Midwestern Democratic orators proclaimed that "every white man in the North, who does not want to be swapped off for a free Nigger, should vote the Democratic ticket."[13]

Many observers regarded the outcome of the elections as a sharp rebuke of the Republicans and of emancipation. Democrats scored a net gain of thirty-two seats in the House. Nearly all of this gain came in the lower North—New York, New Jersey, Pennsylvania, Ohio, Indiana, and Illinois. The Democrats also won the governorships of New York and New Jersey, and gained control of the legislatures in Illinois and Indiana. (Only the fortuitous circumstance that the gubernatorial and legislative elections in Pennsylvania and Ohio were held in odd years and that Republican governors had been elected to four-year terms in Illinois and Indiana in 1860 prevented these state governments from being controlled by Democrats after 1862.) Democrats were exuberant. Typical newspaper headlines proclaimed: "Abolition Slaughtered" and "No Emancipation." According to Ohio Congressman Samuel S. Cox, the election had brought forth a new commandment: "Thou shalt not degrade the white race by such intermixtures as emancipation would bring."[14]

Several historians have concurred in this interpretation of the 1862 elections. "The verdict of the polls," wrote one, "showed clearly that the people of the North were opposed to the Emancipation Proclamation, opposed to governmental encroachment on individual rights, and opposed to conscription."[15] But in fact the elections showed nothing of the kind. They were a setback for the Republicans, but not a defeat. Republicans carried all of New England, the upper North, the two Pacific states, and the border states. To be sure, federal troops excluded secessionist sympathizers from the polls in the border states; but even without these states, the Republicans would have retained control of Congress and of all but two governorships and two state legislatures. If the election was in any sense a referendum on emancipation and on Lincoln's conduct of the war, a majority of Northern voters endorsed these policies.

When Congress convened in December 1862 for its lame-duck session, Republicans emphatically reaffirmed emancipation. First they rejected a Democratic-sponsored House resolution which declared that anyone in the government who proposed to wage war "for the overthrowing or interfering with the rights or established institutions of any of the States" was guilty of "a high crime against the Constitution." Then by a straight party vote the House adopted a resolution endorsing the Emancipation Proclamation.[16] Finally Congress passed a bill to require emancipation as a condition of West Virginia statehood.*

Nevertheless, rumors circulated during December 1862 that Lincoln would withdraw the Emancipation Proclamation. These rumors sprang from the inflated hopes of Democrats following the 1862 elections and gained added force from Lincoln's message to Congress on December 1. The President recommended a constitutional amendment to provide for compensated, gradual (extending to 1900) emancipation in every state "wherein slavery now exists." If Lincoln intended to issue an emancipation proclamation, asked alarmed Republicans, why did he make such a recommendation?

But those who interpreted the message as an alternative to an emancipation proclamation missed its real point. Lincoln also said that no proceedings under the September 22 proclamation would be delayed by his proposal, and that all slaves freed "by the chances of war" would remain "forever free." The President made it clear that one way or another the war must accomplish a new birth of freedom.

> Fellow citizens, *we* cannot escape history. . . . The fiery trial through which we pass, will light us down, in honor or dishonor, to the latest generation. . . . The dogmas of the quiet past, are inadequate to the stormy present. . . . As our case is new, so we must think anew, and act anew. . . . In *giving* freedom to the *slave*, we *assure* freedom to the *free*. . . . We must disenthrall ourselves, and then we shall save our country.[17]

Lincoln privately reassured Republicans that he would not falter on emancipation. "The President is firm," Charles Sumner told Boston friends. "He says that he would not stop the Proclamation if he could, and he could not if he would."[18]

On January 1 Lincoln signed the document, proclaiming freedom to all slaves in the portions of Confederate states not then occupied by Union troops.† South-

---

*The enabling act specified that all persons born after July 4, 1863, should be free; all others under the age of twenty-five would become free on their twenty-fifth birthday. West Virginia incorporated these provisions into its 1863 constitution. But the gradualist features were soon swept aside by the Thirteenth Amendment.

†The portions of the Confederacy exempted from the Proclamation were several counties in Virginia, several parishes in Louisiana, and the entire state of Tennessee. Because these areas (with the exception of eastern

ern leaders damned the proclamation as an infamous incitement to slave insurrection or as a hypocritical Yankee trick, which "emancipated" only those slaves
beyond Northern reach and left the others in slavery. Democratic and conservative reaction in the North ran a similar gamut. A good many radicals were troubled
by the exemption of border states and occupied areas of the Confederacy. They
wriggled uncomfortably under the jibe of the London *Spectator* that the principle
of the proclamation was "not that a human being cannot justly own another, but
that he cannot own him unless he is loyal to the United States."[19]

But such criticism missed the point. The proclamation was a war measure
directed against enemy resources. Under the laws of war, the President and army
had the right to seize these resources; but they had no constitutional power over
slaves not owned by the enemy. Already 100,000 or more contrabands within
Union lines in Tennessee, Louisiana, Virginia, and elsewhere were free by the
realities of war. West Virginia was committed to freedom. Strong emancipation
parties were rising in Missouri, Maryland, and Tennessee that would soon disen-
thrall these states as well. The Emancipation Proclamation announced a new war
aim. Thenceforth the Union army became officially an army of liberation. The
North was now fighting to create a new Union, not to restore the old one.

THE REMOVAL OF McCLELLAN AND BUELL
FROM COMMAND

In September 1862 some Republicans had been apprehensive about how the
Union armies, especially the Army of the Potomac with its hierarchy of Democratic officers, would react to the Emancipation Proclamation. Although there was
reason for worry, few soldiers actually threw down their arms or refused to fight
for black freedom. Much muttering occurred in the ranks, to be sure. A private
in the Army of the Potomac reported that his messmates were saying "they will
not fight to put niggers on a par with white men, that they had been duped &
that they only enlisted for the preservation of the Union & nothing else."[20]

More representative, however, was a letter from the colonel of the 9th Indiana,
who said that while few of his men were abolitionists "there is a desire to destroy
everything that in *aught* gives the rebels strength." Therefore "this army will
sustain the emancipation proclamation and enforce it with the bayonet." Early
in 1863, General in Chief Halleck passed the word to Grant that "the character
of the war has very much changed within the last year. There is now no possible
hope of reconciliation with the rebels. . . . We must conquer the rebels or be
conquered by them. . . . Every slave withdrawn from the enemy is the equivalent
of a white man put *hors de combat.* "[21]

But McClellan and some of his fellow officers in the Army of the Potomac

Tennessee) were occupied by Union troops and governed by military or civil authorities appointed or sanctioned
by the President, they were in effect part of the Union and therefore not subject to the Emancipation
Proclamation, which as a war measure could apply only to enemy territory. Eastern Tennessee was exempted
because Lincoln considered its white inhabitants loyal to the Union.

Lincoln with McClellan and Officers Near the Antietam Battlefield,
October 3, 1862   *(Reproduced from the Collections of the Library of*
Congress)

reacted to the Emancipation Proclamation just as their Republican critics feared
they would. McClellan privately condemned it for "inaugurating servile war."
General Fitz-John Porter called it "the absurd proclamation of a political coward"
and said that it was "resented in the army" by fighting men who were "tired of
the war and wish to see it ended soon and honorably."[22] Some officers even urged
McClellan to march the army on Washington to compel a reversal of the proclamation. A staff officer admitted having said that Lee's army had not been destroyed at Sharpsburg because "that is not the game; the object is that neither
army shall get much advantage of the other; that both shall be kept in the field
till they are exhausted, when we will make a compromise and save slavery."
Lincoln cashiered the officer, and explained: "I thought his silly, treasonable
expressions were 'staff talk' and I wished to make an example."[23] McClellan felt
that this "staff talk" was becoming such a problem that he issued a special order
on October 7 pointing out that it was the government's duty to make policy and
the army's to execute it. At the same time, however, McClellan included in this
order a none too subtle reference to the upcoming congressional elections: "the
remedy for political errors, if they are committed, is to be found only in the action
of the people at the polls."[24]

Although McClellan's Democratic politics obviously hurt him with the administration, it was his military shortcomings that finally brought about his downfall. Believing that he had fought a "masterpiece" at Antietam, the general at first expected to have things his own way. Three days after the battle he wrote to his wife: "I have insisted that Stanton shall be removed & that Halleck shall give way to me as Comdr. in Chief. . . . The only safety for the country & for me is to get rid of the lot of them."[25] Rarely had even McClellan been so blind to reality. The truth was that his failure to follow up Antietam vigorously was soon to end his military career. Telegram after telegram from Washington urged him to give the Rebels a knockout punch while they were still groggy. Back to Washington went as many telegrams full of reasons for delay: the enemy outnumbered him; he must drill the new recruits; and most amazing of all in view of the condition of Lee's army, he could not march until his men were provided with new clothing and shoes!

Lincoln visited the army October 1–4 and personally urged McClellan to get moving. After returning to Washington, the President had Halleck send an order to McClellan that any other general would have considered peremptory: "Cross the Potomac and give battle to the enemy. Your army must move now while the roads are good." Still McClellan did not move. On October 10–12 Stuart's cavalry once more made a circuit around the entire Union army. They raided Pennsylvania as far north as Chambersburg, evaded the Union horsemen sent after them, and brought away 1,200 horses and dozens of prisoners with the loss of only two troopers. When several days later McClellan explained that his advance must be further delayed until he could replace worn-out horses, Lincoln fired back a sarcastic telegram: "Will you pardon me for asking what the horses of your army have done since the battle of Antietam that fatigues anything?"[26]

McClellan's angry response to this goading was expressed in a letter to his wife: "The good of the country requires me to submit to all this from men whom I know to be greatly my inferior socially, intellectually, and morally! There never was a truer epithet applied to a certain individual than that of the 'Gorilla.' "[27] As McClellan was writing this letter, his army was finally beginning to move. But it took six days to cross the Potomac (which Lee's army had crossed in one night after Antietam), and another seven to move fifty miles south to the vicinity of Warrenton, Virginia. Lee divided his smaller force and placed Longstreet's corps between the enemy and Richmond, while Jackson stayed in the valley on McClellan's flank.

Once again the fast-marching Rebels had taken the initiative away from the ponderous Yankees. Lincoln's patience snapped. On November 7 he relieved McClellan from command of the Army of the Potomac and appointed a reluctant Burnside in his place. The soldiers gave McClellan an emotional farewell, but the renewed mutterings by some officers about a march on Washington came to nothing. To his private secretary Lincoln explained his decision: "I peremptorily ordered him to advance. . . . [He kept] delaying on little pretexts of wanting this and that. I began to fear he was playing false—that he did not want to hurt the enemy. I saw how he could intercept the enemy on the way to Richmond. I determined to make that the test. If he let them get away I would remove him. He did so & I relieved him."[28]

Another general who let the enemy get away was also relieved at the end of October. Like McClellan, Don Carlos Buell was a Democrat who made no secret of his opposition to emancipation. But unlike McClellan he was unpopular with his troops, who realized that they had not been used well in the Perryville campaign. When the exhausted and outnumbered Confederates retreated from Kentucky to Chattanooga, Lincoln urged Buell to go after them, smash them, and secure east Tennessee for the Union. But even though more than half of Buell's Army of the Ohio had not fought at Perryville, the general considered it necessary to refit and reorganize before he could renew the offensive. This sounded like McClellan. The exasperated President could not "understand why we cannot march as the enemy marches, live as he lives, and fight as he fights, unless we admit the inferiority of our troops and our generals."[29] Because Buell would not march and fight as Lincoln wished, the President replaced him with William S. Rose-crans. With this change of command the name of the army was also changed to the Army of the Cumberland; about this time its Confederate opponents also changed their name from the Army of Mississippi to the Army of Tennessee.

EUROPE AND THE WAR, 1862

The summer and fall of 1862 were punctuated by flurries of diplomatic activity whose rhythms were dictated by the changing military situation. Lee's victories in Virginia seemed to confirm European opinion that the Confederacy could never be conquered. When news of the Seven Days battles reached France, Napoleon III instructed his foreign secretary: "Demandez au gouvernement anglais s'il ne croit pas le moment venu de reconnaître le Sud." On July 18 the British Parliament debated a motion for recognition of the Confederacy. Although the motion was withdrawn as premature, the debate convinced Foreign Secretary Lord Russell that "the great majority are in favor of the South." Chancellor of the Exchequer William Gladstone wrote on July 26 that "it is indeed much to be desired that this bloody and purposeless conflict should cease." Gladstone later said in a speech at Newcastle that "Jefferson Davis and other leaders of the South have made an army; they are making, it appears, a navy; and they have made what is more than either, they have made a nation." Coming from such an influential source, this was taken as a signal that Britain was about to recognize the Confederacy. The American legation in London was plunged into gloom. "The current here [is] rising every hour and running harder against us than at any time since the Trent affair," wrote Henry Adams, son and secretary of Charles Francis Adams, the American minister to Britain.[30]

News of the second battle of Bull Run and of Lee's invasion of Maryland caused the Southern current to run even faster. Russell suggested to Prime Minister Palmerston a joint British and French offer of mediation. If the North refused, he wrote on September 17, "we ought ourselves to recognize the Southern States as an independent State." Palmerston was more cautious. He wanted to await the outcome of the battle then raging in Maryland. "If the Federals sustain a great Defeat [the North] may be brought to a more reasonable State of Mind [and] be at once ready for Mediation, and the Iron should be struck while it is hot. If, on the other hand, they should have the best of it, we may wait awhile and see what may follow."[31]

The results of the battle of Antietam reinforced Palmerston's caution. Although the idea of mediation remained alive for several more weeks, Palmerston now opposed immediate action. "The whole matter is full of difficulties," he wrote in October, "and can only be cleared up by some more decided events between the contending armies. . . . We must continue merely to be lookers-on till the war shall have taken a more decided turn."[32] When Napoleon III suggested at the end of October that France, Britain, and Russia jointly propose a six-month armistice and a suspension of the blockade, pro-Union Russia refused. The British cabinet discussed a joint French-British overture in November; but only Gladstone and Russell favored it, and no action was taken.

As the meaning of Antietam and the Emancipation Proclamation sank in, it became clear that antislavery Britain could not recognize a proslavery Confederacy whose prospects for victory no longer appeared bright. A dramatic upsurge of pro-Northern opinion took place in Britain. On January 23, Henry Adams wrote from London to his brother in the Army of the Potomac: "The Emancipation Proclamation has done more for us here than all our former victories and all our diplomacy. It is creating an almost convulsive reaction in our favor. . . . We are much encouraged and in high spirits. If only you at home don't have disasters, we will give such a checkmate to the foreign hopes of the rebels as they have never yet had."[33]

But Union arms did suffer more disasters in the winter and spring of 1862–1863. Confederate hopes rose, and Northern morale correspondingly plummeted once again.

Eighteen

The Winter of
Northern Discontent

THE BATTLE OF FREDERICKSBURG

In Virginia the newly appointed commander of the Army of the Potomac, Ambrose E. Burnside, seemed ready in November 1862 to apply Lincoln's formula for military success—hard marching and hard fighting. Instead of continuing southward from Warrenton using the vulnerable Orange and Alexandria Railroad as his supply line, Burnside proposed to feint in that direction while he moved most of his army to Falmouth, across the Rappahannock from Fredericksburg. There he could be supplied by water and a short, secure rail line; and from there he could cross the river to march directly on Richmond. Burnside moved rapidly; his leading corps covered the forty miles to Falmouth in two days, and the whole army was there by November 19. The swiftness of this maneuver surprised Lee, who for several days lost track of Burnside's whereabouts. The Yankees for once seemed to have stolen a march on the Rebels.

But when the Federals reached Falmouth things began to go wrong. The pontoons Burnside had ordered for bridging the Rappahannock had unaccountably gone astray. (Pontoons were flat-bottomed boats anchored in a line to support a floating bridge across rivers too deep to ford.) The pontoons did not arrive until the end of November—the result of bungling by Halleck and several engineer officers—and this allowed Lee to concentrate his army on the heights behind Fredericksburg before the Federals could bridge the river. A Union reconnaissance in force fourteen miles downriver found the Confederates too strong for an unopposed crossing there, so Burnside went ahead with his plan to cross at Fredericksburg itself. Under cover of fog before dawn on December 11 the engineers began to place the pontoons. When the fog lifted, Rebel sharpshooters hiding in buildings along the bank began to pick them off. Union artillery shelled the town, but snipers still fired from the rubble. Finally, volunteers from three blue regiments crossed in boats for an assault that drove the sharpshooters away in street-by-street fighting. The bridges were completed, and next day the huge army crossed the river to deploy for an attack as soon as the fog lifted on December 13.

Lee placed his 74,000 men along seven miles of hills west and south of the town. Swampy ground near the river on the left and steep, rough terrain in the center prevented Federal attacks at those points, so the main defenses were concentrated at Marye's Heights directly behind the town, held by Longstreet's corps, and at Prospect Hill, held by Jackson, three miles to the south. The 113,000 Union troops were organized in three "grand divisions" of two corps each. The left grand division under General William B. Franklin was to attack Jackson's position, the right grand division under Edwin V. Sumner was to assault Marye's Heights, and Hooker's center division was to function as a reserve to exploit breakthroughs.

The Federals first attacked Jackson's position. A blue division commanded by George Gordon Meade temporarily pierced the Rebel line before being driven back by a fierce counterattack. With proper support, Meade might have broken through the Confederate right; but Franklin never managed to get more than half of the 50,000 men under his command into action despite imperative orders from Burnside in midafternoon to renew the attack with his whole force.

Franklin's failure on the Union left spoiled any slim chance for a Northern victory that day, for the odds on the right were hopeless. Longstreet's riflemen were posted along a sunken road behind a stone wall at the base of Marye's Heights. Artillery on the heights commanded the half-mile stretch of open ground over which Union attackers had to advance. As one of Longstreet's officers put it: "A chicken could not live on that field when we open on it." The blueclad soldiers were no chickens. They launched seven courageous but futile assaults against Marye's Heights. "It can hardly be in human nature for men to show more valor, or generals to manifest less judgment," wrote a newspaper correspondent. A New York infantryman said that "we might as well have tried to take Hell."[1]

When the blessedly early December dark finally fell, the ground in front of the stone wall was covered for acres with dead and dying men. The Union army had suffered 12,600 casualties, the Confederates fewer than 5,000. And nothing had been achieved. While the wounded endured untold agonies during the freezing night, Burnside was beside himself with grief for his bleeding army and anger at Franklin's failure to exploit his opening on the Union left. Burnside's subordinates talked him out of the wild idea of personally leading a charge next day at the head of his old corps. After a truce to bury the dead, the Federals pulled back over the river on the night of December 15.

A CRISIS OF CONFIDENCE IN THE NORTH

While the South breathed a sigh of relief after Fredericksburg, Northern despair became acute. *Harper's Weekly* cried out that the people were filled with anguish. "They have borne, silently and grimly, imbecility, treachery, failure, privation, loss

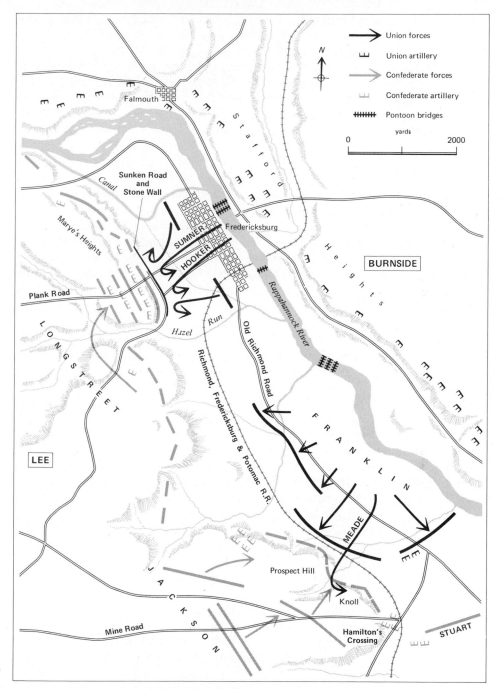

THE BATTLE OF FREDERICKSBURG, DECEMBER 13, 1862

of friends and means, almost every suffering which can afflict a brave people. But they cannot be expected to suffer that such massacres as this at Fredericksburg shall be repeated." Quartermaster General Montgomery Meigs wrote that "exhaustion steals over the country. Confidence and hope are dying." A feeling of defeatism overcame even such staunch radicals as Joseph Medill, editor of the *Chicago Tribune,* who feared that the Rebels could not be beaten and that "an armistice is bound to come during the year '63." When Lincoln learned of the outcome at Fredericksburg, he said to an associate: "If there is a worse place than Hell, I am in it."[2]

Lincoln's hell was made worse by a political crisis that Fredericksburg brought to a head. The military defeat was a catalyst for all the discontent and rumors festering in Washington during those dark December days. Republican dissatisfaction with the administration's conduct of affairs focused specifically on Secretary of State Seward. Distrusted by radicals since his role in compromise efforts during the secession winter of 1860–1861, Seward was believed to be the "evil genius" of the cabinet, the "unseen hand" whose conservative influence over Lincoln had undermined vigorous presidential leadership—especially on questions concerning slavery and the appointment of army commanders. In two long caucus meetings on December 16 and 17, every Republican senator but one voted to request a reorganization of the cabinet to secure "unity of purpose and action." This resolution was aimed at Seward. It was inspired by Secretary of the Treasury Chase, Seward's main rival in the cabinet and a close associate of radical senators whose power would be enhanced if the senatorial scheme succeeded.

This affair was the gravest challenge thus far to Lincoln's leadership. It also created a constitutional crisis of the first order. If Lincoln "caved in" to the senatorial demand, as he put it, he would lose control of his administration. The United States would move closer to a parliamentary form of government. When word of the senatorial caucus leaked out, new rumors swept Washington that the whole cabinet, perhaps even Lincoln himself, would resign. The President was "awfully shaken" by the crisis. Branding the charge of Seward's "malign influence" an "absurd lie," Lincoln unburdened himself to a friend. "What do these men want? . . . They wish to get rid of me, and I am sometimes half disposed to gratify them. . . . Since I heard last night of the proceedings of the caucus I have been more distressed than by any event of my life. . . . We are now on the brink of destruction. It appears to me the Almighty is against us, and I can hardly see a ray of hope."[3]

Lincoln had regained his composure by the time he met with a delegation of eight senators on December 19. Seward had already submitted his resignation in order to relieve the pressure, but Lincoln did not reveal this. He listened with little comment to the senators' speeches "attributing to Mr. Seward a lukewarmness in the conduct of the war, and seeming to consider him the real cause of our failures." Without committing himself, the President invited the delegation back the next day for further discussions. When they returned, Lincoln exhibited his political virtuosity in a bravura performance. The senators were surprised to find that the President had arranged to have the entire cabinet on hand except Seward. In a tactful but forceful speech, Lincoln said that whenever possible he consulted the cabinet about important decisions but that he alone made the decisions; that members of the cabinet sometimes disagreed but that all supported a policy when it had been decided upon; and that Seward was a valuable member of the administration. Then the President turned to the cabinet for confirmation. All eyes fastened on Chase, who was neatly put on the spot. Chase had told the senators that Seward was responsible for cabinet disharmony; if he now denied it he would lose face with them, but if he reaffirmed it he would lose the confidence of the President. Chase mumbled a brief endorsement of Lincoln's statement but tried to save face by expressing regret that major decisions were not more fully discussed by the cabinet. Deflated by the whole experience and disappointed with Chase, the senators knew that Lincoln had won.

Much embarrassed, Chase next day came to the White House to offer his resignation. "Let me have it," said the President eagerly. Chase reluctantly handed over his letter of resignation; Lincoln read it and said triumphantly: "This cuts the Gordian knot. I can dispose of this subject now without difficulty." The Republican senators could not have Seward's resignation without losing Chase as well. Lincoln used a characteristic metaphor to describe his triumph: "Now I can ride; I have a pumpkin in each end of my bag." The President refused both resignations; the cabinet remained unchanged; the crisis was over; the murky political atmosphere suddenly cleared. This was not the first confrontation between the President and congressional Republicans, nor was it the last. But on this occasion Lincoln proved himself master. And he did so without making any enemies. It was an instructive lesson in political skill.[4]

THE WAR IN THE WEST: VICKSBURG

Military news from the West offered little encouragement to offset Northern gloom following Fredericksburg in the East. The Confederates had reorganized their western command structure after the failure of the Kentucky invasion in 1862. Joseph Johnston came to Chattanooga in November to take overall charge of the Western Department, giving the Confederacy unity of command in that theater. General John C. Pemberton, a native of Pennsylvania with two brothers in the Union army, went to Vicksburg as head of Confederate forces in Mississippi. Bragg remained in command of the Army of Tennessee, which concentrated at Murfreesboro thirty miles south of Nashville. West of the Mississippi, the Confederates had 25,000 troops in Arkansas. One thin gleam of cheer to the Union cause occurred on December 7 at Prairie Grove in northwest Arkansas, where 10,000 of these Rebel troops attacked two Union divisions only to be surprised and driven off when another blue division suddenly materialized on the Confederate flank. The victory at Prairie Grove kept northern Arkansas under Union control, but the Confederates remained strong enough to prevent a thrust at Little Rock. The main Union efforts in the West were to be directed against Vicksburg and against Bragg's army in central Tennessee.

The initial Union thrusts at Vicksburg were intended to come from three directions simultaneously.* They failed because of divided command and alert Rebel responses. As commander of the Union Department of the Tennessee, Grant launched an overland invasion through northern Mississippi to attack the river fortress from the rear. In the meantime, Lincoln appointed Nathaniel P. Banks to succeed the controversial Benjamin Butler as commander of Union troops in Louisiana. Lincoln wanted Banks to lead an expedition up the Mississippi to attack Vicksburg from the south while other Union forces besieged it from the north. But the administrative problems of occupied Louisiana and the strong Confederate fort at Port Hudson prevented Banks from sending any force farther north than Baton Rouge. Without informing Grant, Lincoln also authorized another political general, John A. McClernand of Illinois, to command a down-river expedition from Memphis against Vicksburg. When Grant learned of this, he demanded clarification of his authority in the Mississippi theater. The government assured him that he had control of all 75,000 troops in his department, which included the territory between the Tennessee and Mississippi rivers as far south as Vicksburg. Distrusting McClernand, Grant sent Sherman to take charge of the troops assembling in Memphis for McClernand's expedition. When McClernand arrived at Memphis in late December, he discovered that instead of having his own army he was merely a corps commander under Grant and that Sherman had already taken his corps downriver for an attack on the Vicksburg defenses to be coordinated with Grant's overland invasion. McClernand was furious; but Lincoln sustained Grant's authority, and there was nothing McClernand could do about it. The West Pointer Grant had scored a victory over the politician McClernand.

Competition also existed between Confederate Generals Van Dorn and Forrest, but it took a different form. In mid-December they led simultaneous cavalry raids against Grant's supply line. With 2,100 men Forrest eluded numerous Union patrols, killed, wounded, or captured more than 2,000 Federals, cut the railroad and telegraph for a stretch of sixty miles north of Jackson, Tennessee, captured 10,000 rifles and other equipment, and got away with the loss of only 500 men. Meanwhile Van Dorn's 3,500 cavalry forced the surrender of the Union garrison at Holly Springs and destroyed Grant's supply depot at that place. Once again small cavalry forces proved their ability to paralyze a large army dependent on a rail supply line deep in enemy territory. Grant was forced to call off his advance on Vicksburg and return to Tennessee.

Grant's change of plans endangered Sherman's part of the campaign, for his river-based attack was keyed to the expectation that the Confederates would weaken their Vicksburg defenses in meeting Grant's rear attack. With Forrest having cut the telegraph, Sherman had no way of knowing that Grant had been stopped. The Rebels concentrated 14,000 troops on the Chickasaw bluffs three miles north of Vicksburg. Sherman had to occupy these bluffs if he was to reach dry land for a move against Vicksburg itself. Although the Union attackers

*Maps of the campaign against Vicksburg appear on pp. 314 and 315.

outnumbered the defenders by more than two to one, the Confederates were entrenched on high ground with ample artillery to cover the sandbars over which the Federal infantry must cross the swamp-bordered bayou. The Union assault on December 29 was hopeless from the start. Sherman's four divisions suffered nearly 1,800 casualties to the Confederates' 200. The Yankees withdrew to their marshy, disease-ridden camp twenty miles upriver from Vicksburg, while the Northern public learned that yet another December offensive had been snuffed out.

THE WAR IN THE WEST: THE BATTLE OF STONE'S RIVER

For a time it appeared that the third major Union offensive in December would also come to grief. When Rosecrans took over the Army of the Cumberland on October 30, he knew that the administration expected him to drive the Rebels out of central Tennessee. After many delays caused by cavalry raids in their rear, Rosecrans's 42,000 troops marched from Nashville the day after Christmas to confront Bragg's 36,000-strong Army of Tennessee at Murfreesboro. They found the Confederates drawn up astride Stone's River, a shallow stream a mile northwest of town. On the night of December 30 the two armies bivouacked only a few hundred yards apart. Their bands engaged in a musical battle in the still winter air, one side blaring out "Dixie" in challenge to the other's "Yankee Doodle," and so on. Finally one band began to play "Home Sweet Home." Others took it up until all the bands in both armies were playing and thousands of soldiers, Yankees and Rebels together, sang the familiar words. Perhaps some of them wondered at the tragic irony of a war in which they could sing together one night and butcher each other on the morrow.

For Bragg had no intention of retreating or even of remaining on the defensive. He concentrated most of his army on the left for a dawn attack against the Union right—with the intention of rolling it up, pinning the Federals against the river, and cutting them off from their supply line. The Confederates struck at dawn December 31, once again catching the Yankees at breakfast as they had at Donelson and Shiloh. The rebel yell echoed through the scrub cedars and cleared fields as two blue divisions on the Union right crumpled under the onslaught. Gray cavalry got in the Union rear and caused havoc among supply and ammunition wagons. But Rosecrans rose to the challenge of disaster. He personally rode back and forth along the front lines rallying troops; his chief of staff, riding beside him, was decapitated by a cannonball. Sheridan's division on the Union right center stood firm, giving Rosecrans time to form a new line in front of the Nashville Pike. There the Confederate attack stalled before noon.

The fighting had been among the hardest of the war. The roar of artillery and rifles was so loud that soldiers picked cotton from the stalks and stuffed it into their ears. On the Union left center, fragments of several brigades held a patch of woods along the railroad known as the Round Forest. This became the hinge of the reorganized Union line, and Bragg decided to launch an all-out attack to break it. To do the job he brought across the river the large division commanded

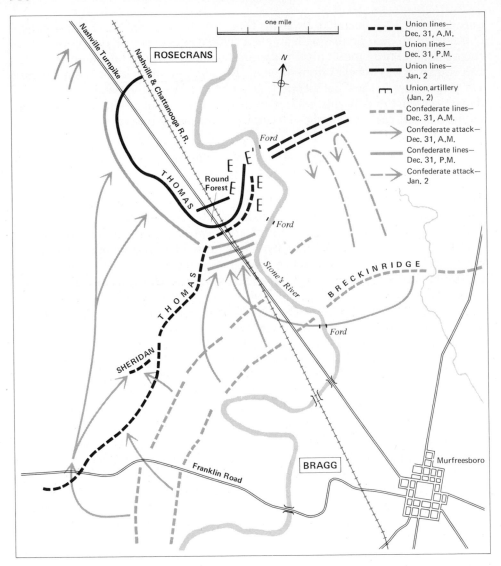

THE BATTLE OF STONE'S RIVER, DEC. 31–JAN. 2

by John C. Breckinridge. This division hurled itself against the Round Forest during the afternoon but was repulsed time after time with heavy loss.

No bands played on the field that night; instead, this New Year's Eve was filled with the groans and cries of the wounded. Bragg wired Richmond that he had won a great victory, and indeed it appeared that he had. He also said that "the enemy is falling back," but the enemy was not. Some of Rosecrans's generals advised him to retreat, but "Old Rosy" (as his troops called him) decided to hold on. There was little fighting next day, though both armies shifted a division to the east side of the river. When he discovered the Federals still in place on January 2, Bragg ordered (over the objections of his subordinates) an assault on the Union troops east of the river. Breckinridge's division drove the blue infantry off the hill, but the Union artillery—fifty-eight guns massed across the river—hit the Rebels in the flank at point-blank range and cut them to pieces.

Next day the torn armies held their positions, knowing that one side or the other would soon have to retreat. The combined casualty rate was the highest of the war: the Confederates had lost 33 percent of their men either killed, wounded, or missing; the Federals 31 percent. Bragg's generals had lost confidence in him; and Southern soldiers were suffering from a lack of supplies and from the incessant winter rains. The Union army, however, had received new supplies from Nashville and appeared ready to stay in position forever. So on the night of January 3–4, the Confederates began withdrawing to a new line behind the Duck River, thirty-five miles to the south. And there they went into winter quarters.

Thus did Rosecrans snatch victory from the jaws of defeat. Northern morale, depressed by the debacle at Fredericksburg and the failure before Vicksburg, rose at the news from Stone's River, despite the heavy casualties. Lincoln was profoundly grateful. "God bless you and all with you," he wired Rosecrans. "I can never forget, whilst I remember anything," the President later wrote the general, that "you gave us a hard victory which, had there been a defeat instead, the nation could scarcely have lived over."[5]

THE VICKSBURG CAMPAIGN: PHASE TWO

During the four months after Stone's River, there were no major battles on any front as the armies waited for spring to dry the roads. Grant spent this time trying fruitlessly to get his army on high ground east of the Mississippi for a campaign against Vicksburg. His greatest obstacle was topography. Vicksburg was built on a 200-foot bluff that gave its artillery command of the river and made the idea of frontal assault suicidal. West of the river a maze of bayous and swamps blocked military operations except at low water, and the winter of 1862–1863 was exceptionally wet. East of the river and extending in a 250-mile arc from Vicksburg to Memphis was a line of hills that enclosed the Delta, a strip of low-lying land averaging sixty miles in width. Today it is rich, well-drained farmland; but in 1863 much of it was a network of swamps, rivers, and junglelike forests. Only east and south of Vicksburg was there dry land suitable for military operations. Grant's problem was to get there with a large enough army—and its supplies—to defeat the enemy, capture the fortress, and reestablish contact with the Union fleet, which controlled the river north of Vicksburg.

On the map the simplest way to reach that dry land would appear to be an overland invasion from Tennessee, but Grant had already tried that without success. And to move back upriver to Memphis and start over again by land would look to the North like a retreat. For better or worse, then, the campaign against Vicksburg would be based on the river. Grant came downriver in late January to take command personally of the troops encamped on the west bank just above

Vicksburg because in his absence the distrusted McClernand was the ranking general.

A Winter of Failures

During the winter, Grant tried five different routes to get his army and supplies across the river. Three involved attempts to bypass the Vicksburg batteries in order to get gunboats, transports, and troops below the city for a secure crossing: (1) Sherman's corps renewed excavation of the canal started the previous summer, but they abandoned the effort in March when rising water flooded the area without cutting the hoped-for deepwater channel through the canal. (2) Other troops started a separate canal several miles to the north to link the river with a series of bayous that rejoined the Mississippi below Vicksburg, but the bayous proved too shallow for anything but the lightest transports. (3) Another corps began an amibitious project to open a 400-mile route from Lake Providence, far above Vicksburg, through a series of bayous and rivers all the way to the Red River far below. After expending enormous labor sawing off trees below the water, the army abandoned this route also (because it was suitable only for shallow-draft steamboats) in favor of two apparently more promising efforts to flank Vicksburg on the north by transporting troops through the endless waterways of the Delta.

The first of these, the Yazoo Pass expedition, blew up a levee opposite Helena, which enabled gunboats to enter a labyrinth of rivers tributary to the Yazoo. These treacherous waterways, where gunboats constantly ran aground and low-hanging branches banged against their smokestacks, caused the naval officer in charge to suffer a nervous breakdown. At a narrow part of the channel, where the gunboats could not maneuver, the Confederates concentrated heavy artillery and loosed a barrage that forced the Yankee fleet to turn back. Finally there was the Steele's Bayou expedition, another attempt to get the navy through the interconnected waterways of the Delta. David Porter, now commander of the Mississippi River Squadron, took eleven gunboats on this venture through twisted channels scarcely wider than the boats themselves. As the strange flotilla penetrated deeper into the jungle, Rebel axemen felled trees across the river ahead of and behind the boats. For a time it appeared that they might trap and capture the whole fleet. But Sherman disembarked his infantry, drove the Confederates off, and the weary sailors maneuvered their tree-battered craft back to the Mississippi.

Success in the Spring

Despite these setbacks, Grant never lost confidence that he would take Vicksburg. No campaign better illustrated his coolness under pressure, his will to succeed, and his quiet ability to impart that will to subordinates. By late March he had matured a plan that had been forming in his mind for some time. Since the attempts to bypass Vicksburg had failed, he would have Porter run the gunboats and supply boats right past the batteries while the troops marched down the west bank to rendezvous with the fleet below Vicksburg. There the men would be ferried across for a campaign against the soft underbelly of Pemberton's defenses. It was a simple plan but a daring one. Once the operation began there was no turning back; for once across the river, Grant would be cut off from his base until he could fight his way back to the Mississippi at or above Vicksburg.

Sherman and Porter opposed the plan, while Lincoln was skeptical. But like Lee, Grant was a great general because he was willing to take great risks. He sent two of his three corps southward on April 5. They made their arduous way through bottomless mud, towing makeshift rafts through the bayous, building bridges, corduroying roads, and cutting new roads as they went. On the moonless night of April 16–17, twelve of Porter's boats drifted quietly downriver toward Vicksburg. Suddenly the sky was lit by bonfires set along the banks by Rebel spotters. The heavy guns of Vicksburg opened on the fleet as the boats churned at full speed past the four-mile gauntlet of shot and shell. Every boat was hit; most were set afire; one sank. But the others got through with the loss of only one man. A few nights later, six transports and twelve barges tried the same feat with less luck— six of the barges and one transport (containing medical supplies) went to the bottom, but all crewmen were rescued.

Grant now had most of his army south of Vicksburg with enough supplies to support it for a while. The troops were ferried across to the high ground at Bruinsburg, thirty-five miles south of Vicksburg. As he later recounted, Grant experienced

> a degree of relief scarcely ever equaled since. . . . I was now in the enemy's country, with a vast river and the stronghold of Vicksburg between me and my base of supplies. But I was on dry ground on the same side of the river with the enemy. All the campaigns, labors, hardships, and exposures, from the month of December previous to this time . . . were for the accomplishment of this one object.[6]

Grant's landing in Mississippi was unopposed because he had ordered two diversionary movements that deceived Pemberton into dispersing most of his troops elsewhere. On the day that Grant crossed the river with two of his corps, Sherman with the other feinted an attack north of Vicksburg in the vicinity of Chickasaw Bluffs. At the same time, Colonel Benjamin Grierson was leading one of the most spectacular cavalry raids of the war. A former music teacher from Illinois, Grierson had built a fine cavalry brigade which demonstrated that Union horsemen were finally coming up to the Confederate standard. Starting with 1,700 men, Grierson pounded down into Mississippi toward Pemberton's railroad supply line east of Jackson. Constantly driving off the Confederate cavalry sent after him, Grierson's troopers tore up fifty miles of railroad and lured a division of Confederate infantry into a futile effort to trap them. The Yankees finally reached Union lines at Baton Rouge sixteen days and six hundred miles from their starting point, having killed or wounded one hundred Rebels and captured five hundred at a cost of only twenty-four men.

It was an exploit worthy of Forrest or Stuart at their best. It also meant that when Grant's 23,000 men reached Port Gibson on May 1 there were only 8,000

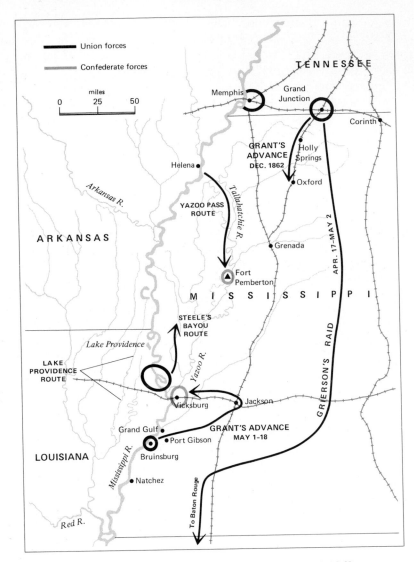

THE VICKSBURG CAMPAIGN, DEC. 1862–MAY 1863

Confederates to meet them. After the Federals had smashed through these defenders, Grant brought Sherman's corps downriver. He now had 44,000 men to
oppose Pemberton's 32,000 plus a few thousand troops that Johnston was desperately trying to assemble in Jackson, the state capital. Grant ordered wagons and
vehicles seized from nearby plantations to be filled with ammunition and other
essential supplies, and told his troops to fill their haversacks with all the rations
they could carry; then he cut loose from his river base and his telegraph communications with the North. His army would "live off the country" until it could fight
its way back to Vicksburg.

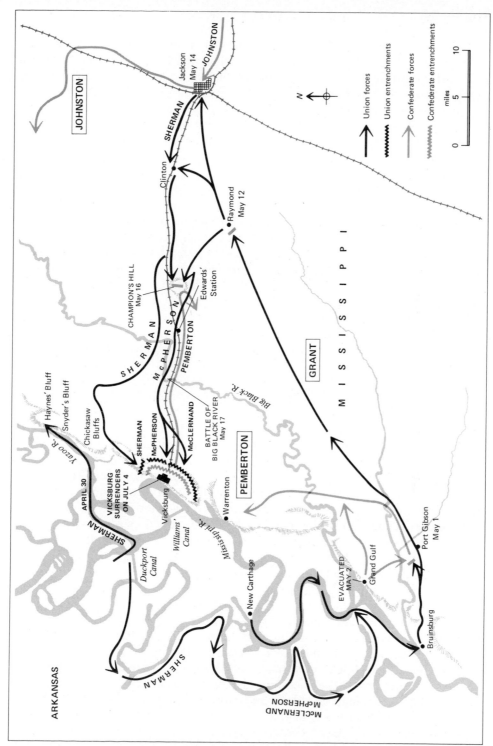

THE VICKSBURG CAMPAIGN, MAY–JULY 1863

For the next two weeks Grant disappeared from sight, so far as anyone in the North could see. During that time his army marched 180 miles, fought and won four battles against separate enemy forces that, if combined, would have been nearly as large as Grant's own, and penned the Confederates up in the Vicksburg defenses. In the words of a British military historian, this campaign was "a brilliant vindication of the tactical maxim to hit hard, hit often, and keep on hitting."[7]

The Confederates were confused by the swiftness and unexpected direction of Grant's movements. Instead of marching directly against Vicksburg, he struck eastward toward Jackson. Grant's strategy was to seize the capital, defeat Johnston there, and having abolished this threat to his rear, to turn west and defeat the main Southern army near Vicksburg. In their attempts to counter these moves the Confederates suffered from divided counsel. Johnston urged Pemberton to move out and join forces with him to attack Grant as far from Vicksburg as possible. But Pemberton had orders from Jefferson Davis to hold Vicksburg at all costs, so he refused to venture far from the river. A native of Pennsylvania who had chosen to side with his wife's Virginia compatriots, Pemberton was reluctant to provoke suspicions of his loyalty to the Confederacy by taking undue risks. On May 12 one Union corps cut up a small Confederate detachment at Raymond, just west of Jackson. On the 14th two corps drove Johnston's scratch army out of Jackson. Sherman's corps remained to wreck the city's railroad and industrial facilities, while Grant turned westward with the rest of his army to strike Pemberton. That luckless general had been edging southward with the idea of cutting Grant's (nonexistent) supply line. On May 16 the two Union corps (29,000 men) ran into part of Pemberton's army (21,000) at Champion's Hill, about halfway between Jackson and Vicksburg.

The ensuing battle was the most decisive of the campaign. It could have been even more decisive but for McClernand's poor generalship. While General James B. McPherson's corps attacked vigorously on the Union right, McClernand was slow and hesitant on the left. Pemberton shifted troops to the points of heaviest fighting, where attacks and counterattacks surged back and forth. As Rebel regiments began falling back in disorder, Pemberton decided to withdraw. One of his divisions was cut off and was forced to escape to the southeast, away from Vicksburg. Not counting this division, Pemberton lost 3,851 men in the battle (to Grant's 2,441). But Grant thought he might have destroyed more of the Rebel force if McClernand had been more alert.

Next day the advancing Yankees came up against the Confederate rear guard at the Big Black River, ten miles east of Vicksburg. A headlong assault routed the unnerved defenders, most of whom retreated over the river, burning the bridge and leaving behind 1,700 men to be captured by the Federals. Ignoring yet another appeal from Johnston to march northward for a junction with his army, Pemberton withdrew to the Vicksburg defenses and called in scattered brigades that had been guarding the bluffs and river crossings nearby. Explaining his decision to defend Vicksburg, Pemberton wrote: "I still conceive it to be the most important point in the Confederacy."[8]

Grant's reinforced army of 45,000 surrounded Vicksburg on the land side, while

Union gunboats cut it off from the river. Believing the Confederates demoralized by their defeats, Grant on May 19 ordered an assault against the Vicksburg trenches. But the Rebels had recovered their morale, and for the first time in the campaign they repulsed the bluecoats. This seemed to confirm the maxim that one soldier in trenches was the equal of at least three in the open. The Vicksburg trenches and fortifications were the strongest defensive works of the war. They were situated on a ridge fronted by deep gullies and protected by felled trees whose branches entangled enemy attackers.

Despite this, Grant decided to launch another assault on May 22, preceded by careful preparation and artillery bombardment. He wanted to avoid a siege during the sickly summer months. He also feared that a prolonged siege would enable Johnston to build up a strong army in his rear. At 10 A.M. on the 22nd, all three corps launched a simultaneous attack along a four-mile front. The attackers made temporary penetrations of the enemy works at several points but could not hold them against murderous Confederate volleys. In the two assaults of May 19 and 22, the Federals lost as many men (about 4,200) as in the previous three weeks of marching and fighting.

The repulse of these assaults compelled Grant to settle down to a siege. The dramatic May campaign of movement and battle was over. But even at its height, this campaign had attracted less public attention in both North and South than events in the Virginia theater.

JOE HOOKER AND THE "FINEST ARMY ON THE PLANET"

Morale in the Army of the Potomac had dropped to rock bottom after the defeat at Fredericksburg. Four McClellanite generals complained directly to Lincoln of Burnside's incompetence. One of the complainers was William B. Franklin, who as commander of the left wing had failed to exploit the only Union breakthrough in the battle. Several anti-McClellan officers also criticized Burnside, especially General Hooker, who indulged in loose talk to newspaper reporters about Burnside's bungling, the administration's stupidity, and the need for a "dictator" to run the country. Much of this feeling filtered down into the ranks. A soldier from Maine wrote that "the great cause of liberty has been managed by Knaves and fools the whole show has been corruption, the result disaster, shame and disgrace." To make matters worse, Burnside was a poor administrator. With all the resources of a rich country at his back and army warehouses bulging with supplies, troops in winter quarters at Falmouth suffered from poor food, poor medical care, slack discipline, and sickness—including even scurvy. Desertions increased in January 1863 to at least 200 a day. An officer described this winter of 1862–1863 as "the Valley Forge of the war."[9]

The final straw was an aborted campaign that became famous as the "Mud March." Determined to recoup his fortunes, Burnside ordered that the army move up the Rappahannock to cross the river and flank the Confederates above Fredericksburg. The general's detractors opposed the plan. "Franklin has talked so much

Co. C, 110th Pennsylvania Infantry After the Battle of
Fredericksburg. This regiment suffered heavy casualties; at the time
this photograph was taken, the full complement of one hundred men
in Co. C was down to about twenty-five. Note the weary slouch of
the enlisted men in contrast to the ramrod-straight posture of the
officer, who was probably an old-army man. *(Reproduced from the
Collections of the Library of Congress)*

and so loudly to this effect," wrote one officer, "that he has completely demoralized his whole command and so rendered failure doubly sure. His conduct has been such that he surely deserves to be broken."[10] The movement began on dry roads amid unusually benign winter weather on January 20. But that night a heavy rain turned the roads into ooze and bogged down the whole army hub-deep in mud. Triple-teams of horses could not budge the artillery or the pontoon wagons. Rebel soldiers across the river watched all this with glee and held up mocking signs with arrows pointing "This Way to Richmond."

After two days, Burnside gave it up and ordered the army back to camp. He then went to Washington and threatened to resign unless Lincoln approved the dismissal of troublemaking generals, beginning with Franklin and Hooker. Lincoln did transfer Franklin and several other generals out of the Army of the Potomac.

But recognizing that Burnside had lost the confidence of his men, the President also accepted Burnside's resignation and assigned Hooker to the command!

This action was less startling than it appeared. Although he had intrigued against Burnside, Hooker was popular with the troops and the public. Lincoln knew that he had a reputation as a drinker and a womanizer (the slang term "hooker" for a shot of whiskey and for a prostitute allegedly derives from Hooker); but he also knew him as an aggressive, hard-driving general and hoped he could infuse this spirit into the army. With the appointment Lincoln also gave Hooker an admonitory letter: "I have heard, in such a way as to believe it, of your recently saying that both the Army and the Government needed a Dictator. Of course it was not *for* this, but in spite of it, that I have given you the command. Only those generals who gain successes, can set up dictators. What I now ask of you is military success, and I will risk the dictatorship."[11]

Hooker started well. He shook up the commissary and quartermaster services, upgraded the food, cleaned the filthy camps, improved the field hospitals, and cut the sick rate in half. He tightened discipline but at the same time granted furloughs liberally. He abolished the grand divisions, reinstituted the old corps, and increased unit pride by devising insignia badges for each corps. He increased the efficiency of the cavalry by reorganizing it into one corps instead of leaving it scattered by brigades or regiments throughout the army. Morale rose, desertions declined, and many absentees rejoined the colors after Lincoln on March 10 promised amnesty to deserters who returned to the army. Within two months Hooker produced a remarkable transformation in the army's spirit. A soldier put it best: "Under Hooker, we began to *live.*"[12]

Never modest, Hooker boasted that he had created "the finest army on the planet." The question was not whether he would take Richmond, he told the President, but when. He hoped that God Almighty would have mercy on the Rebels because Joe Hooker would have none. This gasconade disturbed Lincoln. It reminded him ominously of John Pope. A shrewd judge of character, the President feared that Hooker's boasting was a cloak to mask his insecurity. He remarked pointedly that "the hen is the wisest of all the animal creation because she never cackles until the egg is laid." Lincoln may have heard the old army story that Hooker was a superb poker player "until it came to the point where he should go a thousand better, and then he would flunk." When the President visited the army in April, his parting words to Hooker were: "In your next fight, put in all your men."[13]

THE BATTLE OF CHANCELLORSVILLE

In none of its previous battles had the Army of the Potomac used its full strength. If Hooker had followed Lincoln's advice, he might have won a great victory with his army of 115,000, nearly twice the 60,000 Lee had with him along the Rappahannock (Longstreet had taken two divisions for detached service on the Virginia–North Carolina border). The Army of Northern Virginia had also gone through a hard winter. Men were on reduced rations, and horses were dying because all the forage in Virginia's fought-over countryside had been consumed. But the soldiers' morale remained high. They had constructed twenty-five miles of trenches along the river, which gave them confidence that they could hold off any number of Yankees.

Hooker had no intention of repeating Burnside's futile frontal assaults. He devised an excellent tactical plan and executed it well—up to a point. Leaving two-fifths of his infantry near Fredericksburg to feint another direct assault, he marched the rest far upriver where they swarmed across the fords, captured the surprised Confederate pickets, and moved eastward to close in on the Rebel rear. (Meanwhile Hooker had sent most of his rejuvenated cavalry on a deep raid to cut Lee's supply line. This turned out to be a mistake because the raid did little serious damage and left Hooker short of cavalry for reconnaissance in the coming battle.) On the evening of April 30, 40,000 bluecoats were still in Lee's front at Fredericksburg while 70,000 were only eight or ten miles from his rear in the vicinity of Chancellorsville, a crossroads hostelry in the Wilderness of Virginia, an area of thick second-growth forest and tangled underbrush with few clearings.

Hooker and his generals were jubilant. The 5th Corps commander George Gordon Meade declared: "Hurrah for old Joe! We're on Lee's flank and he doesn't know it."[14] This was not quite true; Lee knew where the Federals were, but he faced a dilemma in deciding what to do about it. His only apparent choices were to retreat toward Richmond, which would expose his army to attacks on both flanks, or to face the army about to meet the larger threat from Chancellorsville, which would expose him to a rear attack from the force at Fredericksburg.

Typically, Lee did neither. Once again he took a bold risk by dividing his army, leaving 10,000 men under Jubal Early to hold the Fredericksburg trenches and marching the rest toward Chancellorsville. The Federals there moved eastward two miles on May 1 to the open country beyond the Wilderness. But when they clashed with advance Confederate units, Hooker suddenly ordered his troops back to defensive positions near Chancellorsville. His corps commanders protested, for this meant surrendering the initiative to Lee. It also meant that the dense woods of the Wilderness would neutralize Union numerical and artillery supremacy. Many theories have been advanced to explain this strange decision by a general previously known as "Fighting Joe." The most likely explanation is that faced with the responsibility of commanding an entire army in a showdown battle, Hooker lost his nerve. The poker player who faltered when it was time to raise his opponent a thousand was not the man to raise a gambler like Lee when the stakes were much greater.

From the afternoon of May 1, Hooker was psychologically "a whipped man," as one of his generals later wrote. Once again Lee read his enemy's weakness like a book. Stuart's cavalry discovered that Hooker's right flank three miles west of Chancellorsville was "in the air." Although the Confederate army was already divided, Lee decided to divide it again. On May 2 he sent Jackson with 28,000 men on a roundabout fourteen-mile march to attack the Union flank, while the remaining 18,000 Confederate infantry stood wary watch against three times their number. It was Lee's riskiest gamble yet, for if Hooker discovered it he could drive a wedge between these two parts of Lee's army before Jackson could get his troops deployed for an attack on Hooker's right.

Federal scouts detected Jackson's movements, and Hooker warned General Oliver O. Howard, commander of the 11th Corps holding the right flank, to strengthen his defenses. But instead of ordering an all-out assault on Jackson's marchers as they crossed his front, Hooker sent only two divisions on a reconnaissance in force. Reports from this reconnaissance that Jackson's troops were moving southward (see map) convinced Hooker that the Confederates were retreating! Both Hooker and Howard thereupon relaxed their vigilance, despite repeated warnings by Union pickets in Howard's corps that the Rebels were building up to something off in the woods.

Many of the 12,000 men in the 11th Corps were playing cards or cooking supper at 5:30 when Jackson's screaming Rebels burst out of the woods and crumbled the Union flank like a dry leaf. The 11th Corps contained many German-American regiments. In the eyes of the rest of the army they had a poor reputation, which this day's fighting did nothing to improve. Some of the regiments fought stubbornly after their initial surprise, but they never had a chance to regain formation. The Confederates pushed them back more than two miles before various blue brigades formed a solid line and brought the onslaught to a halt at dark. Eager to cut the Federals off from the river, Jackson rode ahead to reconnoiter for a night attack. As he was returning to his own lines a jumpy Confederate company, thinking that Jackson's party were Union cavalry, loosed a volley that wounded the general. Early the next morning his left arm was amputated; when Lee learned of this he said: "He has lost his left arm; but I have lost my right arm."[15]

Despite the success of Jackson's attack, Hooker still had a good chance to defeat Lee the next day. The two parts of the Confederate army in the Wilderness were separated by the Union forces, which outnumbered them and held the high ground at Hazel Grove, one of the few clearings where artillery could operate effectively. Under the mistaken assumption that Hazel Grove was an exposed salient, Hooker committed his greatest blunder when he ordered it abandoned at dawn. The alert Stuart, temporarily commanding Jackson's corps, quickly moved fifty guns to the hill, from where they pounded the Union defenses while the Confederate infantry launched repeated assaults. The bluecoats gave ground grudgingly, inflicting heavy casualties.

Only half of Hooker's force was engaged, but forgetting Lincoln's advice to "put in all your men," the general refused to order two idle corps into action. During the fighting Hooker was stunned when a shell struck a column of the Chancellor House on which he was leaning. Although groggy, he would not turn the army over to the senior corps commander, who was eager to throw every Union division into the battle. In midmorning the Federals fell back to a new position north of Chancellorsville.

Meanwhile in Fredericksburg, the 25,000 remaining bluecoats had finally carried the heights beyond the town. When Lee learned that this force was coming

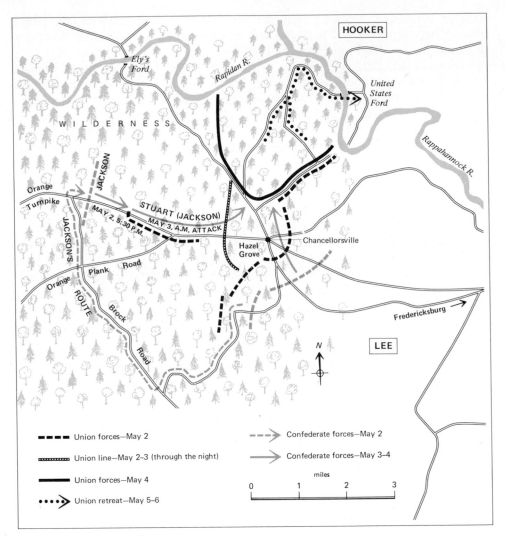

CHANCELLORSVILLE, MAY 2–6, 1863

up on his rear, he once again divided his army at Chancellorsville, leaving Stuart with 25,000 men to contain the 75,000 Federals there while he marched with the rest to reinforce Early's 10,000. In sharp fighting halfway between Chancellorsville and Fredericksburg on May 3–4, the Confederates drove the outnumbered Unionists or this front across the river while Hooker remained idle with his large force only a few miles to the west. Lee then returned to confront Hooker, who gave up the battle and crossed to the north bank of the Rappahannock on May 6.

A Portion of the Confederate Line at the Stone Wall Below Marye's
Heights at Fredericksburg, Carried by Union Troops on May 3,
1863. The photographer took this picture only twenty minutes after
the Yankee assault carried the trenches.   *(Reproduced from the
Collections of the Library of Congress)*

The defeat was a bitter, humiliating one for "the finest army on the planet."
But it was primarily Hooker rather than the army who was defeated. Morale in
the ranks did not suffer after this battle as after Fredericksburg, despite the 17,000
Union casualties (compared with 13,000 Confederate) in four days of fighting.
Chancellorsville has been called "Lee's greatest masterpiece," but that was so
mainly because Hooker's battlefield generalship was the worst of the war. And in
the end the South may have lost more than it gained despite its great victory, for
on May 10 Jackson died of pneumonia, which had set in after he was wounded.

Lincoln received the news of Chancellorsville with an "ashen" face, according
to a visitor. "My God! my God!" he exclaimed. "What will the country say?"[16]
Coming on the heels of the other failures in this winter of despair (so far as the
public knew, Grant was still bogged down in the bayous near Vicksburg), Chancellorsville might be a mortal blow to the Union cause. But instead, it turned out
to be the darkness before the dawn. In the summer and fall of 1863 several crucial
Union victories would turn the conflict in favor of the North.

Nineteen

The Second Turning Point: Gettysburg, Vicksburg, and Chattanooga

THE GETTYSBURG CAMPAIGN

Southern elation over the victory at Chancellorsville masked intensifying problems for the Confederacy. The blockade was tightening; inflation was worsening; Grant was closing in on Vicksburg; Banks was approaching Port Hudson; Rosecrans appeared ready to push Bragg out of central Tennessee; the Federals were preparing a combined army-navy operation against Charleston; and the Army of the Potomac remained poised on the north bank of the Rappahannock. On all fronts the South was hemmed in by superior numbers.

During May, the Confederate cabinet and leading generals held several conferences to hammer out a strategy for dealing with this situation. Longstreet proposed that he take two divisions west to reinforce Bragg for an offensive against Rosecrans. If successful, such an effort would not only liberate Tennessee but also force Grant to relax his grip on Vicksburg. But Lee opposed this plan. The railroads were too rickety to carry a large force to the West, he said; the coming summer would compel the unacclimated Northern troops at Vicksburg to retreat anyway; the most important theater was Virginia, where instead of being weakened the Army of Northern Virginia should be reinforced for another invasion of the North. This would relieve the threat to Richmond, enable the army to supply itself from the rich Pennsylvania countryside, reduce the pressure on Confederate armies in the West by forcing Union armies there to send reinforcements to the East, strengthen the Peace Democrats in the North by demonstrating the unbeatable power of the South, reopen the question of European recognition of the Confederacy, and perhaps accomplish the capture of Washington or other Northern cities. Lee's great prestige enabled him to carry his point. The government approved his plan for an invasion.

Lee has been criticized for his narrow preoccupation with the Virginia theater. A Virginian who had gone to war to defend his state, he lacked a large strategic vision encompassing the South as a whole. The Confederacy was losing the war in the West, even if it appeared to be winning in Virginia. Lee's belief that an invasion of Pennsylvania would force Grant and Rosecrans to weaken their grip in the West was wishful thinking. On the other hand, had it not been for Lee's extraordinary tactical victories in Virginia, the South might have lost the war earlier. And if the Confederates had won the ensuing battle of Gettysburg, nothing would ever have been heard of the defects in Lee's strategic vision.

The return of Longstreet's divisions to the army and reinforcements from elsewhere brought Lee's strength up to 75,000 men. Early in June they began to move. Trying to penetrate Stuart's cavalry screen to find out what the Rebels were up to, Union horsemen crossed the Rappahannock June 9 and precipitated the largest cavalry battle of the war at Brandy Station, near Culpeper. Although eventually driven back across the river, the Yankee troopers gave a good account of themselves. Richmond newspapers reproached Stuart and his "puffed up cavalry" for having been surprised at Brandy Station. This criticism rankled the South's *beau sabreur*. His eagerness to erase the stain by another dramatic ride was to have serious consequences for the forthcoming campaign.

But at first all went well. The advance Confederate units (Jackson's old corps, now commanded by Richard Ewell), captured or scattered Union garrisons at Winchester and elswhere in the Shenandoah Valley, and crossed the Potomac in mid-June. Hooker suggested to Lincoln that since the Confederates were moving north, he should move south to capture Richmond. Lincoln vetoed this proposal, and gave Hooker some sound strategic advice: "I think *Lee's army,* and not *Richmond,* is your true objective point."[1] Although Hooker moved quickly to keep his army between the Confederates and Washington, he began to complain that the Rebels outnumbered him, that the government was not supporting him, and that he could never win unless he had the administration's confidence. This sounded distressingly like McClellan. Lincoln began to suspect that Hooker was afraid to fight Lee again. The President had earlier considered removing Hooker from command; when the general submitted his resignation over a quarrel with Halleck about the Harper's Ferry garrison, Lincoln accepted it and on June 28 appointed a surprised George Gordon Meade to the command.

The Confederate invasion had the opposite effect on Northern opinion from what Lee had expected. Instead of encouraging the antiwar faction, it spurred an outburst of fury among most Northerners that quelled the Copperheads into silence. The invaders had siezed all the cattle, horses, wagons, food, and shoes they could find (paying or promising to pay in Confederate money) and levied tribute on towns they occupied. They had also captured scores of Pennsylvania blacks and sent them south into slavery. All of this roused Northerners to the same pitch of anger and hatred that Southerners had experienced when defending *their* soil.

On the day Meade assumed command, two of Lee's three corps were at Chambersburg; part of Ewell's corps was at York and the rest near Harrisburg. Stuart's cavalry had taken off on a deep raid around the Union rear. Similar raids against McClellan had made Stuart famous, but this one would earn him only rebuke for depriving Lee of his "eyes" when he most needed them. Lee hoped to cross the Susquehanna and rip up the Pennsylvania Railroad between Harrisburg and Lancaster. But in Stuart's absence he did not know where the Union army was. When a scout reported that it was across the Potomac and heading north, Lee hurriedly sent couriers to call in his scattered divisions. Lee intended to concentrate at Cashtown, a village eight miles west of Gettysburg. Meade had disposed his army to cover all the approaches to Washington and Baltimore. Neither had planned to fight at Gettysburg. But early on the morning of July 1 a Confederate infantry brigade on its way to seize shoes in Gettysburg clashed with two Union cavalry brigades west of the town. The Northern cavalry commander, John Buford, had recognized the strategic importance of this town, where a dozen roads converged from every point on the compass. Buford dismounted his troopers to hold back the charging Rebels, while couriers on both sides pounded up the roads to summon reinforcements. Thus began the most crucial battle in American history.

THE BATTLE OF GETTYSBURG

Since they were closer to Gettysburg, the Confederates were able to achieve a faster concentration. They got 25,000 men into action July 1 against the Union's 19,000. Through the long hours of that day it was a story of outnumbered bluecoats desperately holding off repeated gray attacks before finally giving way. In midmorning the tough Union 1st Corps came up to relieve Buford's cavalry and stop the slashing Confederate attacks of A. P. Hill's corps west of the town. The commander of the 1st Corps, John F. Reynolds, was killed by a sharpshooter. During the early afternoon the Union 11th Corps arrived and took up a position north of the town, where they met Ewell's troops coming down from the north. Outgunned along both flanks, the luckless Union "German Corps" (see p. 321) was once again routed by Jackson's old corps, causing the Union position west of Gettysburg also to collapse after some of the war's hardest fighting. Northern troops retreated in disorder through the town to take up a position on Cemetery Hill. Ironically, a sign on the cemetery gate read: "All persons found using firearms in these grounds will be prosecuted with the utmost rigor of the law."

Lee arrived at Gettysburg in midafternoon. Still without Stuart and uncertain where the rest of the Union army was, he was reluctant to bring on a general engagement. But the success of his troops changed his mind. He gave Ewell discretionary orders to take Cemetery Hill "if practicable." When Jackson had commanded this corps such an order would have produced an all-out assault. But Ewell hesitated. He knew that the Federals had dug in on the hill and placed a lot of artillery up there, and in the end he decided not to attack. As darkness fell, one of the many "ifs" of Gettysburg was already being debated: If Ewell had attacked Cemetery Hill on July 1, could he have taken it, and if he had, would the outcome of the battle and of the war have been the same?

During the night and next morning, most of the remaining troops in both

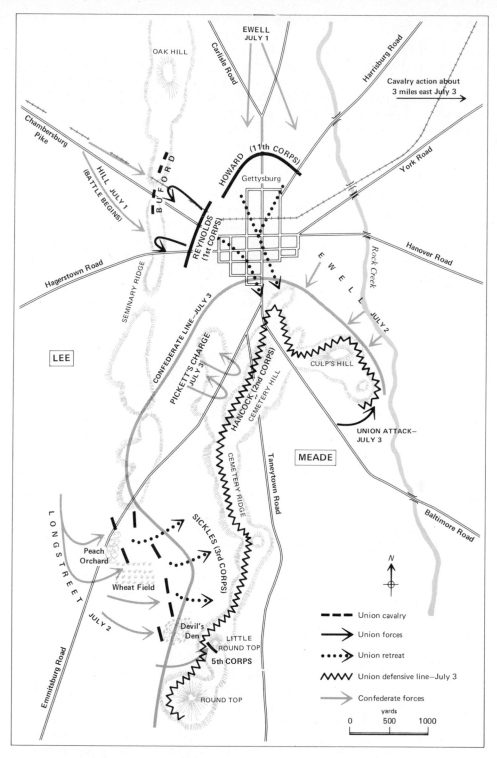

GETTYSBURG, JULY 1–3, 1863

armies reached the battlefield. The Federal position resembled a fishhook, with the barbed end curving from Culp's Hill to Cemetery Hill and the shank running southward along low-lying Cemetery Ridge to the eye at two other hills, Little Round Top and Round Top. With Culp's Hill and the Round Tops anchoring the flanks, and the convex shape of the line allowing reinforcements to be shifted rapidly from one point to another, the Union line was admirably suited to defense. The concave Confederate line was nearly twice as long, and communication from one part to another was difficult.

After studying the Union position on the morning of July 2, Longstreet concluded that it was too strong to be attacked. He urged Lee to make a flanking march to the south, where the Confederates could get between the Union army and Washington, pick a good defensive position of their own, and force Meade to attack them. But Lee's fighting blood was up. He believed his army invincible. Without adequate cavalry, a flanking movement such as Longstreet advocated would be dangerous. With limited supplies and a vulnerable line of communications, Lee thought that he had to fight or retreat. Therefore he rejected Longstreet's advice and resolved to attack the Union flanks. Ewell still thought the right flank too strong, so Lee ordered Longstreet to make the primary assault on the Union left while Ewell, at the sound of Longstreet's artillery, was to make a secondary attack on Cemetery and Culp's hills to prevent Meade from shifting reinforcements to his left.

Because Longstreet did not believe in Lee's plan, his leadership of the attack lacked enthusiasm; and because the most direct route to the attack point was under observation from a Union signal station, Longstreet's troops had to countermarch on a different route and did not attack until late afternoon. Commanding the Union 3rd Corps holding the Federal left was Daniel Sickles, an ex-Tammany politician who had achieved notoriety when he murdered his wife's lover. Contrary to orders, Sickles had advanced his corps from the low ground at the south end of Cemetery Ridge to higher ground along the Emmitsburg road, creating a salient in the Union line. Sickles' advance had left Little Round Top undefended. When Union General Gouverneur K. Warren discovered this, he realized that Confederate capture of the hill would allow Rebel artillery to enfilade the entire Union line. Warren quickly rushed two brigades of the 5th Corps to Little Round Top minutes ahead of the charging Confederates. Desperate fighting raged back and forth across the rocky slopes of the hill. The Yankees held on to Little Round Top, but Sickles' salient to the northwest was driven back in vicious fighting at places that became famous: the Peach Orchard; the Wheat Field; and Devil's Den, a maze of boulders across a boggy creek from Little Round Top. Confederate units attacked with great élan but little coordination, brigades went in piecemeal, giving Union officers time to shift reinforcements to threatened points. The main Federal line on Cemetery Ridge held firm. By dusk the exhausted Rebels on the right had given up the attack.

Over on the left, Ewell's guns had opened when Longstreet began his attack, but instead of sending his infantry against Culp's and Cemetery hills, Ewell engaged in a fruitless three-hour artillery duel with Union batteries. When his

(Reproduced from the Collections of the Library of Congress)

These photos were taken by Northern photographers Alexander Gardner and Timothy O'Sullivan on July 5, three days after the soldiers had been killed and just before the burial crews began their grisly task of gathering and burying the bloated and mangled corpses. One picture shows Union soldiers killed in the assault of Longstreet's corps near the wheat field. The other focuses on a Rebel soldier blown apart by a shell in the same sector of the battlefield.

(Reproduced from the Collections of the Library of Congress)

infantry finally went forward, two brigades penetrated the Union defenses on the east side of Cemetery Hill (held by the hapless 11th Corps) and another occupied some Union trenches on the southern slope of Culp's Hill that had been vacated earlier by troops sent to reinforce the Union left. But in Ewell's sector also a lack of coordination among the attacking brigades robbed the Confederates of any chance to exploit their breakthrough. The successful attacks had come at dusk, and they were unsupported; Union reinforcements drove the Rebels off Cemetery Hill and stopped them short of the summit of Culp's.

A. P. Hill's corps had been crippled the first day; Longstreet's (except George Pickett's division, which did not arrive until evening) was mangled the second day. Longstreet again pleaded with Lee to maneuver around the Federal left. But Lee would not hear of it. He knew that three Federal corps (1st, 3rd, and 11th) had been equally mauled in two days of fighting. In a rare failure of insight into the psychology of his opponents, Lee believed that Union morale had been sapped by these losses. He also thought that the attacks on the Union flanks had forced Meade to weaken his center. Over Longstreet's objections Lee decided to mass three divisions, led by Pickett's fresh troops, for an assault on the Union center. It was a poor decision. Northern morale was high; Meade expected the attack on his center; and the point selected for attack was held by two divisions of Winfield Scott Hancock's 2nd Corps, some of the best troops in the Army of the Potomac.

Before Pickett's charge on the third day at Gettysburg, however, shooting broke out at dawn on Culp's Hill, where the Federals had attacked to regain their lost trenches. In six hours of hard fighting they not only won the trenches but drove most of the Rebels off the hill altogether. An eerie silence fell upon the field at noon. Longstreet was massing 143 guns to soften up the Union center prior to the infantry assault. Stuart's cavalry, which had arrived only the night before, swung out to the east of the battlefield to come in behind the Union center when Pickett hit it in front. But Stuart's troopers never got closer than two and a half miles to the Union rear, for they were intercepted and defeated by Union cavalry in a three-hour clash distinguished by the headlong charges of a blue brigade commanded by twenty-three year old General George Armstrong Custer.

About one o'clock two signal guns shattered the silence at Gettysburg. Suddenly the air was filled with Confederate shells. Union batteries replied, and the heaviest artillery duel of the war ensued. At first the Confederate shelling was accurate and damaging, but as the guns' recoils dug their trails into the ground the shots began to go high, falling in the rear of the Union infantry crouched behind a stone wall and breastworks. The smoke was so thick that Southern artillery observers could not tell the effect of their fire. After more than an hour, many Union batteries began to fall silent, in order to conserve ammunition for the expected Confederate assault and to deceive the Rebels into thinking that the blue artillery had been disabled.

The ruse worked. Confederate cannoneers believed their fire had knocked out the Yankee batteries. Just before three o'clock the Southern artillery ceased firing and the gray infantry stepped out. As 13,000 Rebels approached the Union lines in parade-ground order, the blue artillery suddenly belched forth, cutting great gaps in the Confederate ranks. Then the Northern infantry fired volley after volley into the thinning Southern columns. A handful of Rebels charged over the stone wall but were immediately shot down or captured. Two of the three brigade commanders in Pickett's own division were killed and the third badly wounded. All thirteen of his colonels were killed or wounded. The casualties among officers in several other brigades were almost as high. Scarcely half of the attackers in the war's most famous charge returned to their own lines, where General Lee rode among them trying to console them with the words: "It's all my fault." "You must help me." "All good men must rally."

Aftermath of the Battle

Lee and Longstreet worked feverishly to patch up a defensive line to receive the expected Union counterattack. But no counterattack came. The wounded Hancock pleaded with Meade to go over to the offensive. But Meade, a careful, cautious man who had been in command only six days, three of them fighting for his army's life, was in no mood to take chances. He feared that his troops were too exhausted and disabled by casualties to take the offensive. It was true that the Union army was badly hurt, with 3,155 killed, 14,529 wounded, and 5,365 missing —a total casualty figure of 23,049, more than a quarter of the 86,000 effectives in his army. The battlefield presented a scene of carnage unparalleled in the war, for thousands of dead and dying horses mingled with the dead and dying men. But Meade had 20,000 reserves who had seen little action in the three days of fighting. A more aggressive general than Meade might have used these fresh troops to spearhead a counterattack. The Confederates had been hurt worse than the Federals. They had nearly run out of artillery ammunition, seventeen of their fifty-two generals had been killed or wounded, and between 25,000 and 28,000 of their men were casualties—more than a third of the 75,000 effectives engaged in the battle.

Meade's caution did not end with the battle itself. After remaining in position during July 4, Lee's army began the sad retreat to Virginia in a rainstorm exactly one month after it had started north with such high hopes. From the outset Lincoln had viewed the Confederate invasion more as an opportunity than as a threat—an opportunity to cripple and perhaps to destroy the Rebel army far from its home base. At the President's urging, General in Chief Halleck sent repeated messages to Meade instructing him to "push forward, and fight Lee before he can cross the Potomac."[2] Union cavalry harassed Lee's retreat and destroyed his pontoon bridge over the Potomac. Since the river was too high from recent rains to be forded, Lee was in a tight spot. Straggling and desertions had reduced his army to 42,000 effectives, while reinforcements had brought Meade's strength back up to 85,000. Yet Meade, personally exhausted and in an ill temper from Halleck's prodding messages, followed Lee slowly and hesitated to attack the fortified lines that the Confederates had constructed at Williamsport while their engineers worked with desperate haste to build a new bridge. On the night of July

13–14 the Rebels escaped across the river over their new bridge with the loss of only a few hundred of their rear guard.

When Lincoln learned of this he was inconsolable. "On only one or two occasions have I ever seen the President so troubled, so dejected and discouraged," wrote Secretary of the Navy Gideon Welles. "We had them in our grasp," said Lincoln. "We had only to stretch forth our hands and they were ours. And nothing I could say or do could make the Army move."[3] When Halleck sent word to Meade of the President's dissatisfaction, the testy general offered his resignation. This was a serious matter, for despite his slowness Meade had won great public acclaim for Gettysburg. An administration that sacked a general after such a victory would look foolish, if not worse. Halleck reassured Meade of the government's confidence in him and refused to accept his resignation. Lincoln sat down to write Meade a letter to assuage the general's anger. But the President's own unhappiness caused the letter to come out differently than he intended, so he never sent it. "My dear general," he wrote after congratulating Meade on his victory. "I do not believe you appreciate the magnitude of the misfortune involved in Lee's escape. He was within your easy grasp, and to have closed upon him would, in connection with our other late successes, have ended the war. As it is, the war will be prolonged indefinitely."[4]

The "other late successes" to which Lincoln alluded were the capture of Vicksburg and Port Hudson, and Rosecrans's expulsion of Bragg from central Tennessee.

UNION VICTORIES IN THE WEST

The Fall of Vicksburg and Port Hudson

At Vicksburg the Union army had inexorably tightened its siege lines during the six weeks after the unsuccessful assault of May 22 (see p. 317). Engineers tunneled under the Confederate line and exploded a mine on June 25, but the supporting attack failed to achieve a breakthrough. Another mine was readied for July 6, when Grant planned an all-out assault, but before then the Rebels had had enough. Reduced to quarter rations, subjected to artillery and mortar bombardment around the clock and sharpshooter fire during the day, the garrison was exhausted and near starvation. Civilians who had remained in Vicksburg lived in caves and shared the soldiers' meager diet, supplemented toward the end with mule meat and rats. Their only hope for salvation was Joseph Johnston, who had organized odds and ends of troops into an army of 30,000 men poised across the Big Black River twenty miles to the east. But Johnston lacked sufficient supplies, weapons, and transportation for these men, while Grant's lines had been reinforced to 70,000 tough, well-armed veterans. Johnston reported to Richmond on June 15: "I consider saving Vicksburg hopeless."[5]

So did many of the besieged Vicksburg soldiers, who on June 28 sent General Pemberton a petition that concluded: "If you can't feed us, you had better surrender."[6] On July 3 Pemberton came through the lines under a flag of truce to discuss surrender terms with Grant. Neither, of course, knew of the climactic events taking place at that moment far away in Pennsylvania. The Vicksburg garrison formally surrendered July 4. The 30,000 Confederate prisoners were paroled (that is, they pledged not to bear arms until exchanged), and many of them drifted away to their homes never to fight again.

Before dark on July 4, Sherman took 50,000 men to go after Johnston's hovering army. These Confederates retreated to Jackson, where Johnston hoped to induce Sherman to hurl his infantry against the strong entrenchments. But after some sharp skirmishing, Sherman began to surround the city in order to starve out the defenders, as at Vicksburg. This was just what Johnston feared, so on the night of July 16 he withdrew stealthily, abandoning central Mississippi to the Federals.

Nor was this the full extent of Confederate losses. Union General Banks had besieged Port Hudson on May 23 with 15,000 soldiers and several warships of Farragut's fleet. The trenches and the natural defenses of ravines, woods, and bayous surrounding Port Hudson rivaled those of Vicksburg. Banks tried two assaults, on May 27 and June 14, both of which were repulsed with Union casualties ten times greater than those of the defenders. After the second assault, Banks was content to starve out the garrison, which suffered even more from hunger than Vicksburg. One Confederate soldier wrote in his diary that the men had eaten "all the beef—all the mules—all the Dogs—and all the Rats."[7] The news of Vicksburg's surrender gave the Port Hudson commander no choice but to do likewise, on July 8. The Confederacy was cut in twain. The Mississippi River was now a Union highway. On July 16 a merchant steamboat tied up at the wharf in New Orleans, having traveled unmolested from St. Louis. Rebel snipers on the riverbanks were still to be feared, but Lincoln was essentially correct when he announced that "the Father of Waters again goes unvexed to the sea."[8]

Grant's Vicksburg campaign is generally regarded as the most successful of the war. With casualties of less than 10,000, his army had killed or wounded 10,000 of the enemy and captured another 37,000 (30,000 at Vicksburg and 7,000 previously), including fifteen generals. They had also taken 172 cannon and 60,000 rifles. A distinguished British military historian has written that "we must go back to the campaigns of Napoleon to find equally brilliant results accomplished in the same space of time with such small loss." Lincoln was delighted with the outcome at Vicksburg, so different from the lost opportunity after Gettysburg. "Grant is my man," said the President, "and I am his the rest of the war."[9]

The losses at Gettysburg and Vicksburg shook the Confederacy to its foundations. "I see no prospect now of the South ever sustaining itself," wrote a Confederate private captured at Vicksburg. "We have Lost the Mississippi and our nation is Divided and they is not a nuf left to fight for." A Rebel soldier who had fought at Gettysburg wrote afterward to his sister: "We got a bad whiping. . . . They are awhiping us . . . at every point. . . . I hope they would make peace so that we that is alive yet would get home agane." The loss of Vicksburg left Jefferson Davis "in the depths of gloom. . . . We are now in the darkest hour of our political existence." And Confederate Ordnance Chief Josiah Gorgas wrote in his diary on July 28, 1863:

> Events have succeeded one another with disastrous rapidity. One brief month ago we were apparently at the point of success. Lee was in Pennsylvania threatening Harrisburgh, and even Philadelphia. Vicksburgh seemed to laugh all Grant's efforts to scorn. . . . Now the picture is just as sombre as it was bright then. . . . It seems incredible that human power could effect such a change in so brief a space. Yesterday we rode on the pinnacle of success—today absolute ruin seems to be our portion. The Confederacy totters to its destruction.[10]

The Confederates Retreat From Tennessee

Added to the Southern list of woes in July 1863 was the retreat of Braxton Bragg's army from central Tennessee. After the battle of Stone's River at the end of 1862 (see pp. 309–311), the two bruised armies had shadowboxed warily with each other south of Murfreesboro for nearly six months. Although Rosecrans's Army of the Cumberland had nearly twice as many infantry regiments as the Army of Tennessee, the Confederates were superior in cavalry. Nathan Bedford Forrest and Joseph Wheeler led several mounted raids against Rosecrans's communications, while John Hunt Morgan began a spectacular but relatively unproductive raid that carried him all the way into Indiana and Ohio before he and most of his men were finally captured. Guerrillas also played havoc with the Federals' supply lines. In retaliation, Rosecrans sent a mule-mounted raid (he was short of horses) deep into the Confederate rear to cut the railroad between Chattanooga and Atlanta, but Forrest caught up with the raiders in Alabama and captured them.

Washington put increasing pressure on Rosecrans to begin his campaign against Bragg. Just as Lincoln's patience was about to run out, Rosecrans finally got moving on June 24. Once started, he maneuvered his 63,000 men with speed and skill despite rain that fell steadily for two weeks. The 45,000 Confederates held a strong defensive position behind four gaps in the Cumberland foothills. Feinting with his cavalry and one infantry corps toward the western gaps, Rosecrans sent three corps through and around the other gaps with such force and swiftness that the Confederates were knocked aside or flanked almost before they knew what had hit them.

Forced back to Tullahoma, Bragg received another rude surprise when a blue brigade of mounted infantry armed with new seven-shot Spencer carbines got around to the Confederate rear and threatened their rail lifeline. Once again Bragg fell back, this time all the way to Chattanooga. In little more than a week's time and at a cost of only 560 casualties, Rosecrans had pushed the enemy almost into Georgia. Piqued by dispatches from Washington announcing the great victories at Gettysburg and Vicksburg, Rosecrans wired back that he hoped the War Department would not overlook his own achievement just "because it is not written in letters of blood."[11]

Chattanooga was a city of great strategic importance. Situated in a gap carved by the Tennessee River through the Cumberland Mountains, the city formed the junction of the Confederacy's two east-west railroads and the gateway both to east Tennessee and to the war industries of Georgia. Having already split the Confederacy in two with the capture of Vicksburg, Northern armies could split it in three by a penetration into Georgia via Chattanooga.

Lincoln prodded Rosecrans to attack the Confederates in Chattanooga quickly while they were off balance. But the stiff-backed general insisted that he could not advance until all the railroads and bridges were repaired and new supply bases fully stocked. Rosecrans also wanted his left flank protected by a simultaneous advance of another Union army from Kentucky to Knoxville. This was the newly formed Army of the Ohio, commanded by Ambrose E. Burnside, who had been sent to the West after removal from command of the Army of the Potomac. In mid-August both Union armies began to advance. Burnside's 24,000 troops compelled the outnumbered Confederate defenders of Knoxville to surrender or retreat. Most of them joined Bragg's main army around Chattanooga. Burnside entered Knoxville September 3, finally achieving Lincoln's cherished goal of liberating east Tennessee.

Meanwhile Rosecrans again demonstrated his ability to move a large army quickly and cleverly once he got started. Feinting with three brigades toward the crossings above Chattanooga, Rosecrans crossed most of his troops over the Tennessee River at several places below the city. Deceived by the feint and bewildered by "the popping out of the rats from so many holes," Bragg realized that his formidable defenses in Chattanooga had been flanked by the appearance of Union divisions south of the city.[12] As the Federals drove eastward across rugged mountain passes toward Bragg's lifeline, the Western and Atlantic Railroad, the Confederate general evacuated Chattanooga September 9.

THE BATTLE OF CHICKAMAUGA

For the second time in two months Rosecrans had maneuvered Bragg out of a strategically important position. But now the fortunes of war began to turn. Bragg reached into his own bag of tricks. He sent "deserters" into Union lines with planted stories of Confederate demoralization and retreat. Rosecrans pressed forward eagerly to cut off this supposed retreat. He sent each of his three corps through separate mountain gaps twenty miles apart. But instead of retreating, Bragg was concentrating his army southeast of Chattanooga for strikes against the isolated Union fragments. He had already been reinforced by two divisions from Johnston in Mississippi. This brought Bragg's numbers almost to a par with Rosecrans's. And at an important conference in Richmond, Davis and Lee decided to send Longstreet with two more divisions to Bragg. The Confederate railroad administration mobilized its scanty resources to transport 12,000 men and all their equipment, artillery, and animals from Virginia to northern Georgia. Since the direct route through Knoxville was blocked by Burnside's troops, the Confederate reinforcements had to be sent 965 roundabout miles via Atlanta over broken-down lines of varying gauges. The process took ten days; fewer than two-thirds of the troops arrived in time for the battle, but they made a decisive difference.

Before Longstreet arrived, Bragg had three chances to trap fragments of Rosecrans's separated army, but each time his corps commanders found excuses for failing to obey attack orders. These abortive Confederate maneuvers alerted Rosecrans to his danger. He ordered a concentration of his own forces in the valley of Chickamauga Creek a dozen miles south of Chattanooga. As the first of Longstreet's regiments detrained on September 18, Confederate units forced their way across the Chickamauga in an attempt to turn the Union left and cut the Federals off from their base at Chattanooga. Next morning a full battle erupted. The fighting was some of the most vicious but confused of the war. Much of the battlefield was covered with heavy woods and dense undergrowth. Visibility was limited; brigades and divisions fought in isolation from one another, with little apparent relationship to any overall battle plan. A Union general described Chickamauga as "a mad, irregular battle, very much resembling guerrilla warfare on a vast scale."[13]

Although neither side gained any advantage on September 19, several division-size Confederate attacks had forced the Federals to contract their lines. Most of the pressure had been on the Union left, commanded by General George H. Thomas. Thomas expected the Confederates to attack his corps again in the morning and persuaded Rosecrans to strengthen the left. Bragg did indeed intend to hit the Union left; but his attack on the morning of September 20 started sluggishly, and with the help of reinforcements Thomas stopped the repeated Confederate assaults with heavy loss to both sides.

Then a lucky break turned the battle in the Confederates' favor. A Union staff officer, failing to see a blue division in line amid the smoke and trees, reported a gap on the Federal right. Rosecrans ordered another division to close this supposed gap, thereby creating a true gap when the latter division pulled out of line to plug the nonexistent one. By coincidence, Longstreet just then launched an assault directly at the breach created by this false Union move. The yelling Rebels burst through the gap at noon, cutting off two blue divisions from the rest of the army, rolling up the right flank of the remainder, and threatening to come in on the rear of Thomas's forces while they were desperately engaged in their front. Rosecrans was caught in the rout of the Union right and fled with the broken divisions to Chattanooga. But Thomas kept his head and kept two-thirds of the army on the field. With the aid of two reserve brigades whose timely arrival staved off total disaster, he formed a new line on the Union right and repulsed several all-out Confederate attacks. That night the Federals withdrew toward Chattanooga. For his superb generalship Thomas was thereafter known as "the Rock of Chickamauga."

Chickamauga was an important Confederate tactical victory. "We have met with a severe disaster," Rosecrans wired Washington. When the news reached Richmond, a government clerk wrote exultantly in his diary: "The effects of this great victory will be electrical. The whole South will be filled again with patriotic fervor, and in the North there will be a corresponding depression. . . . Surely the

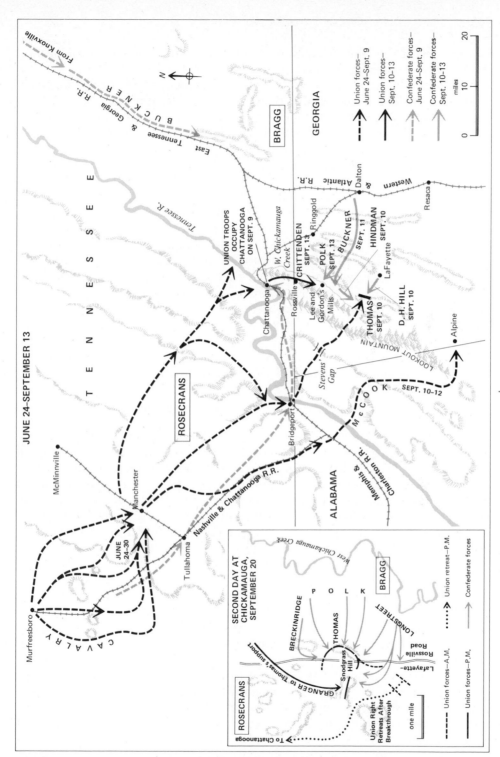

MURFREESBORO TO CHICKAMAUGA, 1863

Government of the United States must now see the impossibility of subjugating the Southern people, spread over such a vast extent of territory."[14]

But the Southern triumph was purchased at the cost of 18,454 casualties, nearly 30 percent of the force engaged. Union casualties were nearly as great (16,170); but the North could replace its losses while the South could not. Chickamauga turned out to be the last significant offensive victory by any Confederate army. And it also proved to be a triumph without strategic consequences. Rosecrans still held Chattanooga, for Bragg had failed to follow up his victory.

Mutual recriminations racked the Confederate high command. All of Bragg's leading generals accused their commander of poor battlefield tactics because he had not exploited Longstreet's breakthrough and had not renewed the attack next day while the Federals were still disorganized. For his part the quarrelsome, fault-finding Bragg accused several subordinates of slowness or refusal to obey orders. He dismissed two corps commanders. The bickering grew so bad that Jefferson Davis made the long trip from Richmond to Bragg's headquarters to resolve the ugly dispute. The Confederate president handled the affair in the worst possible way. In Bragg's presence he asked each of the chief generals whether he thought the army needed a new leader. Each said yes, whereupon Davis decided to keep Bragg in command! Two of the South's premier generals, Johnston and Beauregard, were available for the post, but Davis disliked both of them; he continued to hold a high opinion of Bragg that was shared by few others.

THE BATTLES OF CHATTANOOGA

Lincoln handled his command problems after Chickamauga with more deftness. The Confederates had bottled up Rosecrans in Chattanooga: Bragg's forces had occupied Missionary Ridge east of the city and placed artillery on the brow of massive Lookout Mountain, which commanded all approaches from the south and west. The only supply line open to the Yankees was a circuitous road over mountains to the north, all but impassable in wet weather and vulnerable to Rebel cavalry in all weather. Nevertheless, the Union government decided to reinforce Rosecrans. The War Department ordered 17,000 troops under Sherman to move eastward from Mississippi and transferred 20,000 men of the Army of the Potomac 1,200 miles by rail from Virginia to Chattanooga. Lincoln reactivated Joseph Hooker to command the two Army of the Potomac corps in their new theater of war. The transfer of these troops was the most impressive logistic achievement of the war. The North sent nearly twice as many men from Virginia to Tennessee over a greater distance in less time than the Confederates had done the previous month.

But there was no point putting these men into Chattanooga so long as the troops already there could not be supplied. The Army of the Cumberland was in danger of slow starvation. By mid-October thousands of horses had died and the men were reduced to quarter rations. Rosecrans seemed paralyzed by his defeat at Chickamauga and unable to cope with the crisis. On October 17 Lincoln placed all of the Union military departments between the Appalachians and the Mississippi under the overall command of General Grant. Grant's first action was to replace Rosecrans with Thomas as commander of the Army of the Cumberland. His second was to go personally to Chattanooga. As one officer later wrote, when Grant arrived "we began to see things move. We felt that everything came from a plan."[15] Grant put in motion a previously designed operation to break the supply blockade. While one blue brigade drifted silently downriver on bridge pontoons to Brown's Ferry on the night of October 27, two other columns marched overland to attack Rebel outposts guarding approach roads to the ferry. At dawn the Federals struck, drove away the Confederates, repelled a counterattack, laid the bridge over the river, and thereby established a new supply route (dubbed "the Cracker Line" by hungry bluecoats) beyond the range of Confederate artillery on Lookout Mountain.

Having stationed insufficient force in Lookout Valley to prevent this coup, Bragg committed a bigger mistake on November 4 when, at President Davis's behest, he sent Longstreet with 15,000 men (followed later by 5,000 more) to drive Burnside out of Knoxville. Longstreet himself thought this a foolish move, for it reduced Bragg's strength to 45,000 at a time when the arrival of Hooker's troops boosted Federal strength to nearly 60,000. Longstreet also considered his force too small for the job assigned to it. And so it proved. The Confederate attack on the Knoxville defenses November 29 was repulsed with heavy Southern losses.

Back in Chattanooga the arrival of Sherman with another 17,000 men of the Army of the Tennessee on November 15 gave the Federals the initiative. For the only time in the war, parts of the Union's three main armies—the Cumberland, the Tennessee, and the Potomac—operated in concert, with Grant as commander of the combined forces. Bragg held a six-mile line on 400-foot high Missionary Ridge with trenches at the base and the top and an unfinished line of rifle-pits halfway up the steep slope. Three Confederate brigades held 2,000-foot high Lookout Mountain. All Civil War experience taught that a frontal assault against Missionary Ridge would be suicidal, so Grant's battle plan called for Sherman's four divisions of the Army of the Tennessee to make a flank attack against the north end of the ridge while Hooker with three divisions was to force his way over or around Lookout Mountain, cross the intervening valley to Missionary Ridge, and attack the Rebel left flank there. Thomas's Army of the Cumberland was assigned the secondary role of threatening the Confederate center to prevent reinforcements from being sent to either flank. Eager to avenge their defeat at Chickamauga, Thomas's troops chafed under this passive role and burned to make Grant eat his words that "they could not be got out of their trenches to assume the offensive."[16]

Hooker's divisions carried out their initial assignment handsomely on November 24, driving the outnumbered Rebels off Lookout Mountain in a series of skirmishes obscured by a fog that caused the fighting there to be labeled "The Battle Above the Clouds." Next morning the fog dissolved at sunrise to reveal the Stars and Stripes flying from the pinnacle of Lookout Mountain in full view of both armies. Meanwhile Sherman's divisions had run into trouble. Having gained the crest of one hill at the north end of Missionary Ridge, they discovered that

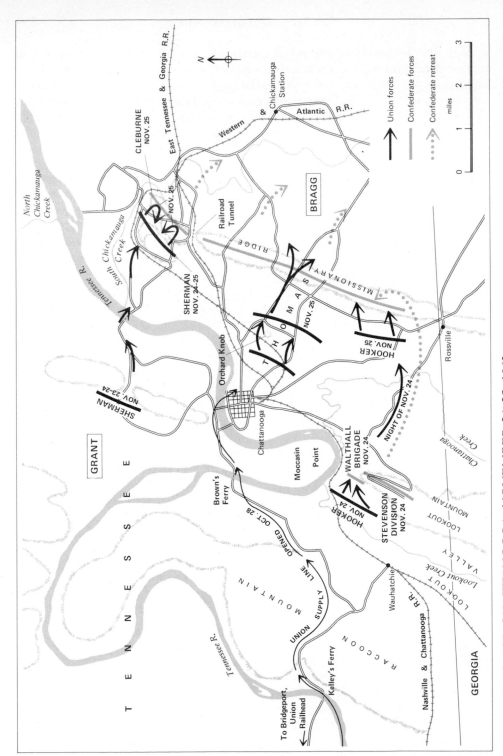

THE BATTLES FOR CHATTANOOGA, NOVEMBER 24-25, 1863

it was only a spur separated by a rock-strewn ravine from the main ridge defended by Patrick Cleburne's oversize division, the best unit in Bragg's army. Sherman's battle-hardened westerners assaulted this position without success on the morning of November 25. Grant sent reinforcements, but still Sherman got nowhere.

As Hooker finally approached the opposite end of Missionary Ridge after being delayed several hours by the destruction of the bridge over Chattanooga Creek, Grant ordered Thomas to make a diversionary attack against the first line of Rebel trenches at the base of Missionary Ridge. Led by two of the divisions that had been routed at Chickamauga, Thomas's boys moved out with spirit and took these lower trenches. Once there, however, they were exposed to fire from the Confederates in the second and third lines of trenches at the midpoint and top of the ridge. Some of the blue regiments began to move up the slope. Soon the whole line swept forward with exultant yells and cleared the second line of trenches. "Who ordered those men up the hill?" Grant asked angrily. No one had ordered it. The only orders were the impromptu commands of front-line officers after their men had already started. As Grant and Thomas watched in amazement from their command post a mile in the rear, the blue line swarmed all the way to the top of the ridge in an assault apparently more hopeless than Pickett's at Gettysburg.

But Bragg's engineer officers had made the mistake of locating the upper trenches on the topographical crest of the ridge rather than several yards lower on the "military crest," from which the line of fire would not have been blocked by intervening swells in the ground. The oncoming Yankees therefore found ravines and dips through which they could advance under cover until they got close enough to enfilade the Rebel defenses. Suddenly seized with panic, the Confederates broke and ran or surrendered, by thousands. The victorious Federals were "completely and frantically drunk with excitement," wrote an officer. They yelled "Chickamauga! Chickamauga!" in derisive triumph as they watched the graybacks rush "wildly down the hill and into the woods, tossing away knapsacks, muskets, and blankets as they ran."

Believing that "an army was never whipped as badly as Bragg's was," Grant hoped to organize a vigorous pursuit to finish off the Rebels. But Cleburne's division, which had not yielded an inch, conducted an effective rear-guard action that enabled Bragg to establish a strong defensive line near Dalton, Georgia, twenty-five miles to the south. After some skirmishing, both armies went into winter quarters as harsh weather came on.[17]

The storming of Missionary Ridge was one of the most remarkable feats of the war. As Grant said with a smile when someone mentioned that Bragg had believed the position impregnable: "Well, it *was* impregnable."[18] The Army of the Cumberland had fully redeemed Chickamauga. More than that, it had completed the cycle of victories begun at Vicksburg and Gettysburg that broke the Confederacy's back, though some of the war's bloodiest fighting still lay ahead. The loss of Chattanooga had also sealed Bragg's fate. The general admitted privately to Davis that "the disaster admits of no palliation, and is justly disparaging to me as a commander. . . . I fear we both erred in the conclusion for me to retain command here after the clamor raised against me."[19] Davis reluctantly appointed Joseph Johnston to succeed Bragg as commander of the Army of Tennessee.

The victory at Chattanooga confirmed Grant as the Union's greatest general. From there he went on in March 1864 to become general in chief of all Union armies. The other three generals who with Grant became the architects of final Union victory—Sherman, Thomas, and Sheridan—also fought at Chattanooga. All four came out of the western theater; two of them, Grant and Sheridan, went east in 1864 to try their victory formula with the Army of the Potomac.

THE WAR AND FOREIGN POLICY, 1863

In January 1863, Henry Adams had written from London that Confederate hopes of foreign recognition were dead unless Union arms suffered another disaster. Chancellorsville was such a disaster. Lee's subsequent invasion of Pennsylvania and Grant's initial failure to take Vicksburg revived the efforts for recognition. On June 22, Napoleon III discussed with pro-Confederate members of the British Parliament a movement for joint recognition of the South. Unfortunately for this movement, the man selected to present the motion in Parliament was John Roebuck, whom Henry Adams aptly described as "rather more than three-quarters mad." In a rambling speech on June 30 Roebuck indiscreetly revealed the details of his talk with Napoleon III. Parliament erupted in chauvinistic anger at the idea of following French leadership. Palmerston denied that the government had received any official communications from Paris on this matter (this was a bit of casuistry). Napoleon was chagrined by Roebuck's breach of confidence, and the whole affair ended in a fiasco that discredited Roebuck in particular and pro-Confederate partisans in general. Then came news of Gettysburg and of the fall of Vicksburg, which gave the *coup de grâce* to Southern hopes in Britain. "It is now conceded at once that all idea of intervention is at an end," wrote Henry Adams on July 23. "The only remaining chance of collision is in the case of the ironclads. We are looking after them with considerable energy, and I think we shall settle them."[20]

The Laird Rams

Adams's reference to ironclads concerned the "Laird rams," which provoked a near crisis in Anglo-American relations in 1863. The source of the trouble lay in Britain's equivocal interpretation of her own Neutrality Act of 1819, which forbade the "equipping, furnishing, fitting out, or arming" of warships to be used against any nation with which Britain was at peace. In June 1861, the Georgian James D. Bulloch had arrived in Liverpool with a mission to buy or build warships for the Confederacy. A tough, clever agent, Bulloch did a remarkable job with limited resources. He contracted for the construction of two powerful commerce raiders that eventually became the *Florida* and the *Alabama*. Between them these raiders sank or captured more than a hundred American merchant ships (see p. 175). Bulloch's antagonist in Liverpool was U.S. Consul Thomas H. Dudley, who employed spies, informers, and double agents to amass evidence that these and other vessels were being built as Confederate warships in violation of British law. Bulloch countered with agents of his own who forged registry papers, fed Dudley's informers false information, and created such a fog of doubt that the true purpose of these ships could not be legally proved before they left England.

The British applied a narrow, technical interpretation of their neutrality law. So long as the ships were built but not "fitted out and armed" as warships in British territory, said Foreign Secretary Lord Russell, they did not violate the law. The *Florida* left Liverpool unarmed and was later converted to a commerce raider in the Bahamas (which itself *was* British territory). By July 1862 the evidence that "No. 290" would do the same was so strong that Russell ordered her seized. But while the order was being delayed by legal quibbles and bureaucratic negligence, Bulloch got wind of it from a double agent and sent the completed ship to sea on a "trial run" before the seizure order arrived. The ship never returned to port; she sailed to the Azores, where by prearrangement she was fitted out as a commerce destroyer and began her career as the *Alabama*.

Bulloch had also contracted with the Laird shipbuilding firm for the construction of two ironclad warships equipped with seven-foot underwater iron spikes attached to their prows. More powerful than anything afloat, these "Laird rams" were designed to destroy the wooden ships of the Union blockade fleet. Bulloch did everything possible to disguise their true purpose. He even transferred their ownership to a French firm, which ostensibly bought them for the Pasha of Egypt! But Dudley's spies piled up a mountain of evidence that they were being built for the Confederacy. All through the summer of 1863, American Minister Charles Francis Adams bombarded the Foreign Office with veiled threats of war if the rams were allowed to escape. Russell replied lamely that he could do nothing in the absence of airtight evidence. On September 5, Adams penned an angry note that concluded with the words: "It would be superfluous in me to point out to your Lordship that this is war."[21]

Next day the British government detained the ships, and later it purchased them for the Royal Navy. When the diplomatic correspondence was published, Adams became something of a hero in the United States, for it appeared that his "this is war" note had forced John Bull to back down. In fact, the British government had decided to detain the rams two days before receiving Adams's note. But Adams did deserve much of the credit for the outcome. His firm protests during the preceding months together with Seward's equally firm line with the British minister in Washington kept unrelenting pressure on the British government. English merchants and naval officers, fearing the consequences in a future war if a neutral United States built destroyers for Britain's enemies, also brought pressure to bear on Her Majesty's government.

To the Confederacy, the seizure of the Laird rams came as a crowning blow in a year filled with foreign policy disappointments. All hope for British recognition and mediation had vanished. Now the opportunity to build warships in Britain seemed to be disappearing as well. In frustration, the Confederacy expelled British consuls (who were still officially accredited to the United States) from

Southern cities and transferred Commissioner James Mason from London to Paris. This was the equivalent of breaking off diplomatic relations, but it hurt Britain not at all and did nothing for the Confederacy except perhaps to salve its injured dignity. From now on Confederate diplomacy would be focused on France.

Intrigues in Mexico

Affairs in that quarter initially seemed promising. The French Emperor's sympathies were notoriously pro-Southern. Since 1862 Napoleon III had been involved in an imperial adventure in Mexico whose success would be imperiled by Union victory. Mexican political and financial instability in 1861 had provoked a joint military expedition by Britain, France, and Spain to collect debts owed by Mexico to foreign creditors. Britain and Spain withdrew their troops in 1862 after negotiating a settlement. But Napoleon III imposed impossible demands on the weak Mexican government and sent additional troops (35,000 by 1863), who seized Mexico City and overthrew the liberal leader Benito Juarez in June 1863.

Meanwhile the Confederacy had concluded quasi-alliances with anti-Juarez chieftains in the northern provinces of Mexico, who profited from the contraband trade across the Texas border. By 1863, a key goal of Southern diplomacy was an agreement with France whereby the Confederacy would recognize a French-controlled regime in Mexico in return for French recognition of the Confederacy. When Napoleon III engineered the selection of Archduke Ferdinand Maximilian of Austria as emperor of Mexico, Confederate envoys approached Maximilian with proposals for an alliance. Although the Austrian was willing, his master Napoleon III did not really want to risk war with the United States. Secretary of State Seward skillfully steered American foreign policy between the two extremes of a surrender of the Monroe Doctrine or an open rupture with France. He warned Napoleon III politely but firmly that the United States would not tolerate foreign interference in Mexico, but at the same time he dropped vague hints that his country might recognize Maximilian if France continued to refuse recognition of the Confederacy.

This carrot-and-stick approach worked. Increasingly embroiled in European conflicts, Napoleon III gradually lost interest in Mexico. He held Confederate envoys at arm's length and clamped down on the construction of Southern warships in France. The last serious Confederate bid for European recognition and support had failed. And after the collapse of the Confederacy in 1865, Napoleon III's Mexican adventure had a tragic denouement for the naive Maximilian. The United States sent 50,000 battle-hardened veterans to the Texas-Mexican border after Appomattox, while Seward put increasing pressure on France to pull her troops out of Mexico. When France did so in 1867, Maximilian's government fell and Maximilian himself was executed by Juarez's partisans.

Twenty

War Issues
and Politics in 1863

Northern military victories in the second half of 1863 powerfully affected domestic politics in both the Union and the Confederacy. North of the Potomac, these victories reversed the erosion of home-front support for the war that had been accelerating during the first half of the year. Gettysburg in particular produced joyous celebration and renewed confidence in the North. "The results of this victory are priceless," wrote a New Yorker when he learned the outcome of the battle in Pennsylvania. "Government is strengthened fourfold at home and abroad. . . . Copperheads are palsied and dumb for the moment at least."[1] But before Gettysburg, the Copperheads had grown in strength until they threatened social disruption, political realignment, and a faltering of the Northern war effort.

VALLANDIGHAM AND THE COPPERHEAD DRIVE
FOR POWER

In the spring of 1863, Clement L. Vallandigham was campaigning for the Democratic gubernatorial nomination in Ohio. Looking for an issue to propel himself into martyrdom and the nomination, he found an unwitting ally in General Burnside,.whose political judgment proved to be no wiser than his military judgment had been at Fredericksburg. After his removal from command of the Army of the Potomac, Burnside had been appointed head of the Department of the Ohio, with headquarters at Cincinnati.* There he found himself in the heart of

*Both the Union and Confederate armies established territorial organizations known as "departments." Each department was headed by a commanding general who was responsible for military operations and for army administrative duties within his territorial jurisdiction. The boundaries and names of some departments changed

Copperhead country during a period of rising antiwar sentiment. On April 19 he issued "General Order No. 38," which declared that "treason" in his department would no longer be tolerated.

In a speech on May 1, Vallandigham deliberately challenged this order by repeating all the themes he had been stating for months: the war was a wicked failure; the Emancipation Proclamation should be repudiated; conscription and the suspension of *habeas corpus* were unconstitutional; "King Lincoln" ought to be dethroned by the voters; and the North ought to stop fighting, declare an armistice, and invite the Confederates to a peace conference to restore the old Union, without New England if necessary. By Burnside's definition this was treason. At 2 A.M. on May 5, a company of soldiers broke into Vallandigham's home in Dayton and arrested him.

A review of political events in the North during the previous five months will provide background for an understanding of this action. Although historians disagree on the size of Vallandigham's following, it was large enough to constitute a threat to the Northern will to continue the war during this winter of discontent. Scores of Democratic politicians and editors were urging resistance to emancipation, the draft, even the war itself. A former governor of Illinois declared that "with the objectives announced in this [emancipation] proclamation as the avowed purpose of the war, the South cannot and ought not to be subdued." A Democratic editor in Iowa considered the Emancipation Proclamation cause for a counterrevolution in the North. If the people "possessed a tithe of the spirit which animated Rome when Cataline was expelled," he wrote, "they would hurl [Lincoln] into the Potomac [along with] Cabinet, Congress, and all." Several Democratic county conventions in the Midwest resolved that "an experience of two years has taught us, that the Union can never be restored by force of arms," called for a "cessation of hostilities," and pledged defiantly that "we will not render support to the present Administration in carrying on its wicked abolition crusade against the South; . . . we will *resist* to the *death* all attempts to draft any of our citizens into the army." Nor were such sentiments confined to Midwestern Democrats. A large meeting of party faithful in New York resolved that "this war of the General Government against the South is illegal, being unconstitutional, and should not be sustained." And Horatio Seymour, a lukewarm War Democrat whose election as governor of New York had propelled him to national party leadership, said in his inaugural address that the "bloody, barbarous, revolutionary" emancipation policy would ruin the country.[2]

Talk is cheap, and much of this rhetoric was little more than loose talk. But such talk could be dangerous when it led to action, as it did in Illinois and Indiana. The 1862 elections in these states had produced Democratic legislatures that

frequently—a source of great confusion to students of the war. The most active Union departments were those in the war zones and in the occupied portions of the Confederacy. But the Union border states and the Northern states themselves were also organized into military departments, where troops were responsible for repelling invasions, quelling internal uprisings, preventing espionage and sabotage, and enforcing conscription. In 1863, the Department of the Ohio comprised the states of Ohio, Illinois, Indiana, Michigan, and Kentucky east of the Tennessee River.

confronted Republican governors (elected in 1860) in a bitter showdown over war policy. The lower houses of both legislatures adopted resolutions calling for an armistice and a peace conference. The Illinois house even named commissioners to such a conference. The Indiana legislature contemptuously rejected Republican Governor Oliver P. Morton's annual message and voted instead to endorse the "exalted and patriotic sentiments" of New York's Governor Seymour. Democrats in both states introduced bills that could have resulted in the withdrawal of state troops from the war.

Governor Richard Yates of Illinois ended the threat in his state by invoking an obscure constitutional clause to adjourn the legislature. Indiana's Governor Morton could not do this, nor could he successfully veto any bills, for Indiana's constitution required only a simple majority to override a veto. But the same constitution specified that two-thirds of the legislature must be present to constitute a quorum. With Morton's connivance, Republicans absented themselves from the state senate to deny a quorum. For two years the iron-willed Morton ran the state without a legislature—and without any appropriations. He financed state operations with loans from banks and railroads, grants from Republican counties, and a subsidy of $250,000 from the War Department. This was an unconstitutional, revolutionary procedure, but these were revolutionary times. "If the Cause fails," Morton reminded Secretary of War Stanton, "you and I will be covered with prosecutions, imprisoned, driven from the country." "If the Cause fails," replied Stanton melodramatically, "I do not care to live."[3]

The Peace Democrats had an impact in Richmond as well as in Northern states. A Confederate War Department clerk reported in February 1863 that "several citizens from Illinois and Indiana" had arrived in the Southern capital

> to consult our government on the best means of terminating the war; or, that failing, to propose some mode of adjustment between the Northwestern States and the Confederacy, and new combination against the Yankee [i.e., New England] States and the Federal administration. . . . I have no doubt, if the war continues throughout the year, we shall have the spectacle of more Northern men fighting against the United States Government than slaves fighting against the South.[4]

Copperhead newspapers openly encouraged desertion from the army. Men who read these newspapers wrote such letters as the following to their sons in the army: "I am sorry you are engaged in this . . . unholy, unconstitutional, and hellish war . . . which has no other purpose but to free the negroes and enslave the whites. . . . Come home, if you have to desert, you will be protected." Desertions were highest among troops from Copperhead areas. Declaring that they would "lie in the woods until moss grew on their backs rather than help free the slaves," all but thirty-five men of the 128th Illinois deserted early in 1863. When the 109th Illinois learned of the Emancipation Proclamation, half of its men deserted and the other half became so insubordinate that General Grant disbanded the regiment. Both regiments came from the Butternut counties of southern Illinois.[5]

To counter the Peace Democrats, Republicans and War Democrats organized loyalist societies and publication agencies to rally support for the war. These organizations coalesced into the National Union League (dominated by Republicans) and the Loyal League (primarily War Democrats) in 1863. Their first successes occurred in the spring elections of that year,* especially in New Hampshire and Connecticut, where Democrats were making strong efforts to elect antiwar governors. These elections presented a crucial challenge to Republicans. If Peace Democrats could win in New England, they would certainly win elsewhere. Union leagues mobilized all their resources, the national government used its patronage to the utmost, and the War Department furloughed home soldiers to vote (experience had shown that front-line soldiers voted overwhelmingly Republican). Even with all this help, the Republicans won just 51.6 percent of the vote in Connecticut and 43.8 percent in New Hampshire. Only the presence of a third-party War Democratic candidate in the latter state denied the Peace Democrat a majority and threw the contest into the legislature, which elected the Republican candidate.

It was in this political atmosphere filled with rumors of conspiracies that Burnside arrested Vallandigham for speaking against the war. A military commission sentenced the Ohioan to imprisonment for the duration of the conflict. A federal judge refused to issue a writ to release Vallandigham to the custody of civil courts. Democrats—and even some Republicans—denounced these proceedings. The government's action was "cowardly, brutal, infamous," said Governor Seymour of New York. "It is not merely a step toward revolution, it *is* revolution. . . . It establishes military despotism. . . . If it is upheld, our liberties are overthrown."[6]

Ohio Democrats unanimously nominated the martyred Vallandigham for governor. Although Lincoln was embarrassed by this affair, he refused to repudiate General Burnside or the military commission that had convicted Vallandigham. Instead, with a shrewd stroke, the President tarnished the Copperhead's martyrdom by commuting his sentence from imprisonment to banishment. Federal troops escorted Vallandigham under flag of truce to General Bragg's lines in Tennessee, where the Confederates reluctantly accepted this dubious gift.

Vallandigham escaped from the South on a blockade runner and went to Canada, from where he tried to direct his gubernatorial campaign in Ohio. The lesson of his exile was driven home by Edward Everett Hale's popular short story "The Man Without a Country." Vallandigham's lawyers took the case to the Supreme Court, where they argued that the trial of a civilian by a military court outside the war zone was unconstitutional. But in February 1864 the Court refused to review the proceedings of the military commission, thereby in effect upholding Vallandigham's conviction.†

---

*Unlike today, states then held state elections at various times of the year—some in the spring, some in August, September, or October, and several (as now) in November.

†In 1866, after the passions of war had partly cooled, the Supreme Court overturned a similar military conviction in 1864 of an Indiana Copperhead, Lambdin P. Milligan, on the grounds that when the civil courts are functioning, civilians must be tried therein even in wartime. This principle would have voided Vallandigham's conviction. But the effect of the Court's decision on Vallandigham was moot, since he had returned

BLACK MEN IN BLUE

The Vallandigham affair occurred amid a rising crescendo of Democratic Negro-phobia. The administration's decision to recruit black regiments swelled the crescendo. "This is a government of white men, made by white men for white men, to be administered, protected, defended, and maintained by white men," thundered a Democratic congressman in opposition to a black soldier bill in February 1863. Forty-three Democratic congressmen signed a round robin con-demning the enlistment of black soldiers as part of a wicked Republican plot to establish "the equality of the black and white races."[7]

In a way they were right. One result of black soldiers fighting for the North was to advance the revolution of freedom a long step toward equality. This had been the purpose of Northern blacks and abolitionists who had urged the enlist-ment of black soldiers in the first place. As Frederick Douglass put it: "Once let the black man get upon his person the brass letters, U.S.; let him get an eagle on his button, and a musket on his shoulder and bullets in his pocket, and there is no power on earth which can deny that he has earned the right to citizenship."[8]

Although blacks had fought as soldiers in the Revolution and in the War of 1812, they were quickly disarmed afterward. A federal law of 1792 banned black men from the state militias, and no blacks had ever been allowed to enlist in the regular army. When antislavery generals in 1862 undertook to enroll black soldiers in Kansas and in occupied portions of Louisiana and South Carolina, the adminis-tration refused to sustain them. So long as the North was fighting only to restore the Union—the old Union—the Lincoln administration felt obliged to keep it "a white man's war."

Blacks in the Navy

The navy, however, had always had some black sailors. From the beginning of the war, the Union navy took whatever men it could get, including free blacks from Northern seaports and contraband slaves from the South. Most of these men served in menial capacities as firemen and coal heavers. But some performed combat duty. As early as August 1861, a contraband gun crew manned one of the guns on the flagship *Minnesota* in the successful attack on the Hatteras Inlet forts. Nine months later a South Carolina slave, Robert Smalls, achieved one of the best-publicized exploits of the war when he commandeered the Confederate vessel *Planter* in the Charleston harbor and ran it out to the Union blockading fleet. "Captain" Smalls served as a pilot in the Union navy for the rest of the war and went on to a prominent political career afterward. In all, several thousand black men served in the Union navy. They played a vital part in the war at sea.[9]

---

to Ohio in 1864 and had been allowed by the Lincoln administration to remain there undisturbed and even to participate actively in politics (see p. 437).

Recruitment of Black Soldiers

Black involvement in the navy encouraged those Republicans who by 1862 wanted to enlist blacks to fight on land as well. What better way to employ able-bodied contrabands than to arm them to fight for the Union—and for their own freedom? This argument became even more compelling when the shortage of Northern white volunteers caused the government to order a militia draft in the summer of 1862. Two laws enacted on July 17, 1862, set the stage for the enlistment of black soldiers. One section of the confiscation act authorized the President to employ contrabands for the suppression of the rebellion "in such manner as he may judge best." And a section of the militia act authorized the enrollment of blacks for "any military or naval service for which they may be found competent."[10]

Neither of these laws required the President to enlist blacks as soldiers. For the time being Lincoln chose to interpret them as granting him authority to enroll contrabands as laborers—which of course the army had been doing for more than a year. But Lincoln had probably made up his mind to arm blacks and was waiting for the right moment to announce it. In this, he followed the same course as he had during the ten weeks between his decision and announcement of an emancipation policy (see pp. 278–279). On August 4, 1862, the President told a delegation from Indiana that "to arm the negroes would turn 50,000 bayonets from the loyal Border States against us that were for us." He said the same to a Chicago delegation six weeks later. But meanwhile, on August 25, Secretary of War Stanton had quietly authorized the Union commander on the South Carolina coastal islands to recruit 5,000 freedmen as soldiers.[11]

By early 1863, Lincoln had become an enthusiastic proponent of enlisting black soldiers. "The colored population is the great *available* and yet *unavailed of,* force for restoring the Union," the President told the military governor of Tennessee in March. "The bare sight of 50,000 armed and drilled black soldiers upon the banks of the Mississippi, would end the rebellion at once. And who doubts that we can present that sight, if we but take hold in earnest?"[12]

The administration proceeded to back these words with action. The War Department created the Bureau of Colored Troops to coordinate recruiting. In Louisiana, General Banks began to form a "Corps d'Afrique." A Northern abolitionist who had organized two black regiments for Massachusetts, George L. Stearns, took his recruiting service to Nashville to enroll black soldiers there. Generals in occupied Virginia and North Carolina formed black regiments. Most important of all, the government sent General Lorenzo Thomas to the Mississippi Valley to recruit freedmen as soldiers. A desk general with no prior field service, Thomas proved remarkably successful at his task. He combined administrative ability with the tact necessary to persuade hard-bitten, race-conscious Western soldiers to accept the new policy. By the end of the war Thomas had raised 76,000 black troops, 41 percent of the total.

In the spring of 1863, an Illinois soldier in Grant's army wrote that "an honest confession is good for the soul. . . . A year ago last January I didn't like to hear anything of emancipation. Last fall, accepted confiscation of rebels' Negroes quietly. In January took to emancipation readily, and now . . . am becoming so [color] blind that I can't see why they will not make soldiers. . . . I almost begin to think of applying for a position in a [black] regiment myself."[13] This man's "confession" hints at one of the conditions that made black regiments acceptable: all commissioned officers and some NCOs were to be white men. The chance for a commission helped convert many a white soldier to the policy of arming blacks—and also produced some racist officers who had little regard for the men they led.

The appointment of white officers could be justified at first on the ground that few blacks had any military experience. In regiments composed of former slaves, few of the soldiers were even literate. But black regiments recruited in the North also had white officers, even though some black soldiers in these regiments were potential officer material. And as time went on, the reluctance to promote capable black men from the ranks was clearly a result of race prejudice. Abolitionists and black leaders attacked this discriminatory policy, but they achieved limited success. In the 166 black regiments organized during the war, fewer than 100 black officers were commissioned (exclusive of surgeons and chaplains), none higher than captain.

Another discrimination that prevailed until 1864 was a difference in pay between black and white soldiers. Under the militia act of 1862 the pay of blacks was fixed at $10 monthly, while white privates received $13 plus a $3.50 clothing allowance. Abolitionists eloquently denounced this discrimination. Frederick Douglass obtained an interview with Lincoln on August 10, 1863, to protest inequalities in pay and status. As Douglass later remembered it, the President told him that

> the employment of colored troops at all was a great gain to the colored people—that the measure could not have been successfully adopted at the beginning of the war, that the wisdom of making colored men soldiers was still doubted—that their enlistment was a serious offense to popular prejudice . . . that they were not to receive the same pay as white soldiers seemed a necessary concession to smooth the way to their employment at all as soldiers.[14]

Although partly remedied in 1864, the inequality of pay was only one of several signs that black regiments were considered second-class soldiers. Some regiments functioned initially as labor battalions to dig trenches, load and unload supplies, and perform heavy fatigue duty for white troops. Even when organized in combat units, black soldiers often carried inferior arms and equipment. Lincoln originally planned to use black troops to garrison forts, protect supply dumps and wagon trains, and perform rear-area duties, thereby releasing white regiments for front-line operations. Three considerations underlay this idea: (1) skepticism about whether blacks would make good combat soldiers; (2) a belief that freedmen were better acclimated to garrison duty in the deep South, where Northern soldiers suffered much sickness; and (3) rear-area duties would reduce the possibility of capture.

(U.S. Army Military History Institute)

(Reproduced from the Collections of the Library of Congress)

Black Sailors and Soldiers. The first photo (p. 352, top) shows the racially mixed crew of the Union gunboat *Hunchback,* which operated along the coastal rivers in Virginia and North Carolina. The second photo (p. 352, bottom) is of Co. E. of the 4th U. S. Colored Troops. The third (left) shows two black soldiers on picket duty posing for the photographer in a firing position.

(Reproduced from the Collections of the Library of Congress)

This last factor was a serious matter, for the Confederate government had threatened captured officers and men of black regiments with death or enslavement. In retaliation, Lincoln on July 30, 1863, issued an executive order stating that for every Union prisoner killed in violation of the laws of war a Rebel captive would be similarly executed, and for every Union soldier enslaved a Confederate prisoner would be placed at hard labor. This order had only part of the desired effect. The Confederacy did not execute captured officers of black regiments, and it generally treated captured blacks who had been free before the war as normal prisoners of war. But several instances occurred of the murder of black soldiers after their surrender in action, mostly notably at Fort Pillow, Tennessee, on April 12, 1864. A few captured freedmen were evidently executed, some were returned as slaves to their former masters, and some black captives were put to forced labor on Confederate fortifications. Because of the difficulty of obtaining accurate information on Southern treatment of black captives, the Lincoln administration did not implement eye-for-an-eye retaliation. The Confederacy also refused to exchange black prisoners, thereby bringing to a halt the prisoner exchange program and contributing to the tragic overcowding and high death rate of war prisoners in 1864 (for more on this, see pp. 450–456).

The substitution of black for white troops in fatigue, labor, and garrison duty helped win over white soldiers to the arming of blacks. But it also placed a stigma of inferiority on black regiments. The stereotype of the shuffling, banjo-strumming, happy-go-lucky darky caused many Northerners to doubt the martial potential of blacks. Even some abolitionists wondered whether slaves who had been conditioned all their lives to fear and obey whites would stand in battle against those same whites. Loyal Northerners "have generally become willing that [blacks] should fight," said the *New York Tribune* on May 1, 1863, "but the great majority have no faith that they will really do so. Many hope they will prove cowards and sneaks—others greatly fear it." Colonels of black regiments pleaded with generals to send them into combat to give the men a chance to prove themselves.

Black Soldiers in Combat

Two actions involving black troops in the Vicksburg campaign converted many white skeptics. On May 27 two Louisiana black regiments participated in an assault on Port Hudson, the Confederate stronghold downriver from Vicksburg. Although the assault was repulsed with heavy Union casualties, the courageous fighting of the black soldiers opened many Northern eyes. One white officer wrote: "You have no idea how my prejudices with regard to Negro troops have been dispelled by the battle the other day." The *New York Times* commented that this battle "settles the question that the negro race can fight." Eleven days later, newly organized contraband regiments at Milliken's Bend on the Mississippi above Vicksburg helped beat off a Confederate attempt to smash through Union defenses west of the river. "The bravery of the blacks in the battle at Milliken's Bend completely revolutionized the sentiment of the army with regard to the employment of negro troops," wrote the assistant secretary of war, who was with Grant's army. "I heard prominent officers who formerly in private had sneered at the idea of the negroes fighting express themselves after that as heartily in favor of it."[15]

Although blacks fought in several major actions during the next two years, they continued to do more garrison and fatigue duty and less fighting than white troops. This was reflected in the casualty rates of the two groups. Nearly 6 percent of white Union troops were killed in action, compared with 1.5 percent for black soldiers. On the other hand, the rate of death from disease among black troops (19 percent) was almost twice as high as among Northern white soldiers. As garrison troops, many black regiments had no chance for combat but suffered from the high disease rates typical of soldiers confined to one place, where their water supply turned foul and they built up deadly accumulations of bacteria. Black regiments also received poorer medical care than whites. There were few black surgeons to draw upon (only eight were commissioned), and white doctors were not notably eager to volunteer for black units.

By October 1863, fifty-eight black regiments had been organized. Much of the initial Northern opposition to them had faded. Indeed, Union recruiters in the occupied South sometimes used press-gang techniques to round up unwilling or bewildered contrabands and draft them into the army. In the North, even Irish Americans had come to see some advantages in black men stopping Rebel bullets that might otherwise come their way. This was the theme of a popular song by "Private Miles O'Reilly" (Irish-born journalist and army officer Charles G. Halpine) entitled "Sambo's Right to be Kilt":

> Some tell us 'tis a burnin shame
>   To make the naygers fight;
> An' that the thrade of bein' kilt
>   Belongs but to the white;
> But as for me, upon my soul!
>   So liberal are we here,
> I'll let Sambo be murthered instead of myself
>   On every day in the year.
>
> On every day in the year, boys,
>   And in every hour of the day;
> The right to be kilt I'll divide wid him,
>   An' divil a word I'll say.[16]

By 1864 the Democratic position on black soldiers had retreated to opposing equal pay, bounties, and status for them. The black man's only right, it seemed, was the right to be killed. At the prodding of abolitionists, congressional Republicans finally passed a bill in June 1864 to equalize the pay of white and black soldiers. But the opposition had forced some compromises in this legislation. To obtain conservative Republican support, congressional leaders had to accept a bill making equal pay retroactive only to January 1, 1864, except for blacks who had been free before the war; they would receive equal pay from the date of their enlistment. The legislation also failed to equalize federal bounties for soldiers who had been slaves. Other forms of discrimination also persisted to the war's end. Yet even with all of these injustices, the enrollment of 179,000 black soldiers (and perhaps as many as 10,000 black sailors) was of crucial significance for the future. By fighting for the Union, black men would help to achieve freedom for their race. By helping the North win the war, they would also help win equal citizenship for blacks after the war.

CONSCRIPTION IN THE NORTH

By early 1863 it had become clear that the North, like the South a year earlier (see pp. 181–182), would be compelled to adopt conscription. The militia draft of the previous fall had been the handwriting on the wall. The enlistment terms of the nine-month men recruited then (ninety regiments) would expire in mid-1863. The same was true of forty regiments of two-year men who had enlisted in 1861. Although some of these men could be expected to reenlist, scarcely any new recruits were coming forward. Therefore the Enrollment Act of March 3, 1863, made every able-bodied male citizen (plus aliens who had filed for naturalization) aged twenty to forty-five eligible for the draft.

Although ostensibly a conscription law, the real purpose of the Enrollment Act was to stimulate volunteering. Under the presidential calls for men that preceded each Union draft (July 1863 and March, July, and December 1864), the War Department assigned each congressional district a quota based on a percentage of its eligible males minus the number of men who had already served in the army. But each district was given fifty days to fill this quota with volunteers. Drafting would be resorted to for only the number of men short of the quota. State and local officials used all the means at their command to secure sufficient volunteers to escape the stigma of conscription.

The principal means of stimulating volunteering were bounties. In time, this became one of the worst evils of the Union's recruiting system (largely avoided in the South because the Confederacy, lacking money, relied more on compulsion than inducement*). As the supply of recruits dwindled, competition for volunteers compelled districts to raise the bidding. Wealthy districts enticed men away from their home districts to enlist where they could get the most money. In October 1863 the federal government got into the act with a $300 bounty for three-year volunteers. By 1864 it was possible for recruits in some districts to parlay federal, state, and local bounties into a total payment of more than $1,000. Northern governments paid out more than half a billion dollars in bounties during the war. A large number of "bounty brokers" sprang up to obtain recruits (and to take a share of their bounties as a commission). The system also generated a class of "bounty jumpers," who enlisted in one district, collected their bounty, deserted, and repeated the process somewhere else. Some recruits got away with this several times; one claimed to have done it thirty-two times.

Equally notorious were the practices of substitution and commutation. The Union draft law, unlike its Confederate counterpart, contained no provision for occupational exemptions. Only those who were medically unfit or the sole support of widows, indigent parents, orphan siblings, or motherless children were exempt. But the Northern law did follow the initial Confederate example of allowing a drafted man to provide a substitute. To prevent the price of substitutes from rising to astronomical heights as it had in the South, the law permitted a drafted man the alternative of paying a $300 commutation fee, which exempted him from that particular draft but not from future drafts.

Although the idea of buying oneself out of the draft seems shocking today, in 1863 it was sanctioned by long precedent. Inevitably, however, fraud and accusations of injustice became associated with these practices. "Substitute brokers" grew rich by collecting a percentage of the substitute's hire price. Collusion

---

*Several Southern states and counties offered small bounties, usually $50, to volunteers. The Confederate Congress authorized an additional $50 for three-year volunteers on December 11, 1861, and voted on February 17, 1864, to give every enlisted man a $100 bond.

between brokers and examining surgeons sent unfit recruits to the army. Veteran volunteers who were risking their lives resented a system that permitted others to buy their way out of the risk. These veterans often ostracized substitutes who joined their units. Officers reported mixed but mostly negative opinions of the soldierly qualities of substitutes, whose desertion rate appears to have been higher than average.

The commutation privilege also provoked resentment. Since few blue-collar workingmen could come up with $300 (at least half a year's wages), the system discriminated against them. As in the South earlier, the cry arose that it was a rich man's war and a poor man's fight. In response to growing protests, Congress in July 1864 abolished commutation except for conscientious objectors. But as opponents of this move had predicted, the price of substitutes immediately soared, and fewer poor men than before could afford to buy their way out of the draft.

The Civil War draft has generally been accounted a costly, sordid failure. Only 46,000 men were drafted directly into the Union army, and another 118,000 furnished substitutes. Taken together, these 164,000 men, along with several thousand from earlier militia drafts, constituted fewer than 10 percent of the Union soldiers. Thus conscription does indeed appear to have been a failure. But when one recalls that the real purpose of the draft was to stimulate volunteering, a different picture emerges. Nearly a million men enlisted or reenlisted voluntarily during the two years that the draft was in effect. Thus the most recent student of Union conscription has concluded that, with all its defects, the system worked.[17] But it worked with such creaking inefficiency and injustice that it became a model of how not to conduct a draft in future wars.

A SOCIOECONOMIC PROFILE OF CIVIL WAR SOLDIERS

Was the Civil War in fact a rich man's war and a poor man's fight? Data on the civilian occupations of Union and Confederate soldiers cast doubt on this popular notion. Table 20.1 (p. 359) compares the occupations of Union soldiers prior to their enlistment with the occupations of all males in the states from which the soldiers came.[18] At first glance the stereotype of a "poor man's fight" seems to be confirmed, for the white-collar and professional occupations appear to have been underrepresented in the army. But it should be remembered that most soldiers were young men (the median age was 24, and nearly two-fifths of the soldiers were 21 or younger at the time of enlistment), whereas the 1860 occupational profile represents men of *all* ages. Studies of occupational mobility in nineteenth-century America have shown that a substantial number of young men starting out as laborers or farm laborers moved into the white-collar or professional classes later in life. When this is taken into account, the Union army appears to have been quite representative of the Northern population. If anything, unskilled laborers were underrepresented—partly because of the underrepresentation of Irish Americans, which is discussed below.

Occupational data on Confederate soldiers are scanty. The only scholar to study this subject has been Bell Wiley, who drew a sample of 9,057 men from the company rolls of regiments from seven states. The results are presented in Table 20.2. From this sample it appears that unskilled laborers were underrepresented in the Confederate army, while the white-collar and particularly the professional categories were, given the youth of soldiers, proportionally overrepresented.

Unless the farmers who enlisted in both armies were poorer than those who stayed home (which from other evidence seems unlikely, despite the notorious but statistically unimportant "20-Negro" draft exemption in the Confederacy), these occupational samples indicate that in neither North nor South was it especially a poor man's fight.

Another long-lived Civil War myth is that the Yankees recruited an army of "foreigners" to do their fighting. "Yankees indeed!" said an indignant Southern woman to a New York officer in 1864. "Your whole army is made up of Irish, Dutch, and negroes." The *Richmond Examiner* declared that the Union army was composed mainly of "the riff-raff of Germany and Ireland." Nearly a century later a Southern historian still insisted that "the majority of Yankee soldiers were foreign hirelings."[19]

But the facts are quite different. Of the 2,100,000 men in the Union army and navy, an estimated 500,000 (24 percent) were foreign-born and 190,000 (9 percent) were black. Not only did immigrants constitute a minority of the Northern soldiers, but they were actually underrepresented in proportion to their share of the male population of military age. While 26 percent of the white soldiers in the Union army were foreign-born, 31 percent of the white males of military age residing in the Union states had been born abroad. One possible explanation for this underrepresentation of immigrants is that nondeclarant aliens were not subject to the draft, so immigrants who had not yet filed for citizenship were free from the compulsion of conscription. The data we have indicate that two of the four principal ethnic groups among the foreign-born—the British and German Protestants—enlisted in proportion to their percentage of the male population, but that the Irish and German Catholics did not. The reason for this may have been the overwhelming commitment of Catholics to the Democratic party and their opposition to what became an increasingly Republican and antislavery war.[20]

Since 90 percent of the foreign-born lived in the states that remained in the Union, the number and proportion of immigrants were of course much greater in the Union army than in the Confederate army. But the widely held belief that "with very few exceptions" Confederate regiments were "composed exclusively of native-born Americans" is also a myth. The careful scholarship of Ella Lonn has yielded data indicating that 9 or 10 percent of the Confederate soldiers were foreign-born. Since only 7½ percent of the males of military age in the South were immigrants, this means that the foreign-born were proportionately overrepresented in the Southern armies in contrast to their underrepresentation in the Northern forces.[21] The reason for this is not clear. It may be related to the higher percentage of substitutes in the Confederate army, who were drawn partly from

Table 20.1

PREVIOUS OCCUPATIONS OF SAMPLES OF WHITE UNION SOLDIERS
COMPARED WITH 1860 OCCUPATIONS OF ALL MALES IN UNION
STATES FROM WHICH THE SOLDIERS CAME

Occupational Categories	Union Soldiers (U.S. Sanitary Commission Sample)	Union Soldiers (Bell Wiley Sample)	All Males (From 1860 Census)
Farmers and farm laborers	47.5%	47.8%	42.9%
Skilled laborers	25.1	25.2	24.9
Unskilled laborers	15.9	15.1	16.7
White-collar and commercial	5.1	7.8	10.0
Professional	3.2	2.9	3.5
Miscellaneous and Unknown	3.2	1.2	2.0

Table 20.2

PREVIOUS OCCUPATIONS OF CONFEDERATE SOLDIERS FROM
ALABAMA, ARKANSAS, GEORGIA, LOUISIANA, MISSISSIPPI, NORTH
CAROLINA, VIRGINIA COMPARED WITH 1860 OCCUPATIONS OF
WHITE MALES IN THESE STATES

Occupational Categories	Confederate Soldiers	White Males (From 1860 Census)
Planters, farmers, and farm laborers	61.5%	57.5%
Skilled laborers	14.1	15.7
Unskilled laborers	8.5	12.7
White-collar and commercial	7.0	8.3
Professional	5.2	5.0
Miscellaneous and Unknown	3.7	.8

the immigrant aliens not subject to the draft, and partly to the South's failure to
use black soldiers, whose enlistment in the Union army reduced the pressure on
the foreign-born manpower pool.

DRAFT RESISTANCE AND RIOTS IN THE NORTH

Although the poor and the foreign-born did not bear a disproportionate burden of the fighting, the social and psychological impact of conscription fell most heavily on these groups. The Union draft became a catalyst for Democratic and ethnocultural opposition to the war. Democratic newspapers and politicians whipped up anti-draft sentiment. The prospect of being drafted into a war to free the slaves was doubly infuriating to the Negrophobic Democratic constituency. Antidraft protests in some cities flared into violence. Armed bands in several Butternut districts of the Midwest attacked and murdered draft officials.

The twin sparks of antidraft and antiblack discontent set off a major explosion in New York City. Rioting began on July 13, 1863. Mobs of Irish workingmen and women roamed the streets, burned the draft office, sacked and burned the homes of prominent Republicans, and tried unsuccessfully to demolish the *New York Tribune* building. The mob's chief target was the black population. Chanting "kill the naygers," they lynched at least a dozen blacks and burned down the Colored Orphan Asylum. Because most of the militia had gone to Pennsylvania for the Gettysburg campaign, the city was especially vulnerable to the snowballing violence. On the fourth day of rioting, the police and several regiments of soldiers that had been rushed to New York from Pennsylvania finally brought the city under control. Units from the Army of the Potomac shot down rioters as coolly as they had shot down Rebels at Gettysburg two weeks earlier. The toll of the riot was staggering. Contemporary estimates of the number killed ranged up to 1,200, but recent research has scaled this down to about 120, most of them rioters killed by police and troops. It was the worst riot in American history. It vividly exposed the complex racial, ethnic, and class tensions that lay close to the surface of American society.

One result of the riot was a renewed surge of anti-Irish feeling among middle- and upper-class New Yorkers. This was in turn part of a general wave of revulsion against Peace Democrats in the months after July 1863. Even non-Copperhead Democrats were caught in this backlash. Governor Seymour's reputation suffered most. Rushing to the city on the second day of violence, he had tried to calm the rioters with a speech in which he began by addressing them as "my friends." Republican newspapers never let him forget this slip. Indeed, many Northerners considered Seymour responsible for having inspired the riot with his speeches denouncing emancipation and conscription.

After the antidraft violence in New York and elsewhere had died down, the draft went forward. Although Northern war weariness and defeatism would once again produce a rise in Copperhead prospects in the summer of 1864, never again would the Peace Democrats be as strong as they were in the spring of 1863. Even before the New York riots, antiwar sentiment had begun to decline in most parts of the North because of the Union successes at Gettysburg and Vicksburg. Northern attitudes toward emancipation and black people also turned a corner in a positive direction in July 1863, not least because of the contribution of black regiments to the Union cause.

EMANCIPATION CONFIRMED

On July 18, two days after the New York draft riots had subsided, two Union brigades assaulted a Confederate earthwork known as Fort Wagner, guarding the entrance to Charleston harbor. Part of an unsuccessful campaign to capture Charleston, the attack was beaten back with heavy loss. This was hardly unusual in Civil War battles. What made this attack unique, however, was that it was led by a black regiment, the 54th Massachusetts. The courageous fighting of the 54th and its long casualty list made the regiment famous. Coming only days after white rioters had marched through New York City attacking blacks, this example of black soldiers giving their lives for the Union could not have been more dramatic. Every Republican newspaper drew the obvious moral: black men who fought for the Union were more deserving of rights than white men who rioted against it. This battle "made Fort Wagner such a name to the colored race as Bunker Hill had been for ninety years to the white Yankees," observed the *New York Tribune*. "Through the cannon smoke of that dark night," said the *Atlantic Monthly*, "the manhood of the colored race shines before many eyes that would not see."[22]

Until July 1863 the proponents of emancipation and black soldiers had been on the defensive. Now they could go over to the offensive, just in time for the vital state elections to be held in the fall of 1863. Radical editors and orators spoke with a new tone of boldness and pride. No longer was emancipation a political liability. No longer was it to be defended only as a military necessity. Republicans now championed it as a long-delayed revolution of justice and right. The theme of heroic black soldiers and cowardly Copperhead traitors became a staple of Republican rhetoric. Lincoln himself set the tone in a public letter on August 26 that became an important document in the forthcoming political campaign. Addressing the foes of emancipation, the President wrote:

> You say you will not fight to free negroes. Some of them seem willing to fight for you. . . . Some of the commanders of our armies in the field who have given us our most important successes, believe the emancipation policy, and the use of colored troops, constitute the heaviest blow yet dealt to the rebellion.* . . . [When final victory is achieved] there will be some black men who can remember that, with silent tongue, and clenched teeth, and steady eye, and well-poised bayonet, they have helped mankind on to this great consummation; while, I fear, there will be some white ones, unable to forget that, with malignant heart, and deceitful speech, they have strove to hinder it.[23]

Although some Peace Democrats dimly perceived the changed current of Northern opinion, they still tried to swim in the same old direction. In the words of a Democratic newspaper headline, their platform for the 1863 fall elections was:

---

*This was a reference to a letter from Grant to Lincoln on August 23: "I have given the subject of arming the negro my hearty support. This, with the emancipation of the negro, is the heaviest blow yet given the Confederacy. . . . By arming the negro we have added a powerful ally. They will make good soldiers and taking them from the enemy weakens him in the same proportion they strengthen us." (Lincoln Papers, Library of Congress.)

"No Abolitionism, No Emancipation, No Negro Equality." Democratic campaign speakers rang all the changes on the "nigger-worshipping Republican party." Young girls at party rallies in Ohio carried banners bearing the slogan: "Father, save us from Negro Equality."[24]

The most important fall elections were those in Ohio and Pennsylvania. All eyes focused on Ohio, where the exiled Clement Vallandigham directed his campaign for governor from Windsor, Canada. The Democratic gubernatorial candidate in Pennsylvania was State Supreme Court Justice George E. Woodward, a Copperhead sympathizer. These elections, and less publicized contests elsewhere, became virtual referendums on Lincoln's war policies. The President was "nervous" about the outcome, according to Gideon Welles. "He told me that he had more anxiety in regard to the election results . . . than he had in 1860 when he was chosen."[25] His anxiety was soon dispelled. The elections proved to be a ringing endorsement of the administration. Republicans swept the board everywhere, especially in Ohio, where Vallandigham went down to a crushing defeat by more than 100,000 votes. The Republicans won three-fourths of the seats in the next Ohio legislature. Even in Horatio Seymour's New York, the Republicans carried nearly two-thirds of the legislative districts.

As in the spring elections, the soldier vote was important for Republicans. Several states had arranged for their soldiers to cast absentee ballots. In addition, the War Department had again furloughed home thousands of soldiers to states that did not permit absentee voting, especially Pennsylvania and New York. While this temporarily weakened the Army of the Potomac, the administration considered political victory well worth the military risk. The fighting men voted 92 percent for the Republican candidates (compared with 56 percent of the "home voters"). Ohio soldiers cast only 5 percent of their ballots for Vallandigham.[26] The soldier vote seemed to confirm the Republican thesis that patriotism equaled Republicanism.

The 1863 fall elections advanced the cause of emancipation. If the Emancipation Proclamation had been submitted to a referendum a year earlier, said an Illinois newspaper in December 1863, "there is little doubt that the voice of a majority would have been against it. And yet not a year has passed before it is approved by an overwhelming majority." Early in 1864, an upper-class New Yorker wrote that "the change of opinion on this slavery question since 1860 is a great historical fact. . . . Who could have predicted it? . . . God pardon our blindness of three years ago." In his annual message to Congress in December 1863, Lincoln admitted that the Emancipation Proclamation had been followed by "dark and doubtful days." But since the fall elections "the crisis which threatened to divide the friends of the Union is past."[27]

One sign of this change was the growing prestige of abolitionists. After crying in the wilderness for so many years, they suddenly found themselves prophets with honor. Contrasting the mobs that had attacked abolitionists in 1860 with the cheers that greeted them now, the *New York Tribune* observed: "It is not often that history presents such violent contrasts in such rapid succession." The veteran abolitionist Lewis Tappan reflected that "all true reformers have been ridiculed

& despised in their own day. We are coming out of the slanderous valley sooner than most reformers have done, for we have lived to hear old opponents say, 'I was wrong.' "[28]

Perhaps the best comment on 1863 as the *annus mirabilis* was an entry in the diary of a Baltimore free black: "This year has brought about many changes that at the beginning were or would have been thought impossible. The close of the year finds me a soldier for the cause of my race. May God bless the cause, and enable me in the coming year to forward it on."[29]

POLITICAL DISAFFECTION WITHIN THE CONFEDERACY

If the events of the latter half of 1863 boosted the cause of Union and emancipation in the North, they intensified the long-festering bitterness of political divisiveness in the South.

The Old South had been as proud of its political leadership as of its military prowess. The section that had produced Washington, Jefferson, Madison, Jackson, Calhoun, and Clay (born in Virginia) was confident that its statesmen as well as its soldiers would put the Yankees to shame. With such high expectations, the reality of mediocre political leadership came as a shock to many Southerners. In no other sphere except the mobilization of economic resources was Northern superiority so clear as in the mobilization of political leadership. The example of state governors is instructive. Several governors in the South proved more obstructive than constructive, in sharp contrast to the energizing role of Northern governors, especially Andrew of Massachusetts, Morton of Indiana, and Curtin of Pennsylvania.

The Confederate Congress also made few positive contributions to the war effort. Much of its legislation was too little and too late. An outstanding example was the failure to pass a comprehensive tax measure until halfway through the war. Some important laws were repealed or amended so often that confusion reigned and enforcement became impossible. Congressmen expended much time and energy in grandiloquent or billingsgate oratory, procedural details, and personal quarrels. Both houses met often in secret session and published no record of their debates. This produced exaggerated and disquieting rumors of what went on behind the closed doors. But Vice President Stephens said sarcastically that perhaps it was best Congress met in secret session "and so kept from the public some of the most disgraceful scenes ever enacted by a legislative body."[30]

Many of these "disgraceful scenes" resulted from the oversized Southern sense of honor and penchant for violence. Two of the Confederacy's most famous politicians, Benjamin Hill of Georgia and William L. Yancey of Alabama, became embroiled in a name-calling Senate debate one day in 1863 that ended with Hill throwing an ink bottle at Yancey, cutting open his cheek. Congressman Henry S. Foote of Tennessee had several fights with other congressmen in which he brandished a variety of weapons, including his fists, an umbrella, a bowie knife, and a revolver. In April 1863, the journal clerk of the House shot and killed the chief clerk in Richmond's capitol square. To make matters worse, the public drunkenness of several congressmen became a notorious feature of Richmond life. "Some malign influence seems to preside over your councils," wrote an influential South Carolinian to Robert M. T. Hunter, president pro tem of the Senate, in 1863. "Pardon me, is the majority always drunk? The People are beginning to think so."[31] By 1863 the reputation of Congress had sunk to a low point from which it never recovered.

Having been schooled for decades in the tactics of obstruction when the South was part of the United States, Confederate politicians found it hard to shed old habits. After a visit to Richmond in 1863, an Alabamian concluded that "many men who were highly gifted in tearing down the old government are worth but little in building up a new one."[32] Then, too, the army rather than Congress attracted many of the Confederacy's ablest leaders. Several members of the Confederate constitutional convention and the provisional Congress went into the army in 1861. Less experienced men took their places. Fewer than one-third of the Confederate lawmakers had previously served in the U.S. Congress. By way of comparison, more than half the members of the wartime Union Congresses had served there before.

The Confederate cabinet also suffered from the greater attractiveness of military service. Two of Davis's initial choices for cabinet posts declined the appointments to accept a brigadier's commission instead. Two others resigned from the cabinet in 1861 to put on a uniform. Except for Judah P. Benjamin, who was successively attorney general, secretary of war, and secretary of state, the Confederate cabinet contained no men equal in ability and stature to Seward, Chase, Stanton, and Welles in Lincoln's cabinet. Critics of the Davis administration described the cabinet as a "farce" or a "ridiculous cipher." These descriptions were unjust. Nevertheless, the cabinet was a relatively undistinguished body that, like Congress, contributed little toward solving the Confederacy's pressing problems. High turnover hindered administrative efficiency. Sixteen different men served in the six cabinet posts, compared with twelve men in the seven positions of the Union cabinet. The Confederacy had five secretaries of war and three secretaries of state, compared with the Union's two and one in these vital offices.

Criticism of Jefferson Davis

Southern criticisms of Congress and the cabinet were as nothing compared with the abuse heaped on Jefferson Davis. The president was a "false and hypocritical . . . wretch," wrote the powerful Robert Toombs. A prominent Mississippian considered Davis "a miserable, stupid, one-eyed, dyspeptic, arrogant tyrant."[33] Davis's most bitter enemies were Georgians, especially vice president Alexander Stephens and his half brother Linton. "Mr. Davis is *mad,* infatuated," wrote Linton Stephens. "He is a *little, conceited, hypocritical, snivelling, canting, malicious, ambitious, dogged* knave and fool." Although Alexander Stephens considered Davis "weak and vacillating, timid, petulant, peevish, obstinate," he claimed to have "no more feeling of resentment toward him" than toward "my poor old blind and deaf dog." Modern historians avoid such vitriolic criticisms. But some of them agree with David M. Potter, who wrote that Davis's leadership constituted "a record of personal failure significant enough to have had a bearing on the course of the war. . . . If the Union and Confederacy had exchanged presidents with one another, the Confederacy might have won its independence."[34]

But no single person can be made to bear such a load of blame for Confederate defeat. Many of the South's wartime problems were beyond the president's control. Nevertheless, it is true that Davis had important defects as a leader. Austere, humorless, wracked by pain from neuralgia and dyspepsia that grew worse as wartime pressures mounted, he often offended others with ill-tempered, biting remarks. He had a knack for making enemies. As an administrator, he wasted time and energy on minor details. He held long cabinet meetings that "from his uncontrollable tendency to digression," wrote Secretary of the Navy Mallory, "consumed four or five hours without determining anything; while the desk of every chief of a Department was covered with papers demanding his attention."[35] A West Point graduate whose first ambition had been to command the Confederate armies, Davis tried to run the War Department himself. Two of the five secretaries of war went to Davis "for instructions about every little matter";[36] another resigned after Davis reversed a decision about which the secretary had *not* consulted the president. Unlike Lincoln, Davis was more concerned with proving himself right than with getting results. He was unable to admit mistakes, and he lacked Lincoln's ability to work with critics and with those who disagreed about the best means toward a common end. Davis also lacked Lincoln's political acumen, his common touch, his talent for communicating with all classes of people, and his eloquence in defining the purpose and meaning of the war.

Significant opposition to Davis did not surface until the second year of the war. Basking in the aftermath of victory at Bull Run, the administration enjoyed smooth sailing in the latter half of 1861. Organized political parties had disappeared during the secession crisis. With a common concern for unity against the Yankees, Southern Democrats and Whigs by mutual consent did not revive their party organizations. No candidates opposed Davis and Stephens in the November 1861 presidential election. Congressional candidates in this election ran without opposition in many districts. The campaign generated no issues, and voting was light. When Davis took the oath of office during a rainstorm on February 22, 1862 (until then he had been provisional president), the government still presented a facade of nonpartisan unity.

But that rainstorm would prove to be an omen of things to come. Military reverses and policy actions provoked the emergence of an antiadministration faction in the spring of 1862. Forts Henry and Donelson and Roanoke Island had fallen to blue armies just before Davis was inaugurated. On the day after the inauguration, Nashville surrendered to the Federals. New Orleans, Memphis, and most of Tennessee soon followed. Davis's own Mississippi plantation was taken over by the Yankees. Inflation was beginning to tighten its fatal grip on the Southern economy. Congress enacted the unpopular Conscription Act in April.

Jefferson Davis
*(Reproduced from the
Collections of the Library of
Congress)*

Even more controversial was a law passed on February 27, 1862, which authorized the president to suspend the writ of *habeas corpus.*

HABEAS CORPUS AND STATES' RIGHTS IN THE CONFEDERACY

In 1861 some Confederate military commanders, like their Union counterparts, arrested civilians for disloyal activities and refused to surrender them to the courts when presented with writs of *habeas corpus.* The Davis administration neither sanctioned nor disavowed these acts. Faced with Grant's invasion of Tennessee and McClellan's imminent invasion of Virginia in February 1862, the Confederate Congress empowered Davis to suspend the writ "in such cities, towns and military districts as shall, in his judgment, be in such danger of attack by the enemy as to require the declaration of martial law for their effective defence."[37] Davis thereupon proclaimed martial law in several parts of the Confederacy. Southern generals in some western districts did the same on their own authority. Davis rebuked them and revoked their actions, but in the crisis of invasion and battle in the West, orders of revocation from Richmond carried little weight. In August 1862, General Bragg even proclaimed martial law in Atlanta, far from the battlefront, because of its importance as a transport and supply center.

These actions aroused cries of protest from Southerners who feared that "military despotism" would undermine the constitutional liberties they were fighting for. "Away with the idea of getting independence first, and looking for liberty afterwards," said vice president Stephens. "Our liberties, once lost, may be lost forever." Stephens urged state governors to "denounce and condemn the wicked act." Joseph Brown of Georgia was the first to do so, calling the suspension of civil liberties "high-handed usurpation."[38]

Because of such protests, Congress allowed the law to expire in February 1863. During the next year, several state judges issued writs to release men charged with desertion, disloyalty, or draft evasion. This made it impossible for Confederate officials in some areas to enforce conscription. The situation became desperate following the defeats at Vicksburg, Gettysburg, and Chattanooga. Desertion increased, and secret Unionist societies became more bold in upcountry districts. In February 1864, Congress complied with Davis's pleas for a new act to suspend *habeas corpus* but specified that the law would expire on July 31.

Davis possessed the authority to suspend the writ of *habeas corpus* for a total period of only eighteen months. And he used the authority more sparingly than Lincoln, who unlike the Confederate president had exercised this power for nearly two years before obtaining congressional sanction for it in March 1863. Nevertheless, this issue stirred up at least as much antiadministration rancor in the Confederacy as in the Union. Along with conscription and the impressment of supplies, it fueled the emergence of opposition factions that hindered the government's effectiveness in the last half of the war.

Opposition Leaders

Although every state contained antiadministration spokesmen, opposition centered in North Carolina and especially in Georgia. Governor Zebulon Vance of North Carolina was jealous of his state's prerogatives. He quarreled with the administration over everything—from the appointment of generals from North Carolina to the use of cargo space on state-owned blockade runners. In Georgia a trio of powerful politicians—Toombs, Stephens, and Brown—evolved into the most outspoken antiadministration bloc. Disappointed at his failure to be elected president of the Confederacy, Toombs had tried the army without much success. He resigned his brigadier's commission in March 1863 and thereafter became a bitter critic of Davis. Vice president Stephens left Richmond in 1862 and rarely returned during the rest of the war, preferring to remain in Georgia and snipe at every measure that increased Jefferson Davis's "dictatorial power." Governor Brown was a political maverick whose growing dislike of "centralizing" war measures drove him to obstructive resistance.

Whatever their motives, opponents of Davis cloaked their opposition in the rhetorical garb of states' rights. "My position is the position of the old State Rights leaders from the days of 1798 to the present," wrote Brown in 1862. "I entered into this revolution to contribute my mite to sustain the rights of states and prevent the consolidation of the Government, and I am still a rebel till this object is accomplished, no matter who may be in power."[39] States' rights was such a deeply ingrained principle in the South that even the demands of total war could not fully overcome it. Jefferson Davis, Robert E. Lee, and other Confederate leaders who urged the necessity of conscription, martial law, and other centralizing measures put realism above ancient principle. But Stephens and his associates were unwilling to do so. As the plight of the Confederacy grew worse in the final years of the war, political dissension increased. Instead of pulling together in the face of crisis, the Confederacy pulled apart.

THE DISADVANTAGES OF NO-PARTY POLITICS

The Lincoln administration also confronted strong opposition, which grew more powerful during periods of military defeat. But a vital difference in the structure of Union and Confederate politics tempered Northern divisiveness: the North had political parties, the South did not. The absence of parties in the South paradoxically produced an opposition that became unmanageable precisely *because* it was nonpartisan. Without the institution of parties, the opposition became personal, factional, and sometimes irresponsible. Under the Confederate constitution, Davis was ineligible for reelection, so he had no motive to create a party organization. In the absence of a party with its ties of loyalty, patronage, and self-interest, Davis had no institutional means to rally support for his policies. The November 1863 congressional elections were conducted on a nonpartisan basis. The record of the Davis administration was the major issue, but candidates announced for or against government policies on an individual, not a party basis. Instead of being channeled through an identifiable organization, the opposition came from every direction and was difficult to counter. Openly antiadministration candidates scored significant gains in the congressional elections, though they fell short of gaining control of the House by about fifteen seats and of the Senate by two seats. But while the Davis administration preserved a narrow majority in Congress, the lack of a party organization made it hard to mobilize that majority.

In the North, by contrast, Lincoln was the leader of a vigorous, well-organized party. Moreover, the existence of an equally well organized opposition served to unify the Republicans on crucial issues. While Lincoln faced criticism from radical Republicans, the momentum of the war pushed moderates toward the radical policies of emancipation and total war, uniting the party in elections and in important congressional votes. Nearly all the Northern state governors were Republicans, which created ties of loyalty and mutual interest between the states and the national government.

By 1863, the economic impact of the war had augmented Northern strengths and exacerbated Southern weaknesses. The Confederacy was losing the war on the home front as well as on the battlefront.

Twenty-one

Behind the Lines

THE ECONOMIC IMPACT OF THE WAR IN THE NORTH

Union military and diplomatic successes in 1863 were matched by a booming economy. As the South grew weaker from invasion and destruction, the North grew stronger from the stimulus of war production and victory. "It was a favorite theory of the rebel leaders, at the beginning of the rebellion, that the withdrawal of Southern trade from the North would . . . 'make grass grow in the streets of New York,' "* commented the *New York Sun* toward the war's end. But the "vast increase of Northern and military trade" more than made up for the loss of Southern business. "There never was a time in the history of New York when business prosperity was more general . . . than within the last two or three years."[1]

Agriculture

The war record of Northern agriculture was especially impressive. American wheat production had increased 73 percent during the decade 1849–1859. Yet despite secession of the South and disruption in the loyal border states, the Union states grew more wheat in 1862 and again in 1863 than the entire country had grown in the previous record year of 1859. Corn production also increased in the North-

---

*This had indeed been a Southern theory. Several Southern newspapers in June 1861 had reprinted an editorial from the *Louisville Courier* entitled "Grass in Their Streets." One person claimed to have seen grass actually growing in a busy New York street. Others described New York's "silent streets, the deserted hotels. . . . The glory of the once-proud metropolis is gone . . . for the trade of the South will never return. . . . Gotham must fall." (*Richmond Daily Examiner*, June 4, July 16, 1861, quoted in Rembert Patrick, *Jefferson Davis and His Cabinet* [Baton Rouge, 1944], pp. 17–19.)

ern states to above prewar levels. Because of crop failures in western Europe from 1860 to 1862, American exports of wheat, corn, pork, and beef actually doubled during the war, even as the Union army consumed more food per man than any previous army in history.

The unique achievement of increasing exports during an internal war occurred while one-third of the normal farm labor force was absent in the army. The expanded use of machinery in Northern agriculture made this possible. The 1850s had been a decade of rapid mechanization in grain farming, and the production of reapers and mowers tripled during the war. The addition of a self-raking device to many reapers represented a further labor-saving advance. Reapers, mowers, and other implements enabled women and children to make up for the absence of their menfolk at the front. "Yesterday I saw the wife of one of our parishioners driving the team in a reaper; her husband is at Vicksburg," wrote an Illinois clergyman in 1863. Another observer wrote:

> So perfect is machinery that men seem to be of less necessity. . . . We have seen, within the past few weeks, a stout matron whose sons are in the army, with her team cutting hay. . . . She cut seven acres with ease in a day, riding leisurely upon her cutter. This circumstance is indicative of the great revolution which machinery is making in production.[2]

"Revolution" was not quite the right word to describe farm mechanization. Rather it was a war-induced *acceleration* of prewar modernizing trends. The same things were happening in other aspects of food production and processing. Canned fruits and vegetables and condensed milk had made their first appearance before the war. But the needs of the Union armies gave these industries a crucial boost. The output of canned fruits and vegetables grew from five million to thirty million cans in the 1860s. Gail Borden had established his first condensed milk plant in 1859. Army contracts enabled him to expand production to 17,000 quarts per month by the summer of 1862. A year later, his plants were producing this much each day.[3]

Transportation

The transport sector of the economy performed almost as well as agriculture. All forms of internal water transport increased in volume, despite the closing of the Mississippi in the early part of the war. Heavy military traffic moved on the river networks above Vicksburg to support Union armies in the western theater. The east-west Great Lakes and canal traffic continued to grow, especially with the large grain shipments destined for armies in the eastern theater and for export. The Erie Canal carried 54 percent more tonnage annually during the war than in the 1850s. This growth of internal water commerce plus the demands of the Union navy caused a boom in shipbuilding, even though Confederate commerce raiders drove most of the merchant marine off the high seas. The United States built almost twice as much merchant tonnage in the four war years as in the previous four years of peace. The 1864 total was not exceeded until 1908.[4]

Rolling Stock of the U. S. Military Railroads at Alexandria, Virginia
(Reproduced from the original in the Henry E. Huntington Library and Art Gallery.)

Large as it was, the wartime expansion of water transport was outstripped by the railroads. The railroad construction boom of the 1850s had produced excess capacity, especially west of the Alleghenies; but the demands of war soon pushed the railroads to and beyond their capacity. Several Northern roads doubled their traffic volume between 1860 and 1865. Some also doubled their earnings. A few paid dividends for the first time. Of all major Northern railroads, only the Baltimore and Ohio was vulnerable to enemy destruction. But even the B&O benefited from increased wartime traffic.

Heavy war traffic compelled the double tracking of busy corridors, the building of new bridges across several rivers, the standardization of gauges or the adding of a third rail or extra car wheels so that frieght could be shipped across lines of different gauges without transloading, and the construction of union terminals to avoid delays in transferring freight or passengers across a city from one railroad to another. Much of the pressure for such improvements came from the government. In January 1862, Congress authorized the President to take control of any railroad "when in his judgment the public safety may require it." Although Lincoln rarely invoked this authority, its existence provided an inducement for railroads to give priority to military traffic. The government made heavy demands on the four different railroads in the corridor between Washington and New York. These companies double tracked much of their line and connected their tracks through Philadelphia in 1863. Nevertheless, the New York–Washington corridor remained something of a bottleneck throughout the war. Although several Northern officials talked of building a government-owned through line there, nothing came of the idea.

But in the occupied South, the War Department went into the railroad business in a big way. The United States Military Railroads, created in February 1862, began life with a few miles of line in northern Virginia. As invading Union armies lengthened their supply lines, the USMRR took over additional captured Southern railroads and built new ones. By war's end the USMRR was operating 2,105 miles of track with 419 engines and 6,330 cars, making it the largest railroad in the world at that time.

Industry

While the war stimulated the transport sector of the economy, its impact on Northern industry was uneven. The largest single industry, cotton textiles, suffered a 74 percent decline in output because of the war-created cotton famine. This was only partly offset by the woollen industry's doubling of production. The second largest consumer industry, shoe manufacturing, was hit hard by loss of its Southern market, though army contracts soon filled much of the gap. Loss of the Southern market also injured other industries in the first year or two of fighting, until war production brought a boom in 1863–1864. Iron production dropped by 14 percent in the first two years of war but by 1864 had reached a level for the Union states alone 29 percent higher than for the entire country in the previous record year of 1856. Coal production dropped in 1861 before rising to a new high in later years, so that the output of Northern coal mines alone was 21 percent greater during 1861–1865 than that of Northern and Southern mines combined during 1856–1860. Other war-related industries—firearms, gunpowder, leather (for horse and mule harnesses), copper (for rifle percussion caps), wagon building, and others —grew rapidly from the beginning of the war. These industries helped the manufacturing index for the Union states alone to rise by 1864 to a level 13 percent higher than that for the country as a whole in 1860.

The war also accelerated the spread of mechanization and the factory system. As one of the first American industries to adopt the principle of machine-made interchangeable parts a half century earlier, firearms production was capable of rapid expansion during the war despite shortages of skilled workers. The experiences of two other Northern industries illustrate how the war quickened the trend toward mechanization. The invention of the sewing machine had established the ready-made clothing business by the 1850s. But the sudden wartime demand for army uniforms acted as a catalyst for further mechanization and standardization. The number of sewing machines doubled between 1860 and 1865. The War Department furnished clothing manufacturers with a series of graduated measurements for soldiers. This led to the concept of standard "sizes" for uniforms and, after the war, for civilian clothes. The war also accelerated the application of new technology to the production of shoes. A generation earlier, the making of shoes had begun to move from the small shop to the factory. The adaptation of the sewing machine to leather had accelerated this process in the 1850s, and in 1858 a Massachusetts inventor, Lyman Blake, had patented an improved machine to sew the uppers to soles. The war created a market for Blake's invention because the old method of hand sewing was too slow for filling army contracts, especially since many skilled shoemakers had joined the army. In 1862 the Massachusetts entrepreneur Gordon McKay purchased and improved Blake's patent and began selling the machines to shoe manufacturers. By the end of 1863 these machines had stitched two and a half million shoes.

The Civil War and Economic Growth

These and other war-fueled changes in the Northern economy prompted an earlier generation of historians to proclaim that the Civil War launched the industrial revolution in America. This was part of what Charles and Mary Beard meant when they labeled the Civil War "the Second American Revolution." But in recent decades economic historians have attacked this thesis on two fronts. They have argued that (1) the basic innovations that produced economic modernization had taken place from the 1820s to the 1850s, and while the war may have accelerated some of these trends it produced no fundamental changes of direction; and (2) the decade of the 1860s witnessed an actual slowing of the rate of economic growth and therefore the war may have retarded rather than promoted industrialization.[5]

The first of these arguments is persuasive. The transportation revolution, the factory, the American system of mass production, and most of the technological innovations of nineteenth-century industrialization antedated the war. Clearly, then, the Civil War did not *begin* the modernization of the American economy. The war was a triumph for modernization, but not a cause of it.

The second argument also appears valid at first glance. By most statistical indexes, the rate of American economic growth was lower in the 1860s than in any other decade between 1840 and 1930. The commodity output of the American economy increased 51 percent in the 1840s, 62 percent in the 1850s, 62 percent in the 1870s, 63 percent in the 1880s, and 36 percent in the 1890s—but only 22 percent in the 1860s. Output per capita actually decreased by 3 percent in the 1860s, compared with an average decennial increase of 20 percent in the other five decades. Value added by manufacture increased only 25 percent during the 1860s, compared with a decennial average increase of 94 percent for the rest of the nineteenth century after 1839. Agricultural output grew 15 percent in the 1860s, compared with a 35 percent average growth for the other decades. Only 1,000 miles per year of new railroad were built during the war, compared with an annual average of 3,000 miles for the rest of the period from 1850 to 1873. Taken together, these statistics, according to a leading economic historian, "support a conclusion that the Civil War retarded American industrial growth."[6]

But the statistics in the foregoing paragraph include the South. Given the war's enormous destruction of resources, productive capacity, and consumer buying power in the South, it is hardly surprising that the 1860s were a decade of low growth for the country as a whole. While the Union states experienced a high growth rate during the war, economic dislocation in the Confederacy more than counterbalanced that growth. The accelerated growth rate after the war reflected in part the rebuilding of the shattered Southern economy and represented a catching-up process after the lag of the 1860s. Between 1840 and 1860, the per capita commodity output of the American economy had increased an average of 1.45 percent annually. After the slight decline of the 1860s, the per capita growth rate between 1870 and 1880 averaged 2.6 percent a year. After 1880 the rate dropped to under 2 percent again. Thus the per capita output of the American economy in 1880 stood at the same level as if the 1840–1860 rate had steadily continued and the Civil War had never occurred.[7]

In a statistical sense, then, the war neither accelerated nor retarded the long-term growth rate. But it did radically alter the sectional distribution of wealth and output. In 1860 the per capita wealth of white Southerners had been 95 percent higher than that of Northern whites; by 1870 Northern per capita wealth was 44 percent greater than that of Southern whites. In 1860 the per capita commodity output (including agriculture) of North and South had been about equal; by 1870 the North's per capita output was 56 percent greater than the South's. In 1860 the South's share of national wealth had been 30 percent; by 1870 it was 12 percent.[8]

Non-Military Wartime Legislation

Sectional shifts in political power were equally dramatic. The war freed not only the slaves; it also freed modernizing Northern capitalism from the shadow of Southern ideology. The consequences of this liberation became evident as early as 1862. Wartime financial legislation created a uniform currency (the greenbacks and national banknotes) and a national banking structure. The absence of Southern Democrats from Congress also made possible the passage in 1862 of three important laws that reflected Whig-Republican modernizing purposes: the Homestead Act, the Land-grant College Act, and the Pacific Railroad Act.

The Homestead Act granted ownership of 160 acres of public land to a settler after five years of residence on his claim. A key plank in the 1860 Republican platform, "free land" had a long history as a cause frustrated by Southerners in Congress and by President Buchanan's veto in 1860. Freed of the Southern incubus, Republicans enacted the measure on May 20, 1862. Before the war's end, nearly 20,000 farmers had taken up three million acres under the law, which eventually accounted for the settlement and ownership of more than eighty million acres.

The Land-grant College Act (generally known as the Morrill Act after its sponsor, Congressman Justin Morrill of Vermont) laid the groundwork for several great universities. The Morrill Act, based on the principle of proportional representation, granted to a state 30,000 acres of public land for each congressman and senator. The proceeds from the sale of this land were to be used for the establishment in each state of at least one college for the teaching of "agricultural and mechanical arts." For a generation, educational reformers had urged such a measure to make higher education more relevant to the economic pursuits of most Americans, but Southerners and Democrats had previously blocked it. Buchanan had vetoed a land-grant bill in 1859. Lincoln signed the Morrill Act on July 2, 1862. In its impact on higher education, this was the most important instance of federal aid to education in American history.

The Pacific railroad bill had enjoyed bipartisan support in the 1850s but had bogged down in sectional disputes over whether the tracks should follow a southern or northern route. This question was settled by the South's secession. The bill enacted on July 1, 1862, stipulated an eastern terminus at Omaha and a western terminus at San Francisco Bay. It provided a minimum grant of 6,400 acres of public land (later doubled) and $16,000 in federal loans for each mile of railroad built. From this act grew the Union Pacific and Central Pacific (later Southern Pacific) railroads, which joined their tracks at Promontory, Utah, in 1869. In 1864, Congress chartered the Northern Pacific Railroad (St. Paul to Seattle) and authorized even larger land grants. These and subsequent land grants to other railroads ultimately totaled 120 million acres.

In practice, these three laws sometimes conflicted with one another. The goal of free land for settlers was at times frustrated by grants to railroads or states, which held the land as collateral for bank loans or sold it to the highest bidder. But the Republicans who passed these laws intended them as complementary measures to advance the cause of free-soil modernizing capitalism: the Homestead Act offered farmers capital in the form of land; the Morrill Act was an investment in human capital that would help these farmers—and "mechanics"—become more prosperous and productive; and the land grants and loans to railroads injected large doses of social overhead capital into the economy.

The 37th Congress (1861–1863) enacted legislation that permanently altered the social and economic landscape. The Legal Tender Act, the National Bank Act, the Homestead Act, the Morrill Act, the Pacific Railroad Act, the Internal Revenue Act, and the Confiscation Act represented the triumph of modernizing capitalism. By confirming this triumph, Northern victory in the war produced an expansive optimism. "The truth is, the close of the war with our resources unimpaired," wrote Senator John Sherman to his brother in 1865, "gives an elevation, a scope to the ideas of leading capitalists, far higher than anything ever undertaken in this country before. They talk of millions as confidently as formerly of thousands."[9]

Labor and the War

One group in the North that viewed this wartime expansiveness with skepticism were blue-collar workers. More than one-third of them were foreign-born, primarily Irish, who lacked enthusiasm for Republican war aims and policies. A good many workers refused to join the middle-class applause for the triumph of modernizing capitalism, especially when they did not fully share in the wartime prosperity.

Wage increases lagged 20 percent or more behind price increases until the final months of the war, when wages began to catch up.

One reason for this wage lag was a change in the composition of the labor force. More than half a million skilled and semiskilled workers enlisted in the Union army. To replace them, employers hired or promoted semiskilled and unskilled persons, including women and boys. In 1860, women constituted perhaps a quarter of the manufacturing labor force, concentrated mainly in textiles and garment making; but during the war, the proportion of women rose to at least a third. Women and other replacements for skilled male workers were paid less for the same work, and because they lacked experience in these jobs, their productivity was also lower—which helps to explain the 3 percent decline in per capita output during the 1860s.

Workers occasionally went on strike for higher wages to keep up with the rising cost of living. Many of these strikes were successful, especially those conducted by skilled and semiskilled workers in 1863–1864. Thereafter, the wages of most skilled workers remained abreast of the cost of living. It was mainly the semiskilled and unskilled, especially women, whose earnings fell further and further behind. The national government rarely intervened in strikes unless military operations were affected. Union officers in the border states and occupied Tennessee did use troops to prevent or break up strikes on several occasions. The government also sent two companies of soldiers to arrest strike leaders at the Parrott gun factory in Cold Spring, New York, in March 1864 (this on the eve of the 1864 military campaigns in which Parrott-made artillery was to play a vital role).

Successful wartime strikes produced a new feeling of unity and strength among skilled workers. Most strikes, and the unions that grew out of them, were spontaneous and local; but from these emerged a number of national unions, which became the basis for an upsurge of labor activism after the war. From a low point in the late 1850s, labor union membership rose sharply until the early 1870s, when a larger percentage of the industrial labor force belonged to unions than at any other time in the nineteenth century.

Most foreign-born workers were Democrats who shared the party's hostility to modernization and emancipation; while most native-born workers were Republicans who approved the free-labor ideology even to the extent of rejoicing in emancipation. Several labor leaders articulated the same views as radical Republicans concerning the need to destroy the oppressive premodern labor system of the South and to give all workers equal opportunity and equality under law. They agreed with the sentiments expressed by the International Workingmen's Association in an address to Abraham Lincoln written by Karl Marx in January 1865:

> The workingmen of Europe feel sure that, as the American War of Independence initiated a new era of ascendancy for the middle class, so the American anti-slavery war will do for the working classes. They consider it an earnest of the epoch to come that it fell to the lot of Abraham Lincoln, the single-minded son of the working class, to lead the country through the matchless struggle for the rescue of an enchained race and the reconstruction of a social world.[10]

Several abolitionists and radical Republicans became active in postwar labor reform movements, most notably Wendell Phillips and Benjamin Butler. But the postwar era revealed a growing difference between Republicans and labor leaders in their understanding of the free-labor ideology. The workers moved beyond the Republican belief in equality of rights and opportunity. They began to demand, in the words of labor leader Ira Steward, an "equal *share* in the wealth their industry creates. (italics added)"[11] By 1870, two-thirds of working Americans were wage earners rather than self-employed. To many of them, the free-labor ideology of competitive capitalism, individualism, social mobility, self-made men, and the harmony of classes seemed increasingly irrelevant to their dependent, wage-earning status. They were becoming conscious of labor as a special interest group, a separate class whose needs conflicted with the privileges of capital. The Civil War was both a climactic triumph of the free-labor ideology and the catalyst of a more class-conscious labor movement that eventually rejected this ideology as serving the interests of conservative capitalism.

ECONOMIC DISCONTENT IN THE SOUTH

The twin disasters at Gettysburg and Vicksburg aggravated the worst home-front problems of the Confederacy: shortages and inflation. Prices rose 58 percent in the ensuing three months. "A poor woman yesterday applied to a merchant in Carey Street to purchase a barrel of flour," wrote a Richmond diarist on October 22, 1863. "The price he demanded was $70. 'My God!' exclaimed she, 'how can I pay such prices? I have seven children; what shall I do?' 'I don't know, madam,' said he, coolly, 'unless you eat your children.' "[12]

Four months later flour in Richmond cost $250 a barrel. Caught in a cruel dilemma whose causes they ill understood, many Southerners sought scapegoats for their misery. The most common targets were "speculators" and "extortioners," who were thought to have cornered supplies in order to profit from the consequent rise in prices. The press and pulpit rang with denunciations of these "contemptible wretches," who would "bottle the universal air and sell it at so much a bottle" if they could. Jefferson Davis spoke out against "the attempt of groveling speculators to forestall the market and make money out of the lifeblood of our defenders." As in the case of other people at other times, some Southerners focused their anger on Jewish merchants who had, in the words of Confederate congressmen, "swarmed here as the locusts of Egypt. They ate up the substance of the country, they exhausted its supplies, they monopolized its trade. . . . The end of the war [will] probably find nearly all the property of the Confederacy in the hands of Jewish Shylocks."[13]

There were "speculators" in the Confederacy, of course; but most merchants, whether Jew or Gentile, were trying to make an honest living in difficult times. They were more the victims than the cause of inflation. Though they may have sold goods at a 50 percent profit, they gained little if the general price level had increased 45 percent between the time they bought and sold the goods. Several Confederate states passed laws "to suppress monopolies," by which they meant wholesalers who allegedly profited from cornering the market in necessities. The Confederate tax law of April 1863 assessed a retroactive 10 percent levy on the profits of wholesalers. None of these laws was enforceable because proof of conspiracy and assessment of profit were virtually impossible amid the financial chaos of the Confederacy.

The Impressment Act of 1863 was also aimed in part at speculators. Because farmers and merchants often refused to sell food and supplies to the army at prices set by the government, commissary and quartermaster officers resorted to the impressment of supplies. This produced bitter outcries. To remedy abuses and regularize the process, Congress on March 26, 1863, passed "An Act to Regulate Impressments," which laid down guidelines for impressment officers and provided for arbitration whenever these officers could not agree with the seller on what constituted a fair price. Like so much Confederate financial legislation, however, this law failed to accomplish its purpose. With the spurt of inflation after Gettysburg and Vicksburg, the disparity between the impressment price and the market price widened to an unbridgeable gap. Indeed, farmers were becoming reluctant to accept Confederate money at any price. Army officers desperate for supplies seized what they wanted and offered the angry farmer an IOU receipt. At the end of the war, an estimated half billion dollars of these unpaid receipts were outstanding.

The impressment policy intensified rather than relieved shortages and inflation, because many farmers hid their crops and drove their livestock into the woods when impressment officers came near. Others refused to plant a crop at all. Impressment also turned many Southerners against the Confederacy. Farmers in a Louisiana district expressed a widely shared sentiment when they told a Confederate officer "that they would prefer seeing the Yankees to seeing our cavalry." Nearly every Southern governor denounced impressment. States' rights advocates, particularly Governor Joseph Brown of Georgia, did everything they could to harass impressment officers. Davis's political enemies used impressment as one of the main issues in their attacks on the administration. "It is far better for a free people to be vanquished in open combat with the invader," thundered William L. Yancey, than to "yield liberties and their constitutional safeguards to the stealthy progress of . . . military dictatorship."[14] But no matter how despicable, impressment was necessary in large parts of the South; without it the army would have been hard-pressed to obtain any supplies.

TRADING WITH THE ENEMY

Another apparently necessary evil in the Confederacy was trade with the Yankees. Trading with the enemy is as old as war. Americans had proven themselves adept at it during the Revolution and in the War of 1812. They proved even more adept in the Civil War, which offered greater temptations and opportunities than most wars. The South had large quantities of a commodity much in demand—cotton —and a great need for shoes, salt, medicine, munitions, and other goods that had to be obtained mainly from the outside world. The North and South had been economically interdependent before the war, and all the regulations of govern-ments and generals could not stop a commerce more profitable in war than it had ever been in peace. When cotton could be bought for 10 or 20 cents a pound in Memphis or New Orleans and sold for 80 cents in Boston or New York, and when salt could be obtained for $1.25 a sack in the North and sold for $60 in the Confederacy, enterprising men would find a way to trade cotton for salt. While the Confederacy embargoed cotton exports, Southerners sold cotton to Yankee or European speculators and Confederate officials looked the other way because the gold and greenbacks this brought in could buy guns and shoes. And while the Union government blockaded the South, it allowed—or at least did not suppress —a trade that partly undermined the blockade.

In 1861 both governments had officially prohibited trade with the enemy. But across a frontier a thousand miles long, much of it running through border states whose allegiance was divided, there was a great deal of smuggling through lonely woods and across unpatrolled rivers in the dark of night. Illicit trade was carried on by sea as well. New York merchants shipped war goods to Bermuda or Nassau, where they were transshipped to blockade runners for Wilmington or Charleston.

With the Union conquest of large areas of the South in 1862, opportunities for contraband trade vastly increased. Under the dictum that "commerce should follow the flag," the Treasury Department issued permits for legitimate trade in occupied territory. This liberal trade policy had two purposes: to restore normal commercial activity in conquered areas and to woo Southern citizens back into the Union—for in theory, only those who took an oath of allegiance could sell cotton or purchase goods from the North. In practice, the permit system never worked well. Hordes of unlicensed as well as licensed traders flocked into occupied areas with greenbacks, gold, bacon, shoes, blankets—or even gunpowder—to exchange for cotton sold by planters or agents, some of whom had taken the oath of allegiance in good faith but many of whom had not. Through Memphis flowed a huge trade in contraband goods that made their way into Rebel lines and did much to sustain Confederate forces in Mississippi and Tennessee during 1862–1863.

Generals Grant and Sherman deplored this commerce. "We cannot carry on a war and trade with a people at the same time," wrote Sherman.[15] He issued a number of orders to limit or stop the trade; but some of them were overridden by Washington, and others proved impossible to enforce. Southern women were effective smugglers in this age of hoop skirts and multiple petticoats. One search of a Memphis woman whose crinolines looked suspicious revealed that tied to her girdle were twelve pairs of boots containing medicine, whiskey, and other items. On another occasion, an elaborate funeral procession in Memphis bore a coffin from the city that turned out to be full of medicine for General Van Dorn's Confederate army.

More serious was the participation of Northern soldiers in this trade. The lure of profits or bribes "has to an alarming extent corrupted and demoralized the army," lamented a War Department official sent to investigate affairs in Mem-phis. "Every colonel, captain, or quartermaster is in secret partnership with some operator in cotton; every soldier dreams of adding a bale of cotton to his monthly pay." In 1863, Grant wrote that this commerce "is weakening us of at least 33 percent of our force. . . . I will venture that no honest man has made money in West Tennessee in the last year, whilst many fortunes have been made there during that time."[16]

Some of the Northern merchants who flocked to Memphis were Jewish, which caused Grant to issue on December 17, 1862, one of the most ill-considered orders of his career: "The Jews, as a class violating every regulation of trade established by the Treasury Department and also [military] orders, are hereby expelled from the department within twenty-four hours from the receipt of this order." Grant's action roused something of a storm in the North. Within three weeks came word from Washington to revoke the order, which Grant promptly did. "The President has no objection to your expelling traitors and Jew peddlers" who traded with the enemy, Halleck informed Grant, but since the order "proscribed an entire religious class, some of whom are fighting in our ranks, the President deemed it necessary to revoke it."[17]*

One top Union general who did nothing to discourage trade with the enemy —indeed, quite the contrary if his critics are to be believed—was Benjamin Butler, commander of the occupying forces in New Orleans from April to December 1862.

Butler was one of the most ambiguous and controversial figures of the war. His rule in New Orleans earned him international notoriety and the undying hatred of Southerners. One of his first acts was to issue an order that any woman who continued to insult Union soldiers "shall be regarded and held liable to be treated as a woman of the town plying her avocation."† A few weeks later, Butler executed a civilian who had torn down the United States flag from a public building. As far away as London and Paris these actions increased foreign sympathy for the Confederacy. Closer to home, one of the mildest epithets that Southerners applied to Butler was "Beast." Jefferson Davis issued a proclamation branding him an outlaw and ordering that if captured he was "to be immediately executed by hanging."[18]

But Beast Butler gave New Orleans the most efficient and healthful administration it had ever known. He cleaned up the foul sewers, established new drainage systems and health regulations, and embarked on an ambitious public works program that provided jobs for the poor and the unemployed. Much of the funds

---

*Several other Union commanders, including Sherman, also singled out Jewish traders for condemnation. Some Confederate officials did the same. These "Jew extortioners," wrote a War Department clerk in Richmond, "have injured our cause more than the armies of Lincoln." (John B. Jones, *A Rebel War Clerk's Diary at the Confederate States Capital*, 2 vols. [New York, 1935; first printed Philadelphia, 1866], I, 221.) These comments were as irrational as such attitudes usually are, for only a fraction of the traders and speculators were Jewish. Like all wars, the Civil War had its seamy as well as heroic side, its profiteers as well as patriots, but neither the former nor the latter belonged predominantly to any class or ethnic group.

†Although perhaps ill-advised, this order was issued after considerable provocation. New Orleans women insulted Northern soldiers in every conceivable fashion. The last straw was when a lady in the French Quarter emptied the contents of a chamber pot on Admiral Farragut's head.

Benjamin Butler
(Reproduced from the Collections of the Library of Congress)

for this program came from Butler's confiscation of public and private Confederate property, actions which earned him another nickname, "Spoons" Butler, because he and his officers allegedly stole Southerners' silver.

Butler also took steps to revive the city's economy from its blockade-induced depression. But much of the trade he promoted involved the exchange of cotton and sugar for such military items as salt, shoes, and provisions that found their way to the Confederate army. The unsavory atmosphere of corruption and profiteering that permeated New Orleans won Butler an unenviable reputation. Nothing illegal was ever proved against the general himself (a frustrated Treasury agent reported that Butler was "such a smart man, that it would, in any case, be difficult to discover what he wished to conceal"). But his brother Andrew, who had accompanied him to New Orleans as a colonel, reportedly made a fortune by means that would not bear examination.[19]

A few days after General Nathaniel Banks replaced Butler in December 1862, a citizen offered him a bribe of $100,000 if he would approve a deal, already cleared by Confederate authorities, for a trade of Southern cotton for Northern salt. The astonished Banks wrote sadly in a private letter: "I never despaired of my country until I came here. . . . Everybody connected with the government has been employed in stealing other people's property. Sugar, silver plate, horses, carriages, everything they could lay their hands on. There has been open trade with the enemy. . . . We can never succeed, under such direction—our people must give up stealing or give up the country." Banks curbed the worst abuses, but he could never entirely stop the contraband trade. A foreign observer wrote that even "a Chinese wall from the Atlantic to the Pacific" could not stop the traffic when so much money was at stake.[20]

In March 1863, the Union Congress passed the Captured Property Act, which was intended to diminish private trading by making all Confederate-owned cotton subject to seizure by the government. In January 1864, the Treasury issued strict regulations to govern the purchase of non-Confederate cotton (that is, cotton owned by persons who had taken the oath of allegiance). In July 1864, Congress abolished the permit system by which civilians had carried on trade in occupied territory.

But these laws and regulations had little impact on the illicit trade. The administration enforced them in such a way as to allow the continued payment for cotton with cash, which then found its way into Confederate hands. Lincoln permitted this because he believed that cotton purchased by Northerners benefited the Union more and the Confederacy less than the same cotton exported through the blockade to Europe. The President explained his reasoning to one irate general who had tried to suppress the cotton trade in his department. Cotton prices had risen to more than six times their prewar level, noted Lincoln. "And yet the enemy gets through at least one sixth part as much in a given period, say a year, as if there were no blockade, and receives as much for it, as he would for a full crop in time of peace," enabling the South to earn foreign exchange for the purchase of arms and supplies. It was therefore "not merely a concession to private interest and pecuniary greed" to allow private traders to buy cotton, because every bale that went North was one less available for export. "Better give him *guns* for it than let him, as now, get both guns and ammunition for it."[21]

Confederate generals were no more successful in stopping the trade than were their Union opposites. Southern civilians near Union lines were quick to take the oath of allegiance in order to sell cotton. And just as bribes tempted Northern soldiers to look the other way when contraband supplies went through the lines, "a pair of boots and a bottle of whisky" accomplished the same purpose with Confederate pickets. Everyone involved was "corrupted and demoralized," complained a Confederate officer. "The fact is that cotton, instead of contributing to our strength, has been the greatest element of our weakness here. Yankee gold is fast accomplishing what Yankee arms could never achieve—the subjugation of [our] people." The Confederate government agreed—in theory. "All trade with the enemy is demoralizing and illegal, and should, of course, be discountenanced," wrote the Secretary of War in Richmond. "But at the same time . . . the Army cannot be subsisted without permitting trade to some extent." Jefferson Davis reluctantly sanctioned the commerce, but only if "the necessity should be absolute."[22]

For the South, the necessity was nearly always absolute. The contraband trade

unquestionably helped the Confederacy more than the Union, Lincoln's arguments and the complaints of Confederate officers to the contrary notwithstanding.
The judgment of historian James Ford Rhodes on the trade seems fair: "For the
South it was a necessary evil; for the North it was an evil and not a necessary
one."[23] It was also an evil that contributed to the climate of corruption and
profiteering that marred the postwar decade.

DISEASE AND MEDICAL CARE IN CIVIL WAR ARMIES

Disease was the principal killer of Civil War soldiers. Two soldiers died of disease
for every one killed in battle. And for every man who died of disease, scores of
others were on the sicklist at any given time. Sickness and physical disability were
the main reasons why the initial 1,000-man enrollment in a regiment was often
cut in half by the time the unit first went into battle.

Physical examinations of recruits were often cursory and sometimes nonexistent. In July 1862 an investigation of Union enlistment procedures concluded that
"the careless and superficial medical inspection of recruits made at least 25 per
cent of the volunteer army raised last year not only utterly useless, but a positive
incumbrance."[24] Medical examinations thereafter became more rigorous. But
even healthy recruits had a hard time staying healthy when they were exposed to
the new disease environment created by the crowding together of thousands of
men. In both armies, soldiers from rural areas proved to be more susceptible to
disease than those from cities, who had already been exposed to many of the
bacteria that struck down farm boys. Recruits from the Midwestern states in the
Union army suffered a disease mortality rate 43 percent higher than those from
the more urban states of the Northeast.

Disease hit Civil War armies in two waves. The first was an epidemic of
childhood maladies—mainly measles and mumps—that many men encountered
for the first time. Though rarely fatal, these illnesses could temporarily incapaci-
tate large numbers of new troops. The second wave consisted of camp and
campaign diseases caused by bad water, bad food, exposure, and mosquitoes.
These included the principal killer diseases of the Civil War: dysentery and
diarrhea, typhoid, and malaria. Primitive or careless sanitation in army camps
often contaminated the water and left wastes exposed to flies and rodents. Even
when medical officers ordered proper sanitary procedures, soldiers sometimes paid
little attention. "Our poor sick, I know, suffer much," wrote Robert E. Lee in
1861, but."they bring it on themselves by not doing what they are told. They are
worse than children, for the latter can be forced."[25]

Because the Civil War soldier was ten times more likely to die of disease and
eight times more likely to die from a battlefield wound than the American soldier
in World War I, numerous historians have concluded that "the medical services
represent one of the Civil War's most dismal failures."[26] The war certainly had
its share of incompetent or drunken surgeons, bureaucratic blundering in the army
medical corps, officers careless of their men's health, and medical old-fogyism. But
these represented only one side of the story. *By the standards of the time,* Civil

War medical care and army health were unusually good. Although the ratio of disease to battle deaths was two to one, this compared favorably with ratios of seven to one in the Mexican War (1846–1848) and six to one in the Spanish-American War (1898). The ratio for the British army in the Crimean War (1854–1856) was nearly four to one; in the Napoleonic Wars it had been eight to one. The allied armies in the Crimea had a disease mortality of 25 percent in less than two years, compared with the Civil War armies' 13 percent in four years (10 percent for the Union army, 20 percent for the Confederates). The U.S. surgeon general was right when he wrote proudly that the Union army's mortality rate from disease and wounds was "lower than had been observed in the experience of any army since the world began."[27]

But by twentieth-century standards the morbidity and mortality rates of Civil War armies are shocking. As the wartime surgeon general later explained with benefit of hindsight, "the Civil War was fought at the end of the medical Middle Ages."[28] Louis Pasteur, Joseph Lister, and other Europeans were just beginning the research in bacteriology that within a generation would revolutionize medical knowledge. Civil War doctors did not know what caused dysentery, or typhoid, or malaria. Ideas concerning the importance of sanitation or good water or balanced diet were in their infancy. Scarcely anyone was aware of the need to sterilize surgical instruments to prevent infection. Doctors knew no better because of the primitive state of their art. Their ignorance was not personal, but a fact of history.

Although the Civil War did not produce any striking advances in medical knowledge, it did generate important innovations in army medical care. Inadequate and amateurish in 1861, the medical services were greatly expanded and professionalized by 1863. When Fort Sumter fell, the surgeon general of the United States was an eighty-year-old veteran of the War of 1812. His successor, aged sixty-four, was equally complacent with the somnolent bureaucracy of the old army. But from the time of the appointment of thirty-three-year-old William A. Hammond as surgeon general in April 1862, the Union Army Medical Bureau was blessed with vigorous, progressive leadership. So was its Confederate counterpart, within the limits of its smaller resources. In April 1861, the U.S. army had only 113 surgeons, of whom 24 resigned to go with the South. By the war's end, more than 15,000 surgeons had served in the Union and Confederate forces. Before the war, the army had no general hospitals; in 1865 there were more than 350, many of them of the new "pavilion" type that became the standard military hospital for half a century.

During the first year or more of the war, procedures for battlefield treatment of the wounded were chaotic. Regimental musicians (many of them younger than eighteen), cooks, teamsters, and other noncombatants were detailed as stretcher-bearers; and civilians were frequently employed as ambulance drivers. More often than not these men and boys bolted in panic when the fighting became hot, leaving the wounded to lie untended for hours or days. Consequently, combat soldiers would often drop out of line to carry wounded friends to the rear, thus reducing the army's fighting strength. To remedy this situation, General McClellan in August 1862 authorized the creation of a trained ambulance corps for the Army of the Potomac. This worked so well that it was adopted by other Union armies and finally mandated by Congress in March 1864. Members of the ambulance corps moved over the battlefield during and after the fighting, administered first aid to wounded soldiers, carried them to brigade or division field hospitals in the rear, and drove the horse-drawn ambulances that evacuated the wounded from field to base hospitals. The Confederates developed a similar "infirmary corps." These units became models for most armies of the world down to World War I.

Much of the pressure for creation of the ambulance corps and for other reforms came from the United States Sanitary Commission. This organization was an example of what Alexis de Tocqueville had described as the American genius for founding voluntary associations to perform tasks that in Europe were usually performed by the state or the church. Organized early in the war, the Sanitary Commission sought government sanction as a civilian agency to help the Army Medical Bureau prevent the health problems that had decimated the British and French armies in the Crimea. After overcoming the army's hostility to "meddling" civilians, the Sanitary Commission received official War Department recognition in June 1861.

The Sanitary Commission became the principal agency through which Northern women aided the war effort. Although its national officers and most of its salaried agents were men, the volunteer workers who ran its 7,000 local auxiliaries, collected supplies, organized the great "Sanitary Fairs" to raise money, and worked as nurses were mostly women. The commission established depots for the distribution of clothing, food, and medicine to the army. It provided meals and lodging to convalescent and furloughed soldiers on their way to and from the front. It sent sanitary inspectors to regimental camps to instruct officers and men in such matters as latrines, drainage, water supply, and cooking. It supplied soldiers with vegetables, an item often lacking in the standard army ration. It gathered emergency stockpiles of medicines and bandages and rushed them to battlefield hospitals. It sent its own nurses and doctors to work in army hospitals. It chartered ships to evacuate wounded from Shiloh and from the Virginia peninsula in 1862, and provided ambulance service on the peninsula when the army's ambulances proved inadequate.

Sanitary Commission officials criticized the surgeon general and his staff in 1861 as "venerable do-nothings and senile obstructionists." The old-army establishment retaliated with angry cries against "sensation preachers, village doctors, and strong-minded women."[29] But so popular was the Sanitary Commission with the soldiers, so obvious its effectiveness, and so great its influence in Congress that it was able to push through a bill to reorganize the Medical Bureau and to secure Hammond's appointment as surgeon general in 1862. This inaugurated an era of partnership between the Medical Bureau and the commission productive of such reforms as the ambulance corps.*

Other voluntary associations supplemented the work of the Sanitary Commis-

---

*The commission and General Hammond ran afoul of Secretary of War Edwin M. Stanton in 1863 for reasons not entirely clear. Stanton sometimes obstructed the commission's activities. He disliked Hammond and forced his dismissal in 1864. By then, however, the reforms Hammond had instituted had become standard army procedure.

sion. Several state societies provided services for soldiers and support for their families. The Western Sanitary Commission, a separate organization, carried on relief and medical work for Union troops in Missouri and Arkansas. The Roman Catholic Sisters of Charity supplied army hospitals with the best-trained nurses in the country. In November 1861 a group of Protestant ministers and YMCA officials organized the Christian Commission to carry YMCA principles to the front. Within a year this commission had emerged as a large organization that gave more than spiritual comfort to the troops. Christian Commission volunteers provided food and nursing care to wounded soldiers, supplied most of the books and pamphlets in hospital libraries, and distributed blankets, warm clothing, and even medicines to convalescent soldiers. Such activities sometimes brought them into rivalry with the Sanitary Commission, whose more secular leadership frowned on the evangelical enthusiasm of the Christian Commission.

The contribution of volunteer agencies to the Union army's health was significant. They also had a long-term impact on medical history. The Sanitary Commission evolved a philosophy of scientific inquiry, hard-headed efficiency, and disciplined humanitarianism that became a hallmark of postwar philanthropy. It provided the model for the American Public Health Association, founded in 1872 by men who had been active in the Sanitary Commission. The APHA played an important role in the subsequent modernization of American medicine and public health.

Organized relief and medical work in the South was less centralized than in the North. No counterpart of the Sanitary or Christian commissions existed in the Confederacy, though local soldiers' aid and hospital relief societies sprang up everywhere. These societies performed valuable services, but Confederate soldiers nevertheless fared less well in medical care than their Union counterparts. One of every six wounded Rebels died of his wounds, compared with one of seven Yankees. The percentage of Confederate soldiers who died of disease was twice that of Union soldiers (it should be noted that the percentage killed in action was also twice as large). This was less the fault of the Confederate medical corps than of the shortages, economic breakdowns, and destruction of resources that plagued all aspects of the Confederate war effort. Sick or wounded soldiers could not get enough food or the right kind of food. Although most accounts also mention shortages of medicines caused by the Union blockade, the fullest study of Confederate medical services maintains that domestic manufacture and illicit trade with the North largely remedied these shortages.[30] But the gradual collapse of Southern railroads caused deficiencies when and where medicines were most needed.

WOMEN AND MEDICAL CARE

In both North and South, women played a vital role in Civil War medicine. Not only did they do most of the hard work in civilian volunteer agencies, but many thousands also served as professional and volunteer nurses in army hospitals. One woman, Mary Walker, served as a surgeon in the Union army in 1864. She was captured in Georgia by the Confederates, who expressed amazement "at the sight of a *thing* that nothing but the debased and depraved Yankee nation could produce."[31]

The male hostility that Walker had to overcome before receiving her appointment was encountered on a smaller scale by women who volunteered as nurses. Nevertheless, the illustrious example of Florence Nightingale in the Crimean War had begun to dignify the profession of nursing, which previously had been stigmatized as a menial occupation. Women were assumed to possess finer and gentler natures than men and were therefore thought to make the best nurses. Yet a somewhat contradictory feeling also existed in 1861, especially in the South, that the rough, masculine, and embarrassingly physical atmosphere of a military hospital was no place for a respectable woman, particularly if she was young, pretty, and unmarried. The Union government in June 1861 appointed Dorothea Dix, the famous reformer of asylums for the insane, as superintendent of female nurses. Dix specified that all nursing applicants must be "plain in appearance" and at least thirty years old. "Dragon Dix . . . won't accept the services of any *pretty* nurses," complained one disappointed applicant. "Just think of putting such an old thing over everyone else. . . . Some fool man did it."[32] Women who managed to pass Dix's scrutiny had to contend with the prejudices of army surgeons such as the one who complained that every preacher in the North "would recommend the most troublesome old maid in his congregation as an experienced nurse." The surgeon said he had been plagued by several of these women, "each one with spectacles on her nose and an earnest gaze in her eyes, to see the man she was to take possession of." An increase in the death rate occurred at the hospital after they arrived, he added, "probably caused by the spectacles."[33]

Northern women slowly overcame such prejudices. They were aided by an order of Surgeon General Hammond in July 1862 that at least one-third of the nurses in army general hospitals must be women (most of the rest were detailed or convalescent soldiers). About 3,200 women served as army nurses in the North, one-quarter of the total number of nurses. The South was slower to use "respectable" white women as army nurses, though many slave women served in army hospitals from the beginning. Not until September 1862 did the Confederate Congress officially authorize women nurses. Thereafter the Southern army welcomed them, though white women constituted a smaller proportion of army nurses in the Confederacy than in the Union. But in both North and South, additional thousands of women worked as hospital volunteers or as employees of the Sanitary Commission, Christian Commission, and the like. Some of the volunteers were Lady Bountiful types and disliked by the soldiers, but most were dedicated, hard-working people who earned respect and praise from officers and men.

Women nurses worked mainly in general hospitals away from the fighting front. But some also shared the hardships and dangers of field hospitals. Clara Barton, later the founder of the American Red Cross, served in numerous Union battlefield hospitals. Several women labored at the base hospitals after Shiloh and during the fighting near Richmond in the summer of 1862. Many Northern women came to Gettysburg in 1863, where they helped care for thousands of

(University of Rochester Medical Center)

Treatment of Union Wounded. (Clockwise from top left)

A photograph of a simulated amputation, taken at the Union army base, Fortress Monroe, Virginia, in 1861. The "patient's" face is blocked by the surgeon's assistant, who is holding the leg with a clamp while the surgeon pretends to saw it off. The spectators are soldiers in a Zouave regiment. The second and third photos show amputees and other

(Reproduced from the Collections of the Library of Congress)

wounded Union soldiers convalescing outside the base hospital at Fredericksburg. Notice the Sanitary Commission nurse sitting in the doorway. The fourth photo was taken at the Armory Square military hospital in Washington, an example of the pavilion-style hospitals built during the war. This clean, cheerful hospital ward shows Union medical care at its best.

(Reproduced from the Collections of the Library of Congress)

(Massachusetts Commandery Military Order of the Loyal Legion and the U.S. Army Military History Institute)

Confederate as well as Union wounded. Mary Ann Bickerdyke was the best known of the front-line women nurses. A widow from Illinois known affectionately to soldiers as "Mother Bickerdyke," she made the health of enlisted men in the Army of the Tennessee her special concern. With the support of Generals Grant and

Sherman, she overcame opposition from surgeons and high-ranking officers. She was one of the few civilians whom Sherman allowed with his army, and she won the lifelong respect of this crusty general.

The work of women as nurses in the Civil War advanced the professional status of nursing in the United States, just as Florence Nightingale's work in the Crimean War had done in Britain. In 1861, the Women's Central Relief Association set up a training program for nurses in New York City. Several other nursing schools were founded in Northern cities during or soon after the war. In this respect, also, the Civil War gave an important impulse to the modernization and professionalization of medicine.

Twenty-two

Wartime Reconstruction and the Freedmen

On December 8, 1863, Lincoln issued a "Proclamation of Amnesty and Reconstruction." Under his constitutional authority to grant pardons for offenses against the United States, he offered "full pardon" and restoration of property "except as to slaves" to those engaged in rebellion who would swear an oath of allegiance to the United States and to all laws and proclamations concerning slavery. (Civil and diplomatic officials of the Confederate government, high army and navy officers, and certain other prominent Confederates were exempted from this offer.) Whenever in any state the number of voters taking the oath reached 10 percent of the number who had voted in the 1860 election, this loyal nucleus could reestablish a state government to which Lincoln promised executive recognition. "Any provision which may be adopted by such State government in relation to the freed people of such State, which shall recognize and declare their permanent freedom, provide for their education, and which may yet be consistent, as a temporary arrangement, with their present condition as a laboring, landless, and homeless class, will not be objected to by the national Executive." To Congress, of course, belonged the right to determine whether the representatives and senators from such states would be seated.[1]

This document was the product of much thought. Addressing itself to the main social and political issues of the war, it laid down the following policies: (1) acceptance of the degree of emancipation accomplished thus far was to be a prerequisite of reconstruction; (2) for the time being, however, Southern states might enact contract labor laws or other measures to bring order out of the chaos caused by sudden emancipation; (3) political restoration of states to the Union was to be a relatively easy process that would impose no harsh punishments for treason, confiscate no property except slaves, and require no more than 10 percent of the voting population to begin the process.

Lincoln formulated these provisions in the context of Northern military success during the second half of 1863. Union troops now occupied nearly all of Tennessee and large parts of Louisiana, Arkansas, Mississippi, and Virginia. A policy for the restoration (or "reconstruction") of elected civil governments in these areas had become necessary. Lincoln's proclamation was designed to meet this necessity. In addition, the President hoped that his liberal promise of amnesty would cause many lukewarm Confederates to renew their allegiance to the Union and thereby further weaken the Confederacy. But these complex provisions divided the Republican party and produced a confrontation between President and Congress. To unravel the complexities requires an analysis of three separate but interrelated issues: emancipation, the status of the freedmen, and political reconstruction.

EMANCIPATION

Although all Republicans wanted to make emancipation a condition of reconstruction, many of them—including Lincoln—doubted whether wartime actions against slavery would remain legally in effect after the war was over. Based on the war power to seize enemy property, those actions might not have constitutional validity in peacetime. Republicans generally agreed that those slaves who had come within Union lines had been freed by the confiscation acts, by the Emancipation Proclamation, or by the military orders of Union commanders in the occupied South—such as those of General Nathaniel Banks, which abrogated the slave code of Louisiana's antebellum Constitution. Lincoln said repeatedly that so long as he was President no person who had been freed would be returned to slavery. But would the courts sustain this position after the war? What about the three million slaves in the Confederacy who had not come within Union lines, and the half million in the border states to whom these measures did not apply? And even if abolition became a condition of reconstruction, there was nothing in the Constitution to prevent a state from reestablishing slavery once it was back in the Union.

By the end of 1863, Republicans had concluded that the only safe course was a constitutional amendment to abolish slavery everywhere. "Such alone can meet and cover all cavils," said Lincoln.[2] In April 1864, the Senate passed the Thirteenth Amendment by a vote of 38 to 6, with two Democrats joining the Republican majority. But Democratic gains in the 1862 congressional elections enabled Northern Democrats and border-state conservatives to block passage in the House, where the 93-to-65 vote for the amendment (with only three Democrats voting aye) on June 15, 1864, fell thirteen votes short of the necessary two-thirds.[3]

Passage of the Thirteenth Amendment by the House would have to await the next session of Congress, after Republican victory in the presidential election of 1864 showed the direction of Northern opinion (see pp. 466–467). Meanwhile, the initiative for further constitutional steps toward emancipation went over to the border states and to occupied portions of Confederate states. Two years earlier, the border states had turned down an offer of compensated, gradual emancipation. Now the issue was immediate, uncompensated abolition. As Lincoln had predicted in 1862, the "abrasion" of total war had been grinding up the institution of slavery in these states until little but the legal shell was left.

In Maryland and Missouri, the absence of many proslavery men who were fighting in the Confederate armies and the disfranchisement of other Confederate sympathizers by their refusal to take a loyalty oath enabled antislavery Union men to gain political control of these states in 1864. Even so, the struggle for emancipation was close. On June 24 a Maryland constitutional convention adopted an amendment abolishing slavery. In the referendum on the new constitution, a majority of civilian voters actually voted against the abolition amendment, and only a vote of 2,633 to 263 in its favor by Maryland Union soldiers provided the razor-thin margin for ratification of the amendment on October 13, 1864. In Missouri, a state constitutional convention passed an abolition amendment on January 11, 1865. Once again, the referendum on the new constitution (which contained several other controversial features, including wholesale disfranchisement of Rebel sympathizers) was characterized by an exceedingly close vote. Only a majority of the soldier votes in favor of the constitution overcame a slight majority of the civilian votes against it to produce a margin of 1,862 votes for ratification out of a total of 85,478 votes cast.

The closeness of these votes and the disfranchisement of many men who would otherwise have voted against the new constitutions meant that emancipation in Maryland and Missouri was scarcely the "voluntary" measure that Lincoln had initially hoped for. The same can be said of the other three states that abolished slavery before the end of the war: Louisiana, Arkansas, and Tennessee. In 1864, constitutional conventions with delegates from the occupied portions of Louisiana and Arkansas abolished slavery as part of their reorganization under Lincoln's "10 percent plan" of reconstruction, and the eligible voters dutifully ratified the new constitutions. A convention in Tennessee adopted an emancipation amendment on January 10, 1865, and Unionist Tennessee voters ratified it on February 22. Although a larger percentage of voters took part in this election than in Louisiana and Arkansas, the total still fell far short of a majority of all potential voters.

In most parts of these five states, the commercially oriented urban population and the prosperous nonslaveholding farmers generally supported the movements for emancipation. In Maryland, for example, the conflict over abolition took place between what an historian later described as "the static, agricultural, society of the tidewater counties" and "the growing commercial, industrial, and farm interests of the north and west." The narrow victory for emancipation, according to one of its proponents from Baltimore, pointed toward a "new alliance with Northern progress and prosperity."[4]

The strength of the tradition-oriented Democrats prevented the development of strong emancipation movements in Kentucky and Delaware, even though the latter was virtually a free state with fewer than 2,000 of its 22,000 black people in slavery. Formal emancipation did not occur in Kentucky and Delaware until the Thirteenth Amendment was ratified eight months after the end of the war.

THE STATUS OF THE FREEDMEN

No single generalization can encompass the variety of ways in which freedom came to the slaves. Many thousands became "contrabands" when their masters fled before invading Northern armies and the slaves stayed behind to welcome the Yankees as liberators. Other slaves, learning of the proximity of blueclad regiments, left the plantations and made their way to Union lines. Tens of thousands trailed Sherman's army as it sliced through Georgia and the Carolinas in 1864–1865 (see p. 462). Some slaves helped Northern soldiers loot the Big House; others helped the Missis bury the silver. Trusted house servants and drivers were often the first to desert the plantation for the Yankees; others remained faithful to Ol' Massa to the end. Many contrabands served as guides and scouts for Union commanders; others feigned ignorance or refused to give information to the invaders. Only one generalization is safe: most slaves welcomed freedom, no matter how ambiguous or disillusioning it proved to be. By the war's end, perhaps one and a half million of the three and a half million slaves in the Confederacy had been directly affected by Northern invasion, and more than half a million of these were within areas of firm Union control.

The Union government never developed a uniform, consistent, considered wartime policy for dealing with these half million contrabands. Authority was fragmented among the army, the Treasury Department (which controlled confiscated property), and various missionary and freedmen's societies organized in the North to bring relief and education to the freedmen. The army officers in command of occupation forces held ultimate power. From their initial attempts to cope with the influx of contrabands, some semblance of a "policy" emerged. In its early stages this policy was attended with much confusion, hardship, and injustice.

The contrabands crowded into improvised camps, where exposure and disease took a fearful toll. Yankee soldiers sometimes "confiscated" the meager worldly goods the blacks had managed to bring with them. Sexual contacts between soldiers and black women caused the spread of venereal diseases. To bring order out of chaos, to prevent demoralization of the troops and exploitation of the contrabands, Union commanders established separate freedmen's villages, appointed army officers as superintendents of freedmen, detailed squads of soldiers to protect these villages against Yankee exploiters and Confederate guerrillas (this became a major function of black regiments), supplied rations, clothing, and medicine to the freedmen, called upon missionary and voluntary associations in the North for help, and moved as quickly as possible to mobilize able-bodied contrabands as laborers and eventually as soldiers.

In all of this, the army's first priority was military efficiency. Humanitarianism was distinctly secondary. The army did not conceive of itself as a reform society. Its chief purpose was to organize the contrabands in such a way as to minimize their interference with military operations and to maximize their labor for support of these operations. The army and navy used contrabands as teamsters, stevedores, pioneers (construction workers), hospital orderlies and nurses, cooks, laundresses, servants, woodchoppers to cut fuel, and so on.

The only difference between these jobs and the same kinds of work that slaves did for the Confederate army was that Union laborers were free and received wages. But sometimes this was a distinction with little difference. While Confederate officers impressed black laborers without their consent, Union officers often did the same. Contraband laborers for the Union theoretically received wages, but many of them seldom saw a dollar because their wages had been deducted for clothing, family support, rations, or medical care. And while Confederate officers or overseers may have been harsh taskmasters, some Yankee provost marshals, quartermasters, and freedmen's superintendents matched them in this respect. Many contrabands could be excused for wondering what difference there was between their old status and the new one.

The same question could be asked by a good many freedmen who worked on plantations seized by the Union invaders. Some lessees of these plantations were dollar-hungry Yankees; others were Southerners who had taken the oath of allegiance. In the lower Mississippi valley, a number of planters took the oath and continued to operate their own plantations with their former slaves, the only difference being the payment of wages. But the same things seemed to happen to these wages as to those of black army laborers. A white Northern worker might have had trouble recognizing the system as free labor. Under regulations issued by General Nathaniel Banks for occupied Louisiana, and copied by army officers in the Mississippi valley north of Louisiana (two-thirds of the freedmen under organized Union control lived in these two areas), labor was defined as "a public duty," idleness and vagrancy as "a crime." All able-bodied freedmen not otherwise employed were required to labor on the public works. A contraband could choose his employer; but once he signed a contract, he must remain with this employer for the full year of the contract. The regulations stipulated minimum wages plus rations and housing. But so many deductions were allowed for clothing, medical care, days lost because of illness, and the like, that in effect most plantation hands wound up working for room and board. Provost marshals were ordered to enforce the "continuous and faithful service, respectful deportment, correct discipline and perfect subordination" of the workers.[5] Abolitionists denounced these regulations as a parody of free labor. Their anger was intensified by revelations of the bad character of many white lessees and of collusion between them and some provost marshals, who functioned much as the old slave patrol had done.

But this was only one side of the story. Some army officers were men of compassion and concern for the freedmen's welfare. This was especially true of Colonel John Eaton, an army chaplain appointed by Grant as head of freedmen's policy in the Mississippi valley, and of General Rufus Saxton, military governor of the South Carolina and Georgia offshore islands. Many of the freedmen in occupied territory, particularly those with skills, commanded good wages. The army intervened as often to protect workers from abuses by planters as to enforce planter discipline over workers. Not all plantation lessees were Simon Legrees. The very concept of written contracts and wages was itself new in the plantation South. It was a major step from a quasi-feudal toward a modern free-labor society.

Not all captured plantations were leased to private parties. Many remained under government control. Freedmen on these plantations worked under the direction of superintendents sent by the Northern freedmen's aid societies. This was the common pattern on the South Carolina offshore islands and in occupied portions of Virginia and North Carolina. These superintendents, unlike lessees or owners, often had more interest in helping the contrabands make the transition to freedom than in making a profit on the crop. But the profit motive also existed. A major theme of the proslavery argument had been the necessity of slavery for the South's staple-crop economy. Northern antislavery people were eager to demonstrate the profitability of free black labor. Although the chaos and disruption of war reduced crop yields below antebellum standards, the war-inflated price of cotton assured profits to most growers—so antislavery people pronounced the free-labor experiment a success.

To be sure, the practice of organizing plantation workers under white supervision—whether that of benevolent "superintendents" or profit-maximizing lessees—was only another form of paternalism. But the officers and civilians who confronted the masses of uprooted, ragged, suffering contrabands believed that they faced a condition, not a theory. After the army had drained off most of the able-bodied adult male contrabands as laborers and soldiers, the freedmen's superintendents were left with women and children and the aged and infirm. Some degree of paternalism was inevitable in these circumstances. The alternative would have been neglect and an appalling death rate that would have been cause for greater condemnation than the charge of paternalism.

As it was, the mortality rate in contraband camps was perhaps as high as 25 percent during the war. Shocking as this may seem, it becomes less so when compared to the nearly 20 percent disease death rates of Confederate soldiers and black Union soldiers, who included no old people or children in their ranks. White refugees displaced by the war also suffered awesome mortality rates. The worst ravages of disease and death among contrabands occurred *before* the Union armies and philanthropic societies acted to organize, discipline, and succor these black refugees. One reason for their determination to put all able-bodied contrabands to work was to disperse them away from the unhealthy camps, where congestion, dirt, and epidemics took a grim toll.

The Question of Land for Freedmen

An obvious alternative to the paternalism of white superintendents or lessees was to lease or sell confiscated lands directly to the freedmen. This was urged by Northern radicals and increasingly practiced in the occupied South. By the last year of the war, nearly 20 percent of the agricultural land under Union control was being independently farmed by blacks. The outstanding example of this occurred on the plantations of Jefferson Davis and his brother Joseph at Davis Bend south of Vicksburg. In 1864 and 1865 black farmers, many of them former slaves of the Confederacy's president, leased several thousand acres at Davis Bend and raised successful cotton and food crops. They cleared a profit of $159,000 on the 1865 cotton crop. These freedmen formed a self-governing colony with black sheriffs and justices of the peace elected by themselves. Freedmen in other parts of the South, especially the offshore islands, were able to buy land during the war.

Such opportunities gave black people a small start toward the status of independent farmers—a status that had become their chief aspiration. Most abolitionists and radical Republicans also envisioned a future South of landowning black farmers. But this vision encountered powerful obstacles. While the freedmen on the offshore islands bought 5,000 acres in 1863–1864, for example, Northern investors bought 20,000 acres (some of this land was later resold to blacks). Many of these Northern purchasers, like Northern lessees elsewhere, foreshadowed the postwar attitude of Southern planters in their preference for a landless black labor force rather than a small-holding black yeomanry.

The Constitution seemed to bar genuine land reform in the South. In July 1862, Lincoln had threatened to veto the second Confiscation Act because, in his view, its expropriation of real estate owned by Confederates violated the constitutional ban on bills of attainder that worked a forfeiture of property beyond the life of offenders.* At the President's insistence, Congress passed an explanatory resolution abrogating any intention to attaint the heirs of Confederates. This of course nullified the value of the Confiscation Act as an instrument of land redistribution. The Direct Tax Act of 1861, under which offshore island lands had been sold for nonpayment of taxes, offered another possibility for reallocating Southern land; but formidable legal and administrative problems loomed there as well.

Radicals were impatient with what they regarded as constitutional quibbles. "By all the laws and usages of civilized nations," said one abolitionist, "rebels against a government forfeit their property." Without land the freedmen would be only half free. "To be safe, peaceable, and permanent," insisted radicals, reconstruction "must be primarily economical and industrial; it must commence by planting a loyal population in the South, not only as its cultivators but as its rightful and actual owners. . . . No such thing as a free, democratic society can exist in any country where all lands are owned by one class of men and cultivated by another."[6]

Lincoln's amnesty proclamation in December 1863 further undermined the chances of land reform by restoring property (except slaves) to Confederates who took the oath of allegiance. Although several thousand Southerners were excluded from this offer of pardon, Lincoln held open the possibility of including them later. "If the President can restore to these traitors all their rights to the land," said one angry abolitionist, "the Confiscation Act is a farce, and the war will have been a gigantic failure."[7]

Early in 1864, radical Congressman George W. Julian introduced a bill to

*Article III, Section 3 of the Constitution states: "The Congress shall have Power to declare the Punishment of Treason, but no Attainder of Treason shall work Corruption of Blood, or Forfeiture except during the Life of the Person attainted." The second Confiscation Act had provided for the seizure of the property of Confederates as a punishment for their treason against the United States. But since this provision would have prevented the children of those so punished from inheriting this property ("corruption of blood"), Lincoln threatened to veto it unless Congress modified the act to prevent this. Since the English precedents on which this section of the Constitution was based applied only to real estate, Lincoln believed that property in slaves would be exempt from the ban on corruption of blood—in other words, slaves could be legally confiscated, but land could not.

extend the homestead act of 1862 to abandoned and confiscated lands in the South. Julian's bill would have granted forty or eighty acres to each head of a freed family, Southern Unionist, and Union army veteran. Although this proposal seemed to conflict with Lincoln's policy, Julian claimed to have secured the President's agreement to sign a repeal of the 1862 resolution limiting confiscation to the life of the offender. Whatever the truth of this claim, the House and Senate each passed in different forms a repeal of the 1862 resolution. But constitutional scruples and the conservatism of some Republicans, who hesitated to tamper with the property rights even of Rebels, prevented final passage of the repeal or of Julian's land redistribution bill. The closest that Congress would come to such legislation was a provision in the law of March 3, 1865, creating a Freedmen's Bureau. This provision stipulated that forty acres of abandoned or confiscated land could be leased to each Southern freedman or Unionist with an option to buy after three years with "such title thereto as the United States can convey."[8]

A large land redistribution program was already under way when Congress passed this bill. Ironically, the man who initiated it—William Tecumseh Sherman —had little use for radicals or freedmen. When Sherman's army reached Savannah in December 1864 after its march through Georgia, thousands of ragged freedmen were straggling in its wake (see p. 462). After a conference with twenty black leaders, who told him that "the way we can best take care of ourselves is to have land," Sherman issued a special order on January 16 designating the coastline and riverbanks thirty miles inland from Charleston to Jacksonville as an area for the resettlement of freedmen on forty acres of land per family. They would receive "possessory titles" to this land until Congress "shall regulate the title." By the end of June 1865, the army had settled more than 40,000 freedmen in this area. The future would determine whether Congress was capable of converting the "possessory titles" into true ownership.[9]

Freedmen's Education

Land ownership was one prop of the radical vision of the future; another was education. In the end, the quest for education was more successful than the quest for land. The Northern crusade to plant schools in the South was one modernizing innovation that really took hold in the former Confederacy.

A Northern missionary in occupied Louisiana wrote in 1863 that he was surrounded by

> negroes in uniform, negroes in rags, negroes in frame houses, negroes living in tents, negroes living in rail pens covered with brush, and negroes living under brush piles without any rails, negroes living on the bare ground with the sky for their covering; all hopeful . . . every one pleading to be taught, willing to do anything for learning. They are never out of our rooms, and their cry is for "Books! Books!" and "when will school begin?"[10]

Abolitionists took the lead in forming freedmen's aid societies all over the North. "The duty of abolitionists to their clients will not cease with the technical abolition of slavery," wrote one. Freedmen's education was the next stage of the movement. "Our duty is to *see the negro through*."[11] Freedmen's aid societies sent at least a thousand teachers during the war, who planted schools in occupied territory. These teachers were the forerunners of 2,000 more who came South in the early postwar years. "We have come to do anti-slavery work, and we think it noble work and mean to do it nobly," wrote one of the first Northern teachers to arrive at Beaufort, South Carolina, in 1862. A generation later, the black leader W. E. B. Du Bois wrote that these missionary teachers, three-quarters of them women, were unsung Civil War heroines and heroes who "fought the most wonderful peace-battle of the 19th century. . . . [They] came not to keep the Negroes in their places, but to raise them out of the defilement of the places where slavery had wallowed them. . . . This was the gift of New England to the freed Negro."[12]

Not all of the teachers were white. The first freedmen's school, established at Fortress Monroe, Virginia, in September 1861, was taught by a free black woman. During the 1860s, perhaps 20 percent of the 4,000 teachers in freedmen's schools were black. Southern blacks founded and supported many of these schools from their own resources.

As Du Bois implied, however, freedmen's education was predominantly a New England enterprise. Three-fifths of the white teachers were born in New England. The largest of the freedmen's societies was the American Missionary Association (Congregational), which received most of its support from New England. The strongest of the secular societies was the New England Freedmen's Aid Society. One teacher wrote that he conceived of his mission as the founding in Alabama of "a real New England civilization." Another hoped that the Yankee school-marm's crusade would furnish enough teachers "to make a New England of the whole South."[13]

The Northern teachers conceived of education as being much broader than the three R's. They hoped to implant in the South the values of the Protestant ethic and the free-labor ideology. At the core of these values was the concept of the necessity and nobility of work. Yankee missionaries condemned the coercive labor regulations of some Union commanders in the occupied South. They believed that the work ethic must be internalized through education, not imposed externally by compulsion. The best kind of discipline was *self-*discipline. The freedmen "need to be held to the Puritan doctrine of the dignity of labor," wrote one abolitionist missionary. Slavery had degraded the nobility of work by associating it with bondage. To help the freedmen "unlearn the teachings of slavery," the schools drilled students in "lessons of industry, of domestic management and thrift"; they taught that "industry is commendable and indispensable to freedom, and indolence both wicked and degrading." Freed slaves, the missionaries believed, needed "the New England church and school to . . . beget order, sobriety, purity, and faith" and teach them to become "like Northerners, in industry, economy, and thrift."[14]

The freedmen's schools reached an estimated 200,000 blacks during the war. After Appomattox, the expanded freedmen's education program reached a much larger number. These schools began an assault on illiteracy that was later con-

(Reproduced from the Collections of the Library of Congress)

The photograph above shows contraband laborers building a stockade in Union-occupied Alexandria, Virginia. Note that the blacks are doing the work while whites stand around and supervise. The right-hand photo shows the integrated teaching staff of a freedmen's school near Norfolk, Virginia.

(Massachusetts Commandery Military Order of the Loyal Legion and the U.S. Army Military History Institute)

tinued by the South's new public school system, built on the foundations of Northern missionary schools.

An important partner of the privately supported freedmen's societies was the Freedmen's Bureau, which spent a third of its budget from 1865 to 1870 on schools. Its full name was the Bureau of Refugees, Freedmen, and Abandoned Lands. First proposed in 1863, the Bureau's establishment was delayed until March 3, 1865, by disagreement between the House and Senate over whether it should be in the War or Treasury Department. Congress finally placed it in the War Department. The Bureau's operations were modeled on the army's wartime experience in the occupied South. It functioned as a relief agency for displaced refugees of both races; it drafted and enforced labor contracts between planters and freedmen; and it cooperated with voluntary associations in the operation of freedmen's schools.

The Government and the Freedmen

The record of the Union government toward the freedmen was a mixture of success and failure, humanitarianism and exploitation, kindness and cruelty. The government's policy often seemed confused and shortsighted; but the government was faced with an unprecedented situation. The emancipation of four million slaves and the reconstruction of a slave society torn apart by civil war were totally new experiences. No models existed to guide those who had to deal with them. There was no tradition of government responsibility for a huge refugee population, no bureaucracy to administer a large welfare and employment program. The Union army and government were groping in the dark. They created the precedents. No other society in history had liberated so many slaves in so short a time; no other army had ever carried through such a social revolution. No other country had established a Freedmen's Bureau to deal with the problems of emancipated slaves; no other society had poured so much effort and money into the education of ex-slaves. Small as these efforts may have been, they were revolutionary by the standards of their time.

POLITICAL RECONSTRUCTION

The fate of any freedmen's policy depended ultimately on the conditions of political reconstruction. Lincoln preferred a moderate approach to this question. The President was an old Whig of the Henry Clay school. He had enjoyed cordial relations with Southern Whigs in antebellum days. He knew that many of these men had been conditional Unionists in 1861. His 10 percent reconstruction plan was an appeal to these old Whigs and other Unionists to come forward and reassert their allegiance to the Union. For Lincoln, the task of reconstruction was one of restoration rather than revolution. Not restoration of the Union "as it was," to be sure, for the new Union would not have slavery. But the President was willing to permit pardoned Southern leaders to "adopt some practical system" to cushion the shock of the "total revolution of labor" and thus enable blacks and whites to "gradually live themselves out of their old relation to each other."[15]

Abolitionists and radicals did not want to cushion the shock of revolution. "The whole social system of the Gulf States [must] be taken to pieces," said Wendell Phillips. "This is primarily a social revolution. . . . The war can only be ended by annihilating that Oligarchy which formed and rules the South and makes the war —by annihilating a state of society."[16] Next to Phillips, Congressman Thaddeus Stevens was the most outspoken advocate of reconstruction as revolution. Described by contemporary European observers as "the Robespierre, Danton, and Marat" of one of the "most radical revolutions known to history," Stevens declared that reconstruction must "revolutionize Southern institutions, habits, and manners. . . . The foundations of their institutions . . . must be broken up and relaid, or all our blood and treasure have been spent in vain."[17]

Such sentiments were shared by many radical officers and officials in the occupied South. Northern values and institutions must prevail after the war, wrote a Massachusetts colonel in South Carolina, and they could do this only by "changing, revolutionizing, absorbing the institutions, life, and manners of the conquered people." A Treasury agent in Louisiana said in 1864 that "there [can] be no middle ground in a revolution. It must work a radical change in society; such [has] been the history of every great revolution."[18] But moderates also cited history to support their *evolutionary* approach. "The history of the world," wrote General Banks (in charge of Lincoln's reconstruction program in Louisiana), "shows that revolutions which are not controlled and held within reasonable limits, produce counter-revolutions."[19]

These contrasting viewpoints framed the struggle within the Republican party over the terms of reconstruction during the first half of 1864. The outcome was a stalemate, but the contest came close to splitting the party and threatening Lincoln's reelection.

Lincoln's policy was based on his theory of the indissoluble Union. Since the states could not legally secede, they were still in the Union. The task of reconstruction, therefore, was to establish a process whereby loyal citizens could regain control of their states. In a practical sense, however, the Confederate states were unquestionably *out* of the Union. Most congressional Republicans did not wish to allow former Rebels to come back into the Union merely by taking a loyalty oath. Distrusting former Confederates, Republicans wished to entrust reconstruction only to undoubted Unionists. They intended to impose conditions that would guarantee the freedom and civil rights of blacks. To justify such interference with the constitutional rights of states, they developed a variety of theories. Thaddeus Stevens declared that since the Southern states had indeed gone out of the Union they should be treated under international law as "conquered provinces." This was too radical for most Republicans, who leaned toward Charles Sumner's argument that by seceding, Southern states had committed "state suicide." Having thus forfeited their rights under the Constitution, they had reverted to the status of territories that could be readmitted as states only when they met the conditions laid down by Congress. But this concept of territorialization was also too strong for some Republicans. More than one-fourth of the House Republicans joined with Democrats and border-state congressmen to defeat a territorialization reconstruction measure in 1862.

Meanwhile, Lincoln had seized the initiative from Congress by appointing military governors for the occupied portions of four Confederate states in 1862. Although this was a pragmatic response to the need for an interim authority to administer occupied territory, Lincoln clearly intended it as a first step toward presidential reconstruction (that is, the shaping of reconstruction policy by executive decision rather than by congressional legislation). At the same time, moderate Republicans in Congress worked out an ingenious alternative to territorialization. Article IV, Section 4, of the Constitution specifies that "the United States shall guarantee to every State in this Union a Republican form of Government." The framers had intended "republican" to mean only nonmonarchical. But like other parts of the Constitution, this phrase was capable of new interpretations to fit changing conditions. For Republicans in 1863, rebellion and slavery could be construed as denials of a republican form of government. To be sure, this raised certain awkward questions. If slavery was unrepublican in Confederate states, what about loyal border states? Nevertheless, by 1863 a consensus had emerged among Republicans to base reconstruction on this clause of the Constitution. Neither the congressional idea of territorialization nor the presidential theory of indestructible states disappeared, but both were subsumed under the concept of a republican form of government, whose ambiguity could justify almost anything.

But the phrase "republican form of government" did not abolish the differences between Lincoln's approach and that of the radicals. The President's policy of pardoning Rebels and letting them take part in reconstruction, said Wendell Phillips, "leaves the large landed proprietors of the South still to domineer over its politics, and makes the negro's freedom a mere sham." Once these pardoned Confederates regained power, warned Phillips, "the Revolution may be easily checked with the aid of the Administration, which is willing that the negro should be free but seeks nothing else for him. . . . What McClellan was on the battle-field —'Do as little hurt as possible!'—Lincoln is in civil affairs—'Make as little change as possible!'"[20]

Not only did radicals want land reform in the South; many of them began to urge black suffrage as well. They did so on grounds of both justice and expediency. For a generation, abolitionists had been trying to win equal voting rights for blacks in the North; they were now prepared to extend that struggle to the South. Unless enfranchised, they said, the freed slaves would never be able to protect themselves against a political counterrevolution by the old master class. Abolitionists also maintained that the freedmen constituted the only large bloc of unconditional Unionists in the lower South. Without their voting power, a reconstructed state would stand on a fragile foundation of loyalty. Was it justice or sound policy to deny the ballot to men who had worked and fought for the Union while giving this precious right to men who had fought against it? "The negro has earned land, education, rights," Phillips told packed lecture halls in early 1864. "Before we leave him, we ought to leave him on his own soil, in his own house, with the ballot and the school-house within reach. Unless we have done it, the North has let the cunning of politics filch the fruits of war."[21]

This doctrine was too advanced for most Republicans in 1864. The Northern electorate, only recently converted to emancipation as a war measure, was scarcely ready yet for political equality. But if at this time only the most radical spokesmen publicly favored black suffrage, the history of the war indicated that where the radicals led, a majority of Republicans would eventually follow. Salmon P. Chase wrote after private talks with several Republicans in the last weeks of 1863: "I find that almost all who are willing to have the colored men fight are willing to have them vote."[22]

Louisiana

Events in Louisiana brought the differing approaches of Lincoln and the radicals toward reconstruction into sharp perspective. In New Orleans, a substantial portion of the middle class and the skilled artisan class, which included some of the 10,000 antebellum free Negroes, provided the nucleus for a genuinely radical reconstruction. Many of these people had opposed secession. They had little stake in slavery and less liking for it. In 1863 their political leaders formed the Free State General Committee and urged the calling of a convention to write a new state constitution. "It seems to me as though I was in a new world," wrote a Treasury agent working with the Free State Committee. "A large majority are as radical as we ever were. A colored delegation of intelligent free men were admitted, which was more than would have been done in Ohio."[23] General Banks, however, favored the moderate Unionist faction in Louisiana over the radical Free State Committee. Instead of calling a constitutional convention as the radicals wished, Banks set up an election of state officers and congressmen under the antebellum constitution, modified by a military order which abolished slavery. Eager to hasten the reconstruction process in Louisiana as a model for other states, Lincoln told Banks to go ahead.

Banks was in a position to influence the results of the election. The Union army controlled the voter registration process. Banks dispensed patronage to leaders of the moderate faction. Many voters would think twice before going against the wishes of the general in command of the occupation forces. Not surprisingly, the moderates easily won the election held on February 22, 1864. Banks's role in this outcome angered the radical Free State men and alienated powerful congressional Republicans. To repair some of the damage, Lincoln urged Banks to put pressure on the moderates to frame a liberal state constitution at the convention now scheduled for April. Meanwhile the Free State committee sent two leaders of the New Orleans black community to Washington bearing a petition for black suffrage. Impressed by the education and eloquence of these men, Lincoln wrote a letter to Michael Hahn, newly elected governor of occupied Louisiana. The constitutional convention would decide the qualifications for voters in the new era. "I barely suggest for your private consideration," wrote the President, "whether some of the colored people may not be let in—as, for instance, the very intelligent, and especially those who have fought gallantly in our ranks. They would probably help, in some trying time to come, to keep the jewel of liberty within the family of freedom."[24]

This letter demonstrated Lincoln's readiness to meet the radicals halfway. But he needed to do more than "barely suggest" black suffrage to get it adopted in Louisiana. Despite pressure from Banks, the convention gave the legislature only discretionary power to enfranchise blacks in the future. The new constitution did prohibit slavery and create a public school system for both races. But this did not mollify radicals. The ratification vote on the constitution represented only 10 percent of the adult white males in the state. Congressional Republicans considered this too slender a basis for reconstruction, especially since none of the radicals —the most reliable Unionists—were part of Louisiana's new government. If this was the showcase of Lincoln's reconstruction policy, a growing number of congressional Republicans wanted no part of it.

The Wade-Davis Bill

But Congress had some recourse—it had the power to exclude representatives from Louisiana, and it did so. It also denied admission to congressmen elected under Lincoln's policy from occupied portions of Arkansas, and it refused to count the electoral votes from both of these states, as well as those from Tennessee, in the 1864 presidential election. Going beyond these negative actions, Congress tried to regain the initiative on reconstruction. "Everybody abounds in schemes for settling the troubles in the rebel states," wrote one jaded congressman, "and at least six plans a day are offered in the shape of a Bill."[25] After nearly five months of debate, the Republicans on July 2, 1864, passed a bill sponsored by Congressman Henry Winter Davis of Maryland and Senator Benjamin Wade of Ohio. The Wade-Davis measure differed from Lincoln's program in several important respects: instead of requiring only 10 percent of the voters to take an oath of allegiance to begin the process, it required 50 percent; instead of allowing this group to elect new state officers, it mandated the election, first, of delegates to a constitutional convention; instead of permitting all whites who took an oath of future loyalty to vote in such an election, it enfranchised only those who could take the "iron-clad oath" swearing that they had never voluntarily supported the rebellion; and it enacted specific legal safeguards of the freedmen's liberty, which were to be enforced by federal courts.

Like Lincoln's program, however, the Wade-Davis bill confined the reconstruction process to white voters. At one point in its progress through the congressional labyrinth, the bill had enfranchised all "loyal" men; but in the last-minute rush to get it passed before adjournment, Wade consented to a white-only amendment to save the bill. Most radicals (the radicals constituted about one-third of the Republican congressmen and senators at this time) would probably have preferred to include black suffrage. But they went along with the deletion in order to have some program with which "to go before the country" in the forthcoming elections. They also expected the 50 percent requirement and the stringent restrictions on white voters to postpone reconstruction until the war was over, when the increasing radicalism of the North might sustain a black suffrage requirement.

Despite the nearly unanimous vote of congressional Republicans for the Wade-Davis bill, Lincoln exercised the little-used constitutional provision for a pocket veto, whereby the president can kill a bill passed at the end of a session merely by refusing to sign it. Lincoln issued a statement explaining his action: he was unwilling to approve a measure that would commit him to any single plan of restoration, especially since it would destroy the fragile governments of Louisiana and Arkansas that he was trying to nurse along. But Lincoln stated a willingness to enforce the Wade-Davis plan in any state "choosing to adopt it"—surely a remote possibility when the milder presidential plan was available as an alternative.[26]

Goaded to fury by Lincoln's cool defiance of Congress, Wade and Davis published a blistering manifesto on August 5. "Congress passed a bill; the President refused to approve it, and then by proclamation puts as much of it in force as he sees fit. . . . A more studied outrage on the legislative authority of the people has never been perpetrated." Throwing down the gauntlet in behalf of congressional Republicans, Wade and Davis warned Lincoln that "if he wishes our support, he must confine himself to his Executive duties—to obey and to execute, not to make the laws—to suppress by arms armed rebellion, and leave political reorganization to Congress."[27]

RECONSTRUCTION AND PRESIDENTIAL POLITICS

Seldom has a president been so sharply attacked by leaders of his own party in the midst of a political campaign whose outcome might determine the nation's life. But this came as little surprise, for the reconstruction issue had long been embroiled in intraparty factionalism. In early 1864, Lincoln's renomination had been by no means assured. The prevailing tradition was a one-term presidency. No president had been elected to a second term since 1832, and no incumbent had been renominated by his party since 1840. Several Republicans believed themselves at least as well qualified as Lincoln for the office.

Foremost among these was Salmon P. Chase, whose ambition overwhelmed his judgment. Chase used Treasury patronage to build a political machine for his nomination in 1864. This effort won the support of radicals disenchanted with Lincoln's reconstruction policy. But Chase's supporters played their hand so badly that once again, as in the cabinet crisis of December 1862 (see pp. 306–307), the secretary was outsmarted and humiliated. In early February, a pro-Chase pamphlet entitled *The Next Presidential Election* circulated in the Midwest under the frank of prominent Republican congressmen. Several days later Chase's manager, Senator Samuel C. Pomeroy of Kansas, sent out a "strictly private" circular touting the secretary's presidential potential. The Pomeroy Circular was soon leaked to the press. The reaction to these documents turned the premature Chase boom into a boomerang. Lincoln proved to have greater support in the party than expected. While Chase had been creating a machine in the Treasury Department, the President had used the patronage of other departments to build a strong organization in nearly every Northern state. Republican legislatures or conventions in fourteen states—including Chase's home state of Ohio—passed resolutions endorsing Lincoln's renomination. The Republican National Committee did the same. The Chase movement collapsed.*

The hopes of some anti-Lincoln radicals next focused on General John C. Frémont. After resigning his Shenandoah Valley command in June 1862, Frémont had cooled his heels in New York "awaiting orders." Ever since his abortive emancipation edict of 1861 in Missouri, he had been something of a hero to abolitionists and radical German Americans. Representatives of these groups met on May 31 in Cleveland to nominate Frémont for president on a platform calling for a constitutional amendment to "secure to all men absolute equality before the law" and to distribute confiscated Rebel land "among the soldiers and settlers."[28]

But this apparently radical platform was tainted by evidence that Democrats had infiltrated the movement. The convention's vice-presidential nominee was General John Cochrane, a lifelong Democrat. One plank of the platform condemned the administration's suppression of free speech and suspension of *habeas corpus*—which were Democratic issues. The convention named itself the "Radical Democratic party," which pretty well summed up this political marriage of strange bedfellows. Although some abolitionists followed Wendell Phillips in supporting Frémont's candidacy, most concurred with William Lloyd Garrison's observation that Frémont had become the catspaw of wily War Democrats hoping to divide and conquer the Republicans. No prominent Republican endorsed Frémont.

When the Republican national convention met in Baltimore on June 7, Lincoln's managers had matters well in hand. Only the radical Missouri delegation opposed the President's renomination. Calling itself the National Union party to broaden its appeal, the convention nominated the Tennessee War Democrat Andrew Johnson for vice president. Avoiding the knotty problem of reconstruction, the platform endorsed Lincoln's war measures, rejected any peace terms except unconditional surrender of the Confederacy, and endorsed a constitutional amendment to abolish slavery.

This demonstration of party harmony concealed persistent divisions caused by the reconstruction issue. At least one-third of the congressional Republicans were unhappy with Lincoln's nomination. Behind the scenes, several radicals continued to maneuver for some way to replace Lincoln with a more acceptable nominee. The President's pocket veto of the reconstruction bill had crystallized Republican discontent. The Wade-Davis Manifesto formed part of an ill-coordinated scheme for a new convention to nominate General Benjamin Butler for president. War Democrats were expected to rally behind this ticket, Frémont would withdraw his

---

*The embarrassed Chase offered to resign after the Pomeroy Circular became public, but Lincoln preferred to keep him in the cabinet, where he would be less of a threat to the President's renomination. Four months later, however, when Chase again offered his resignation over a patronage dispute, Lincoln—now safely renominated—accepted it.

candidacy, and recognizing the inevitable, Lincoln himself would then step down.

In the murky political atmosphere of August 1864 a good many intelligent men actually believed that such a fantastic scheme could work. To understand why, we must turn to the story of the 1864 military campaigns. For in the final analysis, it was not the issue of reconstruction but the issues of war and peace on which the 1864 election turned. The high hopes for military victory with which the North had begun the year had turned to despair as Grant and Sherman appeared to be stymied before Richmond and Atlanta, after fighting a series of battles with staggering casualties. By August, war weariness and defeatism had settled over the Northern political landscape like a heavy fog in which people blindly groped their way.

Twenty-three

Military Stalemate, 1864

The apparent reversal of military fortunes in the summer of 1864 was all the more shocking to the North because the Confederacy's prospects had appeared so bleak at the beginning of the year. With fewer than half as many men under arms as the North, the South had no more reserves of manpower to draw on while the North could mobilize hundreds of thousands of new volunteers and draftees. Tennessee was wholly occupied by Union troops, the Trans-Mississippi Department was cut off from the rest of the Confederacy, the railroad system of the South was in shambles, and supplies of all kinds were lacking. Southern leaders were quarreling with one another over responsibility for the defeats of 1863, and powerful Northern armies were poised for the kill. A Confederate War Department official wrote in his diary on November 6, 1863: "I have never actually despaired of the cause . . . [but now] steadfastness is yielding to a sense of hopelessness."[1]

But all was not so hopeless as it seemed. Morale among front-line Confederate troops remained high, aided by a wave of religious revivals in the winter camps. Southern soldiers were nearly all veterans, while the expiration of Northern three-year enlistments in 1864 foretold a decline in the fighting quality of blue regiments. True, many Confederate three-year enlistments also expired in 1864, but a recent amendment to the conscription law required all of these men to reenlist.

In contrast, Northern men whose enlistments expired were free to leave the army. If all of them did so, nearly half of the combat troops—by far the best half, veterans with three years' experience—would melt away. Instead of compelling these men to reenlist, the Union government relied on persuasion and inducement: an appeal to patriotism and pride, plus a thirty-day furlough and a $300 federal bounty (in addition to state and local bounties for many soldiers) to those who reenlisted. More than half of the three-year veterans reenlisted,* some with fanfare and parades, but most, perhaps, in the spirit expressed by two privates in a Massachusetts regiment that had fought in all the Army of the Potomac's major battles and suffered heavy losses. "They use a man here," said one, "just the same as they do a turkey at a shooting match, fire at it all day and if they don't kill it raffle it off in the evening; so with us, if they can't kill you in three years they want you for three more—but I will stay." And his messmate added: "If new men won't finish the job, old men must."[2]

Without these "veteran volunteers" (who wore a special chevron on their sleeves), the Union armies would have become hollow shells in 1864. This was all the more true because of the unpromising character of many new recruits. Bounty men, substitutes, and conscripts poured into the camps of veteran regiments to bring them up to strength. The boys of '61 were appalled by these "off-scourings of northern slums," these "dregs of every nation . . . branded felons . . . thieves, burglars and vagabonds." With some exaggeration, a New Hampshire veteran wrote that "such another depraved, vice-hardened and desperate set of human beings never before disgraced an army." Another old soldier remarked that "if those fellows are trusted on picket, the army will soon be in hell."[3] Many of the new soldiers deserted as soon as they got a chance. "The men we have been getting in this way nearly all desert," Grant informed the War Department in September 1864, "and out of five reported North as having enlisted we don't get more than one effective soldier."[4] These factors reduced the North's numerical superiority much below appearances. Coupled with the South's advantages of fighting on the defensive, they went a long way toward evening the odds for Confederate survival.

UNION MILITARY STRATEGY IN 1864

In 1864 the North developed a unified command system to coordinate strategy on all fronts. This had been Lincoln's purpose when he appointed Halleck general in chief in 1862, but Halleck had abdicated the responsibility. In March 1864, Grant came to Washington to assume Halleck's title.† But Grant had no intention of becoming a desk general. He thenceforth made his headquarters with the Army of the Potomac, becoming in effect its strategic field commander while Meade remained its titular and tactical commander. Halleck agreeably stepped down to become chief of staff. He stayed in Washington, where his office served as a communications and operations center for Grant's orders to the far-flung armies under his control.

Lincoln at last had a general in chief whose strategic ideas accorded with his own. He could trust Grant to act decisively without the constant prodding neces-

---

*Approximately half of the three-year veterans in the Army of the Potomac reenlisted. The percentage of reenlistments in the western armies was higher.

†Congress had revived the rank of lieutenant general, previously held only by George Washington (Winfield Scott had held this rank by brevet only). Lincoln promoted Grant to lieutenant general and appointed him general in chief of all the armies.

**Lieutenant-General
Ulysses S. Grant at His
Field Headquarters,
1864** *(Reproduced from the
Collections of the Library of
Congress)*

sary with previous commanders in the Virginia theater. Grant believed that in the past the various Union armies had "acted independently and without concert, like a balky team, no two ever pulling together."[5] This had allowed the Confederates to shift troops from one point to another to meet the most pressing danger. For two years Lincoln had been trying to get his armies to advance simultaneously on several fronts, and now Grant worked out such an overall plan. He issued orders to five Union armies stretched over a thousand miles of front to begin coordinated campaigns as early in the spring as possible.

The Army of the Potomac, with about 115,000 men, would attack the 64,000-strong Army of Northern Virginia. "Lee's Army will be your objective point," Grant told Meade. "Wherever Lee goes, there you will go also."[6] Two small armies in Virginia would operate on the perimeters of the main action: Benjamin Butler was to move from Fortress Monroe up the James River with 30,000 men to threaten Richmond from the south and prevent reinforcements from being sent to Lee. At the same time Franz Sigel, now in command of the scattered Union forces in West Virginia, was to move up the Shenandoah Valley to prevent its resources and defenders from going to Lee's aid. As Lincoln aptly described the auxiliary role of Butler and Sigel: "Those not skinning can hold a leg."[7]

Next to Virginia, the most important theater would be Georgia, where Sherman's 100,000 faced Johnston's 50,000 (reinforced to 65,000 as the campaign began). Grant directed Sherman "to move against Johnston's army, to break it up and to get into the interior of the enemy's country as far as you can, inflicting all the damage you can against their war resources."[8] Banks was to move from New Orleans against Mobile, and after capturing that important port he was to strike northeast through Alabama into Georgia to cooperate with Sherman in a pincers movement that would crush all Confederate resistance in that area.

FAILURE OF THE AUXILIARY CAMPAIGNS

Like most military plans, however, this one went awry, partly because the Confederate armies still had a great deal of defensive punch, but also because the Union's political generals—Banks, Butler, and Sigel—did not do their jobs. Indeed, Banks's Mobile campaign did not even get started, though this was not entirely his fault.

The Red River Campaign

Ever since the fall of Vicksburg, Grant and Banks had wanted to move against Mobile. But Lincoln had ordered Banks's Army of the Gulf to invade Texas instead. The President desired a Union military presence in Texas as a warning to France, which was in the process of setting up a puppet government in Mexico. Banks had been unable to do more than plant the flag in a few enclaves along the Texas Gulf coast in 1863. But in March 1864 he undertook an ambitious campaign up the Red River of Louisiana, with the intention of capturing Shreveport and using it as a jumping-off point for an expedition into Texas.

The Confederates had 30,000 combat troops scattered in various detachments around the Trans-Mississippi Department under the overall command of Edmund Kirby Smith. The main Rebel force in Louisiana was commanded by Richard Taylor, son of former President Zachary Taylor. Banks had an army of 27,000 men (10,000 of them borrowed from Sherman), supported by a powerful fleet of river ironclads under Admiral David Porter. Cooperating with Banks was a Union army of 15,000 moving south from Little Rock. From the outset, Grant had considered this campaign a wasteful diversion. He ordered Banks to get it over with quickly, garrison Shreveport, and return most of his troops to New Orleans to launch the campaign against Mobile. But Banks started late and conducted his campaign poorly. On April 8, Taylor's forces routed Banks's advance divisions at Sabine Crossroads, forty miles south of Shreveport. Next day the Federals made a stand at Pleasant Hill and struck the pursuing Confederates a sharp blow.

A vigorous general might have followed up this tactical victory with a fast march to Shreveport, but Banks decided instead to retreat. He had learned that the Union column from Arkansas could not link up with him because bad roads and Confederate cavalry had forced it back to Little Rock. Worse still, the abnormally low Red River was dropping fast and threatening to maroon Porter's entire fleet above the rapids at Alexandria. Calamity was averted by a Wisonsin colonel with a lumbering background, who supervised the construction of a series of ingenious dams that floated the fleet over the rapids. Banks's army returned downriver too late for a drive against Mobile, and the 10,000 troops borrowed from Sherman went to Mississippi to cope with Forrest instead of joining Sherman in Georgia. Lincoln's Texas campaign never even made it to Texas. The Confederates still controlled Texas, northern Louisiana, and southern Arkansas. And with French support, Maximilian had become emperor of Mexico (see p. 344). Banks was relieved of field command, though he remained in charge of the military administration of southern Louisiana.

The James River and Shenandoah Valley Campaigns

While Banks was coming to grief in Louisiana, Butler and Sigel were failing to carry out their part of Grant's strategy in Virginia. Butler brought his 30,000 well-armed troops up the James River and landed fifteen miles south of Richmond on May 5. From there he might have cut the railroads linking Richmond to the South, occupied Petersburg, or even smashed his way into the capital itself against the scratch force of 5,000 troops and an equal number of government clerks serving as emergency militia. Any of these actions would have crippled Lee, then engaged in a desperate battle with Grant sixty miles to the north; for the railroad between Richmond and Petersburg was Lee's lifeline.

In the end, Butler failed to accomplish any of these objectives. Instead of attacking boldly with their overwhelming superiority, Butler's troops entrenched, tore up only a few miles of track, then advanced cautiously toward Richmond on May 12. General Beauregard, in charge of the capital's defenses, had by then assembled an army equal in size to Butler's mobile force (about 18,000 men). Beauregard launched a counterattack on May 16 near Drewry's Bluff, seven miles from Richmond. Although both sides suffered heavy casualties, the Federals were forced back to their trenches across the narrow neck of land between the James and Appomattox rivers just north of Petersburg. The Confederates then entrenched their own line across the neck. As Grant later put it, Butler's army was "as completely shut off from further operations directly against Richmond as if it had been in a bottle strongly corked."[9] Not only had Butler failed to strike a blow against Lee's rear; he could not even prevent Beauregard from sending nearly 7,000 reinforcements to the hard-pressed Army of Northern Virginia.

Despite this sorry performance, Butler's political influence was too great for Lincoln to remove him from command. But the hapless Franz Sigel did not escape this fate. Advancing up the Shenandoah Valley, Sigel was attacked and defeated at New Market on May 15 by a Confederate force of 5,000 in a battle remembered chiefly for a spirited charge by 247 teen-age cadets from the Virginia Military Institute. Sigel had failed in his dual mission—to cut the railroad from the valley to Richmond and to prevent reinforcements being sent to Lee. On May 21 Lincoln relieved him of command.

THE WILDERNESS AND SPOTSYLVANIA

Having planned that Butler and Sigel would each hold a Rebel leg while the Army of the Potomac did the skinning, Grant now realized that this army would have to do the whole job by itself. It would be no easy task, for in two weeks of fighting the Army of the Potomac had already suffered more casualties than in any comparable period of the war.

On May 4 the blue divisions began crossing the Rapidan for a campaign that the North expected would win the war within a month or two. Grant intended

A Grisly Omen. These skeletons of Union soldiers killed at Chancellorsville in May 1863, their shallow graves uncovered by erosion or animals, greeted living Union soldiers exactly a year later, at the beginning of the Wilderness campaign. The Wilderness promised to turn many of them into skeletons as well. *(Reproduced from the Collections of the Library of Congress)*

to move around Lee's right to force his army out of its trenches and into open battle. Lee accepted the challenge, but he planned to hit the Yankees in the flank before they emerged from the dense second-growth forest known as the Wilderness, where Federal numerical and artillery superiority would count for little. It was in the Wilderness that Lee had brought Joe Hooker to grief exactly one year earlier in the battle of Chancellorsville. He hoped to repeat the performance with Grant.

The Battle of the Wilderness

On May 5, Lee's advance units came into contact with Grant's southward-marching men. The surprised Federals faced right and attacked, bringing on two days of vicious fighting in woods so thick that soldiers seldom saw their enemies but fired at the spot where the sound and smoke indicated they were. Whole brigades got lost in the forest; officers had little control over the confused movements of their men; muzzle flashes from thousands of rifles set the underbrush on fire; scores of wounded men burned to death. Most of the fighting surged back and forth near the intersections of the two main roads through the Wilderness. At the end of the first day Union forces still held the vital intersections.

That night Grant ordered Winfield Scott Hancock, commander of the army's crack 2nd Corps, to throw everything he had into an assault on the Confederate right at dawn. The Union generals knew that Longstreet's corps had not come up in time for the first day's fighting. They hoped to roll up Lee's flank before Longstreet could arrive next morning. At first Hancock's attack on May 6 went well. It drove the Rebel right back a mile to a small clearing where Lee had his command post. On the verge of a smashing success, the blue brigades became disorganized by their advance through the tangled woods. At just that moment, the leading units of Longstreet's fresh troops double-timed into the clearing from the opposite side. Agitated by his brush with disaster, Lee tried personally to lead these troops against the re-forming Yankee line. But the gray soldiers shouted "General Lee to the rear" and restrained him, while Longstreet calmly directed a counterattack that rocked the Federals back on their heels.

Later in the morning Longstreet sent part of his corps along the cut of an unfinished railroad, from which they launched a surprise assault on Hancock's exposed flank. Now it was the Confederates' turn to lose all cohesion as they drove the Yankees back through the woods. Riding forward to reconnoiter, Longstreet was shot by his own men in the confusion of smoke and noise. (In a similar accident Stonewall Jackson had been shot a year earlier less than four miles from the spot where Longstreet fell. Longstreet survived but was out of action for five months.) Thereafter most of the steam went out of the Confederate attack on this flank, as Hancock got his men behind breastworks protecting the road intersection. There they repulsed a final Rebel assault in late afternoon. Near twilight, a Confederate attack three miles to the north bent the other Union flank back at right angles and captured several hundred prisoners, including two generals.

It was a situation reminiscent of Chancellorsville, when a successful Rebel assault on the Union right near this same spot had been a prelude to defeat. But Grant was no Joe Hooker. When an overwrought brigadier rushed up and said, "General Grant, this is a crisis. . . . I know Lee's methods well by past experience; he will throw his whole army between us and the Rapidan, and cut us off completely from our communications," Grant replied with some asperity: "I am heartily tired of hearing about what Lee is going to do. Some of you always seem to think he is suddenly going to turn a double somersault, and land on our rear and on both flanks at the same time. Go back to your command, and try to think what we are going to do ourselves, instead of what Lee is going to do."[10]

Grant suited action to words. The Union right was stabilized, darkness fell, and next day—May 7—both armies lay exhausted behind their breastworks. In two days of fighting the Federals had suffered more than 17,000 casualties, the Confederates an estimated 11,000—about 17 percent of each army. Once again Lee had won an apparent victory over superior numbers. In the past each time this had happened, the Army of the Potomac had retreated. Weary veterans were certain it would be the same this time. "Most of us," wrote one soldier, "thought it was another Chancellorsville, and that next day we should recross the river." During the day the movement of supply wagons and artillery toward the rear seemed to confirm this expectation. But when night fell and the men received orders to march *south,* the realization suddenly dawned that whether the Wilderness had been a victory or a defeat, this army was no longer going to retreat. Even though they had just been through hell and the move southward promised more hell, the smoke-grimed Yanks felt a sense of elation. "Our spirits rose," one of them later recalled. "We marched free. The men began to sing." Before the campaign began, Grant had promised Lincoln that "whatever happens, there will be no turning back." Now the eastern troops learned that this general from the West meant to infuse his own brand of aggressiveness into the Army of the Potomac. When Grant cantered unobtrusively along the road next to the 5th Corps on the night of May 7–8, the men recognized him and sent up a cheer—not the parade-ground cheer of McClellan's time, but the veteran's yell of hard-earned respect.[11]

The Battles of Spotsylvania

Grant's objective was the crossroads at Spotsylvania Courthouse a few miles southeast of the Wilderness. There his communications through Fredericksburg would be safe, and with the Union army poised between Lee and Richmond, the Rebels would be forced to fight in open territory on ground of Grant's choosing. But Lee foiled the move. He had ordered Longstreet's corps, now commanded by Richard Anderson, to make a forced march to Spotsylvania on the night of May 7–8. While Anderson marched swiftly, the leading Union divisions were delayed by Rebel cavalry and by their own cavalry blocking the road. On the morning of May 8, Anderson's men scrambled behind hastily improvised breastworks north of Spotsylvania just in time to turn back a Federal assault. As more troops on both sides filed into line, exhausted after their all-night march, Grant renewed the

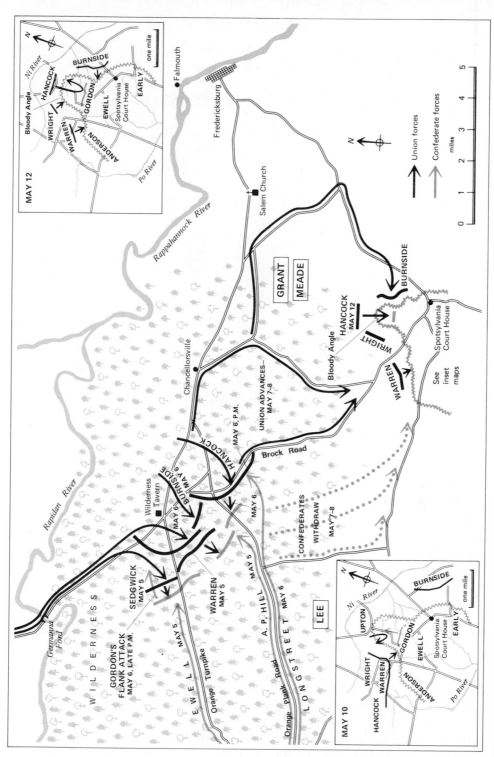

THE WILDERNESS AND SPOTSYLVANIA, MAY 5–12, 1864

Generals in the Army of the Potomac's 2nd Corps in 1864. Seated is Winfield Scott Hancock, commander of the corps. Standing are the division commanders (from left to right): Francis C. Barlow, David B. Birney, and John Gibbon. All four men had been wounded the previous summer at Gettysburg, where they had played key roles in Union victory. They returned to uniform in time to play equally important roles in the Wilderness.

(Reproduced from the Collections of the Library of Congress)

attack without avail. The bluecoats had lost the race for Spotsylvania.

The ragged men in gray, by now masters of entrenchment, threw up formidable breastworks along a five-mile line of trenches covering Spotsylvania in the shape of a huge inverted U. Grant tried to flank the west end of this line, but Lee shifted troops to meet this threat. Believing that the Confederate center was thereby weakened, Grant ordered two assaults on the afternoon of May 10. The first was repulsed, but the other, led by twenty-four-year-old Colonel Emory Upton, achieved a temporary breakthrough. Organizing his twelve specially-picked regiments in four compact lines under cover of woods 200 yards from the Rebel trenches, Upton took them across no-man's land at a sprint. Yelling like maniacs, the Yankees overran the works before the Confederates could fire more than a couple of volleys. But the failure of a supporting division to exploit this opening enabled the Rebels to organize a counterattack that drove Upton back with heavy losses.

Upton's temporary success won him promotion to brigadier general and persuaded Grant to try the same tactics with a whole corps. Upton had hit the northwest face of a salient in the Confederate line dubbed the "mule shoe" because of its shape. Grant decided to launch a large-scale assault against the tip of the salient, considered the weakest point because its convexity caused the fire of defenders to diverge. At 4:30 A.M. on May 12, Hancock's 2nd Corps burst out of the rain and fog and overran the Confederate trenches with unexpected ease. The yelling bluecoats swept forward a half mile, capturing twenty guns and three thousand prisoners. But their very success disorganized the Federals into an exultant, yelling mob. Before their officers could reorganize them, a Confederate counterattack blunted the Union advance. Once more Lee tried to lead this counterattack personally, but with the sure knowledge that if he was killed or captured their cause was lost, the soldiers again shouted "General Lee to the rear" as they went forward at a run. Hancock's men were driven back to the trenches they had initially captured, which they held against repeated gray attacks.

While this was going on, the Union 6th Corps assaulted the Confederate trenches a few hundred yards down the west side of the salient. Here was the famous "Bloody Angle," where some of the most savage fighting of the war took place. Blue and gray slugged it out for endless hours in the rain. Fighting madness turned men into killing machines. Individual soldiers would leap up onto the parapets of the trenches and fire down into them as fast as comrades could pass loaded rifles up to them. When one was shot down another would jump up to take his place. Killed and wounded men lay in the trenches three deep, where some of them were trampled entirely under the muck of mud and blood. The intensity of firing blasted trees and logs into splinters; minie balls cut down one oak nearly two feet thick. "I never expect to be fully believed when I tell what I saw of the horrors of Spotsylvania," wrote an officer in the 6th Corps, "because I should be loath to believe it myself were the case reversed."[12] All day and through half the night, the Confederates grimly held these trenches while Lee's engineers worked desperately to complete a new line a mile to the rear. When the fighting finally stopped after midnight and the Rebels abandoned the mule shoe, the Federals had suffered 7,000 casualties and the Confederates nearly as many, most of them along a quarter mile of trenches.

Grant had dented but failed to break Lee's defenses. He now attempted to maneuver the Confederates out of these defenses, first by swinging half the army around the Rebel right and then countermarching for an attack on the left flank. Continual rain slowed these movements, while Lee was able to shift troops on his shorter interior lines to counter them. Although intermittent heavy fighting occurred during this week of maneuvering, which brought total Union and Confederate casualties at Spotsylvania to about 18,000 and 11,000 respectively, there were no more battles like those of May 10 and 12. During one of the lulls, a Union staff officer reflected on the fraternization between pickets of the two armies:

> These men are incomprehensible—now standing from daylight to dark killing and wounding each other by thousands, and now making jokes and exchanging newspapers! . . . The great staples of conversation are the size and quality of rations, the marches they have made, and the regiments they have fought against. All sense of personal spite is sunk in the immensity of the contest.[13]

On May 11, Grant had sent a dispatch to Washington promising "to fight it out on this line if it takes all summer." Northern newspapers picked up this phrase and garnished it with exaggerated reports of Union success at Spotsylvania. These reports, said one veteran correspondent, produced "delirium" in the North; "everybody seemed to think that the war was coming to an end right away."[14] Lincoln was distressed by such attitudes, for he feared that the end was still far off and that excessive optimism now might lead to a severe letdown later, especially when the casualty lists came in.

FROM SPOTSYLVANIA TO COLD HARBOR

Grant's determination to fight it out at Spotsylvania was based on the assumption that Butler and Sigel would so disrupt Lee's supply lines and threaten his rear that the Rebels would have to come out of their trenches to fight or retreat. On May 9 Grant had also sent the Union cavalry, 10,000 strong and now commanded by fiery Phil Sheridan, on a raid deep in Lee's rear. The blue troopers destroyed supply depots, tore up miles of track, bested the outnumbered Rebel horsemen in several engagements, killed Jeb Stuart and another Confederate general, and broke through the outer defenses of Richmond before being driven off. It was a spectacular raid, and if Butler and Sigel had not suffered their humiliating defeats at precisely this time, the Army of Northern Virginia might well have been cut off and forced out of its trenches. But the damage from Sheridan's raid was soon repaired (though the loss of Stuart was irreparable), and Lee's supply lines remained open.

Grant learned the bad news about Butler and Sigel at the same time that his tactical maneuvers of May 14–19 were failing to dislodge Lee. The Union commander therefore ordered another long flanking movement to place his army between Lee and Richmond. But once again Lee anticipated the move and marched his army twenty miles southward to entrench a strong line behind the North Anna River before the Federals got there. After probing the Confederate defenses, Grant decided not to risk an assault. Instead, he again moved to his left and crossed the Pamunkey River on May 28. Once more he found the Rebels already entrenched behind Totopotomy Creek, less than ten miles northeast of Richmond. So yet again—for the fifth time in the campaign—Grant sidled to the left in an attempt to turn Lee's flank. Sheridan's cavalry seized a dusty, desolate crossroads known as Cold Harbor* and held it against Confederate infantry until their own infantry came up. Lee desperately shifted his line to the right; more Yankee foot soldiers arrived and drove back the Confederate line on the evening of June 1. Grant ordered an all-out attack at dawn next morning to smash through the Rebels before they could fully entrench. But half of the Union army was still on the road, trying to make forced night marches over poorly mapped terrain in stifling heat. One corps got lost and finally staggered into line long after dawn. Many of the men were too weary even to stay awake, much less to fight, and Grant

*So named because the tavern there provided drinks and overnight accommodations but no hot meals.

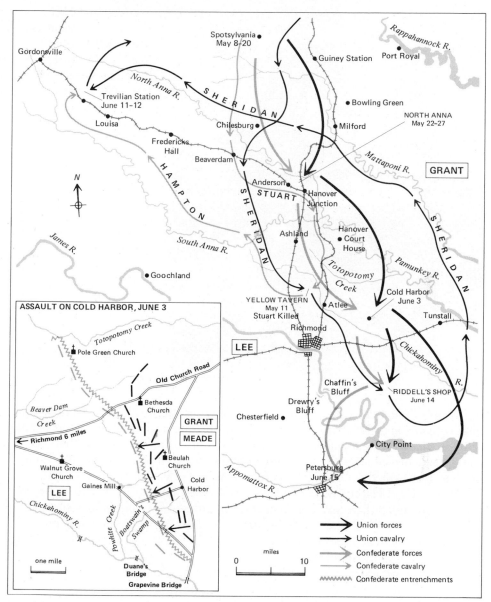

FROM SPOTSYLVANIA TO PETERSBURG, MAY–JUNE 1864

had to postpone the attack for twenty-four hours. This gave the 59,000 gray soldiers all the time they needed to entrench a six-mile line with its flanks protected by the Totopotomy and Chickahominy.

Despite the strength of the Confederate defenses, Grant decided to go ahead with his attack. He had run out of room to maneuver, for another flanking move

Sheridan and His Cavalry Commanders. (From left to right:) Wesley Merritt, Philip Sheridan, George Crook, James W. Forsyth, George Armstrong Custer. *(Reproduced from the Collections of the Library of Congress)*

would only drive the Rebels into their even stronger Richmond fortifications. The blue veterans knew what to expect at dawn on June 3. The night before, many of them pinned slips of paper with name and address on their coats so their bodies could be identified after the battle. One soldier wrote in his diary: "June 3. Cold Harbor. I was killed." The diary was found on his body after the battle. The June 3 attack at Cold Harbor was one of the most costly failures of the war. "I regret this assault more than any one I have ever ordered," Grant said afterward.[15] Delivered by 50,000 Union troops against three miles of the Confederate line held by 30,000 defenders, the attack was decimated by massed frontal and enfilading fire from the dug-in Rebel infantry and artillery. Seven thousand Union soldiers were killed or wounded, most of them in the first few minutes; the Confederates lost only 1,500.

THE SHENANDOAH VALLEY AND PETERSBURG

Some historians have mistakenly described Grant's campaign against Lee as a war of attrition. Grant's hammering assaults, they argue, demonstrated that he was willing to accept heavy losses because he knew they could be replaced while Lee's could not. In the end it worked out that way, but not because Grant intended it. He had planned a war of maneuver and open battle. It was Lee who turned

The Grim Harvest of War. This photograph was taken in April 1865 at the Cold Harbor battlefield, where a reburial detail exhumed the remains of Union soldiers killed the previous June for interment in a national cemetery at Cold Harbor.   *(Reproduced from the Collections of the Library of Congress)*

it into a war of attrition. Once the boldest and most offensive-minded of generals, Lee could no longer risk his limited manpower in battle outside the trenches. The Confederates could no longer hope to "win" the war with the tactics or strategy of Chancellorsville or Gettysburg. By remaining on the defensive, however, they could hope to hang on long enough and to inflict losses enough on the Yankees to make *them* give up trying to win. This strategy was beginning to work in June 1864. In the North, many who had expressed extravagant hopes that Grant would win the war in a month now denounced the general as a "butcher." The Copperheads came to life and began to declaim that the Republicans would persist in this insane war to liberate the slaves until every white man was killed—unless the voters elected a Peace Democrat as president in November.

For political as well as military reasons, therefore, Grant wanted to avoid a war of attrition and siege. Once again he planned a series of coordinated maneuvers to cut Lee's communications, flank him out of his trenches, and force him into the open for a showdown battle. But once more he was frustrated by the Confederates' quick response to his moves and by the poor performance of some of his own generals.

Out in the Shenandoah Valley, General David Hunter had replaced Sigel as commander of the Union forces. Although a West Point graduate and a professional soldier, Hunter was also a radical antislavery man who was appointed to this command in part to gratify radical Republicans. Grant ordered Hunter to advance up the valley, to cut its railroad links with Richmond, and to destroy the Confederate supply depot at Lynchburg. Meanwhile Grant sent part of Sheridan's cavalry to tear up the railroad east of the valley. After accomplishing this, Sheridan was to join Hunter for a raid on the James River Canal and the railroads southwest of Richmond. At the same time, the Army of the Potomac would cross the James southeast of Richmond to cut Lee's rail links through Petersburg and to crush the Army of Northern Virginia when it fought to protect these lifelines, as it must.

Hunter started well. He routed a small Confederate force at Piedmont and started to move quickly toward Lynchburg. Exasperated by guerrilla attacks on their supplies, his ill-disciplined soldiers looted and burned as they went along. They burned the Virginia Military Institute in Lexington on June 11, an action that infuriated Southerners everywhere. Alarmed by this threat to his rear, Lee dispatched more than 10,000 troops under Jubal Early to attack Hunter and sent most of his cavalry to intercept Sheridan. Now commanded by Wade Hampton of South Carolina, the Rebel cavalry clashed with the Yankee horsemen June 11–12 in a drawn battle near Trevilian Station. Learning that Hunter was ninety miles away from him behind the Blue Ridge Mountains, Sheridan abandoned the attempt to join him and returned eastward after doing only minor damage to the railroads. Meanwhile the Confederates under Early had moved faster than Hunter. They concentrated at Lynchburg a force as large as Hunter's and repelled weak Federal attacks there on June 18. Short of supplies and ammunition, with Confederate cavalry and guerrillas across his escape route to the north, Hunter retreated into West Virginia. Not only had he failed in the mission Grant had set for him; he had left the whole Shenandoah Valley open to Early's veterans.

Before Grant learned of Hunter's and Sheridan's rebuffs, his own maneuver against Petersburg had also miscarried. The operation started brilliantly. On the night of June 12–13 the Army of the Potomac silently pulled out of its trenches at Cold Harbor and moved southward. For three days Lee remained in the dark about Grant's movements. Thinking that this was another short-range flanking maneuver, the Confederates entrenched a new line east of Richmond and skirmished with the Union cavalry screen while Yankee engineer troops built the longest pontoon bridge in history (2,200 feet) across the James River. By June 15, two blue corps were south of the river and the rest were on their way while Lee's entire army was still on the north side. General Beauregard held the formidable Petersburg defenses with only 2,500 troops against the oncoming 18th Corps, which outnumbered him by seven to one. If Petersburg fell, Richmond would have to be evacuated, Lee's army would be cut off—and perhaps the war would be over.

But with this opportunity in their hands, Union corps commanders fumbled. Coming up to the Petersburg defenses on the afternoon of June 15, General William F. Smith's 18th Corps carried part of the thinly defended line. One of the Union's few successes that day was the capture of two artillery batteries by a division of black soldiers. There was irony in this, for two years earlier Smith had been one of McClellan's protégés—a Democrat and an opponent of emancipation who had been transferred out of the Army of the Potomac in the reshuffle after Fredericksburg. Now back in Virginia with a chance to redeem himself by leading his white and black troops into Petersburg, he hesitated, overestimated Rebel strength, waited for the 2nd Corps to join him, and then decided against making a night attack in the bright moonlight.

More such failures occurred during the next three days. Although Beauregard received reinforcements from Lee's army, the bluecoats still outnumbered him by four or five to one on June 16. A Northern assault late that day carried part of the enemy line; but lack of coordination among the various Union corps enabled Beauregard to prevent a breakthrough. The story was the same next day, for though the Yankees captured more positions and it seemed to Beauregard that "the last hour of the Confederacy had arrived," poor staff work down the chain

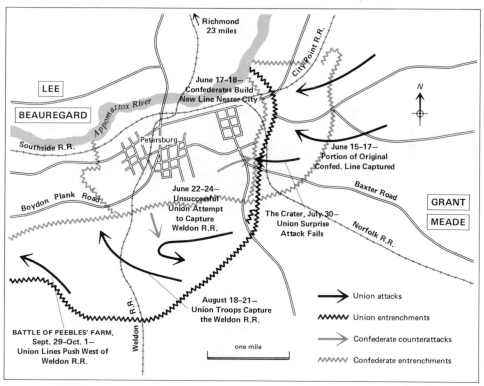

PETERSBURG, 1864

of command in the Union army produced delays and contradictory orders that paralyzed the advance. That night Beauregard pulled his line back another mile, almost to the outskirts of Petersburg, while Lee marched the rest of his lean veterans to these trenches as fast as they could go. Grant planned an assault for June 18, before all of them could arrive. As on previous days he left the tactical arrangements to Meade. This may have been a mistake, for once again the command system of the Army of the Potomac operated sluggishly. The short-tempered Meade finally sent bristling messages to his generals: "I find it useless to appoint an hour to effect cooperation. . . . What additional orders to attack you require I cannot imagine. . . . Finding it impossible to effect cooperation by appointing an hour for attack, I have sent an order to each corps commander to attack at all hazards and without reference to each other."[16]

Part of the problem was that officers and men alike were infected with what might be termed the "Cold Harbor syndrome"—a reluctance to make head-on assaults against trenches. "The men feel just at present a great horror and dread of attacking earthworks again," said one general; while another wrote that the soldiers had been "foolishly and wantonly sacrificed" in suicidal attacks against trenches. On the afternoon of June 18, a veteran unit refused to obey an order to charge a strongly held point in the Confederate line, and yelled to a regiment of new men preparing for the assault: "Lie down, you damn fools, you can't take them forts!" The rookies went in anyway, and lost 632 of their 850 men.[17]

Grant and Meade finally called off the attacks. The Federals had bungled their chance to take Petersburg before Confederate reinforcements made it impossible. The Yankees lost more than 11,000 men in four days of fighting, the Rebels fewer than half that many. The Army of the Potomac had been bled white in the fighting from the Wilderness to Petersburg, suffering about 64,000 casualties, which by grim coincidence equaled the number of combat troops in Lee's army at the beginning of the campaign. These losses, plus the expiration of service for another 18,000 men during the spring and summer, caused the Army of the Potomac to lose its fighting edge. Lee had also lost half of his original army; but the remainder, plus reinforcements and Beauregard's veterans, were protected by miles of elaborate trenches, redans, forts, and abatis. Grant reluctantly settled down for the siege he had hoped to avoid. The Union cavalry and infantry made periodic raids to cut Lee's rail and road communications south of Petersburg. Although these actions achieved only partial success, they did worsen Lee's already serious supply problems. Grant also extended his entrenched lines inexorably south and west, to force Lee to thin his defenses by stretching his own lines.

The Battle of the Crater

The most promising Federal bid to break these defenses—the famous battle of the Crater—ended in tragic fiasco, once again illustrating the bad luck and incompetent officers that plagued the Army of the Potomac. Holding a section of the Union line opposite a Confederate artillery redan was the 48th Pennsylvania, containing many coal miners from Schuylkill County. One day the regiment's colonel, Henry Pleasants, overheard a soldier say that "we could blow that damned fort out of existence if we could run a mine shaft under it."[18] A civil engineer, Pleasants liked the idea and persuaded General Burnside (now a corps commander in the army that had once been his) to endorse it. Meade's engineers scoffed at the project as "claptrap and nonsense," for the shaft would have to run more than 500 feet to reach Confederate lines, requiring ventilation holes that the Rebels would be sure to see. But Pleasants devised an ingenious (and invisible) ventilation system, and his men drove the shaft under the enemy lines without any help from the army's engineer corps. They then filled it with four tons of gunpowder.

Initially skeptical, Grant grew hopeful that the mine would blow a hole in the Confederate trenches through which a heavy assault could roll up the lines right and left and drive straight into Petersburg itself. In Burnside's 9th Corps were three white divisions that had seen hard fighting since the Wilderness, and one black division that had seen no real combat at all. Despite the successful record of black troops on several fronts, including the June 15 attack on the outer defenses of Petersburg, most officers in the Army of the Potomac still doubted their fighting ability. Old prejudices died hard. But Burnside, a New Englander with antislavery sympathies, decided to give his black division special assault training to lead the attack. The soldiers reacted with enthusiasm to this assignment. "Both officers and men," wrote one of the brigade commanders, "were eager to show the white troops what the colored division could do."[19]

The explosion of the mine was scheduled for the predawn darkness of July 30. The black division was ready to lead off, but at the last minute Meade, with Grant's approval, ordered the white divisions to be sent in first. The generals evidently still distrusted the combat reliability of this division; moreover, they did not want to be accused of using black soldiers as cannon fodder. Testifying later before the Committee on the Conduct of the War, Grant said that if black troops had led the assault and the battle turned out badly, it would have been said "that we were shoving those people ahead to get killed because we did not care anything about them. But that could not be said if we put white troops in front."[20]

Deflated by Meade's order to change the attack formation, Burnside provided poor tactical leadership. The mine blew 300 Rebels high into the air and blasted a hole 170 feet long, 60 feet wide, and 30 feet deep. It was the most awesome spectacle of the war. For 200 yards on either side of the crater the stupefied Confederates abandoned their trenches and ran for the rear. But from then on everything went wrong for the Federals. Unprepared for its mission, the leading white division went forward in disorganized fashion while its commander stayed in the rear calming his nerves by swilling rum begged from the surgeon. The bluecoats came to the edge of the crater, gaped at the sight, and milled around in confusion. Many of them went *into* the crater instead of fanning out right and left and forming for a further advance. Generals in the rear sent up more troops; the crater became packed with disorganized men; the Confederates recovered from the shock, brought up artillery, and fired at Yankees in the crater as at fish in a barrel; the Southern infantry counterattacked and pushed back the few Federal units that had moved out from the crater. By the time the black division went into action, the battle was lost. Soldiers had to push their way through panic-stricken white troops streaming to the rear. The blacks fought well under the circumstances and suffered more casualties than any other division, but they too were driven back in confusion. Many Rebel soldiers, enraged beyond reason that the Yankees had sent former slaves against them, bayoneted or shot black men who were trying to surrender.

Admitting failure, Grant finally called off the attack. "It was the saddest affair I have witnessed in the war," he wired Washington. "Such opportunity for carrying fortifications I have never seen and do not expect again to have." Confederate General William Mahone, who organized the counterattack, wrote that for an hour after the explosion "there was nothing to prevent the . . . cutting [of] the Confederate army in twain . . . opening wide the gates to the rear of the Confederate capital."[21] After the Crater, the siege at Petersburg went on about as before. A huge hole in the ground remains to this day as a monument to a lost opportunity.

Early's Raid on Washington

This fiasco did not exhaust the Union's bitter cup of defeat during July 1864. On the same day as the battle of the Crater (July 30), Confederate cavalry from the Shenandoah Valley rode into the town of Chambersburg, Pennsylvania and burned most of it to the ground when its citizens refused to pay a tribute of $500,000. This was Jubal Early's parting shot in a raid that had carried his small army to the outskirts of Washington itself three weeks earlier. After Early had driven David Hunter's Union forces out of the valley in June, his 14,000 gray veterans, many of whom had fought in the valley under Jackson, marched northward in an attempt to repeat Jackson's 1862 strategy of relieving the pressure on Richmond by threatening Washington. The Rebels crossed the Potomac July 5, scattered a scratch force of Federals at the Monocacy River east of Frederick on July 9, and came up to the fortifications northwest of Washington itself on July 11. The defenses were manned initially by a handful of troops plus hastily mobilized government clerks and raw militia, for Grant had combed out most of the garrison for front-line service in Virginia. In response to the government's call for help, Grant sent the 6th Corps from Petersburg. These tough veterans filed into the works on the afternoon of July 11. After studying the situation, Early decided that he had better retreat to Virginia before being crushed between these troops in his front and Hunter's force, finally on its way from West Virginia, in his rear.

To Lincoln's and Grant's disgust, Early got away safely after burning the house of Postmaster General Blair in Maryland and levying $220,000 on the cities of Hagerstown and Frederick in addition to burning Chambersburg. Union pursuit was hampered by conflicts of authority among generals commanding four separate departments. In early August, Grant cut through this red tape by abolishing these departments and sending Sheridan to the valley as overall commander of a newly created Department and Army of the Shenandoah, consisting of the 6th Corps and two cavalry divisions from the Army of the Potomac, Hunter's former Army of West Virginia, and two divisions transferred from the Louisiana theater. Grant ordered the hard-driving Sheridan to go after Early and "follow him to the death." Since the Shenandoah Valley was a source of food for Lee's army and a favorite stamping ground for guerrillas, Grant also told Sheridan to destroy the valley's crops so thoroughly that "crows flying over it for the balance of the season will have to carry their provender with them."[22]

THE ATLANTA CAMPAIGN, MAY–JULY 1864

Sheridan would do just that, but first he had to organize his new command. Far to the south, another general who would soon achieve fame as a destroyer of Confederate resources was also resting and reorganizing in preparation for a final move against Atlanta. In three months, Sherman's army had inflicted nearly 28,000 casualties on the Confederates while suffering only 25,000 themselves. In Virginia, by comparison, while the Confederates had lost about 36,000, they had exacted nearly twice that number in return.

Overview of the Campaign

This contrast in casualty ratios reflected the different tactics in the two theaters. Grant and Lee both favored attack and all-out battle as a means of destroying the enemy. Sherman and Johnston engaged in a war of maneuver. Rather than assault the Confederates' strong defensive positions, Sherman executed a series of flanking movements that forced Johnston repeatedly to fall back to protect his communications. Only once, at Kenesaw Mountain, did Sherman order a frontal assault, with no more success than Grant at Cold Harbor. Although Johnston retreated toward Atlanta as Lee did toward Richmond, such maneuvers in Virginia usually occurred *after* big battles; in Georgia they occurred *without* large-scale fighting. Johnston lost fewer men in the first month of his campaign than Lee did in two days at the Wilderness.

Nearly half of all Confederate casualties in the Atlanta campaign from May through July would occur in the last two weeks of July, after John B. Hood replaced Johnston as commander of the Army of Tennessee. Dissatisfied with Johnston's Fabian strategy, the Confederate government put Hood in his place with the expectation that this hard-fighting transfer from Lee's army would attack and smash the Yankees. Hood did attack, three times, but it was the Yankees who did the smashing. Hood's battered army returned to its trenches, while Sherman settled down for a siege of Atlanta.

The strategy of the Atlanta campaign was dictated by railroads and topography. Atlanta's importance as a rail junction (and manufacturing center) made it a Union objective that came to overshadow Sherman's primary goal of destroying the Confederate army. The mountainous ridges and steep valleys of northern Georgia formed defensive barriers far stronger than the rolling countryside and sluggish rivers of eastern Virginia. For their supplies, both armies in Georgia were tied to the same rickety single-track railroad running between Chattanooga and Atlanta. Neither army could operate for long out of reach of this railroad; both Sherman and Johnston had to protect the tracks in their rear at all costs. As Johnston retreated, his supply line grew shorter and more secure while Sherman's grew longer and more vulnerable. But the Yankee repair crews became so proficient that they could rebuild bridges and re-lay rails almost as fast as the Rebels destroyed them.

Narrative of the Campaign

Sherman's combat forces of 100,000 men were grouped in three separate "armies": 61,000 in the Army of the Cumberland under George Thomas; 25,000 in what had once been Sherman's Army of the Tennessee, now commanded by James B. McPherson; and the small Army of the Ohio under John M. Schofield. Johnston's Army of Tennessee numbered 50,000 effectives (soon to be reinforced by 15,000 from Alabama). At the beginning of May they were entrenched along a rugged, sheer-faced ridge straddling the railroad twenty-five miles south of Chattanooga. Sherman had no intention of assaulting this "terrible door of death." Instead, Thomas and Schofield feinted at the Confederate line while McPherson's fast-marching army swung wide to the right through a mountain gap south of Johnston's left flank to cut the railroad at Resaca. One of the most promising young generals in the army, who had won Grant's and Sherman's praise as a corps commander in the Vicksburg campaign, McPherson performed the first part of his assignment flawlessly. His troops burst through the thinly defended gap on May 9 with a chance to sever Johnston's lifeline and catch the Confederates in a pincers. "I've got Joe Johnston dead!" cried Sherman when he learned of this success.

But McPherson found the Resaca defenses held by the advance brigades of the Alabama reinforcements, whose numbers he overestimated. Instead of attacking, the Federals skirmished cautiously. Thus alerted to this danger on his flank, Johnston skillfully withdrew his whole army on the night of May 12–13 to a prepared defensive position covering Resaca. Although McPherson's caution was justified by his discretionary orders, Sherman was disappointed. "Well, Mac, you missed the opportunity of your life," Sherman told him. But despite this failure, McPherson remained Sherman's most trusted subordinate.[23]

For three days the two armies probed for an opening in each other's lines around Resaca. While this was going on, Sherman sent part of McPherson's army on another swing to the right. Johnston again fell back to protect his rear. The Confederates stopped briefly fifteen miles to the south, at Adairsville, and skirmished with the pursuing bluecoats before continuing ten miles farther to Cassville, where they turned to fight. Sherman's forces were now spread over a twenty-mile front. On May 19 Johnston planned to attack Schofield's isolated corps on the Union left. He ordered Hood's corps to roll up Schofield's flank while Leonidas Polk's corps held him in front. Hood had come to Georgia with Longstreet for

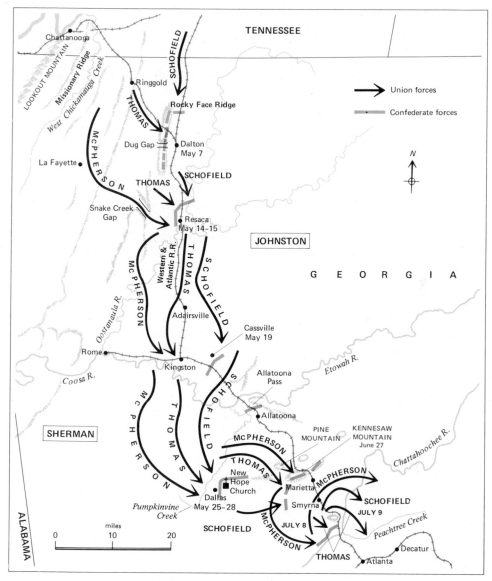

THE CAMPAIGN FOR ATLANTA, MAY–JULY 1864

the battle of Chickamauga the previous September and had remained there after Longstreet returned to Virginia. Hood's left arm was crippled from a Gettysburg wound, and his right leg had been amputated at Chickamauga. But these wounds did not abate his pugnacity. During the Atlanta campaign, he complained of Johnston's tendency to retreat without fighting. But given the chance on May 19 to fight, Hood muffed it. Alarmed by a false report of enemy infantry on his flank, he went on the defensive. Johnston's plan for a counterattack had to be scrapped. Again the Confederates fell back, first to a line behind Cassville, then eight miles farther south to a strong position on a high ridge behind the Etowah River at Allatoona pass.

In two weeks of much marching and little fighting, the Atlanta campaign had begun to resemble the intricate steps of a minuet. The two armies faced each other; Sherman sidestepped gracefully to his right and forward, Johnston stepped back to conform, and after nodding to each other they repeated the process. Johnston stepped back each time to trenches previously dug by slaves. As the Yankees came up to each new position they constructed their own network of trenches and log breastworks. Sherman organized freed slaves into a "pioneer corps" to assist this work. Southern newspapers began to criticize Johnston for his constant retreats. But the general's defenders pointed out that he was trading space for time and luring Sherman deeper into hostile territory, where sooner or later the Yankees would dash themselves to pieces against the trenches.

Instead of obliging Johnston by attacking at Allatoona, Sherman filled his wagons with twenty days' rations, cut loose from the railroad, and sent his whole army around Johnston's left flank toward the road junction at Dallas, Georgia— fifteen miles in Johnston's rear and only thirty miles from Atlanta. Johnston's efficient cavalry detected the move, and once again the Confederates marched swiftly to entrench a new line near Dallas before the Federals got there. For several days at the end of May the two armies fought and skirmished in this vicinity, especially around a Methodist meeting house called New Hope Church but renamed "Hell-Hole" by the Yankees. Thick pine woods made this area as difficult for offensive operations as the Wilderness in Virginia. Adding to Sherman's discomfiture were heavy rains, which began in late May and continued for a month, turning the red clay roads into bottomless mire and crippling the armies' mobility. Sherman side-stepped his lines a mile or two eastward each day. Johnston conformed to every move until by the second week of June both armies were again astride the railroad with the Confederate right anchored on Kenesaw Mountain just north of Marietta.

During these maneuvers the volatile Sherman grew edgy. Although the Confederates had retreated seventy miles, the wily Johnston had used the terrain skillfully to avoid the open, decisive battle that Sherman sought. Meanwhile far away in Mississippi, Forrest's cavalry routed a force twice its size at Brice's Crossroads on June 10. Fearing that Forrest would now move into Tennessee to cut the railroad between Nashville and Chattanooga, Sherman ordered two infantry divisions plus cavalry to move out from Memphis "and follow Forrest to the death, if it cost 10,000 lives and breaks the Treasury. There never will be peace in Tennessee till Forrest is dead."[24] The Union troops drew Forrest into battle at Tupelo, Mississippi, and defeated him. Forrest was wounded during the fighting, but refused to conform to Sherman's wish and later returned to action.

The neutralization of Forrest temporarily relieved Sherman of concern about Tennessee. But Johnston was still entrenched along a seven-mile line in his front, blocking the way to Atlanta. Sherman decided to make a head-on assault. His reasons for doing so are not entirely clear. He was apparently worried that this campaign of maneuver and entrenchment was robbing his men of their fighting edge. "A fresh furrow in a plowed field will stop the whole column, and all begin to entrench," he complained. "We are on the offensive and . . . must assail and not defend."[25] Sherman reasoned that Johnston must have weakened his center to protect his flanks against another turning maneuver, so he ordered an attack on the Rebel center June 27. The main assaults were carried out by three divisions against two hills south of Kenesaw Mountain proper, while the rest of the army feinted against the mountain and the flanks. But Johnston was not caught napping. His troops repelled the blue attacks with a loss of only 600 men while inflicting five times that many casualties.

These losses were small compared with those in Virginia, but costly enough to cause Sherman to renew his flanking tactics. Once more he sent McPherson on a wide swing around the Confederate left. Once more Johnston fell back, this time to a position north of the Chattahoochee River only eight miles from Atlanta. Instead of attacking this line as Johnston hoped he would, Sherman sent cavalry to his right on a pretended search for a crossing in that direction and massed Schofield's army to force a crossing on the opposite flank. Schofield surprised the Rebel pickets and pushed his corps across a quickly built pontoon bridge before Johnston was aware of the danger. One corps of McPherson's mobile Midwestern-ers followed, proving that they could move to their left as well as to their right. With nearly a third of the Union army across the river on his flank, Johnston abandoned his line and withdrew behind Peachtree Creek on the night of July 9–10.

Removal of Johnston From Command

Southern criticism of Johnston rose to a crescendo. Hostility between Johnston and Jefferson Davis had been smoldering since 1861. As Davis saw it, in 1862 Johnston had retreated all the way up the Virginia peninsula to Richmond and might have lost the capital had not fortune put Robert E. Lee in his place. In 1863 Johnston had failed to come to the aid of Vicksburg's besieged defenders. Now he had been driven all the way back to Atlanta without a real battle. The Confederate cabinet unanimously recommended the general's removal from command. "Johnston is determined not to fight," said Secretary of State Judah Benjamin. "It is of no use to re-enforce him, he is not going to fight."[26]

Johnston later insisted that he had planned to attack the Federals as they crossed Peachtree Creek. But at the time he refused to commit himself to any specific course of action. In reply to a telegram from Davis on July 16, Johnston said that his plan must "depend upon that of the enemy. It is mainly to watch for an opportunity to fight for advantage. We are trying to put Atlanta in condition to be held . . . by the Georgia militia, that army movements may be freer and wider." To the administration, Johnston's last sentence implied an intention to abandon Atlanta, just as a year earlier he had ordered Pemberton to give up Vicksburg. The consequences of losing Atlanta would be enormous. In the eyes of both North and South, the city had become a symbol of Confederate resistance second only to Richmond. Johnston's apparent unwillingness to defend the city or to strike Sherman a blow sealed his fate. On July 17 the secretary of war informed him that "as you have failed to arrest the advance of the enemy to the vicinity of Atlanta, far in the interior of Georgia . . . you are hereby relieved of command." Hood took over the army.[27]

This action was controversial then and remains so today. Johnston was popular with his troops, who appreciated the Fabian strategy that kept the army intact and minimized casualties. Many officers distrusted Hood's aggressiveness. Sherman later wrote that "the Confederate Government rendered us most valuable service" by removing Johnston. Hood's reputation as an offensive fighter, said Sherman, "was just what we wanted . . . to fight in open ground, on any thing like equal terms, instead of being forced to run up against prepared intrenchments."[28] Many historians have criticized Davis for removing Johnston. But their appraisals, like Sherman's, have benefited from hindsight. Political and military circumstances made it as difficult for Davis to retain Johnston in command in 1864 as it had been for Lincoln to keep McClellan in 1862.

The Battles for Atlanta

The conditions of Hood's appointment virtually compelled him to attack as soon as possible. After crossing the Chattahoochee, Sherman had sent McPherson on another flanking march to the east to get astride the railroad between Atlanta and the Carolinas, break it up, and prevent any possibility of Lee or Hood reinforcing each other by rail. While McPherson's boys were ripping up the tracks, Hood on July 20 launched an assault on the flank of Thomas's Army of the Cumberland, separated from the other two Union armies by a gap of two miles. Hood hoped to hit two of Thomas's corps while they were crossing Peachtree Creek, but his attack started late, the bluecoats were ready, and the Rebels dashed themselves to pieces against Yankee breastworks. During the night Hood withdrew two miles into the Atlanta fortifications. Sherman invested the city on the north and east. Hood discovered that McPherson's left flank east of the city was in the air, and on the night of July 21–22 he sent a corps on a long march to roll up that flank next morning. The Confederate attack gained some initial success, including the killing of McPherson, but by hard fighting the Army of the Tennessee restored its lines and drove the gray infantry back into the Atlanta defenses with heavy casualties.

Sherman named Oliver O. Howard to succeed McPherson and promptly ordered him to take the Army of the Tennessee on a long swing around the west side of Atlanta to strike toward the city's remaining rail links to the south. At the same time, Sherman sent his cavalry in three columns to tear up the same railroads farther south. Four divisions of Confederate infantry moved out to counter Howard's thrust. In a battle near Ezra Church on July 28, the Yankees for the third time in nine days punished the attackers fearfully. In these three battles Hood lost more than 13,000 men, compared with Union casualties of 6,000. Confederate

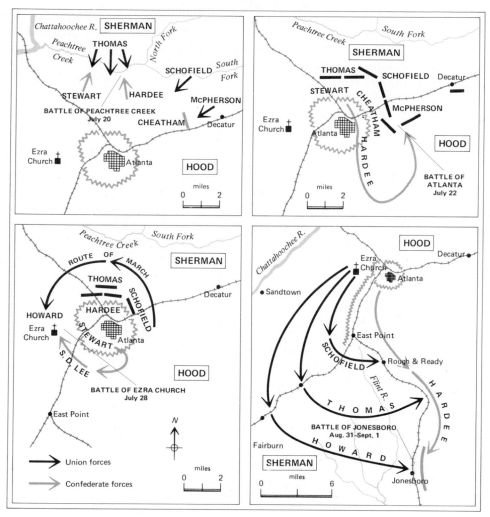

THE BATTLES FOR ATLANTA, JULY 20–SEPT. 1, 1864

morale declined and desertions increased. Less than three weeks after he had given Hood command of the army with tacit orders to attack, Jefferson Davis instructed the general not to risk any more assaults. But Hood's last attack at Ezra Church did halt Howard's envelopment short of the railroad. And Confederate cavalry commander Joseph Wheeler brilliantly countered the mounted Union thrusts (thereby confirming Sherman's low opinion of his own cavalry, which had been frequently outmaneuvered by Rebel horsemen during the campaign). Wheeler divided his mounted force into three columns, each of which headed off and defeated the blue troopers before they could do serious damage to the railroad.

Foiled in his attempts to cut Hood's lifeline and pry him out of Atlanta,

Sherman settled down for an artillery bombardment of the city's defenses while he contemplated his next move. In three months he had driven the Confederates back ninety miles while inflicting more losses on the enemy than suffered by his own army. No other strategic offensive of the war except Grant's Vicksburg campaign accomplished so much at such relatively low cost. One of the foremost military theorists of the twentieth century, the British writer B. H. Liddell Hart, considered Sherman the greatest Civil War general because his employment of mobile tactics and the "indirect approach" in this campaign overcame the bloody stalemate of trench warfare in a fashion that could have been profitably studied by World War I generals.[29]

But in July 1864 little of this was evident to the Northern people, who saw only that Sherman was checked before Atlanta just as Grant was before Petersburg. The hopes of May for quick victory had been drowned in the sorrows of 100,000 Northern battle casualties. "Who shall revive the withered hopes that bloomed at the opening of Grant's campaign?" asked the *New York World.* "Patriotism is played out," declared another Democratic newspaper. "All are tired of this damnable tragedy. . . . Each hour is but sinking us deeper into bankruptcy and desolation."[30] Northern war weariness augured ill for the Republicans in the forthcoming presidential election, which was shaping up as a referendum on the war.

Twenty-four

The Third Turning Point: The Reelection of Lincoln

PEACE FEELERS

Northern war weariness in the summer of 1864 revived the prospects of Peace Democrats. Clement Vallandigham boldly returned from his year-long exile in Canada. Not wanting to martyr him again, Lincoln allowed Vallandigham to stay and to speak out against the war. Democratic district conventions in the Midwest adopted resolutions calling for an armistice and peace negotiations. Democratic congressmen introduced resolutions of similar purport. Although a coalition of Republicans and War Democrats voted down these resolutions, peace sentiment seemed to have gained so much momentum that some Republicans despaired of the party's chances in the fall elections.

The most despairing was Horace Greeley, the eccentric but influential editor of the *New York Tribune*. A radical but also something of a pacifist, Greeley was notorious for his vagaries. He had oscillated between militancy and defeatism since 1860. In early 1864 he supported the Chase-for-President movement because Lincoln was not radical enough. But in midsummer he wrote to the President: "Our bleeding, bankrupt, almost dying country . . . longs for peace— shudders at the prospect of fresh conscriptions,* of further wholesale devastations, and of new rivers of human blood." If the administration did not do something to meet this longing, "we shall be beaten out of sight next November."[1]

Greeley's letter launched one of the most bizarre incidents of the war. Through an intermediary, the *Tribune* editor had learned that Confederate emissaries were in Niagara Falls, Canada, prepared to open peace negotiations. Confederate

---

*On July 18 Lincoln issued a call for 500,000 new volunteers, with deficiencies in district quotas to be filled by a draft in September. When one Copperhead editor read this call, he exulted: "Lincoln is deader than dead." (Frank L. Klement, *The Copperheads in the Middle West* [Chicago, 1960], p. 233.)

agents were indeed at Niagara Falls, but they had no accreditation as peace negotiators. Rather, they were part of the Confederacy's secret service network sent to Canada to plot the escape of Southern prisoners from war prisons, to rig the gold market in New York, to establish contacts with Peace Democrats, and to do anything else they could to undermine the Union war effort. Greeley urged Lincoln to give these "negotiators" safe conduct to Washington. Lincoln had a pretty good idea of what the Rebel agents were up to, but he authorized Greeley to make contact with them and to bring to Washington "any person anywhere professing to have any proposition of Jefferson Davis in writing, for peace, embracing the restoration of the Union and abandonment of slavery."[2]

This put Greeley on the spot, for it made him responsible for verifying the credentials of the negotiators. The editor balked, but Lincoln sent his private secretary, John Hay, to New York to prod Greeley into action. Together Hay and Greeley went to Niagara Falls, where they held two interviews with the Confederate agents. These conversations succeeded only in revealing the Southerners' lack of credentials. Having obtained Lincoln's statement of peace terms, the agents leaked these terms and their own reply to the Associated Press. The Confederate reply was intended for propaganda purposes. Lincoln's terms, it charged, meant further death and destruction, for they precluded negotiations by prescribing conditions known to be unacceptable to the South.

Similar publicity surrounded a second peace mission that occurred simultaneously with the Greeley fiasco. In this case, two unaccredited Northern emissaries sought and obtained an interview with Jefferson Davis to discuss peace terms. The two were free-lance journalist James R. Gilmore and Colonel James Jaquess of the 73rd Illinois Infantry. Jaquess was a Methodist clergyman with a good war record who yearned for an honorable way to stop Christians from slaughtering each other. Lincoln believed that he had nothing to lose and perhaps something to gain from this mission. He allowed Gilmore and Jaquess to pass through the lines to Richmond, where Davis and Secretary of State Judah Benjamin received them on July 17. In a candid interview, the two Northerners conveyed Lincoln's peace terms: Union, abolition, amnesty, and perhaps partial compensation for emancipated slaves. Davis knew that Lincoln could not commit Congress on the last point. But that mattered little, for the Confederate president insisted on no peace terms short of Southern independence. "Amnesty, Sir, applies to criminals," Davis told the emissaries. "We have committed no crime. . . . Extermination [is] preferable to such dishonor. . . . We will [fight] on *unless you acknowledge our right to self-government.*"[3]

Gilmore's account of this meeting was published in a Boston newspaper on July 22—by coincidence the same day that the first detailed reports of the Greeley negotiations were published. In retrospect it became clear that each side in both of these affairs was more interested in scoring propaganda points than in opening serious negotiations. Each president knew that the other's terms were unacceptable. But neither could ignore the significant peace movements among his people. Several peace candidates had won seats in the 1863 Confederate congressional elections; antiwar and pro-Union sentiments in the upcountry districts of North Carolina, Alabama, and elsewhere were stronger than ever; the advocates of peace negotiations included the Confederate vice president himself. By publicizing the unofficial peace missions, each side hoped to show its own people that the enemy's conditions for negotiations would mean the loss of everything they were fighting for: in the case of the South, independence and slavery; in the case of the North, Union and emancipation.

The Confederacy won greater short-run benefits in this propaganda war. Because Lincoln's peace terms included both Union and emancipation, Northern Democrats were able to exploit a belief that the North could have peace if only the government would drop its insistence on emancipation. "Tens of thousands of white men must yet bite the dust to allay the negro mania of the President," ran a typical Democratic editorial. During August this notion gained ground, as stalemate continued on the battlefronts and Northern morale plunged to rock bottom. "The people are wild for peace," wrote the shrewd New York politico Thurlow Weed. "Lincoln's re-election is an impossibility." Bleak reports from Republican state chairmen poured in to Henry J. Raymond, chairman of the Republican National Committee (and also editor of the *New York Times*). "I fear that the desire for peace," wrote Raymond, "aided by the impression that Mr. Lincoln . . . is fighting not for Union but for the abolition of slavery, and by the draft, the tax, the lack of victories . . . will overbear [the administration] and give control of everything to the Opposition."[4]

On August 22, Raymond suggested to Lincoln a plan to counteract the false notion that "we *can* have peace with Union if we would." He urged the President to appoint a commission to offer the Confederates peace on the sole condition of Union, with "all remaining questions" (i.e., slavery and the terms of reconstruction) to be adjusted later. If Davis spurned this offer, as Raymond was sure he would, the rejection would "dispel all the delusions about peace that prevail in the North, silence the clamors and damaging falsehoods of the opposition, [and] . . . reconcile public sentiment to the War, the draft, & the tax as inevitable necessities." Lincoln went so far as to incorporate Raymond's suggestions into a draft of instructions for a peace commission. He also drafted a letter to a Democratic editor that concluded with the words: "If Jefferson Davis wishes to know what I would do if he were to offer peace and re-union, saying nothing about slavery, let him try me."[5]

But Lincoln did not send this letter. Nor did he appoint a peace commission as Raymond had urged. At a meeting on August 25, the President convinced the editor that such a course would be misconstrued in the North as a retreat from emancipation. This would be "worse than losing the Presidential contest—it would be ignominiously surrendering it in advance," for it would alienate antislavery Republicans by seeming to confirm their suspicions of Lincoln's softness on slavery. Beyond that, it would also appear to be a betrayal of the "solemn promise" of freedom embodied in the Emancipation Proclamation.[6]

Lincoln knew about the flurry of meetings among Republican dissidents who hoped to replace him with a different candidate. By the last week of August, these dissidents had gone so far as to prepare a call for a new Republican national convention to nominate another candidate. This movement was motivated partly by radical hostility to Lincoln's reconstruction policy and partly by a despairing

**Abraham Lincoln in
1864** *(Reproduced from
the Collections of the
Library of Congress)*

conviction that the President could not win reelection. Lincoln shared the latter
conviction. On August 23 he wrote the following memorandum and asked his
cabinet to endorse it, sight unseen: "This morning, as for some days past, it seems
exceedingly probable that this Administration will not be re-elected. Then it will
be my duty to cooperate with the President elect, as to save the Union between
the election and the inauguration; as he will have secured his election on such
ground that he cannot possibly save it afterwards."[7]

THE DEMOCRATS NOMINATE McCLELLAN

When he wrote these words, Lincoln expected the Democrats to nominate
McClellan on a peace platform. After his removal from command of the Army
of the Potomac in November 1862, McClellan had lived quietly in New Jersey
and New York. Many of his friends had worked for his restoration to command,
and failing in that had urged him to seek vindication through politics. In the fall
of 1863, McClellan declared his open opposition to the administration by publicly
endorsing the Democratic candidate for governor of Pennsylvania, and by the end
of the year he had discreetly made known his availability for the Presidency.

McClellan's views on the war had not changed since 1862. He still opposed emancipation but favored restoration of the Union by military victory. This made him objectionable to the peace wing of the party, which favored an armistice followed by negotiations. Peace Democrats launched a last-minute effort to nominate Governor Horatio Seymour of New York, but when that fell short they had no choice but to accept McClellan.

Meeting in Chicago August 29–31, the Democratic convention "bridged the crack" between the party's two wings by nominating McClellan while allowing Peace Democrats to write the platform and name the vice-presidential candidate (George Pendleton of Ohio). The platform denounced "arbitrary military arrest," "suppression of freedom of speech and of the press," and "disregard of State rights" (i.e., slavery). The key plank declared that "after four years of failure to restore the Union by the experiment of war . . . [we] demand that immediate efforts be made for a cessation of hostilities, with a view to an ultimate convention of the states, or other peaceable means, to the end that, at the earliest practicable moment, peace may be restored on the basis of the Federal Union."[8]

This plank presented McClellan with a dilemma. Could he run on a platform that put peace first and Union second? Beset by pressures from both wings of the party, McClellan agonized over the wording of his letter of acceptance. The first two drafts endorsed the idea of an armistice, qualified by a proviso that fighting would be renewed if negotiations broke down. But the general's War Democratic friends convinced him that this would be seen as a capitulation to the Confederacy, for few intelligent men believed that if once stopped the war could be started again. Thus the final version of McClellan's letter reversed the platform's priorities: Union first, then peace. When "our present adversaries are ready for peace, upon the basis of the Union," negotiations could begin in "a spirit of conciliation and compromise. . . . The Union is the one condition of peace—we ask no more."[9]

This letter satisfied most War Democrats and upset some Peace Democrats to the extent that they contemplated a bolt. But they had nowhere else to go, so most of them, including Vallandigham, remained in the fold. In their campaign speeches, the Peace Democrats emphasized the platform while the War Democrats stressed McClellan's letter. This schizophrenia gave Republicans a field day. "The truth is," said a Republican orator, "neither you nor I, nor the Democrats themselves, can tell whether they have a peace platform or a war platform. . . . Upon the whole it is both peace and war, that is peace with the rebels but war against their own government."[10]

The Democratic convention helped put an end to Republican divisions. Faced with a tangible threat from a party half opposed to the war and wholly opposed to emancipation, radicals suddenly realized that Lincoln was their only alternative to disaster. The President's insistence on abolition as a condition of peace now began to work in his favor among antislavery people. The plans for a new Republican convention perished. On September 22, Frémont withdrew his third-party candidacy. The next day, Lincoln requested and received the resignation of Postmaster General Montgomery Blair. The Blair family was identified with conservative Republican factions in Maryland and Missouri. Montgomery Blair had been quietly reestablishing old Democratic ties. Radicals suspected that the Blairs had gained a dangerous influence in the administration. Lincoln's request for Blair's resignation was the quid pro quo for Frémont's withdrawal. Republicans went into the campaign as a united party.

MOBILE BAY

On the very day that Lincoln had written his defeatist memorandum of August 23, the final act in a three-week drama at Mobile Bay closed this port to blockade runners. It also chalked up the first of a string of Union victories that would end the summer of Northern discontent and mock the Democrats' description of the war as a failure.

After Farragut's fleet had run the forts below New Orleans and captured that city in April 1862, the next obvious salt-water target was Mobile. But Farragut's warships were needed for operations on the Mississippi, and Grant's plans for a campaign against Mobile after the fall of Vicksburg were aborted by Banks's miscarried Red River expedition (see pp. 412–413). Not until the summer of 1864 could troops and ships be spared for Mobile. The city lay at the head of a bay whose entrance thirty miles to the south was protected by three forts, a minefield, and four gunboats—including the huge ironclad *Tennessee.* Farragut assembled fourteen wooden ships and four ironclads to hammer the forts from the sea while 5,500 blue soldiers invested them by land. On the morning of August 5, the Union fleet engaged the forts in a spectacular duel of heavy guns. Suddenly the leading Union ironclad blew up and sank, the victim of a mine. This brought the fleet to a halt under a punishing fire from the two largest forts. But Farragut took his wooden flagship *Hartford* to the head of the line, where he gave the order that immortalized him in the annals of the U.S. navy: "Damn the torpedoes! Full speed ahead!"* The *Hartford* pushed through the minefield safely; the fleet followed; and after passing into Mobile Bay beyond range of the forts, the Union ships turned their attention to the plucky Confederate gunboats and pounded them into submission. Even the redoubtable *Tennessee,* her rudder chains shot away and her commander wounded, was forced to surrender. By 10 A.M. the Federals controlled the waters of Mobile Bay; during the next eighteen days they forced the forts one after another to surrender. The city of Mobile itself remained in Southern hands, but isolated from the sea it was thereafter of little use to the Confederacy.

THE FALL OF ATLANTA

Important as it was, the victory at Mobile Bay was eclipsed by the capture of Atlanta. After the battles of late July, both armies had sidestepped their trenches southwest from the city, Hood to protect his railroads, and Sherman in an attempt to get at them. In desperation Hood sent his cavalry to cut Sherman's rail

---

*Whether Farragut shouted these exact words is uncertain. But it is certain that he ordered the fleet through the minefield, with his flagship in the lead.

communications, but Union crews repaired the damage. On August 25 Sherman launched his final stroke. Pivoting on its right wing, the blue army swung counterclockwise in another flanking move. Completely hoodwinked, Hood thought that his cavalry raid had forced the Federals to fall back. He telegraphed news of his great victory to Richmond, while special trains carried cheering Georgians into Atlanta for a celebration.

But even as the celebrants entered the city, the bluecoats reached the railroads twenty miles to the south and began making "Sherman neckties" of the rails—by heating them over bonfires of ties and wrapping them around trees. Finally alerted to his danger by reports from his cavalry, Hood sent two corps to attack the Union troops at Jonesboro. But the Federals, although outnumbered, repulsed the Confederates on August 31. Next day they counterattacked and drove the Rebels away. In imminent danger of being surrounded, Hood evacuated the rest of his army and the Georgia militia from Atlanta on the night of September 1–2, after burning everything of military value in the city. The Federals marched into Atlanta next day and Sherman telegraphed Washington: "Atlanta is ours, and fairly won."

This news electrified the North. "Glorious news this morning—*Atlanta taken at last!!!*" wrote a New Yorker on September 3. "It is (coming at this political crisis) the greatest event of the war." Newspapers praised Sherman as the greatest general since Napoleon. Lincoln, Grant, and Halleck sent effusive congratulations to the red-haired general, whose Atlanta campaign, the President predicted, would become "famous in the annals of war."[11] Overlooked in this chorus of praise was the escape of Hood's army. But the symbolic importance of Atlanta had become so great that the political consequences of its fall eclipsed all else. One Republican newspaper capsulized these consequences in its headline on the fall of Atlanta: "Old Abe's Reply to the Chicago Convention. Is the War a Failure?" The *Richmond Examiner* sadly made the same point from the Southern viewpoint. The "disaster at Atlanta," it lamented, came "in the very nick of time" to "save the party of Lincoln from irretrievable ruin. . . . It will obscure the prospect of peace, late so bright. It will also diffuse gloom over the South."[12] In this war of peoples as well as of armies, such a political achievement more than balanced the military survival of Hood's battered and depleted force.

SHERIDAN IN THE VALLEY

The next bad news for the South came from the Shenandoah Valley. Jubal Early's summer campaign in that vale of Union defeats, climaxed by his march to the outskirts of Washington itself, was one reason why so many Northerners had considered the war a failure. After Grant had sent Sheridan in August to whip Early and lay waste the valley's resources, the two opposing armies in the valley had sparred and skirmished for a month. In contrapuntal harmony, the Army of the Potomac meanwhile attacked first the left of the Confederate lines before Richmond and then the right below Petersburg, forcing Lee to recall a division from the valley and giving Sheridan a two to one numerical advantage over Early.

On September 19, Sheridan attacked the Confederate defenses east and north of Winchester. A botched order that tangled one Union corps in its own wagon train caused the fight to go badly for the Federals at first. But with superb battlefield leadership, Sheridan straightened out the mess and sent his cavalry in a picture-book charge against the Rebel flanks while the infantry assaulted the center. Early's left flank crumpled, while the stubborn defenders in the center fell back step by step through the town and then streamed southward through the night to organize a new defensive position along a ridge known as Fisher's Hill, two miles south of Strasburg.

Sheridan came after the Confederates without letup. On September 22, he sent one of his three infantry corps to work its way around the Confederate left at Fisher's Hill while the other two demonstrated in front. Near sunset the flanking corps emerged yelling from the woods to mow down the surprised Confederates on that end, while two miles away their blue comrades converted the demonstration into an attack that sent the whole Rebel line reeling in retreat. Casualties in these two battles were equal on each side—about 5,500—but this represented a loss of nearly one-third of Early's army. The broken Confederates retreated all the way to Brown's Gap eighty miles south of Winchester.

These victories further strengthened Lincoln's reelection bid. James A. Garfield, formerly a general and now a congressman from Ohio, wrote on September 23 that "Sheridan has made a speech in the Shenandoah Valley more powerful and valuable to the Union cause than all the stumpers in the Republic."[13]

Sheridan did not rest on his laurels. His 35,000 men moved up the valley like a swarm of locusts, carrying out the second part of Grant's orders. On October 7 Sheridan reported: "I have destroyed over 2,000 barns filled with wheat, hay, and farming implements; over seventy mills filled with flour and wheat; have driven in front of the army over 4,000 head of stock, and have killed and issued to the troops not less than 3,000 sheep." This was just the beginning. By the time he was done, said Sheridan, "the Valley, from Winchester up to Staunton, ninety-two miles, will have little in it for man or beast."[14]

Here was total war in earnest. Nor was the destruction all on one side. Rebel guerrillas swarmed in the rear of Sheridan's army burning wagon trains and shooting hundreds of teamsters, couriers, and stragglers. The guerrillas forced Sheridan to detach a third of his front-line force and prevented him from carrying out Grant's original orders to move east across the Blue Ridge and come up on Lee's rear at Petersburg. The bushwhackers also provoked Federal troops into a scorched-earth retaliation that went far beyond Sheridan's initial orders to destroy only property of military value. Thousands of valley residents—Rebel, Unionist, and neutral alike—became penniless, ragged refugees.

Having destroyed the valley's resources, Sheridan withdrew northward in mid-October and prepared to return the 6th Corps to Grant. But the irrepressible Early refused to be counted out. He had been reinforced to three-fifths of the enemy's strength. While Sheridan was in Washington conferring on future plans for his army, Early planned to launch a surprise attack across the north fork of the Shenandoah River against the Union left behind Cedar Creek, near

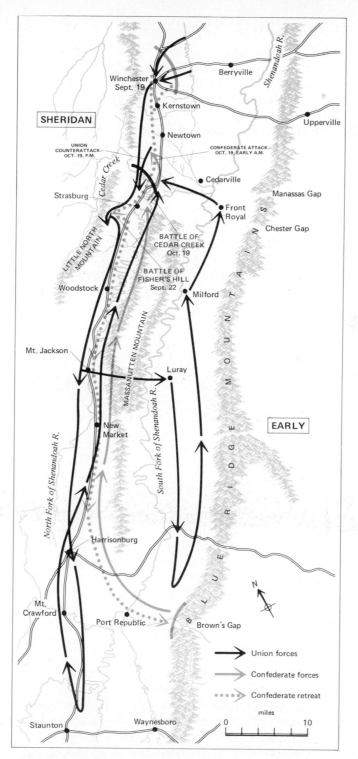

SHERIDAN'S SHENANDOAH VALLEY CAMPAIGN, 1864

Middletown. Three divisions of gray infantry moved silently into position on the night of October 18–19 and overran the tents of the 8th Corps at dawn. Seven thousand bluecoats fled to the rear in panic. It was the most effective surprise attack of the war. The Rebels kept going and drove the other two Union corps back four miles.

But then the attack ran out of steam. Believing that he had won a great victory, Early did little to stop his men from breaking ranks to plunder the Yankee camps. But half of the blue divisions had not been routed, and the rest were re-forming under the electrifying leadership of Sheridan. The Union commander had returned to Winchester the previous afternoon. When the sounds of battle fifteen miles to the south reached him on the morning of October 19, he mounted his horse and galloped toward the battlefield in a ride soon to be celebrated in song and story. As he rode, Sheridan encountered stragglers streaming toward the rear, who stopped and cheered when they saw him. "God *damn* you, don't cheer me!" Sheridan yelled at them. "If you love your country, come up to the front! God *damn* you, don't cheer me! There's lots of fight in you men yet! Come up, God damn you! Come up!"[15]

They continued to cheer, but they also turned around and followed him. The effect of this man's presence on the beaten army was extraordinary. By midafternoon, Sheridan had gotten the stragglers into line and organized a counterattack against the disorganized Confederates. By nightfall, the blue tide had not only washed back over the four miles lost in the morning but had driven the enemy eight miles farther south. Early's army, thrice routed in a month, virtually ceased to exist as a fighting force. For all practical purposes the war in the valley was over except for Rebel guerrilla actions, which continued to tie down large Union detachments.

The Petersburg Front

Sherman and Sheridan had given the Confederacy a one-two punch; now Grant hoped to follow up with a knockout blow. At the end of September, the Army of the Potomac had struck both ends of Lee's line simultaneously. North of the James the Federals captured Fort Harrison, part of the Richmond defenses, but had been unable to achieve a breakthrough either there or southwest of Petersburg. Again at the end of October, Grant unsuccessfully attacked both flanks. This time the hardest fighting occurred on the Petersburg front, where Union forces tried an end run around the Confederate trenches to strike the railroad entering Petersburg from the west. But Lee's ragged veterans foiled the move and drove the Federals back with heavy losses.

In most of these actions, the new troops in the Army of the Potomac—substitutes, draftees, and bounty men—performed poorly. Large numbers of them surrendered without putting up much of a fight. This was especially true in the once-proud 2nd Corps, which had suffered by far the greatest number of casualties in the bloodletting from the Wilderness to Petersburg. Not until the 6th Corps and Sheridan's cavalry could return from the valley would the Army of the

Potomac be capable of real offensive action. Grant failed to strike his knockout blow; but he had forced Lee again to stretch his defensive lines, which now extended thirty-five miles—from the Williamsburg Road east of Richmond to Hatcher's Run southwest of Petersburg. Lee warned Davis that his lines were so thin that unless reinforced "I fear a great calamity will befall us."[16] But the onset of Virginia's coldest winter of the war curtailed operations and postponed the calamity until spring.

THE COPPERHEAD ISSUE IN THE 1864 ELECTION

As military victories cleared away the political clouds, Republicans lost no opportunity to accuse their opponents of disloyalty. At its mildest, this tactic consisted of arguments that the Rebels desired McClellan's election. Republicans made much of Grant's dispatches from the Petersburg front. "The enemy are exceedingly anxious to hold out until after the Presidential election," wrote Grant. "They hope for a counter revolution. . . . Deserters come into our lines daily who tell us that the men are nearly universally tired of the war, and that desertions would be much more frequent, but they believe peace will be negotiated after the fall elections."[17]

Grant and the Republicans may have been more right than they realized. Confederate leaders did indeed believe that McClellan's election would ensure the success of their cause. Vice President Stephens considered the Democratic platform "the first ray of light I have seen from the North since the war began." A Southern army surgeon assumed that if McClellan won, "the war is over. The thought is indescribable. May we not be disappointed." A Confederate secret service agent in Canada sent to Richmond a report on the Northern Democrats: "The platform means peace, unconditionally. . . . McClellan will be under the control of the true peace men. . . . At all events, he is committed by the platform to cease hostilities and to try negotiations. . . . An armistice will inevitably result in peace. The war cannot be renewed if once stopped, even for a short time."[18]

Republicans also did their best to identify Democrats with the antiwar secret societies in the North. The largest of these shadowy organizations had been the Knights of the Golden Circle, which faded away in 1863 when revelations of its ties with the Confederacy destroyed its usefulness. It was replaced by the Order of American Knights, whose membership was concentrated in the southern Midwest. Most members of this order seem in turn to have been absorbed by the Sons of Liberty, formed in February 1864 with none other than Clement Vallandigham as Supreme Grand Commander.

Federal agents infiltrated the Sons of Liberty and compiled a long list of charges against it, which were published in time for Republican use in the 1864 campaign. Among other things, the organization was said to have entered into a conspiracy with Confederate agents to capture a Union warship on Lake Erie, to liberate Southern prisoners of war at several Midwestern prison camps, to burn Northern cities, to stir up antidraft resistance, to foment an armed uprising to form a "Northwest Confederacy," and in general to raise so much hell that Yankee armies in the South would have to come home to deal with the civil war in their rear. Union detectives arrested numerous leaders of these alleged plots, especially in Indiana. Among those tried by a military commission in that state was one Lambdin P. Milligan, whose conviction was reversed two years later in a famous Supreme Court ruling that civilians could not be tried by military tribunals when the civil courts were open.

Republican orators, editors, and pamphleteers drew upon these exposés to link the Democratic party with treason. After all, was not Vallandigham the commander of the Sons of Liberty, and had he not written the Democratic platform? "REBELLION IN THE NORTH!! EXTRAORDINARY DISCLOSURE! Val's Plan to Overthrow the Government! Peace Party Plot!" ran a typical Republican headline. Pamphlets rolled off the presses with such titles as: *Copperhead Conspiracy in the North-West: An Exposé of the Treasonable Order of the Sons of Liberty.* So pervasive was this theme that the Republicans fixed the Copperhead label on the entire Democratic party, a handicap from which the party did not recover for a generation.

Several historians have discounted the stories of Copperhead conspiracies as "a figment of Republican imagination . . . a political apparition." Without question the Republicans exaggerated or fabricated many of these conspiracies. On the other hand, evidence for some of them was a good deal more than mere "lies, conjecture and political malignancy," as one historian has termed it.[19] Perhaps the sworn testimony of Union detectives or of Copperheads who turned state's evidence should be taken with a grain of salt; but the official reports of Confederate agents cannot be disregarded. Several reports from agents in Canada turned up in captured Confederate archives after the war. These documents revealed that several hundred thousand dollars had been distributed to Midwestern Democrats, including candidates for state offices: the nominee for governor of Illinois had accepted $40,000 from a Canadian-based Confederate agent, and two large peace rallies in Illinois had been financed largely by Rebel gold. Detectives found caches of weapons paid for with Confederate secret service money in the homes of Copperheads. There were several plots to free Confederate prisoners, including one to stage an uprising in Chicago during the Democratic national convention to cover the liberation of war prisoners from nearby Camp Douglas.

Most of these fantastic plots, of course, never succeeded. This was owing to two factors: the loose security of the secret societies, which allowed federal agents to infiltrate them; and the inability of Northern conspirators to mobilize more than a handful of men when the time came for real action. Numerous Confederate agents showed up at the Chicago Democratic convention, but the expected legions of armed Copperheads never appeared. The disillusioned Southerners concluded that the Northern peace movement was all talk and no action. The only major operations that took place were those carried out by Confederate agents on their own: a raid across the border on October 19, 1864, that netted $200,000 from the banks of St. Albans, Vermont; and an attempt on November 25 to burn several New York hotels and other buildings, which fizzled out when the nineteen fires set by Southern agents were extinguished after damaging only a few buildings.[20]

The fullest summary of these activities was Jacob Thompson's report to the Confederate secretary of state on December 3, 1864. Thompson was a Mississippian who had been secretary of the interior under Buchanan. His prewar affiliations with Northern Democrats made him an ideal person to head the secret service in Canada. He established contacts with several Peace Democrats, including Vallandigham. "I was received among them with cordiality, and the greatest confidence [was] at once extended to me." Thompson detailed his distribution of $300,000 to purchase arms, hold meetings, and subsidize newspapers. "Money has been advanced to Mr. Churchill, of Cincinnati, to organize a corps for the purpose of incendiarism in that city," he wrote. Thompson had faith in arson as a weapon against the North: "A great amount of property has been burned" (this was an exaggeration), and "[we must continue] to burn whenever it is practicable, and thus make the men of property feel their insecurity and tire them out with the war." Indeed, Thompson was preparing to burn his own records, for "I have so many papers in my possession, which in the hands of the enemy would utterly ruin and destroy very many of the prominent men in the North."[21]

One can readily imagine what use Republicans would have made of this document had they possessed it in 1864. As it was, Democratic "treason" was their most effective issue. Democrats retaliated with charges of "tyranny"; but this and other standard party issues—inflation, debt, corruption, conscription, violation of civil liberties—failed to catch fire. So did personal attacks on Lincoln such as the following, which appeared in a New York Catholic weekly: "Abe Lincoln— passing the question as to his taint of Negro blood . . . is altogether an imbecile. . . . He is brutal in all his habits. . . . He is filthy. He is obscene. . . . He is an animal!"[22]

Even racism had lost much of its potency as a Democratic issue. This was not for lack of trying. Democratic newspapers published snide speculations on Lincoln's black ancestry. Campaign orators rang all the changes on "the negro-loving, negro-hugging worshippers of old Abe." A pair of reporters for the leading Democratic paper, the *New York World*, added a new twist when they wrote anonymously a pamphlet entitled *Miscegenation: The Theory of the Blending of the Races, Applied to the American White Man and Negro.* The pamphlet, purportedly written by an abolitionist, advocated miscegenation (a new word, coined by the real authors) as a solution of the race problem. It predicted that if Republicans won the election they would carry the war into its next stage, "a war looking, as its final fruit, to the blending of the white and the black." Democrats did all they could to exploit the miscegenation issue with doggerel poetry, salacious political cartoons portraying black men kissing white women in the "millenium of abolitionism" after Lincoln's reelection, sensational stories of New England schoolmarms in the occupied South who had produced mulatto babies, and the like. But there is little evidence that all this won many new voters for the Democrats. On the contrary, it may have turned some intelligent voters away in disgust.[23]

THE PRISONERS OF WAR ISSUE

One issue indirectly connected with race, which the Democrats exploited only slightly, was the matter of prisoner of war exchanges. The Democratic platform denounced the administration's "shameful disregard" of "our fellow-citizens who now are, and long have been, prisoners of war in a suffering condition."[24] The plight of war prisoners, especially in Georgia's notorious Andersonville prison, was one reason for Northern war weariness in the summer of 1864. Democrats attributed the breakdown in prisoner exchanges to Republican insistence on the equal treatment of black prisoners. But the Democrats did not make much of this issue, probably because they felt it might backfire. Most Northerners bitterly blamed the South for the suffering of Union prisoners. A party already regarded as pro-Southern was not likely to win many friends on this issue.

The emotional and often misunderstood question of war prisons and prisoner exchanges reached a crisis in 1864. The overcrowding and the appalling death rate at Andersonville became a scandal in both North and South. The stockade was built in early 1864 to accommodate 15,000 prisoners, but by August it was packed with nearly 33,000 men. Thirteen thousand prisoners died at Andersonville. The commandant of the prison, Henry Wirz, was later convicted of war crimes and hanged. Some historians consider Wirz's conviction a miscarriage of justice resulting from the North's need for a scapegoat. They maintain that Northern captives fared no worse on the average than Southern prisoners in Northern camps. Union prisoners received the same rations as Confederate soldiers; if these were meager by 1864, it was because the Yankees had destroyed so many of the South's resources. And so far as Andersonville was concerned, its horrors were the product of a breakdown in exchanges for which, according to this view, the North was responsible.

These are complex questions. It is true that Northern propaganda exaggerated the conditions in Southern prisons. Prisoner memoirs were one of the most sensationalized forms of Civil War literature. It is hard to separate fact from fiction in these memoirs, most of which were written by Northerners. The following might be a fair generalization: with the exception of Andersonville, average conditions at Southern prisons were not much worse than those at Northern prisons. In truth, these conditions were usually bad. Prisoners on both sides suffered from poor sanitary facilities, bad water, disease, trigger-happy guards, boredom, and mental depression. Insufficient clothing and blankets caused cold-weather distress among unacclimated Confederate prisoners at Camp Douglas near Lake Michigan, on Johnson's Island in Lake Erie, and at Elmira, New York. On the other hand, with respect to food and shelter the Confederate prisoners in the North fared better than their Yankee counterparts in the South. While Northern prison camps housed captured Rebels in barracks,* several Confederate camps—including the two largest, Andersonville and Belle Isle (an island in the James River near Richmond)—provided no shelter, and prisoners suffered from exposure. Medical care for prisoners on both sides was probably no worse than for

*An exception was the prison camp at Point Lookout, Maryland, where prisoners lived in tents.

soldiers in general—which is to say that by modern standards it was poor. But shortages of medicine in the South (for which the Union blockade was partly responsible) affected Yankee prisoners as it did Southern soldiers and civilians.

These factors—poorer food, inadequate shelter, and shortages of medicine—help to explain why the death rate for Union captives in Southern prisons was at least 28 percent higher than for Confederate prisoners in the North.* Another way of analyzing the figures shows that Confederate prisoners were 29 percent less likely to die in Yankee prisons than to die of disease in their own army, while Union prisoners were 68 percent more likely to die in Southern prisons than in their own army. No evidence exists to support Northern charges of deliberate Confederate cruelty to prisoners. The difference in death rates can be accounted for primarily by the collapse of the Southern economy in the war's last year, when the number of prisoners reached its maximum.

On the other hand, it is as hard for the modern historian as it was for Northerners in 1864 to understand why Union prisoners at Andersonville were not allowed to build huts out of wood from the abundant pine forests that surrounded the prison. This would have saved many lives. One Georgia woman was shocked by what she saw at Andersonville. "My heart aches for the poor wretches, Yankees though they are, and I am afraid that God will suffer some terrible retribution to fall upon us for letting such things happen. If the Yankees ever should come to South-West Georgia . . . and see the graves there, God have mercy on the land!"

"And yet, what can we do?" she continued. "The Yankees themselves are really more to blame than we, for they won't exchange these prisoners, and our poor, hard-pressed Confederacy has not the means to provide for them, when our own soldiers are starving in the field."[25] The breakdown in the prisoner exchange program was indeed the main reason for the overcrowding of prisons in 1864, but the responsibility for this breakdown was more complex than the Georgia woman implied.

During the war's first year, Lincoln had refused to negotiate an exchange cartel lest this be construed as official recognition of the Confederacy. But field commanders arranged many informal exchanges. The large number of prisoners captured by both sides in 1862 increased the pressure on the Union government to accept a cartel, which it finally did in July. By the terms of this agreement, each side exchanged its prisoners for an equal number held by the enemy, with the surplus on one side or the other to be released on parole until formally exchanged.

---

*Like most Civil War statistics, data on prisoners are at best inexact; this is especially true for the South because so many Confederate records were destroyed or lost during the evacuation of Richmond in April 1865. The most reliable figures indicate that of the 194,743 Union soldiers imprisoned for various lengths of time, 30,218 (15.5 percent) died in prison, while of the 214,865 imprisoned Confederates 25,976 (12.1 percent) died in captivity. Thus the death rate for Union prisoners was 28 percent higher than for Confederates. (General F. C. Ainsworth, Chief of the U.S. Record and Pension Office, to James Ford Rhodes, June 29, 1903, in James Ford Rhodes, *History of the United States From the Compromise of 1850*, 7 vols. [New York, 1893–1906], V, 507–8.) Other, less reliable, figures show a Union death rate of 17.8 percent, which would have been 48 percent higher than the Confederate rate cited in this same report. (*O.R.*, Ser. 2, Vol. 8, pp. 946–48.) For a discussion of this question, see William B. Hesseltine, *Civil War Prisons: A Study in War Psychology* (Columbus, Ohio, 1930), pp. 254–56.

(Reproduced from the Collections of the Library of Congress)

War Prisoners and Prisons. The first photo in this series (above) shows a group of captured Confederate cavalrymen in Virginia in 1864. Note the contrast between the well-uniformed Union guards and the nondescript clothing of many Rebels. The men in the second photograph (p. 453, top) are Confederate war prisoners at Camp Douglas near Chicago. Note the heated barracks and the healthy appearance of the prisoners. Such photographs gave Northern viewers a not wildly inaccurate impression of good treatment of Southern prisoners, which they contrasted with the sufferings of Union prisoners at Andersonville, who are seen in the next two pictures. The third photograph (p. 453, bottom) shows the flimsy shelters rigged up by prisoners at Andersonville from whatever materials they had at hand. The sluggish stream in the foreground served as both sewer and water supply for the prisoners, some of whom are staring at the camera in the fourth picture (p. 454, top). These Andersonville photographs, taken by a Southern cameraman in August 1864 at the height of the stockade's prisoner population, were published after the war in the North, where they exacerbated public anger over the prisoner treatment issue, an issue that perpetuated sectional bitterness long after the war. The fifth photograph (p. 454, bottom) added to

(Chicago Historical Society)

(Reproduced from the
Collections of the Library of
Congress)

this bitterness. This man was among several Union prisoners in
similar condition at Belle Isle prison camp near Richmond who were
returned to Union lines under special exchange in 1864. Although
hardly typical of Union prisoners, the condition of these prisoners—
whose photographs were published in the North—reinforced
Northern beliefs in the Confederacy's fiendish treatment of captured
Yankees.

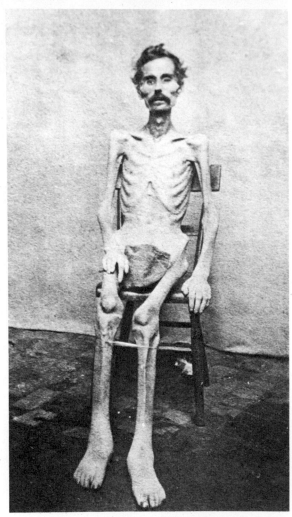

Under this cartel, the war prisons were almost emptied by the fall of 1862. But the agreement broke down in 1863. The initial cause of this breakdown was the Confederacy's response to the Emancipation Proclamation and to the Union army's enlistment of black soldiers. Condemning these actions as "the most execrable measure recorded in the history of guilty man," Jefferson Davis announced that henceforth the officers of black regiments plus all Union officers captured in states affected by the Emancipation Proclamation would be turned over to state governments to be executed as "criminals engaged in servile insurrection." Captured black soldiers were also to be turned over to "the respective States to which they belong to be dealt with according to the laws of said States." The Confederate Congress endorsed these policies, which were of course a violation of the cartel, to say nothing of their other qualities. To ensure that the Confederates did not carry out these measures, Union Secretary of War Stanton ordered all exchanges of Confederate officers stopped so that these captives could be held as hostages against the Confederate threat to execute Union prisoners.[26]

Although official exchanges of officers largely came to an end by June 1863, some exchanges and paroling of enlisted men continued. Grant and Banks paroled the 36,000 men captured at Vicksburg and Port Hudson in July, but soon thereafter the Confederate War Department put thousands of these men back into the army (in time for some of them to fight in the battles at Chattanooga). The Union government regarded this as an outrageous violation of the cartel. Disputes about it brought all exchanges to a halt. By December 1863, 26,000 Confederate prisoners were being held in the North and 13,000 bluecoats in the South—numbers large enough to create pressure for a renewal of exchanges. But the Southern refusal to include captured black soldiers and their officers in any exchange proved a major obstacle. The Confederate exchange agent declared that the South would "die in the last ditch" before "giving up the right to send slaves back to slavery as property recaptured." In reply, Stanton insisted that for the North to negotiate a Jim Crow cartel would be "a shameful dishonor. . . . When [the Rebels] agree to exchange all alike there will be no difficulty."[27]

There matters stood while the battles of May–July 1864 poured an unprecedented number of prisoners into overcrowded stockades. In August, the Confederates offered a man-for-man exchange but again refused to assure Union authorities that captured freedmen would be included.[28] By this time Grant had become convinced that any exchange would benefit the Confederacy more than the Union. "It is hard on our men held in Southern prisons not to exchange them," he wrote, "but it is humanity to those left in the ranks to fight our battles." Every exchanged Confederate "becomes an active soldier against us at once," whereas most of the released Yankees would go home or into the hospital because of expired enlistments or broken-down health. "We have got to fight until the military power of the South is exhausted, and if we release or exchange prisoners captured it simply becomes a war of extermination."[29]

These statements are often cited as proof that the Union insistence on equal treatment for black prisoners was merely a cover for the real reason it refused an exchange—to wear down the Confederacy by attrition. Thus, the argument goes, the North rather than the South was responsible for the horrors of Andersonville.

But the evidence does not sustain this thesis. When Lee on October 1 suggested a man-for-man exchange of prisoners held in Virginia, Grant provisionally accepted a partial exchange but asked Lee for assurance that black soldiers would be included. When Lee replied that "negroes belonging to our citizens are not considered subjects of exchange and were not included in my proposition," Grant closed the affair with the statement that since the Union government was "bound to secure to all persons received into her armies the rights due to soldiers," Lee's refusal to grant blacks those rights "induces me to decline making the exchanges you ask."[30] When the two opposing secretaries of the navy worked out an arrangement in October 1864 for the exchange of captured sailors, the Lincoln administration insisted that black personnel be included—and they were. This was the first real break in the exchange impasse. During the winter of 1864–1865 the two sides exchanged thousands of sick and wounded prisoners without regard to color. In January 1865, the Confederate exchange agent offered to exchange "all" prisoners, and this offer the Union government accepted.[31] The Confederacy was about to enroll slaves in its own armies (see pp. 477–478), and since the continued refusal to exchange black prisoners would then have become an anachronism, it was quietly abandoned. During February and March 1865, the exchanges went forward at the rate of nearly a thousand men per day—until the war's end in April liberated all remaining prisoners.

THE REELECTION OF LINCOLN

The 1864 election was a referendum on the war and emancipation. No one could be entirely sure what the consequences of a Democratic victory would be: Confederate independence; restoration of the Union with slavery; or something else. But the consequences of a Republican victory were certain: the doom of slavery and the continuation of war until the South surrendered. Knowing this, voters went to the polls on November 8 and reelected Lincoln by a majority of 212 to 21 in the electoral college. McClellan carried only New Jersey, Kentucky, and Delaware. Lincoln's majority of 55 percent of the popular vote was a healthy increase from the 48 percent he had received in the same states four years earlier. Only one free state (New Jersey) elected a Democratic governor in 1864. Republicans gained control of all the state legislatures lost in 1862 and won an extraordinary 145 of the 185 seats in the next House of Representatives (the Senate would have a 42-to-10 Republican majority). Seldom in American history has one party won such a lopsided victory in congressional elections. The Republican gains over 1860 came mainly from the soldier vote (discussed later in this section) and from the border states, where troops excluded secessionist voters and may have intimidated some potential McClellan voters.

One remarkable fact about the 1864 election was that it took place at all. No other country before World War II held general elections in the midst of war. Britain twice in the twentieth century canceled elections because of wartime emergencies. The American experiment of holding an election during a *civil* war whose result would determine the nation's future is unique in history. Yet no one in 1864 proposed to postpone the election. As Lincoln himself explained: "We can not have free government without elections; and if the rebellion could force us to forego, or postpone a national election, it might fairly claim to have already conquered and ruined us." The outcome, said Lincoln after his reelection, proved that "a people's government can sustain a national election in the midst of a great civil war."[32]

Equally remarkable was the soldier vote in 1864. No other society had tried the experiment of letting its fighting men vote in an election that might decide whether they were to continue fighting. By 1864, eighteen states had made it possible for their troops to vote in the field. Six of these provided that soldier votes should be deposited with other votes, leaving twelve states in which the army vote would be separately tabulated. The remaining Northern states—most notably Illinois and Indiana—made no provision for absentee voting by soldiers. Democrats in Illinois and Indiana had blocked such legislation, for with good reason they feared the soldier vote. Although McClellan's name still evoked enthusiasm among many officers and men in the Army of the Potomac, few soldiers wished to vote for a party that declared the war a failure. A Democratic victory, wrote one veteran officer, would mean "inglorious peace and shame, the old truckling subserviency to Southern domination." Another soldier, a lifelong Democrat, said that "we all want peace, but none *any* but an *honorable* one. I had rather stay out here a lifetime (much as I dislike it) than consent to a division of our country."[33]

Republicans considered the soldier vote crucial in certain states. As Commander in Chief, Lincoln could do something about this. Military operations came to a halt in early November as thousands of soldiers from states without absentee balloting received furloughs to go home and vote. Democrats charged fraud in Indiana, where thousands of Republican votes were said to have been cast by out-of-state soldiers. On the other hand, Democratic commissioners from New York who went to the front to collect soldier votes were arrested and convicted (one of them having confessed) of stuffing ballot boxes with forged McClellan votes. There were other accusations of fraud and harassment, but on the whole the army vote was marred by no more irregularities than normal in nineteenth-century elections. Lincoln won an extraordinary 78 percent of the separately tabulated soldier vote (119,754 out of 154,045). The Republican majority was probably as large among soldiers who went home to vote or whose ballots were not separately counted. Even in the Army of the Potomac, only 29 percent of the men voted for McClellan.

The soldier vote provided the margin of Republican victory in several congressional districts. It probably also provided Lincoln's margin in New York and Connecticut (and possibly in Indiana and Maryland). Although the President would have won without the army vote, the four-to-one Republican majority of soldier ballots was an impressive mandate for Lincoln's policy of war to victory. The men who would have to do the fighting had voted by a far larger margin than the folks at home to finish the job.[34]

The message of Lincoln's reelection was clear to everyone. "The overwhelming majority received by Mr. Lincoln and the quiet with which the election went off will prove a terrible damper to the Rebels," wrote Grant to a friend. "It will be worth more than a victory in the field both in its effect on the Rebels and in its influence abroad." Union soldiers in the trenches at Petersburg "cheered until they were hoarse" when they heard the news of Lincoln's victory. "At a point where the lines came within a few rods of each other," wrote a Yankee private, "our men heard a voice from behind the rebel breastworks. 'Say, Yank.' 'Hilloa, Johnny.' 'Don't fire, Yank.' 'All right, Johnny.' 'What are you'uns all cheering for?' 'Big victory on our side.' 'What is it, Yank?' came the eager response. 'Old Abe has cleaned all your fellers out up North.' 'You don't say so, Yank?' 'Fact; gobbled the whole concern; there is not peace men enough left in the whole North to make a corporal's guard.' "[35]

McClellan and his friends were disappointed but accepted the outcome with resignation. One of the general's close friends expressed relief that the Democrats would not be saddled with the responsibility for ending the war. "We engaged in an *impossible* fight," he wrote of the election campaign. "We undertook to interrupt a revolution before the completion of its cycle, and we fortunately failed." To the perceptive correspondent of the London *Daily News,* the turn in the tide of Northern opinion since midsummer showed that the North was "silently, calmly, but desperately in earnest . . . in a way the like of which the world never saw before. . . . I am astonished the more I see and hear of the extent and depth of [this] determination . . . to fight to the last."[36]

Richmond also understood the message of Lincoln's reelection. But Jefferson Davis put on a brave official front and insisted that the Confederacy remained "as erect and defiant as ever. Nothing [has] changed in the purpose of its Government, in the indomitable valor of its troops, or in the unquenchable spirit of its people. . . . There is no military success of the enemy which can accomplish its destruction."[37] It was this last-ditch defiance that Sherman set out to break in his famous march from Atlanta to the sea.

Twenty-five

The End of the Confederacy

FROM ATLANTA TO THE SEA

Soon after occupying Atlanta in September, Sherman decided to evacuate most of its civilian population. He wanted to use the city as a military base without the burden of feeding and protecting civilians or of guarding against spies and guerrillas in their midst. "I had seen Memphis, Vicksburg, Natchez, and New Orleans," explained Sherman, "all captured from the enemy, and each at once was garrisoned by a full division of troops, if not more; so that success was actually crippling our armies in the field by detachments to guard and protect the interests of a hostile population."[1]

When Atlanta's mayor and General Hood protested Sherman's "cruelty," the Northern general seized the opportunity to lecture them on the wickedness of rebellion. "War is cruelty and you cannot refine it," Sherman told the mayor. The South had started the war and boasted of its ability to lick the Yankees. "Now that the war comes home to you, you feel very different. You deprecate its horrors, but did not feel them when you sent car-loads of soldiers and ammunition . . . to carry war into Kentucky and Tennessee." The only road to peace was relentless war until the Confederacy surrendered. The evacuation orders for Atlanta "were not designed to meet the humanities of the case, but to prepare for the future struggles in which millions of good people outside Atlanta have a deep interest. We must have peace, not only at Atlanta, but in all America." To Hood, who had denounced Sherman's action as "preeminent in the dark history of war" for "studied and ingenious cruelty," Sherman replied with angry words for "you who, in the midst of peace and prosperity, have plunged a nation into war . . . who dared and badgered us to battle, insulted our flag . . . turned loose your privateers to plunder unarmed ships; expelled Union families by the thousands

459

[and] burned their houses. . . . Talk thus to the marines, but not to me, who have seen these things."[2]

Sherman had long pondered the nature and purpose of this war. He had concluded that "we are not only fighting hostile armies, but a hostile people." Defeat of Southern armies was not enough to win the war; the railroads, factories, and farms that supplied and fed them must be destroyed; the will of the civilian population that sustained the armies must be crushed. Sherman expressed more bluntly than anyone else the meaning of total war. He was ahead of his time in his understanding of psychological warfare, and he was in a position to practice it. "We cannot change the hearts of those people of the South, but we can make war so terrible . . . [and] make them so sick of war that generations would pass away before they would again appeal to it." In Tennessee and Mississippi, Sherman's troops had burned and destroyed everything of military value—and much that was not—within their reach. Now Sherman proposed to do the same in Georgia. He urged Grant to let him cut loose from his base and march his army through the heart of Georgia, living off the land and destroying all the resources not consumed by the army. The psychological impact of such a campaign, said Sherman, would be greater even than its material impact. "If we can march a well-appointed army right through [Jefferson Davis's] territory, it is a demonstration to the world, foreign and domestic, that we have a power which Davis cannot resist. This may not be war, but rather statesmanship."[3]

Lincoln and Grant were reluctant to authorize such a risky move while Hood's army and Forrest's cavalry still roamed in Sherman's rear. With 40,000 men Hood was too weak to attack Sherman; but he was strong enough to move northward along Sherman's communications, gobble up small garrisons, and destroy the railroad back to Chattanooga. In October this was precisely what he tried to do. Sherman followed, leaving one corps to garrison Atlanta. For two weeks the armies skirmished and maneuvered back through the same territory they had fought over from May to August. Forrest's and Wheeler's cavalry also caused havoc in Union-occupied territory from northeast Alabama to western Tennessee.

The Confederate strategy was to force Sherman to abandon Atlanta and disperse his army by chasing the marauding Rebels. But after driving Hood into northern Alabama, Sherman pleaded with Grant not to play the Southern game. "If I turn back now, the whole effect of my campaign will be lost," he said. "It will be a physical impossibility to protect the [rail] roads, now that Hood, Forrest, and Wheeler, and the whole batch of devils, are turned loose without home or habitation. By attempting to hold the roads, we will lose a thousand men monthly and will gain no result." Instead, Sherman proposed to send Thomas with two corps to Tennessee, where with reinforcements and new troops his total force of 60,000 would be more than a match for Hood. Meanwhile Sherman with 62,000 men would "move through Georgia, smashing things to the sea. . . . Instead of being on the defensive, I would be on the offensive. . . . I can make the march, and make Georgia howl!"[4]

Sherman won his point. Grant accepted his trusted subordinate's judgment and approved the march; Thomas returned to Nashville to organize his conglomerate

William Tecumseh Sherman *(Reproduced from the Collections of the Library of Congress)*

army; and Sherman readied his hard-bitten veterans for their march to make Georgia howl. To oppose them, the Confederacy could scrape together no more than a few thousand cavalry and the Georgia militia. Yet Sherman's proposed march of 285 miles to Savannah was one of the most dangerous and unorthodox of military undertakings. "To leave the enemy in his rear, to divide his army, to cut himself adrift from railroad and telegraph, from supplies and reinforcements, and launch not a mere raiding force of cavalry but a great army into a hostile country" was, in the words of a British military expert, "either one of the most brilliant or one of the most foolish things ever performed by a military leader" —depending on how it came out.[5]

The Yankees left Atlanta November 15 after burning everything of military value in the city. Inevitably the flames spread, consuming much of the business district and leveling one-third of Atlanta. As Sherman stood on a hill overlooking the burning city and watched his men march by, a band struck up "John Brown's Body" and the soldiers began to sing. "Never before or since," wrote Sherman a decade later, "have I heard the chorus of 'Glory, glory, hallelujah!' done with more spirit, or in better harmony of time and place."[6] The army moved in four parallel columns of infantry with the cavalry weaving back and forth from one flank to the other. Most of what little fighting occurred was done by the cavalry, which skirmished with Confederate horsemen who tried futilely to obstruct the march. Only once (November 22) did a division of the Georgia militia attack a Yankee infantry brigade, which repulsed it easily and was horrified to discover afterward that the 600 Georgians they had killed or wounded were mostly old men and boys.

The 62,000 bluecoats moved at a leisurely pace of ten miles a day, giving them plenty of time to cut a swath of destruction fifty miles wide through the heart of the Confederacy. The devastation wrought by Sherman's army has become legendary. The legend has much basis in fact. Although Sherman's orders empowered only official foraging parties to gather food and forbade the destruction of civilian property, these orders lost their authority as they filtered down through the ranks. The men were in a devil-may-care mood; they knew about Sherman's philosophy of total war; and officers from the lowliest lieutenant up to Sherman himself were confessedly lax in enforcing discipline. One soldier wrote that "we had a gay old campaign. . . . Destroyed all we could not eat, stole their niggers, burned their cotton & gins, spilled their sorghum, burned & twisted their R. Roads and raised Hell generally."[7]

Much of the unauthorized pillaging and burning of civilian property was carried out by "bummers"—foragers who were not under control of their officers, plus stragglers, deserters (Confederate as well as Union), and native freebooters in the guise of Georgia Unionists. And some of the scorching of Georgia's earth was done by the Rebel cavalry and by the Georgia militia, obeying orders from Richmond to remove all "negroes, horses, cattle and provisions from [the path] of Sherman's army, and burn what you cannot carry. . . . Obstruct and destroy all roads in Sherman's front, flank, and rear, and his army will soon starve in your midst."[8]

One group of Georgians who greeted the bluecoats not as avenging demons but as the army of the Lord were the blacks. Slaves were usually the first property liberated by the Yankee soldiers. Sherman tried to prevent all but able-bodied black males (whom he organized into labor battalions) from following the army, for he worried that thousands of black camp followers would reduce his mobility and consume supplies. But he had limited success. Thousands of freed people—old and young, male and female, sick and lame—fell in with the army. Officers and soldiers took black women into their units as cooks and concubines and hired black men as servants and porters. Three-generation families trailed the army in plantation wagons. Many tragedies accompanied this exodus. An Indiana officer wrote: "Babies tumbled from the backs of mules to which they had been told to cling, and were drowned in the swamps, while mothers stood by the roadside crying for their lost children."[9] Dozens of freedmen drowned trying to cross a river after the army's rear guard had taken up the pontoon bridge. Of at least 25,000 blacks who joined the columns at one time or another, most fell out from weariness, hunger, or sickness. Fewer than 7,000 made it all the way to the coast.

Although myth has exaggerated the ruin that "Sherman's vandals" left in their wake, the sober truth was devastating enough. Sherman estimated the damage "at $100,000,000; at least $20,000,000 of which has inured to our advantage, and the remainder is simple waste and destruction." Georgia would thenceforth send few supplies to Confederate armies. A Southern-born member of Sherman's staff who had initially deplored the destruction eventually came to share his chief's view of its psychological value in producing "among the people of Georgia a thorough conviction of the personal misery which attends war and of the utter helplessness and inability of their rulers to protect them." Sherman had made war "so terrible that when peace comes it will last."[10]

Sherman's march did indeed have this effect on Southern morale. A Georgia editor admitted that "a kind of gloom overshadows the face of many, their minds have lost buoyancy." And a Rebel soldier wrote: "i hev conkludud that the dam fulishness uv tryin to lick shurmin Had better be stoped. we hav bin gettin nuthin but hell & lots uv it ever sinse we saw the dam yankys & I am tirde uv it. . . . Thair thicker an lise on a hen and a dam site ornraier."[11]

The bluecoats came up to Savannah December 10 and found its strong defenses held by 10,000 Confederates. Sherman sent one division to capture Fort McAllister on the Ogeechee River south of Savannah. This reopened the Union army's communications with the outside world, through the navy. Then Sherman closed in on Savannah itself. The Confederates evacuated the city December 21 before the Federals could surround and trap them. In a typically jaunty gesture, Sherman telegraphed Lincoln: "I beg to present you, as a Christmas gift, the city of Savannah, with 150 heavy guns and plenty of ammunition, and also about 25,000 bales of cotton."[12] Published in Northern newspapers on Christmas Eve, this telegram set off another wave of celebration all the more euphoric because it came on the heels of Union victories in Tennessee that had all but wrecked Hood's army.

THE BATTLES OF FRANKLIN AND NASHVILLE

As Sherman moved out of Atlanta in November, Hood moved into Tennessee. His strategy was one of boldness born of desperation. He hoped to draw Sherman after him. Failing that, he intended to take his 39,000 men all the way through Tennessee and Kentucky to the Ohio River and then turn eastward to join Lee in Virginia. To achieve these goals, all he had to do was march 700 miles and defeat Thomas's 60,000 men in Tennessee, beginning with two veteran corps under John Schofield stationed near Pulaski.

Ill-equipped for a winter campaign (thousands of his men wore shoes so poor that they were marching barefoot within two weeks), Hood moved northward on November 19 with Forrest's cavalry leading the way. The Confederates flanked Schofield's smaller force (30,000 men) out of Pulaski. Schofield retreated to the Duck River at Columbia, only forty miles south of Nashville. Hood left two divisions to demonstrate against the Federals at Columbia and sent the cavalry and the rest of his infantry on a long swing around the Union left. Belatedly realizing the danger to his rear, Schofield quickly retreated northward toward Franklin on November 29.

Up to this time everything had gone well for Hood. Most of his army was in Schofield's rear where it could pounce on the retreating Federals. But then

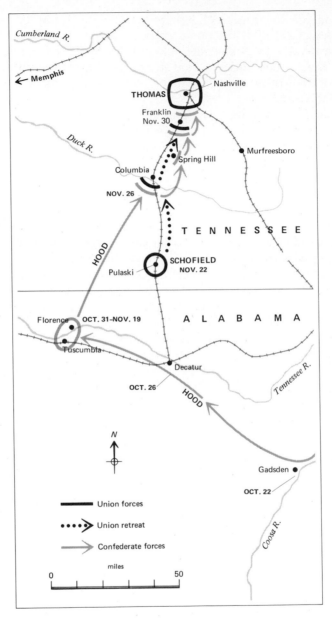

HOOD'S TENNESSEE CAMPAIGN, OCT.–NOV. 1864

everything began to go wrong. A series of contradictory or poorly understood orders caused Hood's corps and division commanders to delay until too late an attack on a single blue division holding the main road at Spring Hill. That night Schofield's whole command escaped silently along this road to Franklin, where

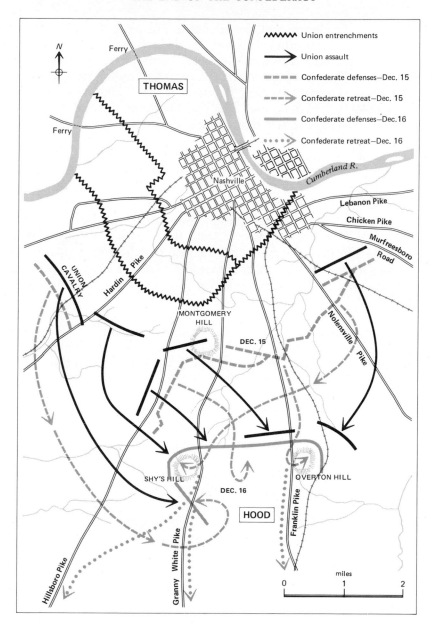

Union entrenchments
Union assault
Confederate defenses—Dec. 15
Confederate retreat—Dec. 15
Confederate defenses—Dec. 16
Confederate retreat—Dec. 16

THOMAS

Ferry

N

Ferry

Nashville

Cumberland R.

Lebanon Pike

Chicken Pike

Murfreesboro Road

UNION CAVALRY

Hardin Pike

MONTGOMERY HILL

DEC. 15

Nolensville Pike

SHY'S HILL

DEC. 16

OVERTON HILL

HOOD

Franklin Pike

Hillsboro Pike

Granny White Pike

miles
0   1   2

NASHVILLE, DECEMBER 15–16, 1864

they entrenched a strong defensive position.

Frustrated and enraged, Hood blamed his subordinates for the lost opportunity at Spring Hill and foolishly ordered a frontal assault at Franklin on November 30. His corps commanders urged him instead to flank the position. But Hood's blood was up; he refused to listen, and almost as if to discipline the army, he ordered the attack to proceed even though two of his divisions were far in the rear and he would not have numerical superiority over the blue veterans waiting behind stout breastworks. The outcome was predictable. The Confederates attacked with reckless valor but were cut to pieces. The total of 6,300 Southern casualties was nearly three times the Federal loss. The casualties among Confederate officers were appalling: twelve generals and fifty-four regimental commanders were killed, wounded, or captured.

His army crippled, Hood's only sensible course was to retreat. Instead, it was Schofield who retreated to join the rest of Thomas's army at Nashville. Hood followed and entrenched his troops on the hills south of the city, but he had run out of options. His forces were too weak to attack the Nashville defenses; it was logistically impossible for them to continue northward; and Hood believed that a retreat would demoralize his army. In truth the army was already demoralized as it awaited the inevitable Union attack. Thomas took his time preparing for this attack—so much time that the impatient Grant was on the verge of removing him from command when, after a further delay caused by an ice storm, the Union troops finally moved out on December 15.

A diversionary attack by a division containing two black brigades held most of one Confederate corps in position on the right, while Thomas launched 40,000 men in a bruising assault against the left. The Rebels hung on grimly through the short December day and withdrew a mile to a new position during the night. Next day the black troops again feinted against the right while the main attack rolled back the left. Dismounted Union cavalry carrying seven-shot Spencer carbines worked their way around to the Confederate rear, while a simultaneous infantry attack in front caused two of Hood's three corps to disintegrate. The Rebels streamed southward in the darkness and rain, which hindered Union pursuit. The battle of Nashville was one of the most crushing Union victories of the war. At the cost of only 3,000 casualties, the Federals had inflicted more than twice that many. The remnants of the shattered Southern army did not stop until they reached Tupelo, Mississippi, where the crestfallen Hood resigned his command in January. Of the 50,000 infantry he had inherited from Johnston in July, fewer than 15,000 were left. Dozens of these men continued to desert every day. For all practical purposes the Army of Tennessee ceased to exist.

ADOPTION OF THE THIRTEENTH AMENDMENT

The destruction of Hood's army coincided with the final step toward the constitutional destruction of slavery. Democratic opposition had defeated the Thirteenth Amendment in the House the previous June. In December, Lincoln urged Democrats to put aside partisanship and join the Republicans in passing the amendment. The next Congress would have a three-fourths Republican majority and would easily pass it. The President was prepared to call the new Congress into special session on March 4, 1865, for this purpose. But he preferred that such a historic achievement be accomplished as a bipartisan measure.

When the amendment came before the House in January, the administration lobbied earnestly to persuade a dozen or more Democrats to change their previous negative votes.

Some Democrats responded favorably. A New York representative reminded his party that it had come to grief in the last election "because we [would] not venture to cut loose from the dead carcass of negro slavery."[13] But most Democrats seemed determined, like Jefferson Davis, to die in the last ditch in defense of the past. Right up to the time of the roll call on January 31, nobody could predict confidently which way it would go. As a few Democrats early in the alphabet voted aye, tense Republican faces began to relax into smiles. Sixteen of the eighty Democrats voted aye; eight others had absented themselves. The vote was 119 to 56—just enough to pass the amendment with two votes to spare. When the result was announced, the most tumultuous celebration in the history of Congress took place. Republican members jumped to their feet and cheered, clapped each other on the back, and shouted triumphant congratulations to their colleagues. In the galleries, black onlookers embraced each other and wept tears of joy. The House voted to take the rest of the day off "in honor of this immortal and sublime event."[14]

Those black celebrants were examples of the great changes wrought by the war; until 1864, black people had not been allowed in congressional galleries. Blacks were also invited to White House receptions in 1865 for the first time. Federal legislation in 1864–1865 prohibited the exclusion of witnesses from federal courts on grounds of race, forbade segregation on streetcars in the District of Columbia, and repealed an 1810 law that had barred blacks from carrying the mail. Several Northern states and cities outlawed segregation in public transportation during or soon after the war. Northern states with black laws—laws that denied blacks certain civil rights—repealed these discriminatory laws between 1863 and 1866. Several states where blacks could not vote scheduled referendums on constitutional amendments to enact black suffrage. Perhaps the most vivid symbol of these changes was an event that occurred February 1, 1865. On that day Chief Justice Salmon P. Chase admitted John Rock of Massachusetts as a practicing lawyer before the U.S. Supreme Court. The only unusual aspect of this proceeding was that Rock was a black man, a member of a race whom Chase's predecessor had eight years earlier declared ineligible for U.S. citizenship.

Within three months after congressional passage of the Thirteenth Amendment, every Northern state legislature but one had ratified it. They were joined by the legislatures of Maryland, Missouri, and West Virginia plus the provisional Unionist legislatures of Louisiana and Tennessee. Only New Jersey, Kentucky, and Delaware—the states carried by McClellan in 1864—refused to ratify the amendment. The rest of the former Confederate states ratified it in the fall of 1865 as a condition of restoration under Andrew Johnson's reconstruction policy. When the amendment became part of the Constitution in December 1865, the institution that had tormented and nearly destroyed the republic existed no more.

DESERTION FROM THE CONFEDERATE ARMIES

While these winds of racial change were blowing over the North in early 1865, the Confederacy was visibly collapsing. Governors Zebulon Vance of North Carolina and Joseph Brown of Georgia stepped up their opposition to the Richmond government. While Lee's poorly clad soldiers suffered from the cold, Vance hoarded 92,000 uniforms and abundant supplies of leather and blankets for the sole use of North Carolina troops. Army desertions rose to alarming proportions. At the end of 1864, more than half of the 400,000 soldiers on the Confederate rolls were absent from the army, many of them deserters. General Beauregard admitted that desertion had become an "epidemic." In one month during the winter, the Army of Northern Virginia lost nearly 8 percent of its combat strength by desertion.

The Civil War desertion rate was high in both armies. Accurate statistics are elusive because of incomplete records and the difficulty of distinguishing between genuine deserters and those who for a variety of reasons were temporarily absent —with or without leave. There appear to have been about 200,000 Union deserters, of whom 80,000 were caught and returned to the army and 147 were executed. At least 104,000 Confederates deserted; 21,000 of them were caught and returned. Deserters thus constituted approximately 9.6 percent of the Union forces and 13 percent of the Confederate forces.

Until the fall of 1864, the desertion rate had been about the same on both sides. It was the "epidemic" of Confederate desertions in the winter of 1864–1865 that lifted the Southern rate higher for the war as a whole. Hunger, cold, and misery at the front, and the desperate plight of soldiers' families back home caused many desertions. Thousands of Confederate soldiers went home in response to such letters from their wives as this one in December 1864: "We haven't got nothing in the house to eat but a little bit o meal. . . . Try to get off and come home and fix us all up some and then you can go back. . . . If you put off a-coming, 'twont be no use to come, for we'll all hands of us be out there in the garden in the grave yard with your ma and mine."[15]

The most important cause of Confederate desertions in the war's final months was the belief that "our cause was hopeless and that further sacrifices were hopeless." A soldier in Lee's army who had previously testified to high morale in the ranks wrote in January 1865 that "the successful and . . . unopposed march of Sherman through Georgia, and the complete defeat of Hood in Tennessee, have changed the whole aspect of affairs." Robert E. Lee was convinced that such "discouraging sentiment" was the main cause of "this defection in troops who have acted so nobly and borne so much. . . . Unless it can be changed, [it] will bring us calamity. . . . Hundreds of men are deserting nightly. . . . I don't know what can be done to put a stop to it."[16]

THE FALL OF FORT FISHER AND THE FAILURE OF PEACE NEGOTIATIONS

Worse was yet to come. Lee's threadbare army drew its meager supplies from the interior of the Carolinas, as yet untouched by invasion, and from Wilmington,

North Carolina, the main port still open to blockade runners. Grant sent an expedition to close off Wilmington, and Sherman set out on his second march of destruction, this one through the Carolinas.

Wilmington was defended by a network of forts at the mouth of the Cape Fear River twenty miles below the city. The most important of these was Fort Fisher, a huge earthwork mounting seventy-five heavy guns. The treacherous channels and the formidable defenses at the mouth of the Cape Fear made it impossible for Union ships to run past the forts as they had at New Orleans and Mobile. Thus Wilmington had remained the principal blockade-running port. In the fall of 1864, the Union command fitted out an army-navy expedition to capture Fort Fisher. Much to Grant's chagrin, Benjamin Butler took command by virtue of his seniority in the Department of North Carolina. Butler conceived the idea of filling an old ship with 215 tons of gunpowder and running it into the shallows to explode next to the fort. This project was a fiasco, for the explosion on the night of December 23 did no damage to the fort. The navy then bombarded Fisher with 640 tons of metal, and Butler landed some of his 6,500 troops. But he decided that the fort was too strong for an assault, and embarked them again.

For Grant this was the last straw. He had long been looking for an excuse to remove Butler from command. With the election over, the administration no longer needed to treat Butler with kid gloves, so on January 8 his checkered military career came to an end. Grant promptly sent another expedition; this one consisted of 8,000 troops (including two black brigades) under General Alfred H. Terry, supported by the largest naval fleet of the war—fifty-eight ships mounting 627 guns. For two days this fleet blitzed Fort Fisher, disabling all but two of its guns. On January 15, 2,000 sailors and marines assaulted Fisher's seaward face while half of the 8,000 army troops circled around to the rear and swarmed over the parapets. With the fall of Fisher the other forts were also evacuated, Yankee ships sailed into the Cape Fear, and the last major Confederate port was sealed off from the world.

Vice president Alexander Stephens considered the loss of Fort Fisher "one of the greatest disasters which had befallen our Cause from the beginning of the war."[17] The disaster brought to a head the growing peace sentiment in the Confederacy. Two weeks after the fall of Fort Fisher, Stephens participated in yet another futile effort to negotiate a peace. In response to unofficial Union overtures borne to Richmond by Francis P. Blair, Jefferson Davis appointed three commissioners headed by Stephens to meet Northern representatives "with a view to secure peace to the two countries." Lincoln expressed his willingness to receive commissioners whom Davis "may informally send to me with the view of securing peace to the people of our one common country."[18]

This crucial difference in wording should have warned the Confederates what to expect. At the nadir of Northern morale six months earlier, Lincoln had insisted on reunion and emancipation as conditions of peace; he was unlikely to recede from this position with Union arms now victorious everywhere. Yet at a meeting with Lincoln and Seward aboard the Union steamer *River Queen* at Hampton Roads, Virginia, on February 3, the Confederate commissioners professed surprise

U.S. Marines. Marines such as these served on board Union naval
ships and participated in such sea-launched attacks as the assault on
Fort Fisher in January 1865.   *(Reproduced from the Collections of the
Library of Congress)*

at Lincoln's refusal to consider even an armistice without prior Southern submission to these terms. On procedural issues—the method of Southern political
restoration, the timing and implementation of emancipation, even the question
of compensation to slaveholders—Lincoln was prepared to be flexible, even at the
cost of opposition within his own party. But on the main issues of reunion and
emancipation he was firm. The Southern commissioners went home empty-
handed. This was probably what Jefferson Davis had expected and wanted, for he
lived in a fog of unreality where victory still seemed possible. Since the North
refused "to permit us to have [peace] on any other basis than our unconditional
submission to their rule," Davis told his Congress, war to the bitter end was the
only honorable alternative.[19]

A month later, Lincoln delivered his second inaugural address. He expressed
again the hope that "this mighty scourge of war may speedily pass away." But with
Old Testament imagery the President suggested that the war was the nation's
punishment for the sin of slavery. "If God wills that it continue, until all the

wealth piled by the bond-man's two hundred and fifty years of unrequited toil shall be sunk, and until every drop of blood drawn with the lash, shall be paid by another drawn with the sword . . . it must be said 'the judgments of the Lord, are true and righteous altogether.' "[20]

SHERMAN'S MARCH THROUGH THE CAROLINAS

In February, Sherman's 60,000 avengers brought the scourge of war to South Carolina in a campaign more devastating than their march from Atlanta to the sea. Sherman's intent was to smash his way through the Carolinas, destroying all war resources in his path and spreading demoralization among the populace as he moved up on Lee's rear to catch the Army of Northern Virginia in a vise between his army and Grant's.

The logistical accomplishments of this march were among the most stunning in the history of warfare. The earlier march through Georgia had taken place against token opposition in dry fall weather along lines parallel to the principal rivers. this one went half again as far and crossed many rain-swollen rivers and swamps in the middle of an unusually wet winter against increasing opposition, as the Rebels desperately scraped together an army in their futile attempt to block the blue bulldozer. Counting rest days and delays caused by skirmishes and fights, Sherman's forces averaged nearly ten miles a day for forty-five days. During twenty-eight of those days rain fell.

The Confederates expected the weather and terrain to stop Sherman. Joseph Johnston believed that "it was absolutely impossible for an army to march across lower portions of the State in winter." But the Yankees did it. Pioneer battalions (100 white soldiers and 75 black pioneers) cut down whole forests to corduroy roads; entire brigades exchanged rifles for spades and axes to build bridges. At night the men—Sherman included—sometimes roosted in trees to escape the flooded ground. Yet in all this, only 2 percent of the army fell sick. When the Federals came to the Salkiehatchie River, Confederate General William J. Hardee assured his superiors: "The Salk is impassable." The bluecoats bridged it and got the army over without loss of a wagon or gun. "I wouldn't have believed it if I hadn't seen it," said Hardee ruefully. Johnston later wrote: "When I learned that Sherman's army was marching through the Salk swamps, making its own corduroy roads at the rate of a dozen miles a day and more, and bringing its artillery and wagons with it, I made up my mind that there had been no such army in existence since the days of Julius Caesar."[21]

Sherman feinted one wing of his army toward Charleston and the other toward Augusta. The Confederates sent reinforcements to both cities. But the Federals pushed straight northward, cutting the railroad between the two cities without going near either. With its communications to the interior cut off, Charleston surrendered on February 18 to the Union forces that had besieged it from the sea for nearly two years. The Union officer who formally received the surrender was the colonel of a black regiment. His men were the first to take possession of the proud city where some of them had been slaves. They marched in singing "John

The Fruits of War. The
first two photographs
(right and below) show
the ruins of Charleston
after Confederate troops
had set fire to large parts
of the city when they
pulled out in February
1865. The photographer
accompanying the Union
occupation forces posed
freed slave children in
one picture and an aged
freedman in the other to
serve as symbols of the
new South rising from
the ashes of the old. The
second two pictures (on
p. 473) show the ruins of
Richmond after the
Confederates set the city

*(Reproduced from the
Collections of the
Library of Congress)*

(U.S. Army Field Artillery and Fort Sill Museum, Fort Sill, Oklahoma)

afire while evacuating it in April 1865. The photographer posed Union soldiers in the rubble of the top picture for similar symbolic purposes.

(Reproduced from the Collections of the Library of Congress)

(Massachusetts Commandery Military Order of the Loyal Legion and the U.S. Army Military History Institute)

Brown's Body" while Charleston's black population cheered mightily. The first task of these occupying troops was to extinguish the fires that evacuating Confederates had set to destroy cotton, military supplies, warehouses, and shipping, but which had spread to other parts of the city.

Queen city of the South, the taproot of secession, Charleston's fall was the most dramatic sign of the Confederacy's collapse. "The disappointment is to me extremely bitter," wrote Jefferson Davis.[22] For abolitionists, a visible symbol of the mighty revolution was the presence in Charleston of George Thompson Garrison, son of the *Liberator*'s editor and a lieutenant in the 55th Massachusetts Colored Infantry. Two months later William Lloyd Garrison himself, along with many other abolitionists, arrived in the city to take part in a ceremonial raising of the Stars and Stripes over Fort Sumter four years to the day after the flag had been lowered in surrender.

Before Sherman began his march into South Carolina, Chief of Staff Halleck had wired him: "Should you capture Charleston, I hope that by some accident the place may be destroyed, and if a little salt should be sown upon its site it may prevent the growth of future crops of nullification and secession."[23] Charleston escaped this fate, but much else in South Carolina did not. In Northern eyes the state deserved special punishment for its fire-eating role in provoking the war. Many Southerners by 1865 shared this viewpoint. During Sherman's march through Georgia, civilians repeatedly said to the Yankees: "Why don't you go over to South Carolina and serve them this way? They started it." The bluecoats were willing. Sherman reported that "the whole army is burning with an insatiable desire to wreak vengeance upon South Carolina. I almost tremble at her fate, but feel that she deserves all that seems in store for her."[24] Sherman's orders in South Carolina were the same as in Georgia: seize or destroy all forage and property of military value, but leave civilian property alone. Bummers respected these orders even less than they had in Georgia, and Sherman did little to restrain them. A Union officer noted that "in Georgia few houses were burned; here few escaped." The soldiers made little distinction between civilian and military property. They "would sometimes stop to tell me that they were sorry for the women and children," wrote a woman whose house was plundered, "but South Carolina must be *destroyed.* South Carolina and her sins was the burden of their song." A pillaging private put it succinctly: "Here is where treason began, and, by God, here is where it shall end!"[25]

The greatest outrage charged against Sherman was the burning of Columbia, the capital of South Carolina. Union soldiers entered Columbia on February 17; by next morning half the city was in ashes. The controversy over responsibility for this act has not yet abated. Southern partisans maintained that the Yankees deliberately put Columbia to the torch. Sherman and his officers insisted that the flames spread from cotton set afire by Confederate cavalry as they evacuated the city. As usual, the truth appears to lie between these claims. Civil order had broken down in Columbia even before Sherman's troops arrived. Great quantities of liquor were stored in the city; Confederate cavalrymen, hoodlums, and slaves had broken into these supplies and were rampaging through the streets, looting and setting fire to cotton. Hundreds of Union soldiers got drunk on February 17; liberated convicts from the jail and escaped Union prisoners from a nearby prisoner-of-war camp joined the inebriated rampage. Sober Union soldiers helped to put out fires started by burning cotton, but when night fell on February 17 and the wind rose to a gale, the social and meteorological combustibility of the city exploded into flame at scores of places. Soldiers and officers, Sherman included, worked through the night to contain the fires, but only a wind shift at 4 A.M.

prevented the entire city from being consumed. No single group—Confederate cavalry, drunken bluecoats, vengeful prisoners, slaves, or criminals—was solely responsible for the burning of Columbia, but neither could any of them be entirely absolved of blame. Columbia was yet another victim of a war that brought more tragedy and destruction to the United States than all its other wars combined.[26]

Sherman's wrecking crew moved on to North Carolina, where they encountered an old antagonist, Joseph E. Johnston. On February 6, Robert E. Lee had become general in chief of the Confederate armies. Although Lee's popularity in the South was so great that he could have assumed dictatorial powers had it been in his character to do so, the only power of his new office that he exercised was to restore Johnston to command. Johnston's task of stopping Sherman was a forlorn hope. By bringing together several scattered units he could muster barely 22,000 men to oppose Sherman's 60,000, soon to be joined by 30,000 bluecoats moving inland from the North Carolina coast. Johnston's only hope was to strike part of Sherman's army while it was isolated from the rest. On March 19 at Bentonville (near Raleigh), Johnston thought he saw his opportunity. With about 17,000 infantry he attacked an equal number of Federals on the left wing of Sherman's advance. The surprised Yankees dug in and held their ground. Next day the rest of Sherman's divisions began to arrive, but before Sherman was ready to order a general assault, the Confederates retreated northward. The Federals went on to Goldsboro to rest and refit after their seven weeks of marching and fighting.

DESTRUCTION OF CONFEDERATE RESOURCES

Behind them Sherman's troops left 425 miles of desolation that would never again support a Rebel army. And even as these weary Union veterans trudged into Goldsboro, two Union armies 700 miles to the southwest launched simultaneous strikes that laid waste the only remaining undamaged part of the Confederacy east of the Mississippi. Forty thousand men moved in two columns from Mobile Bay and Pensacola against the city of Mobile. In a three weeks' campaign they took Mobile and captured or scattered its 10,000 defenders. Meanwhile the twenty-seven-year-old cavalry commander James H. Wilson led the largest, longest, and most destructive cavalry raid of the war from northwest Alabama to southern Georgia. Armed with Spencer seven-shot carbines, Wilson's 13,000 troopers had twice the firepower and three times the mobility of an infantry corps. Smashing their way through Alabama, the blue horsemen defeated Forrest's once-feared cavalry in six engagements, killed or wounded 1,000 Confederates and captured 6,000, and climaxed the 500-mile raid on May 10 by capturing the fleeing Jefferson Davis at Irwinsville, Georgia. Along the way they tore up railroads, wrecked 600 locomotives and freight cars, demolished dozens of munitions factories and arsenals, seized or burned enormous quantities of cotton, and destroyed 300 pieces of artillery and 100,000 small arms.

In 1861 many foreign observers had considered the Confederacy unconquerable because its large area, poor roads, and rugged terrain would defeat an invader just as Russia's vast distances had defeated Napoleon in 1812. But contrary to predictions, the South was not only invaded and conquered, it was utterly destroyed. By 1865 the Union forces had penetrated every corner of 500,000 square miles of the Confederacy (excluding only the peripheral areas of Texas and Florida), a territory as large as France, Spain, and West Germany combined. These forces destroyed two-thirds of the assessed value of Southern wealth, two-fifths of the South's livestock, and one-quarter of her white men between the ages of twenty and forty. More than half the farm machinery was ruined, and the damage to railroads and industries was incalculable. While total Northern wealth increased by 50 percent from 1860 to 1870, Southern wealth decreased by 60 percent (or 30 percent if the slaves are not counted as wealth).[27] These figures provide eloquent testimony to the tragic irony of the South's counterrevolution of 1861 to preserve its way of life. They also testify to the capacity of a modernizing society to overcome the barriers of distance and terrain in history's first "modern" war.

THE RECONSTRUCTION ISSUE IN THE WINTER
OF 1864–1865

While the Confederacy disintegrated, the Northern Congress tried again to define the conditions of reconstruction. Under Lincoln's 10 percent plan (see pp. 391–392), Unionist governments were functioning in occupied portions of Louisiana and Arkansas. A new government was forming in Tennessee. Despite the earlier clash between Lincoln and the radicals over reconstruction, the President now hoped that Congress would recognize these governments. The spirit of Republican harmony growing out of the 1864 election augured well for a compromise between President and Congress. Lincoln's appointment of Salmon P. Chase as chief justice in December was a gesture of good will toward the radicals. So also was a sentence in the President's annual message indicating a willingness to support "more rigorous measures than heretofore" toward the postwar South.[28]

The President and House Republican leaders worked out a compromise whereby Congress would recognize the Lincoln-nurtured governments of Louisiana and Arkansas in return for presidential approval of legislation for the rest of the Confederacy similar to the Wade-Davis bill vetoed the previous July. This compromise measure initially enacted black suffrage in the remaining Southern states, but moderates modified it to enfranchise only black army veterans and literate blacks. During January and February 1865, a bewildering series of committee and floor votes in the House defeated several versions of the bill. Radicals voted against measures that did not enfranchise blacks or that recognized the existing Louisiana government. Conservative Republicans opposed measures that required black suffrage. Democrats voted against all reconstruction bills. As a result, no bill could be passed. In the Senate, an incongruous alliance of Democrats and radicals blocked a proposal to recognize the reconstruction government of Louisiana.[29]

Moderates regretted the breakdown of compromise efforts. But radicals were just as happy to postpone the reconstruction question until the war was over. "In the meantime," wrote a radical congressman, "I hope the nation may be educated up to our demand for universal suffrage."[30] The next Congress, elected in the

Republican sweep of 1864, was sure to be more radical. The President might also become more radical. From 1861 to 1865, Lincoln had moved steadily to the left: from limited war to total war; from gradual, compensated emancipation to immediate, universal abolition; from opposition to the arming of blacks to enthusiastic support for it; from the idea of restoring the Union to the idea of reconstructing it; from the colonization of freed slaves to the enfranchisement of black soldiers and literate blacks. At the close of the war, Lincoln again appeared to be moving closer to the radical position. In a speech on April 11 he reasserted his flexible, pragmatic approach to reconstruction. The Louisiana precedent was not necessarily applicable to other states, said the President, and he was not unalterably committed to it even in Louisiana if this proved "adverse to the public interest." At the end of his speech Lincoln promised "some new announcement" on reconstruction in the near future. But three days later John Wilkes Booth robbed the nation of that announcement forever.[31]

THE CONFEDERATE DECISION TO ARM SLAVES

With most of her territory overrun, her armies melting away, and her economy ruined, the Confederacy in March 1865 was clearly doomed. Yet Davis and Lee still had two cards to play in a desperate bid to stave off the inevitable. The first was the enlistment of slaves in the Confederate army. The second was an effort to unite Lee's and Johnston's 70,000 ragged, half-starved troops to strike Sherman's 90,000 and Grant's 115,000 in succession. Both enterprises were born of fantasy out of despair, but Southern leaders expressed a determination to "die in the last ditch" before they succumbed.

In 1863 the North's enlistment of black soldiers had prompted a few iconoclasts in the South to wonder whether the Confederacy might also tap this reservoir of manpower. General Patrick Cleburne openly suggested the arming of slaves early in 1864, but Jefferson Davis squelched the proposal. It could not stay squelched. As the Confederate armies disintegrated during the winter of 1864–1865, the Southern press and politicians endlessly debated the idea of drafting slaves. By the end of 1864, Davis and his cabinet supported the idea. Two years earlier Davis had denounced the North's arming of contrabands as "the most execrable measure recorded in the history of guilty man." But much had happened since then. As a Confederate diarist put it on Christmas Day, "when the question is between slavery and independence, slavery must go."[32]

But to Southerners for whom the purpose of the war was the defense of slavery, the idea of arming black men was an "inconsistent self-stultification." "What did we go to war for, if not to protect our property?" asked Robert M. T. Hunter of Virginia, president pro tem of the Confederate Senate. Howell Cobb, one of the South's most powerful political generals, insisted that "if slaves will make good soldiers our whole theory of slavery is wrong. . . . The day you make soldiers of them is the beginning of the end of the revolution." Cobb's fellow Georgian Robert Toombs thundered that "the worst calamity that could befall us would be to gain our independence by the valor of our slaves. . . . The day that the army of Virginia allows a negro regiment to enter their lines as soldiers they will be degraded, ruined, and disgraced."[33]

It was Robert E. Lee who finally overcame this opposition. Never a strong proponent of slavery, Lee believed that if emancipated, the slaves would fight for "their country" more readily than for the Yankees. "We must decide whether slavery shall be extinguished by our enemies and the slaves be used against us, or use them ourselves," wrote Lee. "I think we could at least do as well with them as the enemy, and he attaches great importance to their assistance." So great was Lee's prestige (the *Richmond Examiner* said that "the country will not deny to General Lee . . . *anything* he may ask for") that the Confederate Congress on March 13 reluctantly and narrowly passed a bill to enlist black soldiers.[34] Impending disaster converted the counterrevolution of 1861 to the revolution of 1865— but not quite. Despite Lee's recommendation that slave soldiers be freed, the bill did not require this. Whether the slaves would have fought for the South with or without a promise of freedom remained a moot question. Before any regiments could be organized the war was over.

FROM PETERSBURG TO APPOMATTOX

It was over because the Army of the Potomac had finally brought the Army of Northern Virginia to bay. For almost four years, these armies had slaughtered each other across a narrow front of 200 miles while the principal Union armies in the West had marched victoriously through a thousand miles of Rebel territory. This gave rise to a cockiness among Western troops. Lean, hard men from the farms and the frontier, they expressed contempt for the "paper collar" Eastern soldiers. When Western and Eastern Union troops came together they traded insults and sometimes blows. An Indiana private declared in 1863 that "the war would never end were it left to the fighting of the band box army in the east. . . . They have been in but one Confederate state while we have been through five." An Illinois soldier thought that "the Potomac Army is only good to draw greenbacks and occupy winter quarters." For their part, Eastern soldiers considered Western troops an "armed rabble" who owed their military success to the inferiority of the Western Confederate armies. "The Western rebels are nothing but an armed mob," wrote one Army of the Potomac veteran in 1864, "and not anything near so hard to whip as Lee's well disciplined soldiers."[35]

Most historians of the Union armies have accepted the Westerners' image of themselves. And it cannot be denied that from Donelson to Atlanta the Western armies won most of their battles and conquered large chunks of territory while the Army of the Potomac could do no better than a stalemate in Virginia. But this was the result less of differences in the fighting qualities of Eastern and Western soldiers than of differences in the quality of generalship, both Union and Confederate. All four of the Union's best generals—Grant, Sherman, Sheridan, and Thomas—came out of the West. Of the South's most successful generals— Lee, Jackson, Longstreet, Stuart, and Forrest—only Forrest was a Westerner. When Longstreet took part of his corps to Georgia in 1863, he provided the leadership that exploited the breakthrough at Chickamauga, the only clear victory won by the Confederate Army of Tennessee. When the 11th and 12th Corps of the Army of the Potomac went from Virginia to Chattanooga a month later, these troops, considered the weakest units in the Eastern army, became good fighting men in a Western army. It was not the men who had changed but their leaders.

The Western armies did less hard fighting than the Army of the Potomac. Not all contemporaries recognized this. A Wisconsin private who marched with Sherman wrote that "the Potomac Army has no doubt done some hard fighting, but it has been on a different scale than ours, and the most of it was done in the newspapers."[36] He could not have been more wrong. Of the fourteen bloodiest battles of the war (those with combined Union and Confederate casualties of 17,000 or more), ten were fought between the Army of Northern Virginia and the Army of the Potomac. Of the fifty Southern regiments with the highest percentage of battle casualties, forty fought in the Eastern theater. Of the fifty highest-casualty Union regiments, forty-one were in the Eastern armies. Six of the seven Union army corps with the highest battle casualties fought in the Army of the Potomac. This army alone suffered more than half the battle deaths in the entire Union armed forces. The proportion of battle deaths among soldiers from New England and the Middle Atlantic states was 23 percent higher than among those from Western states.[37]

The Fall of Petersburg and Richmond

Although a Westerner, Grant was sensitive to the Army of the Potomac's pride and to its resentment of the Westerners' claims of superiority. Thus he was anxious to finish the war before Sherman's army came up on Lee's rear and took credit for the final victory. Grant's greatest worry now was that he would wake up one morning to find that Lee's army had slipped away during the night to join Johnston in North Carolina. This was precisely what Lee intended to do. Before pulling out of the trenches, however, he gambled on one last assault against Grant's right, east of Petersburg, to compel him to shorten his encircling lines by sending reinforcements from the left. In the predawn darkness of March 25, sham Confederate deserters who had been fraternizing with Union pickets suddenly seized the surprised Yankees and spearheaded an attack that captured Fort Stedman, an earthwork in the Union line. Rebel brigades poured through the gap and soon occupied nearly a mile of Union trenches. But they could not hold them in the face of enfilading artillery fire and an infantry counterattack. By midmorning the Confederates had been driven back with a loss of 4,800 men.

Grant now seized the initiative. He sent two infantry corps and 12,000 cavalry to flank the Confederate right, tear up the last open railroad into Petersburg, and block Lee's escape route to the southwest. At a road junction called Five Forks, Sheridan's cavalry and the 5th Corps on April 1 struck 10,000 Confederates in front and flank and routed them, inflicting more than 5,000 casualties at a cost of only 1,000 to themselves. When Grant learned of Sheridan's success, he ordered an assault all along the Petersburg lines at dawn the next day. The

(U.S. Army Military History Institute)

Victors and Vanquished. Above: Veterans of the 30th Pennsylvania Infantry resting in the trenches after fighting at Petersburg. Right: A fourteen-year-old Confederate soldier killed in the Petersburg trenches during the final Union assault on April 2, 1865. Nothing could testify more powerfully than these two pictures to the contrast in the strength and resources of the two sides at the war's end.

(Reproduced from the Collections of the Library of Congress)

480

remaining Confederates put up a desperate struggle, falling back from one line of trenches to the next during a long and bloody day that cost the Federals 4,000 killed and wounded. Grant hoped to trap Lee's army in Petersburg, but during the night the Rebels escaped across the Appomattox River and retreated westward. Meanwhile the Confederate government and all troops in the area evacuated Richmond after blowing up bridges, factories, and arsenals, and burning all tobacco and government property that could not be removed. By dawn on April 3, Richmond was a blazing inferno.

Among the first Union soldiers to take possession of the city were black troopers of the 5th Massachusetts Cavalry, commanded by Charles Francis Adams, Jr., eldest son of the minister to Britain and grandson of President John Quincy Adams. Once again, as at Charleston, the first task of the occupation troops was to put out the fires, which they had done by nightfall, but only after most of the business and industrial sections of Richmond were destroyed. Next day President Lincoln visited the ruined city, escorted by a troop of black cavalry. Richmond blacks turned out by the thousands to cheer every step of their way. "I know I am free," shouted one, "for I have seen Father Abraham and felt him." A black correspondent of one of the leading Northern newspapers, T. Morris Chester of the *Philadelphia Press*, sat quietly in the Confederate Capitol, writing a dispatch describing the scene. For Richmond whites this was tangible evidence, if any more was needed, of the shattering revolution that had turned their world upside down.[38]

The Road to Appomattox

While these events took place in Richmond, Lee's army of 35,000 was trying to escape from 80,000 Federals in hot pursuit. Sheridan's cavalry and two infantry corps raced parallel to the fleeing Confederates on their left to prevent Lee from turning southward, while two other infantry corps stayed on their rear, picking up hundreds of exhausted Rebel stragglers. On April 6 at Sayler's Creek near Farmville, the Federals cut off and captured 7,000 Confederates after a battle in which the bluecoats lost only 1,200 men. "My God! Has the Army been dissolved?" agonized Lee as he watched the climax of this action. On April 8, Sheridan got in front of what was left of Lee's army and captured two trainloads of rations at Appomattox Station, 100 miles west of Petersburg. When a final Confederate attempt to break through the encircling ring on the morning of April 9 revealed two blue infantry corps in line behind the cavalry, Lee realized that the game was up. One of his artillery officers suggested that the army scatter to the woods and carry on the war as guerrillas. But Lee would have none of this. The guerrillas, he said, "would become mere bands of marauders, and the enemy's cavalry would pursue them and overrun many sections they may [otherwise] never have occasion to visit. We would bring on a state of affairs it would take the country years to recover from." No, said Lee, "there is nothing left for me to do but to go and see General Grant, and I would rather die a thousand deaths."[39]

Lee Surrenders

But go he did, to the house of Wilmer McLean in the village of Appomattox Courthouse. Ironically, McLean had owned a house near Manassas, Virginia, in 1861 that had been used as a Confederate headquarters in the first battle of Bull Run. He had moved to this remote corner of Virginia to escape the ravages of contending armies, only to witness the final act of the war in his living room. Lee arrived resplendent in full-dress uniform; Grant, whose headquarters wagon had not kept up in the mad dash to cut off the Confederates, came to this historic meeting in a faded campaign blouse and with trousers tucked into mud-spattered boots. The only general in American history to capture three separate armies (at Donelson, Vicksburg, and now Appomattox), Grant proposed generous terms that paroled Lee's whole army and allowed them to take their horses or mules home "to put in a crop." As the two generals shook hands, Grant felt "sad and depressed" at "the downfall of a foe who had fought so long and valiantly, and had suffered so much for a cause, though that cause was, I believe, one of the worst for which a people ever fought."[40]

Some Union officers were so awestruck by the news of Lee's surrender that they could hardly believe it. One colonel who had fought in Virginia for three years wrote two weeks after the capitulation at Appomattox: "None of us realize even yet that [Lee] has actually surrendered. I had a sort of impression that we should fight him all our lives." But as news of the surrender spread through Union camps on April 9, the soldiers began to celebrate as if all the Fourths of July in history had been rolled into one. "The air is black with hats and boots, coats, knapsacks, shirts and cartridge boxes," wrote one veteran who tried to describe the scene. "They fall on each others' necks and laugh and cry by turns. Huge, lumbering, bearded men embrace and kiss like schoolgirls, then dance and sing and shout, stand on their heads and play leapfrog with each other." Every band in the army struck up, each trying to outdo the others in volume and spirit.[41] As the telegraph flashed the news of Lee's surrender through the North, which was just recovering from its celebration of the fall of Richmond, new and wilder jubilation broke out.

THE ASSASSINATION OF LINCOLN AND THE END OF THE WAR

Suddenly the rejoicing turned to grief as once more the telegraph clicked out momentous news—but this time news of terrible, grave import—the assassination of Lincoln. On April 14 the careworn fifty-six-year-old President had relaxed by attending a comedy at Ford's Theater. In the middle of the play, John Wilkes Booth had gained entrance to Lincoln's box and shot him in the head. Jumping to the stage (where he broke his leg), Booth shouted "Sic semper tyrannis" and hobbled out a rear door, where he made good his escape on horseback before anyone in the theater could stop him.

The son and brother of famous actors, while a mediocre actor himself, John

Wilkes Booth, aged twenty-six, was a frustrated, unstable egotist thirsting for fame. He had plotted for months to kidnap Lincoln and hold him hostage for concessions to the Confederacy. To help in this mad scheme, he recruited several allies from Washington's underworld of drifters, Rebel spies, and Confederate deserters. The fall of Richmond and Lee's surrender ruined the kidnapping venture, so Booth decided instead to murder Lincoln, Vice President Johnson, and Secretary of State Seward. The accomplice assigned to assassinate Johnson lost his nerve; Seward suffered serious stabbing wounds but survived. On April 26, Union troops finally tracked down the Maryland-born Booth and shot him to death in a burning barn in Virginia. A military court convicted eight accomplices of collusion in the assassination. Four were hanged, and the rest were sentenced to imprisonment at hard labor. In two cases a probable miscarriage of justice occurred: Mary Surratt, keeper of a boardinghouse where Booth planned the kidnapping, was part of his original kidnapping plot but probably unaware of the revised plans for assassination; and Dr. Samuel Mudd, who treated Booth's broken leg, was at most an accessory after the fact. Mrs. Surratt was hanged; Mudd was sentenced to life imprisonment but pardoned (along with the other imprisoned conspirators) in 1869. Their convictions were partly the product of postassassination hysteria and clamors for revenge.*

The Martyred President

On April 15, 1865, Andrew Johnson took the oath as President of a nation in shock and mourning. People wept in the streets for the martyred Lincoln. General Grant wept openly during the funeral services in the White House on April 19. Millions stood silently along the tracks as a nine-car train carried Lincoln's body the thousand miles from Washington back home to Springfield, Illinois. In a nation with an abiding religious heritage, the murder of the President on Good Friday seemed to be more than a coincidence. For black people, especially,

---

*Booth's death before he could stand trial, like that of Lee Harvey Oswald a century later, spawned numerous conspiracy theories to explain who was *really* behind the assassination. Many Northerners believed that Jefferson Davis himself had conspired with Booth; others thought Andrew Johnson was somehow involved. Some contemporaries and later writers have tried to establish links between Booth and Confederate agents operating out of Canada. At least one historian has argued that the mastermind behind the conspiracy was Lafayette C. Baker, a counterintelligence agent in the U.S. War Department who organized and led the pursuit that killed Booth. Another writer insisted that Booth, a secret convert to Roman Catholicism, killed Lincoln at the order of the Jesuits. Most popular of the modern conspiracy theories is the thesis that Secretary of War Stanton plotted the assassination in behalf of a clique of radical Republicans who wanted to get rid of Lincoln because of his "soft" reconstruction policy. Still other writers insist that the man killed in Virginia was not Booth but someone else with his initials who looked like the actor. A recent book and movie manage to blend most of these themes into one grand conspiracy theory that implicates nearly every leading Union and Confederate official, with several Northern bankers thrown in for good measure. (David Balsiger and Charles E. Sellier, Jr., *The Lincoln Conspiracy,* Los Angeles, 1977.) Although a number of ambiguities and unanswered questions remain about the assassination, there is no real evidence to support any of these myths. Booth and his handful of accomplices appear to have acted on their own. And indeed, the man killed in Virginia was John Wilkes Booth. For a summary of various assassination theories, see Lloyd Lewis, *Myths After Lincoln* (New York, 1929), part 2, and Richard N. Current, *The Lincoln Nobody Knows* (New York, 1958), chap. 11.

Lincoln's death at the moment of victory over slavery made of him a Christ-like figure. The event clothed with new meaning the last verse of Julia Ward Howe's "Battle Hymn of the Republic": "As He died to make men holy, Let us die to make men free."

Anger as well as sorrow marked the Northern mood in the weeks after the assassination. There were bitter cries for vengeance against not only the assassination conspirators but against all Confederate leaders, who were considered to be ultimately responsible for the death not only of Lincoln but also of the 360,000 Union soldiers who had been killed in the war. But such cries were contrary to the teachings of the Christ to whom Lincoln was now being compared. They also seemed to be contrary to the moving peroration of Lincoln's second inaugural address: "With malice toward none; with charity for all; with firmness in the right, as God gives us to see the right, let us strive . . . to bind up the nation's wounds [and to achieve] a just, and a lasting peace."[42]

The tension in this passage between "charity" and "firmness" would characterize Northern attitudes toward the South for months after the assassination, just as it had characterized Lincoln's wartime leadership. Lincoln's greatness as President had lain in his ability to resolve these and other tensions in such a manner as to maintain the Northern will to fight through many moments of doubt, discouragement, and division.

Subject to moods of depression (which he called "the hypo"), Lincoln had learned to transcend despair in his personal life just as the Union under his leadership was able to transcend its national despair. The President told anecdotes not only as parables to illustrate points about larger issues, but also to dissolve anxiety in laughter. Lincoln loved to frolic with his two youngest sons, eleven-year-old Willie and eight-year-old Tad. In February 1862, both fell ill, probably with typhoid fever. Tad recovered, but Willie did not; on February 20 he died. (In a sad parallel two years later, five-year-old Joseph Davis, son of the Confederate president, fell from a balcony of the executive mansion in Richmond and died of a skull fracture.) Abraham and Mary Lincoln were almost prostrated with grief at Willie's death. Abraham recovered to face the problems of emancipation, political opposition, and military defeats and to overcome them; Mary suffered a nervous breakdown and never fully regained her mental balance. The anguish in the White House was a microcosm of the ordeal experienced by the nation during Lincoln's four years and six weeks as president. No other president endured such personal affliction while in office; no other president faced such a national crisis. Lincoln's success in surmounting both is a measure of his humanity and his greatness.

The End of the War

During the weeks after Lincoln's death, while President Johnson was trying to get accustomed to his new office and several Confederate armies were still in the field, Secretary of War Stanton was the government's strong man. Brusque and excitable, Stanton feared that the assassination was part of a Rebel plot to overthrow the government. Under his orders, hundreds of Confederate sympathizers were arrested; those implicated in the assassination were harshly treated and their legal rights all but ignored.

In the midst of these events came news of the surrender terms negotiated by Sherman and Johnston. These terms aroused in Stanton a different set of suspicions. An advocate of hard war, Sherman had always hoped for a soft peace once the Rebels were thoroughly whipped. He had opposed the arming of blacks; he had little faith in black equality; he opposed the radical program of reconstruction. In the spirit of what Sherman thought Lincoln's policy would have been, he went far beyond Grant's surrender terms for Lee's army and negotiated with Johnston what amounted to a peace treaty. It provided for the recognition of existing Southern state governments when their officials had taken the oath of allegiance; it allowed disbanded Confederate troops to deposit their arms in state arsenals; and it guaranteed to Southerners "their political rights and franchises, as well as their rights of person and property."

Normally astute and chary of political involvement, Sherman here committed a major blunder. Not only did he exceed his authority, but he also failed to see that this agreement could be interpreted as recognizing insurgent governments, guaranteeing property in slaves, and taking the question of reconstruction out of the hands of the President and Congress. Grant conveyed to Sherman the cabinet's unanimous disapproval of the terms, and Sherman unhesitatingly negotiated a new surrender agreement with Johnston on April 26 that duplicated the Grant-Lee terms. There the matter might have rested except that Stanton, distrustful of Sherman's motives (Democrats were beginning to sing his praises), released to the press a distorted version of the affair that put Sherman in a bad light. Stanton's fears were unfounded; his action, though sincere, was unjust, and Sherman never forgave the Secretary of War.*

Everyone in Washington, Stanton most of all, was under great pressure during the weeks after the assassination. Although Lee had surrendered, Jefferson Davis and his cabinet remained at large, moving southward as fast as the dilapidated railroads could carry them. At every stop Davis exhorted his people to fight on, "operating in the interior," where the enemy's extended lines of communication would "render our triumph certain."[43] Even after Johnston surrendered, Davis spoke of moving the government to the trans-Mississippi states and carrying on the war. To the Union government it appeared that guerrilla warfare might go on for years, turning the South into another Ireland. But most Southerners had had more than enough. Lee's example was stronger than Davis's rallying cries. In Alabama on May 4, General Richard Taylor surrendered the remaining Confederate forces east of the Mississippi. Union cavalry captured Jefferson Davis and his entourage in Georgia on May 10. On May 26 General Edmund Kirby Smith

---

*Stanton's motives and personality have eluded the analytical efforts of many historians. Efficient, incorruptible, hard-working, and intensely dedicated to the Union, he was a superb secretary of war. At the same time, he was secretive, high-strung, brusque, sometimes devious in personal relationships, and often insensitive to the feelings of others.

surrendered the trans-Mississippi army. These events of May brightened the skies in Washington. The problems of peace still lay ahead, but the war was definitely over.

Demobilization of the Union Armies

Two feared consequences of the war did not materialize. (1) There was no bloodbath of vengeance. No Confederates were tried for treason. Jefferson Davis was imprisoned without trial for two years but then released to live a quiet life and write his memoirs. This absence of reprisals was almost unique in the history of rebellions, especially those waged on the scale of this one. (2) The army did not become a power in American life. To be sure, every elected president until 1904 save one (Grover Cleveland) had fought in the Union army and owed his political success in part to his war record. But none of them, not even Grant, was a "military" president; all except Grant were civilians who had sprung to arms in the crisis of 1861 and returned to civilian life as quickly in 1865.

Before they went home, however, the Army of the Potomac and Sherman's army held a Grand Review in Washington on May 23–24. For two days, the armed might of the republic marched in a giant parade down Pennsylvania Avenue before thousands of cheering spectators. As Sherman's long-striding Westerners came swinging by on the second day, some people in the stands began to sing "John Brown's Body." The soldiers picked it up, and soon thousands of voices were thundering the great marching song of the Union armies in a city once trod by slaves. Nothing could have testified more eloquently to the revolution wrought by the war.

After the Grand Review, the victorious veterans scattered quietly to their homes. The Union armies were demobilized with remarkable swiftness. Within two months 641,000 men had been mustered out. The navy shrank from 530 to 117 warships by the end of 1865. By November 1866 only 65,000 men remained in an army that eighteen months earlier had numbered more than a million. Most returning soldiers seemed to readjust quickly to civilian life, apparently without the social and psychological problems that have plagued so many veterans of recent wars. "When I returned home I found that the farm work my father was then engaged in was cutting and shucking corn," wrote an Illinois veteran.

> So, the morning after my arrival, September 29th, I doffed my uniform of first lieutenant, put on some of my father's old clothes, and proceeded to wage war on the standing corn. The feeling I had while engaged in this work was sort of queer. It almost seemed, sometimes, as if I had been away only a day or two, and had just taken up the farm work where I had left off.[44]

THE IMPRINT OF WAR

But in truth, nothing would ever be the same again for this Illinois veteran—or for anyone else in the country. The war left an indelible imprint on the nation's

The Grand Review. The 6th Corps of the Army of the Potomac
marching down Pennsylvania Avenue in the victory parade of May
23, 1865. *(Reproduced from the Collections of the Library of Congress)*

consciousness. A thrice-wounded infantry captain and future Supreme Court
justice put it best: "The generation that carried on the war has been set apart by
its experience," said Oliver Wendell Holmes in 1884. "Through our great good
fortune, in our youth our hearts were touched with fire. It was given to us to learn
at the outset that life is a profound and passionate thing."[45] The Civil War
generated a greater outpouring of memoirs, regimental histories, popular literature, and scholarly studies than any other war in American history—perhaps more
than all of them combined. Civil War roundtables persist into the late twentieth
century. The Civil War monuments on town squares in thousands of communities

far outnumber the monuments to other notable events in the American past. For generations, Southerners dated their history by reference to "before the war" or "since the war"—and nobody had to ask which war they meant. In the 1960s "The Battle Hymn of the Republic" became one of the inspirational songs of the civil rights movement, while the Confederate flag and "Dixie" served as symbols of Southern resistance to that movement.

One reason for the Civil War's profound impact was its human cost. Approximately 620,000 soldiers lost their lives (360,000 Union and 260,000 Confederate), a toll that nearly equals the 680,000 American fighting men killed in all the other wars combined in which the United States has been involved. There was scarcely a family in North or South that did not mourn a relative or friend killed in the war. Until well into the twentieth century, Civil War veterans missing an arm or leg remained a common sight on the streets of American towns and cities. Veterans' organizations—the Grand Army of the Republic and the United Confederate Veterans—kept war memories alive and became potent political forces in their respective sections. In time, heroic myths and romance glazed over the war's grim realities. But these myths themselves, especially in the South, soon became an important reality—a lens through which people viewed their world, providing a perspective that governed their lives.

The Civil War marked a decisive turn in the nature of American nationality. Buried forever was the notion of the Union as a voluntary confederation of sovereign states. The word "Union" gradually gave way to "nation." The name "United States" became construed as a singular rather than plural noun. The war strengthened the national government at the expense of the states. Before 1861, only the post office among federal agencies touched directly the lives of most Americans. Citizens paid their taxes to local or state governments and settled most of their disputes in state courts. For money, they used the notes of banks chartered by state legislatures. When war came in 1861, the President called first on the state militia. State governors took the lead in recruiting, equipping, and officering the volunteer regiments. But the centralizing pressures of war changed all this. By 1863 the War Department prescribed enlistment quotas for states and drafted men directly into the army if states failed to meet the quotas. The President declared martial law and stationed soldiers in every state, where their powers of detention superseded those of state courts. The United States government levied a host of direct taxes and created an internal revenue bureau to collect them. It printed paper money, established a national banking system, and taxed state banknotes out of existence. It confiscated the property and freed the slaves of Southern citizens, and it set up a social welfare agency—the Freedmen's Bureau —to override state law in the governance of the freed people. The first eleven amendments to the Constitution had limited the power of the federal government; the Thirteenth Amendment established a precedent by which the next six amendments restricted state powers or expanded those of the national government.

The war's impact fell most heavily on the South. Emancipation made the deepest dent of all in the social order. Seventy years later, aged ex-slaves interviewed by the Federal Writers Project recalled with vivid clarity the day they had learned of their freedom. For many, it was still the central event of their lives. "Never was no time like 'em befo' or since," said one. "Niggers shoutin' an' clappin' hands an' singin'! Chillun runnin' all over de place beatin' tins an' yellin'. Ev'ybody happy. Sho' did some celebratin'." So sweeping was this transformation that contemporaries described it in the language of revelation and revolution. North Carolina freedmen believed that "these are the times foretold by the Prophets, 'When a Nation shall be born in a day.' "[46] A Memphis newspaper marveled in 1865: "The events of the last five years have produced an entire revolution in the social system of the entire Southern country." The chaplain of a black regiment occupying Wilmington described the whites who stared at the soldiers as uncertain "whether they are actually in another world, or whether this one is turned wrong side out." One black soldier, recognizing his former master among a group of Confederate prisoners he was guarding, shouted a greeting: "Hello, massa; bottom rail on top dis time."[47]

In 1865 the bottom rail did indeed appear to be on top. Whether it would stay there depended on the events of Reconstruction.

Notes

CHAPTER 10

1. Roy P. Basler (ed.), *The Collected Works of Abraham Lincoln*, 9 vols. (New Brunswick, N.J., 1953–1955), IV, 331–32.

2. Henry Steele Commager (ed.), *The Blue and the Gray*, rev. ed. (Indianapolis, 1973), I, 47; Bruce Catton, *The Coming Fury* (Garden City, N.Y., 1961), p. 325.

3. *Chicago Tribune*, May 2, 1861; Henry B. Stanton to Elizabeth Cady Stanton, April ?, 1861, E. C. Stanton Papers, Library of Congress.

4. *War of the Rebellion: A Compilation of the Official Records of the Union and Confederate Armies* (Washington, D.C., 1880–1901), Ser. 3, Vol. 1, pp. 71, 79. Hereinafter cited as *O.R. (Official Records)*.

5. *Ibid.*, pp. 70, 72, 76, 81, 83.

6. Shelby Foote, *The Civil War: A Narrative. Fort Sumter to Perryville* (New York, 1958), p. 51.

7. *Ibid.*, p. 53; Allan Nevins, *The War for the Union: The Improvised War, 1861–1862* (New York, 1959), p. 78.

8. *O.R.*, Ser. 3, Vol. 1, p. 83.

9. Thomas L. Snead, *The Fight for Missouri from the Election of Lincoln to the Death of Lyon* (New York, 1886), pp. 199–200.

10. Jay Monaghan, *Civil War on the Western Border 1854–1865* (New York, 1955), p. 185.

CHAPTER 11

1. Allan Nevins, *The War for the Union: The Improvised War, 1861–1862* (New York, 1959), pp. 75, 95–96, 151; Bell I. Wiley, *The Life of Johnny Reb: The Common Soldier of the Confederacy* (Indianapolis, 1943), p. 310.

2. B. H. Liddell Hart, *Sherman: Soldier, Realist, American* (New York, 1929), pp. 74, 72.

3. Bruce Catton, *Grant Moves South* (Boston, 1960), p. 93.

4. Dunbar Rowland (ed.), *Jefferson Davis, Constitutionalist: His Letters, Papers and Speeches*, 10

vols. (Jackson, Miss., 1923), IX, 543; Thomas Wentworth Higginson, "Regular and Volunteer Officers," *Atlantic Monthly,* 14 (September 1864), 349.

5. Bell I. Wiley, *The Life of Billy Yank: The Common Soldier of the Union* (Indianapolis, 1952), p. 26; Douglas Southall Freeman, *Lee's Lieutenants: A Study in Command,* 3 vols. (New York, 1942–1944), I, 13.

6. Halleck to W. T. Sherman, April 29, 1864, in *O.R.,* Ser. 1, Vol. 34, pt. 3, pp. 332–33.

7. See especially Frank L. Owsley, *King Cotton Diplomacy* (Chicago, 1931).

CHAPTER 12

1. Bell I. Wiley, *The Life of Johnny Reb: The Common Soldier of the Confederacy* (Indianapolis, 1943), pp. 128–29.

2. Hugh C. Bailey, "Disloyalty in Early Confederate Alabama," *Journal of Southern History,* 23 (November 1957), 525.

3. Albert B. Moore, *Conscription and Conflict in the Confederacy* (New York, 1924), pp. 256, 71.

4. Quoted in Richard N. Current, "God and the Strongest Battalions," in David Donald (ed.), *Why the North Won the Civil War* (Baton Rouge, 1960), p. 5.

5. Dunbar Rowland (ed.), *Jefferson Davis, Constitutionalist: His Letters, Papers and Speeches,* 10 vols. (Jackson, Miss., 1923), V, 84.

6. London *Times,* July 18, 1861, August 29, 1862.

7. John Slidell to Samuel L. M. Barlow, July 20, 1861, Judah Benjamin to Barlow, January 8, 1861, S. L. M. Barlow Papers, Henry E. Huntington Library.

8. Bell I. Wiley, *The Life of Billy Yank: The Common Soldier of the Union* (Indianapolis, 1952), p. 283; Douglas Southall Freeman, *Lee's Lieutenants: A Study in Command,* 3 vols. (New York, 1942–1944), III, 146n.

9. Roy P. Basler (ed.), *The Collected Works of Abraham Lincoln,* 9 vols. (New Brunswick, N.J., 1953–1955), V, 505; *O. R.,* Ser. 1, Vol. 12, pt. 3, p. 890.

10. Quoted in Donald, *Why the North Won the Civil War,* p. ix.

11. Franklin Marshall Pierce, *The Battle of Gettysburg* (New York, 1914), pp. 37–38.

12. Thomas L. Livermore, *Numbers and Losses in the Civil War in America* (Boston, 1901).

13. Quoted in J. F. C. Fuller, *Grant and Lee: A Study in Personality and Generalship* (London, 1933), p. 41.

14. Bruce Catton, *Glory Road* (Garden City, N.Y., 1952), p. 170.

15. Catton's introduction to Virgil Carrington Jones, *Gray Ghosts and Rebel Raiders,* (New York, 1956), pp. vii–viii; and Jones's own assertion in *ibid.,* 12.

16. Albert Castel, *The Guerrilla War, 1861–1865* (Gettysburg, 1974).

17. Bruce Catton, *The Coming Fury* (Garden City, N.Y., 1961), p. 413.

18. Jones, *Gray Ghosts and Rebel Raiders,* p. 279.

19. William T. Sherman, *Memoirs of General W. T. Sherman,* 2 vols., 2nd ed. (New York, 1886), I, 365–66.

20. H. C. B. Rogers, *The Confederates and Federals at War* (London, 1973), p. 51.

21. Wiley, *Billy Yank,* p. 63.

22. See especially Robert V. Bruce, *Lincoln and the Tools of War* (Indianapolis, 1956), and Allan Nevins, *The War for the Union: The Improvised War 1861–1862* (New York, 1959), pp. 361–69.

23. *The Civil War Diary of General Josiah Gorgas,* ed. Frank E. Vandiver (University, Ala., 1947), 90–91.

24. Douglas Southall Freeman, *R. E. Lee: A Biography,* 4 vols. (New York, 1934–1935), III, 247.

25. Russell F. Weigley, *Quartermaster-General of the Union Army: A Biography of Montgomery C. Meigs* (New York, 1959), p. 205.

26. Eugene M. Lerner, "The Monetary and Fiscal Problems of the Confederate Government," *Journal of Political Economy*, 62 (December 1954), 520.

27. Bray Hammond, *Sovereignty and an Empty Purse: Banks and Politics in the Civil War* (Princeton, 1970), p. 23.

28. Hugh McCulloch, *Men and Measures of Half a Century* (New York, 1888), p. 201; *Congressional Globe*, 37th Cong., 2nd sess., (1862) 549.

29. Francis Fessenden, *Life and Public Services of William Pitt Fessenden*, 2 vols. (Boston, 1907), I, 194; Chase quoted in Robert P. Sharkey, *Money, Class, and Party: An Economic Study of Civil War and Reconstruction* (Baltimore, 1959), p. 41.

CHAPTER 13

1. *O.R.*, Ser. 1, Vol. 51, pt. 1, pp. 369–70.

2. T. Harry Williams, *Lincoln and His Generals* (New York, 1952), p. 21.

3. Bruce Catton, *Glory Road* (Garden City, N.Y., 1952), p. 57.

4. Joseph E. Johnston, "Responsibilities of the First Bull Run," *Battles and Leaders of the Civil War*, 4 vols. (New York, 1887), I, 252.

5. Kenneth P. Williams, *Lincoln Finds a General: A Military Study of the Civil War*, 5 vols. (New York, 1949–1959), I, 113.

6. George B. McClellan, *McClellan's Own Story* (New York, 1886), pp. 85, 91, 172; Bruce Catton, *Terrible Swift Sword* (Garden City, N.Y., 1963), pp. 80, 84–85.

7. Tyler Dennett (ed.), *Lincoln and the Civil War in the Diaries and Letters of John Hay* (New York, 1939), p. 33.

8. *McClellan's Own Story*, p. 87; Catton, *Terrible Swift Sword*, p. 84; Shelby Foote, *The Civil War: A Narrative. Fort Sumter to Perryville* (New York, 1958), p. 141.

9. Foote, *Fort Sumter to Perryville*, pp. 141–42; *McClellan's Own Story*, p. 176; Dennett, *Lincoln and the Civil War*, p. 34.

10. Montgomery Blair to Francis P. Blair, Sr., October 1, 1861, Blair-Lee Papers, Princeton University Library; McClellan to Samuel L. M. Barlow, November 8, 1861, S. L. M. Barlow Papers, Henry E. Huntington Library.

11. Frank L. Owsley, *King Cotton Diplomacy: Foreign Relations of the Confederate States of America* (Chicago, 1931), pp. 16–23.

12. Robert H. Jones, *Disrupted Decades: The Civil War and Reconstruction Years* (New York, 1973), p. 363.

13. Ephraim D. Adams, *Great Britain and the American Civil War*, 2 vols. (New York, 1925), I, 263.

14. Allan Nevins, *The War for the Union: The Improvised War, 1861–1862* (New York, 1959), p. 388.

CHAPTER 14

1. Roy P. Basler (ed.), *The Collected Works of Abraham Lincoln*, 9 vols. (New Brunswick, N.J., 1953–1955), V, 95; T. Harry Williams, *Lincoln and His Generals* (New York, 1952), pp. 55–56.

2. Ulysses S. Grant, *Personal Memoirs*, 2 vols. (New York, 1885–1886), I, 311.

3. Ephraim D. Adams, *Great Britain and the American Civil War*, 2 vols. (New York, 1925), I, 272–73.

4. Bruce Catton, *Grant Moves South* (Boston, 1960), p. 218; Shelby Foote, *The Civil War: A Narrative. Fort Sumter to Perryville* (New York, 1958), pp. 329, 331.

5. Catton, *Grant Moves South*, p. 247.

6. Kenneth P. Williams, *Lincoln Finds a General: A Military Study of the Civil War*, 5 vols. (New York, 1949–1959), III, 389; Shelby Foote, *The Civil War: A Narrative. Red River to Appomattox* (New York, 1974), p. 398.

7. Bruce Catton, *Terrible Swift Sword* (Garden City, N.Y., 1963), p. 236.

8. *Ibid.*, p. 261.

9. Catton, *Grant Moves South*, p. 371.

CHAPTER 15

1. Roy P. Basler (ed.), *The Collected Works of Abraham Lincoln*, 9 vols. (New Brunswick, N.J., 1953–1955), V, 184–85; Johnston to Robert E. Lee, April 22, 1862, *O.R.*, Ser. 1, Vol. 11, pt. 3, pp. 455–56.

2. Edward T. Downer, *Stonewall Jackson's Shenandoah Valley Campaign, 1862* (Charlottesville, 1959), p. 27.

3. George B. McClellan, *McClellan's Own Story* (New York, 1886), p. 398; T. Harry Williams, *Lincoln and His Generals* (New York, 1952), p. 106.

4. Shelby Foote, *The Civil War: A Narrative. Fort Sumter to Perryville* (New York, 1958), p. 465; Douglas Southall Freeman, *R. E. Lee: A Biography*, 4 vols. (New York, 1934–1935), II, 92.

5. *O.R.*, Ser. 1, Vol. 11, pt. 3, p. 266.

6. *O.R.*, Ser. 1, Vol. 11, pt. 1, p. 61.

7. Daniel H. Hill, "McClellan's Change of Base and Malvern Hill," in *Battles and Leaders of the Civil War*, 4 vols. (New York, 1887), II, 394.

8. Foote, *Fort Sumter to Perryville*, p. 509.

9. Bruce Catton, *Mr. Lincoln's Army* (Garden City, N.Y., 1951), p. 149.

10. *Ibid.*, p. 166.

11. Bell I. Wiley, *The Life of Johnny Reb* (Indianapolis, 1943), pp. 35, 75; Bell I. Wiley, *The Life of Billy Yank* (Indianapolis, 1952), p. 79.

12. Wiley, *Johnny Reb*, pp. 308–9; Wiley, *Billy Yank*, p. 348.

13. Foote, *Fort Sumter to Perryville*, pp. 518–19.

14. Samuel L. M. Barlow to Henry D. Bacon, July 15, 1862, S. L. M. Barlow Papers, Henry E. Huntington Library; Basler, *Works of Lincoln*, V, 292.

15. Basler, *Works of Lincoln*, V, 296–97.

16. *O.R.*, Ser. 1, Vol. 12, pt. 3, pp. 473–74.

17. Douglas Southall Freeman, *R. E. Lee, a Biography*, 4 vols. (New York, 1934–1935), II, 264.

18. *O.R.*, Ser. 1, Vol. 17, pt. 2, p. 150.

19. George B. McClellan, *McClellan's Own Story* (New York, 1886), pp. 487–89.

20. McClellan to Samuel L. M. Barlow, July 23, 1862, Barlow Papers.

21. Stephen E. Ambrose, *Halleck: Lincoln's Chief of Staff* (Baton Rouge, 1962), *passim.*

22. Porter to Manton Marble, August 10, 1862, in T. Harry Williams, *Lincoln and His Generals* (New York, 1952), p. 148.

23. *McClellan's Own Story*, pp. 514–15; Tyler Dennett (ed.), *Lincoln and the Civil War in the Diaries and Letters of John Hay* (New York, 1939), pp. 45, 47; Gideon Welles, *The Diary of Gideon Welles*, ed. Howard K. Beale, 3 vols. (New York, 1960), I, 93–106.

24. Dennett, *Lincoln and the Civil War*, p. 47; Welles, *Diary*, I, 113.

CHAPTER 16

1. Allan Nevins, *The War for the Union: The Improvised War 1861–1862* (New York, 1959), pp. 204, 205.

2. John G. Nicolay and John Hay, *Abraham Lincoln: A History,* 10 vols. (New York, 1890), IX, 119–20.

3. Roy P. Basler (ed.), *The Collected Works of Abraham Lincoln,* 9 vols. (New Brunswick, N.J., 1953–1955), IV, 347, 353–54, 364, 414, 419, V, 241–42.

4. Edward McPherson (ed.), *The Political History of the United States During the Great Rebellion,* 2nd ed. (Washington, D.C., 1865), p. 150.

5. *Chicago Daily Journal,* April 17, 1861, in Howard C. Perkins (ed.), *Northern Editorials on Secession,* 2 vols. (New York, 1942), II, 808–9; Basler, *Works of Lincoln,* VIII, 332.

6. Basler, *Works of Lincoln,* IV, 438; Tyler Dennett (ed.), *Lincoln and the Civil War in the Diaries and Letters of John Hay* (New York, 1939), p. 19.

7. Basler, *Works of Lincoln,* V, 53, VII, 23.

8. Belle B. Sideman and Lillian Friedman (eds.), *Europe Looks at the Civil War* (New York, 1960), pp. 117–18.

9. Basler, *Works of Lincoln,* IV, 263; *Congressional Globe,* 37th Cong., 1st sess., (1861) 222–23.

10. *Saturday Review,* September 14, 1861, quoted in Ephraim D. Adams, *Great Britain and the American Civil War,* 2 vols. (New York, 1925), I, 181; *Economist* (London), September 1861, quoted in Karl Marx and Friedrich Engels, *The Civil War in the United States,* ed. Richard Enmale (New York, 1937), p. 12.

11. Basler, *Works of Lincoln,* II, 255, III, 92.

12. William Lloyd Garrison to Oliver Johnson, April 19, 1861, W. L. Garrison Papers, Boston Public Library; *Douglass' Monthly,* May 1861.

13. Edward L. Pierce, *Memoir and Letters of Charles Sumner,* 4 vols. (Boston, 1877–1893), IV, 49.

14. *Montgomery Advertiser,* November 6, 1861.

15. *Douglass' Monthly,* July 1861.

16. Basler, *Works of Lincoln,* V, 48–49.

17. *Principia,* May 4, 1861.

18. Margaret Shortreed, "The Anti-Slavery Radicals, 1840–1868," *Past and Present,* no. 16 (November 1959), 77.

19. McPherson, *Political History,* pp. 196–98.

20. *Liberator,* December 6, 1861, July 25, 1862.

21. Basler, *Works of Lincoln,* V, 222–23.

22. *Boston Advertiser,* August 20, 1862; Basler, *Works of Lincoln,* V, 317–19; Allan Nevins, *The War for the Union: War Becomes Revolution* (New York, 1960), pp. 148–49.

23. *Douglass' Monthly,* September 1861; Gideon Welles, *The Diary of Gideon Welles,* ed. Howard K. Beale, 3 vols. (New York, 1960), I, 70–71; Francis B. Carpenter, *Six Months at the White House With Abraham Lincoln* (New York, 1866), p. 22.

24. Frank L. Klement, "Economic Aspects of Middle Western Copperheadism," *Historian,* 14 (Autumn 1951), 39–40; Wood Gray, *The Hidden Civil War: The Story of the Copperheads* (New York, 1964; first printed 1942), p. 125.

25. Samuel S. Cox, "Puritanism in Politics," in Samuel S. Cox, *Eight Years in Congress* (New York, 1865), pp. 283, 290; Cuthbert E. Allen, "The Slavery Question in Catholic Newspapers, 1850–1865," U.S. Catholic Historical Society, *Historical Records and Studies,* 26 (1936), 145, 160.

26. Cox, "Puritanism in Politics," p. 283.

27. Joel H. Silbey, *A Respectable Minority: The Democratic Party in the Civil War Era, 1860–*

1868 (New York, 1977), p. 101; Frank L. Klement, *The Limits of Dissent: Clement L. Vallandigham and the Civil War* (Lexington, Ky., 1970), p. 79.

28. *Congressional Globe*, 37th Cong., 2nd sess., (1862) 1923; Samuel L. M. Barlow to Henry D. Bacon, January 23, 1862, Barlow Papers, Henry E. Huntington Library; Benjamin J. Blied, *Catholics and the Civil War* (Milwaukee, 1945), pp. 44–45.

29. V. Jacque Voegeli, *Free but Not Equal: The Midwest and the Negro During the Civil War* (Chicago, 1967), p. 6; Forrest G. Wood, *Black Scare: The Racist Response to Emancipation and Reconstruction* (Berkeley, 1968), p. 35; Frank L. Klement, *The Copperheads in the Middle West* (Chicago, 1960), p. 14.

30. Voegeli, *Free but Not Equal*, pp. 1, 18.

31. Bell I. Wiley, *The Life of Billy Yank* (Indianapolis, 1952), p. 40.

32. *Ibid.*, pp. 42, 109.

33. *Ibid.*, p. 44.

34. *Ibid.*, p. 114.

35. *Ibid.*, p. 112.

36. Basler, *Works of Lincoln*, V, 370–75.

37. Purvis in *New York Tribune*, September 20, 1862; David Donald (ed.), *Inside Lincoln's Cabinet: The Civil War Diaries of Salmon P. Chase* (New York, 1954), p. 112.

38. *Boston Post*, quoted in *Boston Commonwealth*, October 18, 1862.

39. Voegeli, *Free but Not Equal*, p. 45.

40. *National Anti-Slavery Standard*, March 19, 1864.

41. Basler, *Works of Lincoln*, V, 388–89.

42. *Ibid.*, V, 419–25.

CHAPTER 17

1. Bruce Catton, *Terrible Swift Sword* (Garden City, N.Y., 1963), p. 449; T. Harry Williams, *Lincoln and His Generals* (New York, 1952), p. 166.

2. *O.R.*, Ser. 1, Vol. 19, p. 218.

3. Frederick Tilbert, *Antietam* (National Park Service, Washington, D.C., 1961), pp. 36, 39.

4. *O.R.*, Ser. 1, Vol. 19, p. 377.

5. Jay Luvaas, *The Military Legacy of the Civil War: The European Inheritance* (Chicago, 1959), pp. 18–19.

6. George B. McClellan, *McClellan's Own Story* (New York, 1886), p. 612.

7. *O.R.*, Ser. 1, Vol. 16, pt. 2, p. 421.

8. Gideon Welles, *The Diary of Gideon Welles*, ed. Howard K. Beale, 3 vols. (New York, 1960), I, 142–45; John G. Nicolay and John Hay, *Abraham Lincoln: A History*, 10 vols. (New York, 1890), VI, 158–63.

9. Henry G. Pearson, *The Life of John A. Andrew*, 2 vols. (Boston, 1904), II, 51; Samuel May, Jr., to Richard Webb, September 23, 1862, Samuel May, Jr., Papers, Boston Public Library.

10. Roy P. Basler (ed.), *The Collected Works of Abraham Lincoln*, 9 vols. (New Brunswick, N.J., 1953–1955), V, 436–37.

11. *Ibid.*, VI, 263, 266–67.

12. James G. Randall, *Constitutional Problems Under Lincoln*, rev. ed. (Urbana, Ill., 1951), chaps. 6–8, 19–20; quotations from pp. 154, 155, 520.

13. *New York World*, October 18, 1862; V. Jacque Voegeli, *Free but Not Equal: The Midwest and the Negro During the Civil War* (Chicago, 1967), p. 55.

14. Voegeli, *Free but Not Equal*, p. 64.

15. William B. Hesseltine, *Lincoln and the War Governors* (New York, 1948), p. 265.

16. *Congressional Globe*, 37th Cong., 3rd sess., (1862) 15, 92.

17. Basler, *Works of Lincoln*, V, 537.

18. Sumner to Samuel Gridley Howe, December 28, 1862, Sumner-Howe Correspondence, Houghton Library, Harvard University.

19. *Spectator* (London), October 11, 1862.

20. Augustus Auberne to Samuel L. M. Barlow, January 17, 1863, S. L. M. Barlow Papers, Henry E. Huntington Library.

21. Allan Nevins, *The War for the Union: War Becomes Revolution* (New York, 1960), p. 239; *O.R.*, Ser. 1, Vol. 24, pt. 3, p. 157.

22. McClellan to William H. Aspinwall, September 26, 1862, in *Battles and Leaders of the Civil War*, Extra-Illustrated ed., Henry E. Huntington Library, Vol. VIII; Porter to Manton Marble, September 30, 1862, in Nevins, *War Becomes Revolution*, pp. 238–39.

23. Basler, *Works of Lincoln*, V, 442–43, 508–9; Nicolay and Hay, *Abraham Lincoln*, VI, 186–88.

24. *O.R.*, Ser. 1, Vol. 19, pt. 2, pp. 395–96.

25. McClellan to Ellen McClellan, September 20, 1862, McClellan Papers, Library of Congress.

26. *O.R.*, Ser. 1, Vol. 19, pt. 1, p. 72; Basler, *Works of Lincoln*, V, 474.

27. McClellan to Ellen McClellan, undated, McClellan Papers.

28. Tyler Dennett (ed.), *Lincoln and the Civil War in the Diaries and Letters of John Hay* (New York, 1939), pp. 218–19.

29. *O.R.*, Ser. 1, Vol. 16, pt. 2, p. 627.

30. Shelby Foote, *The Civil War: A Narrative. Fort Sumter to Perryville* (New York, 1958), p. 523; D. P. Crook, *Diplomacy During the American Civil War* (New York, 1975), pp. 84, 92; Worthington C. Ford (ed.), *A Cycle of Adams Letters, 1861–1865*, 2 vols. (Boston, 1920), I, 166.

31. Ephraim D. Adams, *Great Britain and the American Civil War*, 2 vols. (New York, 1925), II, 38, 41; Kinley J. Brauer, "British Mediation and the American Civil War: A Reconsideration," *Journal of Southern History*, 38 (February 1972), 57.

32. Adams, *Great Britain and the Civil War*, II, 44.

33. Ford, *Cycle of Adams Letters*, I, 243.

CHAPTER 18

1. James Longstreet, "The Battle of Fredericksburg," in *Battles and Leaders of the Civil War*, 4 vols. (New York, 1887), III, 79; Shelby Foote, *The Civil War: A Narrative. Fredericksburg to Meridian* (New York, 1963), p. 44; Allan Nevins, *The War for the Union: War Becomes Revolution* (New York, 1960), p. 348.

2. *Harper's Weekly*, December 27, 1862; Meigs to Burnside, December 30, 1862, in *O.R.*, Ser. 1, Vol. 21, p. 917; Medill to Elihu Washburne, January 14, 1863, in Nevins, *War Becomes Revolution*, p. 351; Lincoln quoted in William Henry Wadsworth to Samuel L. M. Barlow, December 16, 1862, Barlow Papers, Henry E. Huntington Library.

3. Samuel Wilkeson to Sydney Howard Gay, December 19, 1862, Gay Papers, Columbia University Library; Orville Hickman Browning, *The Diary of Orville Hickman Browning*, ed. Theodore C. Pease and James G. Randall, 2 vols. (Springfield, Ill., 1927–1933), I, 600–601.

4. The best contemporary accounts of this affair are Gideon Welles, *The Diary of Gideon Welles*, ed. Howard K. Beale, I, 194–204, and Pease and Randall, *Diary of Browning*, I, 596–604. The best secondary accounts are Nevins, *War Becomes Revolution*, 350–65, and James G. Randall, *Lincoln the President*, 4 vols. (New York, 1945–1955), II, 241–49.

5. Roy P. Basler (ed.), *The Collected Works of Abraham Lincoln*, 9 vols. (New Brunswick, N.J., 1953–1955), VI, 39, 424.

6. Ulysses S. Grant, *Personal Memoirs,* 2 vols. (New York, 1885–1886), I, 480–81.

7. Frederick E. Whitton, *The Decisive Battles of Modern Times* (London, 1923), p. 45.

8. *O.R.,* Ser. 1, Vol. 24, pt. 1, p. 273.

9. Bell I. Wiley, *The Life of Billy Yank* (Indianapolis, 1952), p. 280; Alan T. Nolan, *The Iron Brigade: A Military History* (New York, 1961), p. 193.

10. Charles S. Wainwright, *A Diary of Battle,* ed. Allan Nevins (New York, 1962), pp. 157–58.

11. Basler, *Works of Lincoln,* VI, 78–79.

12. Bruce Catton, *Glory Road* (Garden City, N.Y., 1952), p. 161.

13. *Ibid.,* p. 157; Darius N. Couch, "The Chancellorsville Campaign," in *Battles and Leaders of the Civil War,* 4 vols. (New York, 1887), III, 155.

14. John Bigelow, *The Campaign of Chancellorsville* (New Haven, 1910), p. 221.

15. Douglas Southall Freeman, *Lee's Lieutenants,* 3 vols. (New York, 1942–1944), II, 669.

16. Noah Brooks, *Washington in Lincoln's Time* (New York, 1896), pp. 57–58.

CHAPTER 19

1. Lincoln to Hooker, June 10, 1863, in Roy P. Basler (ed.), *The Collected Works of Abraham Lincoln,* 9 vols. (New Brunswick, N.J., 1953–1955), VI, 257.

2. *O.R.,* Ser. 1, Vol. 27, pt. 1, p. 83.

3. Gideon Welles, *The Diary of Gideon Welles,* ed. Howard K. Beale, 3 vols. (New York, 1960), I, 371; Tyler Dennett (ed.), *Lincoln and the Civil War in the Diaries and Letters of John Hay* (New York, 1939), p. 67.

4. Basler, *Works of Lincoln,* VI, 327–28.

5. *O.R.,* Ser. 1, Vol. 24, pt. 1, p. 227.

6. Allan Nevins, *The War for the Union: The Organized War 1863–64* (New York, 1971), p. 71.

7. Bell I. Wiley, *The Life of Johnny Reb* (Indianapolis, 1943), p. 94.

8. Basler, *Works of Lincoln,* VI, 409.

9. J. F. C. Fuller, *Grant and Lee* (London, 1933), p. 184; T. Harry Williams, *Lincoln and His Generals* (New York, 1952), p. 272.

10. Bell I. Wiley, *The Road to Appomattox* (Memphis, 1956), pp. 64–65; Dunbar Rowland (ed.), *Jefferson Davis, Constitutionalist,* 10 vols. (Jackson, Miss., 1923), V, 548, 554; Frank Vandiver (ed.), *The Civil War Diary of General Josiah Gorgas* (University, Ala., 1947), p. 55.

11. *O.R.,* Ser. 1, Vol. 23, pt. 2, p. 518.

12. Daniel Harvey Hill, "Chickamauga—The Great Battle of the West," in *Battles and Leaders of the Civil War,* 4 vols. (New York, 1887), III, 644.

13. Bruce Catton, *Never Call Retreat,* Pocket Books ed. (New York 1967), p. 235.

14. *O.R,* Ser. 1, Vol. 30, pt. 1, p. 142; John B. Jones, *A Rebel War Clerk's Diary* (New York, 1935), II, 50.

15. Catton, *Never Call Retreat,* p. 247.

16. Shelby Foote, *The Civil War: A Narrative. Fredericksburg to Meridian* (New York, 1963), p. 843.

17. Quotations in these paragraphs are from *ibid.,* p. 856, and Catton, *Never Call Retreat,* p. 253.

18. Foote, *Fredericksburg to Meridian,* p. 859.

19. *Ibid.,* p. 868.

20. Worthington C. Ford (ed.), *A Cycle of Adams Letters, 1861–1865,* 2 vols. (Boston, 1920), II, 40, 60.

21. Ephraim D. Adams, *Great Britain and the American Civil War,* 2 vols. (New York, 1925), II, 144.

CHAPTER 20

1. Allan Nevins and Milton H. Thomas (eds.), *The Diary of George Templeton Strong, 1835–1875*, 4 vols. (New York, 1952), III, 330.

2. The former Illinois governor, the county Democratic conventions, and the New York meeting are quoted in Wood Gray, *The Hidden Civil War: The Story of the Copperheads* (New York, 1942), pp. 115, 123, 147; the Iowa editor is quoted in Frank L. Klement, *The Copperheads in the Middle West* (Chicago, 1960), p. 44; Seymour is quoted in Allan Nevins, *The War for the Union: War Becomes Revolution* (New York, 1960), p. 394.

3. Albert G. Riddle, *Recollections of War Times* (New York, 1895), p. 321.

4. John B. Jones, *A Rebel War Clerk's Diary*, 2 vols. (New York, 1935), I, 249, 253.

5. Gray, *Hidden Civil War*, p. 133; Bruce Catton, *Glory Road* (Garden City, N.Y., 1952), p. 246.

6. William B. Hesseltine, *Lincoln and the War Governors* (New York, 1948), p. 331.

7. *Congressional Globe*, 37th Cong., 3rd sess., (1863) Appendix, 93; Forrest G. Wood, *Black Scare: The Racist Response to Emancipation and Reconstruction* (Berkeley, 1968), p. 42.

8. *Douglass' Monthly*, August 1863.

9. Herbert Aptheker, "The Negro in the Union Navy," *Journal of Negro History*, 32 (April 1947), 169–200, estimates that blacks constituted one-fourth of the navy personnel. This estimate may be too high. The navy did not designate its personnel by race.

10. Edward McPherson, *The Political History of the United States During the Great Rebellion*, 2nd ed. (Washington, D.C., 1865), pp. 197, 274.

11. Roy P. Basler (ed.), *The Collected Works of Abraham Lincoln*, 9 vols. (New Brunswick, N.J., 1953–1955), V, 357, 423; *O.R.*, Ser. 1, Vol. 14, pp. 377–78.

12. Basler, *Works of Lincoln*, VI, 149–50.

13. Bruce Catton, *Grant Moves South* (Boston, 1960), p. 404.

14. Frederick Douglass, *The Life and Times of Frederick Douglass* (Hartford, 1882), pp. 386–87.

15. *National Intelligencer*, August 24, 1863; *New York Times*, June 11, 1863; Charles A. Dana, *Recollections of the Civil War* (New York, 1898), p. 86.

16. William Hanchett, *Irish: Charles G. Halpine in Civil War America* (Syracuse, 1970), p. 70.

17. Eugene C. Murdock, *Patriotism Limited: The Civil War Draft and the Bounty System* (Kent, Ohio, 1967).

18. The data for the 1860 occupations of males in the Union and Confederate states in Tables 20.1 and 20.2 were compiled from the occupational tables in the 1860 census. The samples of the previous occupations of Union soldiers are from (1) a U.S. Sanitary Commission survey of the occupations of 666,530 Union soldiers from all Union states except Maryland and Delaware; (2) Bell I. Wiley's sample of 13,392 white Union soldiers in 114 companies from all the free states plus Missouri. (California, Oregon, and the territories are not included in these data because they contributed a negligible number of soldiers to Civil War armies.) Both the Sanitary Commission and Wiley samples were drawn from company muster rolls. Both were generally representative of the proportion and distribution of soldiers from the various states. The Sanitary Commission data were reported in Benjamin A. Gould, *Investigations in Military and Anthropological Statistics of American Soldiers* (New York, 1869). I am grateful for the generosity of the late Professor Wiley in supplying me with copies of his research data on the occupations of Union soldiers as well as similar data on the occupations of Confederate soldiers, analyzed in Table 20.2.

19. Southern woman and *Richmond Examiner* quoted in Ella Lonn, *Foreigners in the Union Army and Navy* (Baton Rouge, 1951), p. 576n.; Southern historian quoted in Wiley, *Billy Yank*, p. 428n.

20. Data on the percentage of foreign-born soldiers in the Union army were derived from Gould,

Investigations in Military and Anthropological Statistics of American Soldiers, pp. 15–29; Lonn, *Foreigners in the Union Army and Navy,* esp. pp. 581–82; and Wiley, *Billy Yank,* 306–13. The proportion of foreign-born males of military age in the Union states has been calculated from the population tables of the 1860 and 1870 published census reports.

21. Ella Lonn, *Foreigners in the Confederacy* (Chapel Hill, N.C., 1940), pp. 200–240, esp. pp. 200, 218–20.

22. James M. McPherson, *The Struggle for Equality: Abolitionists and the Negro in the Civil War and Reconstruction* (Princeton, 1964), p. 211.

23. Basler, *Works of Lincoln,* VI, 408–10.

24. Frank L. Klement, *The Limits of Dissent: Clement L. Vallandigham and the Civil War* (Lexington, Ky., 1970), p. 245; V. Jacque Voegeli, *Free but Not Equal* (Chicago, 1967), p. 126.

25. Gideon Welles, *The Diary of Gideon Welles,* ed. Howard K. Beale, 3 vols. (New York, 1960), I, 470.

26. The voting percentages are calculated from the data in *The Tribune Almanac for 1864,* pp. 55–69.

27. Voegeli, *Free but Not Equal,* p. 131; Nevins and Thomas, *The Diary of George Templeton Strong,* III, 408; Basler, *Works of Lincoln,* VII, 49–50.

28. McPherson, *Struggle for Equality,* pp. 85, 132.

29. The Diary of Christopher Fleetwood, Manuscripts Division, Library of Congress.

30. E. Merton Coulter, *The Confederate States of America 1861–1865* (Baton Rouge, 1950), p. 141.

31. Clement Eaton, *A History of the Southern Confederacy,* Collier Books ed. (New York, 1961 [1954]), p. 63.

32. Thomas B. Alexander and Richard E. Beringer, *The Anatomy of the Confederate Congress* (Nashville, 1972), p. 40.

33. Coulter, *Confederate States,* pp. 375, 386.

34. James Z. Rabun, "Alexander Stephens and Jefferson Davis," *American Historical Review,* 58 (1953), 307, 310; A. Stephens to Herschel V. Johnson, April 8, 1864, in *O.R.,* Ser. 4, Vol. 3, p. 280; David M. Potter, "Jefferson Davis and the Political Factors in Confederate Defeat," in David Donald (ed.), *Why the North Won the Civil War* (Baton Rouge, 1960), pp. 102, 112.

35. Joseph T. Durkin, *Stephen R. Mallory: Confederate Navy Chief* (Chapel Hill, N.C., 1954), p. 176.

36. Edward Younger (ed.), *Inside the Confederate Government: The Diary of Robert Garlick Hill Kean* (New York, 1957), p. 100.

37. James M. Mathews (ed.), *Public Laws of the Confederate States of America* (Richmond, 1862), p. 1.

38. Shelby Foote, *The Civil War: A Narrative. Fredericksburg to Meridian* (New York, 1963), p. 951; Curtis A. Amlund, *Federalism in the Southern Confederacy* (Washington, D.C., 1966), p. 106; Allen D. Candler (ed.), *The Confederate Records of the State of Georgia,* 4 vols. (Atlanta, 1909–1911), II, 305.

39. Ulrich B. Phillips (ed.), *The Correspondence of Robert Toombs, Alexander H. Stephens, and Howell Cobb* (Washington, D. C., 1913), p. 598.

CHAPTER 21

1. *New York Sun,* March 24, 1865.

2. Emerson D. Fite, *Social and Industrial Conditions in the North During the Civil War* (New York, 1910), p. 9; George Winston Smith and Charles Judah (eds.), *Life in the North During the Civil War* (Albuquerque, 1966), p. 167.

3. Paul W. Gates, *Agriculture and the Civil War* (New York, 1965), pp. 141, 193; Joe B. Frantz, *Gail Borden: Dairyman to a Nation* (Norman, Okla., 1951), p. 255.

4. These statistics and those in subsequent paragraphs are compiled from the relevant tables in *Historical Statistics of the United States* (Washington, D.C., 1975), and from Ralph Andreano (ed.), *The Economic Impact of the American Civil War* (Cambridge, Mass., 1962), Appendix.

5. See especially Thomas C. Cochran, "Did the Civil War Retard Industrialization?" *Mississippi Valley Historical Review*, 48 (September 1961), 197–210; David T. Gilchrist and W. David Lewis (eds.), *Economic Change in the Civil War Era* (Greenville, Del., 1965); and Stanley L. Engerman, "The Economic Impact of the Civil War," *Explorations in Entrepreneurial History*, 2nd Ser., III (1966), 176–99.

6. Cochran, "Did the Civil War Retard Industrialization?" p. 205.

7. Engerman, "The Economic Impact of the Civil War," p. 184.

8. Lee Soltow, *Men and Wealth in the United States 1850–1870* (New Haven, Conn., 1975), p. 65; Stanley Engerman, "Some Economic Factors in Southern Backwardness in the Nineteenth Century," in John F. Kain and John R. Meyer (eds.), *Essays in Regional Economics* (Cambridge, Mass., 1971), pp. 291, 300.

9. Rachel Sherman Thorndike (ed.), *The Sherman Letters* (New York, 1894), p. 258.

10. Karl Marx and Friedrich Engels, *The Civil War in the United States*, ed. Richard Enmale (New York, 1937), p. 281.

11. David Montgomery, *Beyond Equality: Labor and the Radical Republicans, 1862–1872* (New York, 1967), pp. 90–91.

12. John B. Jones, *A Rebel War Clerk's Diary*, 2 vols. (New York, 1935), II, 78.

13. E. Merton Coulter, *The Confederate States of America 1861–1865* (Baton Rouge, 1950), pp. 225, 231–32, 227.

14. Stephen E. Ambrose, "Yeoman Discontent in the Confederacy," *Civil War History*, 8 (September 1962), 262; Frank L. Owsley, *State Rights in the Confederacy* (Chicago, 1925), p. 229.

15. *O.R.*, Ser. 1, Vol. 17, pt. 2, p. 141.

16. *Ibid.*, Vol. 52, pt. 1, p. 331, Vol. 24, pt. 3, p. 538.

17. *Ibid.*, Vol. 17, pt. 2, pp. 424, 530, 544, Vol. 24, pt. 1, p. 9.

18. Jessie A. Marshall (ed.), *Private and Official Correspondence of General Benjamin F. Butler During the Period of the Civil War*, 5 vols. (Norwood, Mass., 1917), I, 490; Frank Moore (ed.), *The Rebellion Record: A Diary of American Events, With Documents, Narratives, Illustrative Incidents, Poetry, etc.*, 12 vols. (New York, 1862–1868), VI, 291–93.

19. Gerald M. Capers, *Occupied City: New Orleans Under the Federals, 1862–1865* (Lexington, Ky., 1965), pp. 83–84.

20. Banks quoted in Bruce Catton, *Never Call Retreat*, Pocket Books ed. (New York, 1967), p. 68; Coulter, *Confederate States*, p. 287.

21. Roy P. Basler (ed.), *The Collected Works of Abraham Lincoln*, (New Brunswick, N.J., 1953–1955), VIII, 163–64.

22. *O.R.*, Ser. 4, Vol. 2, pp. 151, 173–75, 334–35, Vol. 3, pp. 646–48.

23. James Ford Rhodes, *History of the United States From the Compromise of 1850*, 7 vols. (New York, 1892–1906), V, 420.

24. *O.R.*, Ser. 3, Vol. 2, p. 236.

25. Robert E. Lee, Jr., *Recollections and Letters of General Robert E. Lee* (New York, 1904), p. 46.

26. Peter J. Parish, *The American Civil War* (New York, 1975), p. 147.

27. William Q. Maxwell, *Lincoln's Fifth Wheel: The Political History of the United States Sanitary Commission* (New York, 1956), p. 245. The comparative statistics in this paragraph are from *ibid.*, p. 5; George W. Adams, *Doctors in Blue: The Medical History of the Union Army in*

the Civil War, Collier Books ed. (New York, 1961), p. 169; and E. B. Long, *The Civil War Day by Day: An Almanac, 1861–1865* (Garden City, N.Y., 1971), p. 711.

28. Allan Nevins, *The War for the Union: The Organized War, 1863–1864* (New York, 1971), p. 312.

29. Adams, *Doctors in Blue,* p. 68.

30. H. H. Cunningham, *Doctors in Gray: The Confederate Medical Service* (Baton Rouge, 1958).

31. Mary Elizabeth Massey, *Bonnet Brigades* (New York, 1966), p. 62.

32. *Ibid.,* p. 47.

33. Bruce Catton, *Grant Moves South,* (Boston, 1960), pp. 53–54.

CHAPTER 22

1. Roy P. Basler (ed.), *The Collected Works of Abraham Lincoln* (New Brunswick, N.J., 1953–1955), VII, 53–56.

2. *Ibid.,* p. 380.

3. *Congressional Globe,* 38th Cong., 1st sess. (1864), 2995.

4. Charles L. Wagandt, *The Mighty Revolution: Negro Emancipation in Maryland, 1862–1864* (Baltimore, 1964), p. 264.

5. *O.R.,* Ser. 1, Vol. 15, pp. 666–67, Vol. 34, pt. 2, pp. 227–31, Ser. 3, Vol. 4, pp. 166–70.

6. *Liberator,* February 5, 1864; *Boston Commonwealth,* January 15, 1864; James McKaye, *The Mastership and Its Fruits: The Emancipated Slave Face to Face With His Old Master* (New York, 1864), p. 37.

7. *Boston Commonwealth,* March 4, 1864.

8. George W. Julian, *Political Recollections* (Chicago, 1884), pp. 245–46; *U.S. Statutes at Large,* XIII, 507–9.

9. James M. McPherson, *The Struggle for Equality* (Princeton, 1964), pp. 257–59.

10. *Liberator,* January 8, 1864.

11. *National Anti-Slavery Standard,* January 7, 1865; *Friends' Review,* December 28, 1872.

12. Rupert S. Holland (ed.), *Letters and Diary of Laura M. Towne* (Cambridge, Mass., 1912), p. 8; W. E. B. Du Bois, *The Souls of Black Folk* (New York, 1903), p. 100.

13. James M. McPherson, *The Abolitionist Legacy: From Reconstruction to the NAACP* (Princeton, 1975), pp. 161–63.

14. *Ibid.,* pp. 212, 188.

15. Basler, *Works of Lincoln,* VI, 365, VII, 51.

16. McPherson, *Struggle for Equality,* pp. 370, 249; *Liberator,* August 8, 1862.

17. For a perceptive brief treatment of Stevens, see Eric Foner, "Thaddeus Stevens, Confiscation, and Reconstruction," in Stanley Elkins and Eric McKitrick (eds.), *The Hofstadter Aegis: A Memorial* (New York, 1974), pp. 154–83.

18. H. B. Sargent to John Andrew, January 14, 1862, Andrew Papers, Massachusetts Historical Society; John C. Collins quoted in Peyton McCrary, *Abraham Lincoln and Reconstruction: The Louisiana Experiment* (Princeton, 1978), p. 228.

19. Banks to Lincoln, December 20, 1863, quoted in McCrary, *Lincoln and Reconstruction,* p. 224.

20. Phillips to Benjamin Butler, December 13, 1863, Butler Papers, Library of Congress; Phillips to George W. Julian, March 27, 1864, Giddings-Julian Papers, Library of Congress; *Liberator,* May 20, 1864.

21. *Liberator,* February 5, 1864.

22. Hans L. Trefousse, *The Radical Republicans* (New York, 1969), p. 285.

23. McCrary, *Lincoln and Reconstruction,* p. 199.

24. Basler, *Works of Lincoln*, VII, 243.

25. Herman Belz, *Reconstructing the Union: Theory and Policy During the Civil War* (Ithaca, 1969), p. 173.

26. Basler, *Works of Lincoln*, VII, 433–34.

27. *New York Tribune*, August 5, 1864.

28. *Ibid.*, June 1, 1864.

CHAPTER 23

1. Edward Younger (ed.), *Inside the Confederate Government: The Diary of Robert Garlick Hill Kean* (New York, 1957), p. 119.

2. Bruce Catton, *A Stillness at Appomattox* (Garden City, N.Y., 1957), p. 36.

3. *Ibid.*, pp. 25–29; Bell I. Wiley, *The Life of Billy Yank* (New York, 1952), pp. 343–44.

4. *O.R.*, Ser. 1, Vol. 42, pt. 2, p. 783.

5. *Ibid.*, Vol. 46, pt. 1, p. 11.

6. *Ibid.*, Vol. 33, pp. 827–28.

7. Tyler Dennett (ed.), *Lincoln and the Civil War in the Diaries and Letters of John Hay* (New York, 1939), p. 179.

8. *O.R.*, Ser. 1, Vol. 32, pt. 3, p. 246.

9. *Ibid.*, Vol. 46, pt. 1, p. 20.

10. Horace Porter, *Campaigning With Grant* (New York, 1897), pp. 69–70.

11. Catton, *Stillness at Appomattox*, p. 91; Shelby Foote, *The Civil War: A Narrative. Red River to Appomattox* (New York, 1974), pp. 189–91.

12. Catton, *Stillness at Appomattox*, p. 127.

13. George R. Agassiz (ed.), *Meade's Headquarters, 1863–1865, Letters of Colonel Theodore Lyman* (Boston, 1922), p. 106.

14. *O.R.*, Ser. 1, Vol. 36, pt. 2, p. 627; Noah Brooks, *Washington in Lincoln's Time* (New York, 1895), p. 148.

15. Foote, *Red River to Appomattox*, pp. 290, 294.

16. *O.R.*, Ser. 1, Vol. 40, pt. 2, pp. 167, 179, 205.

17. Catton, *Stillness at Appomattox*, pp. 168, 170, 198.

18. *Ibid.*, p. 220.

19. Dudley T. Cornish, *The Sable Arm: Negro Troops in the Union Army* (New York, 1956), p. 273.

20. *Ibid.*, p. 274.

21. *O.R.*, Ser. 1, Vol. 40, pt. 1, p. 17; William Mahone, "The Crater," in James H. Stine, *History of the Army of the Potomac* (Philadelphia, 1892), pp. 675–76.

22. Bruce Catton, *Grant Takes Command* (Boston, 1969), pp. 343, 347.

23. Lloyd Lewis, *Sherman: Fighting Prophet* (New York, 1932), p. 357.

24. *O.R.*, Ser. 1., Vol. 39, pt. 2, p. 121.

25. *Ibid.*, Vol. 38, pt. 4, p. 507.

26. Bruce Catton, *Never Call Retreat*, Pocket Books ed., (New York, 1967), p. 315.

27. *O.R.*, Ser. 1, Vol. 38, pt. 5, pp. 882–83, 885.

28. William T. Sherman, "The Grand Strategy of the Last Year of the War," in *Battles and Leaders of the Civil War*, 4 vols. (New York, 1887), IV, 253; William T. Sherman, *Memoirs*, 2nd ed. rev., 2 vols. (New York, 1886), II, 72.

29. Basil H. Liddell Hart, *Sherman: Soldier, Realist, American* (New York, 1929), esp. chaps. 16–18.

30. *New York World*, July 12, 1864; Frank L. Klement, *The Copperheads in the Middle West* (Chicago, 1960), p. 233.

CHAPTER 24

1. Greeley to Lincoln, July 7, August 8, 1864, Lincoln Papers, Library of Congress.

2. Roy P. Basler (ed.), *The Collected Works of Abraham Lincoln*, 9 vols. (New Brunswick, N.J., 1953–1955), VII, 435.

3. Edward C. Kirkland, *The Peacemakers of 1864* (New York, 1927), pp. 85–96; Hudson Strode, *Jefferson Davis*, 3 vols. (New York, 1955–1964), III, 74–81.

4. *Columbus Crisis*, August 3, 1864, quoted in V. Jacque Voegeli, *Free but Not Equal* (Chicago, 1967), p. 146; Francis Brown, *Raymond of the Times* (New York, 1951), pp. 259–60.

5. Basler, *Works of Lincoln*, VII, 517–18, 501.

6. *Ibid.*, pp. 518, 500, 507.

7. *Ibid.*, p. 514.

8. Edward McPherson, *The Political History of the United States During the Great Rebellion*, 2nd ed. (Washington, D.C., 1865), pp. 419–20.

9. Charles R. Wilson, "McClellan's Changing Views on the Peace Plank of 1864," *American Historical Review*, 38 (April 1933), 498–505. The three drafts of McClellan's letter showing the transition from peace to Union as the first priority are in the S. L. M. Barlow Papers, Henry E. Huntington Library.

10. William F. Zornow, *Lincoln and the Party Divided* (Norman, Okla., 1954), p. 139.

11. Allan Nevins and Milton H. Thomas (eds.), *The Diary of George Templeton Strong*, 4 vols. (New York, 1952), III, 480–81; Basler, *Works of Lincoln*, VII, 533.

12. Wood Gray, *The Hidden Civil War: The Story of the Copperheads* (New York, 1942), p. 189; Lloyd Lewis, *Sherman: Fighting Prophet* (New York, 1932), p. 409.

13. Bruce Catton, *Never Call Retreat*, Pocket Books ed. (New York, 1967), p. 369.

14. *O.R.*, Ser. 1, Vol. 43, pt. 1; pp. 30–31.

15. Quoted in Catton, *Never Call Retreat*, p. 374, from a letter of a Union army surgeon written on the day of the battle.

16. Clifford Dowdey (ed.), *The Wartime Papers of R. E. Lee* (Boston, 1961), p. 868.

17. Grant to Elihu Washburne, August 16, 1864, quoted in Bruce Catton, *Grant Takes Command* (Boston, 1969), p. 355; Grant to Stanton, September 13, 1864, in *O.R.*, Ser. 3, Vol. 4, p. 713.

18. E. Merton Coulter, *The Confederate States of America* (Baton Rouge, 1950), p. 544; Clement C. Clay to Judah Benjamin, September 12, 1864, in *O.R.*, Ser. 4, Vol. 3, pp. 637–38.

19. Frank L. Klement, *The Copperheads in the Middle West* (Chicago, 1960), p. 205; Frank L. Klement, *The Limits of Dissent: Clement L. Vallandigham and the Civil War* (Lexington, Ky., 1970), p. 294. See also Richard O. Curry, "The Union as It Was: A Critique of Recent Interpretations of the Copperheads," *Civil War History*, 13 (March 1967), 25–39.

20. For a sober summary of the evidence about these activities, see Stephen Z. Starr, "Was There a Northwest Conspiracy?" *The Filson Club Historical Quarterly*, 38 (October 1964), 323–41. Two full-scale studies that tend to exaggerate the dimensions of treasonable Copperhead activities are Gray, *Hidden Civil War*, and George Fort Milton, *Abraham Lincoln and the Fifth Column* (New York, 1942). Of the two, Gray is the more reliable.

21. *O.R.*, Ser. 1, Vol. 43, pt. 2, pp. 930–36.

22. *Freeman's Journal*, August 20, 1864.

23. For a summary of the race issue in the 1864 campaign, see Forrest G. Wood, *Black Scare: The Racist Response to Emancipation and Reconstruction* (Berkeley, 1968), pp. 53–79.

24. McPherson, *Political History of the Rebellion*, p. 420.

25. Eliza Frances Andrews, *The War-Time Journal of a Georgia Girl, 1864–1865* (New York, 1908), pp. 78–79.

26. *O.R.*, Ser. 2, Vol. 5, pp. 797, 808, 940–41, 128, 696.

27. *Ibid.*, Vol. 6, pp. 441–42, 647–49, 226.

28. *Ibid.*, Vol. 7, pp. 578–79, 606, 688, Vol. 8, p. 150; Benjamin F. Butler, *Autobiography* (Boston, 1892), p. 605.

29. *O.R.*, Ser. 2, Vol. 7, pp. 607, 615.

30. *Ibid.*, pp. 906–7, 909, 914.

31. Gideon Welles, *The Diary of Gideon Welles*, ed. Howard K. Beale, 3 vols. (New York, 1960), II, 168–72; *O.R.*, Ser. 2, Vol. 7, p. 1007, Vol. 8, pp. 98, 123, 504.

32. Basler, *Works of Lincoln*, VIII, 101.

33. Bruce Catton, *A Stillness at Appomattox* (Garden City, N.Y., 1957), p. 323; John Berry to Samuel L. M. Barlow, August 27, 1864, Barlow Papers.

34. The best account of the soldier vote is Oscar O. Winther, "The Soldier Vote in the Election of 1864," *New York History*, 25 (1944), 440–58.

35. Catton, *Grant Takes Command*, p. 384; Paul M. Angle and Earl Schenck Miers (eds.), *Tragic Years, 1860–1865* (New York, 1960), p. 920.

36. Samuel L. M. Barlow to Fitz-John Porter, November 17, 1864, Barlow Papers; Allan Nevins, *The War for the Union: The Organized War to Victory, 1864–1865* (New York, 1971), p. 141.

37. Dunbar Rowland (ed.), *Jefferson Davis, Constitutionalist*, 10 vols. (Jackson, Miss., 1923), VI, 386.

CHAPTER 25

1. William T. Sherman, *Memoirs*, 2nd ed. rev., 2 vols., (New York, 1886), II, 111.

2. *Ibid.*, pp. 119–21, 125–27.

3. *O.R.*, Ser. 1, Vol. 39, pt. 3, p. 660; John Bennett Walters, "General William T. Sherman and Total War," *Journal of Southern History*, 14 (August 1948), 463, 470.

4. *O.R.*, Ser. 1, Vol. 39, pt. 3, pp. 162, 202, 595.

5. Lloyd Lewis, *Sherman: Fighting Prophet* (New York, 1932), p. 457; B. H. Liddell Hart, *Sherman* (New York, 1929), p. 330.

6. Sherman, *Memoirs*, II, 179.

7. Bruce Catton, *Never Call Retreat*, Pocket Books ed. (New York, 1967), p. 395.

8. Sherman, *Memoirs*, II, 189.

9. Lewis, *Sherman*, 440.

10. *O.R.*, Ser. 1, vol. 44, p. 13; Lewis, *Sherman*, 451–52.

11. E. Merton Coulter, *The Confederate States of America* (Baton Rouge, 1950), pp. 549–50.

12. *O.R.*, Ser. 1, Vol. 44, p. 783.

13. *Congressional Globe*, 38th Cong., 2nd sess., (1865) 525–26.

14. *Ibid.*, p. 531.

15. Bessie Martin, *Desertion of Alabama Troops From the Confederate Army* (New York, 1932), p. 148.

16. Bell I. Wiley, *The Life of Johnny Reb* (Indianapolis, 1943), p. 134; Ella Lonn, *Desertion During the Civil War* (New York, 1928), p. 28.

17. Alexander Stephens, *A Constitutional View of the Late War Between the States*, 2 vols. (Philadelphia, 1868–1870), II, 619.

18. Roy P. Basler (ed.), *The Collected Works of Abraham Lincoln*, 9 vols. (New Brunswick, N.J., 1953–1955), VIII, 275–76.

19. Dunbar Rowland (ed.), *Jefferson Davis, Constitutionalist*, 10 vols. (Jackson, Miss., 1923), VI, 466. The fullest account of the Hampton Roads conference is in Stephens, *Constitutional View*, II, 599–624.

20. Basler, *Works of Lincoln*, VIII, 333.

21. Lewis, *Sherman*, pp. 484, 490.

22. Rowland (ed.), *Jefferson Davis*, VI, 489.

23. *O.R.*, Ser. 1, Vol. 44, p. 741.

24. Lewis, *Sherman*, p. 446; *O.R.*, Ser. 1, Vol. 44, p. 799.

25. Lewis, *Sherman*, pp. 493, 489; James G. Randall and David Donald, *The Civil War and Reconstruction*, 2nd ed. (Lexington, Mass., 1969), p. 432.

26. The fullest and fairest discussion of this event is Marion Brunson Lucas, *Sherman and the Burning of Columbia* (College Station, Tex., 1976).

27. James L. Sellers, "The Economic Incidence of the Civil War in the South," *Mississippi Valley Historical Review*, 14 (1927), 179–91; Stanley Engerman, "Some Economic Factors in Southern Backwardness in the Nineteenth Century," in John F. Kain and John R. Meyer (eds.), *Essays in Regional Economics* (Cambridge, Mass., 1971), pp. 300–302; *U.S. Census*, 1870, Vol. III, pp. 8–11.

28. Basler, *Works of Lincoln*, VIII, 152.

29. These complex events are chronicled in Herman Belz, *Reconstructing the Union: Theory and Policy During the Civil War* (Ithaca, 1969), chap. 9.

30. *Boston Commonwealth*, March 4, 1865.

31. Basler, *Works of Lincoln*, VIII, 399–405.

32. Edward Younger (ed.), *Inside the Confederate Government: The Diary of Robert Garlick Hill Kean* (New York, 1957), p. 182.

33. Robert F. Durden, *The Gray and the Black: The Confederate Debate on Emancipation* (Baton Rouge, 1972), p. 184; *O.R.*, Ser. 4, Vol. 3, p. 1010; Shelby Foote, *The Civil War: A Narrative. From Meridian to Appomattox* (New York, 1974), pp. 766, 860.

34. *O.R.*, Ser. 4, Vol. 3, p. 1012; James D. McCabe, Jr., *Life and Campaigns of General Robert E. Lee* (Atlanta, 1866), p. 574; Emory Thomas, *The Confederacy as a Revolutionary Experience* (Englewood Cliffs, N.J., 1971), p. 130.

35. Bell I. Wiley, *The Life of Billy Yank* (Indianapolis, 1952), pp. 321–23; Lewis, *Sherman*, p. 362.

36. Wiley, *Billy Yank*, p. 322.

37. These data were compiled from Thomas L. Livermore, *Numbers and Losses in the Civil War* (Boston, 1901), and William F. Fox, *Regimental Losses in the American Civil War* (Albany, 1889).

38. *Philadelphia Press*, April 11, 12, 1865.

39. Douglas Southall Freeman, *R. E. Lee: A Biography*, 4 vols. (New York, 1934–1935), IV, 120–23.

40. Ulysses S. Grant, *Personal Memoirs*, 2 vols. (New York, 1885), II, 489.

41. *War Diary and Letters of Stephen Minot Weld, 1861–1865* (Boston, 1979), p. 396; Bruce Catton, *Grant Takes Command* (Boston, 1969), p. 469.

42. Basler, *Works of Lincoln*, VIII, 333.

43. Rowland, *Jefferson Davis*, VI, 530.

44. Leander Stillwell, *The Story of a Common Soldier, or Army Life in the Civil War* (Erie, Kansas, 1917), p. 154.

45. Oliver Wendell Holmes, Jr., *Speeches* (Boston, 1913), p. 11.

46. Leon F. Litwack, *Been in the Storm So Long: The Aftermath of Slavery* (New York, 1979), p. 171; William McKee Evans, *Ballots and Fence Rails: Reconstruction on the Lower Cape Fear* (New York, 1967), p. 87.

47. Eugene D. Genovese, *Roll, Jordan, Roll: The World the Slaves Made* (New York, 1974), p. 110; Litwack, *Been in the Storm So Long*, pp. 96, 102.

Glossary

Abatis.   A network of felled trees in front of an entrenched position, with branches interlaced and facing the enemy's position to form an obstacle to attacking troops.

Blockade.   A cordon of patrolling warships attempting to prevent vessels from entering or leaving enemy ports.

Bounty.   A payment by the federal, state, or local government to induce men to enlist in the army.

Breastworks.   A barricade of logs, fence-rails, stones, sandbags, or other material to protect fighting on the defensive. When erected in front of trenches, breastworks are covered with the dirt excavated from the trenches.

Breechloader.   A rifle that is loaded at the breech, i.e., the rear of the barrel near the trigger.

Brevet rank.   An honorary appointment of an army or navy officer to a rank above his regular rank, given as a reward for meritorious service but carrying no increase in authority.

Bushwhacker.   Opprobious slang term for an irregular guerrilla soldier who fights from ambush or in hit-and-run attacks.

Caisson.   A two-wheeled horse-drawn vehicle with a large box to carry artillery ammunition.

Cashier.   To cashier an officer is to dismiss him from the service for disciplinary reasons.

Commissary Bureau.   The administrative department of the army responsible for supplying food to the soldiers.

Contraband.   Technically, contraband is enemy property or goods subject to seizure by a belligerent power in war. During the Civil War, "contrabands" became the popular name for freed slaves.

Countermarch.   To reverse the direction of marching troops and return to or near the starting point.

Court martial.   A court of army or navy officers to try persons for offenses under martial (or military) law.

Demonstrate, demonstration.   In military operations, a demonstration is a show of force on a given front without an actual attack, intended to distract enemy attention from the actual point of attack. Similar to a *feint*.

Earthworks.   Military fortifications constructed of earth, sand, gravel, etc.

Enfilade.   To bring an enemy position under fire from the side or end instead of directly or obliquely from the front. The advantage of enfilading fire is twofold; shots that miss the initial target may hit men further down the line; the enemy has difficulty returning the fire effectively without risk of hitting their own men.

Envelop.   To undertake an attack on one or both flanks or the rear of an enemy position; to encircle or surround.

Exchange cartel.   An official agreement between governments at war with each other for the exchange of prisoners of war.

Feint.   A limited attack or movement of troops against one objective to mislead the enemy and cause him to weaken his defenses at the intended point of real attack. Similar to but more aggressive than a *demonstration*.

Field trenches.   Trenches constructed by an army fighting or maneuvering in an active campaign, as opposed to fortifications and trenches protecting a fixed strategic point such as a city.

Flank.   The side or end of a moving or stationary column or line of troops. "To flank" an enemy position is to get around to its side or rear in order to *enfilade* the position. A "flanking march" is the movement of troops to get on the enemy's flank or rear.

Flotilla.   A group of warships and transports acting in concert with one another for a specific purpose. A flotilla generally contains a smaller number of ships than a fleet.

Forage.   As a noun, forage is grass, hay, or grain for horses and mules. Forage was as necessary for a Civil War army as petroleum is for a modern army. The verb "to forage" meant to seek food for humans as well as for animals.

Forced march.   A long march of troops at a fast pace made necessary by an impending battle or other emergency.

Guerrilla warfare.   Guerrillas are members of small armed bands that operate independently of the organized armed forces—often behind enemy lines, where they attack small detachments of enemy troops or destroy supply and transportation facilities. Guerrillas are sometimes civilians who take up arms temporarily and then return to their homes until called upon for another raid.

Martial law. Temporary government of a civilian population by military authorities, accompanied by the suspension or partial suspension of civil liberties and civil courts.

Mortar boat. A specially constructed warship carrying a large mortar. A mortar is a short, large-caliber cannon designed to fire shells at a high angle so that they fall behind defensive fortifications too strong to be breached by direct artillery bombardment.

Muzzleloader. A firearm loaded at the muzzle (end) of the barrel.

Ordnance Bureau. The administrative department of the army responsible for supplying arms and ammunition (ordnance).

Parole. An oath by a captured soldier, given in return for release from captivity, not to bear arms against the captors until formally exchanged for one of the captor's soldiers. To parole a captured soldier is to exact such an oath as a condition of his release.

Picket. A soldier assigned to the perimeter of an army encampment or position to give warning of enemy movements.

Pincers movement. A military operation by two or more cooperating forces to converge on and attack a single enemy force from different directions, thereby catching the enemy in a "pincers."

Prize crew. Crew put on board a captured enemy ship or a neutral ship carrying contraband to bring the capture ship into one of the captor's ports.

Quartermaster. An officer responsible for supplying army units with uniforms, shoes, equipment (exclusive of ordnance), transportation, and forage. The Quatermaster Bureau or Quartermaster Corps is the army administrative department in charge of this function.

Ranger. A soldier engaged in special service detached from organized army units, often operating behind enemy lines to gather information or to destroy facilities. "Ranger" and "guerrilla" were often used interchangeably during the Civil War.

Reconnaissance in force. A tentative or probing attack or other maneuver by a sizeable number of troops, usually a brigade or larger, to gain information about the location, size, and movements of enemy forces.

Redan. Earthworks or breastworks thrown up in front of a cannon in the form of an inverted V to protect the gun and its crew from enemy fire.

Regular. An officer in the peacetime army, or "regular army," as distinguished from a "volunteer" in the "volunteer army" who enlisted for the specific purpose of fighting in the Civil War.

Repeating firearm. A gun that can be fired two or more times before reloading.

Salient. A portion of a defensive line or trench that juts out toward the enemy.

Screen (cavalry). A patrol of the front and flanks of an army to prevent enemy cavalry or scouts from getting close enough to the main army for observation.

Shotted guns. Cannons loaded with live ammunition.

Solid shot. Round cannonballs that do not explode.

Specie.   Coined money, especially gold and silver. Specie payments are payments in coin, or the redemption of paper money on demand with coin equivalent. To suspend specie payments is to refuse to redeem paper money in coin.

To spike (a gun).   To drive in and clinch a spike or nail in the vent (airhole where the powder is ignited) of a muzzleloading cannon in order to prevent the cannon being fired without major repairs.

Transport.   An unarmed ship carrying troops or supplies.

Trooper.   A cavalryman.

Volley.   The simultaneous firing of their guns by an entire unit of soldiers.

Works.   A general term to describe defensive military fortifications of all kinds.

Bibliography

ABBREVIATIONS

AH	Agricultural History
AHR	American Historical Review
CWH	Civil War History
JAH	Journal of American History
JEH	Journal of Economic History
JNH	Journal of Negro History
JSH	Journal of Southern History
MVHR	Mississippi Valley Historical Review
SAQ	South Atlantic Quarterly

BIBLIOGRAPHIES ON THE CIVIL WAR–RECONSTRUCTION ERA

The number of books and articles on the era of the Civil War and Reconstruction is so enormous that the following essay can provide only a selective listing of the most important and useful of them. Students desiring a more detailed bibliography should consult the following: Don E. Fehrenbacher (ed.), *Manifest Destiny and the Coming of the Civil War* (1970); David Donald (ed.), *The Nation in Crisis, 1861–1877* (1969); and the relevant portions of Frank Freidel (ed.), *Harvard Guide to American History*, rev. ed. (1974). The bibliography of James G. Randall and David Donald, *The Civil War and Reconstruction*, 2nd ed. rev. (1969), contains a rich listing of items published before 1969. The December issue each year through 1977 of the quarterly journal *Civil War History* (1954–) classifies articles dealing with the Civil War era published in other journals during the previous year. Each issue of the *Journal of American History* and the May issue each year of the *Journal of Southern History* list articles published in other journals, including many articles on the Civil War era. The ongoing volumes of *Writings in American History* and *America: History and Life*, contain classified listings of books and articles on all aspects of American history.

511

GENERAL WORKS ON THE CIVIL WAR–RECONSTRUCTION ERA

Two eminent historians writing a half-century apart have produced magisterial multivolume narratives of America's sectional trauma: James Ford Rhodes, *History of the United States From the Compromise of 1850 to the McKinley-Bryan Campaign of 1896*, 8 vols. (1892–1919); and Allan Nevins, *Ordeal of the Union*, covering the years 1847–1857, 2 vols. (1947); *The Emergence of Lincoln*, covering 1857–1861, 2 vols. (1950), and *The War for the Union*, 4 vols. (1959–1971). In addition to James G. Randall and David Donald, *The Civil War and Reconstruction*, cited in the first section of this bibliography, other important one-volume studies covering all or part of this period include Peter J. Parish, *The American Civil War* (1975) and William R. Brock, *Conflict and Transformation: The United States 1844–1877* (1973), both by British historians who offer valuable perspectives on the American experience; David M. Potter, *Division and the Stresses of Reunion, 1845–1876* (1973); Robert H. Jones, *Disrupted Decades: The Civil War and Reconstruction Years* (1973); David Herbert Donald, *Liberty and Union* (1978); Arthur C. Cole, *The Irrepressible Conflict 1850–1865* (1934); Elbert B. Smith, *The Death of Slavery: The United States, 1837–1865* (1967); Donald M. Jacobs and Raymond H. Robinson, *America's Testing Time 1848–1877* (1973); Emory M. Thomas, *The American War and Peace 1860–1877* (1973); David Lindsey, *Americans in Conflict: The Civil War and Reconstruction* (1974); Ludwell H. Johnson, *Division and Reunion: America 1848–1877* (1978); Thomas H. O'Connor, *The Disunited States: The Era of Civil War and Reconstruction*, 2nd ed. (1978); and George T. McJimsey, *The Dividing and Reuniting of America: 1848–1877* (1981).

Charles A. Beard and Mary A. Beard's sweeping survey of American history, *The Rise of American Civilization*, 2 vols. (1927), interprets the Civil War as a "Second American Revolution," by which an industrializing North destroyed the agrarian civilization of the Old South. Refinements and modifications of this interpretation can be found in Barrington Moore, *Social Origins of Dictatorship and Democracy* (1966) chap. 3: "The American Civil War: The Last Capitalist Revolution"; Margaret Shortreed, "The Anti-Slavery Radicals, 1840–1868," *Past and Present*, no. 16 (1959), 65–87; and Raimondo Luraghi, *The Rise and Fall of the Plantation South* (1978). Carl N. Degler, "The Two Cultures and the Civil War," in Stanley Coben and Lorman Ratner (eds.), *The Development of an American Culture* (1970), pp. 92–119, emphasizes cultural differences between North and South.

Wilbur J. Cash, *The Mind of the South* (1941), evokes the impact of the sectional conflict on the South; while Robert Penn Warren, *The Legacy of the Civil War* (1964), a book published during the centennial commemoration of the conflict, critically appraises the war's meaning. Several essays in Arthur S. Link and Rembert W. Patrick (eds.), *Writing Southern History: Essays in Historiography in Honor of Fletcher M. Green* (1965), evaluate historical writing about the South during the middle decades of the nineteenth century. Carl N. Degler, *The Other South: Southern Dissenters in the Nineteenth Century* (1974), offers a fresh and enlightening account of Southern whites who resisted the dominant institutions and developments in their region. Roger W. Shugg, *Origins of Class Struggle in Louisiana 1840–1875* (1939), focuses on nonelite whites in one state during the era. Superb insights into the mentality of the South's planter elite can be found in the massive collection of letters from the Jones family of Georgia, Robert M. Myers (ed.), *The Children of Pride* (1972).

Hans L. Trefousse, *The Radical Republicans: Lincoln's Vanguard for Racial Justice* (1969), analyzes the group in the North most committed to an overthrow of the Old South's institutions; while George M. Fredrickson, *The Black Image in the White Mind: The Debate Over Afro-American Character and Destiny, 1817–1914* (1972), traces the evolution of racial ideologies during the era.

Several individual historians have published collections of important and stimulating essays on the Civil War and related themes: C. Vann Woodward, *The Burden of Southern History*, rev. ed. (1968), and *American Counterpoint: Slavery and Racism in the North-South Dialogue* (1971); David M. Potter, *The South and the Sectional Conflict* (1968); David Donald, *Lincoln Reconsidered: Essays on the Civil War Era*, 2nd ed., enl. (1961); Stephen B. Oates, *Our Fiery Trial: Abraham Lincoln, John Brown, and the Civil War Era* (1979); and Eric Foner, *Politics and Ideology in the Age of the Civil War* (1980). The literary critic Edmund Wilson has written a number of provocative essays in *Patriotic Gore: Studies in the Literature of the American Civil War* (1962).

Anthologies of essays and articles by various historians include: Charles Crowe (ed.), *The Age of Civil War and Reconstruction, 1830–1900*, rev. ed. (1975); George M. Fredrickson (ed.), *A Nation Divided: Problems and Issues of the Civil War and Reconstruction* (1975); Robert P. Swierenga, (ed.), *Beyond the Civil War Synthesis: Political Essays on the Civil War Era* (1975); Irwin Unger (ed.), *Essays on the Civil War and Reconstruction* (1970); and Harold D. Woodman (ed.), *The Legacy of the American Civil War* (1973).

The history of political parties and presidential elections during the era is ably covered by several historians in Winifred E. A. Bernhard (ed.), *Political Parties in American History* (1973); Arthur M. Schlesinger, Jr. (ed.), *History of U. S. Political Parties*, 4 vols. (1973), vols. I and II; and Arthur M. Schlesinger, Jr. (ed.), *History of American Presidential Elections*, 4 vols. (1971), vol. II. The maps in Charles O. Paullin, *Atlas of the Historical Geography of the United States* (1932), provide a wealth of important data on the social, economic, and political history of this period. *Historical Statistics of the United States* (1975) and Donald B. Dodd and Wynette S. Dodd (eds.), *Historical Statistics of the South* (1973), are indispensable.

The large literature on Abraham Lincoln provides penetrating insights on the antebellum as well as the war years. The fullest and most scholarly study of Lincoln's career is James G. Randall, *Lincoln the President*, 4 vols. (1945–1955; vol. IV completed by Richard N. Current). Randall published several essays on Lincoln and his times, in *Lincoln the Liberal Statesman* (1947). Two other multivolume biographies of the sixteenth president are John G. Nicolay and John Hay, *Abraham Lincoln: A History*, 10 vols. (1890), by Lincoln's wartime private secretaries; and Carl Sandburg, *Abraham Lincoln: The Prairie Years*, 2 vols. (1926), and *Abraham Lincoln: The War Years*, 4 vols. (1939). Both the Nicolay-Hay and Sandburg biographies perpetuate a number of myths and apocryphal stories about Lincoln that have been discredited by subsequent scholarship. To separate fact from fiction in Lincoln's life, two books are useful: Lloyd Lewis, *Myths After Lincoln* (1929); and Richard N. Current, *The Lincoln Nobody Knows* (1958). Among the many one-volume biographies of Lincoln, the following are the best: Benjamin P. Thomas, *Abraham Lincoln: A Biography* (1952); Reinhard H. Luthin, *The Real Abraham Lincoln* (1960); and Stephen B. Oates, *With Malice Toward None: The Life of Abraham Lincoln* (1977). Three anthologies of essays about Lincoln also contain material of value: Norman Graebner (ed.), *The Enduring Lincoln* (1959); Don E. Fehrenbacher (ed.), *The Leadership of Abraham Lincoln* (1970); and Cullom Davis *et al.* (eds.), *The Public and Private Lincoln: Contemporary Perspectives* (1979). The historical scholarship on Lincoln is summarized and analyzed in Don E. Fehrenbacher, *The Changing Image of Lincoln in American Historiography* (1968). The student of this period will also wish to read Lincoln's own words, which have been published in Roy P. Basler (ed.), *The Collected Works of Abraham Lincoln*, 9 vols. (1953–1955), and *The Collected Works of Abraham Lincoln—Supplement, 1832–1865* (1974). One-volume editions of Lincoln's selected writings and speeches include Roy P. Basler (ed.), *Abraham Lincoln: His Speeches and Writings* (1946); and Paul M. Angle and Earl Schenck Miers (eds.), *The Living Lincoln* (1955).

THE CIVIL WAR

General Works

Several bibliographical guides will introduce the student to the rich and massive literature on the war: Allan Nevins, Bell I. Wiley, and James I. Robertson (eds.), *Civil War Books: A Critical Bibliography*, 2 vols. (1967–1969); Ralph G. Newman and E. B. Long, *A Basic Civil War Library* (1964); James I. Robertson (ed.), *Southern Historical Society Papers, Index-Guide* (1980); and E. Merton Coulter, *Travels in the Confederate States: A Bibliography* (1968). Two multivolume studies by gifted writers who emphasize military aspects of the war will give the interested reader endless hours of pleasure: Bruce Catton, *The Centennial History of the Civil War*, 3 vols. (1961–1965), vol. I: *The Coming Fury*, vol. II: *Terrible Swift Sword*, vol. III: *Never Call Retreat;* and Shelby Foote, *The Civil War: A Narrative*, 3 vols. (1958–1974): vol. I: *Fort Sumter to Perryville*, vol. II: *Fredericksburg to Meridian*, vol. III: *Red River to Appomattox*. Bruce Catton has also written a good one-volume history of the war, *This Hallowed Ground* (1956), which treats mainly military events, as does Earl Schenck Miers, *The Great Rebellion* (1958). Two one-volume histories that concentrate on social history are William L. Barney, *Flawed Victory: A New Perspective on the Civil War* (1975); and Robert Cruden, *The War That Never Ended* (1973).

Most of the one-volume accounts, as well as Catton's *Centennial History*, focus principally on the Union side. But the Confederacy has received its full due of fine one-volume histories: Emory M. Thomas, *The Confederate Nation 1861–1865* (1979); E. Merton Coulter, *The Confederate States of America 1861–1865* (1950); Clement Eaton, *A History of the Southern Confederacy* (1954); Charles P. Roland, *The Confederacy* (1960); and Frank E. Vandiver, *Their Tattered Flags: The Epic of the Confederacy* (1970). See also Jon L. Wakelyn, *Biographical Dictionary of the Confederacy* (1977). Biographies of Jefferson Davis become virtual histories of the Confederacy. See especially Hudson Strode's laudatory *Jefferson Davis*, 3 vols. (1955–1964); and Clement Eaton's more critical *Jefferson Davis* (1977). Davis's own writings can be consulted in Dunbar Rowland (ed.), *Jefferson Davis, Constitutionalist: His Letters, Papers, and Speeches*, 10 vols. (1923). A fascinating perspective by a modern Southern writer is offered in Robert Penn Warren, *Jefferson Davis Gets His Citizenship Back* (1980).

For their wealth of factual data, Mark M. Boatner, *The Civil War Dictionary* (1959), and E. B. Long, *The Civil War Day by Day: An Almanac 1861–1865* (1971), are indispensable for any student of the war.

Contemporary printed materials of all kinds dealing with the war were collected and published by Frank Moore (ed.), *Rebellion Record*, 12 vols. (1861–1868), and have been reprinted in a modern edition (1977). Numerous anthologies of primary sources on the war are available to students: Paul M. Angle and Earl Schenck Miers (eds.), *Tragic Years 1860–1865*, 2 vols. (1960); Henry Steele Commager (ed.), *The Blue and the Gray*, 2 vols. (1950; rev. and abr. ed., 1973); William B. Hesseltine (ed.), *The Tragic Conflict: The Civil War and Reconstruction* (1962); Richard Wheeler (ed.), *Voices of the Civil War* (1976); Richard B. Harwell (ed.), *The Confederate Reader* (1957), and *The Union Reader* (1958); and Charles M. Segal (ed.), *Conversations With Lincoln* (1961).

Many short books, essays, and collections of essays offer interpretations of the meaning of the war or of specific aspects of it: Herbert Aptheker, *The American Civil War* (1961); James A. Rawley, *Turning Points of the Civil War* (1966); Emory M. Thomas, *The Confederacy as a Revolutionary Experience* (1971); Bell I. Wiley, *The Road to Appomattox* (1956); Grady McWhiney (ed.), *Grant, Lee, Lincoln, and the Radicals: Essays on Civil War Leadership* (1964); James I. Robertson (ed.), *Rank and File: Civil War Essays in Honor of Bell Irvin Wiley* (1976); William R. Brock (ed.),

The Civil War (1969); David Donald (ed.), *Why the North Won the Civil War* (1960); Frank E. Vandiver *et al.*, *Essays on the American Civil War* (1968); Henry Steele Commager (ed.), *The Defeat of the Confederacy* (1964); Allan Nevins, "A Major Result of the Civil War," *CWH*, 5 (1959), 237–50; Roy F. Nichols, "The Operation of American Democracy, 1861–1865: Some Questions," *JSH*, 25 (1959), 31–52.

The science of photography and the enterprise of photographers and artists made the Civil War the most lavishly illustrated war in history before the twentieth century. A good introduction to the subject is W. Fletcher Thompson, Jr., *The Image of War: The Pictorial Reporting of the American Civil War* (1960). The most ambitious effort to collect and publish the best of the tens of thousands of war photographs is Francis T. Miller (ed.), *The Photographic History of the Civil War*, 10 vols. (1911; reprinted 1957). A more selective collection, with a higher quality reproduction of the original photographs made possible by modern technology, is Hirst D. Milhollen and Milton Kaplan (eds.), *Divided We Fought: A Pictorial History of the War 1861–1865*, with narrative by David Donald (1952). For excellent selections of the work of one of the war's best photographers, consult Alexander Gardner, *Gardner's Photographic Sketch Book of the Civil War* (1959). Two other fine photographic histories are Bell Irvin Wiley and Hirst D. Milhollen, *They Who Fought Here* (1959); and Bell Irvin Wiley and Hirst D. Milhollen, *Embattled Confederates: An Illustrated History of Southerners at War* (1964). A lavish volume that reproduces photographs as well as drawings and paintings, some in full color, is Richard M. Ketchum (ed.), *The American Heritage Picture History of the Civil War*, with narrative by Bruce Catton (1960). Another volume that combines photographs and drawings is Paul M. Angle, *A Pictorial History of the Civil War Years* (1967). The work of wartime artists and illustrators is beautifully reproduced in Stephen W. Sears (ed.), *The American Heritage Century Collection of Civil War Art* (1974). One of the United States' best nineteenth-century painters worked as an illustrator for *Harper's Weekly* during the war; for a collection of his war drawings and paintings, see Julian Grossman, *Echo of a Distant Drum: Winslow Homer and the Civil War* (1974). The illustrations and text from the Union's two leading illustrated weeklies have been reprinted in modern editions: *Harper's Pictorial History of the Civil War* (1975) and *Frank Leslie's Illustrated History of the Civil War* (1977). William A. Frassanito has movingly re-created the battles of Antietam and Gettysburg through the use of contemporary and modern photographs in two rich volumes: *Antietam: The Photographic Legacy of America's Bloodiest Day* (1978) and *Gettysburg: A Journey in Time* (1975).

Strategies, Commanders, Armies, and Soldiers

John T. Hubbell (ed.), *Battles Lost and Won: Essays from Civil War History* (1975), is a good collection of articles on strategy, tactics, and leadership. Two British scholars wrote perceptive books on the American war that offer a comprative perspective: George W. Redway, *The War of Secession 1861–62* (1910), and H. C. B. Rogers, *The Confederates and Federals at War* (1973). A celebrated Union veteran offered some occasionally acerbic comments on the lessons of the war: Emory Upton, *The Military Policy of the United States* (1904). Modern scholars of military history have placed the Civil War in the context of American wars. See especially T. Harry Williams, *Americans at War* (1962); and Russell Weigley, *Towards an American Army* (1962) and *The American Way of War* (1973). Michael C. C. Adams, *Our Masters the Rebels: A Speculation on Union Military Failure in the East 1861–1865* (1978), advances a stimulating thesis that focuses on the Army of the Potomac's defensive and defeatist psychology. Hans Trefousse, "The Joint Committee on the Conduct of the War: A Reassessment," *CWH*, 10 (1964), 5–19, does much to redeem the reputation of the congressional committee sometimes blamed for hamstringing commanders of the Army of the Potomac.

A good introduction to the historiographical disputes concerning Confederate strategy and leadership is Douglas Southall Freeman, *The South to Posterity: An Introduction to the Writing of Confederate History* (1939). Two detailed studies of Confederate strategy are Thomas L. Connelly and Archer Jones, *The Politics of Command: Factions and Ideas in Confederate Strategy* (1973); and Archer Jones, *Confederate Strategy from Shiloh to Vicksburg* (1961). Edward Hagerman, "The Tactical Thought of R. E. Lee and the Origins of Trench Warfare in the Civil War," *Historian,* 38 (1975), 21–38, is an interesting study. Confederate guerrilla operations are assessed in Albert Castel, *The Guerrilla War* (1974); Virgil Carrington Jones, *Gray Ghosts and Rebel Raiders* (1956); and Richard S. Brownlee, *Gray Ghosts of the Confederacy: Guerrilla Warfare in the West 1861– 1865* (1958). For modern assessments of the legacy of the Civil War for American and European military thinkers, see Thomas C. Leonard, *Above the Battle: War-Making in America From Appomattox to Versailles* (1977); and Jay Luvaas, *The Military Legacy of the Civil War: The European Inheritance* (1959).

Three evaluations of Union military leadership that give Lincoln high marks as a strategist and emphasize his cordial relationship with Grant are Maurice Frederick, *Statesmen and Soldiers of the Civil War: A Study of the Conduct of War* (1926); Colin R. Ballard, *The Military Genius of Abraham Lincoln* (1926); and T. Harry Williams, *Lincoln and His Generals* (1952). See also Herman Hattaway and Archer Jones, "Lincoln as Military Strategist," *CWH,* 26 (Dec. 1980), 293–303. On the Confederate side, Frank E. Vandiver, "Jefferson Davis and Confederate Strategy," in Frank E. Vandiver and Avery Craven (eds.), *The American Tragedy: The Civil War in Retrospect* (1959), assesses Davis's leadership favorably; while Grady McWhiney, "Jefferson Davis and the Art of War," *CWH,* 21 (1975), 101–12, is critical.

Ezra J. Warner, *Generals in Blue: Lives of the Union Commanders* (1964), provides brief biographies of all Union generals. For a perceptive study of Henry W. Halleck's mixed record, see Stephen E. Ambrose, *Halleck: Lincoln's Chief of Staff* (1962). Kenneth P. Williams, *Lincoln Finds a General: A Military Study of the Civil War,* 5 vols. (1949–1959), is highly critical of McClellan and laudatory of Grant; while Warren W. Hassler, *Commanders of the Army of the Potomac* (1962), defends McClellan. The British military historian J. F. C. Fuller rates Grant as superior to Lee and to all other Civil War generals in two books: *The Generalship of Ulysses S. Grant* (1929) and *Grant and Lee: A Study in Personality and Generalship* (1933). See also a study by another British scholar, Alfred H. Burne, *Lee, Grant, and Sherman* (1938). T. Harry Williams, *McClellan, Sherman, and Grant* (1962), finds Grant and Sherman much superior to McClellan. A record of Grant's generalship in his own words can be found in John Y. Simon (ed.), *The Papers of Ulysses S. Grant,* 8 vols. to date, covering events through July 6, 1863 (1967–); and in *The Personal Memoirs of U.S. Grant,* 2 vols. (1885–1886). The best modern narrative of Grant's Civil War career is Bruce Catton, *Grant Moves South* (1960) and *Grant Takes Command* (1969). For Sherman, the best place to start is with his sprightly written autobiography, *Memoirs of General W. T. Sherman,* 2nd ed., 2 vols. (1886). Of the four principal biographies of Sherman, Basil H. Liddell Hart, *Sherman: Soldier, Realist, American* (1929), Lloyd Lewis, *Sherman, Fighting Prophet* (1932), and James M. Merrill, *William Tecumseh Sherman* (1971), are basically sympathetic; while John B. Walters, *Merchant of Terror: General Sherman and Total War* (1973) is hostile. For Sheridan, see his *Personal Memoirs of P. H. Sheridan,* 2 vols. (1888), and Richard O'Connor, *Sheridan the Inevitable* (1953). Freeman Cleaves, *Rock of Chickamauga: The Life of General George H. Thomas* (1948), is an informative biography. Both George B. McClellan, *McClellan's Own Story* (1886), and Warren W. Hassler, *George B. McClellan: The Man Who Saved the Union* (1957), are laudatory, though McClellan includes material in his memoirs that may cause the reader to question his political judgment. For a biography of two other important Union generals, consult William M. Lamers, *The Edge of Glory: A Biography of General William S. Rosecrans, U.S.A.* (1961), and Freeman Cleaves, *Meade of Gettysburg* (1960).

Ezra J. Warner, *Generals in Gray: Lives of the Confederate Commanders* (1959), chronicles the careers of all Confederate generals. Additional material on West Point graduates who went with the South can be found in Eliot Ellsworth, *West Point in the Confederacy* (1941). Frank E. Vandiver, *Rebel Brass: The Confederate Command System* (1956), disentangles a complicated story.

For a magisterial and sympathetic study of the South's greatest hero, read Douglas Southall Freeman, *R. E. Lee: A Biography*, 4 vols. (1934–1935). Thomas L. Connelly, "Robert E. Lee and the Western Confederacy: A Criticism of Lee's Strategic Ability," *CWH*, 15 (1969), 116–32, takes Lee to task for the eastern-oriented narrowness of his strategic vision; while Albert Castel comes to Lee's defense in "The Historian and the General: Thomas L. Connelly Versus Robert E. Lee," *CWH*, 16 (1970), 50–63. Thomas L. Connelly critically traces the Lee legend and uses a psychological approach to probe the general's character and leadership in his provocative *The Marble Man: Robert E. Lee and His Image in American Society* (1977). For additional material on Lee, consult Robert E. Lee, Jr. (ed.), *Recollections and Letters of General Robert E. Lee* (1904); and Clifford Dowdey (ed.), *The Wartime Papers of R. E. Lee* (1961). Lee's principal subordinates in the Army of Northern Virginia are appreciatively analyzed in Douglas Southall Freeman, *Lee's Lieutenants: A Study in Command*, 3 vols. (1942–1944). For the incomparable Stonewall Jackson, the most insightful studies are by the British scholar G. F. R. Henderson, *Stonewall Jackson and the American Civil War*, 2 vols. (1919); and the American Frank E. Vandiver, *Mighty Stonewall* (1957). James Longstreet's memoirs, *From Manassas to Appomattox: Memoirs of the Civil War* (1903; rev. ed., with intro. by James I. Robertson, 1960), contain much material of value. See also Donald B. Sanger and Thomas R. Hay, *James Longstreet* (1952). Other important Confederate generals are treated in T. Harry Williams, *Beauregard: Napoleon in Gray* (1955); Gilbert Govan and James Livingood, *A Different Valor: The Story of General Joseph E. Johnston* (1956); Grady McWhiney, *Braxton Bragg and Confederate Defeat* (1969); Burke Davis, *Jeb Stuart: The Last Cavalier* (1957); and Robert S. Henry, *"First with the Most" Forrest* (1944).

The fullest bibliography of regimental histories and individual accounts of army life and service is Charles E. Dornbusch, *Regimental Publications and Personal Narratives of the Civil War*, 3 vols. (1961–71). Frederick H. Dyer, *A Compendium of the War of the Rebellion*, 3 vols. (1908; new ed. in 2 vols., 1961), contains a great deal of information about Union military units from battalion to army. Another valuable aid to the student of the war's military events is William F. Amann, *Personnel of the Civil War*, 2 vols. (1961). A massive statistical profile of soldiers in the Union army can be found in Benjamin A. Gould, *Investigations in the Military and Anthropological Statistics of American Soldiers* (1869). Ella Lonn, *Foreigners in the Union Army and Navy* (1951), is the fullest account of this subject. Unit casualties in the Union armies, along with a great deal of other information, are provided in William Freeman Fox, *Regimental Losses in the American Civil War 1861–1865* (1889). The most judicious treatment of the sometimes confusing and controversial question of battle casualties is contained in Thomas L. Livermore, *Numbers and Losses in the Civil War* (1901).

The hard-luck but eventually triumphant story of the Army of the Potomac is brilliantly brought to life by Bruce Catton in three volumes: *Mr. Lincoln's Army* (1951), *Glory Road* (1952), and *A Stillness at Appomattox* (1953). Thomas L. Connelly has written a history of the Confederacy's principal western army that is as thorough if less readable: *Army of the Heartland: The Army of Tennessee 1861–1862* (1967) and *Autumn of Glory: The Army of Tennessee 1862–1865* (1971). Of the numerous small-unit histories, two of the best deal respectively with the most celebrated brigades in the Army of the Potomac and the Army of Northern Virginia: Alan T. Nolan, *The Iron Brigade* (1961); and James I. Robertson, *The Stonewall Brigade* (1963). Two genuine classics of Civil War literature are Bell I. Wiley's books on the experiences of common soldiers: *The Life of Johnny Reb* (1943) and *The Life of Billy Yank* (1952). Less scholarly but also valuable is Wiley's illustrated narrative *The Common Soldier of the Civil War* (1975). One of the best of many books by Union veterans about life in the army is John D. Billings, *Hard Tack and Coffee: Or, The Unwritten Story of Army Life* (1887; reprinted 1973). Additional insights on Southern soldiers are offered by David Donald, "The Confederate as a Fighting Man," *JSH*, 25 (1959), 178–93; and Le Grand J. Wilson, *The Confederate Soldier* (1980). Ella Lonn, *Desertion During the Civil War* (1928), and Bessie Martin, *Desertion of Alabama Troops From the Confederate Army* (1932), are detailed studies of this unhappy subject.

Military Campaigns and Battles

There is a huge literature on Civil War battles. Only a sample of the best studies can be cited here. The British military historian J. F. C. Fuller has placed the most important Civil War battles in a larger context in his *Decisive Battles of the U.S.A.* (1942). A durable narrative by a West Point professional is Gustav J. Fieberger, *Campaigns of the American Civil War* (1910). The dispatches, orders, reports, and other official documents that constitute the basic sources for any military history are available in the 128 volumes published by the U.S. government a generation after the war: *War of the Rebellion: A Compilation of the Official Records of the Union and Confederate Armies* (1880–1901). The maps accompanying these official records, by contemporary cartographers, are valuable: George B. Davis *et al.*, *The Official Military Atlas of the Civil War* (1895; reprinted 1978); but the maps in Vincent J. Esposito (ed.), *The West Point Atlas of American Wars*, vol. I (1959), are easier for the modern student to follow. Participants in the war analyzed the major campaigns in *Battles and Leaders of the Civil War*, 4 vols. (1887). For narratives of the cavalry's role and development, three books are worthwhile: Samuel Carter, *The Last Cavaliers: Confederate and Union Cavalry in the Civil War* (1980); Edward C. Longacre, *Mounted Raids of the Civil War* (1975); and Stephen G. Starr, *The Union Cavalry in the Civil War*, vol. I: *From Fort Sumter to Gettysburg* (1979).

The pamphlets issued by the National Park Service to explain the battles whose sites the service maintains provide incisive and concise narratives of these battles: Frank Barnes, *Fort Sumter* (1952); Francis F. Wilshin, *Manassas* (1953); Edwin C. Bearss, *The Fall of Fort Henry* (1963); Edwin C. Bearss, *Unconditional Surrender: The Fall of Fort Donelson* (1962); Albert Dillahunty, *Shiloh* (1955); Joseph P. Cullen, *Richmond National Battlefield Park* (1961); Frederick Tilberg, *Antietam*, rev. ed. (1961); Joseph P. Cullen, *Where a Hundred Thousand Fell: The Battles of Fredericksburg, Chancellorsville, the Wilderness, and Spotsylvania* (1966); Frederick Tilberg, *Gettysburg* (1954); William C. Everhart, *Vicksburg* (1954); James R. Sullivan, *Chickamauga and Chattanooga Battlefields* (1956); and Richard Wayne Lykes, *Campaign for Petersburg* (1970).

The following are the most useful books about particular campaigns and battles, in their chronological order: William C. Davis, *Battle at Bull Run: A History of the First Major Campaign of the Civil War* (1977); James J. Hamilton, *The Battle of Fort Donelson* (1968); Wiley Sword, *Shiloh: Bloody April* (1974); James Lee McDonough, *Shiloh: In Hell Before Night* (1978); Robert G. Tanner, *Stonewall in the Valley* (1976); Clifford Dowdey, *The Seven Days* (1964); Edward J. Stackpole, *From Cedar Mountain to Antietam* (1959); James V. Murfin, *The Gleam of Bayonets: The Battle of Antietam* (1965); James Lee McDonough, *Stones River: Bloody Winter in Tennessee* (1980); John Bigelow, *The Campaign of Chancellorsville* (1910); Edwin B. Coddington, *The Gettysburg Campaign* (1968); Glenn Tucker, *High Tide at Gettysburg* (1958); Earl Schenck Miers and Richard B. Brown (eds.), *Gettysburg* (1948); Samuel Carter, *The Final Fortress: The Campaign for Vicksburg* (1980); Earl Schenck Miers, *Web of Victory: Grant at Vicksburg* (1955); Richard Wheeler (ed.), *The Siege of Vicksburg* (1978); Peter F. Walker, *Vicksburg: A People at War* (1960); Fairfax Downey, *Storming the Gateway: Chattanooga, 1863* (1960); Ludwell H. Johnson, *Red River*

Campaign: Politics and Cotton in the Civil War (1958); Edward Steere, *The Wilderness Campaign* (1960); Clifford Dowdey, *Lee's Last Campaign* (1960); Richard J. Sommers, *Richmond Redeemed: The Siege at Petersburg* (1980); William C. Davis, *The Battle of New Market* (1975); Frank Vandiver, *Jubal's Raid* (1960); Edward J. Stackpole, *Sheridan in the Shenandoah* (1961); Samuel Carter, *The Siege of Atlanta, 1864* (1973); Burke Davis, *Sherman's March* (1980); Richard Wheeler (ed.), *Sherman's March: An Eyewitness History* (1978); John B. Barrett, *Sherman's March Through the Carolinas* (1956); Marion Brunson Lucas, *Sherman and the Burning of Columbia* (1976); Thomas R. Hay, *Hood's Tennessee Campaign* (1929); Stanley F. Horn, *The Decisive Battle of Nashville* (1956); and James P. Jones, *Yankee Blitzkrieg: Wilson's Raid Through Alabama and Georgia* (1976).

The Armies: Organization, Logistics, Medical Care, Prisons

Four studies provide comprehensive coverage of the organization and supply of the Union army: Fred A. Shannon, *The Organization and Administration of the Union Armies 1861–1865*, 2 vols. (1928); A. H. Meneely, *The War Department, 1861* (1928); Benjamin P. Thomas and Harold M. Hyman, *Stanton: The Life and Times of Lincoln's Secretary of War* (1962); and Russell F. Weigley, *Quartermaster-General of the Union Army: A Biography of Montgomery C. Meigs* (1959). There are few comparable studies for the Confederacy, but see Richard D. Goff, *Confederate Supply* (1969). Recruitment and conscription in the Confederacy and Union are treated in Albert B. Moore, *Conscription and Conflict in the Confederacy* (1924); and in Eugene C. Murdock, *Patriotism Limited: The Civil War Draft and the Bounty System* (1967) and *One Million Men: The Civil War Draft in the North* (1971).

Robert V. Bruce, *Lincoln and the Tools of War* (1956), is a fascinating account of the President's role in ordnance innovation. Other valuable volumes dealing with arms and ammunition include Carl L. Davis, *Arming the Union: Small Arms in the Civil War* (1973); William A. Albaugh and Edward N. Simmons, *Confederate Arms* (1957); Frank E. Vandiver, *Ploughshares Into Swords: Josiah Gorgas and Confederate Ordnance* (1952); and Frank E. Vandiver (ed.), *The Civil War Diary of General Josiah Gorgas* (1947). The use of balloons for military reconnaissance is treated in F. Stansbury Haydon, *Aeronautics in the Union and Confederate Armies* (1941). Three volumes provide detailed coverage of the crucial role of railroads in military movements and supply: George E. Turner, *Victory Rode the Rails* (1953); Thomas Weber, *The Northern Railroads in the Civil War* (1952); and Robert C. Black, *The Railroads of the Confederacy* (1952).

The basic medical records of the Union side were compiled by the U.S. War Department, Office of the Surgeon General, *The Medical and Surgical History of the War of the Rebellion*, 6 vols. (1875–1888). Stewart Brooks, *Civil War Medicine* (1966), is a useful brief study. Valuable data and insights are contained in Paul E. Steiner, *Disease in the Civil War* (1968), and in Horace H. Cunningham, *Field Medical Services at the Battles of Manassas* (1968). Two monographs on Union medicine are excellent: George W. Adams, *Doctors in Blue: The Medical History of the Union Army* (1952); and George W. Smith, *Medicines for the Union Army: The United States Army Laboratories During the Civil War* (1962). The role of the Sanitary Commission is analyzed in William Q. Maxwell, *Lincoln's Fifth Wheel: The Political History of the United States Sanitary Commission* (1956). A significant collection that delineates the role of women nurses for the Union is John R. Brumgardt (ed.), *Civil War Nurse: The Diary and Letters of Hannah Ropes* (1980). The work of two Southern women—Kate Cumming and Phoebe Yates Pember—as nurses for the Confederate forces is described in Richard B. Harwell (ed.), *Kate: The Journal of a Confederate Nurse* (1959) and Bell I. Wiley (ed.), *A Southern Woman's Story: Life in Confederate Richmond* (1959). The best—indeed, almost the only—study of Confederate medicine is Horace H. Cunningham, *Doctors in Gray* (1958).

There is no adequate modern study of Civil War prisons and prisoners. The closest approach to adequacy is William B. Hesseltine, *Civil War Prisons* (1930). The entire June 1962 issue (vol. 8) of *Civil War History* is devoted to articles on prisons. The most objective account of Andersonville is Ovid L. Futch, *History of Andersonville Prison* (1968).

The Naval War

Myron J. Smith, *American Civil War Navies: A Bibliography* (1972), provides a list of sources. Also useful is U.S. Department of the Navy, Naval History Division, *Civil War Naval Chronology 1861–1865* (1971). The basic sources for a naval history of the war are the *Official Records of the Union and Confederate Navies in the War of the Rebellion*, 30 vols. (1892–1922). Two readable one-volume narratives are Bern Anderson, *By Sea and by River: The Naval History of the Civil War* (1962); and Howard P. Nash, *A Naval History of the Civil War* (1972). The fullest account is Virgil C. Jones, *The Civil War at Sea*, 3 vols. (1960–1962). For the war's most famous naval battle, consult William C. Davis, *Duel Between the First Ironclads* (1975). Additional references can be found in David R. Smith, *The Monitor and the Merrimac: A Bibliography* (1968). For the river war, three books are valuable: H. Allen Gosnell, *Guns on the Western Waters: The Story of River Gunboats in the Civil War* (1949); John D. Milligan, *Gunboats Down the Mississippi* (1965); and James M. Merrill, *Battle Flags South: The Story of the Civil War Navies on Western Waters* (1970).

Union naval strategy and leadership are treated in Richard S. West, *Mr. Lincoln's Navy* (1957); James M. Merrill, *The Rebel Shore: The Story of Union Sea Power in the Civil War* (1957); Richard West, *Gideon Welles: Lincoln's Navy Department* (1943); John Niven, *Gideon Welles: Lincoln's Secretary of the Navy* (1973); and Charles L. Lewis, *David Glasgow Farragut*, 2 vols. (1941–1943). Rowena Reed, *Combined Operations in the Civil War* (1978), argues that the Union did not exploit its full potential for combined army-navy operations.

For the Confederate navy and its leadership, see Philip Van Doren Stern, *The Confederate Navy* (1962); Tom H. Wells, *The Confederate Navy: A Study in Organization* (1971); William N. Still, *Confederate Shipbuilding* (1969) and *Iron Afloat: The Story of the Confederate Armorclads* (1971); Joseph T. Durkin, *Stephen R. Mallory: Confederate Navy Chief* (1954); and Milton F. Perry, *Infernal Machines: The Story of Confederate Submarine and Mine Warfare* (1965). Two studies tell the story of blockade running: Hamilton Cochran, *Blockade Runners of the Confederacy* (1958); and Frank E. Vandiver, *Confederate Blockade Running Through Bermuda 1861–1865* (1947). For Confederate Cruiser warfare against Northern merchant ships, see George W. Dalzell, *The Flight from the Flag* (1943); Edward C. Boykin, *Ghost Ship of the Confederacy: The Story of the* Alabama *and Her Captain* (1957); and Stanley F. Horn, *Gallant Rebel: The Fabulous Cruise of the C.S.S. Shenandoah* (1947).

Foreign Relations

The most complete treatment of this complex subject is by an Australian historian: David P. Crook, *The North, The South, and the Powers 1861–1865* (1974). An abridged version of this book is titled *Diplomacy During the Civil War* (1975). Essays on the policies of various countries toward the American war can be found in Harold M. Hyman (ed.), *Heard Round the World: The Impact Abroad of the Civil War* (1969). An old but still useful survey of European public opinion is Donaldson Jordan and Edwin J. Pratt, *Europe and the American Civil War* (1931). A good anthology of European opinion is Belle B. Sideman and Lillian Friedman (eds.), *Europe Looks at the Civil War* (1960). For the writings of two subsequently famous Europeans who were intensely interested in the Civil War, see Karl Marx and Friedrich Engels, *The Civil War in the United States*, ed. Richard Enmale (1937); and Saul K. Padover (ed.), *Karl Marx on America and the Civil War* (1972).

Frank O. Owsley, *King Cotton Diplomacy: Foreign Relations of the Confederate States of America* (1931; rev. ed. 1959), is exhaustive but partisan. It should be supplemented by Henry Blumenthal, "Confederate Diplomacy: Popular Notions and International Realities," *JSH*, 32 (1966), 151–71, and by Samuel B. Thompson, *Confederate Purchasing Operations Abroad* (1935). For a fresh perspective on the Union secretary of state, see Norman Ferris, *Desperate Diplomacy: William H. Seward's Foreign Policy, 1861* (1976). A valuable study of an important subject is Stuart L. Bernath, *Squall Across the Atlantic: American Civil War Prize Cases and Diplomacy* (1970).

There is a large literature on the crucial question of Anglo-American relations during the war. The best starting point is Ephraim D. Adams's magisterial but dated *Great Britain and the American Civil War*, 2 vols. (1925). For a more recent study, which covers only the first year of the fighting, see Brian Jenkins, *Britain and the War for the Union* (1974). Robin Winks, *Canada and the United States: The Civil War Years* (1960), deals with a subject that was never absent from the calculations of both Britain and the United States. For the Confederate attempt to build naval ships in Britain, see Frank J. Merli, *Great Britain and the Confederate Navy* (1970). Martin Duberman, *Charles Francis Adams* (1961), is an excellent biography of the American minister in London. See also Worthington C. Ford (ed.), *A Cycle of Adams Letters 1861–1865*, 2 vols. (1920). For a full treatment of a major Anglo-American crisis, consult Norman B. Ferris, *The Trent Affair* (1977). Mary Ellison, *Support for Secession: Lancashire and the American Civil War* (1972), revises previous notions about the Union sympathies of British textile workers. A number of important articles offer revealing insights on British attitudes and policy: Eli Ginzberg, "The Economics of British Neutrality During the American Civil War," *AH*, 10 (1936), 147–56; Max Beloff, "Great Britain and the American Civil War," *History*, 37 (1952), 40–48; Wilbur D. Jones, "The British Conservatives and the American Civil War," *AHR*, 58 (1953), 527–43; Joseph M. Hernon, "British Sympathies in the American Civil War: A Reconsideration," *JSH*, 33 (1967), 356–67; and Kinley J. Brauer, "British Mediation and the American Civil War: A Reconsideration," *JSH*, 38 (1972), 49–64. For relations with France, see Lynn M. Case and Warren F. Spencer, *The United States and France: Civil War Diplomacy* (1970); and Alfred J. Hanna and Kathryn A. Hanna, *Napoleon III and Mexico: American Triumph Over Monarchy* (1971).

The Border States

A still useful study of the border states, which also pays some attention to the southern portions of Midwestern Union states, is Edward C. Smith, *The Borderland in the Civil War* (1927). For Maryland, the best study is Jean H. Baker, *The Politics of Continuity: Maryland Political Parties from 1858 to 1870* (1973). See also Charles B. Clark, "Suppression and Control of Maryland 1861–1865," *Maryland Historical Magazine*, 54 (1959), 241–71. An older, pro-Confederate study of Kentucky is E. Merton Coulter, *The Civil War and Readjustment in Kentucky* (1926). It should be supplemented by William H. Townsend, *Lincoln and the Bluegrass: Slavery and Civil War in Kentucky* (1955); and Lowell Harrison, *The Civil War and Kentucky* (1975). Missouri is well covered in William E. Parrish, *Turbulent Partnership: Missouri and the Union 1861–1865* (1963). See also Hans C. Adamson, *Rebellion in Missouri: 1861* (1961); and Arthur R. Kirkpatrick, "Missouri's Secessionist Government, 1861–1865," *Missouri Historical Review*, 45 (1951), 124–37. The military conflict in the Missouri-Arkansas-Kansas theater is the subject of Jay Monaghan's sprightly *Civil War on the Western Border 1854–1865* (1955). Albert Castel, *A Frontier State at War* (1958), deals primarily with Kansas but covers also the vicious fighting along the Missouri-Kansas border. For West Virginia, the best single study is Richard O. Curry, *A House Divided: A Study of Statehood Politics and the Copperhead Movement in West Virginia* (1964).

Government and Politics in the North

Eric L. McKitrick, "Party Politics and the Union and Confederate War Efforts," in William Nisbet Chambers and Walter Dean Burnham (eds.), *The American Party Systems* (1967), pp. 117–51, is a brilliant comparison of the Union and Confederate political systems. A good brief narrative of Northern wartime politics is James E. Rawley, *The Politics of Union* (1974). Allan Nevins, *The Statesmanship of the Civil War* (1953), contains several thoughtful essays; while James A. Rawley (ed.), *Lincoln and Civil War Politics* (1969), is a useful anthology reflecting various viewpoints. An invaluable collection of laws, congressional votes, and other official government documents is Edward McPherson (ed.), *The Political History of the United States During the Great Rebellion*, 2nd ed. (1865). Burton J. Hendrick, *Lincoln's War Cabinet* (1946), is readable and informative. A great deal of useful information as well as provocative interpretations can be found in William B. Hesseltine, *Lincoln and the War Governors* (1948). Lincoln's skillful use of political patronage is analyzed in Harry J. Carman and Reinhard H. Luthin, *Lincoln and the Patronage* (1943). T. Harry Williams, *Lincoln and the Radicals* (1941), posits a sharp conflict between the President and Republican radicals; while Hans Trefousse, *The Radical Republicans* (1969), emphasizes their cooperation. For thorough biographies of the two leading radical Republicans, read Fawn M. Brodie, *Thaddeus Stevens: Scourge of the South* (1959); and David Donald, *Charles Sumner and the Rights of Man* (1970). The student should also, of course, consult the biographies of Lincoln cited in the section "General Works on the Civil War–Reconstruction Era."

Several studies of Northern states and localities contain important insights and information: John Niven, *Connecticut for the Union* (1965); Eugene H. Roseboom, *The Civil War Era 1850–1873* (1944), on Ohio; Kenneth M. Stampp, *Indiana Politics During the Civil War* (1949); Arthur C. Cole, *The Era of the Civil War 1848–1870* (1919), on Illinois; Richard N. Current, *The History of Wisconsin: The Civil War Era 1848–1873* (1976); and William Dusinberre, *Civil War Issues in Philadelphia 1856–1865* (1965). Margaret Leech, *Reveille in Washington* (1941), chronicles life and politics in the capital during the war. Frank Freidel (ed.), *Union Pamphlets of the Civil War*, 2 vols. (1967) is an invaluable collection of Northern writings.

Of the numerous published diaries of important Northern political leaders, the following are the most significant: Howard K. Beale (ed.), *The Diary of Gideon Welles*, 3 vols. (1960); Tyler Dennett (ed.), *Lincoln and the Civil War in the Diaries and Letters of John Hay* (1939); David Donald (ed.), *Inside Lincoln's Cabinet: The Civil War Diaries of Salmon P. Chase* (1954); and Theodore D. Pease and James G. Randall, eds., *The Diary of Orville Hickman Browning*, 2 vols. (1927–1933).

Northern Democrats, especially the Copperheads, have received a great deal of attention. For a recent survey, read Joel Silbey, *A Respectable Minority: The Democratic Party in the Civil War Era* (1977). Two useful articles are Leonard P. Curry, "Congressional Democrats, 1861–1863," *CWH*, 12 (1966), 213–29; and Jean H. Baker, "A Loyal Opposition: Northern Democrats in the Thirty-seventh Congress," *CWH*, 25 (1979), 139–55. The classic study of the Peace Democrats, which emphasizes their disloyalty to the Union war effort, is Wood Gray, *The Hidden Civil War: The Story of the Copperheads* (1942). See also George Fort Milton, *Abraham Lincoln and the Fifth Column* (1942). Frank L. Klement offers a much more sympathetic treatment, which stresses the anti-industrialist economic ideology of the Peace Democrats, in the following books and articles: *The Copperheads in the Middle West* (1960); *The Limits of Dissent: Clement L. Vallandigham and the Civil War* (1970); "Economic Aspects of Middle Western Copperheadism," *Historian*, 14 (1951), 27–44; and "Middle Western Copperheadism and the Genesis of the Granger Movement," *MVHR*, 38 (1952), 679–94. For other studies that provide insights on the Democrats, consult Henry C. Hubbart, *The Older Middle West 1840–1880* (1936); Eugene Roseboom, "Southern Ohio and the Union, 1863," *MVHR*, 39 (1952), 29–44; and Hubert H. Wubben, *Civil War Iowa and the Copperhead Movement* (1980). Richard O. Curry, "The Union as It Was: A Critique of Recent Interpretations of the 'Copperheads,' " *CWH*, 13 (1967), 25–39, deemphasizes the dimension of disloyalty. But William G. Carleton, "Civil War Dissidence in the North: The Perspective of a Century," *SAQ*, 65 (1966), 390–402, and Stephen Z. Starr, "Was There a Northwest Conspiracy?" *Filson Club Historical Quarterly*, 38 (1964), 323–39, find considerable evidence to buttress the older view of Copperhead antiwar intrigues. For the antiblack sentiments of Democratic and Catholic newspapers, see Ray H. Abrams, "Copperhead Newspapers and the Negro," *JNH*, 20 (1935), 131–52; Joseph George, " 'A Catholic Family Newspaper' Views the Lincoln Administration: John Mullaly's Copperhead Weekly," *CWH*, 24 (June 1978), 112–32; and Cuthbert E. Allen, "The Slavery Question in Catholic Newspapers, 1850–1865," U.S. Catholic Historical Society, *Historical Records and Studies*, 26 (1936), 99–169.

The interrelationships between the peace movement of 1864, the presidential election, and the issues of emancipation and reconstruction are analyzed in Edward C. Kirkland, *The Peacemakers of 1864* (1927); William F. Zornow, *Lincoln and the Party Divided* (1954); Charles R. Wilson, "McClellan's Changing Views on the Peace Plank," *AHR*, 38 (1933), 498–505; and Ludwell H. Johnson, "Lincoln's Solution to the Problem of Peace Terms, 1864–1865," *JSH*, 34 (1968), 576–86. Confederate hopes and expectations regarding the Union presidential election are documented in Larry E. Nelson, *Bullets, Ballots, and Rhetoric: Confederate Policy for the United States Presidential Contest of 1864* (1980). For the soldier vote, see Josiah H. Benton, *Voting in the Field* (1915); and Oscar O. Winther, "The Soldier Vote in the Election of 1864," *New York History*, 25 (1944), 440–58.

Dean Sprague, *Freedom Under Lincoln* (1965), is a critical analysis of the Lincoln administration's curtailment of civil liberties. More approving of the administration is James G. Randall, *Constitutional Problems Under Lincoln*, rev. ed. (1951), which also treats many other legal and constitutional aspects of Union war policy. On these matters, see also Harold M. Hyman, *A More Perfect Union: The Impact of the Civil War and Reconstruction on the Constitution* (1973); and Philip S. Paludan, *A Covenant With Death: The Constitution, Law, and Equality in the Civil War Era* (1975).

Government and Politics in the Confederacy

Two books that analyze the basic structure of the Confederate polity are Charles R. Lee, *The Confederate Constitutions* (1963); and Curtis A. Amlund, *Federalism in the Southern Confederacy* (1966). On the Confederate Congress: Wilfred B. Yearns, *The Confederate Congress* (1960), is a valuable narrative; and Thomas B. Alexander and Richard E. Beringer, *The Anatomy of the Confederate Congress* (1972), is a quantitative analysis. Two books cover thoroughly the cabinet and administrative departments of the Richmond government: Rembert Patrick, *Jefferson Davis and His Cabinet* (1944); and Burton J. Hendrick, *Statesmen of the Lost Cause* (1939). For some indication of the bitter opposition to Jefferson Davis, read James Z. Rabun, "Alexander H. Stephens and Jefferson Davis," *AHR*, 58 (1953), 290–321; and Harrison A. Trexler, "The Davis Administration and the Richmond Press, 1861–1865," *JSH*, 16 (1950), 177–95. Bell I. Wiley, *The Road to Appomattox* (1956), is critical of Confederate political leadership. David M. Potter, "Jefferson Davis and the Political Factors in Confederate Defeat," in David Donald (ed.), *Why the North Won the Civil War* (1960), pp. 91–114, and Paul D. Escott, *After Secession: Jefferson Davis and the Failure of Confederate Nationalism* (1978) focus the criticism specifically on Davis; while Frank E. Vandiver, *Jefferson Davis and the Confederate States* (1964), is a more favorable treatment of the Confederate president. Two diaries yield important insights into the operations of the Richmond government: *John B. Jones, A Rebel War Clerk's Diary* (1866; reprinted 1935); and Edward Younger (ed.), *Inside the Confederate Government: The Diary of Robert Garlick Hill Kean* (1957).

For the classic statement that states' rights undermined the Confederacy, read Frank L. Owsley, *State Rights in the Confederacy* (1925). But Mary S. Ringold, *The Role of State Legislatures in the Confederacy* (1966), argues that most legislatures contributed constructively to the war effort. For an analysis of one particularly divisive issue, see John B. Robbins, "The Confederacy and the Writ of *Habeas Corpus,"* *Georgia Historical Quarterly*, 55 (1971), 83–101. The following books deal with the two most recalcitrant Confederate states and their leaders: T. Conn Bryan, *Confederate Georgia* (1953); Louise B. Hill, *Joseph E. Brown and the Confederacy* (1939); Joseph H. Parks, *Joseph E. Brown of Georgia* (1977); and Richard E. Yates, *The Confederacy and Zeb Vance* (1958). Other states and regions are covered in Charles E. Cauthen, *South Carolina Goes to War 1861–1865* (1950); John K. Bettersworth, *Confederate Mississippi* (1943); and Robert L. Kerby, *Kirby Smith's Confederacy: The Trans-Mississippi 1863–1865* (1972). For disloyalty and Unionism in the South, consult Georgia Lee Tatum, *Disloyalty in the Confederacy* (1934); and Frank W. Klingberg, *The Southern Claims Commission* (1955).

Economy and Society in the Wartime North

The basic study of the Northern home front, still valuable for insights as well as facts, is Emerson D. Fite, *Social and Economic Conditions in the North During the Civil War* (1910). For a good collection of primary sources, consult George W. Smith and Charles Judah (eds.), *Life in the North During the Civil War* (1966). For a review and analysis of the debate over the impact of the war on Northern economic growth, see Harry N. Scheiber, "Economic Change in the Civil War Era: An Analysis of Recent Studies," *CWH*, 11 (1965), 396–411. The most important writings on this question, along with some of the statistics for understanding it, are published in David Gilchrist and W. David Lewis (eds.), *Economic Change in the Civil War Era* (1965); and Ralph Andreano (ed.), *The Economic Impact of the American Civil War*, 2nd ed. (1967). See also Stanley L. Engerman, "The Economic Impact of the Civil War," *Explorations in Entrepreneurial History*, 2nd Ser., 3 (1966), 176–99. For agriculture, the basic works are Paul W. Gates, *Agriculture and the Civil War* (1965), which deals also with the South; and Wayne D. Rasmussen, "The Civil War: A Catalyst of Agricultural Revolution," *AH*, 39 (October 1965), 187–96. On war finance, the fullest study is Bray Hammond, *Sovereignty and an Empty Purse: Banks and Politics in the Civil War* (1970). Leonard P. Curry, *Blueprint for Modern America: Non-Military Legislation of the First Civil War Congress* (1968), analyzes the processes by which financial, banking, homestead, and railroad legislation was passed.

For a newspaper-reading people, reports from the battle front were vital in shaping home-front morale. There are a number of good studies of Civil War journalism: J. Cutler Andrews, *The North Reports the Civil War* (1955); Louis M. Starr, *Bohemian Brigade: Civil War Newsmen in Action* (1954); and Bernard A. Weisberger, *Reporters for the Union* (1953). Of several books on Northern churches and the war, perhaps the most challenging is James H. Moorhead, *American Apocalypse: Yankee Protestants and the Civil War 1860–1869* (1978). See also Benjamin J. Blied, *Catholics and the Civil War* (1945). Two stimulating studies of the war's impact on leading Northern writers and thinkers are George M. Fredrickson, *The Inner Civil War: Northern Intellectuals and the Crisis of the Union* (1965); and Daniel Aaron, *The Unwritten War: American Writers and the Civil War* (1973). On the role of women in several crucial aspects of the war effort, see Agatha Young, *Women and the Crisis: Women of the North in the Civil War* (1959); and Mary Elizabeth Massey, *Bonnet Brigades* (1966), which also treats Southern women.

The social tinder that flamed into the New York draft riots of 1863 is analyzed in Basil L. Lee, *Discontent in New York City 1861–1865* (1943); and Adrian Cook, *The Armies of the Streets: The New York City Draft Riots of 1863* (1974).

Finally, several articles by Ludwell H. Johnson describe the sometimes tawdry but always profitable business of trading with the enemy: "The Butler Expedition of 1861–1862: The Profitable Side of War," *CWH*, 11 (1965), 229–36; "Northern Profit and Profiteers: The Cotton Rings of 1864–1865," *CWH*, 12 (1966), 101–15; "Trading With the Union: The Evolution of Confederate Policy," *Virginia Magazine of History and Biography*, 78 (1970), 308–25; and "Contraband Trade During the Last Year of the Civil War," *MVHR*, 49 (1963), 635–53. See also Joseph H. Parks, "A Confederate Trade Center Under Federal Occupation: Memphis, 1862 to 1865," *JSH*, 7 (1941), 289–314.

Economy and Society in the Confederacy

For a comprehensive overview of this subject, the best study is Charles W. Ramsdell, *Behind the Lines in the Southern Confederacy* (1944). Two collections of documents on the Confederate home front are Albert D. Kirwan (ed.), *The Confederacy* (1959); and W. Buck Yearns and John G. Barrett (eds.), *North Carolina Civil War Documentary* (1980).

For the tangled question of Confederate financial and monetary policy, consult the following: John C. Schwab, *The Confederate States of America 1861–1865: A Financial and Industrial History* (1901); Richard C. Todd, *Confederate Finance* (1954); Eugene M. Lerner, "The Monetary and Fiscal Problems of the Confederate Government," *Journal of Political Economy*, 62 (1954), 506–22, and 63 (1955), 20–40; and Eugene M. Lerner, "Inflation in the Confederacy, 1861–1865," in Milton Friedman (ed.), *Studies in the Quantity Theory of Money* (1956), pp. 163–78. Two studies that argue perhaps too vigorously that the Civil War produced a forced modernization and industrialization of the Southern economy are Raimondo Luraghi, "The Civil War and the Modernization of American Society: Social Structure and Industrial Revolution in the Old South Before and During the War," *CWH*, 18 (1972), 230–50; and Emory M. Thomas, *The Confederacy as a Revolutionary Experience* (1971). For other studies of Confederate economic mobilization see: Lester J. Cappon, "Government and Private Industry in the Southern Confederacy," in *Humanistic Studies in Honor of John Calvin Metcalf* (1941), pp. 151–89; Louise B. Hill, *State Socialism in the Confederate States of America* (1936); Charles B. Dew, *Ironmaker to the Confederacy: Joseph R. Anderson and the Tredegar Iron Works* (1966); Mary Elizabeth Massey, *Ersatz in the Confederacy* (1952); and Ella Lonn, *Salt as a Factor in the Confederacy* (1933). Some idea of the war's devastating economic impact on the South can be gleaned from James L. Sellers, "The Economic Incidence of the Civil War in the South," *MVHR*, 14 (1927), 179–91; Stanley L. Engerman, "Some Economic Factors in Southern Backwardness in the Nineteenth Century," in John F. Kain and John R. Meyer (eds.), *Essays in Regional Economics* (1971), pp. 279–306; and Claudia G. Goldin and Frank K. Lewis, "The Economic Cost of the American Civil War: Estimates and Implications," *JEH*, 35 (1975), 299–326. Gavin Wright, *The Political Economy of the Cotton South* (1978), and Roger L. Ransom and Richard Sutch, *One Kind of Freedom: The Economic Consequences of Emancipation* (1977), emphasize factors other than the war as causes of the South's postwar economic ills.

The sufferings, endurance, and discontent of the Southern people are chronicled in the following: Bell I. Wiley, *The Plain People of the Confederacy* (1943); Stephen E. Ambrose, "Yeoman Discontent in the Confederacy," *CWH*, 8 (1962), 259–68; Paul D. Escott, "Southern Yeomen and the Confederacy," *SAQ*, 77 (1978), 146–58; Mary Elizabeth Massey, *Refugee Life in the Confederacy* (1964); Alfred H. Bill, *The Beleaguered City: Richmond 1861–1865* (1946); Emory M. Thomas, *The Confederate State of Richmond: A Biography of the Capital* (1971); and William J. Kimball, *Starve or Fall: Richmond and Its People 1861–1865* (1976).

Other important studies of the Confederate home front include Ella Lonn, *Foreigners in the Confederacy* (1940); Francis B. Simkins and James W. Patton, *The Women of the Confederacy* (1936); and Bell I. Wiley, *Confederate Women* (1975). On the Southern press, the best book is J. Cutler Andrews, *The South Reports the Civil War* (1970). Finally, a diary and two collections of letters offer unparalleled insights into Southern life during the war: C. Vann Woodward (ed.), *Mary Chesnut's Civil War* (1981); Robert M. Myers (ed.), *The Children of Pride: A True Story of Georgia and the Civil War* (1972); and Betsy Fleet and John D. P. Fuller (eds.), *Green Mount: A Virginia Plantation Family during the Civil War* (1962).

Slaves, Freedmen, and Wartime Reconstruction

For an introduction to this subject, read Clarence L. Mohr, "Southern Blacks in the Civil War: A Century of Historiography," *JNH*, 69 (1974), 177–95. A succinct Marxian interpretation can be found in Herbert Aptheker, *The Negro in the Civil War* (1938). Two readable narratives by Benjamin Quarles are *The Negro in the Civil War* (1953) and *Lincoln and the Negro* (1962). An article and two books by James M. McPherson analyze the active role of abolitionists and blacks in the quest for emancipation and equal rights: "The Civil War and Reconstruction: A Revolution of Racial Equality?" in William G. Shade and Roy C. Herrenkohl (eds.), *Seven on Black: Reflections on the Negro Experience in America* (1969), pp. 49–72; *The Struggle for Equality: Abolitionists and the Negro in the Civil War and Reconstruction* (1964); and *The Negro's Civil War* (1965).

For the role of blacks in the Confederate as well as the Union war effort, the best single study is Bell I. Wiley, *Southern Negroes 1861–1865* (1938). See also James H. Brewer, *The Confederate Negro: Virginia's Craftsmen and Military Laborers 1861–1865* (1969); and David C. Rankin, "The Impact of the Civil War on the Free Colored Community of New Orleans," *Perspectives in American History*, 11 (1977–1978), 379–418. The desperate last-minute move in the Confederacy to emancipate and arm the slaves is chronicled and set in context by Robert F. Durden, *The Gray and the Black: The Confederate Debate on Emancipation* (1972).

John Hope Franklin, *The Emancipation Proclamation* (1963), tells the story of how this momentous decision came about. For Lincoln's thinking and action on emancipation and the race question, see also Hans L. Trefousse (ed.), *Lincoln's Decision for Emancipation* (1975); Don E. Fehrenbacher, "Only His Stepchildren: Lincoln and the Negro," *CWH*, 20 (1974), 293–310; and George M. Fredrickson, "A Man but Not a Brother: Abraham Lincoln and Racial Equality," *JSH*, 41 (1975), 39–58. The process of emancipation in one border state is exhaustively studied in Charles L. Wagandt, *The Mighty Revolution: Negro Emancipation in Maryland 1862–1864* (1964). For the hopes and realities of freedom as experienced by the freedmen, Leon F. Litwack, *Been in the Storm So Long: The Aftermath of Slavery* (1979), is rich in information and insight. Hostile Northern reactions to emancipation are treated in V. Jacque Voegeli, *Free but Not Equal: The Midwest and the Negro during the Civil War* (1967); Forrest G. Wood, *Black Scare: The Racist Response to Emancipation and Reconstruction* (1968); and James M. McPherson (ed.), *Anti-Negro Riots in the North, 1863* (1969). The impact of loss of mastery on slaveholders is sensitively studied in James L. Roark, *Masters Without Slaves: Southern Planters in the Civil War and Reconstruction* (1977).

For black soldiers in the Union army, the best book is Dudley T. Cornish, *The Sable Arm: Negro Troops in the Union Army* (1956). See also Herbert Aptheker, "Negro Casualties in the Civil War," *JNH*, 32 (1947), 10–80. A striking portrait of the transition from slave to soldier is provided by a white abolitionist colonel of a black regiment in Thomas Wentworth Higginson, *Army Life in a Black Regiment* (1869; reprinted 1961). For blacks in the navy, read Herbert Aptheker, "The Negro in the Union Navy," *JNH*, 32 (1947), 169–200. Confederate responses to the Union's arming of black men are analyzed in Brainerd Dyer, "The Treatment of Colored Union Troops by the Confederates, 1861–1865," *JNH*, 20 (1935), 273–86.

Two studies of Lincoln's reconstruction policy provide somewhat contrasting interpretations: Charles H. McCarthy, *Lincoln's Plan of Reconstruction* (1901); and William B. Hesseltine, *Lincon's Plan of Reconstruction* (1960). The fullest study of wartime reconstruction efforts is Herman Belz, *Reconstructing the Union: Theory and Policy During the Civil War* (1969). Belz has also written two perceptive books that focus specifically on Republican policies toward the freedmen: *A New Birth of Freedom: The Republican Party and Freedmen's Rights* (1976) and *Emancipation and Equal Rights: Politics and Constitutionalism in the Civil War Era* (1978). See also David Donald, *The Politics of Reconstruction 1863–1867* (1967).

The complex and important question of federal policy toward freedmen and their former masters in the occupied South has been the subject of several excellent studies, which sometimes disagree concerning the motives and results of Northern policy: Louis S. Gerteis, *From Contraband to Freedman: Federal Policy Toward Southern Blacks, 1861–1865* (1973); Willie Lee Rose, *Rehearsal for Reconstruction: The Port Royal Experiment* (1964); John Eaton, *Grant, Lincoln and the Freedmen* (1907); Steven Joseph Ross, "Freed Soil, Freed Labor, Freed Men: John Eaton and the Davis Bend Experiment," *JSH*, 44 (1978), 213–32; John W. Blassingame, "The Union Army as an Educational Institution for Negroes, 1862–1865," *Journal of Negro Education*, 34 (1965); Peyton McCrary, *Abraham Lincoln and Reconstruction: The Louisiana Experiment* (1978); C. Peter Ripley, *Slaves and Freedmen in Civil War Louisiana* (1976); William F. Messner, *Freedmen and the Ideology of Free Labor: Louisiana 1862–1865* (1978); Thomas J. May, "Continuity and Change in the Labor Program of the Union Army and the Freedmen's Bureau," *CWH*, 17 (1971), 245–54; James T. Currie, *Enclave: Vicksburg and Her Plantations 1863–1870* (1979); and Peter Maslowski, *Treason Must Be Made Odious: Military Occupation and Wartime Reconstruction in Nashville, Tennessee 1862–1865* (1978). For two fascinating collections of letters from Northern whites who went to the South Carolina sea islands during the war to teach the freedmen, read Rupert S. Holland (ed.), *The Letters and Diary of Laura M. Towne* (1912; reprinted 1970); and Elizabeth Ware Pearson (ed.), *Letters from Port Royal 1862–1868* (1906; reprinted 1969).

Index

A Note About the Author

James M. McPherson is Edwards Professor of American History at Princeton University, where he has taught since 1962. He was born in Valley City, North Dakota, in 1936. He received his B.A. from Gustavus Adolphus College in 1958 and his Ph.D. from The Johns Hopkins University in 1963. He has been a Guggenheim Fellow, a National Endowment for the Humanities Fellow, a visiting Fellow at the Henry E. Huntington Library in San Marino, California, and a Fellow at the Center for Advanced Study in the Behavioral Sciences at Stanford. In 1982 he was Commonwealth Fund Lecturer at University College, London.

A specialist in Civil War–Reconstruction history and in the history of race relations, Mr. McPherson is the author of *The Struggle for Equality: Abolitionists and the Negro in the Civil War and Reconstruction* (1964), *The Negro's Civil War* (1965), *Marching Toward Freedom: The Negro in the Civil War* (1968), and *The Abolitionist Legacy: From Reconstruction to the NAACP* (1975).

A Note on the Type

This book was set via computer-driven cathode ray tube in Avanta, a film version of Electra, a type face designed by W. A. Dwiggins. The Electra face is a simple and readable type suitable for printing books by present-day processes. It is not based on any historical model, and hence does not echo any particular time or fashion. Composed by Haddon Craftsmen, Inc. Scranton, Pennsylvania. Printed and bound by R. R. Donnelley & Sons, Co., Crawfordsville, Indiana.

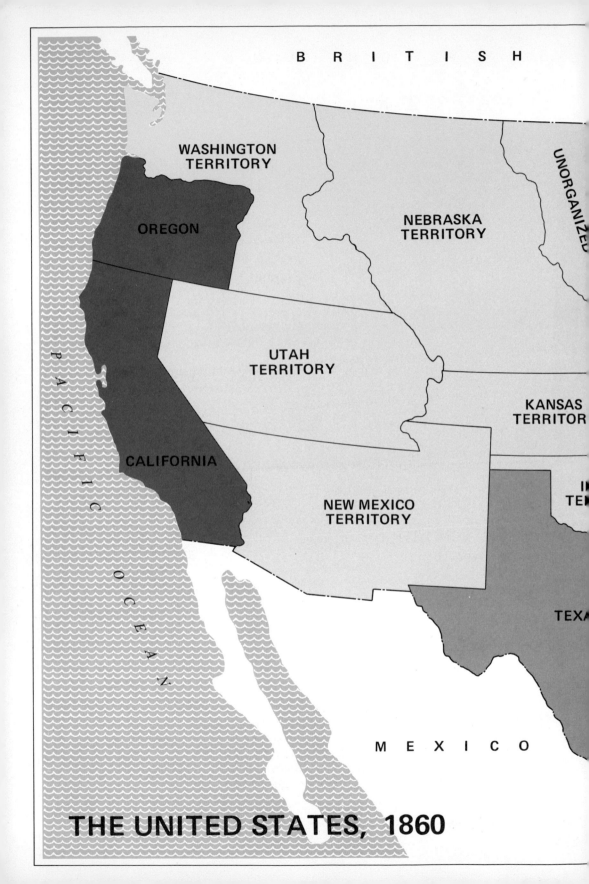

THE UNITED STATES, 1860

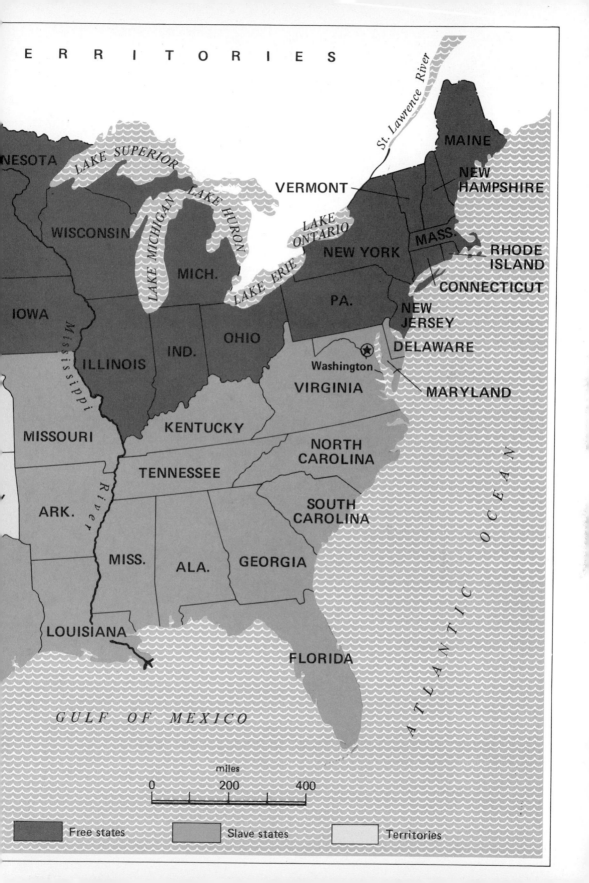

ERRITORIES

St. Lawrence River

MAINE

NEW HAMPSHIRE

NESOTA

LAKE SUPERIOR

VERMONT

WISCONSIN

LAKE MICHIGAN

LAKE HURON

LAKE ONTARIO

NEW YORK

MASS.

RHODE ISLAND

MICH.

LAKE ERIE

CONNECTICUT

IOWA

PA.

NEW JERSEY

ILLINOIS

IND.

OHIO

DELAWARE

Washington

VIRGINIA

MARYLAND

Mississippi

MISSOURI

KENTUCKY

NORTH CAROLINA

TENNESSEE

River

SOUTH CAROLINA

ARK.

MISS.

ALA.

GEORGIA

LOUISIANA

FLORIDA

ATLANTIC OCEAN

GULF OF MEXICO

miles

0   200   400

Free states   Slave states   Territories